Van Abbemuseum

A Companion to Modern and Contemporary Art

Van Abbemuseum

A Companion to Modern and Contemporary Art

Edited by Jan Debbaut and Monique Verhulst

Van Abbemuseum, Eindhoven, 2002

Contents

Introduction

The collection is the cork on which the museum floats
Edy de Wilde

The collection of the Van Abbemuseum is perhaps better known abroad than in its hometown. Over the past twenty years, large parts of it have been exhibited in major cities—in Germany, Greece, Belgium, France, Luxembourg, Spain, Portugal, Israel and even Japan. This interest from abroad may have to do with the fact that, unlike many European capitals, Eindhoven has had—as a provincial town, not centrally located—an internationally oriented museum specializing in modern and contemporary art from as early as 1936. During the last two decades there has been a rapid increase in the creation of museums and centers for contemporary art. The many biennials and international art events as well as the opening of sensational new buildings such as the Guggenheim in Bilbao and the Tate Modern in London have attracted mass-media attention and large crowds. This causes us to forget that public interest in contemporary art is of fairly recent origin and thus highly vulnerable.
By European standards, the founding of an internationally oriented museum for modern and contemporary art in Eindhoven was very early and almost unprecedented. As a result, the Eindhoven museum has become, to some extent, a model or reference by which others have been inspired or guided while studying and developing their own needs.

The definitive museum does not exist. A museum's identity is always determined by a combination of factors: its geographical location and its socio-cultural context, the period during which it came into being and the way in which this took place, the ratio of private and government support, and the means at its disposal. But, above all, it is the outcome of the vision and ideas of people who have worked there and determined its artistic policy over the years. From this point of view it is remarkable that, for more than sixty-five years, the Van Abbemuseum has existed in a city such as Eindhoven and developed into what it is today. In 1936 Eindhoven was a comparatively small and provincial town, even within the Netherlands. Located at some distance from the country's center, it had little cultural identity or heritage. Slowly but surely, thanks to the impact of such companies as Philips and DAF, it has grown from being the provincial center of an agricultural region into a busy industrial city, an urban area with a population of approximately 250,000. Eindhoven is a technology-oriented business town, not a center of tourism. Until recently, similar provincial cities, both in Holland and throughout the rest of Europe, possessed only two kinds of art institutions—if any at all. On the one hand, there was the *kunsthalle* or *palais des beaux arts*: a multifunctional space, used for temporary exhibitions of all kinds. And on the other, the *musée des beaux arts*: the typical provincial museum of art that generally has a diverse collection which is fairly incoherent, in a historical and thematic sense, and which was often created on the basis of bequests and private donations that were merged to form a larger—rather hybrid—whole only at a later date. The department of modern and contemporary art is most often a fairly recent addition to such institutions.

As René Pingen describes further on in this catalogue, the history of the Van Abbemuseum deviates from that norm. In 1936 the museum in Eindhoven was started without an existing building or collection. It was founded by a private person: Henri van Abbe, a wealthy cigar manufacturer and art collector. Van Abbe himself was initially interested in the work of his contemporaries in the province of Brabant. Over the course of time, however, he broadened his view to include contemporary artists from Belgium and France. He seems to have been particularly fascinated by studio visits and by his personal contacts with artists. In 1936 he offered the municipality of Eindhoven—which, at the time, did not have a cultural institution of its own—a museum building which he had built for this purpose at his own expense, commissioning the architect A.J. Kropholler to design it. Kropholler's building for Van Abbe was conceived as a simple, closed and symmetrical structure; its interior layout—calm, well-proportioned exhibition rooms and beautiful top lighting—continues to have an exceptional attraction for many hundreds of artists who have shown their work there over the years. Not only did Henri van Abbe donate the building to Eindhoven; he also gave the town twenty-six paintings from his collection of work by Dutch artists. On this occasion, the city council also purchased fourteen extra works from his collection.

Now, sixty-five years later, the collection consists of a few thousand works, spanning the period from 1900 to the present by way of a number of well-developed ensembles. Important elements include: cubism, De Stijl, Constructivism and the Lissitzky collection, Expressionism, Dutch figurative art between the wars, Cobra, École de Paris, Zero, Neo-Constructivism, the Matter Painters, Minimal Art, Conceptual Art, Arte Povera, German painting of the 1970s and 1980s, and more recently formed ensembles of contemporary sculpture, installations and video art. The collection stands out by way of its integration of Dutch art into an international context. Its importance also lies with the first-rate quality of many individual works, ranging from world-famous paintings such as *Hommage à Apollinaire* (1921) by Chagall and *Die Macht der Musik* (1918) by Kokoschka to more recent works such as *Voglie vedere i miei montagne* (1971) by Beuys, *Tapis de Sable* (1974) by Broodthaers or the installation *Categorical Imperative and Morgue* (1999) by Mike Kelley, which have already become artworks essential to a proper understanding of contemporary developments.

The Van Abbemuseum is a place where definite choices have been made. The aim has never been encyclopedic completeness. There are deliberate emphases which provide a basis for larger, more or less coherent groups of work. With their subjective but coherent artistic choices, my predecessors have always opted for a close and personal relationship with the artist and for a clear—almost organic—link between the development of the exhibitions program and the further expansion of the collection. This constant interaction has transformed the present collection into a natural matrix within which and against which new developments can be tested and compared. The Van Abbemuseum's collection is the cumulative result of activities and ideas that have come about there. It consequently represents not only the history of the art that has been shown in the museum over the years, but also the history of the institution itself and the ideas of people who have worked there.

Looking back, all of my predecessors seem to have had distinct personalities, and their views—concerning museum policy as well as artistic interests and affinities—differed radically. For this very reason, however, their policies for the Van Abbemuseum can be regarded as a constant. In their approaches they consistently opted, with great commitment to their contemporaries, for a fundamental renewal of museum policy. The art of their own generation was of prime importance to them; they remained closely involved in the artistic issues of their time. With modest means it has thus been possible to keep on augmenting the existing collection with new 'chapters' as these took shape and reflected the changing spirit of the age. That is why a relatively small institution has continued to play an ongoing role in the further development of international art.

Over the last ten years we have tried to uphold this attitude. This catalogue introduces, for the first time, the parts of the collection which have been formed recently and which thus demonstrate our commitment to our own generation as well as to younger artists. With the creation of the foundation Promoters of the Van Abbemuseum in 1989 the collection was vigorously developed. Therefore this book should also be seen as an interim report that is deliberately confined, as a kind of introduction, to the major acquisitions and to new emphases. In recent years—a time certainly not noted for its broad, consistently intellectual or social movements—we have been concerned with juxtaposing a number of artists who express extremely individual viewpoints which sometimes conflict with the art scene today. Their 'dialogue' usually takes place beyond the realm of traditional sculpture and painting, with the use of new media and at a point in history that is seen as being a kind of no-man's-land, where the powerful cultural mechanisms of 'modernity' are allegedly worn out and no longer effective. A fragmented worldview and rapid developments in technology and in our visual environment are, once again, pointing to the underlying issue as to the potential and the limits of truly meaningful art. Each artist whose work is collected here explores this matter in an individual manner, subtly and with nuance, without a dogma or manifesto and without forming a clique or dictating behavior. Clearly, we are dealing with the subjective selection of a number of highly diverse artistic personalities whose work we presently consider exciting and significant.

Naturally, one collects and exhibits works of art primarily on the basis of intrinsic qualities and in the hope of arousing interest in those works and the artists. But by presenting a public collection such as this, one also reveals an attitude, a constant commitment to an ever-changing and self-renewing, living culture.

Jan Debbaut
Director Van Abbemuseum

With thanks to the Vereniging Rembrandt, the Mondriaan Foundation, the Van Abbemuseum Promoters Foundation and the Province of Noord- Brabant, which have made many acquisitions possible.

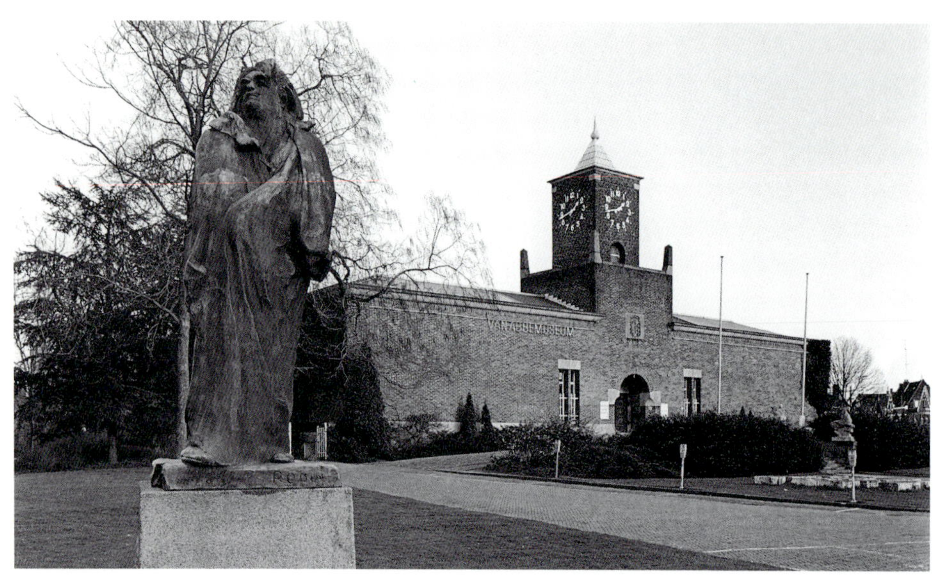

The Van Abbemuseum designed by architect
A.J. Kropholler, 1936

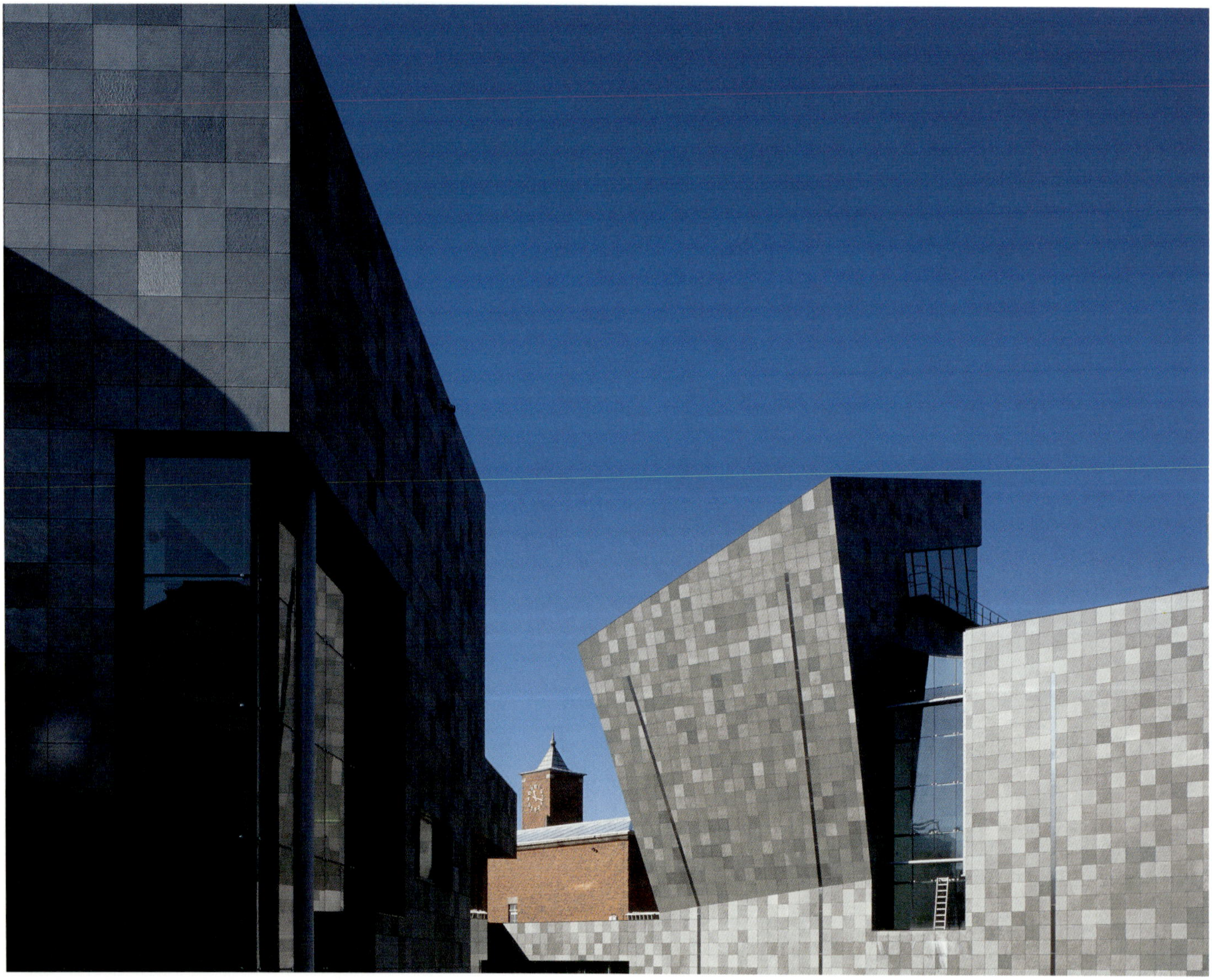

The Van Abbemuseum designed by architect A. Cahen, 1998

A history of the Van Abbemuseum in five episodes

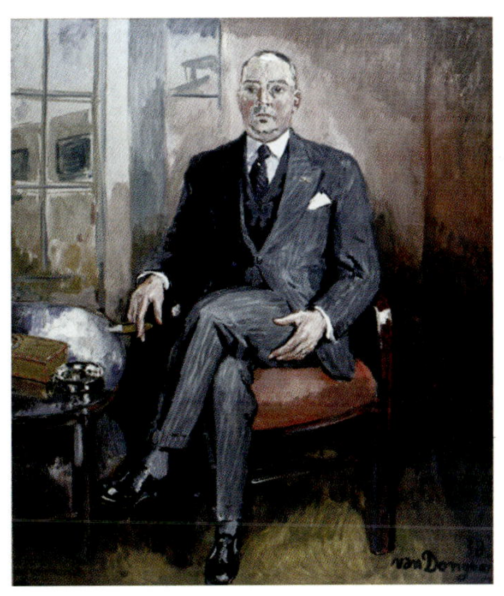

Kees van Dongen, *Portrait Henri van Abbe,* 1938
Collection H.J. van Abbe

1933-1946

On January 30, 1933 Mayor A. Verdijk made a solemn statement at the meeting of Eindhoven's municipal council: one of the local dignitaries, the cigar manufacturer H.J. van Abbe (1880-1940) had offered to donate the city a museum for painting. Included in the offer was Henri Van Abbe's financing of the construction of the museum, the initial acquisitions and even, for some time, operational costs. The town council was astonished by this gesture of Van Abbe which reflected such great "civic virtue, feeling for art and community spirit." It was decided that, in exchange for this, the ground on which the new museum was to be built would be provided free of charge and that the museum would be named after the generous donor.

In 1920 Eindhoven was consolidated with five surrounding towns to form a single municipality, and by 1930 its population nearly doubled to 100,000 inhabitants. That rapid rise in population was brought about by the call for workers made by the *N.V. Philips gloeilampenfabrieken*—the later multinational Philips Electronics—and countless smaller enterprises, particularly in the textile and cigar branches. The economic activity had not yet been matched on a cultural level, however. In that sense, the gift made by Van Abbe was—in the absence of any initiative on the part of the municipality—a fitting gesture. Whether the local authorities were particularly pleased with that during the frugal years of the Depression, however, remains the question. No municipal collection existed and funds were limited, especially due to the payment of unemployment compensation. The fact that a prominent citizen felt called upon to fulfill a civic duty was rather convenient, but the city would not begin to finance the museum in any substantial way until after World War II.

Though the visual arts still lacked a representative institution in Eindhoven, there were in fact quite a number of collectors in the area. Since about 1920 Henri van Abbe had been collecting mainly contemporary art, and his taste gradually seemed to shift from regional painters to highly celebrated Dutch artists of the 1930s, such as Jan Sluijters and Kees van Dongen. These artists were also commissioned to produce family portraits. Work by artists from abroad was acquired for the collection only intermittently and primarily involved Flemish Expressionists such as Constant Permeke, Gustave De Smet and Gustave Van de Woestijne. Van Abbe's preference for realistic painting, ranging from the

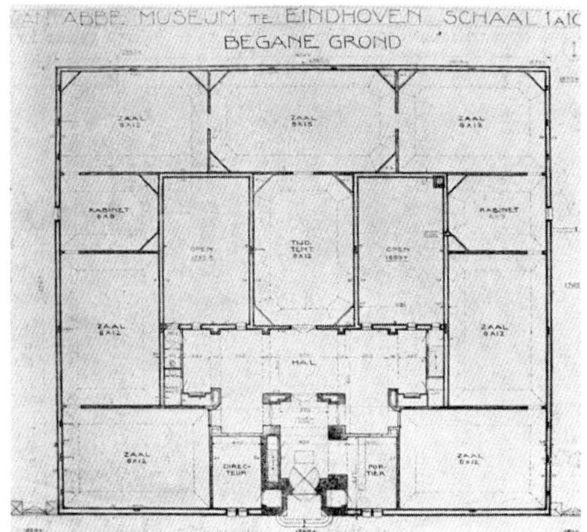

Floor plan of galleries

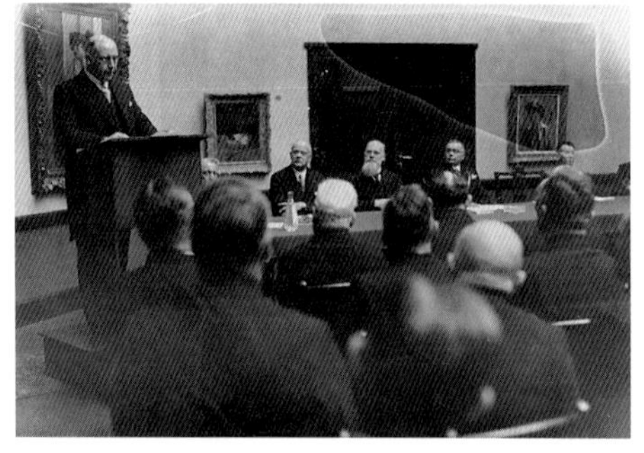

Henri van Abbe giving speech at the opening of the museum on April 18, 1936

expressionistic to the 'magic-realistic', reflected what was considered modern at that time.

After the donation had taken place in 1933, the main issue was to look for a distinguished architect, as Henri van Abbe wished. When it became apparent that the Rotterdam city architect A. van der Steur failed to obtain permission from his superiors—at that point he was very busy with the new building of Museum Boymans—the architect A.J. Kropholler was chosen. His work is regarded as being part of the Delft School. The circumstances of the Depression years and a religious/ethical point of view shaped, to some degree, the Delft School's desire for more conservative architecture and a pure use of traditional methods. In accordance with this, Kropholler presented his final sketch in February 1934. The municipal council responded enthusiastically, and construction began immediately; on September 13, 1935 the new museum was completed. On an area of forty by forty meters, Kropholler had practically windowless walls of red brick erected. A monumental set of stairs, flanked by two rearing horses made by the sculptor John Rädecker, led to the entrance, marked by a stocky tower. All of the rooms—ten in all, including two print rooms—were symmetrically arranged around two inner courts. As would become evident, the rooms were exceptionally well proportioned; in addition to this, the symmetrical lay-out and the incidence of light from above would be praised by future users.

In February 1936 Dr. Wouter Visser (1904), an art historian and specialist in early Christian art, became the museum's first director, hired on the basis of two days per week. This proved to be insufficient, but more time and personnel—the only other employee was a caretaker—were not granted. In order to supplement his meagre income as director, Visser also worked as an archivist and, from 1939 onward, he combined these jobs with a teaching position as well. Trained as a medievalist, Visser could not be considered an outright expert on contemporary art. According to the city's governing board (the mayor and alderman) this was not a problem, however, since purchases would be assessed by a committee of external specialists. This Advisory Committee had already been formed in October 1933 and was comprised of D. Hannema (director of Museum Boymans), C. W. H. Baart (director of Amsterdam's Stedelijk Museum until 1936) and his successor D.C. Röell. Along with this, a Supervisory Board was appointed, and Henri van Abbe was among its members.

The Van Abbemuseum officially opened its doors on April 18, 1936 with the exhibition *Hedendaagsche Nederlandsche Kunst*. With that title Visser clearly indicated the level of the ambitions. Though the Van Abbemuseum was a municipal museum, there was no preference for artists from Eindhoven or the province of North Brabant. The exhibition offered, with its 185 paintings and drawings and twenty-two sculptures by a total of nearly one hundred artists, a fairly complete survey of the modern art which was in vogue at that time. Immediately after the opening, preparations for a second large retrospective exhibition began, this one being dedicated to contemporary Belgian painting and sculpture. That was eventually held in 1937.

With solo exhibitions of work by such artists as Matthieu Wiegman (1936), Toon Kelder (1937), Kees van Dongen and Jan Sluijters (1938) as well as group exhibitions dedicated to the 'Bergen School' (1939), the Groningen group 'De Ploeg' (1940) and others, Visser elaborated on the initial exhibition. The same held true for acquisitions. With the funds set aside by Van Abbe, twenty-six paintings by figures such as Carel Willink, Jan Sluijters, Wim Schuhmacher and Dirk Nijland were purchased for the opening of the museum. All of these paintings came from Van Abbe's private collection. From the exhibition *Hedendaagsche Nederlandsche Kunst* paintings were once again purchased, thirteen in all, by Charles Eyck, Leo Gestel, Gerard Röling and others. The role of the external advisors evidently came to an end after this, and responsibility for the selection of works was taken over by Visser and the Supervisory Board. Visser's proposal to collect paintings of the most important representatives of contemporary movements was adopted, but the number of purchases nevertheless began to decline in 1937. Gaps in the collection were filled as well as possible with lent works. And so even during the 1930s, there was a concern for coherent acquisition and exhibition policies that would reflect contemporary artistic developments, despite the absence of the more avant-garde tendencies. In that respect the solo exhibition of work by Theo van Doesburg (1936) did constitute an exception.

The increasing difficulty with which the Van Abbemuseum operated on a practical level as of 1938, however, is evident. After closing its doors for more than a half year—the municipality needed a space for the judging the designs of the new city hall—the day-to-day state of affairs was seriously hindered by the threat of war. For the sake of security, the collection and loans were brought to the cellar, and the number of visitors to the museum decreased. Even the lectures and art-history courses organized by Visser, which initially drew hundreds of participants, met with a decline in interest. Due to the difficult political and financial circumstances, Visser was unable to prevent the museum from gradually fading into regional isolation.

When the occupation began, the situation became worse. Planned exhibitions were cancelled. Museum Kempenland (specializing in local history) and, later, the air-raid protection service were housed at the Van Abbemuseum. In order to reduce the risk of bomb strikes, the glass roof was covered with green paint, something which must have made the exhibition of paintings rather difficult. Visser seems to have carried out his work with increasing reluctance, and because he had no desire to hold an exhibition of the NSB (Dutch national socialist movement) he resigned in February 1942.

Visser's successor was J.P.G. Peeters, who remained in the position only for a short time due to illness; in March 1943 Louis Vrijdag was appointed director of the Van Abbemuseum. Aside from being a place for exhibitions in which artistic standards were upheld, though the nature of these was sometimes dubious, the Van Abbemuseum also proved to be a platform for propaganda exhibitions under the directorships of Peeters and Vrijdag. After the liberation, Visser was appointed director again, yet this did not last long; as of January 1, 1946 he accepted a post as director of the *Rijksmonumentenzorg* (the 'National Trust' of the Netherlands).

1946-1963

The directorship of Edy de Wilde (1919), who assumed his duties in July 1946, is the start of a new chapter for the Van Abbemuseum. In the aftermath of the war, the cultural awareness of the city gradually developed in connection with the optimistic outlook of the recovery period and the leading position that Eindhoven began to assume as an industrial center in the southern part of the Netherlands. That is not to say, however, that De Wilde was able to realize his plans without a struggle. Initially, the resistance to his involvement with modern art was considerable, and this primarily had to do with the lack of a cultural tradition. Even the 'ground-breaking' work of Visser had been unable to bring about a change in this respect.

Actually De Wilde established the foundations of the collection; in doing so, he largely ignored the prewar collection—a total of roughly seventy paintings by predominantly Dutch artists—as he considered it incomplete and of an inadequate quality. Times had

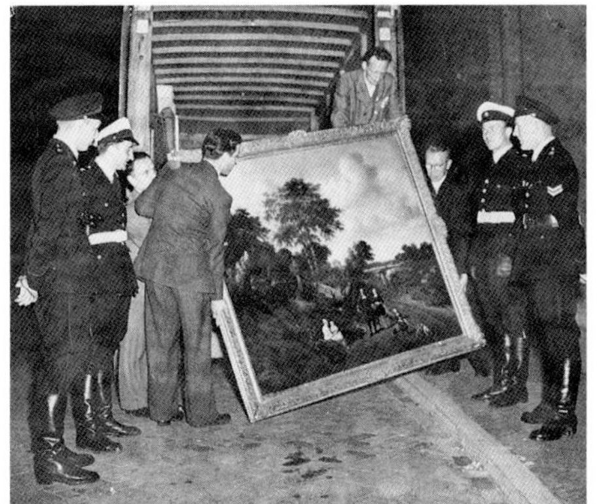

Edy de Wilde (center) accepting artworks for the exhibition *Recuperated Art: A selection of Dutch art treasures returned from Germany, 1946*

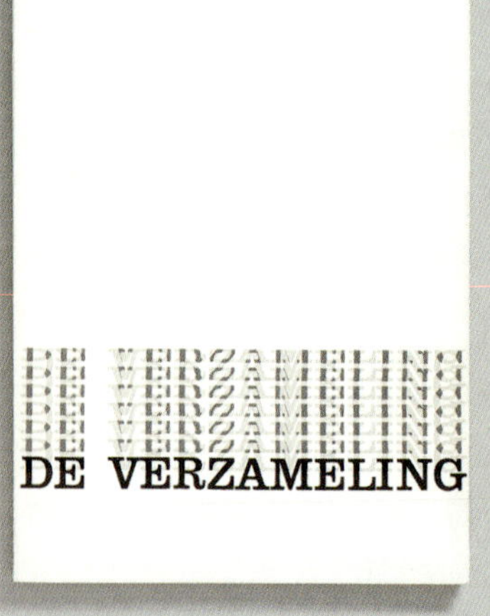
DE VERZAMELING

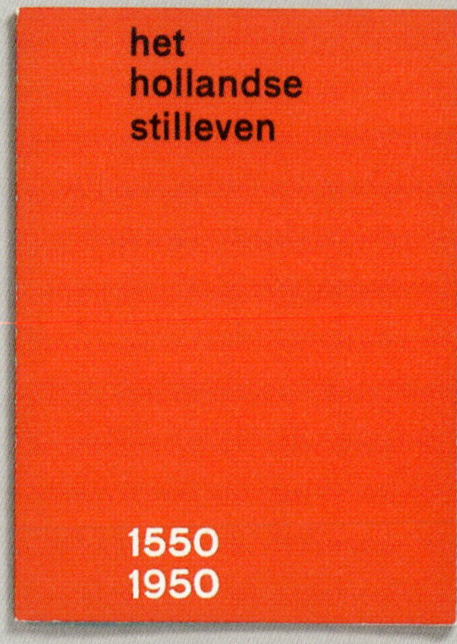
het
hollandse
stilleven
1550
1950

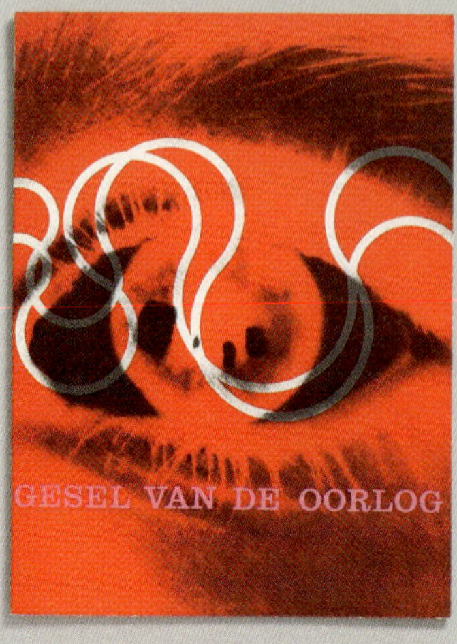
GESEL VAN DE OORLOG

brusselmans

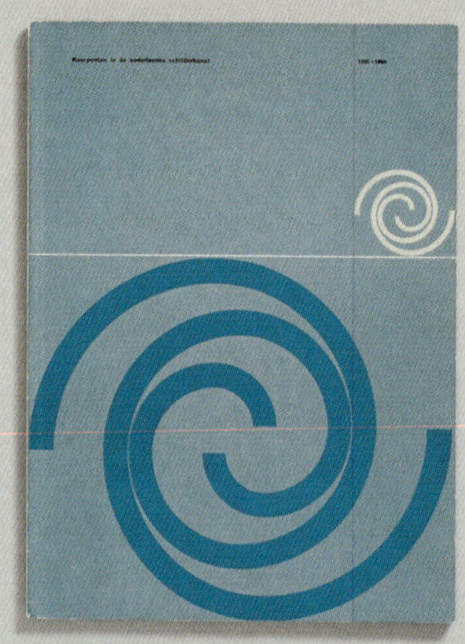

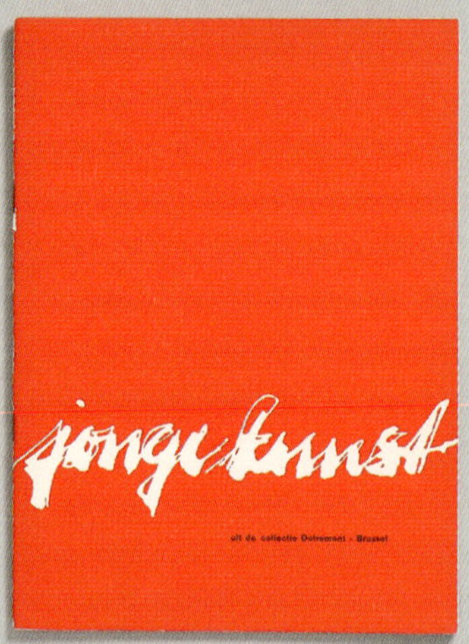
jonge kunst

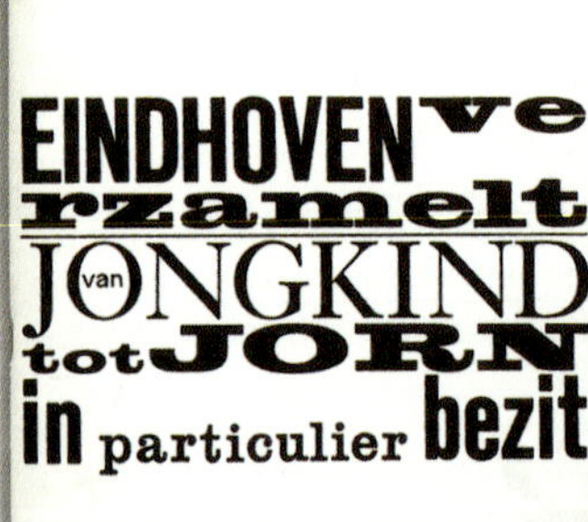
EINDHOVEN ve
rzamelt
van JONGKIND
tot JORN
in particulier bezit

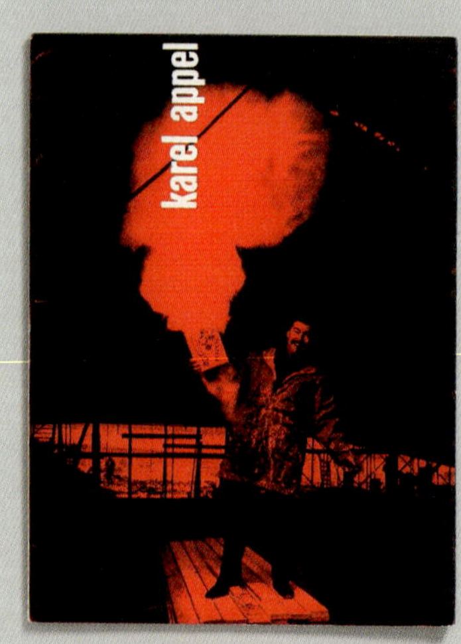
karel appel

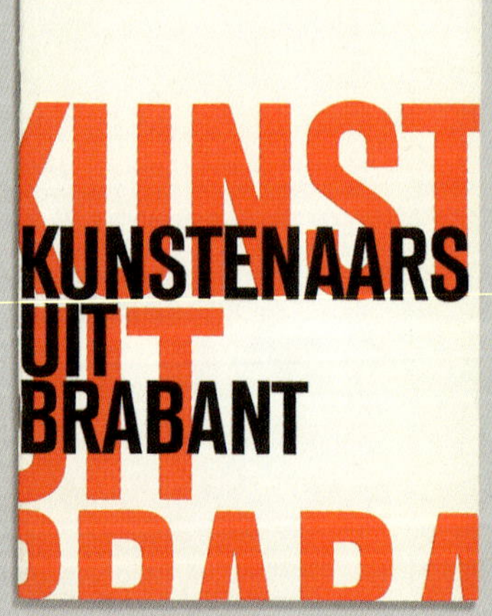
KUNST
KUNSTENAARS
UIT
BRABANT

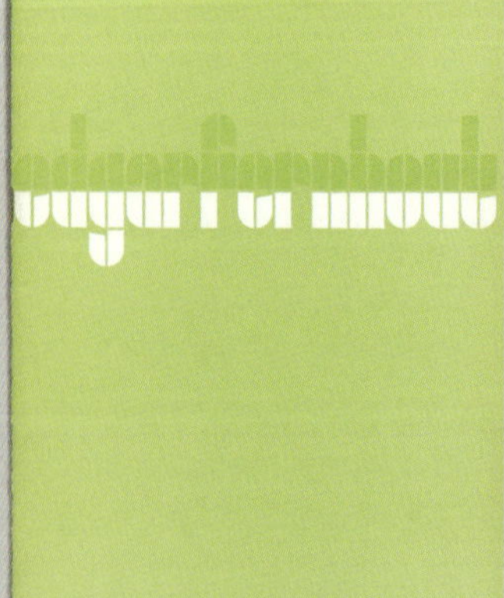
edgar fernhout

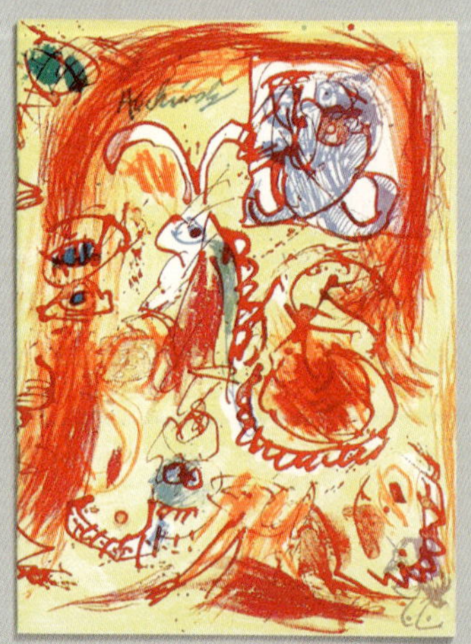

fontana

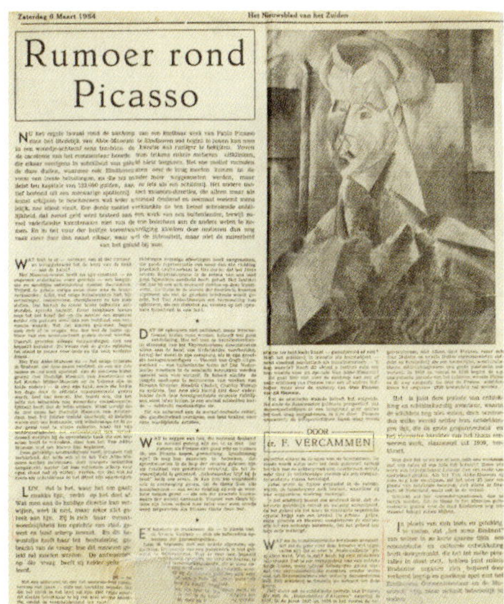

'Commotion surrounding Picasso acquisition', Newspaper article (*Het nieuwsblad van het zuiden*, Saturday, March 6, 1954) on the purchase of Picasso's *Femme en vert*

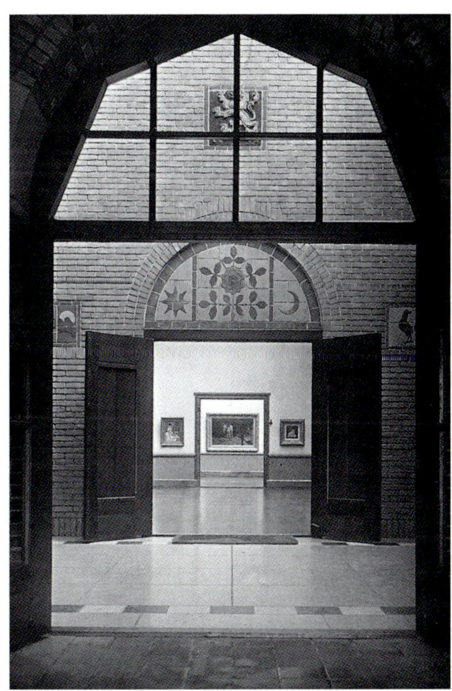

View from entrance hall into the exhibition space (*G.H. Breitner* exhibition, 1956)

Left page
Catalogues produced under the directorship of **Edy de Wilde**, designed by **Wim Crouwel**

changed in an artistic sense and in terms of appreciation, and from the late forties on, the policy of the Van Abbemuseum would become identified more and more with classic modern art and the contemporary avant-garde. In addition to this, De Wilde underscored, with that harsh judgment, the fact that a new status for the museum would require a different vision as well as financial commitments. Though De Wilde's original aim was to form a broad collection of modern Dutch art, this was adjusted in 1951. In his now celebrated speech to the municipal council, he then argued particularly for the internationalization of the collection and for a focus on Expressionism. Only in this way could the museum stand out in relation to the major Dutch museums of modern art.

Despite De Wilde's decision to concentrate on international art of the twentieth century, loans of seventeenth- and nineteenth-century art were, in fact, included in the collection after 1948. Also by means of exhibitions of older art, such as *Herwonnen Kunstbezit* (1946) and *Nederlandse landschapskunst in de 17e eeuw* (1948), he introduced a standard for quality, which was meant to serve as a model for the collection of modern art to be built. In pursuing that objective De Wilde had the support of the Advisory Committee, which was re-appointed in 1949, the initial members including figures such as A.M. Hammacher, director of the Rijksmuseum Kröller-Müller, and Hans Jaffé, curator of the Stedelijk Museum.

There was a less harmonious relationship with the Supervisory Board, which appeared to advocate the idea of a collection that would also include older art. In 1951 this difference of opinion escalated, and due to the 'one-sided' acquisitions of modern art, the Supervisory Board voted to withdraw support for De Wilde's policy. In his speech De Wilde pointed out that the plans for collecting older art could not be realized; quality was always to be the main consideration in forming a collection, and that was unaffordable with older art. Ultimately the conflict was settled by the mayor and aldermen, but it was not until 1955 that an official statement defined the acquisition policy of the Van Abbemuseum as being solely focused on modern art. After this, a new Supervisory Board was also appointed, and De Wilde's policy was indeed supported on the basis of conviction.

The acquisition of *Hommage à Apollinaire* (1912) by Marc Chagall in 1952 prompted some adjustment to the acquisition program as presented to the municipal council in 1951. The painting by Chagall was to be the point of departure for the formation of a 'base collection'. This involved a small group of paintings, representative of the developments in Expressionism as well as Cubism. The collecting of Cubist paintings had not been an option prior to this, but the acquistion of *Hommage à Apollinaire* brought that into the field of vision. Not only is this painting a highlight in the oeuvre of Chagall, but it can also be regarded as a key work within the collection.

Within a very brief period of time, De Wilde managed to collect a considerable number of classic modern masterpieces for this base collection, paintings by artists such as Wassily Kandinsky, Oskar Kokoschka, Robert Delaunay, Piet Mondrian, Georges Braque and Juan Gris. In particular, the purchase of Picasso's *Femme en vert* (1909) led to public commotion, especially owing to the sum of € 51,731 (114,000 guilders) which was paid for it, an outrageous amount of money in 1954. Nevertheless, in January 1954 the municipal council allocated extra credit in order to bring about the completion of the base collection and to finance the acquisition of *Femme en vert*. The vast majority of the municipal council voted to grant the credit, this being initial proof that De Wilde's cautious maneuvers, involving both a firm standpoint and a good sense of the local political situation, were beginning to yield results.

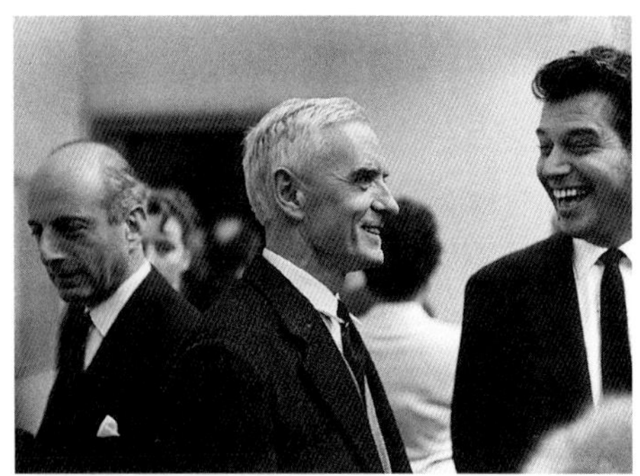

Jean Bazaine (center) speaking with **Edy de Wilde** at the opening of his solo exhibition, 1958

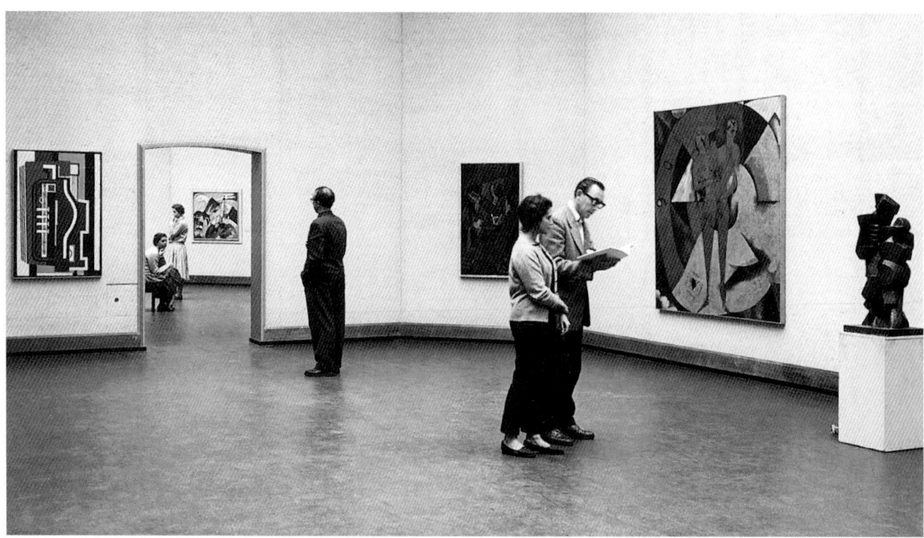

Installation view of the collection, 1957

De Wilde did not allow himself to be thrown off course by the opposition to his policy–on the contrary: in a certain sense, it sharpened him in the making of distinct choices. The fact that modern art was controversial could not be denied, and in this respect the museum was faced with a responsibility to mediate. In 1955 this was stated by him as follows: "The job of a museum is, on the one hand, to educate the public primarily to appreciate the quality of an artwork, secondly to understand the artistic, that is to say intellectual, movements in art. The museum of modern art moreover has the responsibility to bridge the discrepancy between the art that is being produced now and the public's appreciation of it. This makes sense: through a non-rational approach, the intellectual background of our time becomes visible in the work of art. It signifies a moment of consciousness-raising in the development of the personality."[1]

As the base collection was beginning to take shape, De Wilde directed his attention to the formation of a 'transitional group' bridging the base collection and the contemporary art. This group, including paintings by Picasso, Fernand Léger, Max Beckmann, Raoul Dufy, Joan Miró and Max Ernst, also stands out by way of its high quality. At the same time, he certainly did not neglect his great passion, contemporary French painting. The lyrical expressionist work of Jean Bazaine became a *specialité de la maison*, and paintings by Roger Bissière, Alfred Manessier and Serge Poliakoff were also acquired. Art from Paris appeared to be setting the norm in the art world, and as of 1950 it was vitalized to an increasing extent by non-French artists. That, too, is reflected in De Wilde's acquisition policy, resulting in purchases of works by Asger Jorn, Antonio Saura, Hans Hartung and Pierre Alechinsky throughout the second half of the fifties. In addition to works from the realm of Abstract Expressionism, paintings by Jean Dubuffet and Antoni Tàpies, artists who led the way to Matter Painting, were also acquired for the collection.

With the collection of Dutch art, a solid foundation of mainly prewar art was formed (Willink, Sluijters, Charley Toorop, Hendrik Chabot, Herman Kruyder, Bart van der Leck and Piet Mondrian), while from the mid fifties onward, contemporary Dutch art arrived on the scene, the work of Corneille, Karel Appel and Jaap Wagemaker being among the highlights. The guideline throughout all of those years of purchasing foreign as well as Dutch art was the idea that only limitation and distinct choices could lead to a consistent collection.

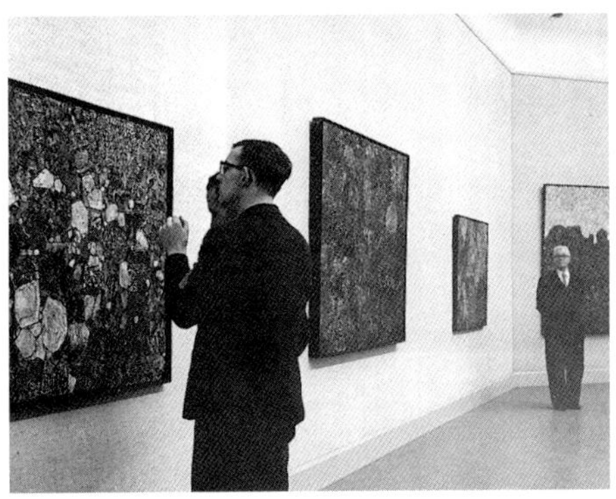
Installation of works by **Dubuffet** at the exhibition *Kompas I: Painters from Paris*, 1961-62

As far as the exhibition policy was concerned, De Wilde took an equally gradual approach. Though the controversial exhibition *Moderne Meesters* (1947) formed a major exception, most of the exhibitions held prior to 1950 included only the work of Dutch artists. After that, the exhibition policy became more international in scope. With *Moderne Franse Religieuze Kunst* (1951) and *11 tijdgenoten uit Parijs* (1953) the leading French art was first introduced, and that perspective was further refined on the basis of solo exhibitions. De Wilde also organized, of course, solo exhibitions of work by important artists in the collection, including Carel Willink (1949), Herman Kruyder (1952), Raoul Dufy, Alfred Manessier (1955), Roger Bissière, Robert Delaunay, Fernand Léger (1957), Jean Bazaine (1958), Jean Dubuffet (1960), Karel Appel and Corneille (1961). Special mention should also be given to *Kompas I* (1961) and *Kompas II* (1962), extensive group exhibitions dealing with the artistic developments in Paris and London, respectively. This series, as well as the group of exhibitions dedicated to Brabant artists held from 1953 onward, would be continued by De Wilde's successor, Jean Leering.

By the time De Wilde was appointed director of Amsterdam's Stedelijk Museum in 1963, the Van Abbemuseum had cast off its provincial image and had come to be one of the leading museums of the Netherlands. The number of visitors had multiplied by seven since his appointment, but De Wilde himself was the first to put this increase into perspective. It was not the public, but the art which came first, as he stated on taking leave of the museum in August 1963: "The point is not to draw thousands to the museum by means of exhibitions ensured of success in advance; the point is that we reach visitors, that the awareness of a different, out-of-the-ordinary world is created, that the imagination is roused. For art is not the beautiful object for sheer enjoyment, but it is the reaction of the artist to the world around him. He gives that world a face, and he makes that world visible. If the museum succeeds in giving the artwork that chance, it has fulfilled its task."[2]

1964-1973

Jean Leering began his work as the new director of the Van Abbemuseum in April 1964. De Wilde's successor proved to be not an experienced museum man but an architectural engineer, fresh from school, whose major feat had been the organization of an international exhibition of religious art during his university days. Though it was initially thought that Leering would follow the course set by De Wilde, he nevertheless very rapidly put the Van Abbemuseum on a track that differed radically from that of his predecessor.

From the very beginning of Leering's policy-forming period, there is a discernible shift in focus from Paris to New York as a leading art center. That is moreover evident from Leering's exhibition program, in view of the solo exhibitions of artists such as Robert Indiana, Christo (1966), Robert Morris (1968), Donald Judd, Keith Sonnier, Andy Warhol (1970), Ad Reinhardt (1972), William Wiley and Bruce Nauman (1973). The *Kompas* (Compass) series reflects that shift as well: *Kompas III* (1967) was dedicated to New York, and the last of these exhibitions *Kompas IV* (1969) dealt with art from the American West Coast. Even so, Leering was not one-sided with respect to nationalities or centers of art, since he was among the few museum directors who also showed an interest in the current German art. This led to exhibitions of work by, for instance, Bernd and Hilla Becher, Joseph Beuys (1968) and Franz Erhard Walther (1972). That concern for German art would continue under Leering's successor Rudi Fuchs.

Despite a strong emphasis on contemporary art—stronger than had been the case with De Wilde—Leering also organized important historical retrospectives. With these he opted for artists whom he viewed as having renewed, present-day significance, such as

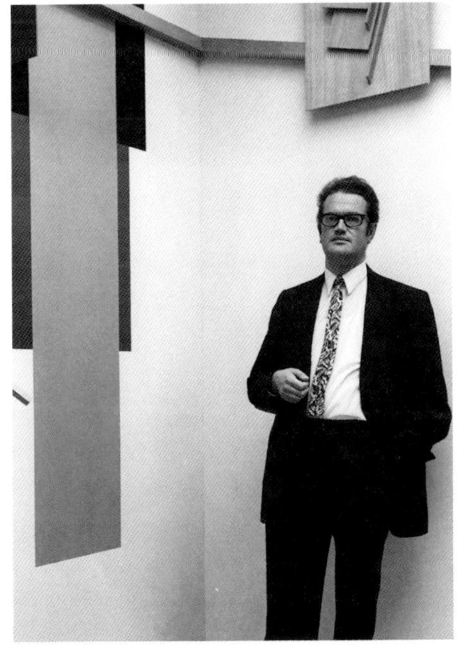
Jean Leering in the reconstruction of the **El Lissitzky** Prounraum

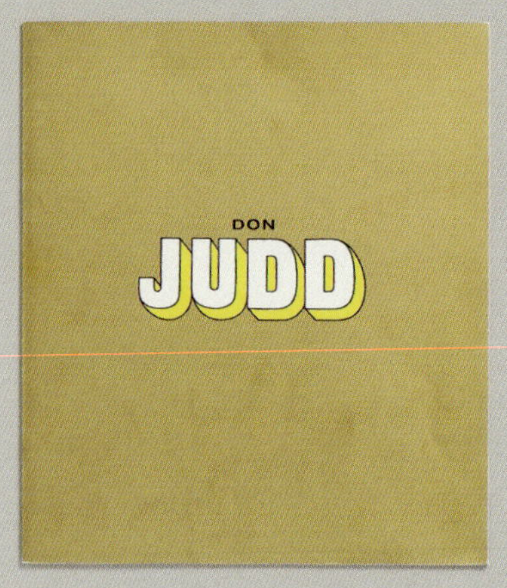
DON
JUDD

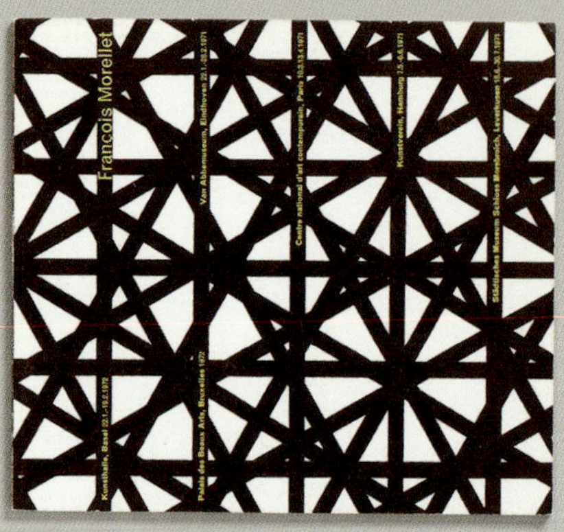
François Morellet

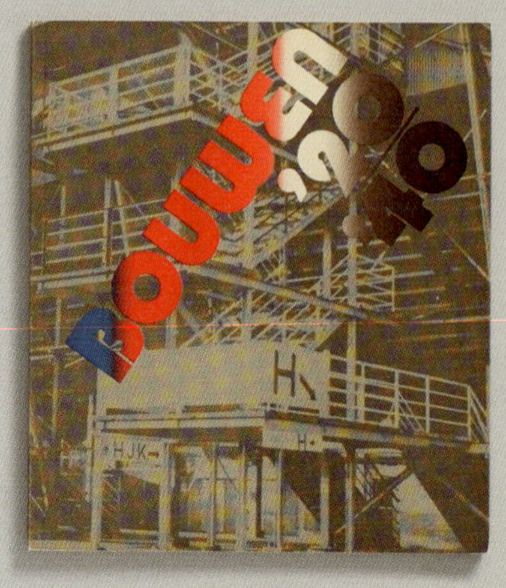
Bouwen?

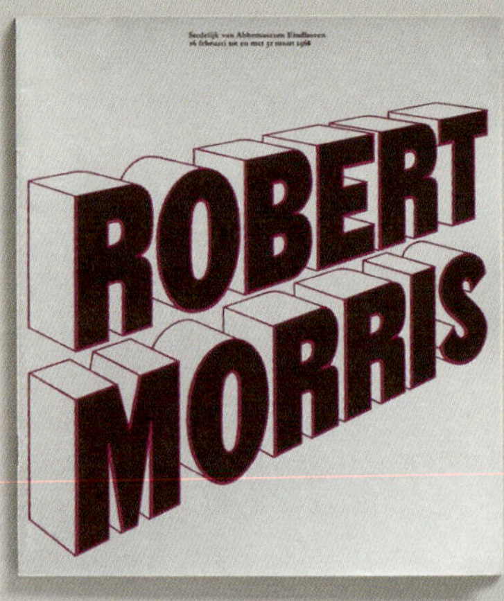
ROBERT
MORRIS

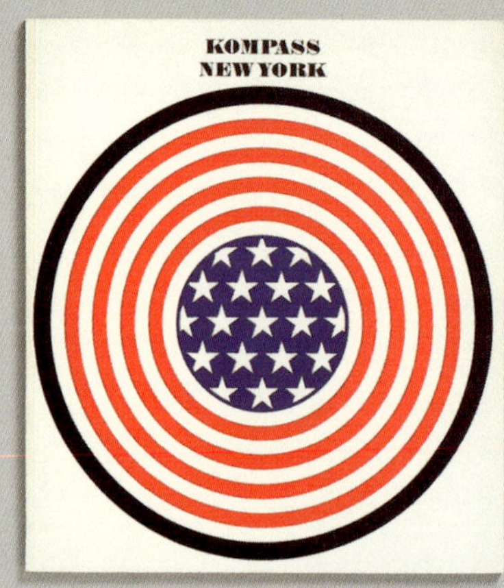
KOMPASS
NEW YORK

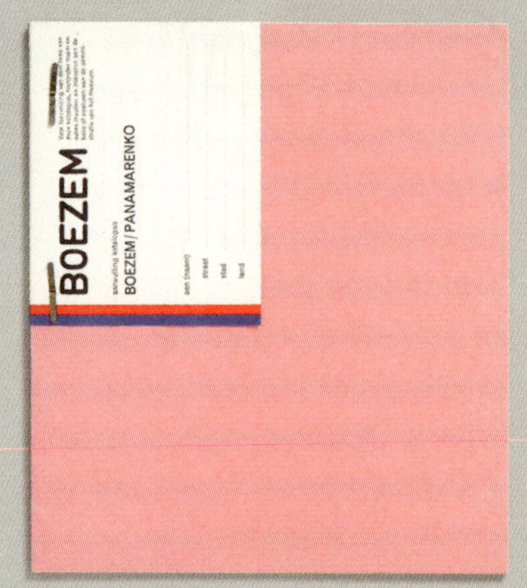
BOEZEM
BOEZEM / PANAMARENKO

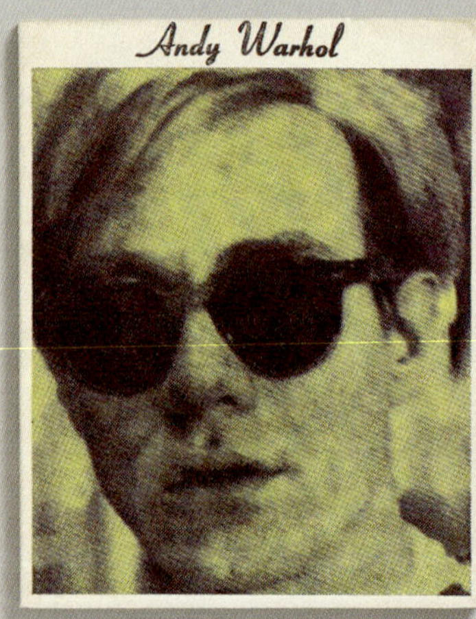
Andy Warhol

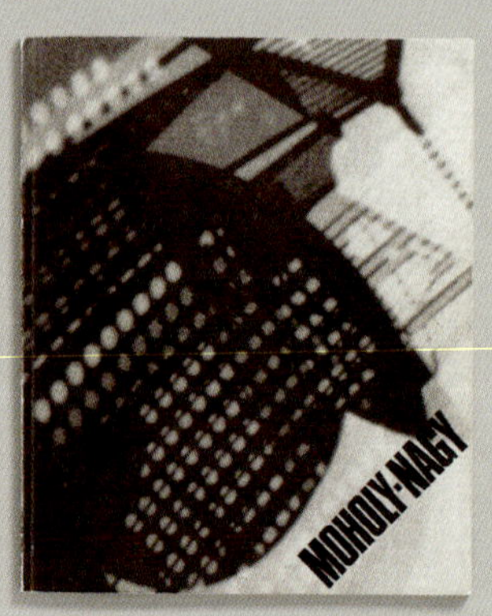
MOHOLY-NAGY

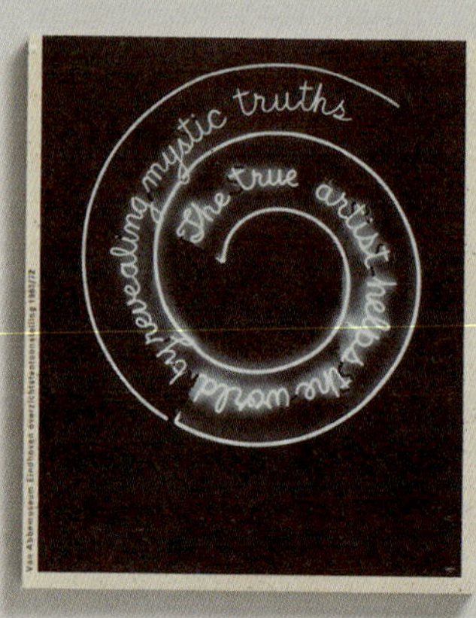
The true artist helps the world by revealing mystic truths

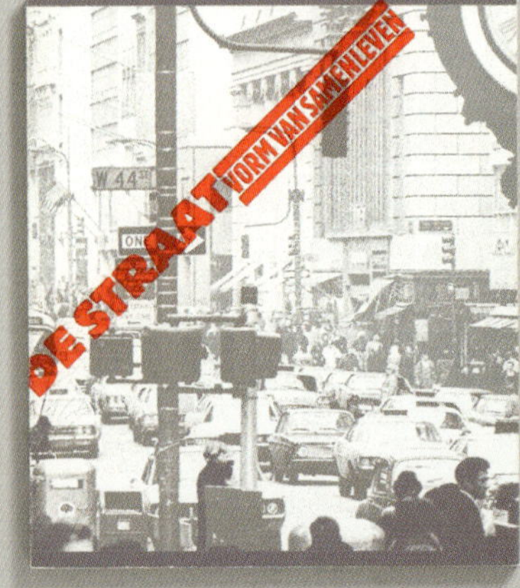
vordemberge
gildewart

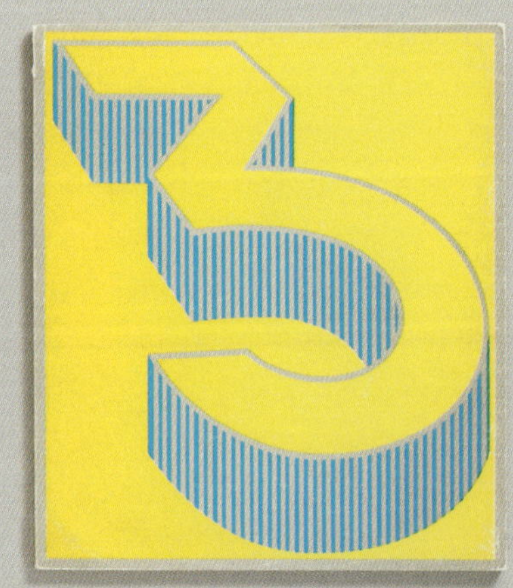
DE STRAAT TONY VAN SCHAYELIJK

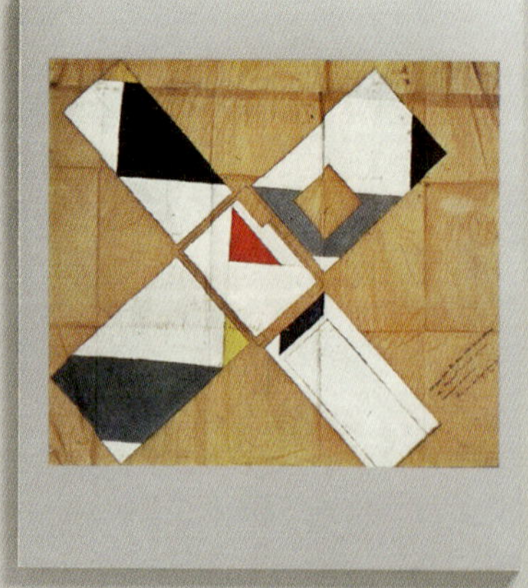

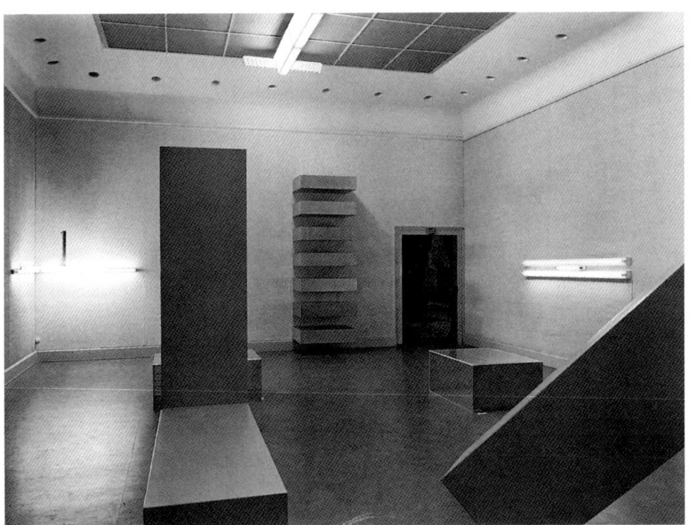

Installation view of works by Dan Flavin, Donald Judd and Robert Morris in the exhibition *Kompas III*, 1967

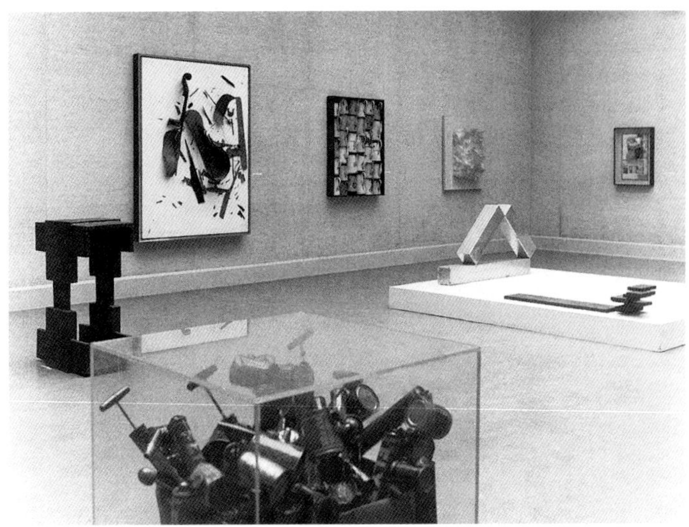

Installation view of the exhibition *Three Blind Mice, the collections Visser, Peeters, Becht*, 1968

'*Situaties Ambiances Environments*' held during the event **Museumfeest**, on September 2, 1967 under the auspices of the Eindhovense museumkring and organized by Jan Lanting and Paul Panhuysen.

Left page
Catalogues produced under the directorship of **Jean Leering**, designed by **Jan van Toorn**

Marcel Duchamp, El Lissitzky (1965), Francis Picabia (1967), László Moholy-Nagy, Theo van Doesburg (1968) and Vladimir Tatlin (1969). That idea–the actualization of history–was also expressed in his acquisition policy. According to Leering, the backgrounds of the most recent movements and tendencies were to be found particularly with De Stijl, Constructivism and Dada. By way of a focus on contemporary art, the collection was "kept open toward the future", while an acquisition policy aimed at the twenties and thirties, chiefly involving Constructivism, firmly anchored the modern movements. Furthermore, this caused De Wilde's 'transitional group' to become broader in scope. Among Leering's first purchases were works by Piero Manzoni, Yves Klein, Lucio Fontana, Heinz Mack, Otto Piene and Günther Uecker. Such acquisitions were not made without a struggle, though, for Leering did have to contend with unwilling members of the Supervisory Board and Advisory Committee just as De Wilde had done throughout his directorship. Then, in 1965, came the first painting by Morris Louis–the Van Abbemuseum was the first museum in Europe to acquire a work by this American artist–followed by work by Frank Stella, Ellsworth Kelly and Larry Poons. Pop Art and *nouveau réalisme* were represented with acquisitions of work by Jim Dine, Robert Indiana, Arman, Martial Raysse, Christo and Jean Tinguely. Parallel to the exhibition policy, the beginnings of a collection of Minimal Art could be seen as early as 1968, with works by Robert Morris, Dan Flavin and Donald Judd. As a result of agreements made during the solo exhibition of Joseph Beuys, *Voglie vedere i miei montagne* became, in 1972, the first large installation of his to be owned by a Dutch museum.

A highpoint in Leering's acquisition policy is, without a doubt, the purchase of eighty-six works by El Lissitzky from the Vordemberge-Leda collection in 1968. These works constituted the largest collection of work by this artist outside of Russia. The legacy of Constructivism and De Stijl–Leering also managed to acquire important work by Moholy-Nagy and Van Doesburg–was further extended by purchases of art by Richard Paul Lohse, Victor Vasarely, Friedrich Vordemberge-Gildewart, François Morellet, Peter Struycken, Ad Dekkers and others. Nor did Leering neglect the Dutch art of that time, for in addition to the last two artists mentioned, the collection also came to include Jan Schoonhoven, JCJ Vanderheyden, Ger van Elk and Jan Dibbets.

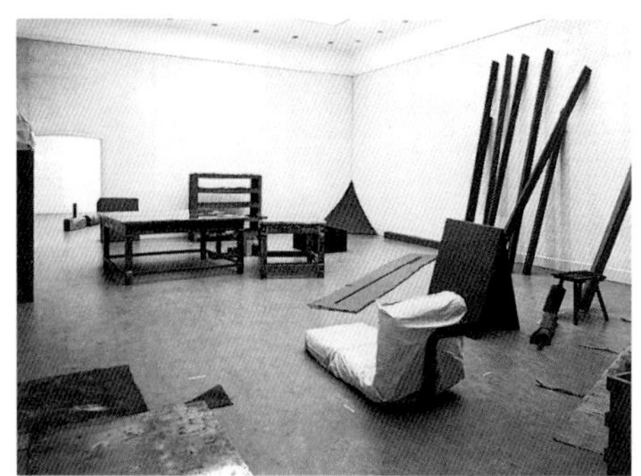

Installation view of the **Joseph Beuys** exhibition, 1968

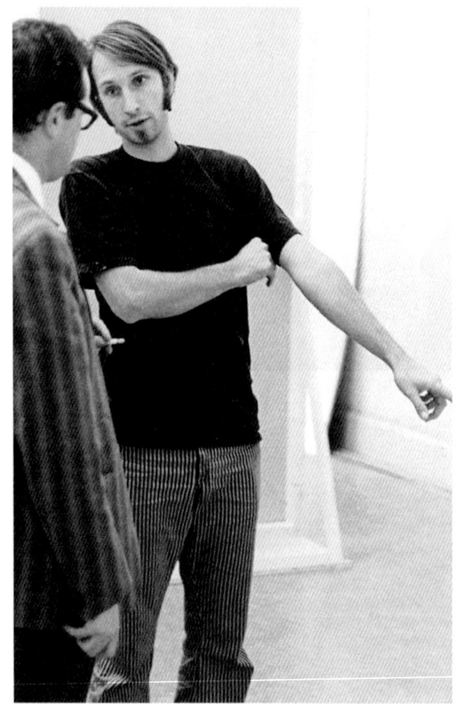

Jean Leering (left) speaking with **Bruce Nauman** during the installation of the exhibition *Kompas IV: Westcoast U.S.A.*, 1969

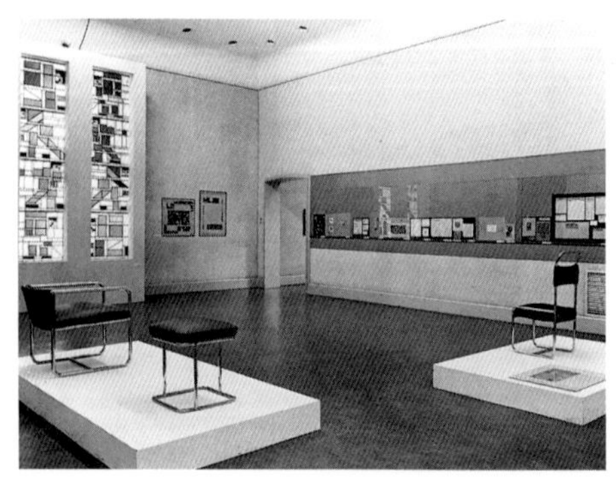

Installation view of the **Theo van Doesburg** exhibition, 1968-69

While Leering had problems with the Supervisory Board as a result of the Christo exhibition in 1966, he was indebted to that very exhibition for his invitation to become part of the organizing committee of *documenta 4* (Kassel, 1968). His prominent membership on this board confirmed his reputation as a progressive museum director with a very keen eye for contemporary art, but at the same time the *documenta* also proved to be a turning point for Leering. After the *documenta*, in Eindhoven, the museum's role in society would be underscored by him to an increasing degree. Certainly nothing new to Leering, the notion of social commitment was thoroughly consistent with the function that he ascribed to art: that of raising a consciousness of structures in reality.

Following the momentous year 1968, the movement advocating greater democratization gained impetus, and artists protested against the goverment's cultural policy. The bourgeois-elitist culture had lost its dominant position, and with this came a change in ideas concerning the 'distribution' of culture. Modern art, in his view, was to be assimilated with the notion of culture, a product of society: "It is no longer sufficient for the museum to be a forum for contemporary art, for it should enable the visitor to become aware of his cultural position within our dynamic society. And that involves conveying the social relevance of art."3

Leering advocated a museum focus on "collective creativity", that is to say "visual phenomena as consequences of (design) processes, which occur in society itself."4 Visual art was entirely linked with individual creativity, while the context of the arts and the problematics of those taking part in them were the main issues of collective creativity. The museum continued to be responsible for providing insight on the cultural context, also when this related to individual creativity. One of the means to achieve this was the 'parallel' exhibition, which enabled the viewer to establish a connection between the artistic problem and a similar situation in the day-to-day world. With the Warhol exhibition, for instance, Eindhoven's local newspaper was analyzed on the basis of Warhol-like traits. This was meant to heighten the impact of those traits on the everyday life of the viewer. During Leering's directorship, ample consideration was given to architecture, and he organized exhibitions on figures such as Adolf Loos (1965), Rob van 't Hoff (1967) and Hans Scharoun (1968). *Cityplan Eindhoven* (1969), dedicated to the urban plan for Eindhoven conceived by the firm Van den Broek en Bakema, dealt primarily with the design as a structural factor in the urban environment. This introduced a shift in focus, also with respect to presentations of architecture, from the individual design to its collective use. The idea that architecture and urban planning were entitled to a socially influential role was further developed with *Bouwen '20-'40. De Nederlandse bijdrage aan het Nieuwe Bouwen* (1971).

The exhibition most consistent with the museum's new function was, in Leering's view, *De Straat. Vorm van samenleven* (1972). The responsibility of the museum no longer being confined to aesthetic development, this exhibition focused on stimulating a public awareness of and participation in socio-cultural processes. As had been the case with *Bouwen '20-'40*, its compilation was placed in the hands of an interdisciplinary work group, as museum organizational policy had also become democratized to a certain degree. With that same goal in mind, Leering invited guest curators to compile five presentations of the collection.

Although there was certainly no intention to banish the expressions of individual artists from the museum, the precise way in which the relationship between collective and individual creativity was to take shape in museum policy remained unclear as yet. At the same time, his policymaking had reached an impasse during the summer of 1973, when his

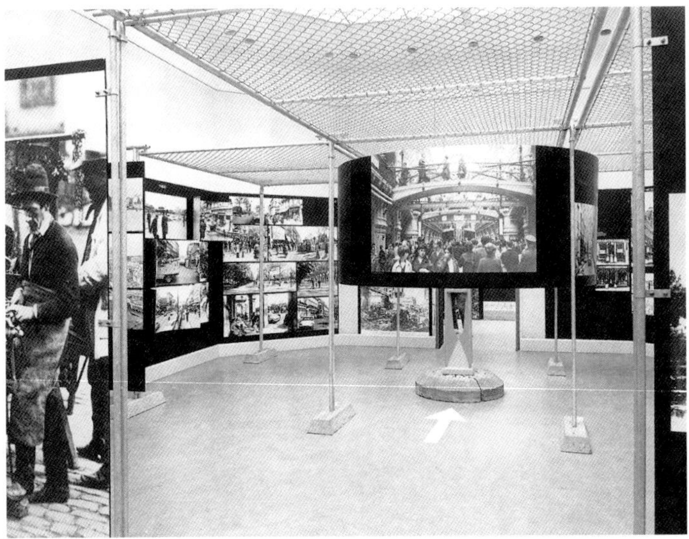

Installation view of the exhibition *De Straat*, 1972

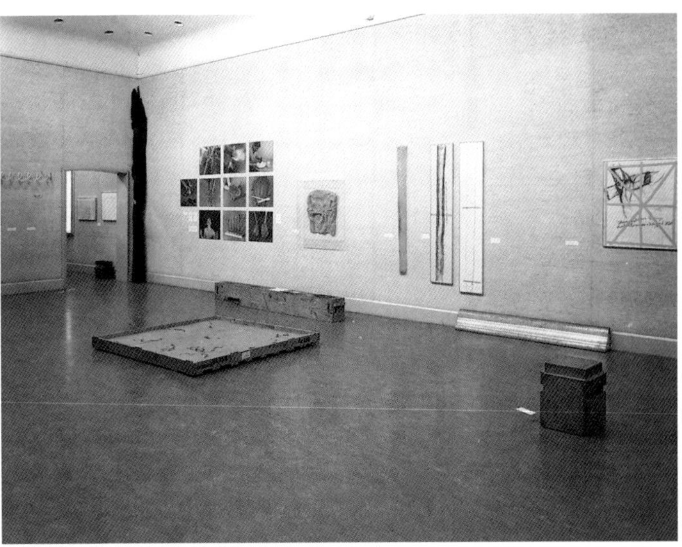

Installation view of the **Bruce Nauman** exhibition, 1973

ideas on the new function of the museum no longer appeared to correspond to those of the mayor and aldermen. Leering submitted his resignation and began as director of Amsterdam's Tropenmuseum on December 1, 1973. There he hoped to be able to give greater consideration to collective creativity.

Whereas De Wilde was considered an outright 'collector', for many years Leering was mainly associated with a directorship aimed at innovative exhibition policy. It was in that realm in particular that his ideas on the new responsibility of the museum were expressed, and that certainly contributed to such an impression. Nonetheless Leering, too, had an exceptionally good eye for quality, and he purchased key works for the collection, sometimes at a very early stage. Leering's socially committed museum policy was unique, and a wish to continue this was expressed within the museum. The question, however, was whether the municipal council held the same opinion.

1975-1987

Rudi Fuchs (1942) came to the helm on February 1, 1975. An art historian and art critic, he had been previously employed as a researcher at the Leidse Kunsthistorisch Instituut. Like De Wilde and Leering, he had never worked in a museum before, yet Fuchs would also develop into one of the leading museum directors of Europe, a position that would be officially recognized by way of his appointment as artistic director of *documenta 7* (Kassel, 1982).

Leering and Fuchs can be regarded as opposites with respect to their views on the function of the museum. For the latter, the prime concern was the autonomy of the art, and for that reason alone the museum could never be an instrument for social change. With the appointment of Fuchs, the municipality made clear to the outside world that it no longer wished to follow the change of course instigated by Leering. Staff members threatened to resign; they preferred Frans Haks (who would later become director of the Groninger Museum) for his commitment to the function of visual art within society. Fuch remained steadfast, and under his authority the points of departure were completely reversed. No longer did the emphasis lay with inspired ideas on 'visual services' and participation–the museum became a haven for 'pure' art.

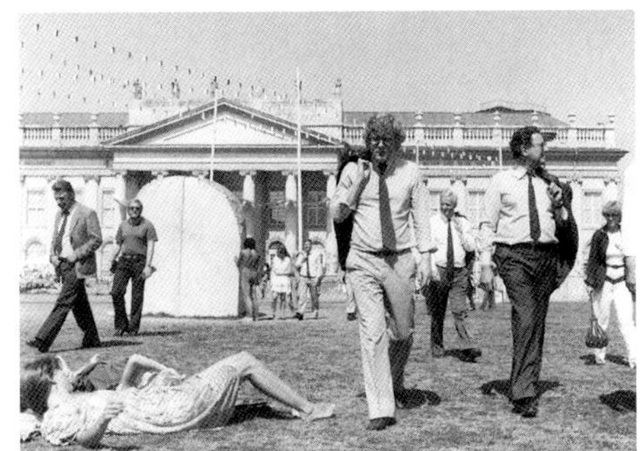

Rudi Fuchs at *documenta 7*, 1982

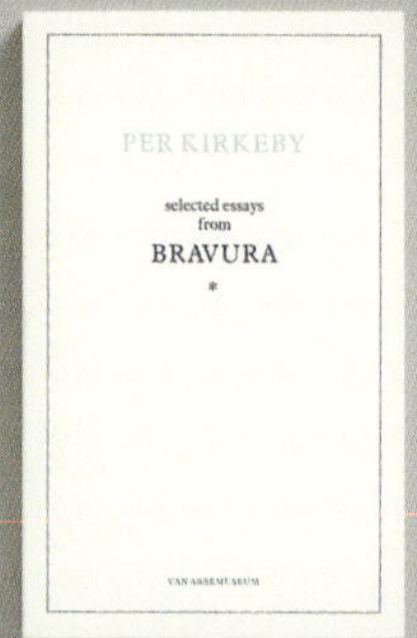
PER KIRKEBY
selected essays
from
BRAVURA
*
VAN ABBEMUSEUM

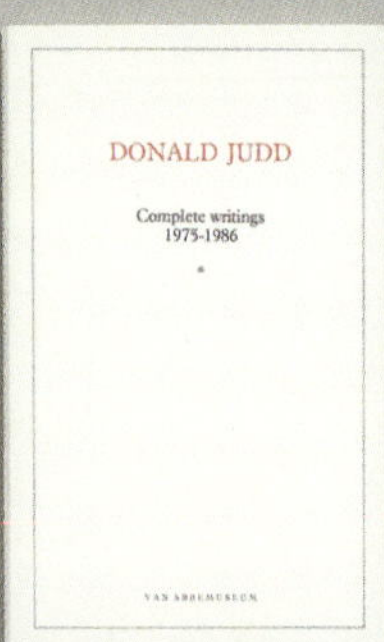
DONALD JUDD
Complete writings
1975-1986
*
VAN ABBEMUSEUM

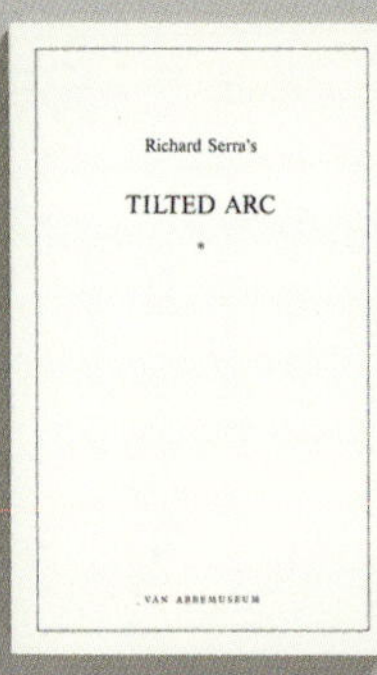
Richard Serra's
TILTED ARC
*
VAN ABBEMUSEUM

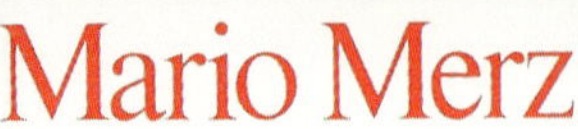
Mario Merz

ARMANDO
VAN ABBEMUSEUM EINDHOVEN

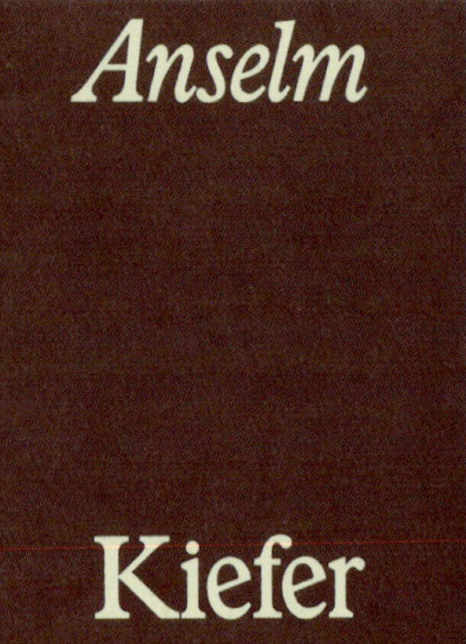
Anselm
Kiefer

Michael Asher

Mario Merz

Jannis Kounellis

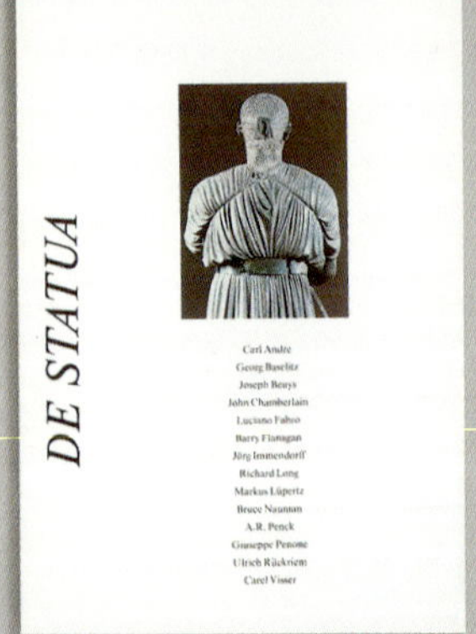
DE STATUA
Carl Andre
Georg Baselitz
Joseph Beuys
John Chamberlain
Luciano Fabro
Barry Flanagan
Jörg Immendorff
Richard Long
Markus Lüpertz
Bruce Nauman
A.R. Penck
Giuseppe Penone
Ulrich Rückriem
Carel Visser

. . . wir betrachteten, wie die Sonne, die kurz
vorher und rund um sich her auch noch von dicken
Regenwolken überzogen war, sich mitten über dem
Meer eine etwas dünnere Stelle wie ein Loch
hineingeschienen hatte. Sie warf ein weiß-
glänzendes Licht auf die Küste der Insel Hven,
ferner ein etwas blässeres auf die schwedische
Küste; einige weiße Segel wurden hell beleuchtet.
Die ganze Natur schien den einen Punkt wie in
Triumph hervorzuheben; alles trat in einen
schwärzlichen Wolkenschatten zurück, und nur
dieses einzelne war wie durch Vorsatz
unbeschreiblich schön und stark erhellt . . .
Uit het Noorden
Edvard Munch / Asger Jorn /
Per Kirkeby

LE CORBEAU ET LE RENARD. LE CORBEAU SONNE. LE PEINTRE EST
ABSENT. LE RENARD SONNE. L'ARCHITECTE EST ABSENT. MÊME
JEU. LE CORBEAU ET LE RENARD SONT ABSENTS. JE ME SOUVIENS
D'EUX, MAIS À PEINE. J'AI OUBLIÉ LES PATTES ET LES MAINS, LES
JEUX ET LES COSTUMES, LES VOIX ET LES CRIS, LA FOURBERIE ET
LA VANITÉ. LE PEINTRE ÉTAIT TOUT COULEURS. L'ARCHITECTE ÉTAIT
EN PIERRE. LE CORBEAU ET LE RENARD ÉTAIENT DE CARACTÈRES
IMPRIMÉS. LE SYSTÈME D. IL Y AVAIT DU CHIEN JUSQUE DANS
LA FOULE. IL PLEUVAIT SUR L'AGORA. L'AGORA ÉTAIT BONDÉE. IL Y
AVAIT UN CHIEN VERT, UN CHIEN ROUGE, UN CHIEN BLANC, UN
CHIEN NOIR ET BLEU, DE CARACTÈRE IMPRIMÉ. JE ME SOUVIENS
D'EUX, MAIS À PEINE. LE RENARD SONNE. LE CORBEAU SONNE.
works from the collection of Annick and Anton Herbert

Christa Dichgans
Lili Dujourie
Marlene Dumas
Lesley Foxcroft
Kees de Goede
Frank van Hemert
Cristina Iglesias
Harald Klingelhöller
Mark Luyten
Juan Muñoz
Katherine Porter
Julião Sarmento
Barbara Schmidt Heins
Gabriele Schmidt-Heins
Didier Vermeiren

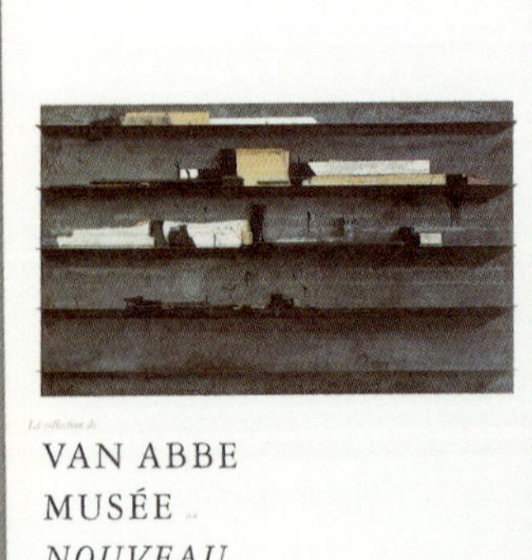
VAN ABBE
MUSÉE
NOUVEAU
MUSÉE

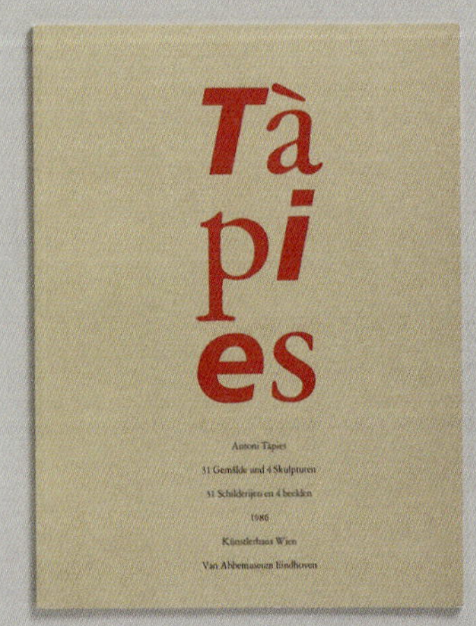
Tà
pi
es
Antoni Tàpies
51 Gemälde und 4 Skulpturen
51 Schilderijen en 4 beelden
1989
Künstlerhaus Wien
Van Abbemuseum Eindhoven

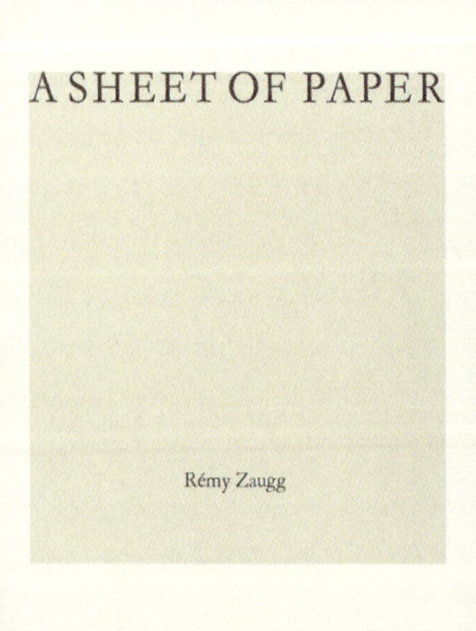
A SHEET OF PAPER
Rémy Zaugg

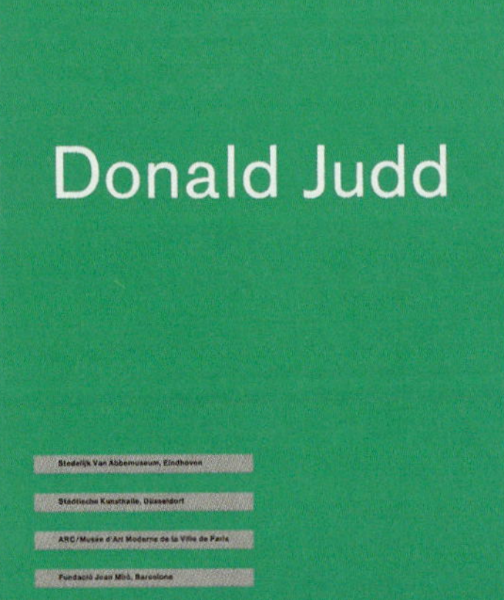
Donald Judd
Stedelijk Van Abbemuseum, Eindhoven
Städtische Kunsthalle, Düsseldorf
ARC/Musée d'Art Moderne de la Ville de Paris
Fundació Joan Miró, Barcelona

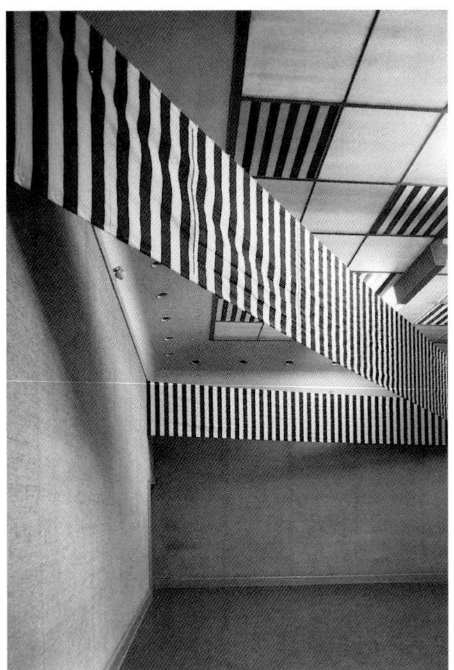

Installation view of the **Daniel Buren** exhibition *Ailleurs/Elders*, 1976

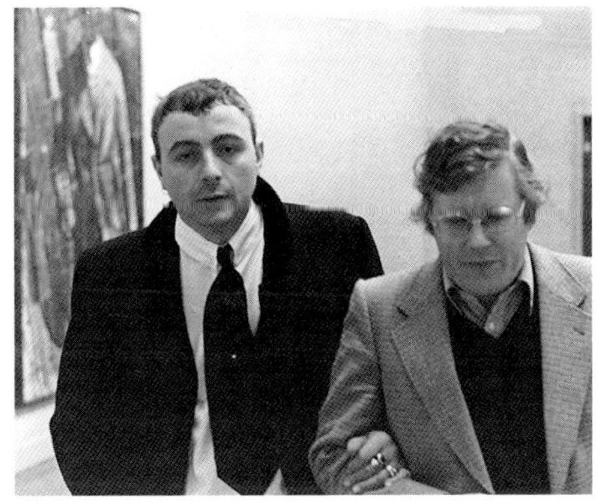

Markus Lüpertz (left) and **Rudi Fuchs** at the opening of the solo exhibition *Markus Lüpertz*, 1977

Catalogues produced under the directorship of **Rudi Fuchs**, designed by **Walter Nikkels**

Ironically, a government memorandum happened to ratify the educational responsibility of Dutch museums in 1976, precisely when the education department of the Van Abbemuseum, which had thrived under Leering, was dissolved. In a certain sense, this was illustrative of Fuchs's policy at that time in view of the fact that the 'socialization' of museums was perhaps most clearly expressed in government emphasis on education as part of socio-cultural development. Contrary to the Leering period, when reaching the public was an essential notion, that of Fuchs was marked by the idea that the loyalty of the museum lay primarily with the art and the artist. The museum could do nothing more than provide "the most exact information, on the circumstances related to the production of a work–so that the work becomes as clearly visible as possible."[5]

While the change of directors in 1964 was accompanied by a shift of focus from Europe to the United States, there now came a shift in the opposite direction: Fuchs became more and more convinced of the wealth of European artistic tradition, which was characterized by countless regional variants. He emphatically made it his task not to confine himself to the dominant 'international style'–the modernist canon which seemed to reach its culmination for the time being in the new American art–but also to draw on other sources, initially less familiar to him. He found these, for the most part, in the southern and central part of Europe, among artists who were literally and figuratively operating on the fringes of modernism. That idea was the basis for his interest in German painters such as Penck, Lüpertz, Baselitz, Immendorff and Kiefer, the *arte povera* artists Giovanni Anselmo, Mario Merz and Jannis Kounellis and the Austrians Arnulf Rainer, Hermann Nitsch and Günter Brus.

The Van Abbemuseum functioned, in Fuchs's view, as an 'arena' where occasionally antithetical ideas on art, ranging from Minimal Art and Conceptual Art to the expressive German painting, were to confront each other. This was an ambitious venture: a 'dialogue' could open up new roads in art. Fuchs's introduction of German painting was considered controversial, because some–including artists exhibiting at the Van Abbemuseum–saw this as a reactionary tendency from an artistic point of view. A guide and interlocutor throughout the rediscovery of this 'other' Europe was Johannes Gachnang, appointed director of the Kunsthalle Bern in 1974. At the end of 1975 Fuchs took over Gachnang's solo exhibition of work by A.R. Penck, and that was the start of a both practical and ideological collaboration. This link was so solid that some began referring to the 'Eindhoven-Bern axis', though frequently London's Whitechapel Art Gallery, headed by Nicholas Serrota, was involved in the joint projects. Quite clearly, the preoccupation with European sensibilities was inspired by the supremacy of American art; European art was imbued with the weight of history, and that is what determined part of its quality.

Whereas De Wilde and Leering were forced, during the early stages of their directorships, to defend their plans for the collection at board meetings, Fuchs scarcely had any problems in that respect. To an even greater extent than Leering, he concentrated on current art, also because the prices on the art market had soared explosively around the time of his arrival and thereby eliminated the possibility of a continued expansion of the historical 'base'. Initially, Fuchs focused on purchases and exhibitions of Conceptual Art–something which, unnoticed by Leering, was viewed by him as being the leading tendency of that time. Over the years this grew into a respectable series including Lawrence Weiner, Daniel Buren, Ian Wilson, Stanley Brouwn, Michael Asher, Robert Barry, Jan Dibbets, Niele Toroni, Joseph Kosuth, Douglas Huebler, On Kawara and John Baldessari. The innovative contributions of British artists in the realm of sculpture were reflected in exhibi-

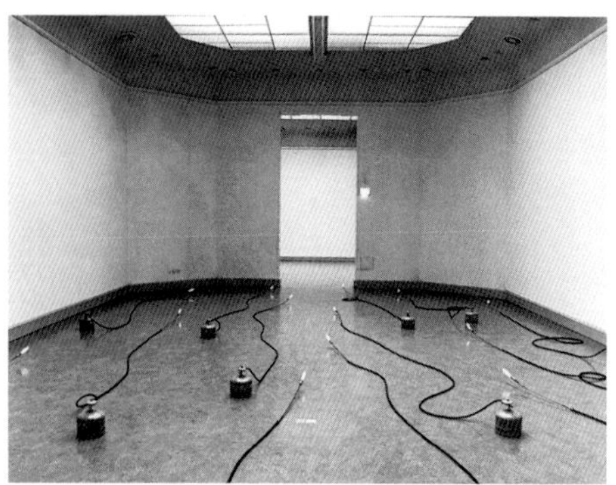

Installation view of the **Jannis Kounellis** exhibition, 1981-82

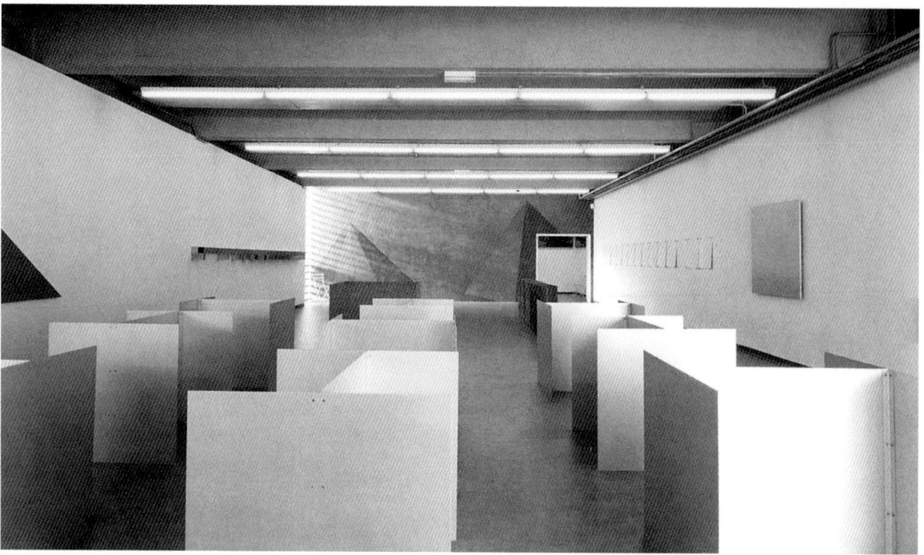

Installation view of the exhibition *Eye Level* at Van Abbe II, 1986

tions and purchases of work by Hamish Fulton, Richard Long, Barry Flanagan and Gilbert & George. In addition to this, the collection of Minimal Art set up by Leering was further developed with acquisitions from Sol LeWitt, Carl Andre, Dan Flavin, Donald Judd and Ulrich Rückriem. In 1977 the more Eurocentric vision began to emerge, first with exhibitions and acquisitions of work by the previously mentioned German painters. The work of Merz, Kounellis, Anselmo and Paolini followed as of 1980, and in 1983 Fuchs's interest in Austrian art started to become visible in the collection. The general premise of the collection policy remained consistent with that of his predecessors: the purchase of individual works of a very high quality, which could provide an impression—albeit incomplete—of the most significant artistic developments of the twentieth century.

Fuchs's directorship was marked by a prominent trend involving theme exhibitions, in which artists were dealt with on the basis of their attitudes and not on the basis of style or formal points of departure. Exhibitions such as *De Statua* (1983), *Uit het Noorden* (1984), *Don Giovanni, Het ijzeren venster* (1985) and *Regenboog* (1987) demonstrated this principle. Fuchs also implemented this idea with presentations of the collection and with *documenta 7*. This approach was intended as a means releasing works from their 'stylistic security' and offering an alternative to the linear model of development and presentation that neatly corresponded to the dialectic notion of culture. Moreover, it was the theme exhibitions, reflecting a great concern for the quality of the individual work of art, which frequently showed Fuchs to have sharp instincts where the installation of work was concerned. He himself preferred to call this the *mise en scène*. The fact that his approach caused artworks and artists to be separated from their (historical) contexts was, for him, not a valid criticism. The very issue was to create *current* possibilities, by which the work of art would boosted and given new meaning. De Wilde's *École de Paris* collection, for instance, was placed in a different light by the paintings of Baselitz, which in turn happened to show connections with the work of Kurt Schwitters. In 1986, however, Fuchs managed to acquire the Schwitters work *Isle of Man* (1941), one of the few historical purchases to be made during his directorship. This would, in his view, provide a basis for the somewhat rootless German painting in the collection.

In 1986 a large part of the collection was being shown in connection with the museum's fiftieth anniversary under the title *Ooghoogte* (Eye Level). This exhibition—on display at three locations—actually underscored the chronic lack of space that had existed for years. Since 1956 the expansion of the museum had been under official consideration, but this was continually postponed, mainly due to the financial priorities of the municipality. A new wing had indeed been realized at the back of the Kropholler building in December 1978. But this had always been meant to serve as a temporary accomodation. A 'collection museum', which Fuchs preferred, was consistent with his wish for deceleration and introspection; to an increasing degree, the present-day art business, with its ever-changing exhibitions and fondness for 'new' and young artists, was regarded by him as being too hectic and fashionable.

Because Fuchs distanced himself more and more from the current scene and, at the same time, displayed unconditional loyalty to 'his' artists, his policy gradually received more criticism in the media throughout the course of the eighties. In a certain sense, that was a logical consequence of his way of working. "Partisanship is the issue in the art world. You're for something or you're against something. When you're for something, you have to propagate it fervently, and the museum is an instrument for this," he had already said in 1978.[6] That same outlook would also be demonstrated by him after 1987 as director of the Haags Gemeentemuseum, a position that he gave up in 1993 to become director of the Stedelijk Museum in Amsterdam.

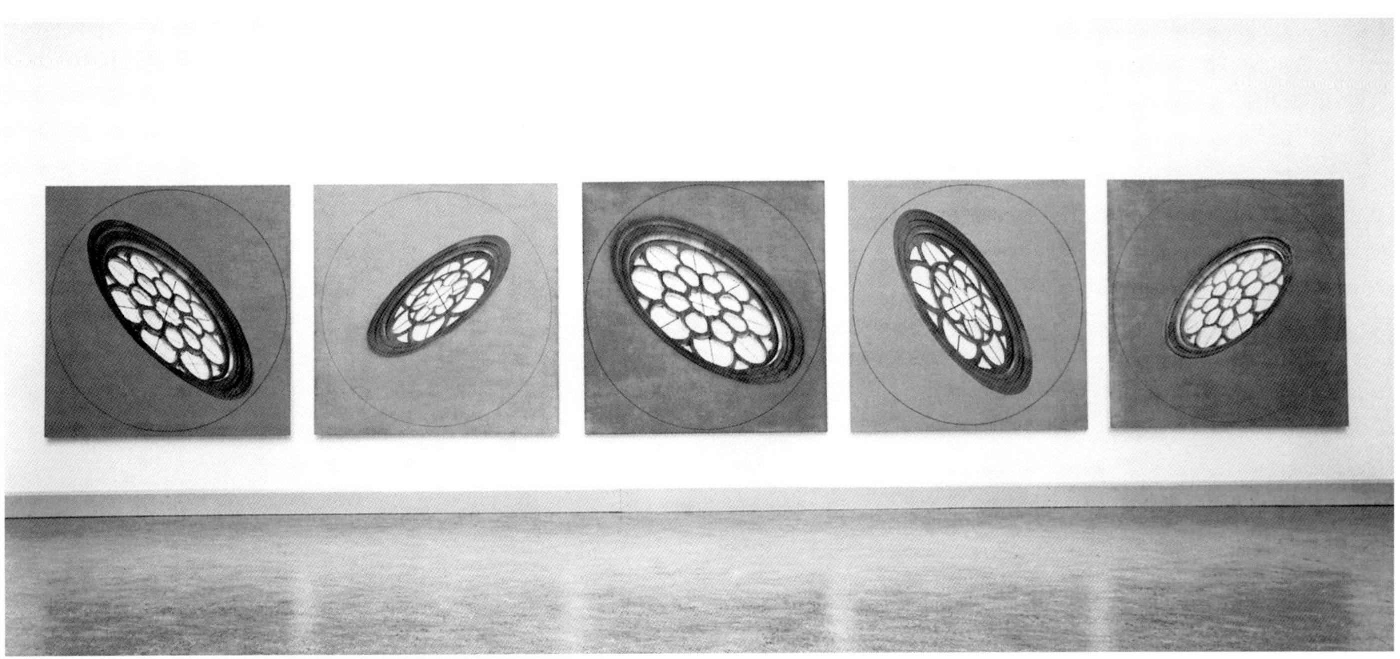

Installation view of the **Jan Dibbets** exhibition, 1988-89

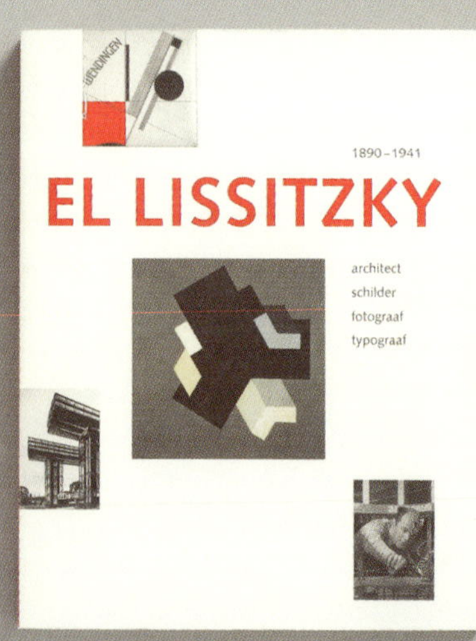

EL LISSITZKY
1890–1941
architect
schilder
fotograaf
typograaf

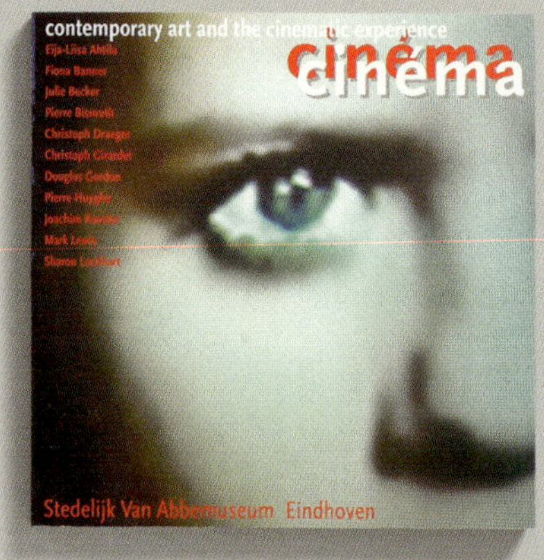

contemporary art and the cinematic experience
cinéma cinéma
Eija-Liisa Ahtila
Fiona Banner
Julie Becker
Pierre Bismuth
Christoph Draeger
Christoph Girardet
Douglas Gordon
Pierre Huyghe
Joachim Koester
Mark Lewis
Sharon Lockhart
Stedelijk Van Abbemuseum Eindhoven

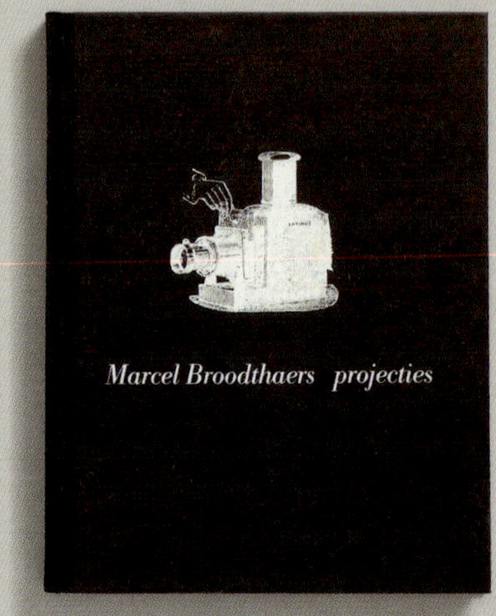

Marcel Broodthaers   projecties

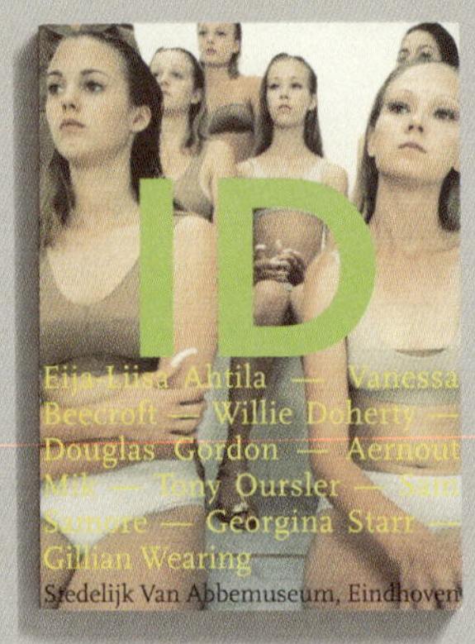

ID
Eija-Liisa Ahtila — Vanessa
Beecroft — Willie Doherty —
Douglas Gordon — Aernout
Mik — Tony Oursler — Sam
Samore — Georgina Starr —
Gillian Wearing
Stedelijk Van Abbemuseum, Eindhoven

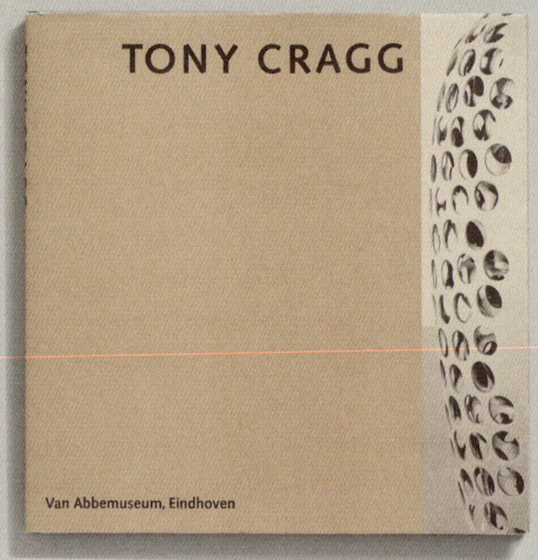

TONY CRAGG
Van Abbemuseum, Eindhoven

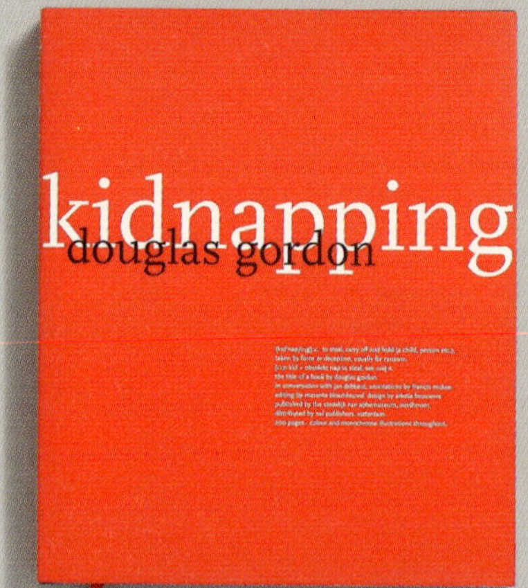

kidnapping
douglas gordon

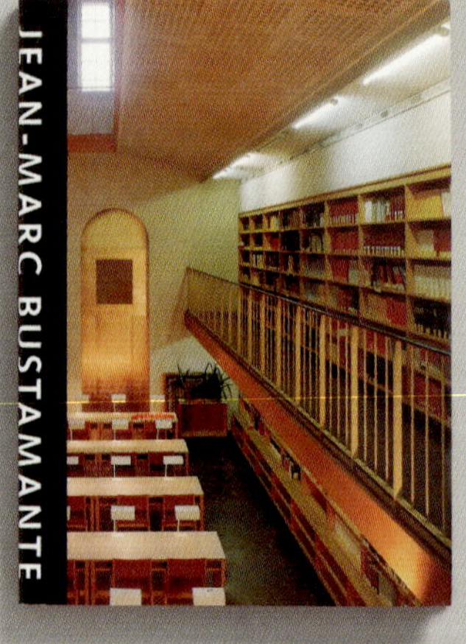

JEAN-MARC BUSTAMANTE

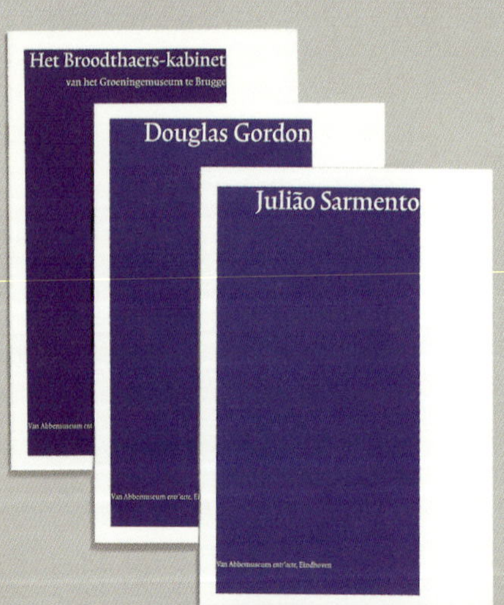

Het Broodthaers-kabinet
van het Groeningemuseum te Brugge
Douglas Gordon
Julião Sarmento
Van Abbemuseum, Eindhoven

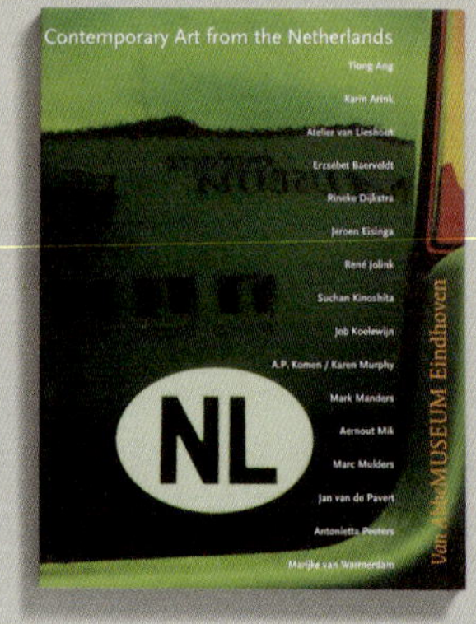

Van Abbemuseum Eindhoven
een
collectie
is ook
maar een
mens
Edy de Wilde
Jean Leering
Rudi Fuchs
Jan Debbaut
over verzamelen

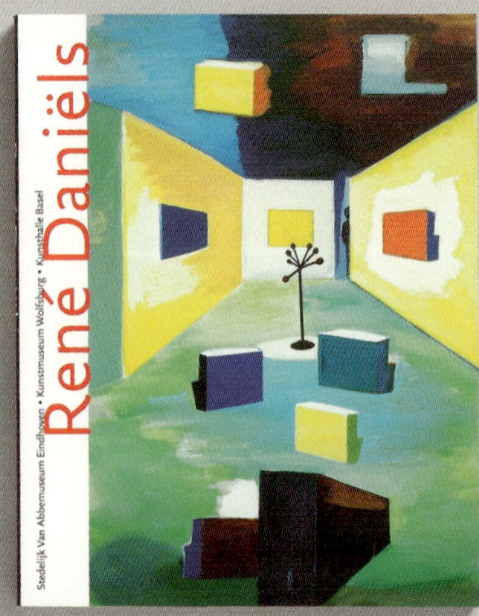

Rene Daniëls
Stedelijk Van Abbemuseum Eindhoven • Kunstmuseum Wolfsburg • Kunsthalle Basel

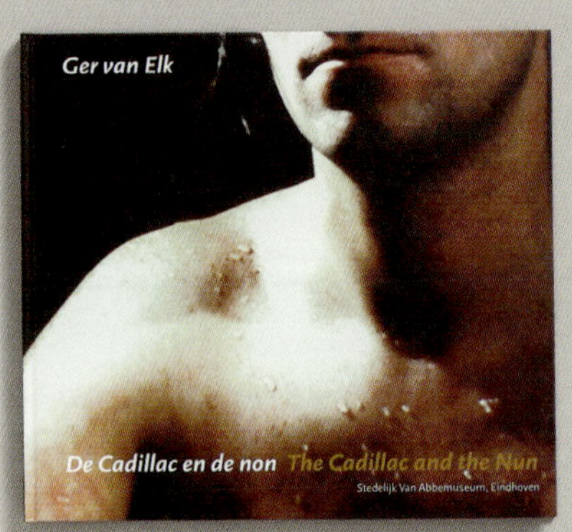

Ger van Elk
De Cadillac en de non   The Cadillac and the Nun
Stedelijk Van Abbemuseum, Eindhoven

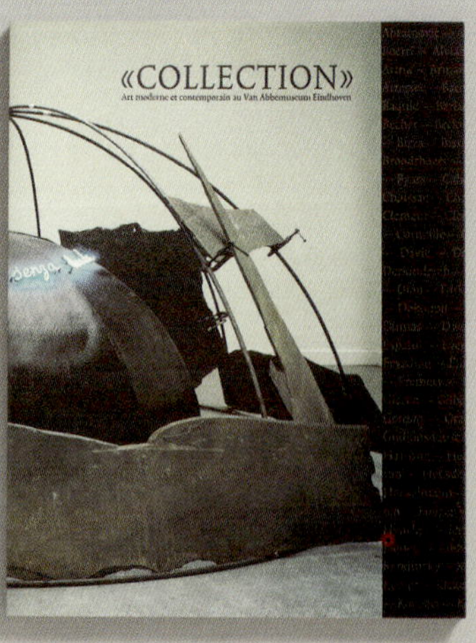

«COLLECTION»
Het moderne en eigentijdse in het Van Abbemuseum Eindhoven

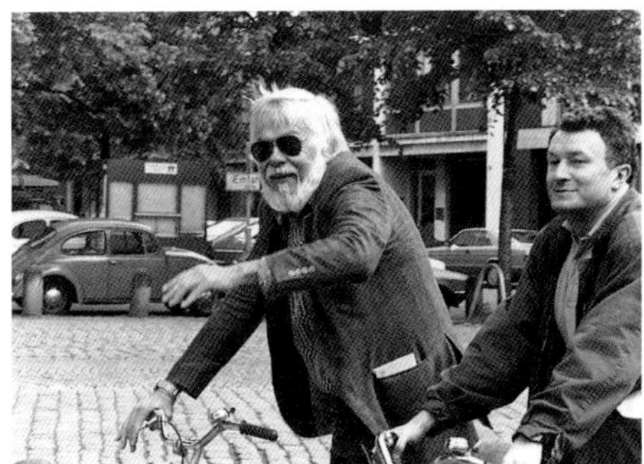

John Baldessari (left) and **Jan Debbaut** at the exhibition
Skulptur Projekte Münster, Münster, 1987

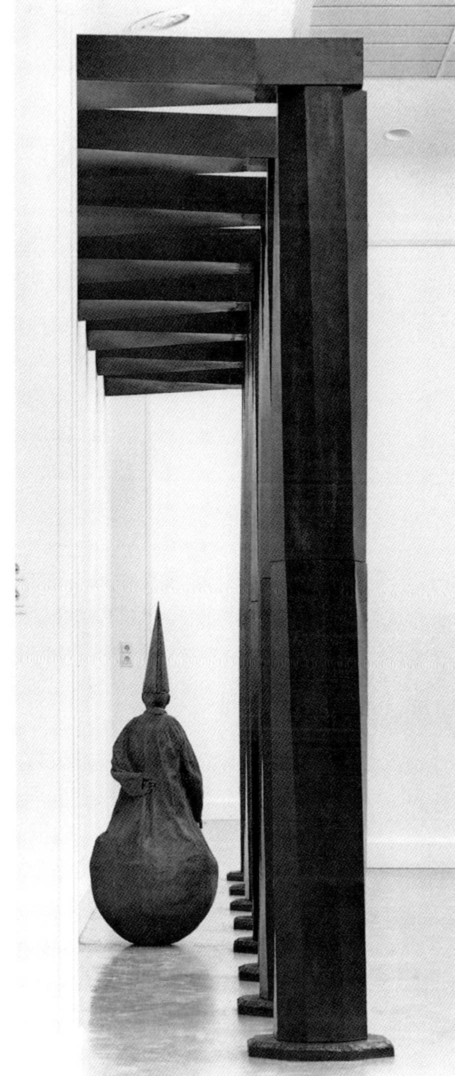

Installation view of the **Juan Muñoz** exhibition, 1991-92

1988-

Jan Debbaut (1949) was appointed to become Fuchs's successor as of January 1, 1988. Debbaut was an old friend of the museum; before assuming a position as director general of the society for exhibitions of the Brussels Paleis voor Schone Kunsten in 1986, he had been employed at the Van Abbemuseum, first as a curator and later also as deputy director.

As far as artistic choices were concerned, Debbaut followed the method that had been well tested in Eindhoven: in 1988 he, too, broke with the policy of his predecessor. After Fuchs had initially compensated for the lack of Conceptual Art and *arte povera*, he, like De Wilde, began to develop an increasingly distinct preference for painting. Debbaut opted, as Fuchs did, for artists of his own generation, but in his view the major artistic problems had shifted from painting to the 'metamorphosis of the object'. This could be seen in a series of exhibitions and purchases of work by artists scarcely known in the Netherlands, such as Tony Cragg, Allan McCollum, Rodney Graham (1989), Harald Klingelhöller, Jan Vercruysse, Thomas Schütte (1990), Juan Muñoz (1991), Jean-Marc Bustamante and Niek Kemps (1992). Not forming a coherent group with a particular style, these choices can be regarded as sharing, at most, a common attitude. In a 1999 interview Debbaut put it as follows: "The depletion of modernism could be felt, and at the end of the eighties an enormous inflation of the art market began. That led to the marketing and 'media-hyping' of postmodernism, just say 'art à la Jeff Koons'. For me, that was too anecdotal and too artificial. The artists of my generation with whom I had an affinity avoided that very media-hype. They attempted to articulate, in an artistic sense, what sort of place or position the object could have, in art or even just in general, each in his own way and within that changing artistic context."[7]

A younger generation of Dutch artists had already been exhibiting under the directorship of Fuchs, and by way of exhibitions and acquisitions Debbaut hoped to renew contacts with René Daniëls, Marlene Dumas, Henk Visch and Pieter Laurens Mol. In connection with the previously mentioned international 'group', the work of Niek Kemps was acquired as well. Resumed consideration was also given to Conceptual Art, and this led to memorable exhibitions on Hanne Darboven, Marcel Broodthaers (1992) and Dan Graham (1993). To a greater extent than Fuchs, Debbaut aimed to fill the existing gaps in the collection. His first purchase was *T-junction* (1998) by Richard Serra, one of the ten room-sized works specially produced for his solo exhibition in Eindhoven. In 1993 this was followed by the Marcel Broodthaers's *Tapis de Sable* (1974) and, later on, retrospective purchases of art by John Baldessari, Bruce Nauman, Ulay & Abramović, Jan Dibbets, Stanley Brouwn and Ger van Elk. The first historical exhibition in more than ten years, dedicated to the work of El Lissitzky, was also held in 1990. With the purchase of a painting by El Lissitzky, *Proun P23 no. 6* (1919) in 1997, a long-cherished wish of Leering had been fulfilled.

Parallel to the development of his artistic policy, Debbaut concentrated on the realization of the new building from 1988 onward. From the very start, he maintained that concurrent activities—a (semi)permanent presentation of the collection along with the organization of changing exhibitions—would be essential, seeing that the museum would otherwise lose its pioneering status on an international level. Since the second half of the seventies, there had been a boom in the construction of museums and art centers within the Netherlands and abroad. The first of these were not very inspiring, as many of them, in Debbaut's view, amounted to high-priced architectonic packaging with very little content. In Eindhoven, on the other hand, an exceptionally high-quality collection had been

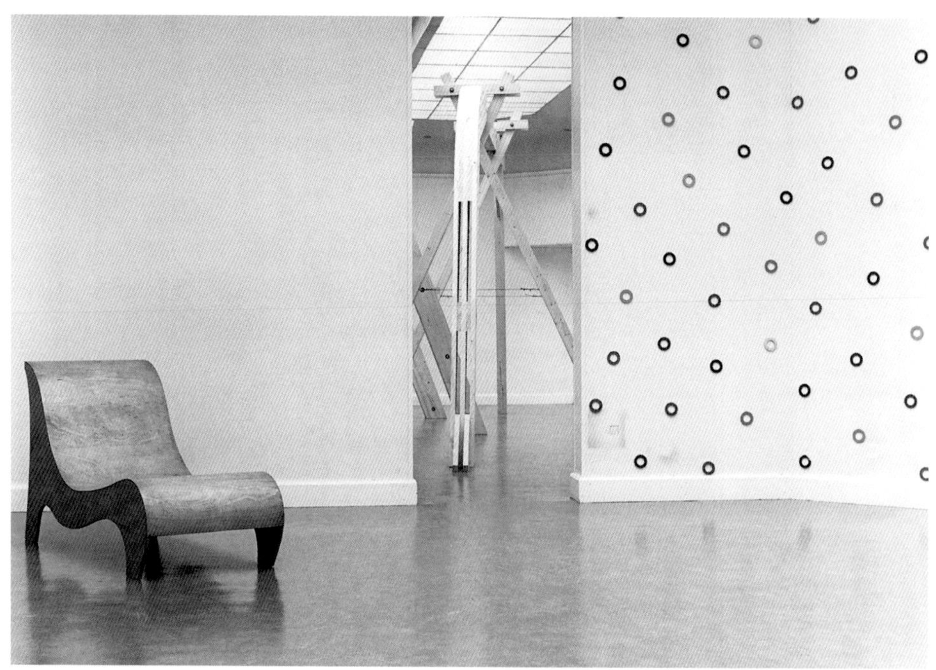

Installation view of the **Thomas Schütte** exhibition, 1990

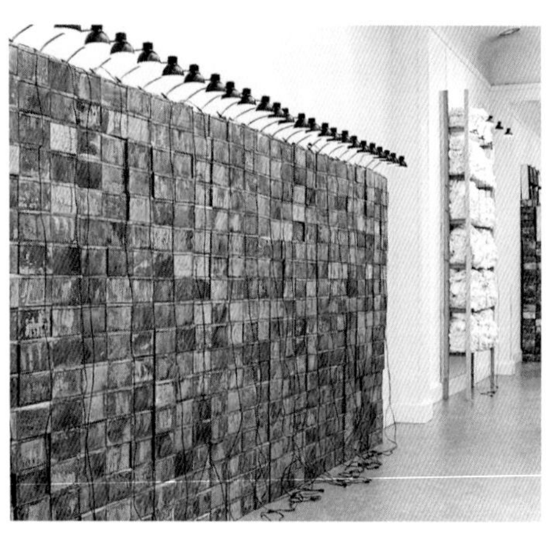

Installation view of the **Christian Boltanski** exhibition, 1990

formed within fifty years, but for at least twenty of those years, the decision-making related to an expansion of the museum's scale as well as a structural increase in the acquisition and exhibition budgets had stagnated. Should the Van Abbemuseum wish to strengthen its progressive position within the changing museum sector, Debbaut argued, an improvement of the accomodations, operation and approach to the public would be an absolute necessity.

As evident from the explicit choices made by successive directors, the museum's small size initially posed no major obstacles to a maintenance of its pioneering role. But as the collection had grown and as proportionally less and less of the collection could be shown, the direct relationship between the collection and the exhibition policies threatened to disintegrate. In Debbaut's view, the collection should be seen as a 'natural breeding ground' against which new developments, presented in changing exhibitions, can be evaluated. In that sense De Wilde's time-honored adage "the collection is the cork on which the museum floats" has lost none of its validity.

Partly as a result of an ambitious investment plan by Debbaut, the years of deadlock had been overcome, and in January 1990 the municipal council expressed its support for a continued development of the museum. One month later the Amsterdam architect Abel Cahen received the assignment to draw up a rough plan for the new building. This did not bring an end to the problems, however. In his design, presented in June 1991, Cahen had opted for an expansion in terms of height, partly in order to maintain the much-praised routing and spatial effect of Kropholler's interior. Various staggered levels were placed on the old building, while a vertical glass shaft and two glass veranda-like constructions were added on the front side as components introducing visual form.

Although the municipal council made credit available for the realization of this design in 1992, construction never began. Through a series of lawsuits initiated by three action groups which fought for the preservation of the Kropholler building, the museum was declared a national monument in 1996. This put an end to Cahen's design once and for

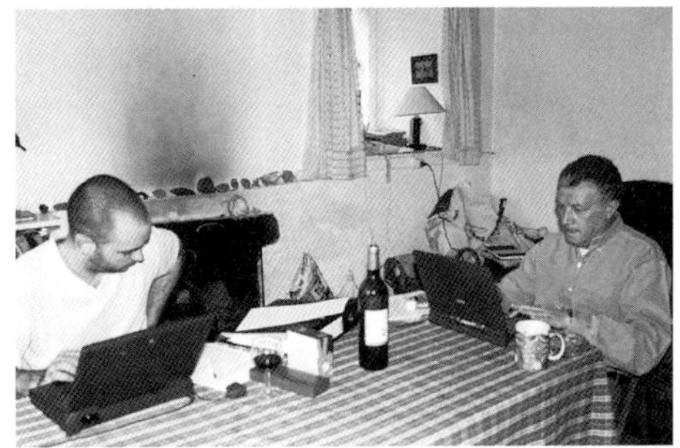

Douglas Gordon (left) and Jan Debbaut during preparations for the publication *Kidnapping*, Inveraray, Scotland, March, 1997

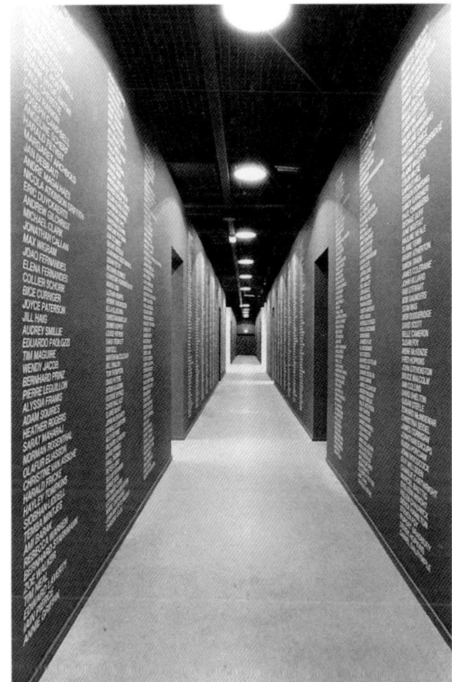

ID exhibition, 1996-97
Douglas Gordon, *List of Names*, 1990-ongoing

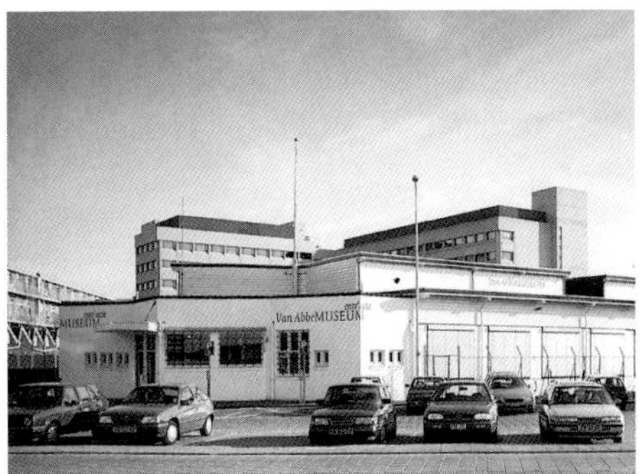

Temporary accomodations of the museum on the Vonderweg, 1995-2002

all. The main objection of those opposing the plan related to the way in which this would affect the building's exterior. In terms of public opinion, the tower had rapidly grown into a nostalgic symbol for all of the characteristic buildings that had been demolished in Eindhoven since the 1960s.

In anticipation of the new building, the museum had moved to a temporary location–the former Philips personnel store on the Vonderweg–as of January 1, 1995. The stay at this location, under the slogan *Van AbbeMUSEUM entr'acte*, was intended for a maximum of two years, but due to new setbacks in connection with the new building, that extended into a period of at least seven years. During that time, a second design by Cahen–providing an expansion, partially below ground level, toward the back and side of the Kropholler building–was approved and executed.

Until the start of *Van AbbeMUSEUM entr'acte* in 1995, Debbaut's policy was mainly associated with the previously mentioned polemics concerning the relevance of visual art on the interface of modernism and postmodernism. After the move and partly owing to the circumstances of this new location, the focus shifted to a somewhat younger generation, the emphasis being placed on audiovisual or somewhat more process-oriented work. Presentations and purchases of work by Tony Oursler, Douglas Gordon (1995), Ann Hamilton (1996) and Marijke van Warmerdam (1997), to name only a few, underscored this tendency. In addition, there came a shift of interest to the American West Coast, including artists such as Mike Kelley (1996) and Jason Rhoades (1998). A reintroduction of the theme exhibitions can also be discerned: *ID* (1996) focused on the idea of identity, *Cinéma Cinéma* (1999) dealt with the filmic experience in visual art, while *Twisted* (2000) raised the issue of contemporary landscape painting, that is to say the construed or artificial form of this.

A flexible approach to the space provided by the industrial building on the Vonderweg

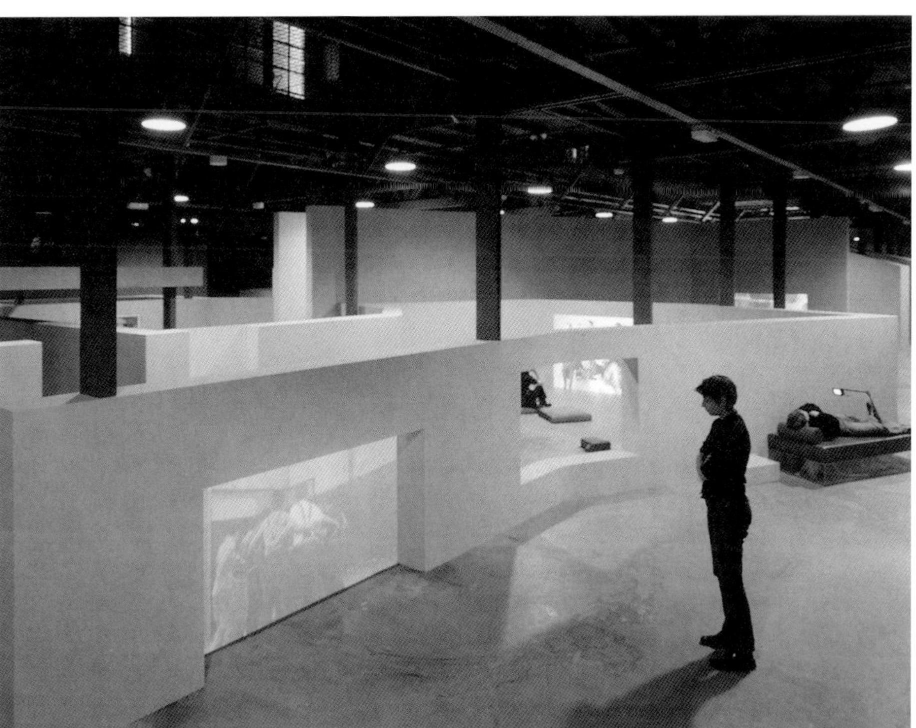

Installation view of the **Aernout Mik** exhibition *Primal Gestures, Minor Roles*, 2000

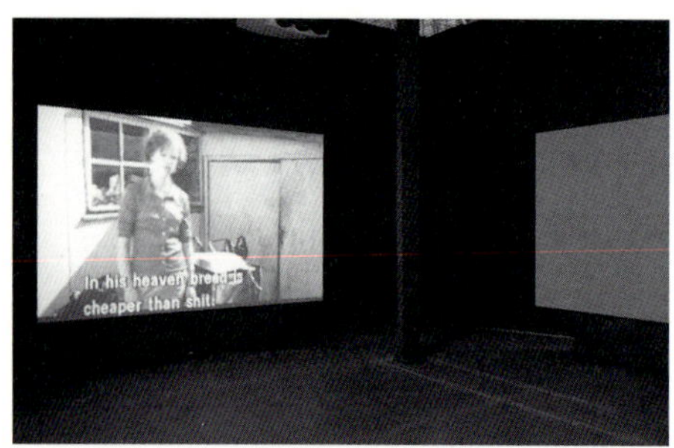

Installation view of the *Cinéma, Cinéma* exhibition 1999
Eija-Liisa Ahtila, *Today*, 1996-97

proved to be of great importance. This made it possible to adapt the layout of the rooms to the concept of each exhibition, the most memorable results of which were the presentations of Aernout Mik (2000) and Pierre Huyghe (2001), artists whose work has also been included in the collection. That different outlook upon the space, together with the idea that the museum can also play a role as co-producer, came to influence perspectives on the spatial structure of the new museum. In this one sees greater variation in scale, and there is also a special space in which artists can experiment, regardless of the deadline of an exhibition.

While the lengthy stay at the temporary building could have led to inertia, Debbaut managed to make use of the less-than-optimal circumstances. With the new museum, the combination of a semi-permanent presentation of the collection and the experiences of spatial concepts generated at *Van AbbeMUSEUM entr'acte* reflects the decision to opt for flexibility and 'the best of both worlds'.

Having reached the age of sixty-five, the Van Abbemuseum is now looking forward to the best years of its life.

René Pingen

1. Letter by E. de Wilde to mayor H.A M.T. Kolfschoten, December 20, 1955.
2. Farewell speech by Edy de Wilde to Eindhoven's 'museum friends' on August 28, 1963.
3. J. Leering, 'De funktie van het museum. Tendens van mausoleum naar "levend museum"', *Intermediair*, June 26, 1970.
4. J. Bremer, J. Ober (eds.), 'Naschrift' in: *De gebruiker en de vormgeving van het leefmilieu. Verslag van een serie discussie-avonden over dit onderwerp, gehouden in het Van Abbemuseum in 1973*, Eindhoven, Stedelijk Van Abbemuseum, 1973
5. R.H. Fuchs, 'De zuiderzeekunst van CRM' *Hollands Diep*, April 23, 1977.
6. P. Peters, 'Rudi Fuchs en zijn omstreden museum. "In de kunst gaat het om partijdigheid. Je bent vóór iets or tegen iets"', *De Tijd*, October 1978.
7. 'Jan Debbaut: "Voor collectioneren moet je soms een lange adem hebben [...] Het is sprinten en marathon lopen tegelijk"', in: C. Berndes, M. Bloemheuvel, J. Debbaut [et.al], *Een collectie is ook maar een mens. Edy de Wilde, Jean Leering, Rudi Fuchs, Jan Debbaut over verzamelen*, Eindhoven, Rotterdam 1999, p. 128-129.

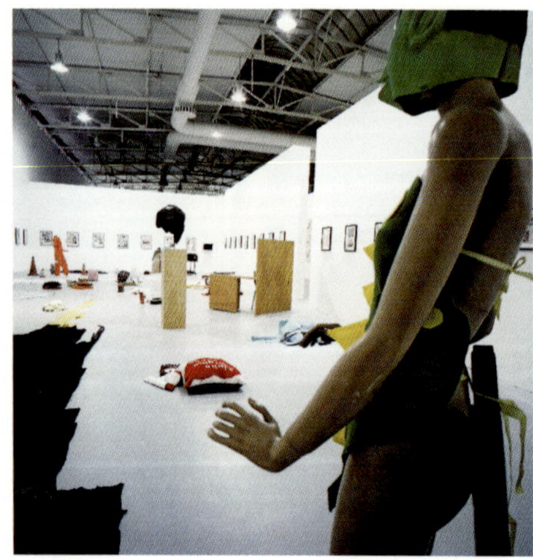

Installation view of the exhibition *Conversation? Recent acquisitions of the Van Abbemuseum*, Athene, 2002. **Mike Kelley**, *Categorical Imperative and Morgue*, 1999 (detail)

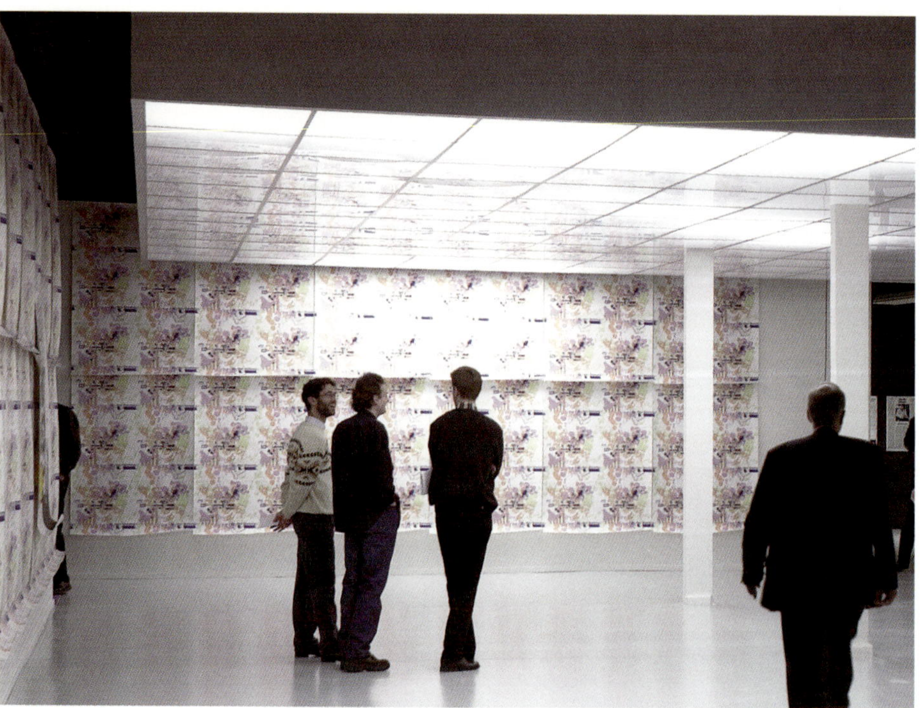

Installation view of the **Pierre Huyghe** exhibition *Interludes, 2001*

Jan Sluijters

Leo Gestel

Herman Kruyder

Hendrik Chabot

Carel Willink

Charley Toorop

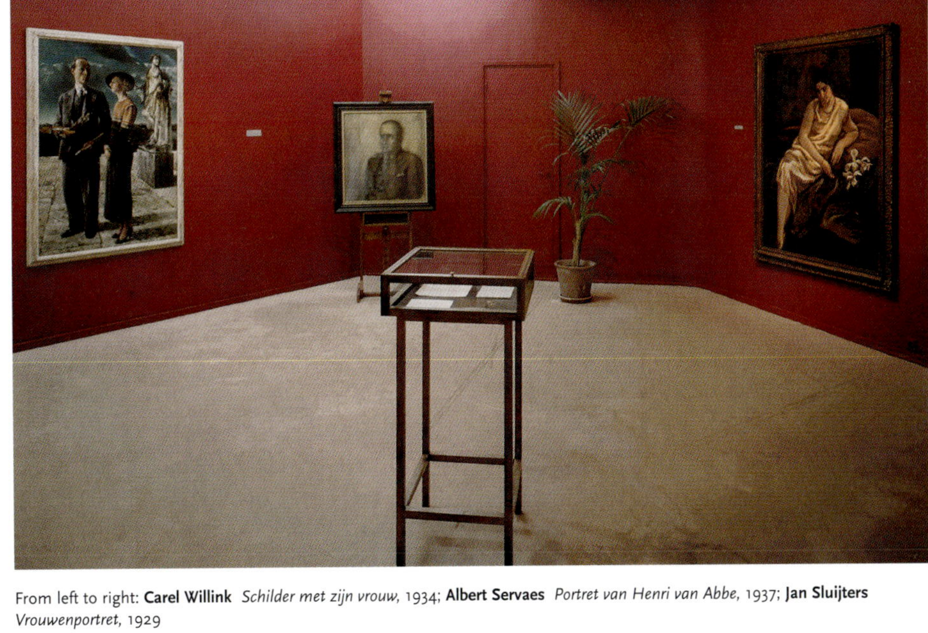

From left to right: **Carel Willink** *Schilder met zijn vrouw*, 1934; **Albert Servaes** *Portret van Henri van Abbe*, 1937; **Jan Sluijters** *Vrouwenportret*, 1929

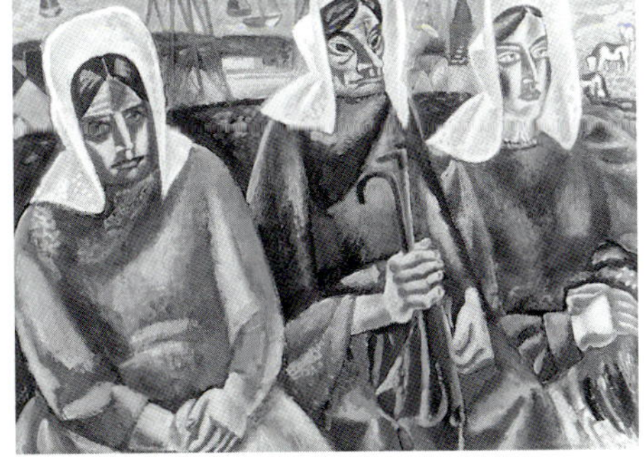

Leo Gestel *Drie Huizer vrouwen*, 1929

When the Eindhoven cigar manufacturer Henri van Abbe presented the city of Eindhoven with a museum building in 1936, the city purchased twenty-six works by contemporary Dutch artists from the collection of Van Abbe as a start of the collection which had yet to be formed. Henri van Abbe collected, for the most part, work by contemporary artists employing a figurative and expressive style. Emphasis lay with the Netherlands and Flanders: Permeke, Sluijters, Gestel, Schuhmacher and Willink. Jan Sluijters and Leo Gestel were pioneers in Dutch modernism, but the choice of three paintings by Sluijters and one by Gestel shows Van Abbe's preference for contemporary, though largely 'traditional' painting.

With respect to the work of Sluijters, not the early paintings such as *Landschap* (1910) and *Lezende vrouw* (1911), highly influenced by French fauvism–both works were later added to the collection by director Edy de Wilde–but much more traditional paintings such as *Vrouwenportret* (1929) and *Vaas met bloemen* (1929) were purchased by him.

The same can be said of Leo Gestel's *Drie Huizer vrouwen* from 1929. This painting, too, is a long way from Gestel's early work, in which he experimented with modernist principles such as Cubism and Futurism. The angularity and lack of perspective in the picture plane of *Drie Huizer vrouwen* do hint at Gestel's 'cubist' roots, but these attributes alone can hardly be called modernist.

In 1904 **Jan Sluijters** and **Leo Gestel** began making frequent trips to Paris in order to keep in touch with the latest developments in painting. Subsequent to an initial joint visit to the city in 1904, they each developed a style which makes use of the 'division' of colors: a technique in which separate strokes of paint are applied to the canvas, often as small dots. Seurat, Signac and Pissarro were the leading protagonists of this style in Paris. They painted in an almost scientific manner, based on optics, physiology and psychology. Gestel and Sluijters used this technique mainly in an impressionistic way, however. Around 1909 their work became more and more removed from visible reality. Together with Mondrian, they now represent the essence of what was referred to by contemporaries as Amsterdam Luminism, a style which displays great formal similarity to the French fauvism of, among others, Maurice De Vlaminck and André Derain. Rather than producing a 'precise copy' of reality, these 'luminists' endeavored, through the use of greatly intensified colors, to portray the inner sensation that an image, a person or a landscape would evoke in them (e.g. *Lezende vrouw* by Jan Sluijters).

After 1912 the two artists underwent the influences of Cubism and Futurism, while World War I gave rise to a more expressionist tendency and an austerity of palette, which had been very bright up to this point. As evident from this development, Gestel and Sluijters soon came to absorb, like many of their contemporaries, a great number of different influences: the constant stream of innovative tendencies throughout the first two decades of the twentieth century should not be underestimated, even in terms of its secondary effect. The peak of artistic ability lay, for both of these artists, precisely in this period. Though beautiful work of high quality was still often produced incidentally after this, their work generally assumed a more subdued and traditional tone. Gestel's oeuvre can, despite its lack of adherence to any distinct style, best be described as a typically Dutch blend of cubist principles and a recognizably expressionist visual language. Sluijters was among the most celebrated Dutch artists of the twenties and thirties. He received numerous portrait assignments (*Vrouwenportret*, 1929). Furthermore, he continued to paint female nudes. These two types of work differed from earlier work due to a more realistic, moderate tone and expression, as well as a complete absence of experimentation.

During the 1920s a new painterly personality, **Herman Kruyder**, entered the Dutch art scene with hesitancy and great personal reticence. His body of work, fairly moderate in size, clearly attests to expressionist influences. The paintings can sooner be regarded as flashes, sudden releases and experiences than parts of a deliberately planned artistic scheme. Though Kruyder did have contacts with other artists, such as Gestel, he lived a secluded existence in the vicinity of Haarlem. His paintings usually exude an atmosphere of enchantment, a

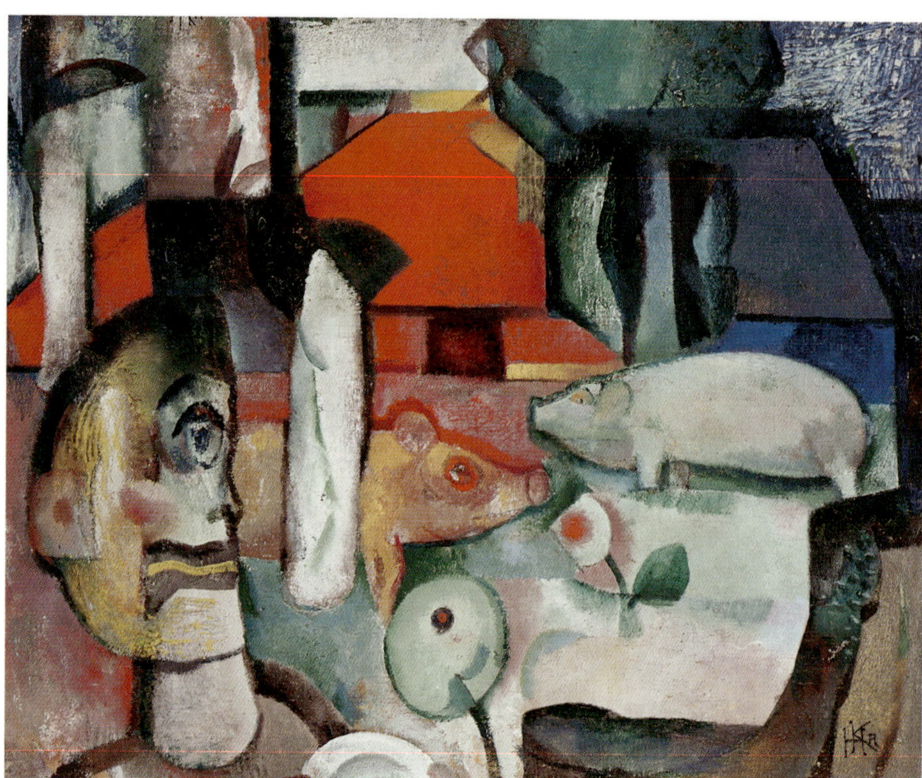

Herman Kruyder *De varkensdoder*, ca. 1925

world of danger, fear and upheaval. The stiff, grinning mask of the butcher in *De varkensdoder* (1925), for instance, disrupts the idyllic image of the countryside. Doubt as to the true meaning of the butcher's presence is heightened by the ambiguous character of a number of motifs in the painting. The knotty tree stumps can also be seen as meat axes. Moreover, the painting derives its tension from the fact that the pictorial space hovers between the two-dimensional and the three-dimensional. From a formal point of view, the visual language of *De varkensdoder* bears some affinity with the vocabulary of the group *Der Blaue Reiter* in terms of the use of color in general, the contrasts in this and the clear contours. The static juxtaposition of motifs and areas of color alludes to the work of the German painter Heinrich Campendonk, who came to live in the Netherlands.

Hendrik Chabot, an artist originally from Brabant, shared Kruyder's fondness for simple country life but employed an entirely different style. Greatly influenced by the Flemish expressionism of Permeke and De Smet, Chabot produced, in austere earthen hues, robust paintings with highly distorted peasant figures. In *Slapende boer* (1936) the perspective has been tilted in such a way that the farmer, in all his pride, virtually emerges

from the canvas. As a socially committed artist who was always occupied with the portrayal of the tragedy of a bare existence, Chabot evidently intended to paint, in a dramatic manner, the dignity and the difficult life of simple rural people. During the war–by then he had been living in Rotterdam for some time–he painted, in the same monumental way, depictions of the many war victims: those in hiding, the hungry, the refugees.

A very different kind of reality emerges in the oppressive works of **Carel Willink**. The houses on a deserted square in the painting

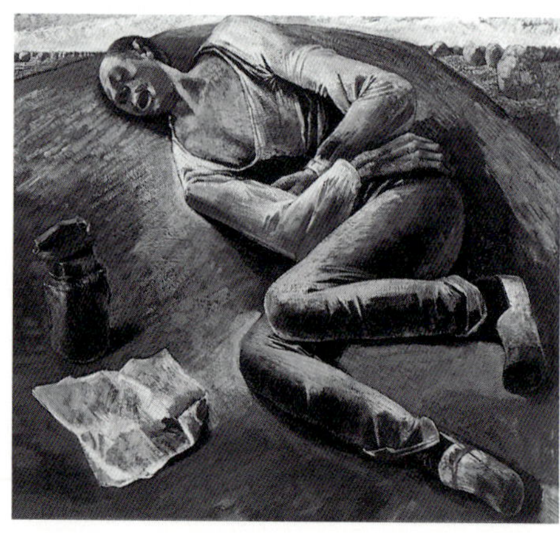

Hendrik Chabot *Slapende boer*, 1936

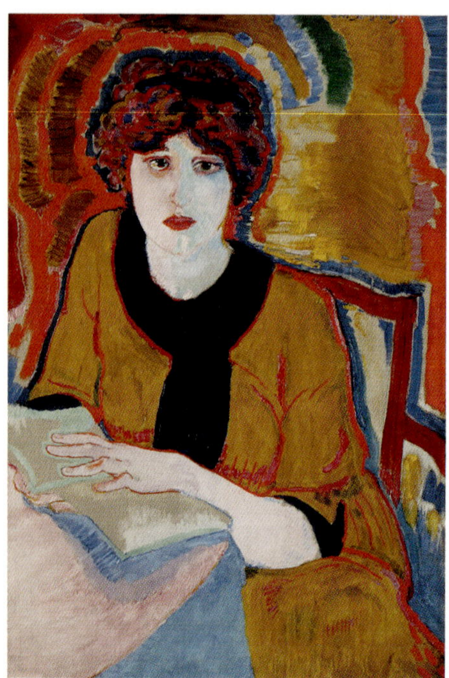

Jan Sluijters *Lezende vrouw*, 1911

Stadsgezicht (1933), for instance, are painted in a highly realistic manner on the one hand, but have a certain unreal quality at the same time. The entire painting is dominated by a vague sense of danger. This is evoked not only by the desolation of the square, but particularly by the harsh light that is cast across the buildings and the ominous dark clouds hovering above the scene. This atmosphere of approaching doom in landscapes and urban scenes painted with photographic precision can be seen in many works by Willink. For this reason, his painting came to be known as 'Magic Realism'. Willink himself preferred to call his art "imaginary realism, reality painted from the imagination." In *Schilder met zijn vrouw* (1934), which originally came from the collection of Henri van Abbe, the realism with which Willink has portrayed himself and his wife has assumed an almost supernatural connotation by way of the peculiar, imaginary quality of the landscape in which they appear.

A different sort of realism can be seen in the

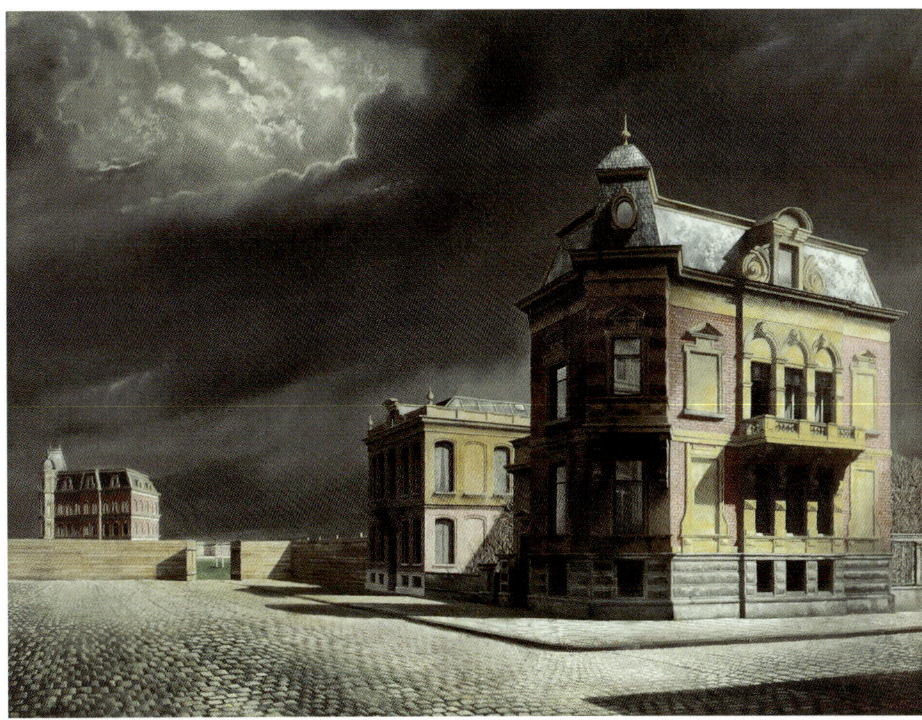

Carel Willink *Stadsgezicht*, 1934

work of **Charley Toorop**. Her portraits, such as *Zelfportret met wintertakken* (1944-45), have less precision in the depiction of reality than those of Willink. Due to the contours, the strong contrasts of light and shade and the use of color, her painterly style is of a much more expressionistic nature. Another striking aspect of this work is the frontal depiction of the portrait subject, who stares at us in a penetrating manner. This effect is further heightened by the pattern of bare branches in the background, parallel to the image surface. Many of her portraits, both those of individuals and of groups, display this frontal approach, which seems to be aimed at bringing about a direct confrontation with the person depicted. Toorop clearly intended to capture the essence of the portrait subject and did not wish to be confined to the surface. Although her paintings do show the same smooth, contained forms that can be seen with the 'magic realists', Toorop's austere forms and simplified colors point to a strong inner tension.

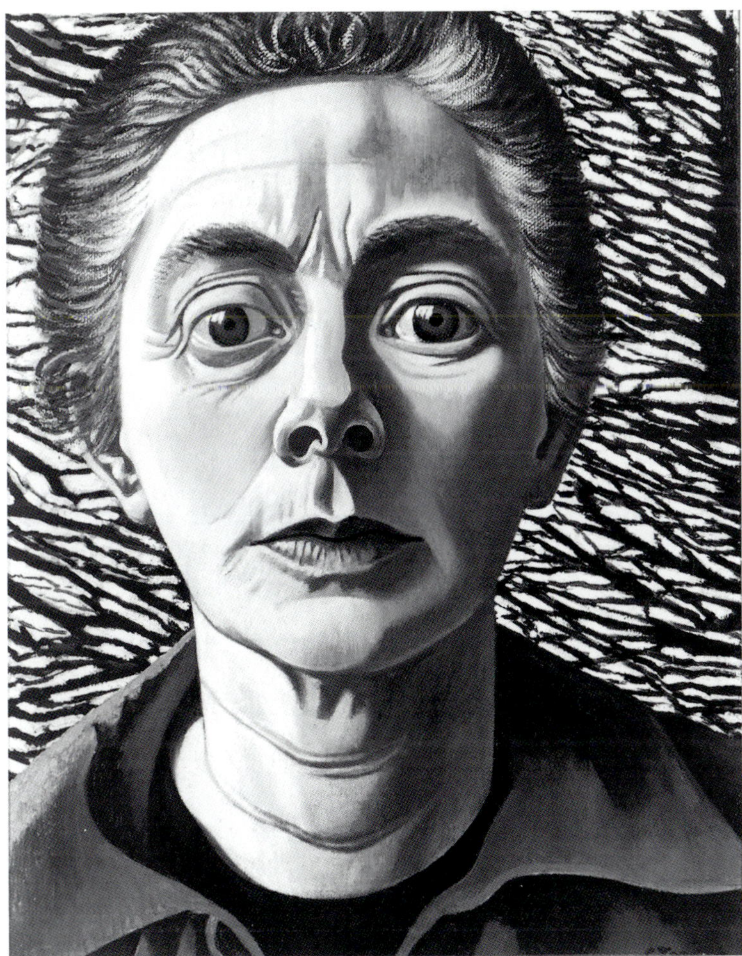

Charley Toorop *Zelfportret met wintertakken, 1944-45*

Wassily Kandinsky
Heinrich Campendonk
Oskar Kokoschka
Max Beckmann
Constant Permeke
Gustave De Smet
Jean Brusselmans

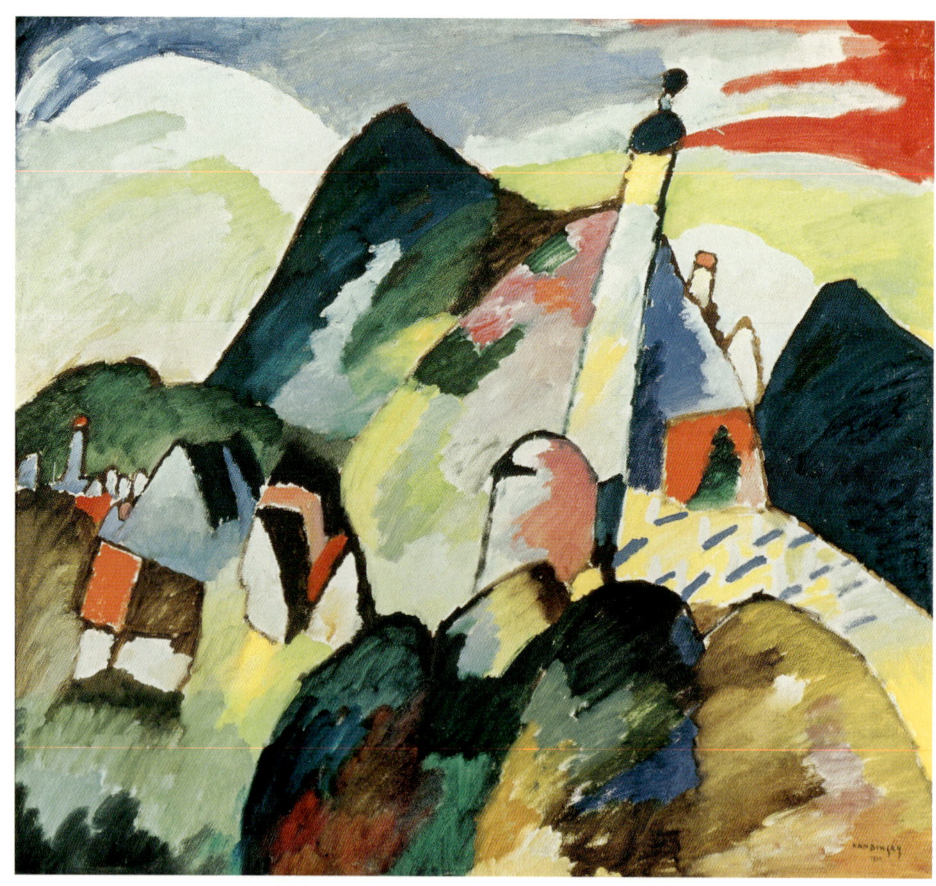

Wassily Kandinsky *Blick auf Murnau mit Kirche*, 1910

The early years of the twentieth century offer a complex view of changes and developments that were taking place at the same time, not only in society, politics, philosophy and science, but also in the visual arts, literature and music. The Impressionists had approached reality in a manner that undermined established ideas on painting, on how things should be rendered. Yet the Impressionists were still concerned with a painterly portrayal of nature as seen by the eye and therefore continued to cling to naturalistic representation.

Only at a slightly later point did Van Gogh and Gauguin provide a more personal, more connotative outlook on their surroundings. Partly by means of their non-naturalist use of color, they aspired to express something more than that which was simply visible. They considered the 'inner eye', the sense of things, more important than sensory perception. Because of that more subjective point of view, the artist came to be regarded more as an individual than as a representative of a style or a movement. When a number of individual artists were working on the basis of the same intentions at the start of the twentieth century, they often joined together to form a group, usually for a brief period and without a great deal of dogmatic deliberation. These groups usually acquired a name through the art criticism of the day. In Paris, for instance, figures such as Matisse, Derain and De Vlaminck developed, between 1904 and 1907, a type of painting–based on the works of Gauguin, Van Gogh, Ensor and Munch–that would give them the name *Les Fauves* (wild animals). They shared a common concern for the symbolic qualities of primitive art, they used pure color in an expressive rather than naturalistic way, and they arranged the image surface into simplified forms and contours. Man's position as an observer of the world underwent a definitive change in Germany, however, due to a number of artists who had come together to form two groups. In 1905 *Die Brücke*, whose leading representatives included Kirchner and Nolde, was founded in Dresden; and in 1911, the group *Der Blaue Reiter*, to which Kandinsky, Macke and Marc belonged, came about in Munich. These artists were the prime figures of Expressionism.

"I value only those artists who are truly artists, that is to say those who consciously or unconsciously, in a thoroughly original form, give shape to the expression of an inner life, those who work only, and can only work, with this in mind," stated **Wassily Kandinsky**. Kandinsky's ideas on what art should be were articulated in his book *Über das Geistige in der Kunst*, which was published in 1912. In 1896 he had come to Munich in order to devote himself to painting, after having ended a career as a lawyer in his native country Russia. From there he made many trips throughout Europe and, in 1906, spent a year in Paris. There he saw the first exhibition of the Fauvists and, once back in Germany,

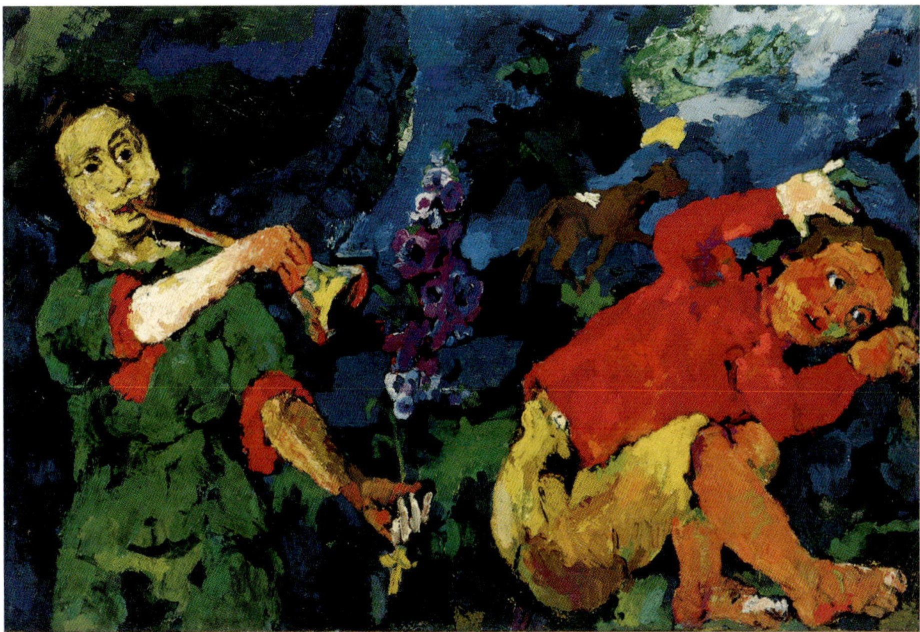

Oskar Kokoschka *Die Macht der Musik*, 1918

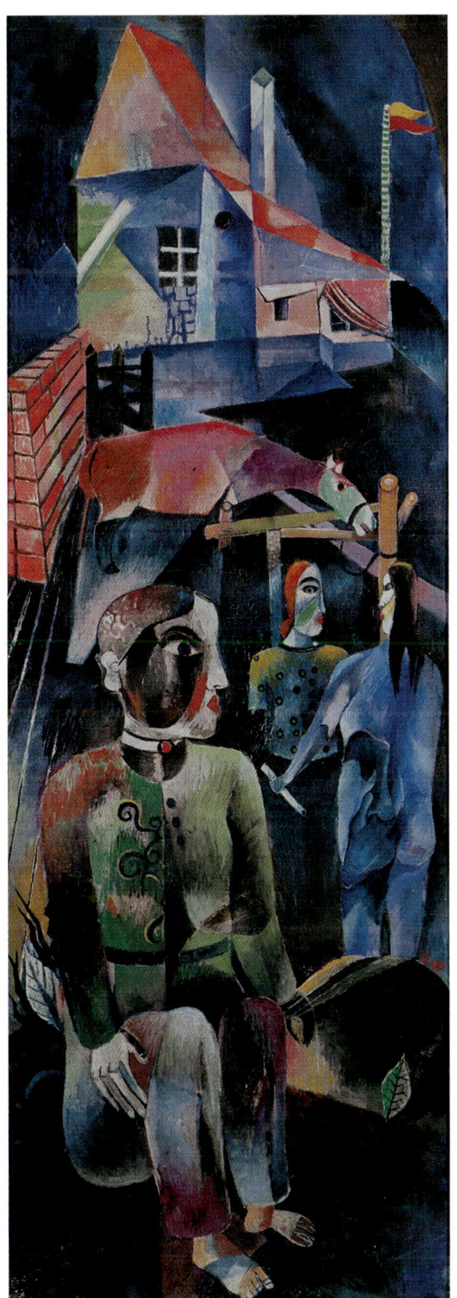

Heinrich Campendonk *Boerderij*, 1919

where he came to settle in Murnau, the Fauvist influence became distinctly evident in his use of color. During this period Kandinsky painted a great many landscapes, among them *Blick auf Murnau mit Kirche* (1910). Though this work remains recognizable as a landscape, the visual means of color and form have taken charge and become free of their representative functions. As such, the visual means themselves become the content, namely that of color and form as phenomena. A mountain, for instance, becomes secondary to the intensity of its blue. This gives rise to an ordering of colored planes, separated from each other by means of vivid contrasts or outlines. In Kandinsky's later abstract work, the line even begins to play an entirely independent role. The activities of *Der Blaue Reiter* went beyond exhibitions of their own work; presentations of work by artists not from Munich, such as Arp, Braque, Klee, Nolde and Picasso, were also organized. The group's broad international base, by which they distinguished themselves from *Die Brücke*, expanded even further due to the publication of an almanac in 1912. Aside from reproductions of paintings, this contained examples of primitive and folk art, children's drawings, Asiatic and African works, medieval sculptures and woodcuts, as well as articles on music written by Schönberg, Berg and Webern. Continually fascinated by the relationship between art and music, Kandinsky wished to instill art with the same independence that he felt in music, and

because of that he opened the way to a new subject for art, based on the 'inner needs' of the artist.

When World War I broke out, *Der Blaue Reiter* ceased to exist and Kandinksy left for Russia, where he witnessed the Revolution. In 1922 he returned to Germany for a teaching position at the Bauhaus, until the Nazis closed this institute in 1933. Having decided to move to Paris after this, Kandinsky continued to live and work there until his death in 1944.

Heinrich Campendonk felt a great affinity for the ideas and the manner of painting cultivated by the artists of *Der Blaue Reiter*. In 1911 he moved to Bavaria in order to join them. The outbreak of World War I brought an end to the collaboration, after which Campendonk worked in isolation for several years. During this period he painted idyllic, rural scenes that express a longing for a lost paradise in which man and the animal world live in harmony with the cosmos. The influences of Gauguin and Rousseau can be discerned in this work. His compositions consist of planes of complementary colors, as in the painting *Boerderij* (1919). In his later work there emerged a calm detachment, and the emphasis came to lie with monumental and decorative design. Unlike Kandinsky, however, Campendonk never arrived at abstraction in his work.

Another influential figure in Expressionism was Herwarth Walden, who began to publish the magazine *Der Sturm* in 1910 and opened a gallery of the same name in Berlin in 1912.

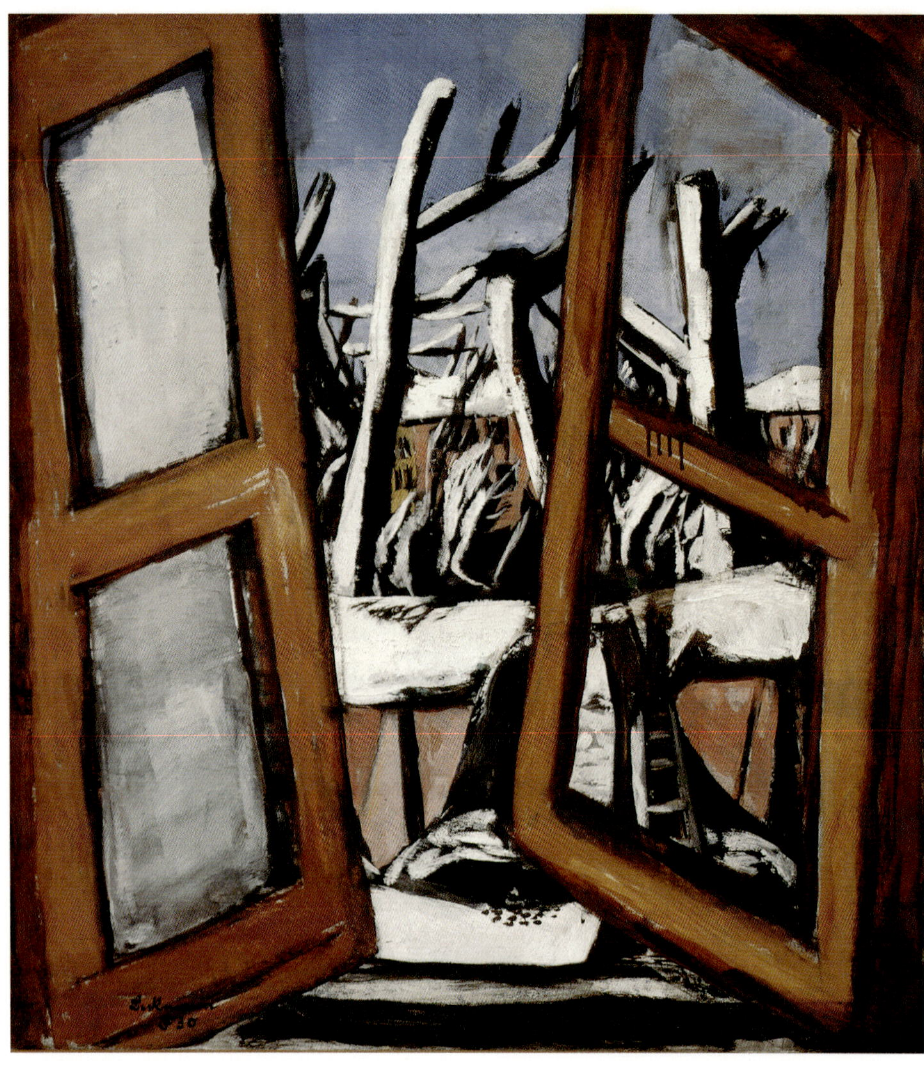

Max Beckmann *Winterbild*, 1930

In *Der Sturm*, Walden published articles by such writers and artists as Apollinaire, Léger and the Italian Futurists, and he brought many of the international modernisms to Berlin by organizing exhibitions that were both influential and symptomatic with respect to German interests. Walden also supported **Oskar Kokoschka**, who had come to Berlin from Vienna in 1910, and held a solo exhibition of his work at Der Sturm in 1912. In his personality and in the nature of the plays that he wrote, Kokoschka showed himself to be the pre-eminent Expressionist. He is thought to have said, "I have never been able to be measured along with others." This sort of individualism was of prime importance to many Expressionists, and it may explain why Expressionism, as a whole, was so diverse and multifaceted. After Kokoschka had recuperated from injuries sustained during World War I, he settled in Dresden in 1918. During that year he painted

Die Macht der Musik (1918). The theme is rendered in bright colors and an emphatic brushstroke: green and yellow, the cooler colors, for the woman playing music and predominantly red for the man entranced by her playing. The density and weight of the paint as matter are clearly evident, and there is no circumscribing by means of line; as a result, the structural and expressive qualities of color are used in a way that differs from that of Kandinsky. The arrangement of planes of color gives the spatial relationship between the figures and the background a certain undefined character, and because of this a certain tangibility arises in the relationship between the painted subject and the flat surface of the canvas.

During the years following World War I, various artists were of the opinion that the enthusiasm of the Expressionists reflected little concern for postwar problems. Prominent individuals from this group, *Neue*

Sachligkeit, included Grosz, Dix and Heartfield. They were bound, on the one hand, by a common sense of resignation and cynicism with respect to the situation in Germany at that time and, on the other, in their artistic ideas, by a common desire for a more sober view of reality. The emphasis on the importance of the visible object, as opposed to the subjective, emotional approach of the Expressionists, makes someone such as **Max Beckmann** very closely related to this *Neue Sachligkeit*. His perception of the problem of evil and of man's existence in postwar society dominated his painted works, largely from around 1920, in which nightmarish scenes are portrayed. Continually fascinated by the very activity of observing and painting, with relentless concern for objects from the world around him, Beckmann also began to paint landscapes, harbor scenes and still lifes with increasing frequency during the 1920s. *Winterbild*, a view of a winter world painted in very forceful, plain forms, dates from 1930. In a lecture given in 1938 at the New Burlington Gallery in London, Beckmann said, "My aim is always to get hold of the magic of reality and to transfer this reality into painting–to make the invisible visible through reality. It may sound paradoxical, but it is, in fact, reality which forms the mystery of our existence. What helps me most in this task is the penetration of space. Height, width and depth are the three phenomena which I must transfer into one plane to form the abstract surface of the picture, and thus to protect myself from the infinity of space (...) When spiritual, metaphysical, material or immaterial events come into my life, I can only fix them by way of painting."

"My form of expression is painting; there are, of course, other means to this end, such as literature, philosophy or music; but as a painter, cursed or blessed with a terrible and vital sensuousness, I must look for wisdom with my eyes. I repeat, with my eyes, for nothing could be more ridiculous or irrelevant than a 'philosophical conception' painted purely intellectually without the terrible fury of the senses grasping each visible form of beauty and ugliness. If from those forms which I have found in the visible, literary subjects result–such as portraits, landscapes or recognizable compositions–they have all originated from the senses, in this case, from the eyes, and each intellectual subject has been transformed again into form, color and space."

Expressionism, as it had crystallized Germany, actually had only a few related

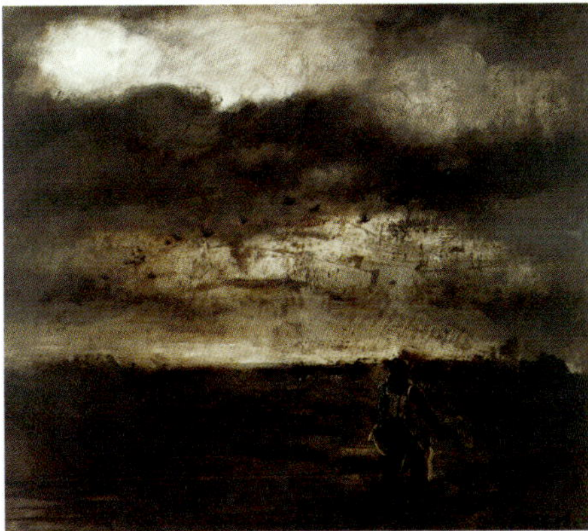

Constant Permeke *De zaaier*, 1935

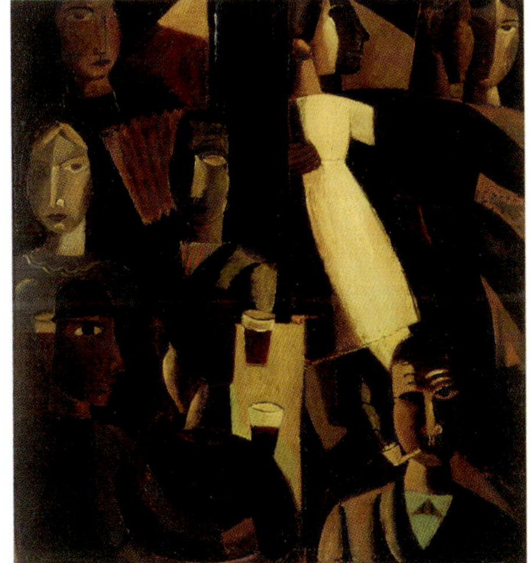

Gustave De Smet *Danslokaal*, 1921

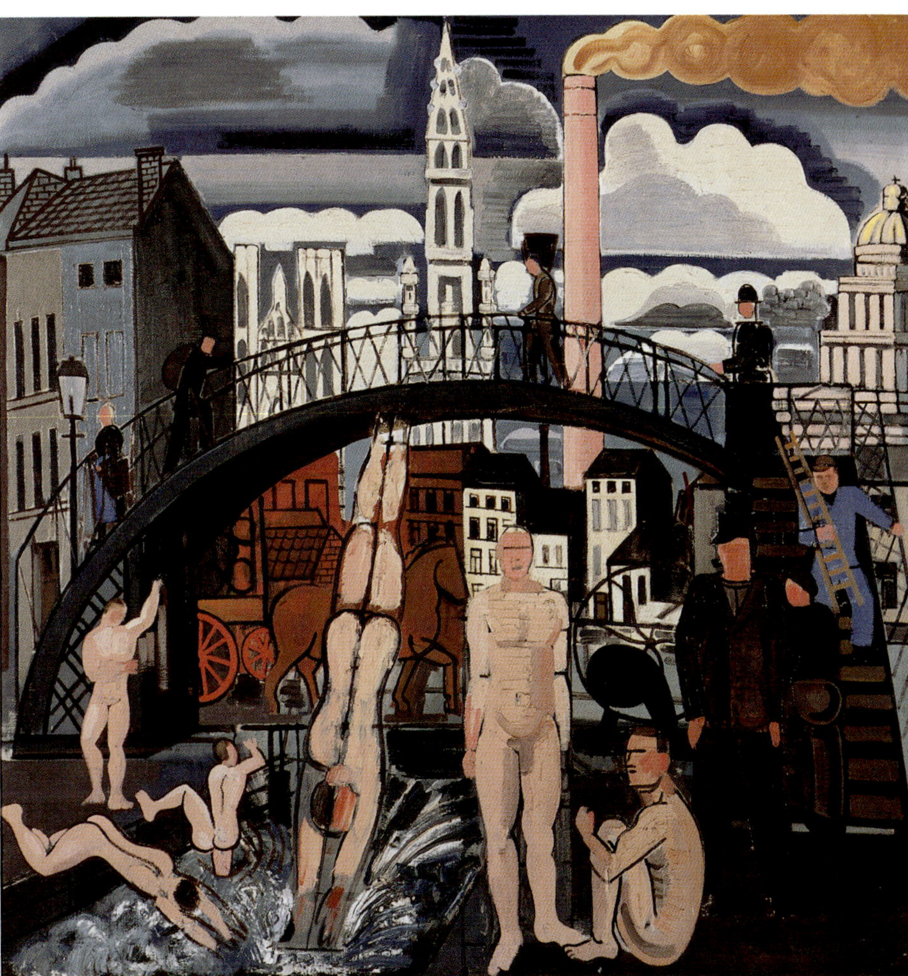

Jean Brusselmans *Le bain des vagabonds*, 1936

artists in Flanders and the Netherlands. In the aftermath of World War I, **Constant Permeke** gave shape to Flemish Expressionism together with Jean Brusselmans, Gustave De Smet and Frits van den Berghe. Permeke 'attacked' the earth with his brush and colors. He sought his subjects in nature and peasant life, in which he could give his temperament and emotions free rein, sometimes with bright hues, then with rich and warm harmonies of earthen colors, as in *De zaaier* (1935). The psychological atmosphere of the landscape shows the artist's sensitivity to nature that is experienced as a kind of cosmic violence. **Gustave De Smet** arrived at his expressive style during World War I, which he spent in exile in the Netherlands. Here he became acquainted with the work of *Der Blaue Reiter* and artists such as Picasso, Braque, Léger and Chagall. Both Cubist and Expressionist influences can be discerned in his work. In 1917 he began to develop a highly personal language of forms and palette, as can be seen

in *Danslokaal* (1921). His human figures are reticent, angular shapes with elongated oval heads, almond-shaped eyes and long straight noses. Tube-shaped arms and legs and cylinder-like necks emphasize the elementary, the universal, rather than the individual. Simplification and austerity are also expressed in his choice of color, which largely consists of subdued, sober hues. Like De Smet, **Jean Brusselmans** also preferred to paint local and everday scenes, landscapes and still lifes. His compositions are simply and clearly structured. The play of lines and planes of color is of considerable importance in his work, yet this always remains subordinate to the image. "In my paintings, a line remains a line. A stroke of color or layer of paint remains what it is. The true painter seeks not an imitation but a higher truth. What interests him is the moral color of the painting, whose full meaning is expressed at once by this. Not only inspiration, but reason, too, gives rise to such color. Art consists of giving light to all things,

even to the thankless and the meagre." The painting *Le bain des vagabonds* (1936) is based on the childhood memory of summer swims with his brother in a branch of the Charleroi Canal. This theme was dealt with by Brusselmans seven years before in a painting of the same title. The footbridge in the background is a favorite motif that crops up frequently in his work.

Pablo Picasso

Georges Braque

Juan Gris

Fernand Léger

Marc Chagall

Robert Delaunay

Jacques Lipchitz

Ossip Zadkine

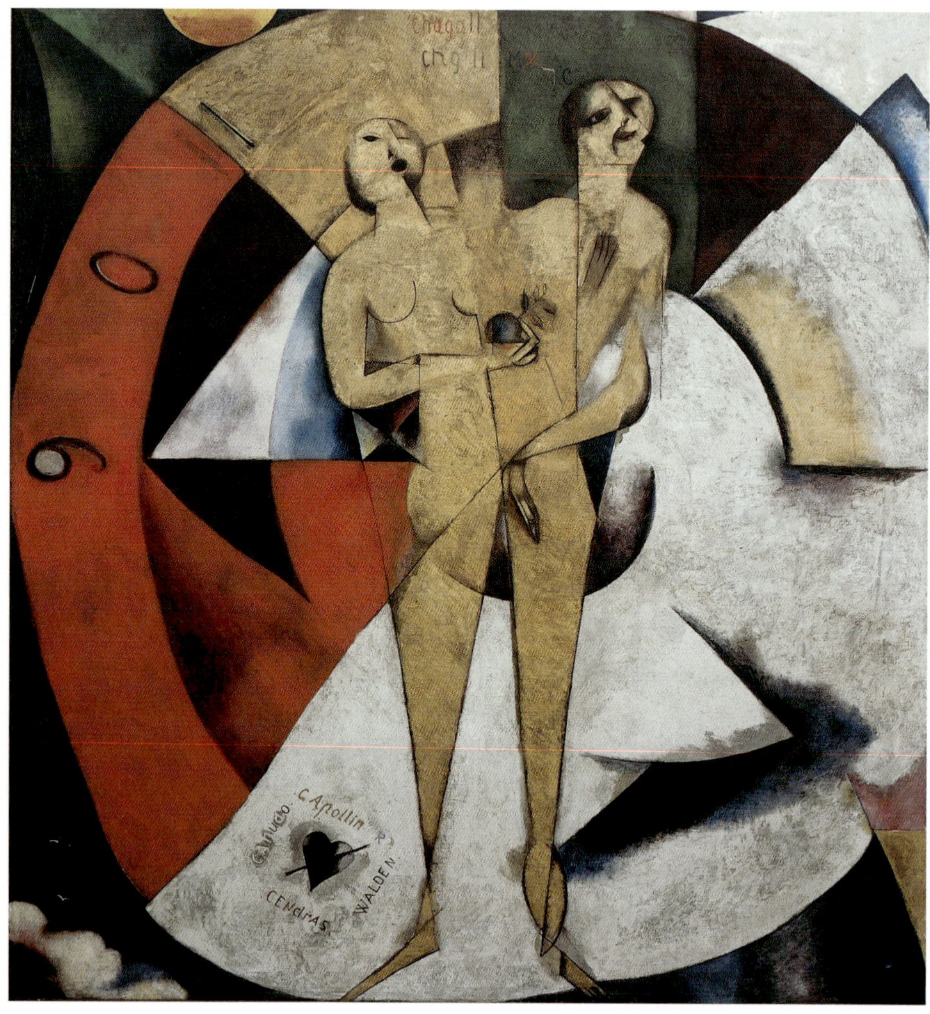

Marc Chagall *Hommage à Apollinaire*, 1911-12

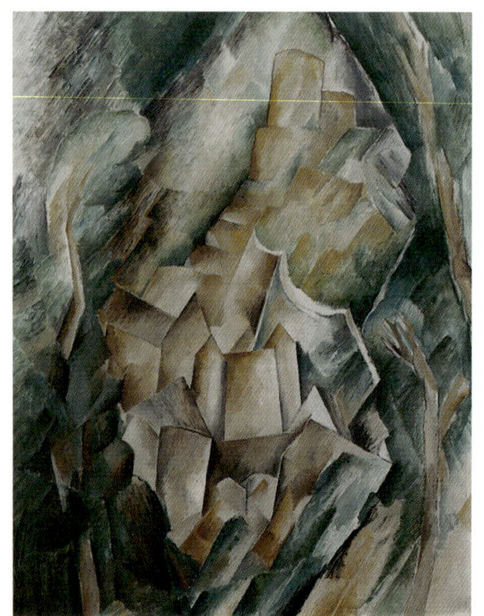

Georges Braque *La Roche-Guyon*, 1909

Cubism has freed modern painting, once and for all, from its classical roots. That has probably been the most significant innovation in the early history of modern art, even though the achievements of Cubism were further radicalized in the abstract painting of Mondrian and others later on. The pioneers and the leading representatives of this influential movement are Picasso and Braque, both of whom are present in the collection of the Van Abbemuseum with several works. The paintings *Femme en vert* by **Pablo Picasso** and *La Roche-Guyon* by **Georges Braque** were both produced in 1909. The works clearly show the drastic nature of the change introduced by these artists in the existing approach to painting and in the rendering of visible reality–in this case a landscape and a female figure.

Picasso took the first steps toward this change in 1906-1907 with the famous painting *Les Demoiselles d'Avignon*. Braque saw this work in Picasso's studio in 1907 and was deeply impressed by it. This encounter led to a huge change in his work. He was shocked by the brutality of the painting but, most of all, fascinated by the completely new way in which form and space were dealt with here by Picasso. This was the start of their common adventurous attempts to create a yet unimagined visual world of forms and spaces, based on their experiences of reality. In this they concentrated not only on a close investigation of the sculptural qualities of their subject, but also on the understanding that an object can be approached from various points of view. It seems as though they collected their visual information by walking around the subject of the painting. Due to this analysis of form, this period of Cubism (1907-1912) is frequently referred to as the analytical one. The main issue was the discovery of the potential to incorporate these countless viewpoints of reality into the surface of one painting and give rise to a new spatial entity. During these years Picasso and Braque developed, in the process of painting on the flat image surface, spatial edifices, constructions and volumes that are of an autonomous nature yet continue to allude to reality. Though they portray an artistic world, one which cannot be perceived in reality as such, the topics of their painting can still be clearly determined. Their paintings are always about a landscape, a human figure, a still life and so on. What interests them in this, however, is a reality that is determined by the consciousness. In 1908 Braque said, "There is no certainty at all, except for that which is understood by the mind." A similar stance is reflected in a later statement: "Things do not even exist in themselves. They exist only through us. One cannot simply depict things. One must penetrate into things, become a thing oneself."

The painterly representation of a subject and the fixed relationship with the space in which it is observed–having been accepted since the Renaissance–ceased have primacy after 1907. The ideas of Picasso and Braque and the bold realization of these in paintings signified a radical turning point in the history of art. During these years, they were laying the foundations for a great many new developments in the twentieth century–Suprematism, Constructivism, De Stijl, Geometric Abstraction, but also Minimal Art and, in a certain sense, even Conceptual Art.

In the work *La Roche-Guyon* (1909) by Braque, we can ascertain without difficulty that this is a landscape consisting of a mass of rock, on which houses and the tower of a castle are built. The greatly simplified forms of the houses, the entry gate, the city walls, the square tower below and the round tower above seem to be separate, independent elements stacked against the steep slope of the rock. Each form is painted from a different angle: from the front, the side, from above and below.

Like Picasso, Braque deliberately opted not to use a central perspective, which had been ordering the painting in a familiar way since the Renaissance. By giving each of the simplified forms (rectangles, triangles, cylinders) a different spatial placement, he was designing a new rhythmic order, which presents a visual idea of the variegated buildings on a rock in an abstract manner. Color was used to a limited degree (greens, ochres, greys) in order to give emphasis to the forms and bring about coherence in their diversity.

With *La Roche-Guyon*, as well as with his other landscapes painted at l'Estaque, it appears that Braque owed a great deal to Cézanne. This primarily relates to his sense of spatial and sculptural qualities.

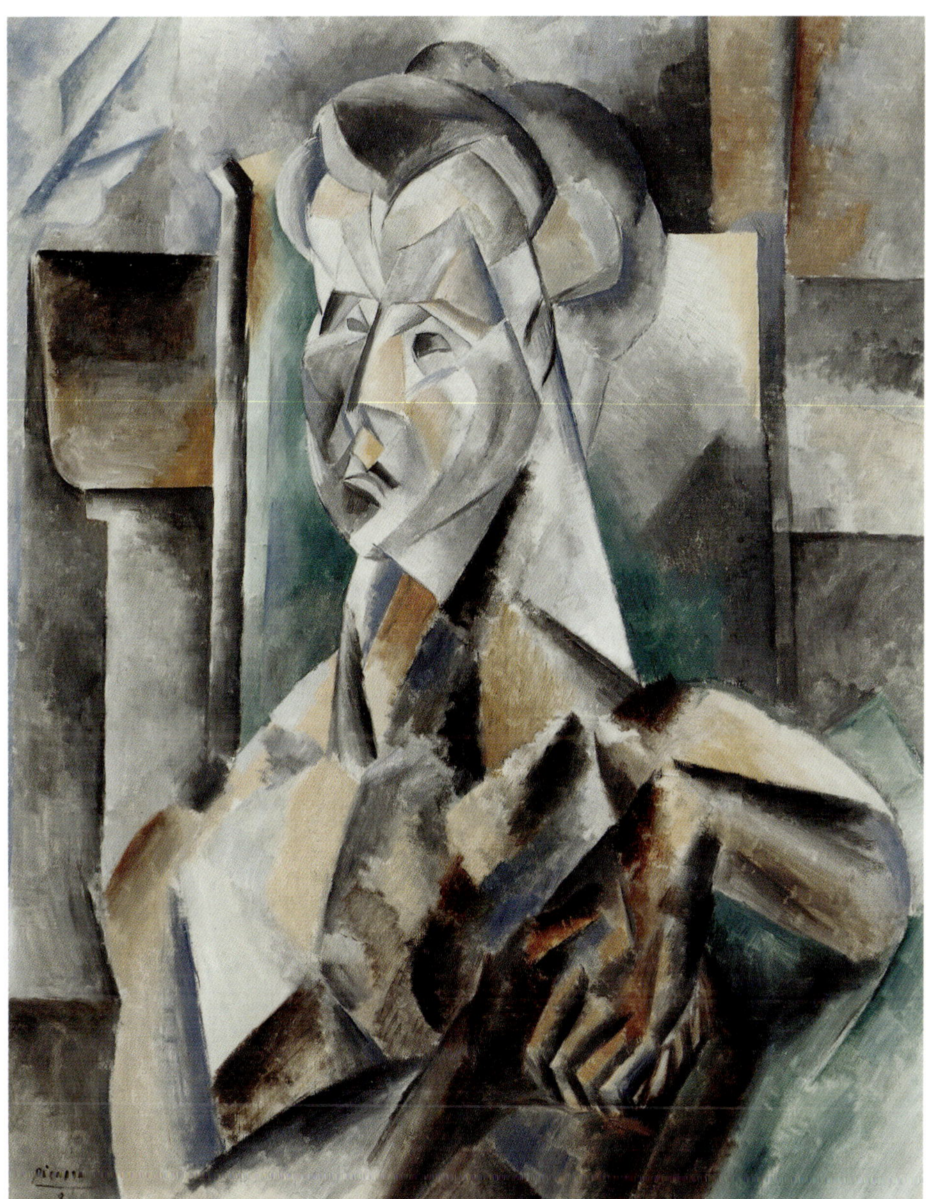

Pablo Picasso *Femme en vert*, 1909

Particularly the arrangement of the spatial elements of a landscape or a still life on a flat surface–Cézanne had already frequently neglected central perspective as though it no longer mattered–must have been of considerable importance to Braque. It is certain that the large retrospective exhibition of Cézanne's work held in Paris in 1907, the same year in which he met Picasso, had an enormous influence on him.

A painting by Braque prompted Matisse to use the term 'Cubist' for the first time in 1908. Shortly following this, the critic Louis Vauxcelles wrote that Braque reduced everything to cubes. Since then the designation 'cubist' has become widely accepted. Initially, the depicted objects were indeed reduced to simple stereometric volumes, such as the cube, the cylinder and the cone. The name 'cubist', however, fails to acknowledge another, equally important visual element of this style: the facet. Paintings by Picasso and Braque are primarily made up of countless facets, small surfaces, delineated by straight or curved lines and having a convex or concave form. It seems as though these small surfaces are painted at a constantly different angle with respect to the vertical surface of the canvas. Sometimes they overlap or merge with each other. This gives rise to a moving relief, which provides a comprehensible image but which, at the same time, is impossible to reconstruct. As such, the eye and the

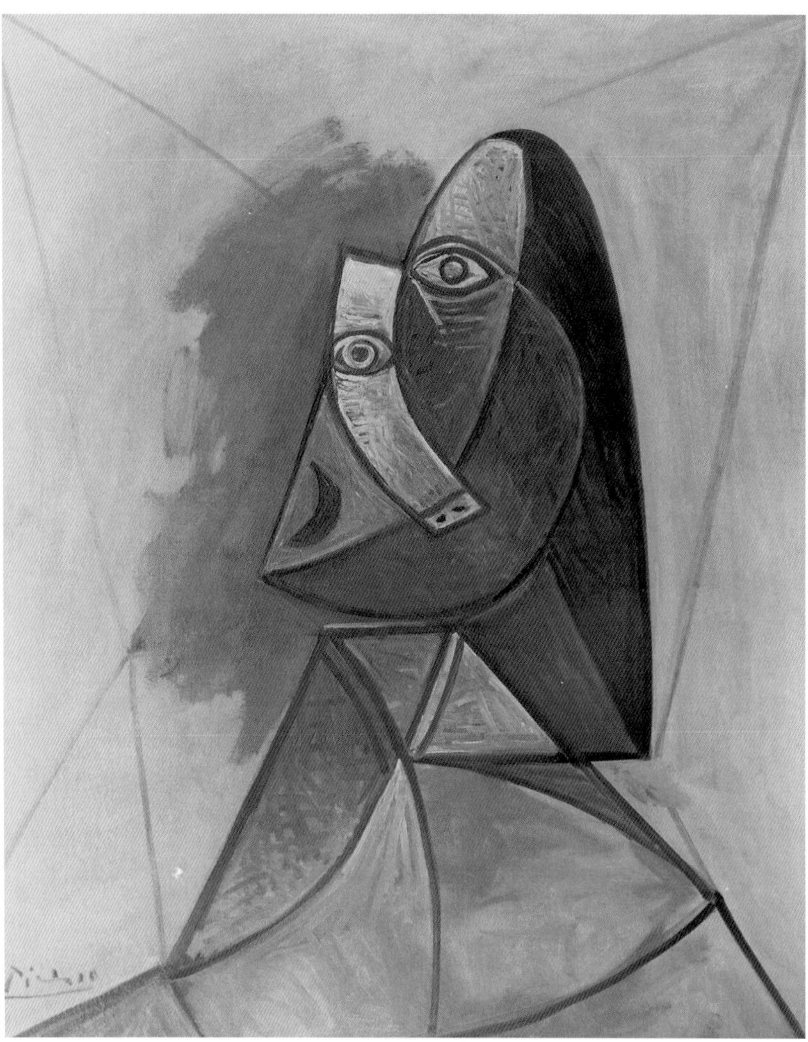

their composition no longer contain any reference to visible reality. But Picasso believed that painting would die if it abandoned the great classical themes–the landscape, the still life, the nude, the portrait–and he was not prepared to give them up. As a result of this, he thwarted, as it were, his own development. Until the early 1920s he remained one of the great revolutionary artists, one of the pioneers of the twentieth century, and the author of paintings which were, in many ways, of great influence for later developments. All of his artistic discoveries were derived, directly or indirectly, from the cubist formula, and inevitably there came a time when the paintings ceased to be inventions and became repetitions or variations. Picasso became a virtuoso: someone who, within the chosen formula, could paint anything, knew how to exploit every possible variant, and whose paintings continually maintained a high level.

The painting *Buste de femme* was made in 1943. If one compares this to the early Cubist painting from the collection (*Femme en vert*, 1909), it is easy to see that basically little has changed: the way in which forms are manipulated and transposed into a greater whole has remained the same for the most part. The forms have, however, become simpler and more robust–they have been drawn and painted with refinement. The painting has a certain elegance.

From analytical cubism, which dissected the forms into their component parts, came synthetic cubism, which then fitted the fragmented reality back together as though it were a puzzle. The Spanish artist **Juan Gris**, who moved to Paris in 1906, quickly became part of Picasso's circle. There he grew, under the influence of Picasso and Braque, into one of the leading representatives of this second period of Cubism. His paintings, mainly still lifes, are the result of a composition of more or less geometric surfaces, derived from the form of depicted objects. Gris provided no analysis of that which was depicted but built, with the elements developed by him on the basis of the subject, a new arrangement of contained surfaces which were placed along side or on top of each other. This gave rise to abstract compositions which only in parts refer to the origins of the image. In *Nature morte* from 1920, for instance, the schematized forms of a guitar, a pipe and a sheet of music are only recognizable in certain segments. A typical aspect of the work of Gris (and a characteristic of synthetic cubism) is the total absence of any suggestion of depth, the complete flatness in terms of

imagination of the viewer are continually roused into great activity. The painting *Femme en vert* (1909) by Picasso possess a great sculptural quality due to this very use of facets with light and shade effects. That he was concerned not only with an abundance of forms, but also with the spatiality of the painting, is evident from the fact that the female figure is completely detached from the background.

Though the way in which Cubist painting arose is, in essence, totally original, there are a number of influences to be discerned, certainly where the language of forms is concerned. For Picasso these are undoubtedly the highly formalized African 'primitive' sculpture, ancient Iberian sculpture, the work of the Spanish painter El Greco and the French naive painter Le Douanier Rousseau, and ultimately Cézanne. The descriptions given to these paintings deal mainly with the formal means, which were introduced by the Cubists: the prime

issue was their development of new visual representation, which owes its existence to freedom of thought, to 'guts' and great powers of imagination. Picasso regarded art first and foremost as a mental adventure: "Art is a lie, which makes us aware of truth." At certain points, Picasso's development shows that typical hesitation between further radicalization and the maintenance of the ultimately limited innovation of Cubism. Picasso was the inventor of Cubism and yet, for all his involvement with this, he was not tied to the 'theory' of Cubism. To a large degree, he was a pragmatist who gave no thought to the consequences that his discoveries could have. If those consequences did not correspond to his instinct for what a good painting was, they simply did not occur to him. Mondrian, someone of an entirely different nature, saw the inevitable consequence of Cubism as being a purely abstract art–an art in which, contrary to Picasso's Cubism, the elements of form and

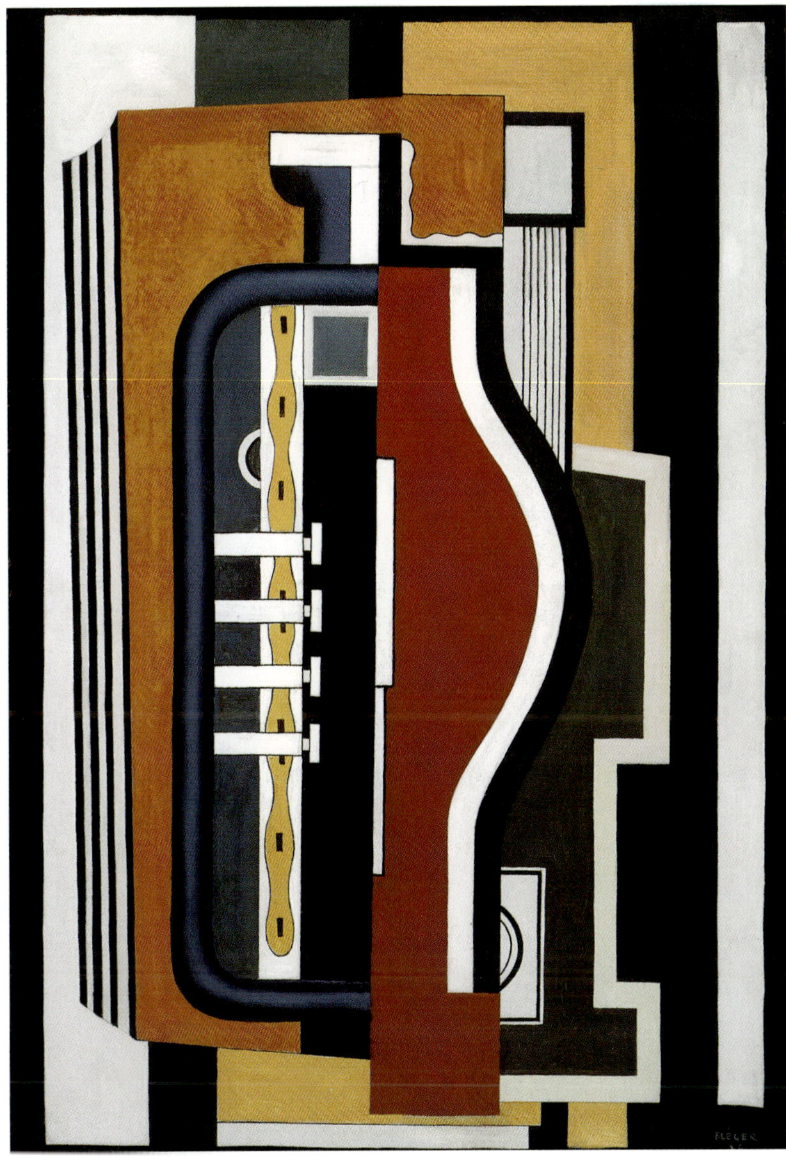

Fernand Léger *L'accordéon*, 1926

depiction. The colors are often confined to subdued greys, dark blue, brown, ochre and black. These usually correspond to the form of the geometric surfaces.
Throughout its various phases, Cubism was concerned with purely artistic problems, such as the composition of the image and structure with respect to color. It had been aimed at the disassembling of the 'object' to be painted in order to arrive at a different artistic order in the painting. Initially, **Fernand Léger** was also an 'analytical' Cubist, and on a very high level, but whereas cubism unravelled the various forms in order to dissect their structure, Léger did this, conversely, in order to give each form more emphasis and dynamics. He therefore put his paintings together in such a way that the sculptural quality of the form was preserved.

"The closeup, which is the new discovery of film, helped me. The object/fragment has its own value; by isolating it, one gives it personality."
L'accordéon (1926) consists of fragments of different musical instruments, which have been overlapped with each other as flat surfaces. Nonetheless, the sculptural quality is maintained due to the contrasts of form and color and due to the sudden contrast of the blue tubular element and the perspectival vertical lines at the left side of the canvas. His experiences in the trenches during World War I, when as a soldier he came into contact with a cross section of the French people (different from the way in which this happens on evening visits to the 'café des artistes') taught him how 'ordinary' people were concerned with tangible things, with

day-to-day objects, rather than with abstract theories. If he wished to produce art for all people, and not only for the elite, he had to find an equivalent for the concrete, direct way in which 'common people' lived.
In addition to this, Léger had a keen interest in modern technology. His works reflect a distinct sympathy for the machine and architecture. This attitude was very closely related to Purism, an artistic discipline in which objects are depicted in their architectural simplicity, inspired by the machine, whose perfect forms were possible only by way of the exclusion of all non-functional parts. Purism, as defined by Amédée Ozenfant and Charles Edouard Jeanneret (better known as Le Courbusier, the great architect) regarded nature not as something mystical but rather as a calculable machine. Nature, they believed, had structural laws, the laws of geometry, underlying its appearances. By constructing the world in harsh contrasts of form and bright colors, Léger stripped it of refinement and outward beauty. The image which came about in this way assumed a value of its own, became autonomous. "In my opinion, sculptural beauty is entirely free of sentimental, descriptive or imitative qualities. Each object, painting, building or ornamental composition has its own intrinsic value, is absolute in the strict sense and independent of whatever it might represent." Though the Russian-born **Marc Chagall** later opted for very different solutions in his work, he too made use of the cubist idiom in his younger years. The painting *Hommage à Apollinaire* (1911-12) was produced during his first period in Paris, from 1910 to 1914. There he soon came to be influenced by the cubist painters and their work. This painting, which is dedicated to the poet Guillaume Apollinaire, a friend and supporter of the Cubists, thus shows distinctly cubist traits. The heads of the two figures have been reduced to orbs, the necks to cones. For the other body parts Chagall used geometric shapes, which schematically indicate the various vantage points. Throughout this painting, whose composition is determined by the circular shape and the centrally placed figures, more or less geometric shapes can be seen. Despite the art-historical significance of its cubist character, this painting is not primarily about Chagall's discovery of these new ideas and forms. It is, above all, the portrayal of his outlook on life, his mystical view of mankind. The main theme could be described as 'man at the center of space and time'.
The two figures are depictions of Adam and

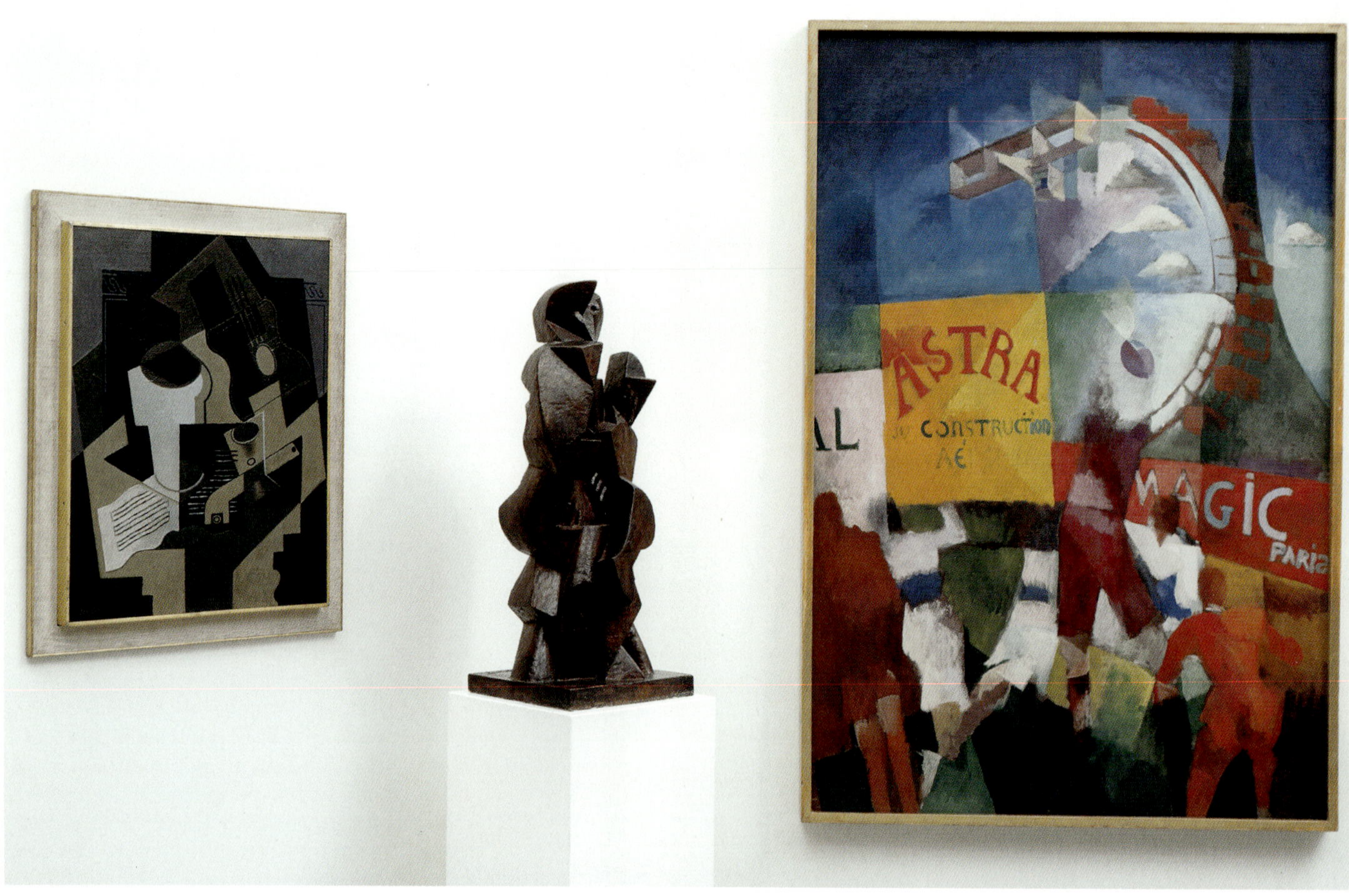

From left to right: **Juan Gris** *Nature morte*, 1920; **Jacques Lipchitz** *Marin et guitare*, 1917-18; **Robert Delaunay** *L'équipe de Cardiff*, 1913

Eve, who function as prototypes of man in the shape of a dual entity. They are standing in the middle of a circle, which suggests both the earth in the universe and the face of a clock. The latter is indicated in a sketchy manner with the digits for 9, (1)0 and 11 o'clock, at the upper left of the circle. Another reference to the idea of time can be inferred from the fact that the earth shows day and night: the left upper half of the circle/orb has been painted in warm colors (red, green, gold) that glow beneath the sun's rays, while the right lower half is predominantly covered with silver and dark blue, colors that are symbolic of night.

Hommage à Apollinaire is one of Chagall's richest and most beautiful paintings. It is a poetic portrayal of man, who is projected into a kind of magic circle, the age-old symbol of the earth and the cosmos. Within this circle Chagall created a fascinating image of rhythmic forms and radiant colors.

That cubism was not a rigid or dogmatic theory is also evident from the work of **Robert Delaunay**, whose painting *L'équipe de Cardiff* (1913) is about subjects such as space,

movement and light. Delaunay dealt with these themes, by way of a number of phenomena which he considered typical of the dynamics of the modern age. Not only does one see fragments of a rugby team in action, but also billboards, a Ferris wheel, an airplane–then still a miracle of technology–and the Eiffel Tower. An essential aspect of this painting is that the impression of movement in space is chiefly brought about by color, supported by the structure of the composition. The dynamics of the rugby players, for instance, is not primarily expressed by their stances referring to action, but much more by the countless colors and color contrasts.

In 1912 Delaunay writes, "The light in nature generates the movement of the colors." And one year later: "I have strived for an architecture of colors, in the hope of realizing the impulses, the conditions of a dynamic poetry and of confining myself in this to the painterly means, free of any literature, free of any descriptive anecdote."

Due to the lyrical nature of his work, which is particularly expressed in the use of color and

light, Apollinaire viewed the work of Delaunay as being among the most important examples of Orphism, a tendency in cubism designated by him.

Among the sculptors who based their work on the principles of cubism, Constantin Brancusi, Alexander Archipenko, Raymond Duchamp-Villon, Henri Laurens, **Jacques Lipchitz** and Ossip Zadkine were the more significant. Most of them, however, produced their first cubist work only after cubism had reached its highpoint in painting. Some sculptors, such as Lipchitz, became linked with cubism by adopting the range of characteristic forms that had already been developed by the painters and by constructing sculptural figures which nearly seem to be translations of figures in paintings. That was one option. For other artists, particularly for the most important sculptor from the first half of the twentieth century, Constantin Brancusi, cubism had a different, less specific yet more universal ideological meaning.

The first cubist sculpture by Lipchitz dates from 1913. During this time, he was living and working in Paris, where he had contact with Picasso and Juan Gris.

Jacques Lipchitz had a preference for subjects such as clowns, pierrots, and guitar-playing seamen. In the sculpture *Marin et guitare* from 1917-18 he has reduced the natural forms into stereometric elements and arranged these again into a spatial composition; due to the shifting, the staggering and the compression of these different volumes, the sculpture possesses a strong rhythmic quality. Lipchitz manages to combine these abstract sculptural forms into an organic and independent whole, which in its vitality is reminiscent of the figure which served as the point of departure.

In 1929 **Ossip Zadkine**–living in Paris, like so many Eastern Europeans of his generation–produced a tall wooden sculpture of a somewhat tragic-looking human figure (*Saint Sébastien*) which was extraordinarily characteristic of the period in which it was made. Zadkine came to Paris shortly after the birth of Cubism. He was therefore not a direct participant in the 'revolution', sooner a gifted user of the new visual language. In view of the fact that the cubist principles had been formulated by painters–first by Picasso and Braque, immediately followed by Gris and Léger–these principles could not simply be transferred to sculpture. The Cubist painters constructed their paintings from small angular surfaces, in order to allow the form in the painting to correspond to the surface that the painting basically was. They sacrificed the resemblance to reality: in their view, a painting could no longer be a depiction of nature. It had to be an autonomous image which was primarily meant to obey the very laws of the medium, the flat, two-dimensional painting. This signified a fundamental breakthrough: the painting no longer served the function of depiction–it now became a reality of its own, an expression, mainly of the artistic vision of the individual artist.

Zadkine falls into the category of Brancusi, where the ideological significance of cubism has particular importance. Just as the Cubists had abandoned the direct observation of nature and were no longer concerned with perspectival space, Zadkine now felt free to interpret the human figure–the 'standard' throughout many centuries of sculpture–in a very liberal manner. The viewpoint from which that free interpretation took place could, of course, vary from one artist to the other, all the more because each viewpoint could be nothing other than a personal choice. Cubism, preceded in that by several late-nineteenth-century artists such as

Cézanne, had freed art from its traditional conventions. Because of this, the 'laws' that would determine just how a painting or sculpture was supposed to look were also gone. From this point on, only the artist as an individual could determine that. Zadkine opted for a minimal stylization of the human figure and, within this, for a concentration on certain instinctive qualities. In *Saint Sébastien* from 1929 he used a piece of wood, a tree trunk, in a clever manner. Hardly needing to do anything to this, he merely gave it the rough form of a figure, in such a way that the body becomes the support for the strangely tilted head. It is especially this contrast, the nearly motionless body juxtaposed with the downcast head, which lends this sculpture its deeply sorrowful, nearly sentimental quality. Many critics have remarked that the tension and the excitement about the new developments in art began to wane at the end of the twenties. The adventurous spirit that had characterized the previous years, particularly the years between 1908 and 1918, was starting to fade. The findings of Cubism had become common knowledge.

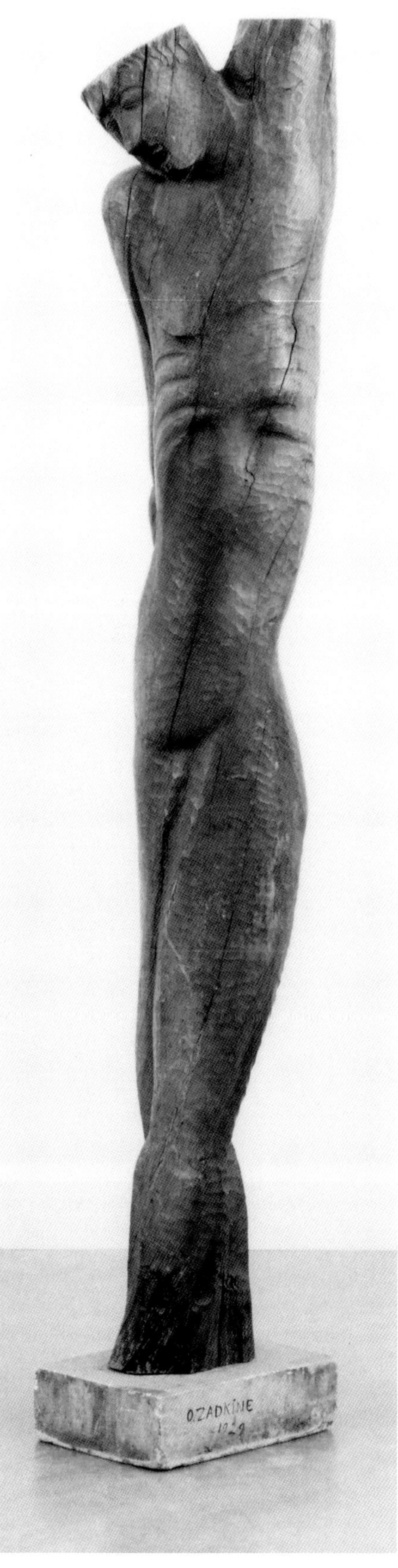

Ossip Zadkine *Saint Sébastien*, 1929

iV

Theo van Doesburg

Piet Mondrian

Bart van der Leck

László Moholy-Nagy

Kurt Schwitters

Friedrich Vordem-
berge-Gildewart

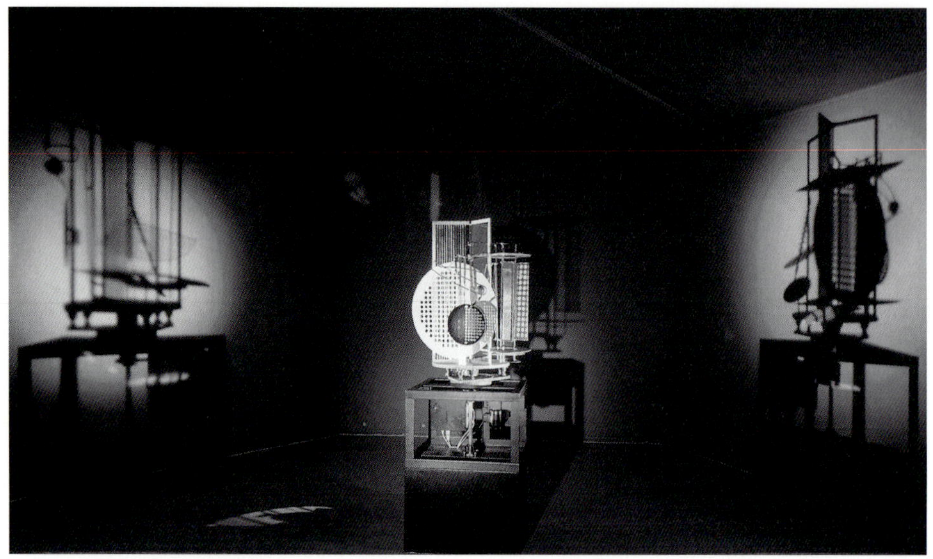

László Moholy-Nagy *Licht-Raum-Modulator*, 1922-30

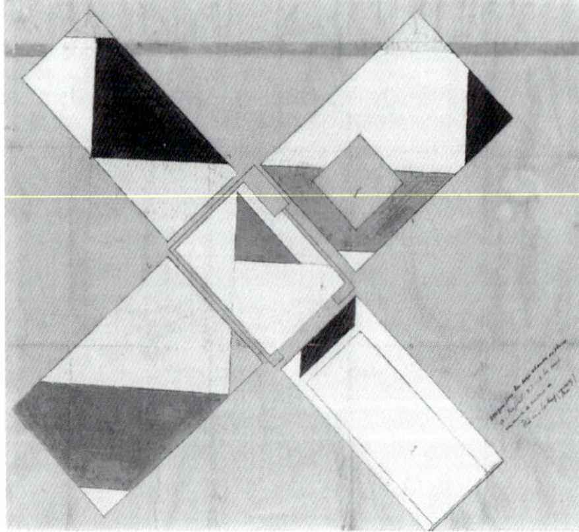

Theo van Doesburg *Ontwerp kleurbeeld van een bloemenkamer,*
1924-25

Cubism, which had reached its highpoint around 1910, had clearly denounced the conventional ways of rendering objects and had even negated them to a certain degree. But, even so, the cubists had worked with visible reality in mind; their compositions referred to visible objects. From the foundations laid by Cubism, with its language of forms, there arose an art that would rigorously break with the subjective rendering of reality. Purely geometric forms became the building blocks for an abstract painting. The artist no longer showed what could already be seen, such as a landscape or a human figure, but rather made something visible. What he attempted to make visible were, above all, the relationships among visual elements: that is to say, such fundamental aspects as the tension between the horizontal and the vertical, the thick and the thin, the high and the low, but also the relationships among colors, among surface, space and rhythm. Art was regarded as an ideological model for harmonious relationships, which were to be attainable for individuals as well as for all other aspects of society. The new painting, produced according to this ideal, which avoided any trace of the material world and was free of all personal influence from the individual artist, would be entirely autonomous and comply only with universal laws.

Since this type of art alluded to much that could not be seen and because it implied that a new ideal harmony could be brought about between man and his environment, there remained a great deal to explain. Artists who often joined together in groups wrote manifestoes, published periodicals and books and gave lectures. All over Europe, movements adhering to these ideals were cropping up; the most revolutionary and far-reaching were being expounded in the Netherlands and in Russia.

In the Netherlands the desire for a new, present-day tradition which would reflect the 'consciousness' of the age brought together a number of artists who jointly expressed several new points of departure in the periodical *De Stijl*, founded in 1917 upon the initiative of Theo van Doesburg. The group included not only painters, but also designers and architects.

Their artistic program also involved abstract film, typography and stage design. People from various disciplines held discussions on the principles of the new visual language, which was to be introduced in all visual phenomena. The first five points of *Manifest I*, quoted from *De Stijl* (II, 1, 1918) and listed below, provide some idea as to the atmosphere in which the diverse principles were being put into words.

"1. There is an old and there is a new consciousness of time. The old centers on the individual. The new centers on the universal. The struggle between individual and universal is manifested in the world-war, as well as in contemporary art.
2. The war is destroying the old world and its content: domination by the individual in every area.
3. The new art has asserted the content of the new consciousness: individual-universal equilibrium.
4. The new consciousness is ready to be to realized in every area, including material life.

5. This realization is obstructed by tradition, dogma, and domination by the individual (the natural)."[1]

The real world, in which the nature of the relationships between format and placement was clear (e.g. a mountain is higher than a house), no longer served as a model. The problem now became: how to place the elements in relation to each other on the image surface. Under the influence of the neo-platonistic philosophy of the mathematician Schoenmaekers, who published *Het nieuwe wereldbeeld* in 1915 and *Beeldende wiskunde* in 1916, those elements were confined to the straight line, the right angle, the primary colors red, yellow and blue, and the primary non-colors white, black and grey. Line, space and color were arranged in the most elementary compositions.

The painting *Composition XXII* (1922) by **Theo van Doesburg** shows a construction of rectangular forms. The planes, which maintain their own concreteness due to their volume and color, have been placed along side each other in such a way that they suggest a spatial movement forward and backward. In this manner of 'building' the painting already hints at Van Doesburg's later activities (1923) in architecture.

The Van Abbemuseum owns a number of replicas and scale models carried out on the basis of Van Doesburg's designs. These were made in connection with the retrospective exhibition *Theo van Doesburg: 1883-1931* in 1968. At that time the museum also received a gift from his widow Nelly van Doesburg, which is titled *Ontwerp kleurbeeld van een bloemenkamer* (1924-25). Van Doesburg designed the 'Chambre des fleurs' in 1924 for a villa in Hyères, property of the Vicomte de Noailles. In this villa was a very small room measuring approximately one by one-and-a-half meters, with a height of about two-and-a-quarter meters. Every morning, the wife of the Vicomte arranged fresh flowers for the salon in this room. Van Doesburg

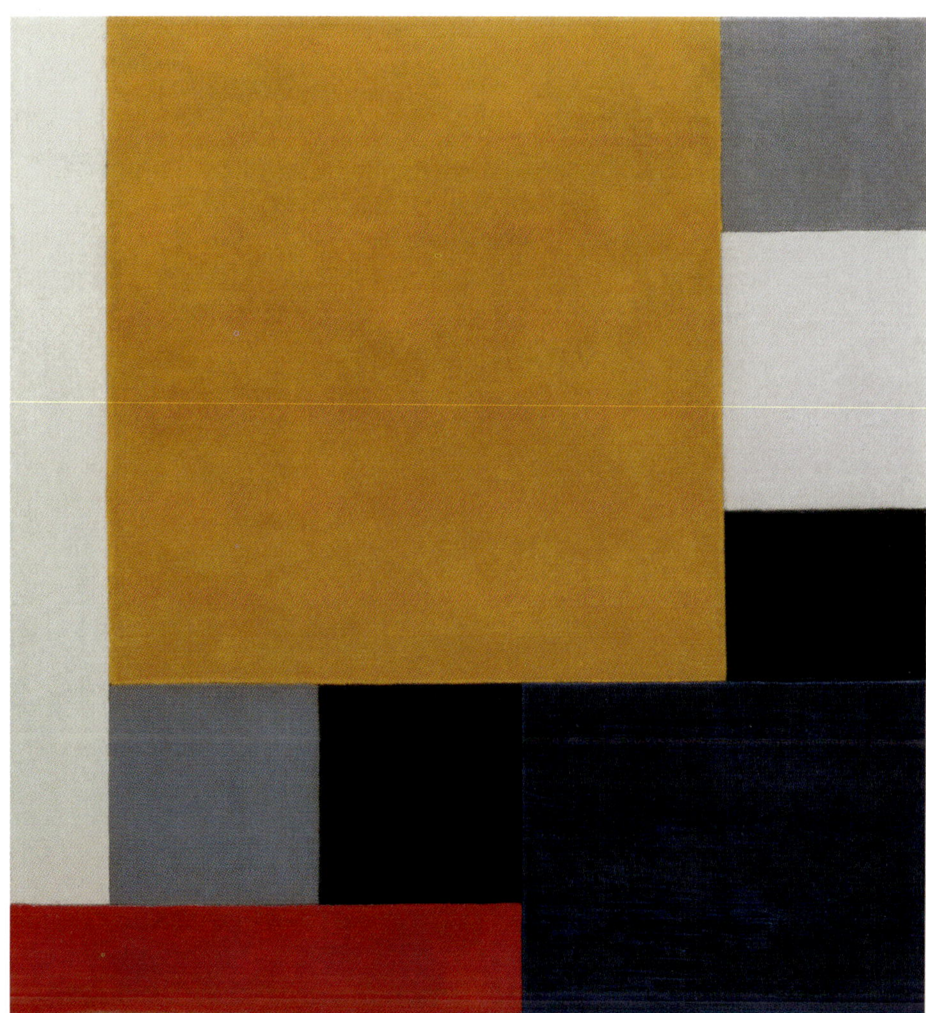

Theo van Doesburg *Compositie XXII*, 1922

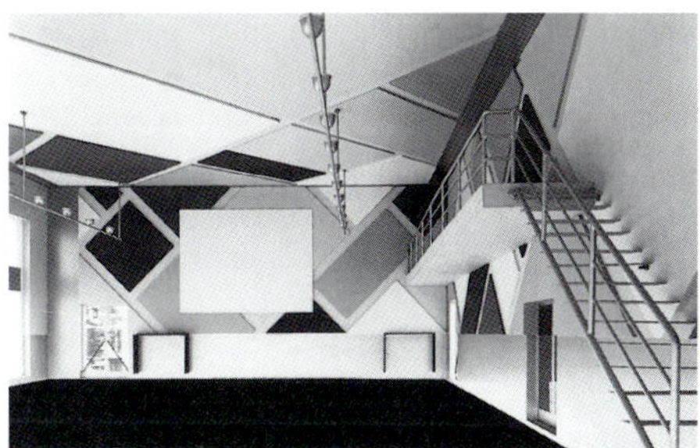

Theo van Doesburg *Interieur grote feestzaal van l'Aubette Strasbourg*, 1928 (reconstruction)

made a color design for this room based on diagonal lines and planes of color. Interestingly, in 1968, the director of the Van Abbemuseum at that time, Jean Leering, discovered that the design had not been carried out according to Van Doesburg's plan. Due to the rather singular way in which he had rendered his idea, the design sketch was interpreted wrongly and applied to the wall in reverse. This mistake was corrected in the reconstruction of the 'Chambre des fleurs' made by the museum.

Van Doesburg's activism and dynamic personality made him the central figure of De Stijl as a movement. He was the one who travelled most and established many contacts so that De Stijl also came to have international prominence within the European avant-garde. After his death in 1931, De Stijl moreover disbanded as a group. The most persuasive and most dogmatic representative of De Stijl was **Piet Mondrian**. In 1911 he saw works by Braque and Picasso

for the first time at an exhibition in Amsterdam. What struck him in these was the concern for the form and the potential to 'spiritualize' form. Up to that point he had, in his paintings of landscapes and trees, been mainly occupied with color as a means of interpreting his experiences and view of reality, in which–strikingly, even at that time–color and contour were being used by him as an indication of the structure and form. On seeing these Cubist paintings, Mondrian was no doubt drawn to the neutrality of the subject, which had been made subordinate to formal experiments. The unique quality of the subject–whether it be a landscape or a building–had come to have little importance to him during these years. Then he was already being guided by the idea of seeking a way which would lead, in the pictorial surface, "from the particular to the universal," as he later expressed this. The cubists exerted such an attractive force on him that, at the end of 1911, he left for

Piet Mondrian *Composition No. II*, 1930

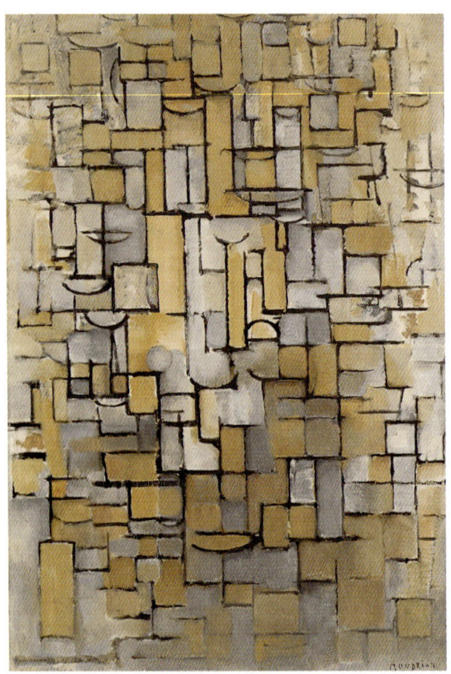

Piet Mondrian *Compositie XIV*, 1913

In the context of his overall development, it is plausible that Mondrian was already seeking, in these paintings, a universal representation of reality, which he attempted to reduce to an abstract network of horizontals and verticals here. He was, however, not yet prepared to opt for absolute form and color, as can be seen with his purely abstract work from 1920 onward, a style which he himself referred to as Neo-Plasticism (Nieuwe Beelding). These paintings can indeed be considered steps in this direction, though.

Mondrian was forced to stay in the Netherlands during World War I, and it was at this time that he came to know Bart van der Leck, Theo van Doesburg and the philosophy of Schoenmaekers as well. In search of universality, he turned away from the figurative element in Cubist painting. New painting was to be concerned with universal issues rather than specific ones. The essence of reality lay in harmony and order. This harmony could be depicted by the artist by means of a comparison of relationships in the elements of the painterly language itself: forms and colors. Mondrian formulated his theories in the essay '*De nieuwe beelding in de schilderkunst*', which was published in *De Stijl* in 1917-1918:

"Painting–which is in essence one and unchangeable–has always manifested itself in very diverse expressions. The expressions of the past–characterized by so many *styles*–differ only by reason of place and time, but fundamentally they are one. However they may differ in appearance, all arose from a single source: the *universal*, the profound essence of all existence. Thus all historical styles have striven toward this single goal: to manifest the *universal*.

Thus all style has a timeless content and a transitory appearance. The timeless (universal) content we can call the universality of style, and its transitory appearance the characteristic or the individuality of style. That style in which individuality best serves the universal will be the greatest: the style in which universal content appears most determinately plastic with be the purest." (*De Stijl I*, 2, pp. 13, 14)

"To see plastically is to perceive consciously, or more precisely, to see profoundly. It is to distinguish, to see truth. It is to compare and therefore to see relationship; or to see relationship and therefore to compare. It is to see things objectively, so far as this is possible. To see plastically is to be plastically active. By seeing plastically we automatically destroy the naturalistic and reconstruct the abstract appearance of things. By seeing plastically we improve, so to speak, our

Paris, where he remained until the summer of 1914. There he produced a series of paintings, which are characterized by horizontal and vertical lines and neutral colors (grey, brown) evidently inspired by the cubists' use of color.

Compositie XIV from 1913 is one of these. Though the origins of this visual motif probably lie with his increasingly abstracted paintings and drawings of trees, or with the structure of the facade of a Gothic cathedral, Mondrian has completely liberated himself from the subject here. He develops a structure of relatively short vertical and horizontal lines, which form many small rectangular planes, interrupted by only a few curved lines. This structure is supported by the rectangle of the image surface. Characteristically, the structure also disintegrates toward the edges: the lines are not cut off by the edges of the painting, and this gives the image a high degree of independence. The edges of the painting do not constitute a 'window' providing a view to an illusionistic space, but are simply the end of the image surface.

ordinary optical vision, and thus convert the individual to the universal. In this way pure plastic vision unites us with the universal. Pure plastic aesthetic vision expresses truth through beauty, therefore still veiled. But such beauty can no longer be the most outward beauty, simply because pure plastic vision sees more profoundly: ordinary vision sees this beauty as abstract." (*De Stijl, II*, 12, p. 135)

After the war Mondrian returned to Paris, where *Composition No.II* (1930) was produced. Contrary to many of his works, no primary color has been used in this painting. Black lines of different widths have been placed asymmetrically, intersecting, on a white background; they structure the white space.

World War II forced Mondrian to leave Europe, and he took up residence in New York, whose dynamics and freshness appealed to him as an atmosphere in which to work. Until his death in 1944, he continued to give shape to his vision of a harmonious balance in more complex and colorful compositions.

Though a member of the *De Stijl* staff since its inception, **Bart van der Leck** was only briefly drawn to the ideology of the group. When he met Mondrian in 1915-1916, he had already arrived at an extensive simplification of forms and colors. Van der Leck was initially trained as a stained-glass artist and did not attend the Rijksacademie van Beeldende Kunsten until a somewhat later age.

On the basis of applied art, he developed a style of his own, rendering his subjects in an increasingly stylized manner. The highest degree of abstraction is to be found in his paintings from 1916-1918, which Van der Leck himself referred to as 'mathematical images'. In addition to black, he used only the colors red, yellow and blue–mostly in rectangular forms. The dogmatic tendency and precision, as shown by Mondrian, was not present in the work of Van der Leck: after 1918 he reverted to more recognizable subjects.

The painting *Compositie (bloeiende tak)* from 1921, is made up of small elements of form that are placed separately in the space of the image surface. Though the image may not be recognizable as such, the title indicates that this relates to a theme derived from reality. In this respect it differs fundamentally from the visual outlook of most members of De Stijl. The first crucial steps toward fully abstract art had already been taken in Russia in 1913. In that year, Malevich painted a black square on a white background, this being the purest

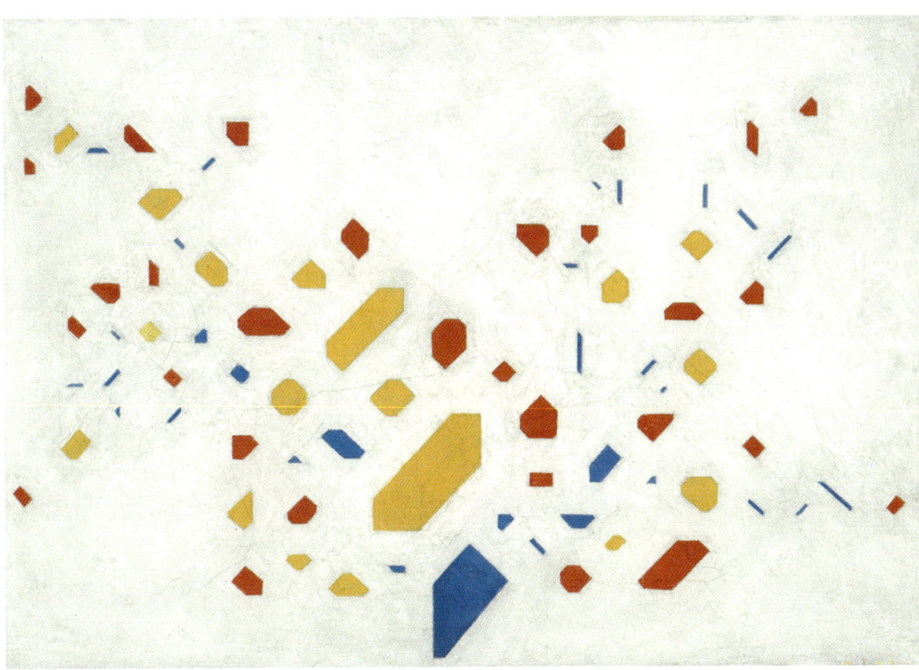

Bart van der Leck *Compositie (bloeiende tak), 1921*

and most radical painting that had ever been seen. Malevich's square was the start of a consistent course toward the definition of the object-free world of Suprematism. Tatlin built–also in 1913–his abstract relief constructions of metal, glass and wood. Together with the work of Pevsner, this constituted the beginnings of Russian Constructivism. An essential aspect of the new language of forms was the use of geometric form (the straight line, the square, the circle and the triangle) as geometry was regarded as the best example of perfect relationships. What particularly linked the Constructivists was the deep conviction that the artist could contribute to the physical and intellectual needs of the entire society. Their aim was to create a new art which would be universal and clear and thereby contribute to a new culture, in which not only the artist but also the scientist and engineer would take part.

Like the artists of De Stijl, the Constructivists believed that the basic principles of this new art should therefore be made applicable to architecture, urban planning, industrial design and typography. This art form, which aimed to anticipate technological and social developments, was initially approved by Trotsky after the Revolution of 1917. After 1925, when Stalin had managed to oust Trotsky from the center of power, it became impossible for many artists, however, to continue working in Russia.

In an extraordinary manner, El Lissitzky placed his artistry and his life in the service of a vision of a new reality and a new society. The Van Abbemuseum owns a large collection (128 works) of Lissitzky's watercolors, gouaches, drawings, typographic designs, experimental prints and one of his most important paintings. For this reason, a separate chapter is dedicated to him in this catalogue.

Die grosse Gefühlsmachine from 1920, a work by the Hungarian artist **László Moholy-Nagy**, attests to a very free notion of Constructivism. In this painting on unprepared linen, all sorts of components–cogwheels, digits, letters–are bursting from a machine and hovering in space. Along side the much more serious Constructivist paintings of Maholy-Nagy, this work has a certain playful look and displays the ironic characteristics of Dadaism.

During the early 1920s, Moholy-Nagy came to Berlin, where he soon became a well-known figure in the avant-garde. In 1923 Walter Gropius invited him to the Bauhaus in Weimar (founded in 1919), where he taught and headed the metal shop until 1928. The many 'isms' of that age came together at the Bauhaus, and it was here that abstraction became more or less institutionalized. The Bauhaus had an educational system which was revolutionary for that time, and underlying it was the idea of a union of applied and fine arts. The arrival of Moholy-Nagy brought an emphasis on the functional and utilitarian aspects of art, which was

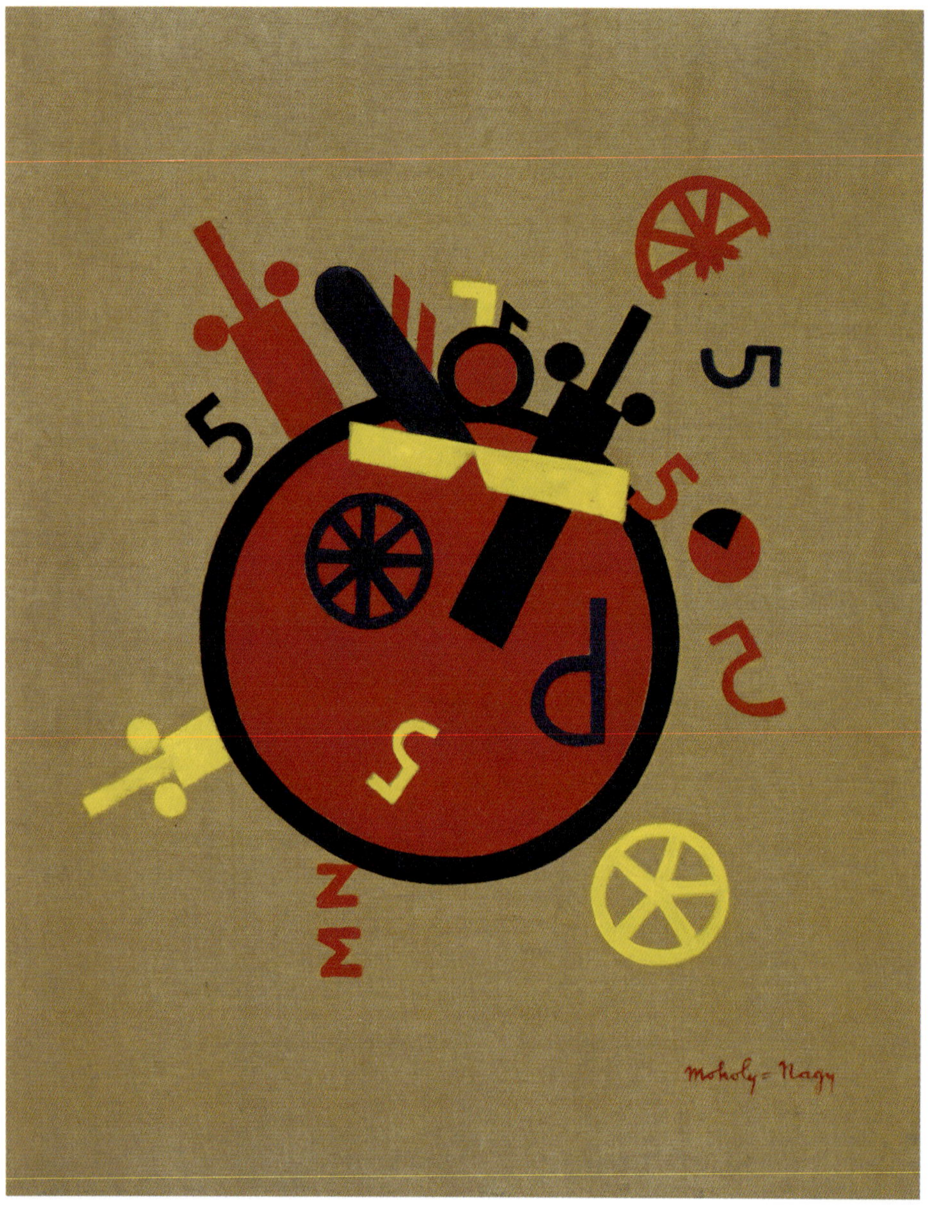

László Moholy-Nagy *Die grosse Gefühlsmaschine*, 1920

by the machine and the automaton and how they themselves can shape their living environment as a result. Giving man a voice, giving him the capacity to understand what goes on in the visible, material world, could also make him free to gain control of decisions, enable him to participate actively in the changes taking place in the technological world and the social forms of this. Moholy-Nagy wanted an art that would be not an indirect part of life but rather an integral part of current changes. In 1937, under the pressure of the political situation in Germany, he travelled to the United States, where he continued his work at the New Bauhaus in Chicago.

Kurt Schwitters–painter, sculptor, designer, writer and poet–has become known particularly for his *Merzplastiken* (constructions) and *Merzbilder* (paintings and collages). Schwitters happened to find the word fragment 'Merz' on a piece of newspaper and used it as a title for his works. The material that he used for these 'Merz' works largely consisted of litter, found objects and scraps of paper, combined with wood, paint or fabric. Schwitters regarded them as creations of fragile beauty that emerged from the ruins of the German culture.

During the 1920s Schwitters came into contact with the ideas of Constructivism and De Stijl. In this period he worked together with his friend El Lissitzky and Theo van Doesburg. Aside from the Merz works, he was now producing several, almost classical-looking, abstract reliefs. Due to the political situation in Germany, Schwitters moved to Norway in 1937 and, fleeing the Nazis, to England in 1940. Here he was held at an internment camp on the Isle of Man, where there were many intellectuals, writers, musicians and artists who had emigrated from Germany. In addition to the portraits of his fellow inmates, Schwitters also made abstract works, such as the oil-on-linoleum *Isle of Man* (1941).

Like Moholy-Nagy, **Friedrich Vordemberge-Gildewart** was among the artists who came into direct contact with the Constructivist tradition at an early point in their careers as painters. He received his training in Hanover, where the art scene was flourishing then. Here he could keep up with the latest developments, partly through encounters with El Lissitzky and Kurt Schwitters. In 1925 he joined De Stijl and, by way of the artists affiliated with this, came to know his comrades on an international level.

The activities of the group *Abstraction-Création*, which had been attempting to combine various tendencies in art through all

expressed in great activities in the realm of industrial design. Moholy-Nagy was an artist who, by continually experimenting with new industrial materials and with light as a visual means, showed his diversity not only in the field of industrial design but also in those of photography, film, kinetics and total theatre. In 1971 the Van Abbemuseum came into the possession of a replica of his *Licht-Raum-Modulator*, which was produced during the years 1922-1930. The light machine itself is comprised of three parts: the electric motor, the transmission and, on top of this, a rotating construction of various forms based on the straight line, the square, the circle and the diagonal–made of glass, plastics and different metal alloys–each of which carries

out its own movement in relation to the others. These movements are lit from different angles by two lamps, and this gives rise to a continually changing play of light on the walls and the ceiling of the space in which the machine has been set up. The work consists of the activities carried out by the visibly moving parts of the machine as well as those of the movements caused by the projection onto the walls. No hidden magical procedure takes place before the viewer, who is himself part of that space: everything that happens–the movement, the light source, the effect–remains visible.

Here one sees Moholy's view as to the attitude of people toward their modern world: how they should relate to a world influenced sorts of exhibitions, also led to a breakthrough and recognition of his work. After a period in which the visual elements–diagonals and triangles–were placed on the canvas in an amazing balance, around the 1950s Vordemberge-Gildewart made compact paintings based on the vertical plane and the vertical line, as in *Komposition no. 176* (1949). This deals with the "organization of the surface through pure verticality."

After having been driven from Germany by the war, Vordemberge-Gildewart returned in 1954 to head the Hochschule für Gestaltung in Ulm, where he wished to carry on the principles of the Bauhaus. There he worked together with a younger generation of abstract artists, which included Richard Paul Lohse, one of the leading personalities of the geometric-structural art from the postwar period.

In the Netherlands, the interest in the elementary principles and the ideals of De Stijl and Constructivism remained lively after the war as well. The exhibition on De Stijl, held in Amsterdam in 1951, and Vordemberge-Gildewart's continued presence in the Netherlands (until 1954) contributed to this. Young artists explored the principles of Mondrian and Van Doesburg and began to formulate their own rules for the structure of a painting.

Note: Excerpts from *De Stijl* translated by Harry Holtzman and Martin S. James in:*The New Art–The New Life, The Collected Writings of Piet Mondrian*, G.K. Hall & Co., Boston), 1986.

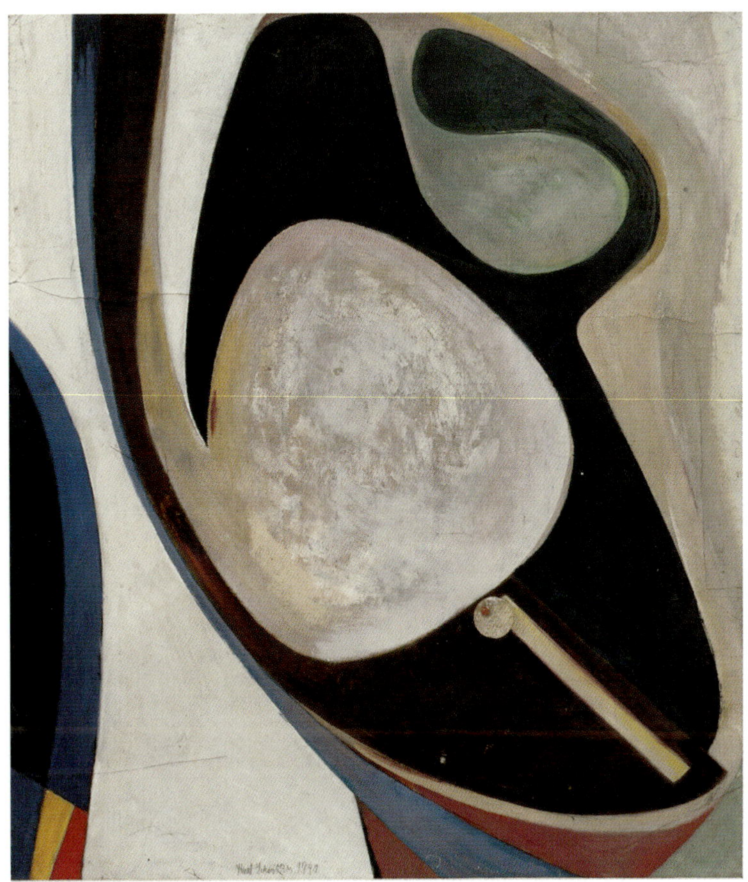

Kurt Schwitters *Isle of Man*, 1941

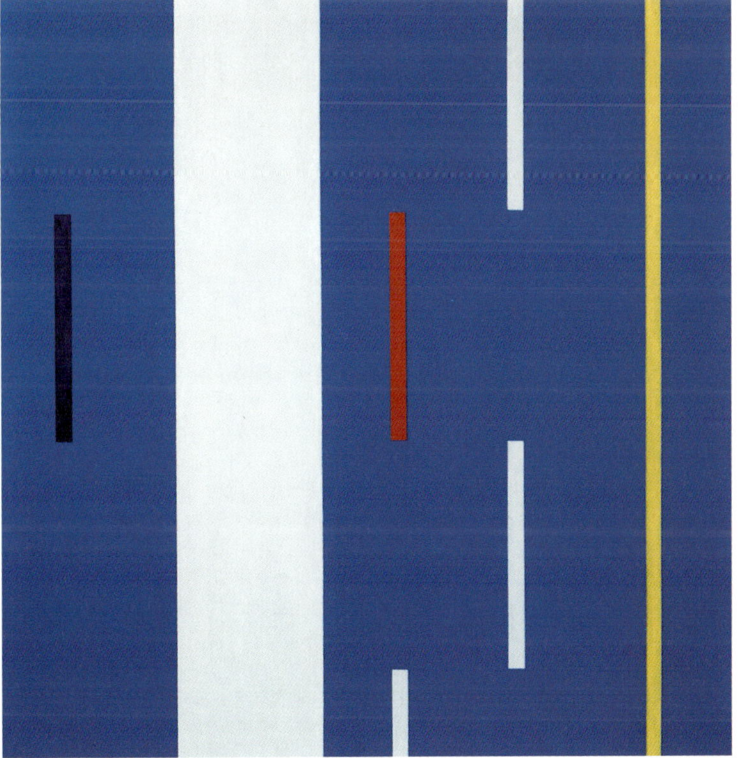

Friedrich Vordemberge-Gildewart *Komposition no. 176*, 1949

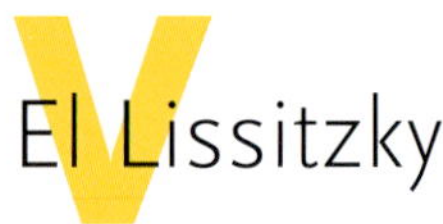

El Lissitzky

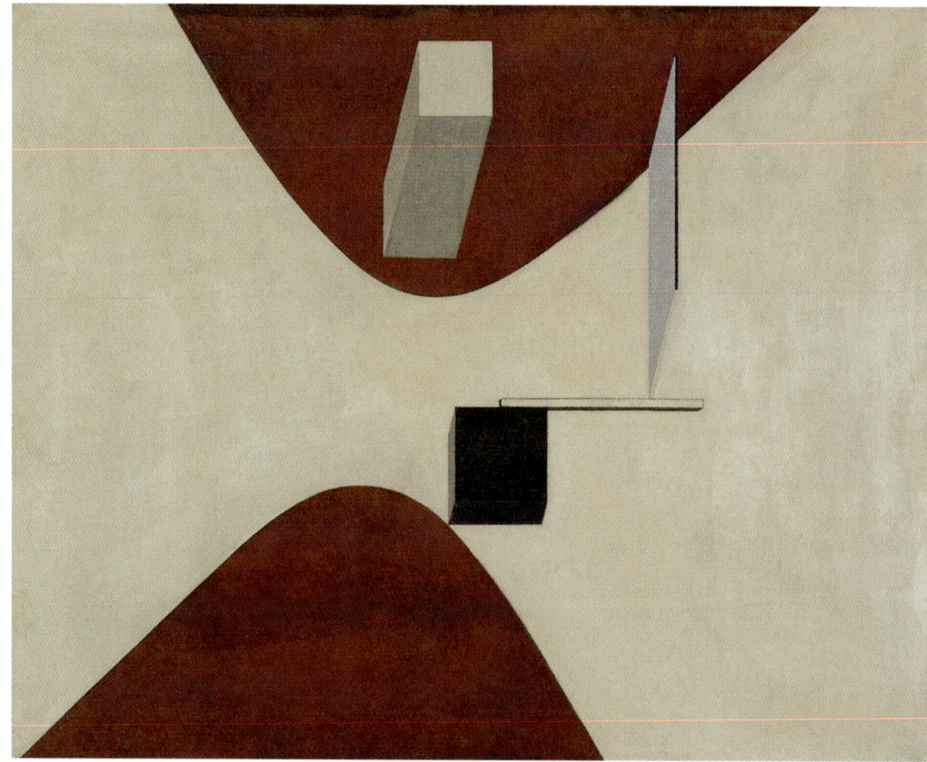

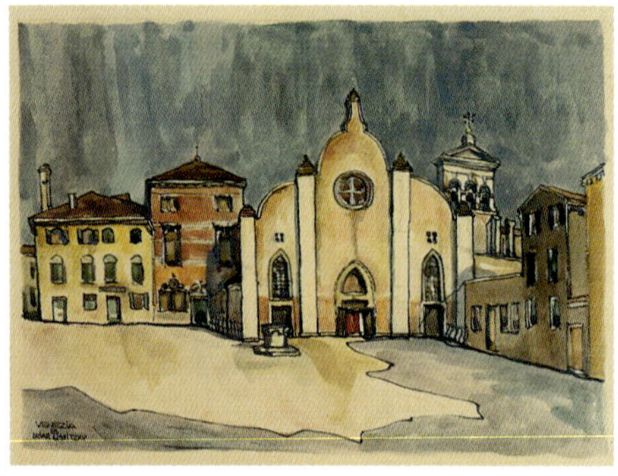

El Lissitzky *Venezia*, 1913

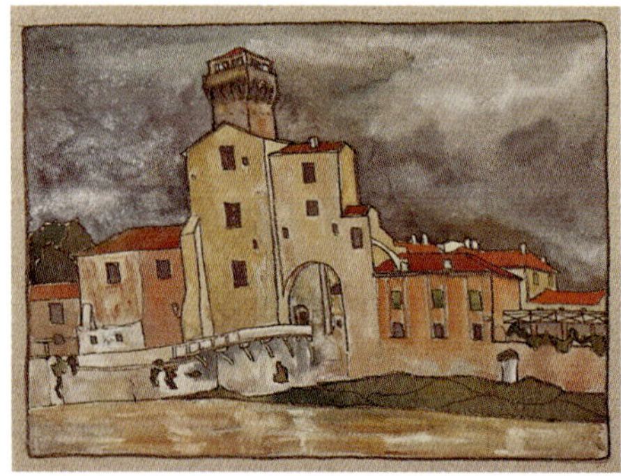

El Lissitzky *Italiaanse stad*, 1913

Together with Kazimir Malevich, Alexander Rodchenko and Vladimir Tatlin, El Lissitzky was among the most prominent representatives of the Russian avant-garde during the early part of the twentieth century. Seeking a new world, a new awareness, these artists aimed to create a new visual language in which a universal, objective reality could be expressed. Lissitzky strove to implement this language in the day-to-day world as well: in architectural and furniture design, typographic design and exhibition design. With all of this, he wished to make a tangible contribution to a new and better society. He shared this ambition with the artists of De Stijl in the Netherlands and those of the Bauhaus in Germany, and had frequent contacts with both from 1921 onward. Lissitzky was born in czarist Russia in 1890 as the son of Jewish parents. After his secondary education, he took the admissions exam for the art academy in St. Petersburg. Having passed, he was nevertheless denied admission because of his Jewish background: only a limited number of Jews were permitted to receive education at schools and universities in Russia every year. Like so many others who suffered this fate, he left for Germany in order to study there. He chose to go to Darmstadt, where he registered at the Polytechnische Hochschule for training as an architect. While studying there, Lissitzky continued to draw: a number of works from that time, including *Venezia* (1913), a drawing of a piazza with a small church, can be found in the collection of the Van Abbemuseum. The drawing came about in connection with a walking journey that Lissitzky had made through northern Italy in 1912.

When World War I broke out, Lissitzky returned to Russia and, in Moscow, studied to become an 'architect-engineer'. After obtaining his diploma in 1917, he was employed at a number of architectural firms. In addition to this, he devoted himself to the design and illustration of Jewish books. The Revolution of 1917 and the fall of the czar heralded a new era for the Jews of Russia. The new government gave them more freedom to express their own identity. Jewish artists studied the Jewish culture and dealt with Jewish themes in their work. Jewish writers wrote stories and plays in Yiddish, and these were illustrated by such figures as El Lissitzky and Marc Chagall.

In 1919 Marc Chagall founded an art academy in Vitebsk. He invited Lissitzky to come there and give lessons in architecture and the graphic arts. It was at this academy that Lissitzky met Kazimir Malevich, who joined the teaching staff shortly after he did. The acquaintance with Malevich and their collaboration from 1919-1920 was of great importance to Lissitzky's development.

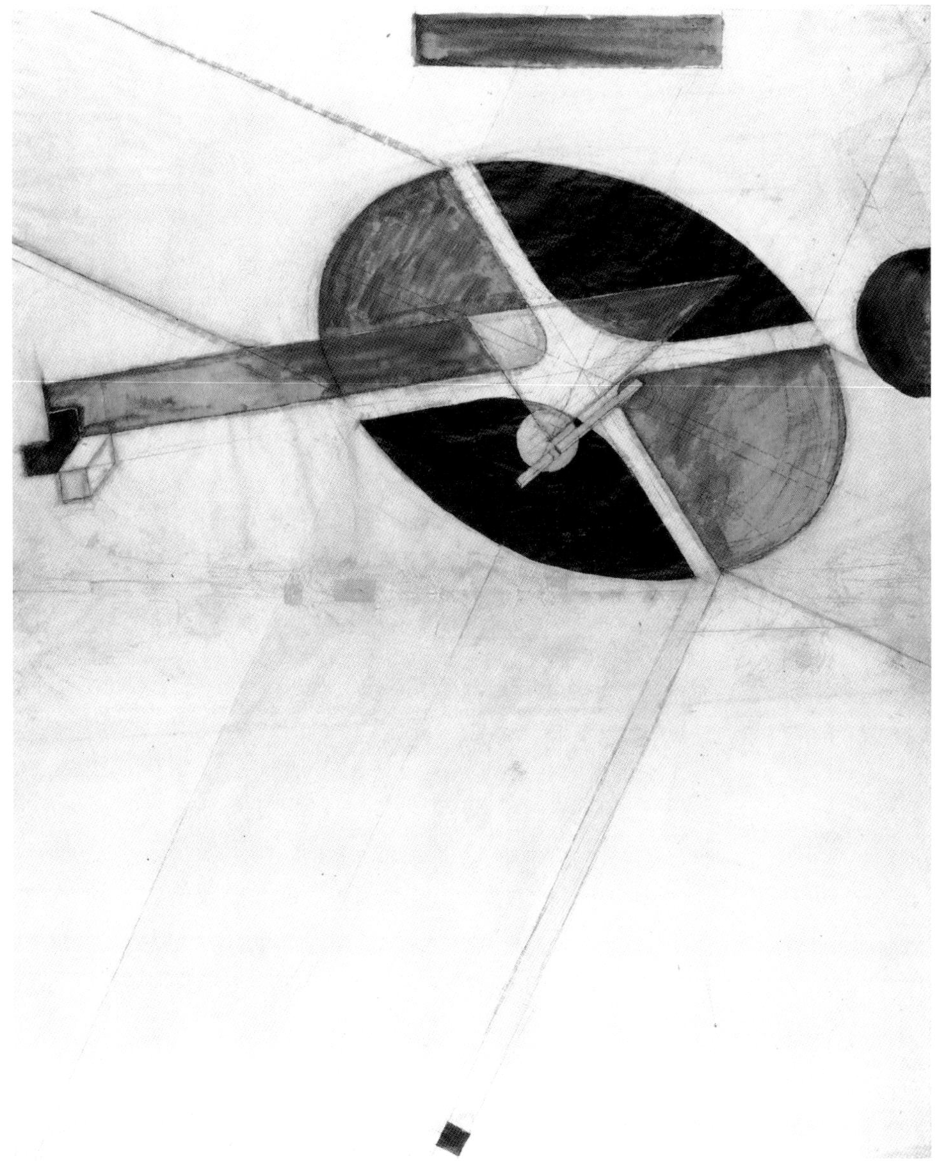

El Lissitzky *Ontwerp voor Proun G7*, ca. 1922-23

Malevich had ceased to depict visible reality around 1915. Influenced by discoveries in the field of physics, he had come to the conclusion that true reality did not consist of matter, but of energy, of forces that interact. In his Suprematist paintings he attempted to portray this reality with the aid of abstract and geometric forms, which he placed against a white ground. To Lissitzky, Suprematism was the theoretical and aesthetic equivalent of social revolution. He considered this art pre-eminently suited to the shaping of a new society and the realization of a universally comprehensible art. In 1919 he began to paint his *Prounen*. These are abstract works in which Lissitzky provided Suprematism's language of forms with a spatial dimension. Geometric planes and volumes seem to hover in an endless space. Forms are overlapped or juxtaposed on the surface, so that they create fields of tension or suggest movement. Movement, not only in all the possible directions of a two-dimensional surface, but also forward, in the direction of the viewer, or backward, away from the viewer. By axonometrically projecting the geometric forms onto the flat surface, Lissitzky attains a suggestion of depth which can be interpreted in many ways and which thereby evokes added tension.

The word *Proun* itself can be interpreted on multiple levels. It could be derived from the Russian *proekt unovisa*, which means 'architectonic design of Unovis. Unovis (Advocates of the new art) was the name that Malevich gave to his students and the teachers at the People's Art School in Vitebsk. Equally plausible are the meanings 'for the champions of the new art' and 'design for the affirmation of the new'. Lissitzky himself never explained the origins or meaning of the word. In 1920 he wrote, "The artist constructs new symbols with his brush. This symbol is not a recognizable form of anything which is already finished, already made, already existent in the world–it is a symbol of a new world, which is being built upon and which exists by way of people." Lissitzky painted most of the *Prounen* between 1919 and 1922. They express his utopian view of the future, in which man–freed from gravity–creates a new, floating world. The *Prounen* can be regarded as a turning point in Lissitzky's oeuvre, and they form the basis for his later work. The language of forms that he developed in his *Prounen*, as a painter and draughtsman, were applied in his activities as a typographer, architect and photographer. The painting *Proun P23, no. 6* from 1919 illustrates this turning point exceptionally well. The work stands out by way of its sobriety, in terms of both form and color; with minimal means Lissitzky manages to achieve maximum expression here. The use of two hyperbolas, which seem to be slightly shifted in relation to each other, gives the composition an intriguing tension. The bar and the plane, both of which protrude straight ahead into the viewer's space, as it were, are characteristic of Lissitzky's visual language. The hyperbola crops up again as a form in various later works in the museum's collection, including *Ontwerp voor Proun G7* and the design for the periodical *MA*. We also see a frequent use of the hyperbola in his later architectural designs.

Around 1923 Lissitzky developed the *Proun* into a three-dimensional model. At the *Grosse Berliner Kunstausstelling* he was given the use of a small, square space. Rather than hanging existing *Proun* paintings, he designed reliefs of *Proun* compositions, and this gave rise, as it were, to a three-dimensional *Proun*. Lissitzky himself said the following about this *Prounenraum*: "(...) The space was designed (as an exhibition space) by using elementary forms and materials: line, surface and rod, cube, sphere, black, white, grey and wood: in addition, surfaces (color) were set flat against the walls, and other surfaces (wood) were placed at right angles to the wall.(...) With this model I wish to clarify a number of principles which I find necessary for the fundamental organization of any space (...) I am aiming for a spatial balance, both active and elementary, that will not be

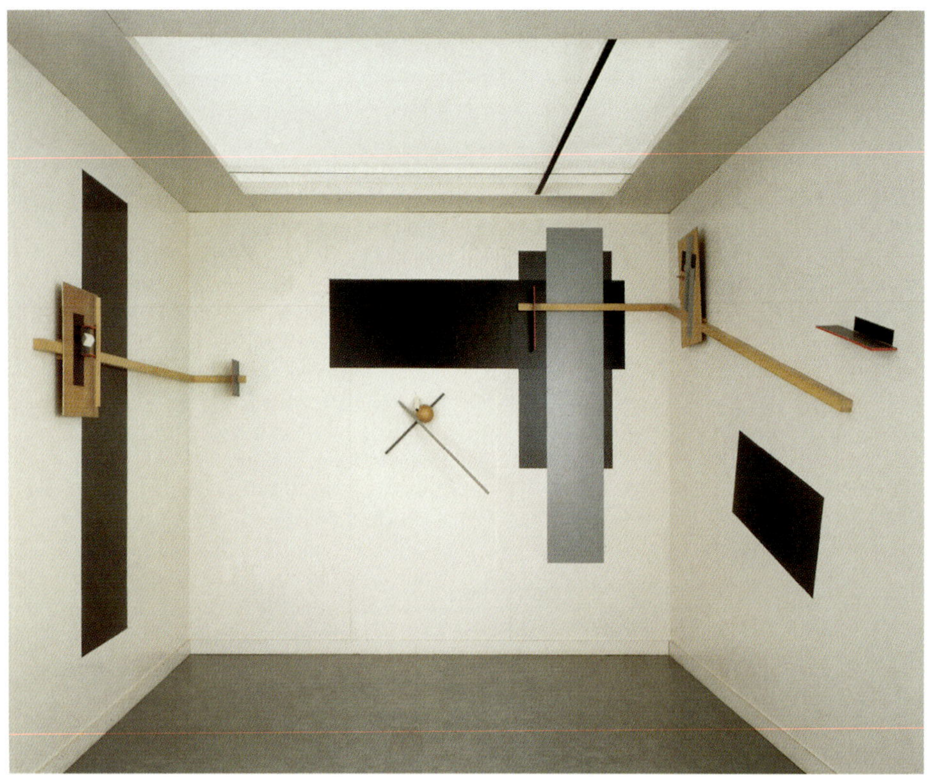

El Lissitzky *Prounenraum*, 1923 (reconstruction 1965)

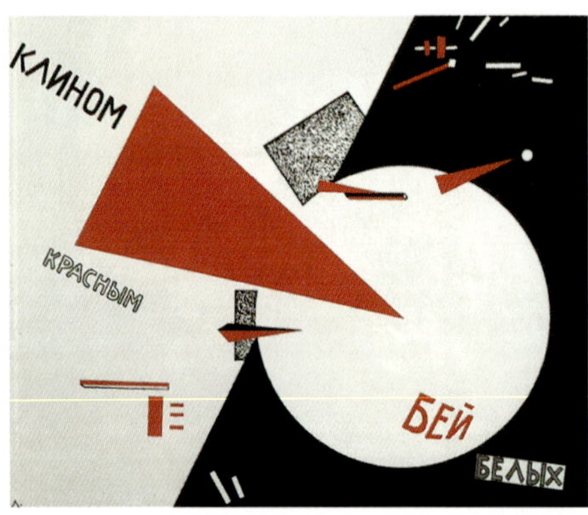

El Lissitzky *Klinom krasnym bej belych*, 1919-20 (reprinted 1966)

made designs for nine electromechanical dolls, which would assume the roles of the actors. One of these is *Neuer* symbolizing the 'new man' with a red square (the mark of Unovis) on its body, and the new society with a black and a red Soviet star on its two heads. The dolls would move across a kind of scaffolding, the *Schaumaschinerie*, operated by one person who would also be responsible for all of the voices. Lissitzky only designed these, preferring to allow others to make them. This never came about, however. An edition of the *Figurinenmappe* as well as a series of sketches and proofs are owned by the Van Abbemuseum. The actual design sketches can be found at the Tretiakov Gallery in Moscow.

After 1921 this spiritually oriented, utopian art was gradually driven away by a more utilitarian type of art: art that served society, the individual artist being subordinate to the community. Lissitzky was not indifferent to this. Convinced of his function as an artist in society and of the contributions that he could make to the reshaping of this, he wrote: "New inventions, which will enable us to move about in space in new ways and with new speeds will bring about a new reality. The static architecture of the Egyptian pyramids has been superseded—our architecture revolves, swims, flies. We are approaching the state of hovering in the air and swaying like a pendulum. I would like to help in discovering and developing of this form of reality."

More and more, Lissitzky served as a kind of cultural representative of the Soviet government in foreign countries. He organized exhibitions and published magazines. In 1922 he was asked to participate on the organization and installation of the *Erste Russische Kunstausstellung* in Berlin, where Westerners could become acquainted with developments in the realm of Russian art. There he met, among others, Van Doesburg, Schwitters, Arp and Moholy-Nagy. Art in the West and movements in Russia had developed separately in a surprisingly parallel manner. Despite the many similarities, there were, however, interesting differences: whereas, in Suprematism, the flat surface of the painting was disrupted by a concentration of spatial tensions that suggest a space that goes beyond that of the painting, De Stijl sought, on the contrary, a flatness in which the bounds of the image surface played an important role. In 1923 the exhibition travelled to the Stedelijk Museum in Amsterdam. Lissitzky went to the Netherlands, held lectures and made contacts

disrupted by the presence of a telephone in it or a standard piece of office furniture. *Space exists for man—man does not exist for space.*" A reconstruction of this *Prounenraum* is owned by the Van Abbemuseum.

An early example of a practical application of his new language of forms is the poster *Klinom krasnym bej belych* (1919-20). Here the abstract elements have assumed concrete meaning. We see how the Red Army wages war against the Whites: a large red wedge forces its way into a white circle, and at the upper right a smaller red wedge besieges a shaded white circle. A use of this language of forms in a very different different context can be seen with *Figurinenmappe Sieg über die Sonne*, for which Lissitzky produced designs in 1920 and which was published in Hanover in 1923. The portfolio contains designs for mechanical dolls, intended for the futuristic opera 'Victory over the Sun' by the painter-poet Alexei Kruchenykh and the painter-composer Michail Matyushin. The story is about the battle against the sun, which is taken prisoner and then replaced by a energy source created by man himself. The opera was performed for the first time in Moscow in 1913. Malevich designed the costumes and the sets. In 1920 it was performed once again by the pupils of Unovis, under the direction of Malevich. As a result of this, Lissitzky

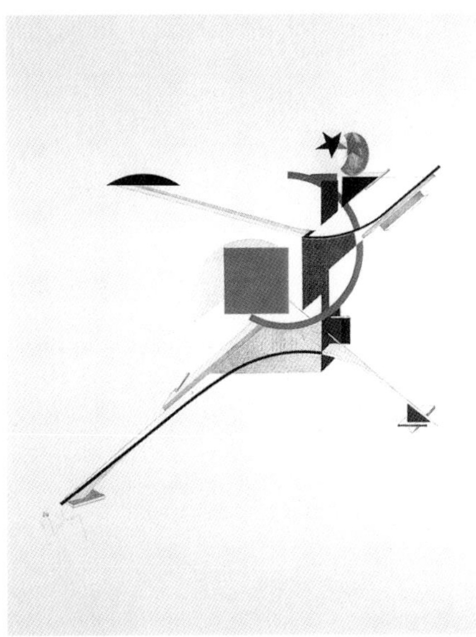

El Lissitzky *Figurinenmappe. Neuer*, 1923

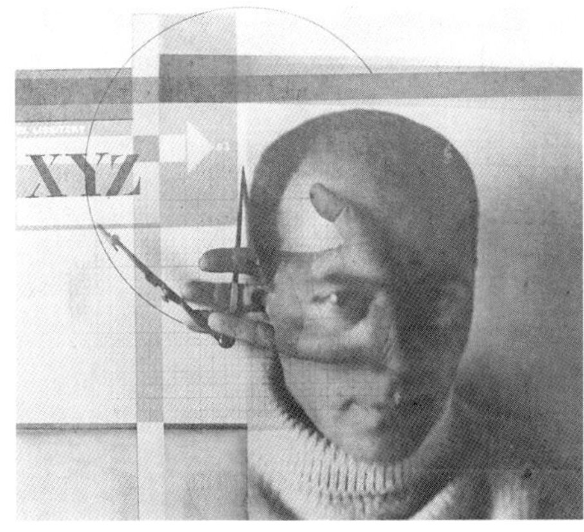

El Lissitzky *Der Konstrukteur (Selbstbildnis)*, 1924

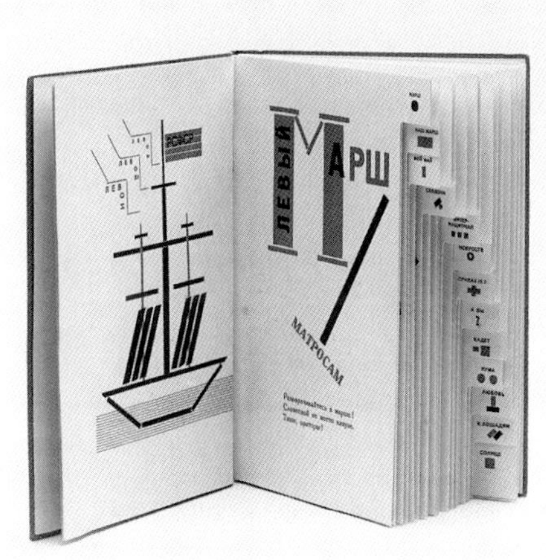

El Lissitzky *Vladimir Majakovski, Dlja golosa*, 1923

there with artists and architects, among them J.J.P. Oud. With him, Lissitzky kept up a correspondence; those letters are also in the collection of the Van Abbemuseum. Together with Van Doesburg, Lissitzky made pronouncements in which they appear to regard art as a universal expression of creative energy that can be used for the betterment of humanity.

In addition to his activities as a cultural ambassador and organizer of exhibitions, Lissitzky was also intensively occupied with the design of various publications. One example of his unconventional design is the small book *Dlja golosa*, from 1923, by the Russian writer Majakovski. The book, which contains thirteen poems, is meant to be read aloud. For the reader's convenience, Lissitzky gave the book a thumb index, a veritable innovation in the field of typography. Each poem has its own title page with an illustration, for which Lissitzky used only typographic elements, such as letters, lines, circles and grids.

Stricken with tuberculosis, Lissitzky was forced to spend time in a sanatorium in Switzerland in 1924. Despite his illness, he remained active and worked on all sorts of projects. No longer painting *Prouns*, he focused more on typography and architecture, on writing articles and experimenting with the medium of photography. In 1925 he returned to Moscow where, until his death in 1941, he devoted himself primarily to installing exhibitions and making publications for the Soviet government. One of these projects was the Soviet pavilion for the *Internationale Press-Ausstellung Pressa* held in Cologne in 1928. In a rare way, he placed his artistry and life in the service of a vision of a new reality and a new society.

The works of Lissitzky constitute a prominent and fundamental part of the Van Abbemuseum's collection. The majority of these were acquired in 1968 by director Jean Leering, a great admirer of and authority on Lissitzky's work. Leering discovered the works in 1965–while preparing an exhibition on Lissitzky–in the collection of Mrs. Vordemberge-Leda in Stuttgart. Aside from drawings, gouaches and lithographs, he found sketches, designs, working plans and proofs, which provided an extraordinarily good impression of the developmental process in Lissitzky's work. The works date predominantly from 1919-1924, the period in which Lissitzky's visual language took shape. On the occasion of the exhibition at the Van Abbemuseum in 1965, the *Prounenraum* was also reconstructed and made part of the collection. During the early seventies Leering broadened this collection with a number of letters, photographs and books designed by Lissitzky from the collection of J.M A. Oud-Dinaux, and in 1986 he donated an example of Lissitzky's photographic self-portrait *Der Konstrukteur (Selbstbildnis)* from 1924. In 1990 the museum organized, in connection with the centenary celebration Lissitzky's year of birth, a large retrospective exhibition of his work, which attested to the immense diversity of his artistry. This diversity was reflected extraordinarily well in the collection of the Van Abbemuseum, with the exception of one aspect: his activities as a painter. The purchase of the work *Proun P23, no. 6* (1919) in 1997 changed this. It crowns the museum's Lissitzky collection. At present the Van Abbemuseum owns the largest collection of Lissitzky's work outside the former Soviet Union.

vi

Roger Bissière

Jean Bazaine

Serge Poliakoff

Alfred Manessier

Sam Francis

Edgar Fernhout

Hans Hartung

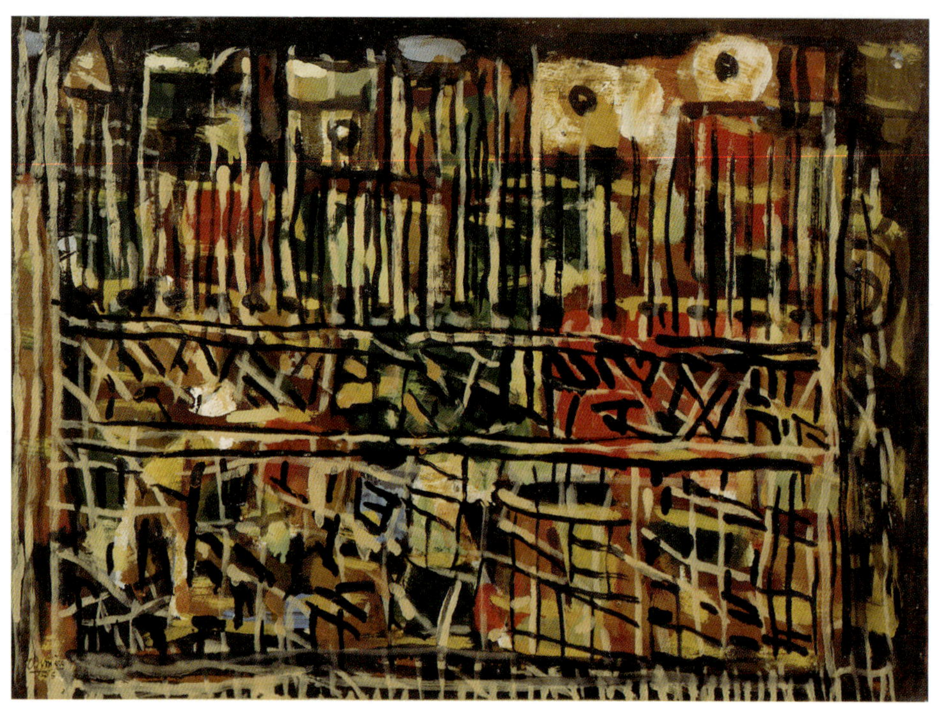

Roger Bissière *Composition*, 1955

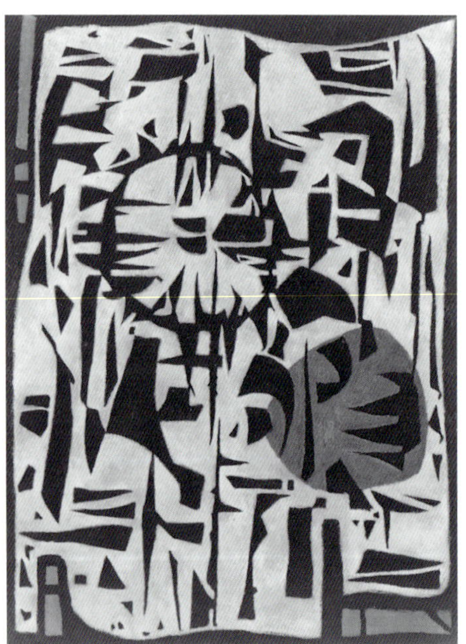

Alfred Manessier *Barabbas*, 1952

The end of World War II brought, in the history of visual art as well, the start of a new age, the age of abstract art. Particularly, non-geometric abstract art, which comes up here and which for the sake of convenience will be referred to as abstract expressionism, flourished during the first fifteen years after the war. The term abstract expressionism is, however, normally used specifically for the postwar developments in the United States (e.g. Gorky, De Kooning, Pollock, Kline and others).

The French painter **Roger Bissière** observed, already in 1948, that abstract expressionist painting was developing very rapidly: "Hundreds of artists from all over the world are suddenly turning away from the more or less innocuous painting of apples and sunsets, in order to head for adventure." Apart from the distinctions among the various tendencies that were emerging in non-geometric abstract art (including *École de Paris*, Cobra, tachism, action painting, American abstract expressionism, *art informel*, matter painting), this period was generally characterized by the attribution of great value to emotions, spontaneity and the subconscious as starting points for the work of art and, beyond this, to the choice of the free form and the act of painting. No lengthy deliberations, no rational rules, no systematic approach, but a spontaneous and direct expression determined the result. The straight line and the monochrome color surface do not appear in this art. The painting is dominated, on the contrary, by an abundance of colors. Frequently, the act of painting and the emotions involved in this are directly evident from the way in which the color and the form are applied.

This stormy development of postwar abstract expressionist art was certainly not a coincidence. Newly acquired freedom and expectations of the future after the oppression of war played, of course, an important role among artists as well. Much greater importance must be given, however, to the influence of certain prewar abstract artists and movements. Specifically surrealism (Max Ernst, Matta and Breton), the lyrical abstraction of Kandinsky and the work of Paul Klee were of special significance in this respect.

In Europe, Paris was the center of abstract painting. There one could find the exhibitions, the galleries, the collectors, the museums and the periodicals (including *Art d'Aujourd'hui*) that presented and fostered this new art. Bissière attracted a group of like-minded artists, who called themselves the *École de Paris*. In addition to Bissière, Jean Bazaine, Alfred Manessier, Serge Poliakoff, Pierre Soulages, Maurice Estève and Gustave Singier are usually included among them. Despite the abstraction which is characteristic of their work, these artists nonetheless aspired to a strong relationship with reality. In the book *Notes sur la Peinture*

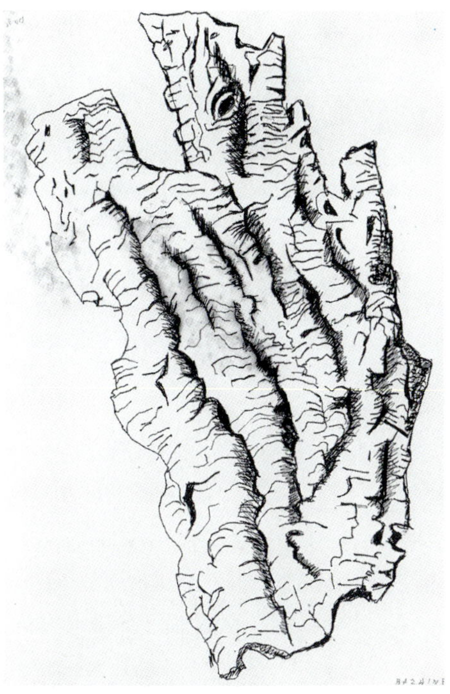

Jean Bazaine *Écorce de chêne-liège*, 1949

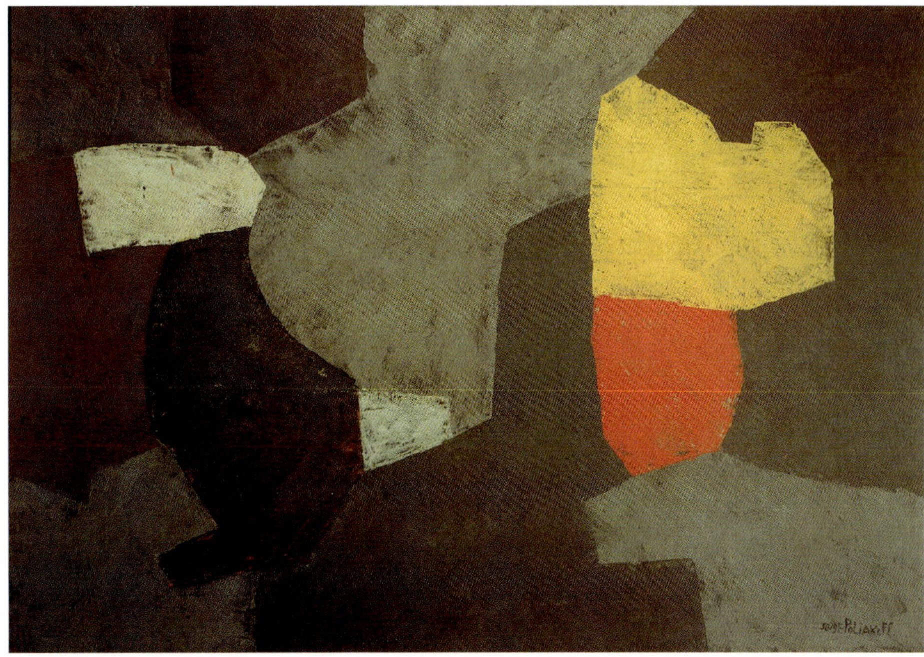

Serge Poliakoff *Composition*, 1956

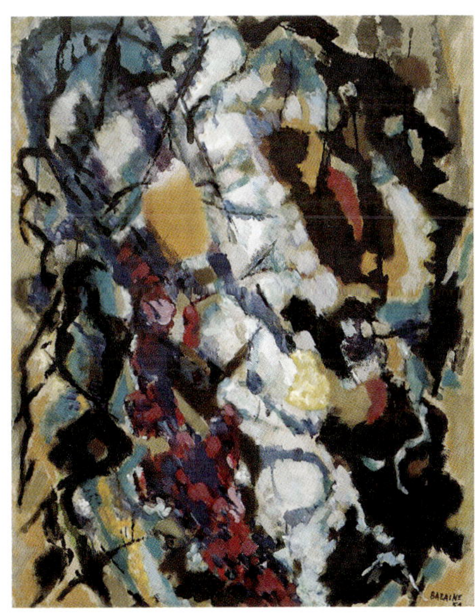

Jean Bazaine *L'orage au jardin*, 1952

d'Aujourd'hui (1948), **Jean Bazaine** wrote that it was the task of visual art to portray the structural unity between man and his environment. What mattered was not the extent to which a work of art was abstract, but whether it epitomized something of the essence of the universe. "We have no choice," Bazaine writes further on. "To systematically deny the existence of the external world is to deny our own existence. That would be a kind of suicide."

Bissière, Bazaine, Manessier, Poliakoff and others therefore dealt with nature or with the cosmos in their work, with the portrayal of that structural unity between man and his environment. The painting was to embody the essence of the universe, and the painter had to show that he could see not only with his eyes, but with his entire body. Bazaine said, "His task is to discern, in the forms, the mystery and the enchantment of that which is unformed, unsaid."

The Russian painter **Serge Poliakoff** took up residence in Paris in 1923 and thereby, under the influence of Kandinsky and Delaunay, gradually began to paint in an abstract manner. His paintings–see *Composition* (1956)–are comprised of closed, fairly austere forms that are pressing against each other. Each plane has a single worked-through, obfuscated color; the colors border each other and thus determine the form of each plane. The flat compositions have an air of natural calm. Poliakoff ascribed mainly a cosmic character to the abstract art of this period.

"While figurative art exists within the framework of the painting and remains within it, abstract art goes beyond that framework in order to create a cosmos." The paintings and drawings of Jean Bazaine have their origins in nature. Though no realistic motif whatsoever can be found in them, his work continues to relate to concrete subjects, such as trees, rocks and clouds. This can also be said about the work *L'orage au jardin* (1952), which provides an abstract visual image of a thunderstorm with daubs and strokes of color, areas of dark and light and a strong diagonal movement. This painting displays a pattern of dappling and areas that are cut off by the edges in a relatively arbitrary manner. All of this extends beyond the painting. The white diagonal streaks could be interpreted as a flash of lightning that casts a bright light across a garden with flowers and plants. Nevertheless, the lightning and the garden are not rendered as being recognizable as such. The painting offers an abstract image of a storm.

The work of **Alfred Manessier** is very religiously oriented. When he began to work in the lyrical abstract style of the *École de Paris* after the war, he developed a system of signs based on the crucifix and the crown of thorns as symbols of Christianity. These symbols are clearly recognizable in the very characteristic painting *Barabbas*. His use of color, initially sober and iridescent, later grew toward dark and more dramatic expression. As with many painters of the *École de Paris*, the work of

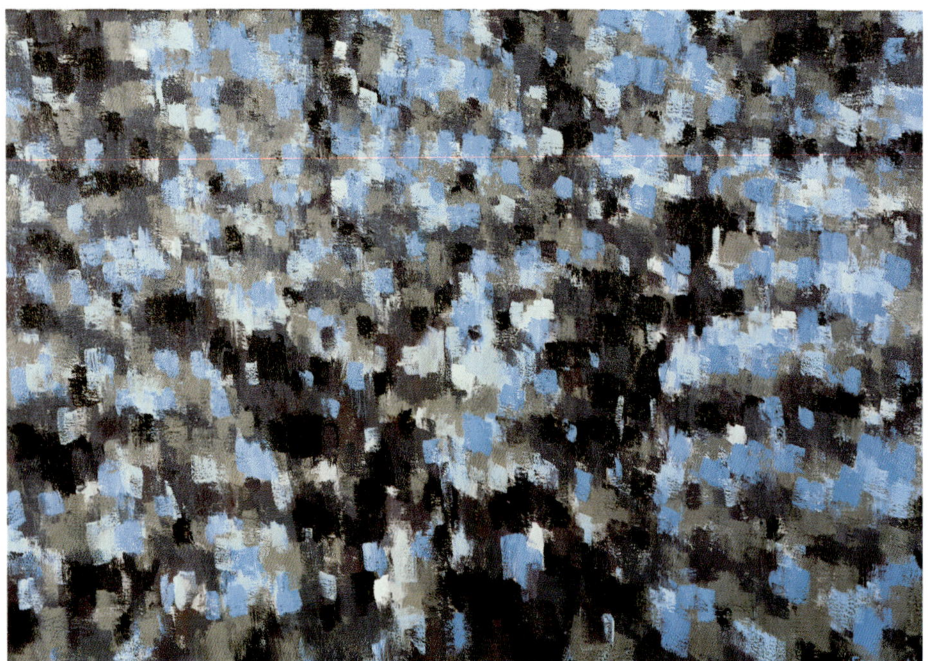

Edgar Fernhout *Herfst*, 1962

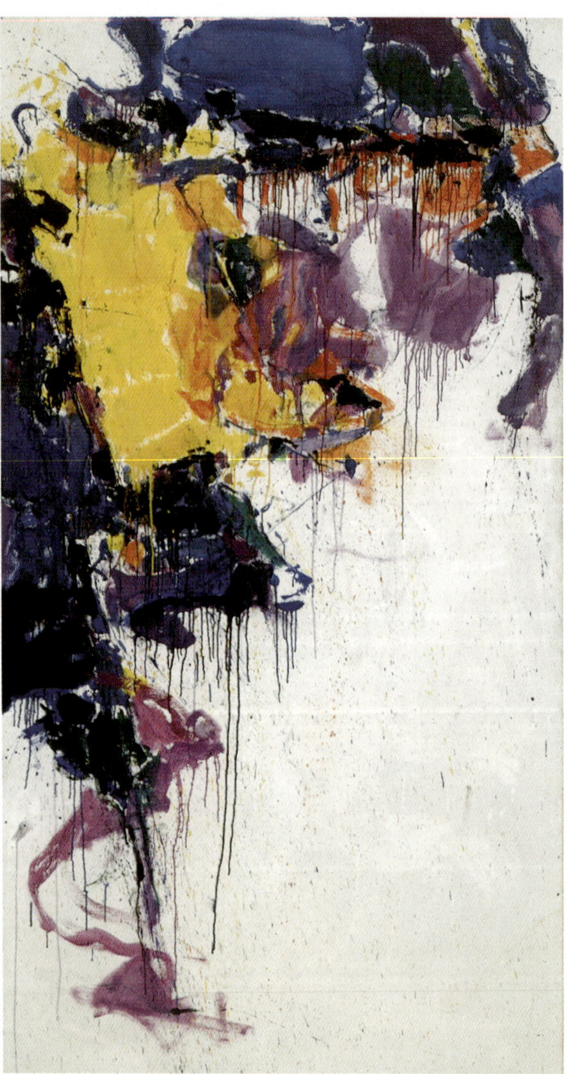

Sam Francis *Peinture*, 1957

Manessier shows no distinction between figuration and abstraction: these are interchangeable and are often used in combination with each other.

In the paintings of the American artist **Sam Francis** there is, just as in the work of Bazaine and Bissière, a link with visible reality. Though not immediately recognizable reflections of nature, their origins lie with a great number of optical impressions and experiences that have been transposed into an entirely new image. After having studied in California, Sam Francis lived in France and Switzerland for many years after 1950 and also lived in Tokyo for a time during 1957. The many impressions absorbed by him during this period and on his travels throughout the world (Europe, Asia, Central America) have undoubtedly contributed to the ultimate look of his paintings. Until 1955, the form had predominance in his work. The painting then shows a pattern made up of planes of color that cover nearly the entire canvas and refer to reflections of water and drifting clouds. As with Bazaine, the image seems limitless, a cutout from an infinite whole. After 1955, however, color became dominant: the forms are generated by the spontaneous application of color. Another characteristic is that since then–perhaps through the influence of art from East Asia–large areas of the canvas are left white. The painting *Peinture* (1957) is a good example of this. Spatters and dripping paint have always been a very deliberately used visual element in Francis's work, as can be seen here. The colors in his paintings after 1955 are vivid and radiant, alternated by several dark areas. They bring to mind the way in which Monet, Bonnard and Matisse used color. This connection with the European tradition probably stems from his contact with the work of these artists during his years in Paris and Bern.

The hovering between an abstract pattern of brushstrokes and the constant tie with nature as a base can also be seen in the work of the Dutch painter **Edgar Fernhout**. Son of the painter Charley Toorop, Fernhout worked on the fringes of the major tendencies and figures in painting from before and after World War II. His entire body of work displays a gradual, consistent growth from sharp realism to considered, sensitive abstraction. His first paintings from the thirties and forties–largely still lifes and interiors–provide a very accurate depiction of reality and attest to intense observation. During the mid fifties, nature (and later the landscape in particular) became the main subject of his paintings. At the same time,

color was being used more independently.
After 1957 his paintings developed into a field
of brushstrokes placed along side and on top
of each other; no longer do they function as a
means to achieve an immediately
recognizable depiction, but as pure color,
which in terms of tone, placement and
gradation, is a painterly translation of the
natural subject serving as the point of
departure. For though the color has, strictly
speaking, become autonomous, Fernhout
emphatically wished to maintain the link
with nature in the paintings from these years.
This is also true with respect to *Herfst* (1962),
which is made up of an endless number of
vertical white, light and dark blue, grey and
black brushstrokes that seem to move across
the canvas in a close relationship with each
other. It is the colors, the interrelationships of
the colors and the active placement of the
brushstrokes which jointly give rise to the
idea of autumn, not in a direct way but as a
form of painterly imagery.
Ultimately Fernhout went farther than the
painters of the *École de Paris*. After 1970, in
particular, he imposed on himself an
increasing limitation of visual means.
Abandoning the continuous link from one
brushstroke to another and applying a
monochrome color field to the canvas, he
allowed the broad strokes of paint to become
situated at varying distances from each other.
By doing so, he created a system or a model
analogous to structures in nature. Due to the
spatial tension among the brushstrokes and
the autonomous strength of the color, there
arises a painting which is free of any
immediate association.
Aside from the typically painterly approach of
the *École de Paris*, these years were also
marked by the work of artists who opted for
the free graphic gesture. One of them was
Hans Hartung, who went to live in Paris in
1935 after his training in Germany. Already
during the early 1930s, under the influence of
Kandinsky and Klee but also Miró and the
'psychic automatism' of the surrealists,
Hartung developed a manner of painting and
drawing that was characterized by an
extremely spontaneous and expressive
execution of line. After 1945, the subjective
element disappeared from his work. The
expressive marks became stylized into
elegant movements, which resulted in
groups of usually intersecting, thick
brushstrokes. This is followed by a form of
calligraphy–as can be seen with the painting
Composition (1956)–which comes about
through a mentally and intuitively guided
motoric movement.

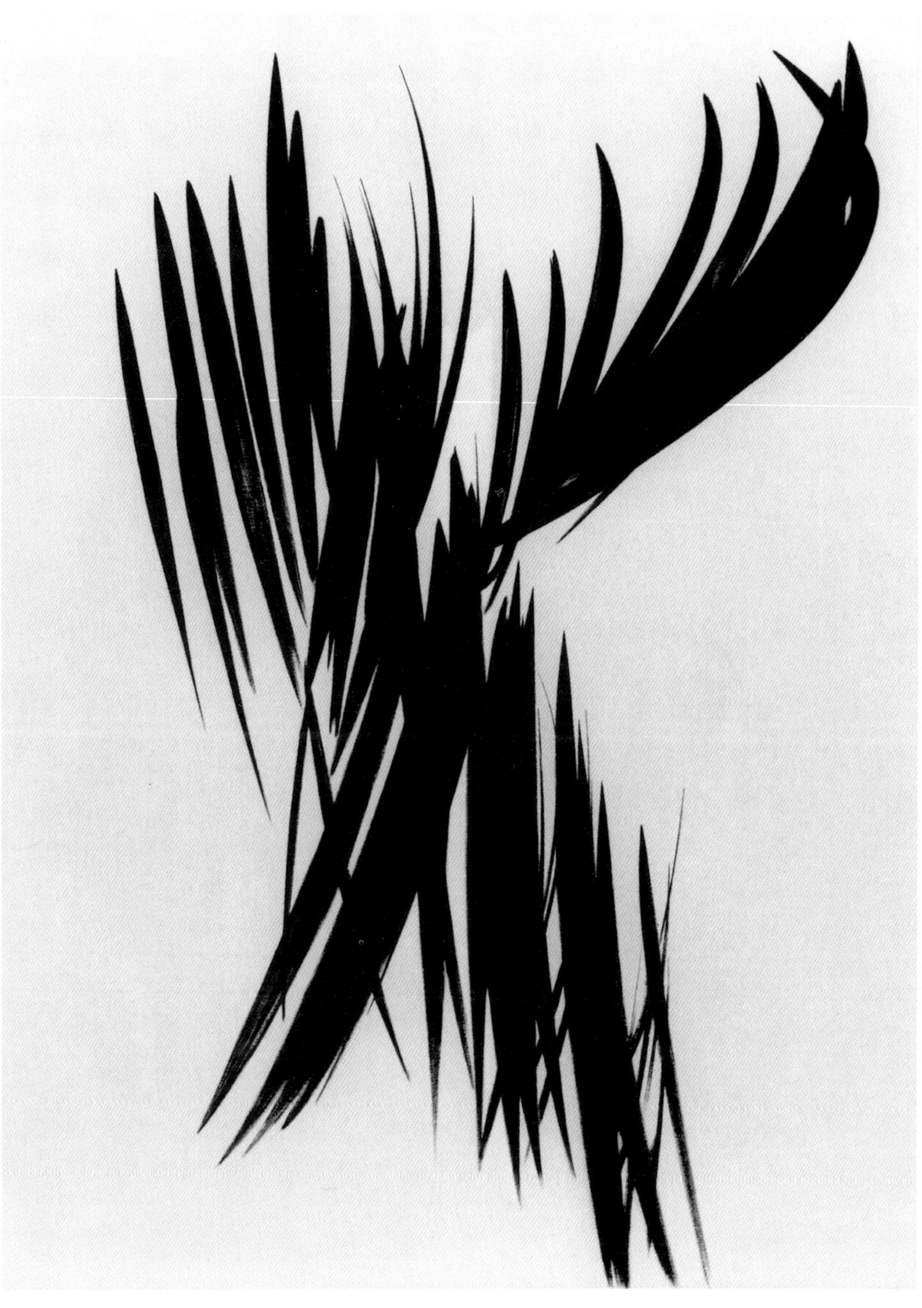

Hans Hartung *Composition*, 1956

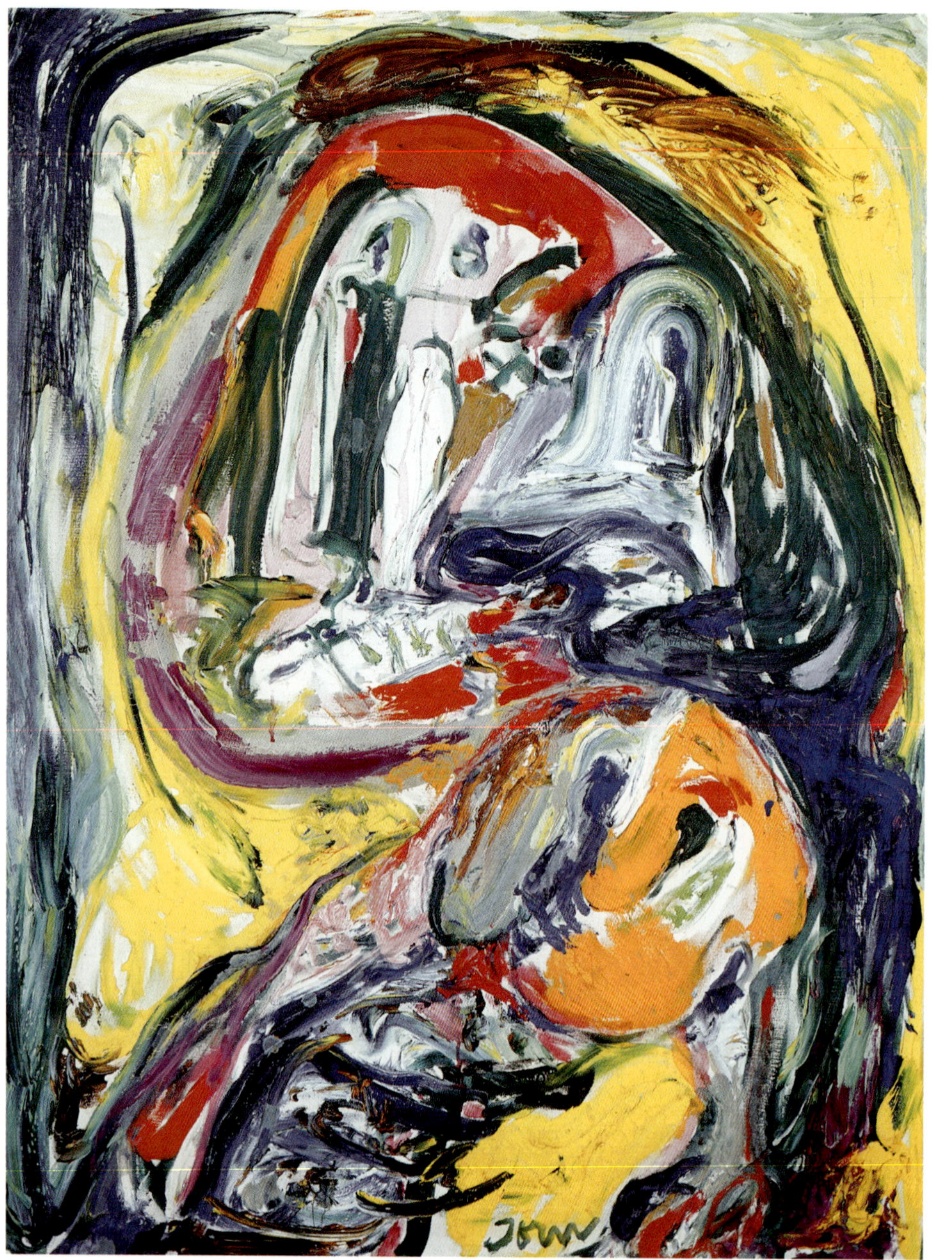

Asger Jorn *Le monde perdu*, 1960

The activities of the Cobra group were typical of the postwar climate in visual art from the Netherlands, Belgium and Denmark. The Dutch Experimental Group and the periodical *Reflex* were founded in Amsterdam in 1948 as forerunners of this. Among the founders of the Experimental Group were Karel Appel, Constant, Corneille, Anton Rooskens and Theo Wolvecamp. In November of that year, a meeting of young 'revolutionary surrealists' was held in Paris, and its participants included Appel, Constant and Corneille. The Dane Asger Jorn and the Belgian writer Christian Dotremont also took part. It was during this convention that the Cobra group was founded. The name Cobra is made up of the first letters of the cities Copenhagen, Brussels and Amsterdam. In addition to the members of the Dutch Experimental Group, the Belgian artist Pierre Alechinsky and the painter/poet Lucebert joined Cobra at a later stage. The ideas and principles of the group were conveyed to others by way of the magazine *Cobra*. The most important issue to be raised by these painters and poets was their urge to create an entirely new art which, free of all previous classical art movements and traditions, would give expression in a visual manner to the most vital and existential motives of man. Not only could one speak of a liberation but, above all, of a–perhaps

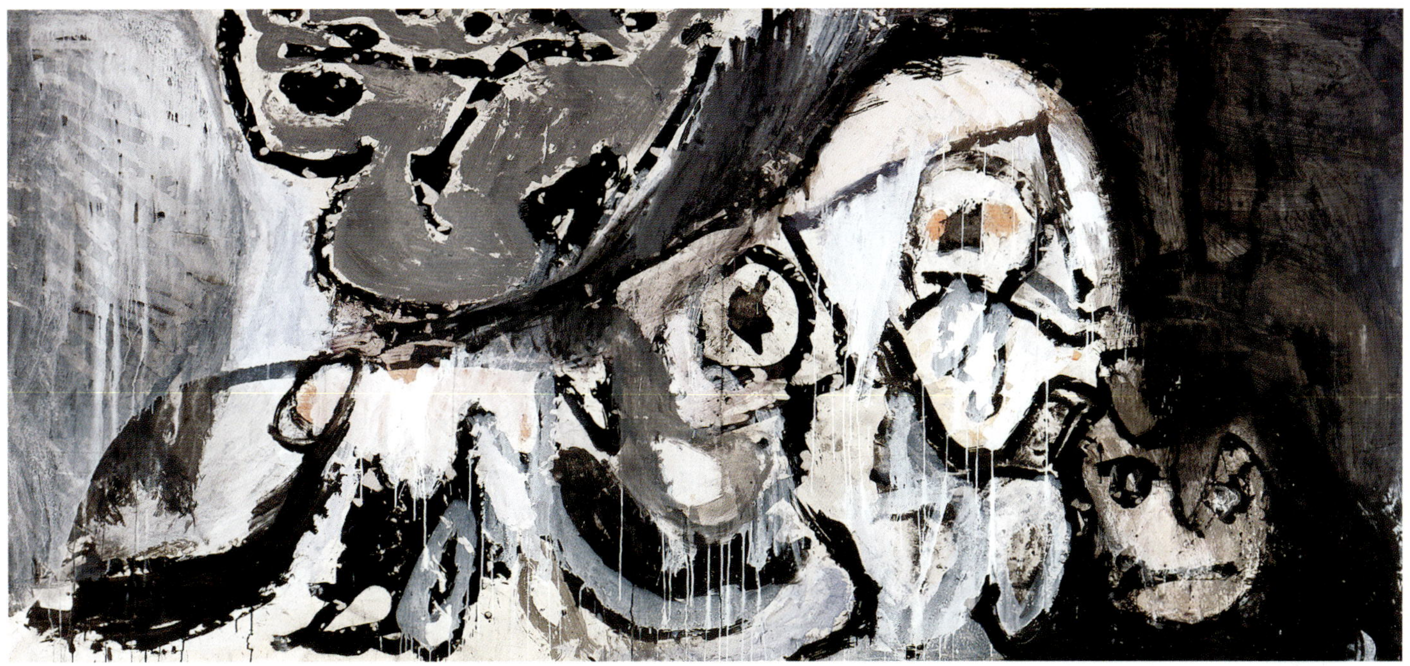

Pierre Alechinsky *Malone meurt*, 1962

Romantic–escape to the 'unspoiled' world of the child and primitive cultures. In a manifesto published in the magazine *Reflex* (1948), spokesman Constant wrote: "A painting is not a construction of colors and lines, but an animal, a night, a scream, a person, or all of that together."
Cobra opposed the formalist tradition from before the war, particularly the geometric abstraction of Suprematism, Constructivism and De Stijl. Dotremont stated it in 1949, at the opening of the first extensive Cobra exhibition organized by the Stedelijk Museum in Amsterdam, as follows: "The general curse of these lousy times, the leash of this age, is formalism."
The Dutch participants were initially inspired by a series of exhibitions, at the Stedelijk Museum in Amsterdam, on the prewar work of Picasso, Chagall, Miró and Klee. For the Cobra artists these modern classics, whose work they had never actually seen before, were an enormous stimulus.
The Danes (in particular Asger Jorn and Carl-Henning Pedersen) had the background of a kind of Scandanavian 'abstract surrealism' that had come about around 1930; in this prime importance was given to irrational creation and a concern for dream worlds and myths, inspired by Nordic folk art. Belgium, too, had a surrealist tradition, including such figures as René Magritte and Paul Delvaux. The work of James Ensor, whose paintings are inhabited by peculiar and frightening creatures, was also of importance. What

mainly interested the younger generation with respect to the work of these surrealistic predecessors was their spontaneity, the active character of their *écriture automatique*, in which one could allow a thought-free stream of images to rise from the subconscious, their sardonic humor and the idea that creativity is not something on which artists have a monopoly.
Though the Dutch were less influenced by surrealism, they shared the ideas of the Danes and the Belgians and were especially interested in the unformed, spontaneous–even crude–nature of children's drawings, drawings by insane people and the art of primitive cultures. In this they found a natural, unconstrained creativity and way of working for which they felt a great affinity. Characteristic of the visual means of Cobra are the many bright and warm colors and the drawing-like manner of painting. The figures and forms often seem to be drawn with a brush and then developed with color. Line is therefore prominent here. The paintings of the Cobra artists are inhabited by human figures, animals–especially birds–and a great number of fantasized creatures, such as fairy-tale figures and trolls. Their paintings show an imaginary world, in which the vital forces of man and pure, childlike depiction play a major role.
The works of Asger Jorn, Pierre Alechinsky and Karel Appel in the collection of the Van Abbemuseum clearly display these

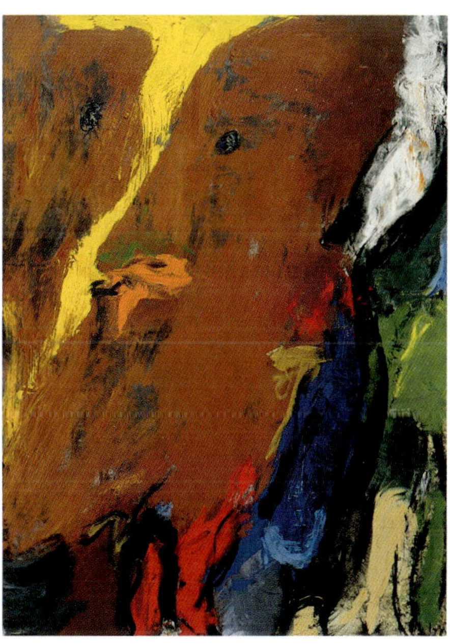

Asger Jorn *Le creux au ventre*, 1960

characteristics: Jorn's contorted faces in bright yellows, blazing reds and rich oranges, Alechinsky's gruesome creatures that break away from the spatters of paint and Appel's tormented figures, which have been drawn on the canvas with paint squeezed directly from the tube.
In 1941 **Asger Jorn** started the periodical *Helhesten* in Copenhagen, together with like-minded artists such as Carl-Henning Pedersen, and in this they articulated ideas

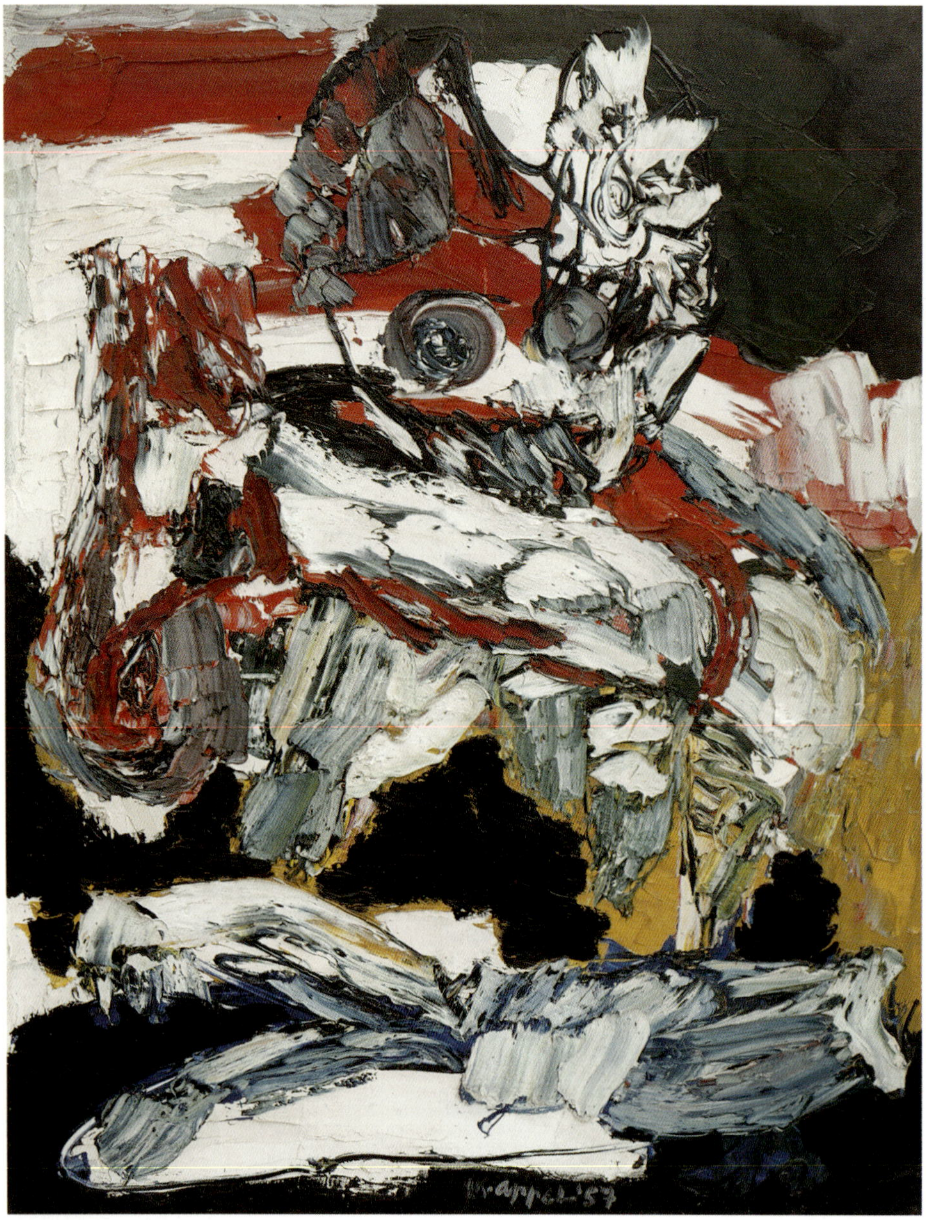

appeared after 1954. Around 1958 his works were inhabited by imaginary creatures and skull-headed figures. But during the 1960s Alechinsky put his intentions, as defined in 1951, into practice; he adopted the method of the Asian calligrapher by drawing, in a concentrated manner, an image based on handwriting.

From the later part of the 1950s onward, the Van Abbemuseum collected the work of Cobra artists. In 1961 the museum organized solo exhibitions of the work of Karel Appel and Corneille. Five paintings by **Karel Appel** are in the museum's collection. These show the development from the figurative/expressionist work (*Paard en fluitist*, 1951) to his almost literal struggle with the paint, in which the conditions of human existence are portrayed with extreme vehemence (*Le cavalier*, 1957).

From 1961 to 1962 Appel produced various sculptures in olive wood. He tells about these in the book *Ik wou dat ik een vogel was*, published in 1990: "I spent the spring and summer of 1961 on the seventy-five-hectare estate *l'Abbaye de Roselande*, owned by Jean Larcade–the director of Galerie Rive Droite in Paris–and made eighteen man-sized sculptures from olive-tree stumps taken from the olive orchard that had been reduced to ashes. Local workmen pulled them out of the ground, roots and all. They were rinsed clean with hot water and took on a new life. After I had worked on them with a chisel and an axe,

Karel Appel *Le cavalier*, 1957

that would later have repercussions within Cobra. The Danes referred to themselves as 'myth-creating' artists and, inspired by ethnographic objects, prehistoric art, Scandinavian myths and the drawings of children, aimed for spontaneous, painterly expression that would result in a new type of folk art. Jorn's paintings from before 1945 show mainly imaginary creatures, grotesque human figures and faces, and only after the Cobra period would his spontaneous painterly style based on automatism come to full blossom. *Le monde perdu* (1960) is typical of his nearly abstract way of working during this period, in which color determines the composition and anthropomorphic forms loom forth, as though by chance, from the active brushstrokes. He himself said the following about this: "I believe that color immediately and totally conveys the content of a painting."

Like other members of Cobra, **Pierre Alechinsky** was fascinated with a personal 'handwriting', and he regarded spontaneous expression as the most direct voice of the human psyche. In 1951 he defined a theoretical context for his work, in which such 'handwriting' serves as the premise and the foundation for painting. A trip to Japan in 1955, for the study of calligraphy, made a deep impression on him and would prove to have a great influence on his later work. Initially his paintings consisted of compositions of abstract spots, in which more movement

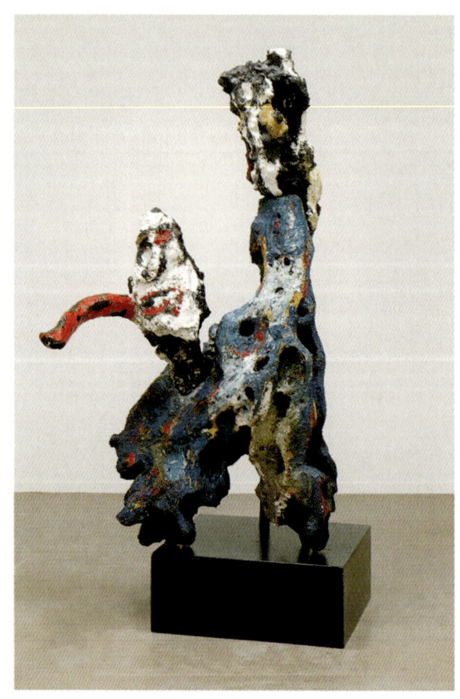

Karel Appel *Sculptuur*, 1961

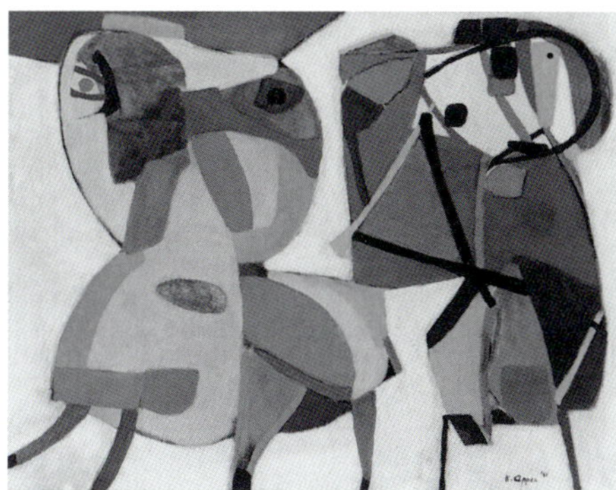

Karel Appel *Paard en fluitist*, 1951

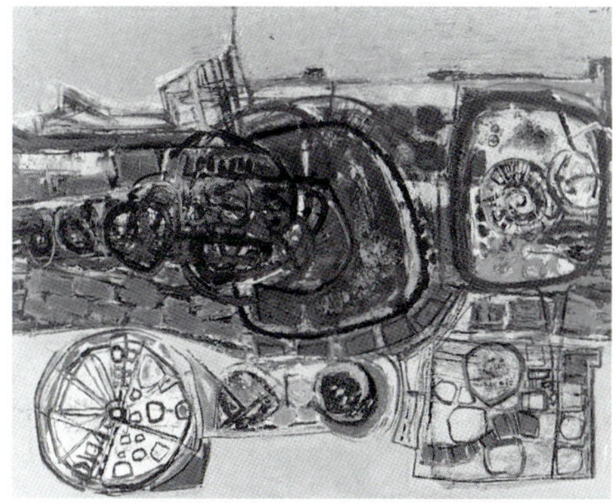

Corneille *Fin des terres*, 1955

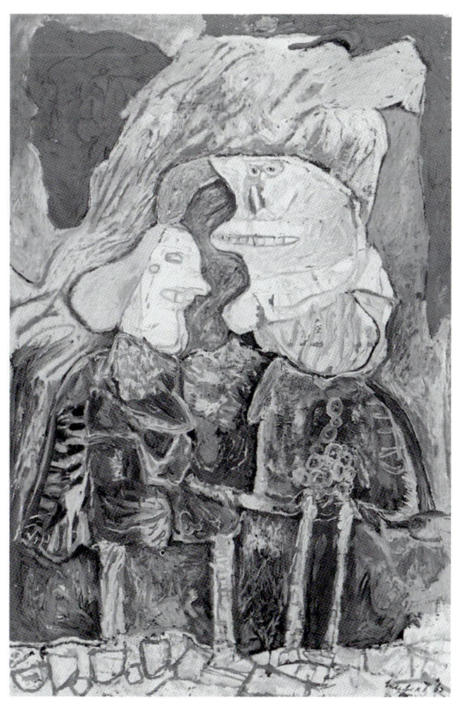

Lucebert *Prinsenpaar*, 1962

they were painted with polyester varnish mixed with pigment–two long summers of hard work." *Sculptuur* from 1961 is one such 'olive' work.

The inspiration that Cobra artists found in children's drawings and primitive art can also be seen with **Corneille**. He believed that these contained the untainted primal images of the human imagination. Until 1950 Corneille painted mainly imaginary creatures, birds and fish. After his move to Paris in 1950, the work became more abstract. Rhythmic lines and geometric forms began to determine the appearance of the image. *Fin des terres*, from 1955, shows the interplay of forces between line, form and color.

Aside from writing poetry, **Lucebert** always drew and, later on, painted as well. He joined the Cobra group in 1949, and a certain affinity with the language of Cobra can be discerned: the energetic movement of the brush, the colorful and variegated palette and a whimsical manner of drawing. During the mid sixties his paintings took on a social connotation. The mythical creatures and animal figures that were painted in a childlike style gave way to human figures which, in contorted positions and often with ghastly facial expressions, were put on the canvas in a gruesome, forceful style.

But it was **Constant**, in particular, who displayed political commitment in his work and, together with Jorn and Dotremont, laid the theoretical foundations for Cobra. In manifestoes he stressed that Cobra should be regarded not only as an artistic but also as a political/revolutionary movement which was paving the way for a Marxist-oriented society. The expressive visual language of Cobra undermined, in his view, the academic/aesthetic norms and would eventually be able to mobilize the dormant creativity of the masses. Around 1950, while living in Paris, Constant became convinced that the mythical world of Cobra had ceased to be consistent with the envisaged social objective. The paintings that he produced after 1950 were no longer filled with childlike figures rendered in cheerful colors; frightening creatures in aggressive environments began to dominate his paintings. When a new threat of war arose in 1950, due to the outbreak of the Korean War, Constant painted a series of canvases in which the violence of war–the destruction and the victims that accompany this–is portrayed in a dramatic manner. Constant combined an immediately recognizable message with an experimental form. The museum owns from this important series: *De oorlog* (from 1950).

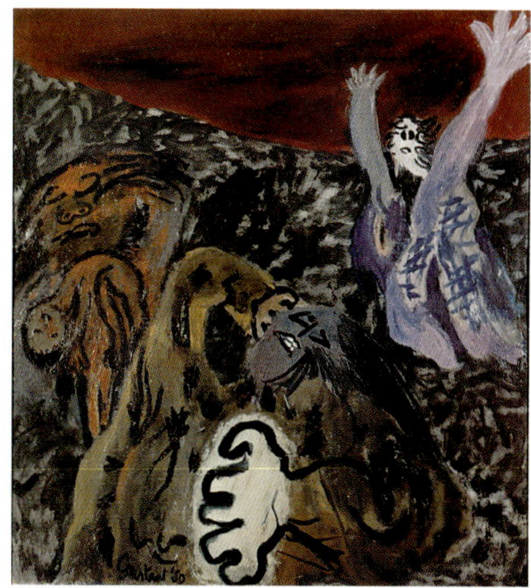

Constant *De oorlog*, 1950

Shortly thereafter, from 1954 to 1969, Constant stopped painting and focused on experimental architectonic design. He created utopian, labyrinth-like constructions which he collectively referred to as 'Nieuw Babylon' (New Babylon). These maquettes served as models for the living environment of the free 'homo ludens' who had a new and creative awareness.

It is characteristic of Cobra, though, that this art never developed into full abstraction and remained much closer to the recognizability of the depiction than the work of the *École de Paris* did, for instance. A more significant difference in the nature of these two movements is that the *École de Paris* could be described as lyrical, poetic and tranquil, while Cobra is often characterized as being bold, blaring and aggressive.

The Cobra painters were much more down-to-earth and direct than those of the *École de Paris*. The ideology of Cobra was much more aimed at the liberation of color and paint–at the setting free of matter–whereas the ideas of the *École de Paris*, having cosmic dimensions, were of a more spiritual nature. Cobra ended its brief existence in 1951, when its actions had achieved the desired effect. Each artist went on to work on an individual basis. Cobra had become a style and had given impetus to a powerful and innovative development in the postwar art of Europe.

viii

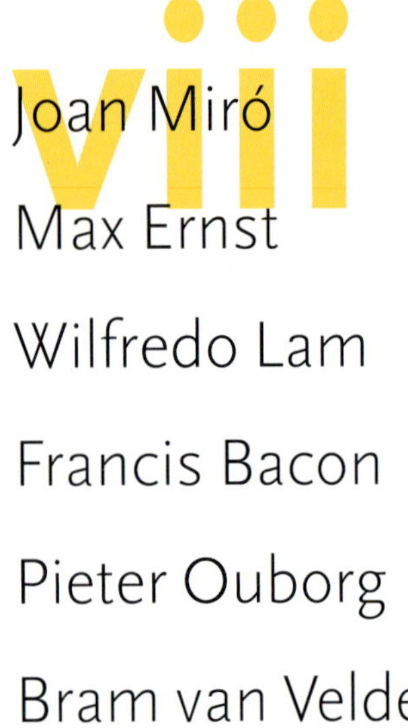

Joan Miró

Max Ernst

Wilfredo Lam

Francis Bacon

Pieter Ouborg

Bram van Velde

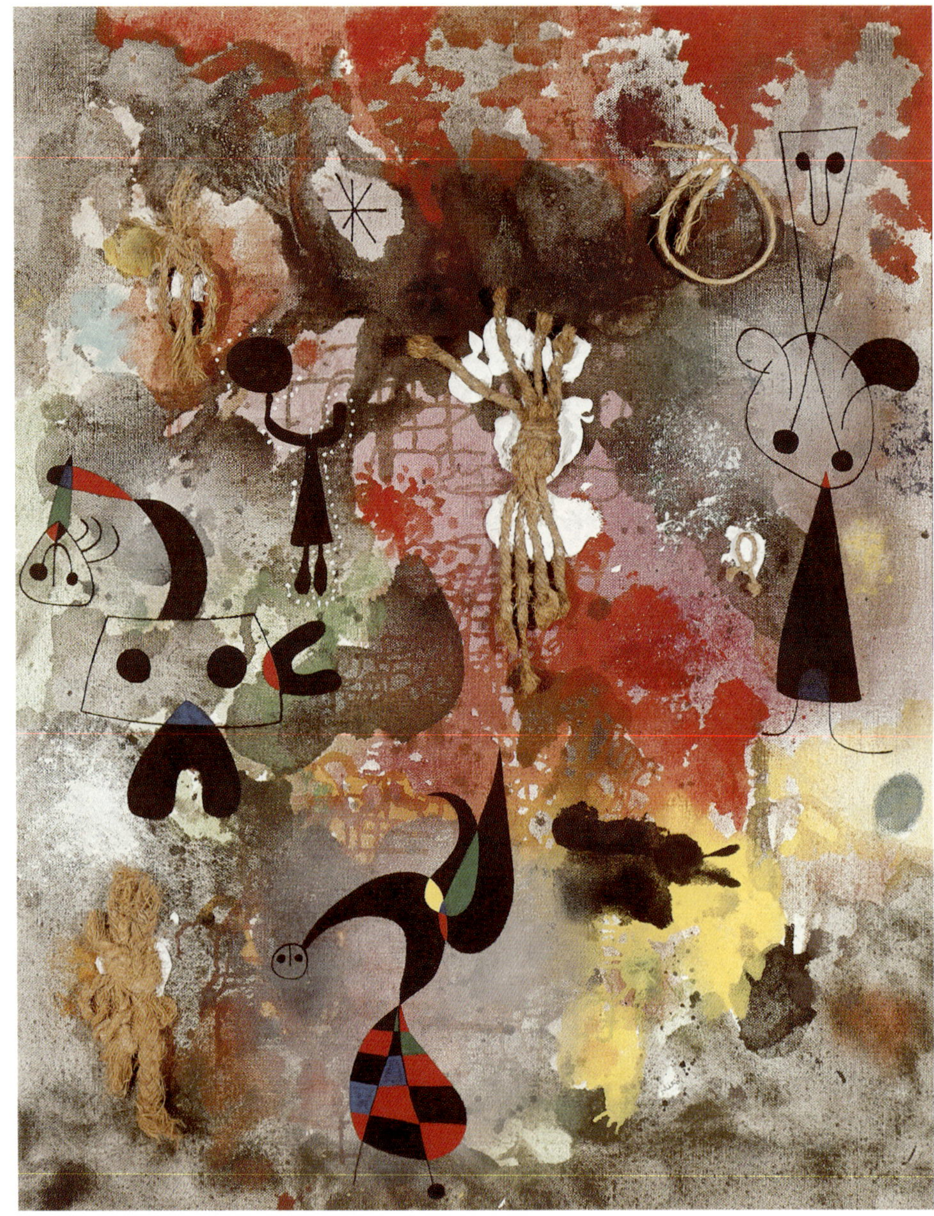

Joan Miró *Composition avec des cordes*, 1950

In visual art, Surrealism was more or less a reaction to the detached, intellectual character of Cubism and artists such as Mondrian, who came after this. The objection to that abstract art was its almost complete exclusion of life, the emotions. Sigmund Freud, whose theories had great influence on Surrealism, had learned that the most profound reality of man could be discovered only through a descent by way of conscious thinking (subject to restrictive social patterns in which certain thoughts, being taboo, are repressed) into the subconscious. Surrealists believed that abstract art was too deliberately constructed to have any truth.

Within Surrealist painting there arose many variants: from the purely figurative, whose major representative was René Magritte, to a nearly abstract one–but then abstract in a manner unlike the art of Mondrian. In an abstract Surrealist painting, like that of **Joan Miró** (who called Mondrian's art a 'deserted house') the forms and the colors flow across the canvas, seemingly without control. But, of course, these paintings have not been made without deliberation. Miró's painting *Composition avec des cordes* from 1950, for example, consists of three layers, each of which has been carefully identified. The first of these, a space of diluted blotches of color, has been identified as 'background', as clouds. Hovering in front of these are a

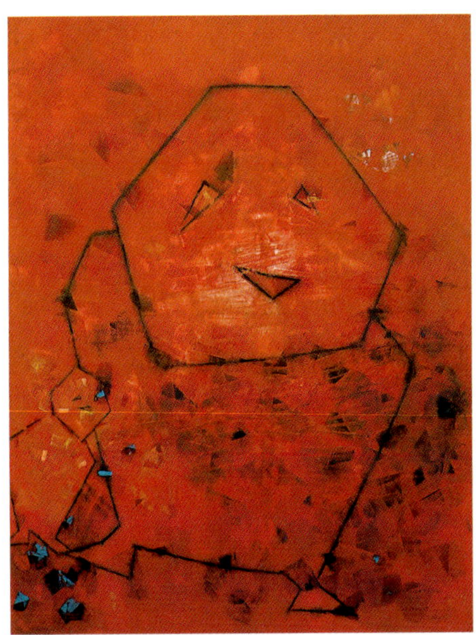

Max Ernst *Interrogation (what kind of bird are you?)*, 1956-58

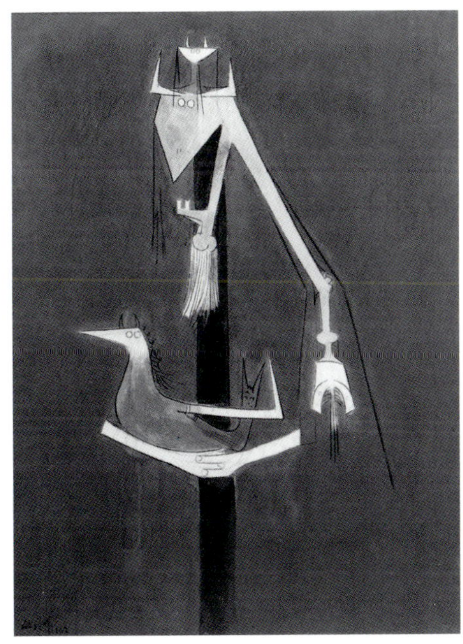

Wilfredo Lam *Figure*, 1962

number of sharply drawn figures, strange tenuous constructions which look like people, then like animals or birds, and which are characteristic of most of Miró's paintings. The third layer is concrete: figures made of rope, attached to the canvas and held together by thick clumps of white distemper. These three layers undermine, as it were, each other's realities: the forms, that of the rope and those that are drawn, for instance, generally display an odd similarity, but they are not the same, if only for the fact that they each have a different material status. As a result, everything in this painting becomes ambiguous, extremely indeterminate: things appear as they do in a dream.

Max Ernst is primarily known for his collages, the best of which were produced during the 1920s, made from fragments of mainly nineteenth-century illustration prints that were reordered into frequently sinister, gruesome and fairy-tale-like images. But he was also, in 1924, the inventor of the frottage technique: by laying a thin piece of paper on a piece of wood, for instance, and rubbing over this with a pencil, one obtains a heightened textural impression of the grain of that wood. Using such isolated fragments, Ernst developed abstract paintings, though many of them have the appearance of landscape–be it a nocturnal moon landscape or a desert scene. Nature, as Ernst saw it, yielded unexpected forms and combinations of forms which he, as an artist, could transform into psychograms by free variation. The frottage technique is Max Ernst's equivalent of the *écriture automatique* propagated by André Breton, Surrealism's leading spokesman.

The painting in the collection of the Van Abbemuseum, *Interrogation (what kind of bird are you?)* from 1956-58, is a later work by Max Ernst. In this painting, the surface is filled with angular red and reddish black brushstrokes: these brushstrokes give rise to several larger forms, outlined in black, which join together into what could be perceived as a bird. The painting is called *Interrogation*, the questioning of the world of forms, but the answer to this–in the form of a question–follows: *what kind of bird are you?* Thus the title holds a typically Surrealist ambiguity: the question can refer to the bird in the painting, but also to the viewer who looks at the painting.

The Cuban painter **Wilfredo Lam** is represented in the museum's collection with the work *Figure* from 1962. Lam came to Europe in 1923 and lived in Spain and in France until 1941. There he encountered, among other art, the works of Hieronymus

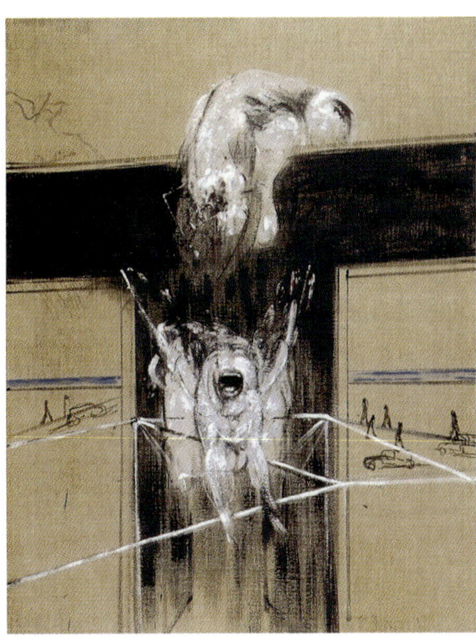

Francis Bacon *Fragment of a Crucifixion*, 1950

Bosch, El Greco, African art and, of course, Cubism and Surrealism. Lam combined the visual language of Cubism and Surrealism into a style of his own, in which primitive and mystical elements predominate.

Via Cubism, Miró, Ernst and Lam found the freedom to produce their later work. On the other hand, Surrealism, too, with its emphasis on the individual and the 'illogical', has also made a contribution which, in terms of importance, goes beyond actual, orthodox Surrealism. As early as the thirties, for instance, and to an even greater extent in later decades, one can speak of combinations of the two points of departure, of hybrid forms and of artists who developed highly personal styles based on those hybrid forms. The work of the British painter **Francis Bacon**, of whom the Van Abbemuseum owns a relatively early work (*Fragment of a Crucifixion*, 1950) is, without a doubt, related to Surrealism; but along with this, Bacon's work has become marked by a sharpness that has nothing to do with the lyrical, enchanted quality of many surrealist paintings. Bacon is the painter of lonely, deformed figures in closed and desolate spaces–figures such as he alone sees them and shows us in barefaced paintings.

With the exception of a few artists, the Netherlands has never had any Surrealist movement of significance during the thirties and forties. During the thirties the magic realism of Carel Willink, Raoul Hynckes and others prevailed as the 'modern' style. That was a figurative style which bore some similarity to the figurative, Belgian Surrealism of that time (René Magritte, Paul

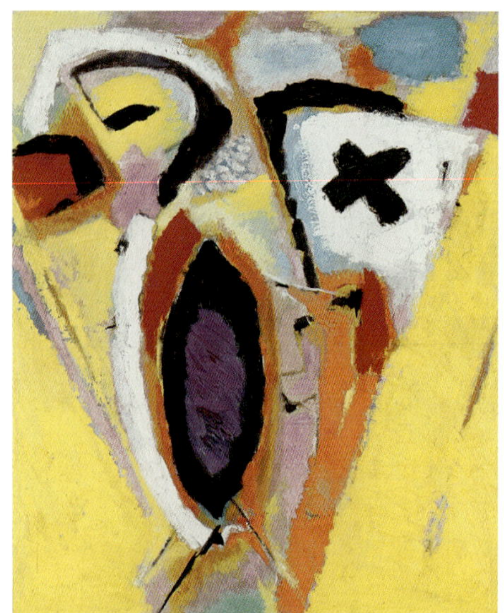

Pieter Ouborg *Figuur,* 1947

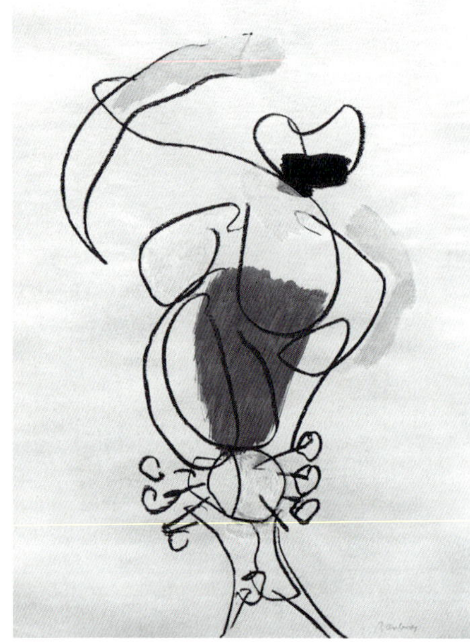

Pieter Ouborg *Schutter,* 1950

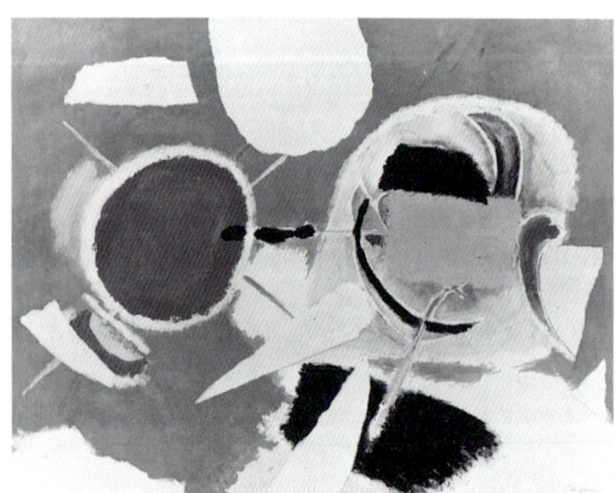

Pieter Ouborg *Zwevend op elkaar stoten,* 1950

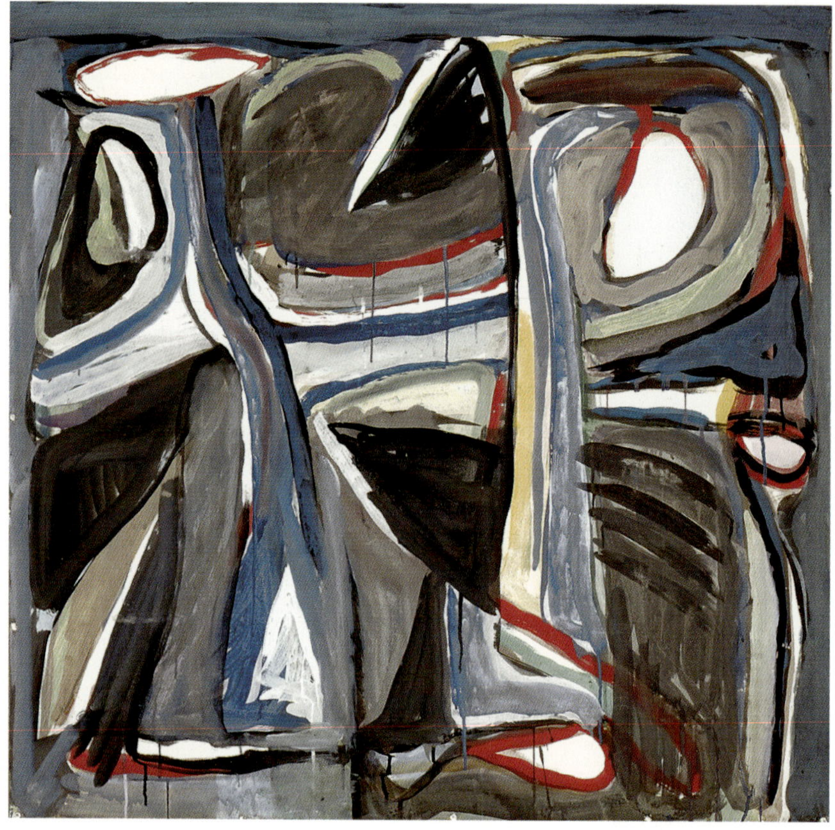

Bram van Velde *Zonder titel,* 1961

Delvaux) but which was quite removed from the most interesting developments in Surrealism: Max Ernst, Joan Miró and André Masson.

The only Dutch painter who worked in this abstract tradition was the artist **Pieter Ouborg**, who did not live in the Netherlands itself but in the Dutch East Indies and who received his information on what was happening in European art primarily by way of Parisian periodicals, such as *Cahiers d'Arts*, which frequently contained reproductions of the recent work of all the masters working there: Picasso, Braque, as well as Masson, Ernst and Miró. With those models and in the relative isolation of a colony, Ouborg worked on a remarkable oeuvre in an abstract surrealist style. The Van Abbemuseum owns a representative group of works by this very unusual loner in modern Dutch art, who never was part of the 'art scene' in his home country and who is only now receiving proper recognition.

Another loner was **Bram van Velde**, a painter living in Paris but from the Netherlands, who developed a personal language based on Cubism. His paintings stand entirely on their own; or rather, they have absorbed a number of 'influences' from the history of modern art and assimilated them in an independent manner. The persistent will to carry on with this individual adventure has a strength in itself and attests to a deep belief in the meaning of painting at a time when the painting was often the subject of criticism. Both Francis Bacon and Bram van Velde are typical representatives of twentieth-century art, which has brought not only dramatic and radical innovations but which has also allowed personal freedom and the unorthodox to be meaningful forms of artistic conduct.

ix

Jean Dubuffet

Gaston Chaissac

Antoni Tàpies

Jaap Wagemaker

Antonio Saura

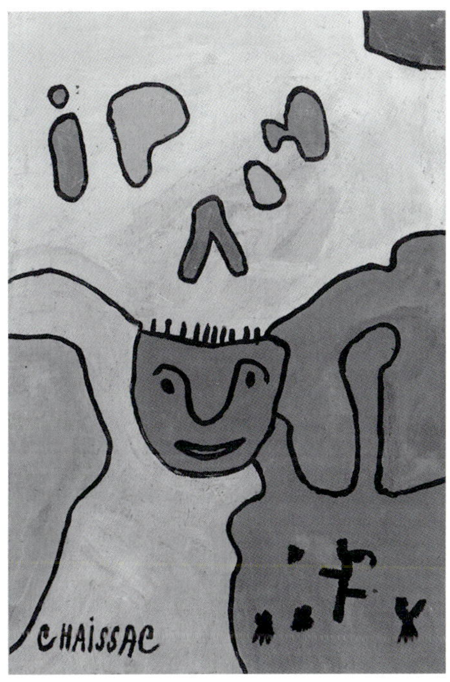

Gaston Chaissac *Le masque*, 1959

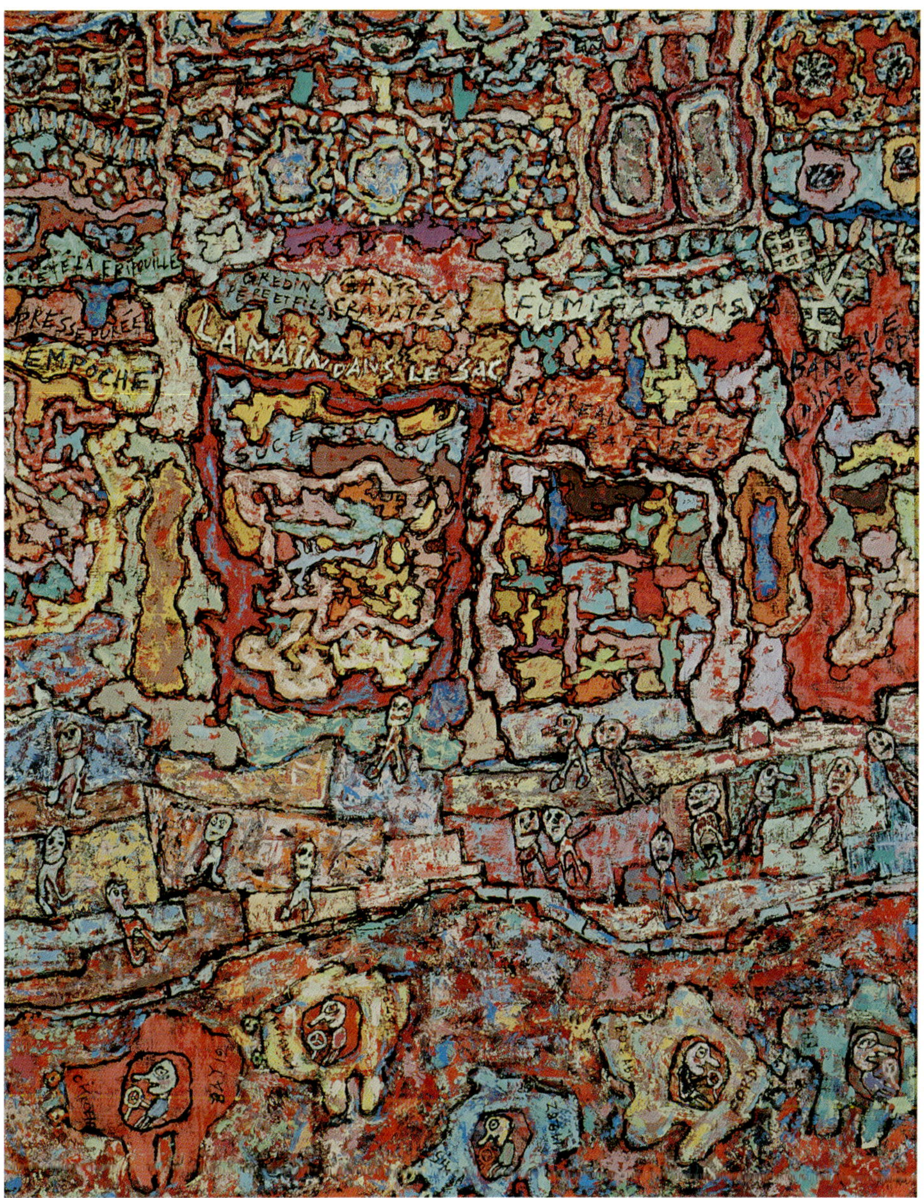

Jean Dubuffet *La main dans le sac*, 1961

In the art produced immediately following the war, an ever-recurrent element is the concern for that which is 'primitive', that is to say–in the context of these times–the instinctive, the non-Western, the absurd, the pure or the unspoiled. This tendency can easily be understood in the aftermath of a war which had cruelly demonstrated the decline and the failure of Western civilization. In work from the Cobra movement as well as in that of Dubuffet and, in a more indirect way, that of artists such as Tàpies and Wagemaker, one can discern a fondness for that which is primitive.

Jean Dubuffet had always shown a considerable preference for a primitive manner of representation. To him, this love of primitive art was a form of principled opposition to Western culture. What appealed to him were such values as "instinct, passion, mood, violence, madness." "Those primitive societies have surely much more respect than Western man for every being of the world; they see man not as the ruler of these beings, but as one of them." Dubuffet was also deeply impressed by the visual expressions of the insane, of children and of primitive peoples. He collected these types of objects and referred to them as *art brut*.

After having abandoned art for many years, Dubuffet began to paint again in 1942. Until 1957 his works were populated with human figures–occasionally animals or objects–which have been painted in a very primitive and highly diagrammatic manner.

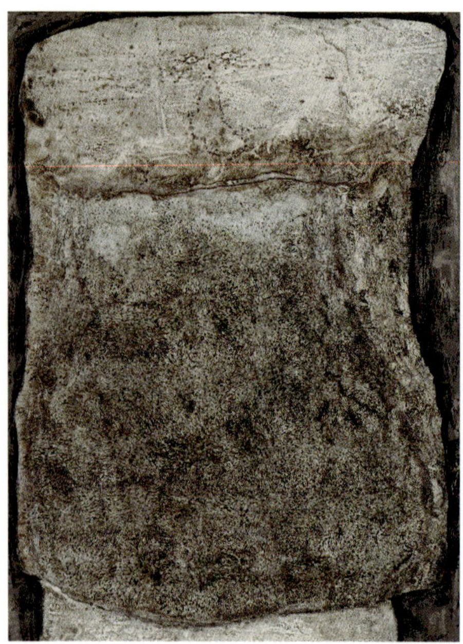

Jean Dubuffet *Barbe des solitudes, 1959*

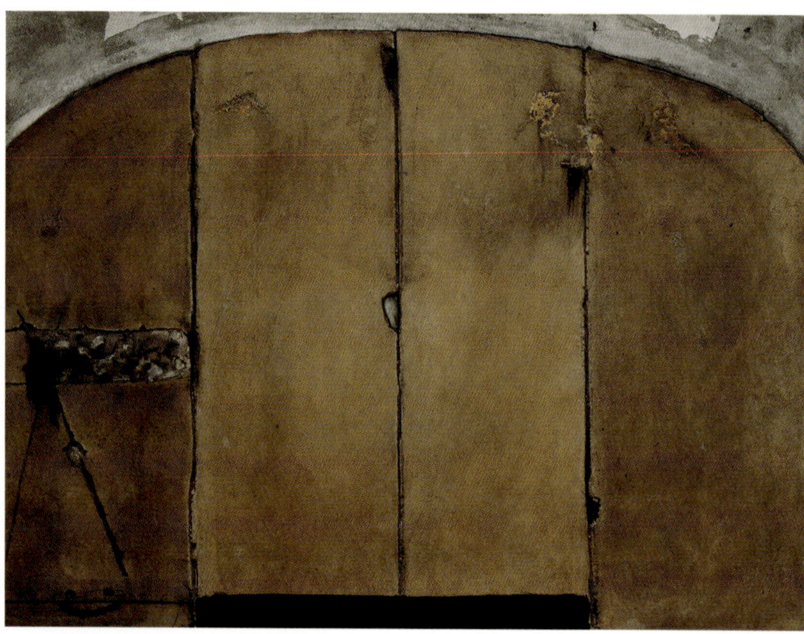

Antoni Tàpies *Double porte beige, 1960*

They reflect a union of man and his natural environment. This work also came to inspire the Cobra painters.

After 1957 Dubuffet produced various series of paintings in which matter–mainly soil, stone, sand, plaster–determines the look of the painting through its visual and tangible qualities. Among the titles of those series are *Célébration du sol, Texturologies, Barbes, Matériologies.* Matter itself was applied to the canvas without much deliberation and according to the principle of chance. Natural materials become the visual means and the content of the painting. The series *Barbes*, of which the painting *Barbe des solitudes* (1959) is a part, also contains a figurative element; these paintings show, in a very simplified manner, the image of a face with a beard, though this has been achieved with the colors and surface structures of sand and stone.

In 1961 a radical change occurred in Dubuffet's work. As a response to 'matter painting'–including his own work–and *art informel*, he began to focus again on man and on human life in an urban environment. He explained this change as follows: "In my paintings there will now be no reference whatsoever to immediately discernible phenomena from the realm of matter. I've had it, once and for all, with the mystical glorification of the material world; I've come to loathe it. (...) I am now enraptured with irreality, I yearn for the nonexistent, for make-believe reality, the antiworld. With my work I have chosen the course of irreality. Rather than those two insane notions, the abstract and the figurative, I experience reality and irreality as being the two poles between which art fluctuates (...)."

The ensuing series *Paris circus*, to which the painting *La main dans le sac* (1961) belongs, shows the life of people in the big city in a childlike and ironic manner. In this particular painting, that is done from a bird's-eye perspective. The inscriptions on the painting suggest that Dubuffet is scrutinizing the dark practices in this metropolis. The people, the streets and houses have been designated with distinct contours and lively colors. These contours will begin to become much heavier with the series *L'hourlope* (1963), thus giving rise to a 'puzzle effect' that will determine the appearance of his later work.

The French painter **Gaston Chaissac** is relatively unknown in the art world. He was self-taught, and his art was far removed from what was going on in established art circles during the thirties and forties. In 1944 Dubuffet was among the first to acknowledge Chaissac's talent and the paradoxes contained in his work. In Chaissac's drawings, paintings and sculptures he discerned an authenticity and directness which he found characteristic of 'outsider' art, of the *art brut* that he sought. Within this context Dubuffet purchased a great number of works by Chaissac for his *art brut* collection. Later Dubuffet would admit that Chaissac's art was, in fact, different from true *art brut,* in the sense that Chaissac, though ill-adjusted and very obstinate, did know exactly what he was doing and did not produce art on the basis of some blind obsession.

Dubuffet's characterization does indicate fairly well, however, where the quality of Chaissac's work lies. Chaissac drew and painted people, faces and mythical creatures in a seemingly naive manner which alluded to the drawings of children. These motifs are made up of simple, elementary forms, usually outlined in black and pieced together like a jigsaw puzzle. Eyes, noses, mouths have been rendered in the most rudimentary way, by means of a line or a dot. Not only does this give the 'characters' an ambivalent nature; it is also reminiscent of sculptures and masks from primitive cultures. Chaissac's images find their strength in a similar sort of simplicity. They stem from his imagination and collectively make up a universe of his own. In addition to his visual work, Chaissac also wrote many literary texts and created *langage dessiné* (drawn language), in which handwriting becomes part of the image. Initially, these were mainly drawings in which text was employed as a kind of calligraphy and line drawing. In later paintings, such as *Le masque* from 1959, elements of this appear again in a more painterly manner. In *Le masque* the letters become forms and the forms letters. Also his signature has a formal quality of its own within the image surface. The way in which Chaissac pieces his forms together seems to anticipate the later work of Dubuffet.

Whereas Matter Painting constituted only a brief phase in Dubuffet's overall development,

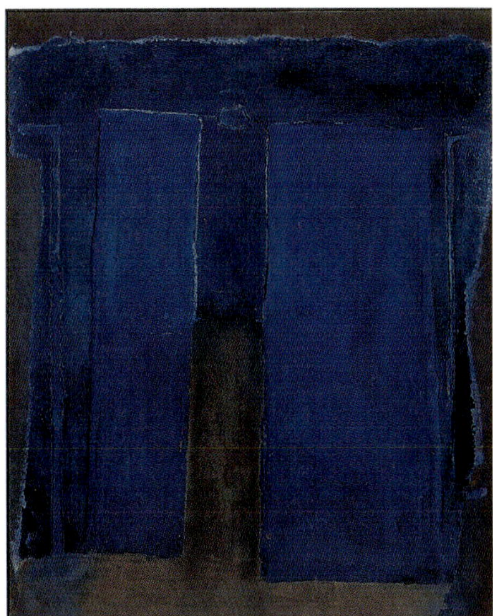

Antoni Tàpies *Blue outremer*, 1958

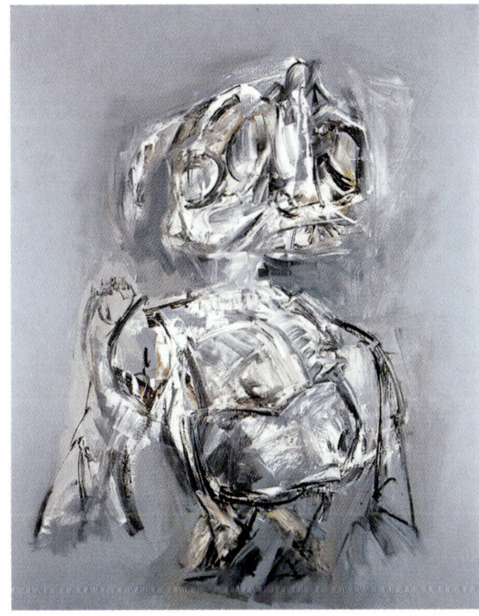

Antonio Saura *Ada*, 1962

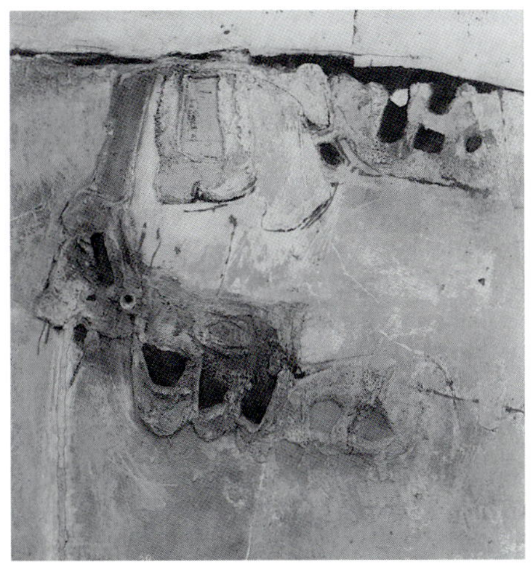

Jaap Wagemaker *Sable gris*, 1960

the idea of matter had fundamental importance, as content and as means, in the work of the Spanish artist **Antoni Tàpies**. Tàpies was, without a doubt, the most prominent representative of Matter Painting. This type of painting flourished particularly during the second half of the 1950s.

The first paintings that Tàpies produced in 1945 are reminiscent of the work of Miró, especially due to the use of materials such as rope, branches, fabric and paper in the form of collages. His concern for matter began to increase after 1953. According to a thought-out architectonic construction, he applied a kind of mortar (a mixture of sand and chalk) onto the canvas. This is how a number of textural surfaces and layers take shape on the canvas. The paint–usually sandy grey or ultramarine blue–is smeared over this and scraped off. Simple, occult symbols are scratched or objects are pressed into the layer that is still soft. Generally speaking, Tàpies attributed great value to the materiality and the surface structure (the tears, holes, irregularities) of his works.

An important theme in his work is the door or the gate. These are always portrayed frontally and in a shut position, as can be seen in the work *Double porte beige* (1960); the massiveness of the composition and the highly developed surface of the painting cause such works to evoke associations with the mysterious beauty of ancient walls.

In the work produced after 1970, matter gave way to the painterly; here the mark and the gesture gained predominance.

There were also a number of interesting 'matter painters' in the Netherlands during the fifties, and among these were Wim de Haan and Bram Bogart. The most prominent was **Jaap Wagemaker**. Having started painting before World War II, in a expressionistic style reminiscent of Kruyder and Chabot, Wagemaker sought, in its aftermath, a personal manner of expression in which matter would play a major role. Until 1955 his work was directly related to that of the Experimental artists: the Cobra artists in the Netherlands. But at some point during the mid fifties, Wagemaker found his own way. Fascinated with the work of Dubuffet, Wols and Fautrier, and influenced by the Italian Alberto Burri, Wagemaker began to create paintings in which he mixed the paint with sand, jute, ash and cement. In these works, matter is both the aim and the means. No longer is it suggested by the paint; it has, in itself, become the content of the work. Like fellow artists Burri and Tàpies, Wagemaker was seeking a kind of primal force that lay hidden, as it were, in the matter.

He himself said the following about this: "In my work, matter is the central focus; I allow the work of art to come about, also in a mental and spiritual sense, on the basis of that matter, so that a connection arises between the matter and the spirit, the content of the painting." Until 1960 the various materials and parts of objects vanished into a single, predominant structure and tonality, as can be seen in *Sable gris* (1960). After 1960 Wagemaker allowed the different materials and objects to speak for themselves: pieces of slate, wood, shell, metal, tubing or jawbone remain recognizable as such.

For the Spanish artist **Antonio Saura**, the gesture of painting had major importance. Limited by the Franco regime in his knowledge of what was going on in the art world, Saura developed, during the early fifties, a type of painting that took inspiration directly from Surrealism, the last significant art movement to have great Spanish influence. Saura experimented with *écriture automatique* and a magic-surrealist language of forms. At the end of the fifties, after having spent time in Paris, Saura (who had yet to turn thirty) discovered his own way of painting, and he would scarcely deviate from this in the years to come. His canvases were more or less evenly colored–usually white, black or grey–and on them he would paint portraits. The faces are entirely made up of separate, wildly brushed strokes, in such a way that no recognizable individuals can be found in them. Though Saura was, at this time, primarily painting women's faces and titling his works with the actual names of women (e.g. *Junca*, 1958 and *Ada*, 1962), the portraits show no individual but rather deformed and caricatural faces.

Saura can be characterized as a classical painter who relates to his mentors from art history–Goya, Velázquez, Picasso and Rembrandt–in a contemporary way.

Piero Manzoni

Yves Klein

Lucio Fontana

Heinz Mack

Otto Piene

Günther Uecker

Jan Schoonhoven

Henk Peeters

Armando

Yves Klein *Monochrome bleu, sans titre (IKB 63)*, 1959

In 1957 a number of radical innovations began to emerge in the visual art of Europe, and these can be seen as a response to the many forms of abstract expressionism (*art informel*, tachism, Cobra, action painting) that arose after World War II. The new developments were marked by a general opposition to the particular and the individual aspects of visual expressions in abstract-expressionist art. Composition, handwriting, expression, spontaneity, the subconscious–as points of departure or motifs–were dismissed by these artists. They endeavored, on the contrary, to give shape to a type of visual art that would be an embodiment of their dynamic sense of reality. The art was to break new ground, create a new sense of freedom that would make it possible to experience the achievements of this age.

Some of these artists formed groups, such as Zero in Germany, Nul in the Netherlands. Their frequent contact with each other and many joint exhibitions and activities contributed to the rapid spread of their ideas among a broader public. They believed that art should concentrate on, and be an affirmation of, the totality of human existence. In their work they attempted to allow art and life, art and reality, to merge. The subject matter of their work included phenomena such as light, movement, order, space and time. The visual means and the materials that they employed were also very

inconsistent with the norm of that time. One of the most striking developments to emerge from this new art was the monochrome painting, that is to say a painting consisting of a single color.

Piero Manzoni first produced such paintings in 1957. He referred to them as *Achromes*, works without color. These are always bright white fields on which no color, no figure, no symbol, no reference whatsoever to reality or to the role of the artist can be found. The work is 'a field of freedom', a white surface with seams or folds.

Manzoni was hereby proclaiming the autonomous presence of this flat white object to be the most significant aspect of his art. In 1960 he wrote, "(...) the question, as far as I'm concerned, is that of rendering a surface integrally white (integrally colorless and neutral) far beyond any pictorial phenomenon or intervention extraneous to the value of the surface. A white that is not a polar landscape, a material in evolution or a beautiful material, a sensation or a symbol or anything else: just a white surface that is simply a white surface and nothing else (a colorless surface that is a colorless surface). Better than that, a surface that simply is: to be (to be complete and to become pure)."

Initially, Manzoni made these *Achromes* from linen drenched in kaolin (fine white clay used for porcelain) and glue. Later he used other materials such as cotton balls, cloth, felt and fiberglass. In many cases, this gave rise to a grid due to the fact that the square pieces of linen were glued or sewn side by side. The artist confined his intervention to the implementation of this simple structure and the choice of the material. Works that possess great independence and a strong physical presence were the result of this.

All of Manzoni's work is governed by ideas that are realized in a very unconventional form. The upside-down pedestal which thereby holds up the world, *Socle du Monde* (1961), is a marvelous example of this. Its conceptual premise causes many to regard it as a link between Dada and conceptual art. Not only because of his works and writings but also due to his countless contacts with such artists as Fontana, Klein, the Zero and Nul groups, Manzoni became a key figure in the art scene of the sixties.

The work of Frenchman **Yves Klein** was highly imbued with the idea that his art would bring about a special degree of freedom and awareness in the viewer. He considered this capacity to render and give rise to such 'sensibility' as being the most important function of his work. The single color was his prime aid in achieving this. He was convinced of the notion that every unmixed color has its own individuality and is able to project an intangible strength. On the basis of this conviction, he began producing monochrome paintings in 1949. "From the mute conversation that follows between the state of things and myself, there arises an impalpable affinity, 'indefinable' as Delacroix would say. This 'indefinable', this ineffable poetic moment is what I wish to capture on my canvas, since my mode of being (notice I don't say, 'of expression') is to paint. (...) Sensing the soul without explaining it, without any vocabulary, and representing this sensation...That, I believe, is what led me to monochromy. To me, the art in painting is to produce, to create freedom in the raw material state."

"What I wanted from the viewer was that 'moment of truth', making it possible to clear the slate of all external influence and to attain a degree of contemplation in which color becomes full and pure sensibility." As early as 1955, Klein was applying paint, made with industrial pigments, to the canvas by means of a roller in order to obtain an even distribution. Soon he ascertained that the color blue possessed the greatest intensity and, in his view, represented an emancipation from materiality.

The endless depth of the blue in the sky is also a phenomenon that inspired him to a singular degree. After lengthy research he developed, in 1955, a deep, radiant ultramarine-blue paint possessing a large degree of the immaterial effect that he sought. Usually he painted on a thin layer of plaster that had been applied to the linen. With this blue–the IKB (International Klein Blue)–he painted a great number of works, including *Monochrome bleu, sans titre (IKB 63)* from 1959. Frequently he applied many layers of paint on top of each other, without nuance, without hues, without drawing: one single shade of blue fills the entire canvas. The blue monochrome was, to Klein, the embodiment, the materialization of the infinite, immeasurable realm of the immaterial, of a cosmic experience, which he usually designated as 'cosmic sensibility' and 'pure energy'.

Later Klein gave expression to this 'cosmic sensibility' in many other forms, for instance by means of the famous exhibition *Le Vide* in 1958, for which he whitewashed the space of gallery Iris Clert in Paris and allowed it to remain empty.

In the work of **Lucio Fontana**, ideas such as color, sound, movement and space are central. In 1949 he began to puncture the canvas of the painting. By doing this he was

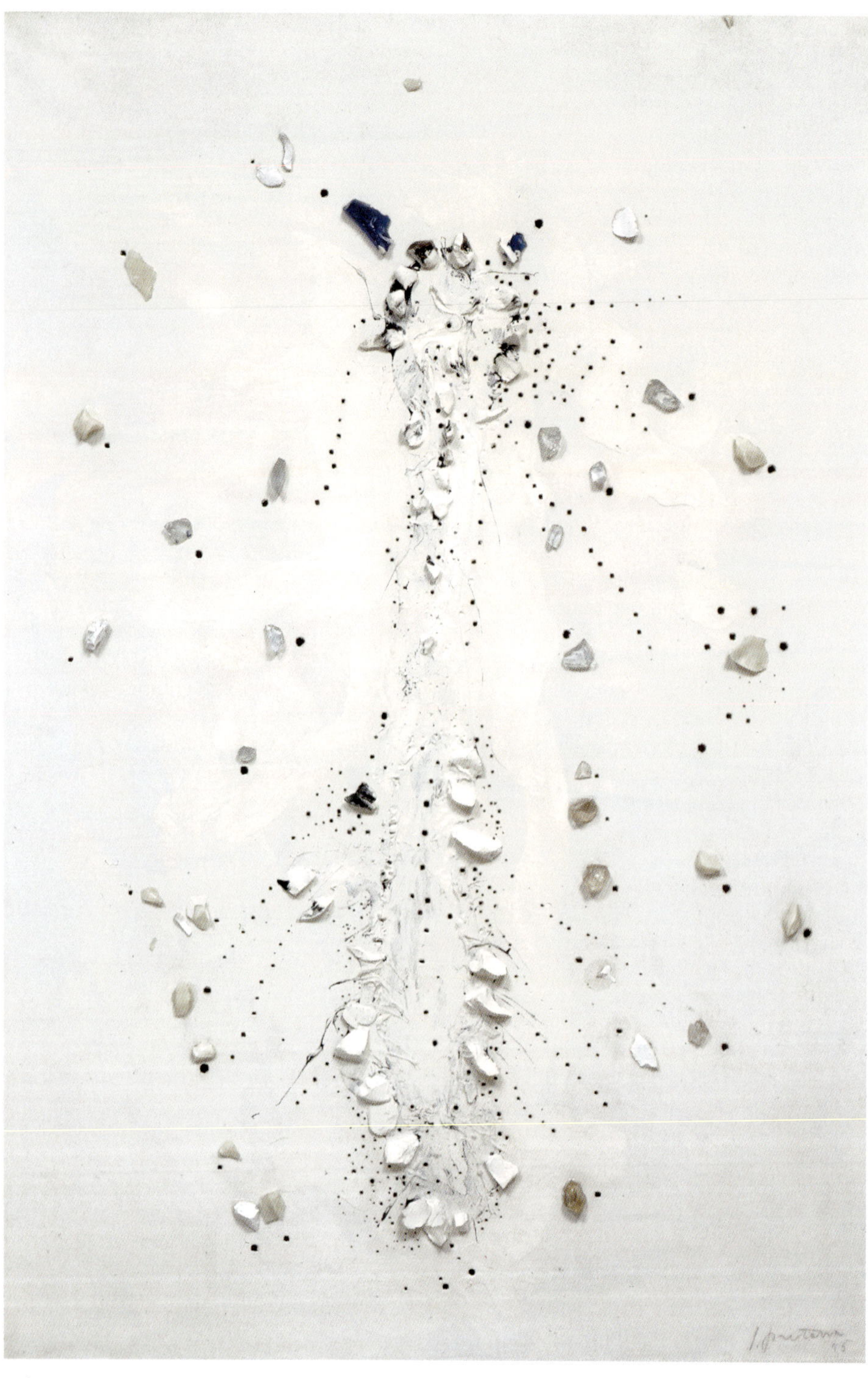

Lucio Fontana *Concetto Spaziale*, 1955

attempting to escape the illusionistic space on the flat surface of the painting, which had dominated painting since the Renaissance. With his piercings Fontana introduced actual space; the work no longer depicted space, but was itself part of it. Fontana referred to his works as *Concetti Spaziali* (spatial concepts). These ideas on the concept of space (*spazialismo*) were explained by him in a number of manifestoes (1948-1953).
In 1958 Fontana began to produce monochrome canvases with razor-sharp slashings, made with great precision and intent, as in *Concetto Spaziale: Attese* (1960). It is a gesture that reveals aggressiveness but also a certain stance-taking, as though it were a manifesto. By slashing the canvas, he demonstrated his view that the easel painting—as it had existed for centuries—was no longer adequate. At the same time, he was literally creating an opening to space. Fontana himself had few words to say about this radical intervention, other than: "All depends upon ideas, upon the cut and the gesture."

Though Fontana did not become affiliated with a group, he had regular contacts with figures such as Klein, Manzoni and the groups Zero and Nul. His work, his environments (dark spaces with ultraviolet neon lighting), his ideas about space and the potential that he saw in a collaboration between visual art, science and technology have had great significance for the development of art during the sixties and seventies.

In Germany, too, artists reacted against abstract expressionism and sought new visual means.

Heinz Mack and **Otto Piene** founded the Zero group in 1958. Günther Uecker joined the group later. The word Zero is taken from the countdown of a rocket launching, the point in time which precedes the actual liftoff. They moreover defined Zero as "the Zone of silence for a new beginning."

The Zero artists made it their aim to produce a new type of art that would focus on the qualities of pure light, movement, simple structures and on white as a concentration of light. Otto Piene wrote, "Light is the first condition for all visibility. Light is the mood of the color. Light is the vital element for both man and the painting."

Particularly the qualities of light that determine space were investigated by them; in this, not only was the effect of daylight used on all sorts of reflecting materials, as was done by Heinz Mack in the work *Silberrotor* (1965), but also artificial light became a visual means. The absoluteness of their basic assumptions, their ideas about space and their choice of the monochrome (primarily white) displays great similarity to the work and the ideas of Lucio Fontana and Yves Klein, whom they regarded as the pioneers.

In 1957 and subsequent years, the artists of the Zero group organized a series of evening exhibitions, on which occasion they published, by way of a catalogue in 1958, the magazine *Zero*, of which three issues were produced. From these publications it becomes evident that they, too, were obsessed with certain aspects of nature (the sky, the sea, the desert) and technology (the launching of a rocket). In their romantic passion for the infinite, the spiritual and the non-material, they showed a lyricism that is

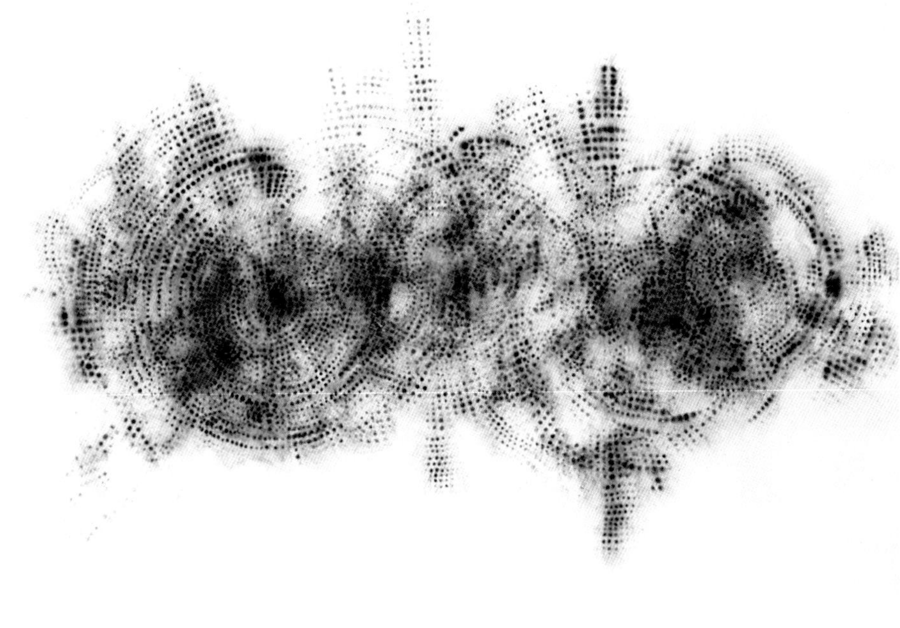

Otto Piene *Rauchzeichnung*, 1959

expressed in their work as well as in their writings. In 1967 the group disbanded.

In the magazine *Zero*, Otto Piene stated that he wished to disrupt the existing confines of art by using air, water, fire and artificial light as visual means. Initially he produced monochrome paintings consisting of grids of light. After that, in 1959, came his smoke paintings and drawings, such as *Rauchzeichnung* (1959). Due to the use of a metal plate, in which holes have been made according to an orderly pattern of concentric circles, the precipitation of the smoke remained behind, on the canvas or the paper, in the form of the pattern.

In 1958 **Günther Uecker** began making 'nail reliefs', which have since become characteristic of his work. These are arrangements of equal elements. The nails have been hammered into a wooden board and painted white. These arrangements first consisted of regular horizontal and vertical rows; later he grouped the nails more loosely and in such a way that their diagonal position creates a fluctuating movement. The relief *Bewegtes Feld* (1964) is an example of this. Through the placement of the nails and the use of white paint, Uecker managed to achieve a light/shade effect that gives the work a certain immaterial quality. The character of his work–the ordering of identical elements, the effects of light, the suggestion of movement–clearly relates to the themes of Zero. Uecker did not join this group, however, until 1961. At a later stage he added, as did Mack, a rotating movement to his reliefs.

Dutch artists such as Armando, Jan Henderikse, Henk Peeters and Jan Schoonhoven felt an affinity with Manzoni, Klein, Fontana and the Zero artists and established the Group Nul in 1961. They, too,

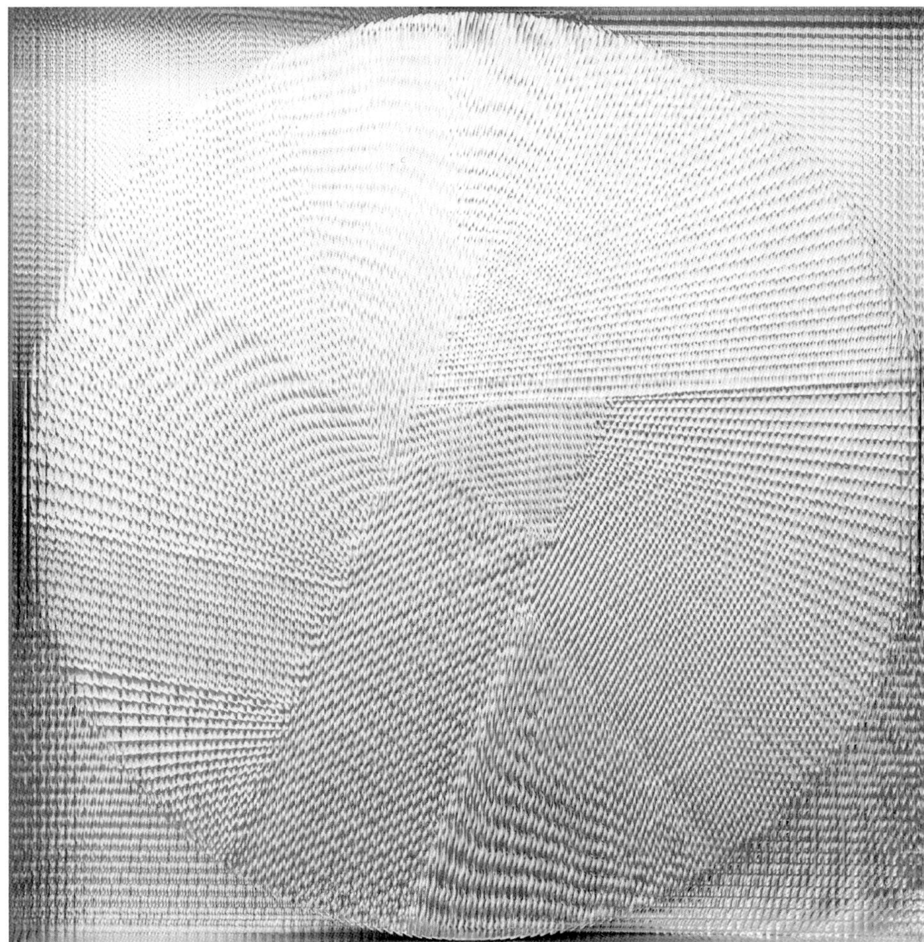

Heinz Mack *Silberrotor*, 1965

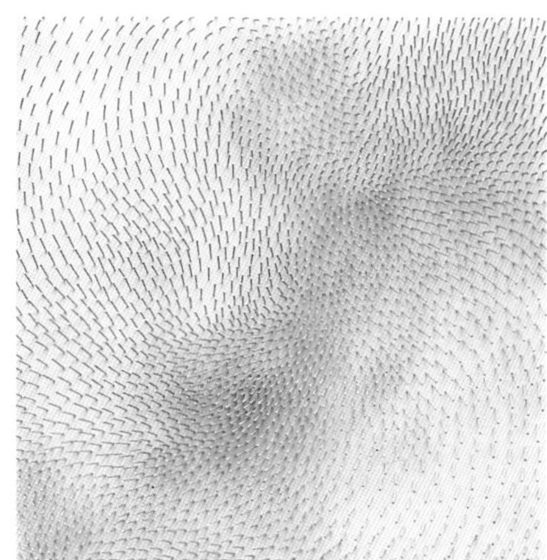

Günther Uecker *Bewegtes Feld*, 1964

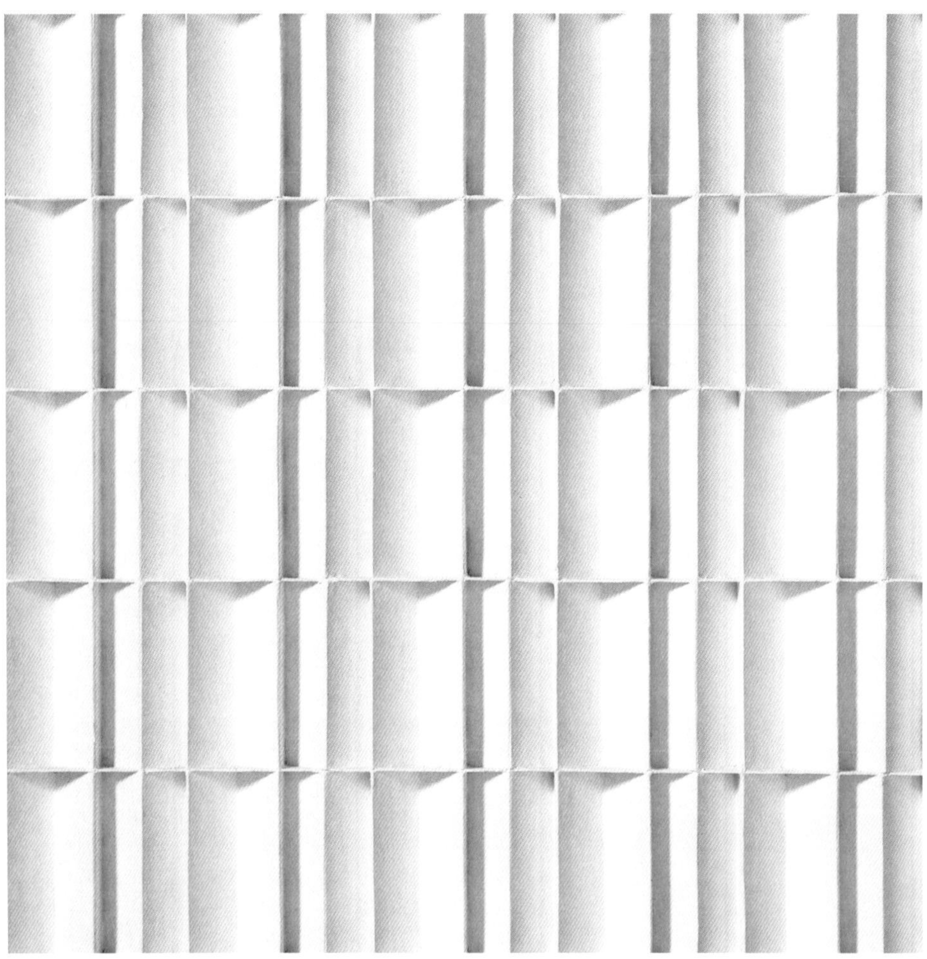

Jan Schoonhoven *R 68-6 (Reliëf VI)*, 1968

sought an art that would be an objective reflection of reality rather than a product of subjective expression. And here, too, the major themes are space, light and movement, as well as a serial arrangement based on the principle of a repetition of identical elements. But unlike Zero, with its lofty, romantic aspirations and its fondness for the immaterial and the spiritual, the Nul movement was always a bit more matter-of-fact and cynical and always focused on an observable, day-to-day reality. Fascinated with technology and contemporary materials, they wished to show reality as it is and open the viewer's eyes to its beauty. In 1965 **Jan Schoonhoven** described the approach and the ideology of Zero and Nul as follows: "Zero is, first and foremost, a new conception of reality, in which the individual role of the artist is confined to a minimum. The Zero artist merely chooses, isolates segments of reality (materials, as well as ideas derived from reality) and shows these in the most neutral way. Fundamental to Zero is the avoidance of personal feelings: the

acceptance of things as they are and not changing them for personal reasons, only introducing changes where necessary in order to show reality in a more intensive way."

This description applies only in part to Schoonhoven's own work, as he, unlike the other members of Group Nul, did not isolate elements from reality but rather constructed the elements himself and thus actually added a new factor to reality in the form of a square or rectangular compartment. The series of vertical and horizontal compartments make up an even field, in which no one part is more important than another. The number of compartments or the size of these is not determined by an internal law. But the edges do indicate the limits of the field and thereby the concreteness of the object.

A significant quality of Schoonhoven's reliefs, and one typical of Zero and Nul, is the effect of light as a result of the surface being painted white. The identical, bright white forms take on a heightened presence due to the light and shade, as can be seen, for

instance, with the work *R 68-6 (Relief VI)* from 1968. It is particularly the traces of the manual labor that become visible due to the light. Each compartment has, because of this handwork, inevitable aberrations and slight surface structures. It is precisely the tension between these sensitive irregularities and the logical order of the whole that determines, to a high degree, the beauty of these reliefs.

Henk Peeters was the spokesman and organizer of Group Nul. Together with Armando, he wrote art-theoretical essays on Nul, founded the magazine *Nul=0* and coordinated various exhibitions. Peeters was aiming, during the early sixties, for an art that was new and fresh. The materials that he used, such as nylon and plastic, were contemporary. Color was banished by him: most of his works are white, grey or black. In the work *62-01* (1962) we see the characteristically Group Nul repetition of isolated segments from reality being implemented in a subtle way. Here Peeters used cotton balls, a material that everyone occasionally uses or has used in daily life. The irregularities of the cotton balls, and the way in which they have been arranged on the surface, yields a playfulness and a lightness that displays dadaist tendencies.

To a greater degree than other members of Group Nul, Peeters initially regarded Nul as a means to fight social injustice and work toward a better society. Unfortunately, this weapon proved to be inadequate. "After 1945 everyone thought: now we'll have another society. That didn't happen, and you got a restoration to the prewar situation. At the end of the fifties, this could be still sustained economically, but not culturally: students, and to a lesser extent artists, were getting ready for other things. We then thought: *now* there will be changes. But that, too, proved not to be the case. From that time on, I stopped painting (…)." In 1965 Group Nul disbanded. Though their art had initially earned a great deal of criticism, during their second exhibition at the Stedelijk Museum in Amsterdam in 1965 their work appeared to have become totally accepted and even applauded. The Nul movement had lost its militant character and, with that, its effectiveness in the struggle for innovation.

Armando is known not only as an artist, but also as a writer and actor. He is fascinated by extreme situations in which human behavior becomes unpredictable and where themes such as violence, guilt and tragedy play a role. His position is that of the outsider, the observer, who renders his findings in words or in images, not in the form of illustration but as metaphor. During the fifties he

Armando *Zwarte bouten op zwart*, 1960

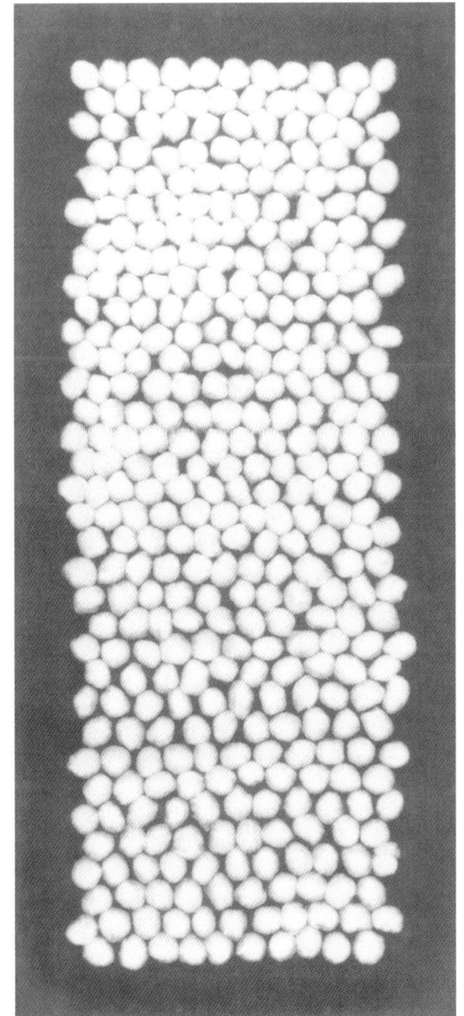

Henk Peeters *62-01*, 1962

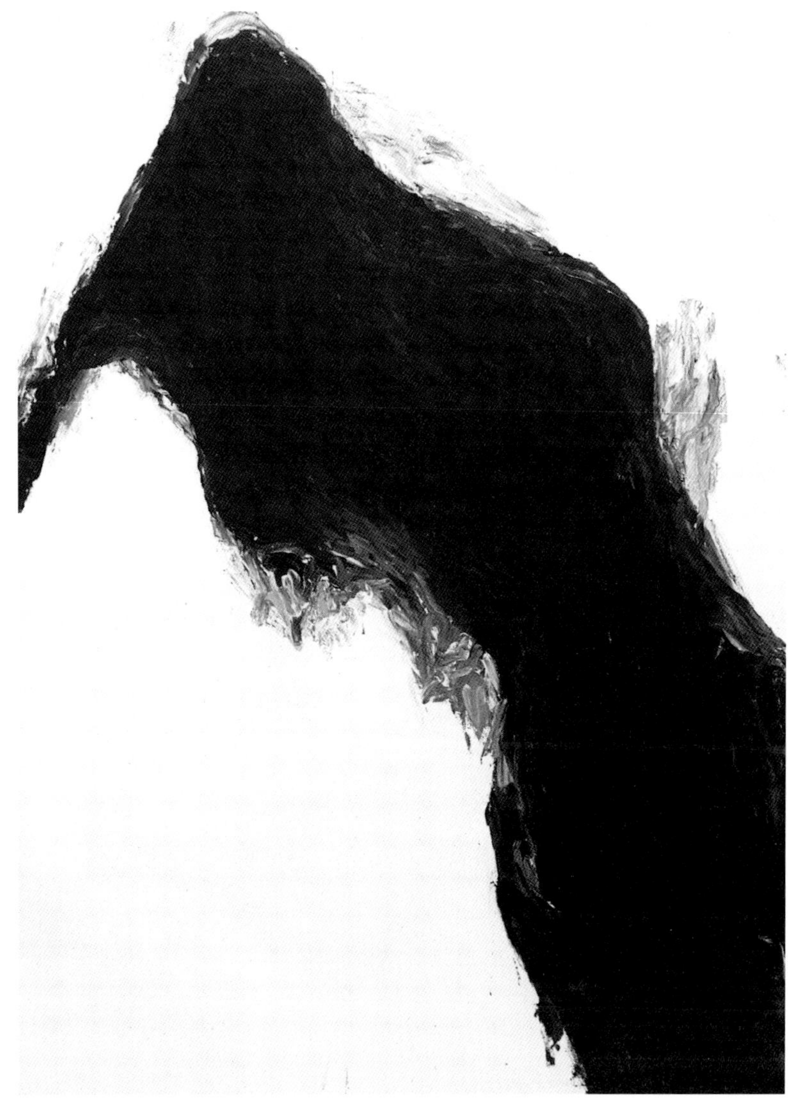

Armando *Fahne*, 1980-81

produced abstract paintings (*peintures criminelles*) and monochromes (*espaces criminelles*). In his Nul period he used harsh, industrial materials and objects such as iron, barbed wire, bolts, rivets and car tires, which he preferred to paint black, as with *Zwarte bouten op zwart* (1960), but also red–the color of blood–or white. "What I found beautiful during that time were voids. I thought vast surfaces with a single color were wonderful: factory sites or barracks, all that nauseating–and grim–regularity. Things like this always have a double meaning for me. It's because the German army was beautiful. Evil that's beautiful. That's what I always had at the back of my mind. Instinctively, I opted for harsh materials; those appealed to me, they fit me." Due to the choice of materials and the technique used, the personal signature of the artist was completely banished during this period. At the end of the sixties, Armando returned to his expressive manner of drawing and painting. This resulted in works–predominantly in black, white and grey–which are marked by an aggressive vehemence. The use of repetition and working in series remained important in this later work as well.

xi

Richard Paul Lohse

Victor Vasarely

François Morellet

Joost Baljeu

Peter Struycken

Bob Bonies

Ad Dekkers

Jan Maaskant

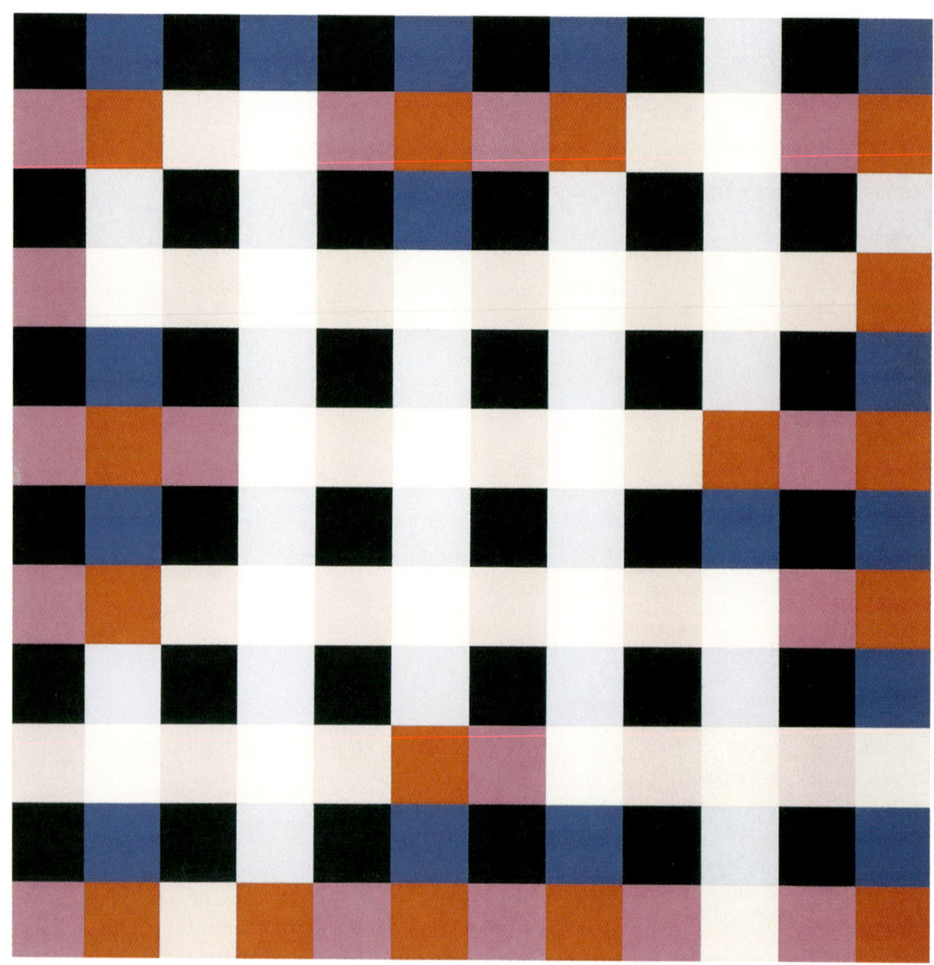

Richard Paul Lohse *Vier gleiche asymmetrische Gruppen innerhalb eines regelmässigen Systems*, 1962-63

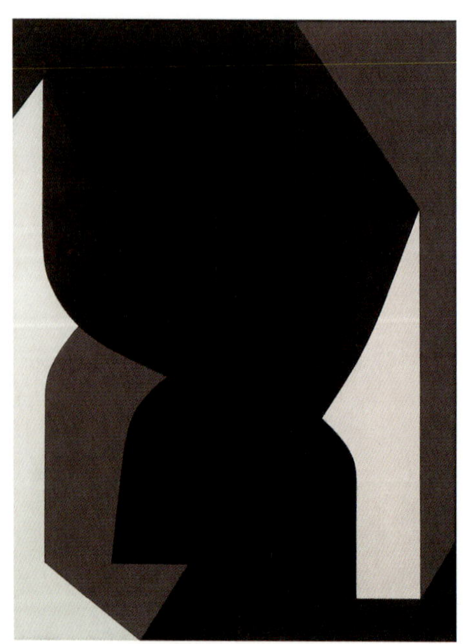

Victor Vasarely *Silur*, 1952-58

The fundamental analysis of painterly problems during the twenties and thirties led, after the war, to the further development of geometric abstraction, art which tended to be based on systems and the patterns arising from these. The work of art became, to an even greater extent, the product of objective points of departure and mathematical precision.

Vier gleiche asymmetrische Gruppen innerhalb eines regelmässigen Systems (1962-63) by the Swiss artist **Richard Paul Lohse** is an example of a painting that has come about on the basis of fundamental rules and meticulous deliberation over the procedure to be used; these rules and the method followed become, in themselves, the content of the painting. In ever-changing combinations Lohse organized, within the image surface and in a predetermined direction, color groups consisting of modules equal in size (i.e. standard elements). Each new rule of the game yielded yet another type of behavior or experience of color and generated new relationships among the given elements.

Lohse ascribed no priority to any form, relationship or color whatsoever; nor did he impose a hierarchical system. He himself referred to his structures as being 'democratic': all of the elements are equivalent and dependent on each other and, as such, constitute an entity. To Lohse, these were more than mere models for painting; he also saw them as being a contribution to the generation of a new and more just society and a better living environment. About this he said the following: "Forms of expression from a nonhierarchical society are accordingly flexible, transparent, and controllable, in terms of both method and result."

Victor Vasarely also belongs to the slightly younger generation of artists who, in the footsteps of Suprematism, De Stijl and Bauhaus, explored the pure elements of form, space and surface during the postwar years. Hungarian by birth, he spent the years 1928 and 1929 studying at the Bauhaus of Budapest, where Moholy-Nagy taught after leaving Weimar. In 1930 Vasarely moved to

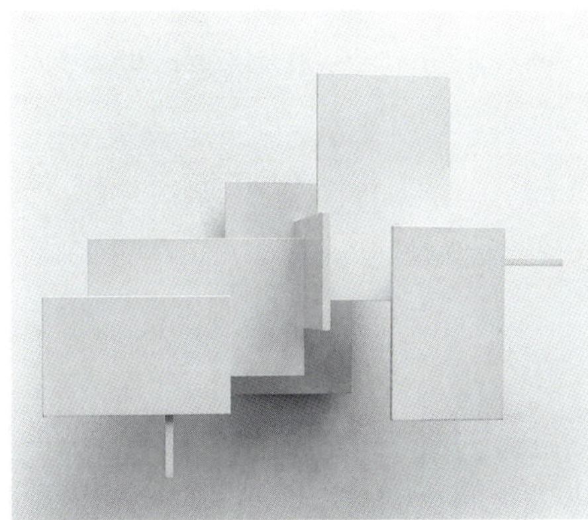

Joost Baljeu *Synthetische constructie W-II, 1957*

Paris. During the initial phase of his work Vasarely did not confine himself to the purely geometric forms of the line, the circle and the rectangle. Derivative forms such as the parabola, the ellipse and the hyperbola can also be found, as in *Silur* (1952-58). Until 1958 he painted more organic forms and units of color that are part of the sculptural space (*espace plastique*); large planes–whose curved forms are juxtaposed–suggest a spatial effect partly due to their gradation in color: a third dimension is thereby introduced. These types of works were the forerunners of paintings and reliefs that Vasarely began to develop into more elementary geometric forms in 1958, thus creating images which were indeed static, but which nonetheless suggested movement. With these works Vasarely opened the way to Kinetic art and 'op art'. The Frenchman **François Morellet** produced

the work *32 Rectangles* (1953) on the basis of structures of repeated patterns, in which the placement of identical elements is staggered. By doing this he wished to eliminate the arbitrary nature of composition, format, matter and color. Around 1960 Morellet began to produce more spatial constructions in which the viewer can become aware of the structure of the system in which optical experiences can become even more varied. In those works there is an even greater demand for the eye to observe in a 'differentiating' manner. By allowing the object to move or allowing the viewer to walk by it, Morellet wanted to show the perspectival changes of regular spatial units.

Later these kinetic works were further developed by him in constructions with artificial lighting, such as *Néon moderne en état de marche* (1973) Simple geometric patterns of colored neon lighting switch on, but in a sequence which has not been determined in advance; just as one image seems to become fixed, this is disrupted by the intervention of another.

In the Netherlands there were also explorations of the principles of constructivism from the twenties and thirties, which gave rise to new rules and structures.

After a period of naturalist painting, **Joost Baljeu** began, in 1954, to investigate elementary matters–such as the relationship between the surface and the color and the balance of horizontal/vertical–in geometric compositions. In 1955 he went on to produce reliefs, prompted by a desire for greater

concreteness and in order to counteract illusionism. From 1955 to 1957 Baljeu made three-dimensional structures in a single color (white), because he believed that a variety of colors interfered with the volumes of the construction. The work *Synthetische constructie W-II* (1957) dates from that period. Baljeu articulated his ideas in the periodical *Structure*, which he founded in 1958 and whose participants included prominent constructivist artists from other countries, including Great Britain, France and Switzerland. From this manner of thinking in a constructivist language of forms, it was a fairly natural progression for Baljeu to become concerned with architecture and the constructed environment, the creation of spaces and volumes in which people move about, and with the relationship between those people and their surroundings. This latter aspect would offer the potential for art to function directly within society.

The exploration of continually different types of visual structures, based on the implementation of different rules, takes place according to a programmed procedure in the work of **Peter Struycken**. The painting *Cluster 12* (1971-75) is one of a series of sixteen that were produced according to a computer program named Cluster. This series deals mainly with the placement of colors, their variants and their interconnections. Struycken introduces this program as follows: "The computer program Cluster contains a number of conditions and rules by which visual matter can be ordered. In the computer program the conditions and rules

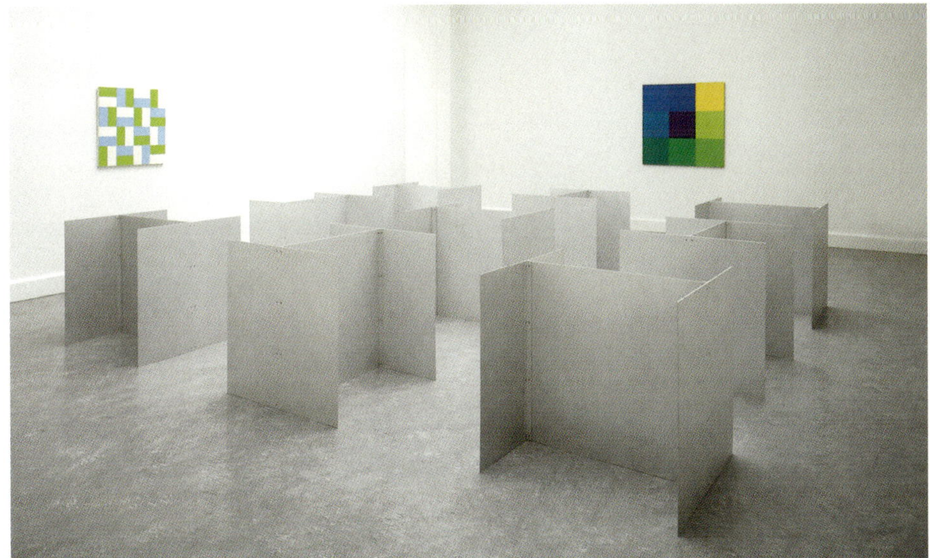

Robert Morris *9 H-shapes, 1968;* **François Morellet** *32 Rectangles, 1953;* **Richard Paul Lohse** *Bewegung von Gelb über Grün und Blau zu Violett, 1958-73*

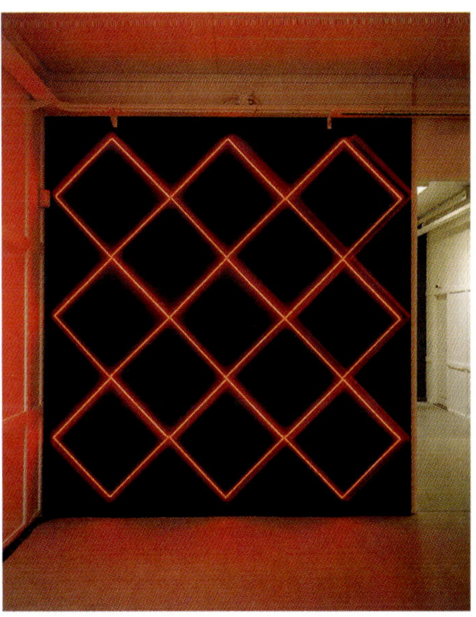

François Morellet *Néon moderne en état de marche, 1973*

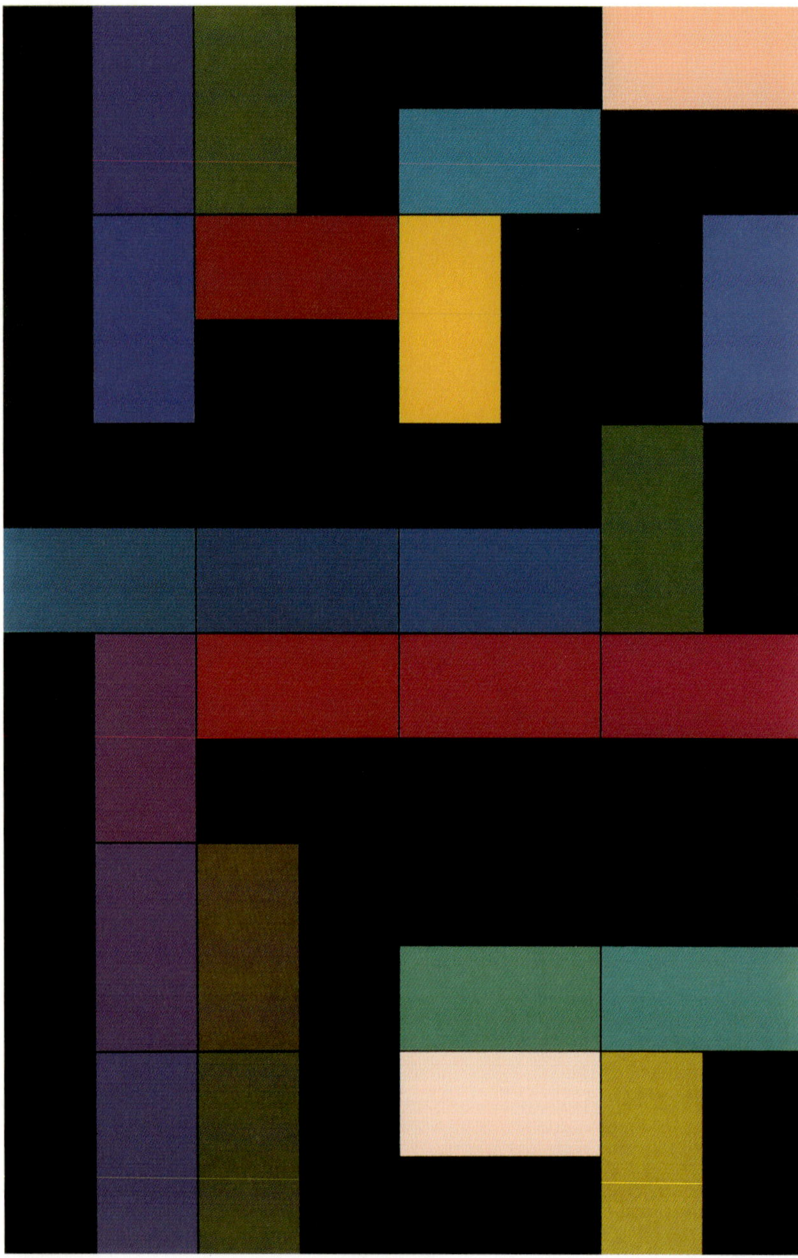

Peter Struycken *Cluster 12, 1971-75*

about by the use of a systematic structure. Geometric planes are ordered according to a particular system. In order to arrive at a painting of the greatest possible clarity, Bonies has 'limited' himself to the colors red, blue, yellow, green and white. The colors are applied to the canvas in an even and monochrome manner. And the shifting, doubling or tilting of the geometric planes according a particular system gives rise to what are called 'shaped canvases': the contour of the painting is no longer a square or a rectangle but another geometric form which causes the image, often made up of many parts, to expand in space.

The painting *Dyptiek* (1972) by Bonies is not a 'shaped canvas' but rather consists of two rectangular canvases, the left and right parts of which have the same planar division. That which is painted white on one half of the one canvas has been given a color on the other half, so that if the two parts were overlapped, the existing geometric planes would be enlarged or extended.

Ad Dekkers investigated not only the effects of visual elements on each other, but also (and primarily) the material quality of the painting as an object: its form, its delineation, surface and material. With earlier illusionistic painting, such object-like characteristics never struck the eye, because the image, that which was depicted on the picture plane, had prime importance; the painting functioned as a window through which one saw a depicted reality. In his approach to illusionism as being antithetical to the concreteness of the painting, Dekkers arrived at the making of reliefs, as it allowed him to become removed from illusionism: the relief itself involved, after all, a third dimension. In a relief he could show that third dimension in a concrete manner, as in *Variatie op cirkels nr. III* (1965). Initially, Dekkers produced reliefs that consisted of stacks of geometric forms on a base surface; later he developed, from this, reliefs with linear grooves and saw cuts. Within the boundaries (the edges) and the surface of a wooden board, he sawed slots which began to behave like lines–concrete, spatial lines–on the surface. At first he placed these slots symmetrically within a square surface, as the center line of the square for instance, and later he began to introduce only a part of such a line and leave an increasing part of the surface untouched. In yet another phase he allowed the saw cuts to begin deep in the board and gradually rise to the surface; this caused a greater disruption of the board's mass. Throughout the entire oeuvre of Dekkers, surface and line have always been

are phrased in an explicit and logical manner. When applied to visual matter, they prove to grant their own specific characteristics to its coherence. The most important aspect that arises in this is, on the one hand, the interaction between the formal system which is free of value and has no expression or other visual aesthetic quality and, on the other, the visual results which offer an abundance of visual information and which can no longer be interpreted as being 'free of value'. While, on a visual level, one ascribes different values to the different results, one is also aware of their formal capacities on the program level." Each painting is an ordering of visual means

in terms of their interrelationships. This ordering has a nature of its own (it can, for example, be intuitive) or is based, as had been stated earlier by Lohse and Morellet, on a controllable system or on a controllable structure. By visual means, Struycken is referring to surface, circumscribing line, hue, color intensity, color saturation, material, texture and movement. The way in which these elements form a visual structure together is determined by a controllable procedure (just as in the past, for instance, mathematical perspective was used in order to portray space).

The paintings of **Bob Bonies** are also brought

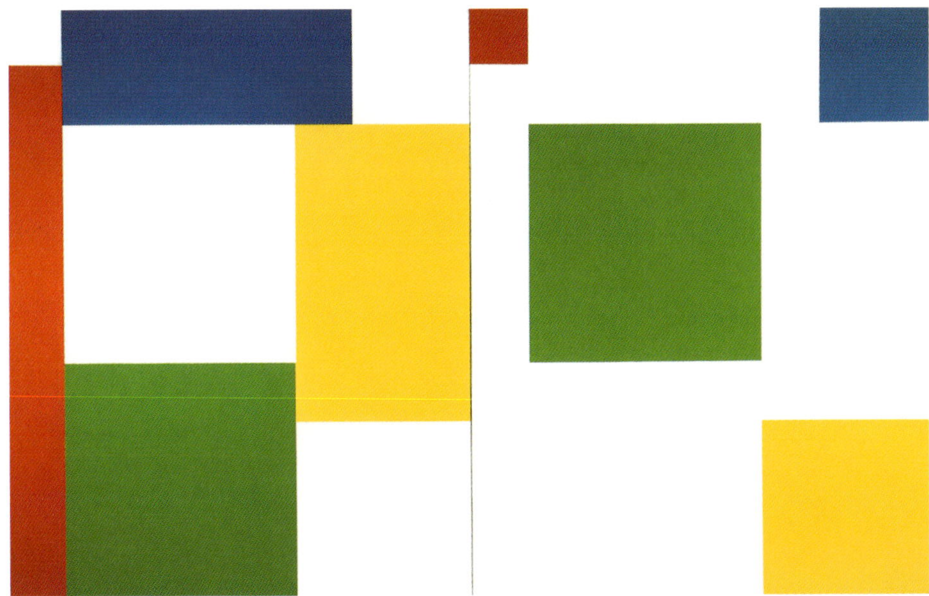

Bob Bonies *Dyptiek,* 1972

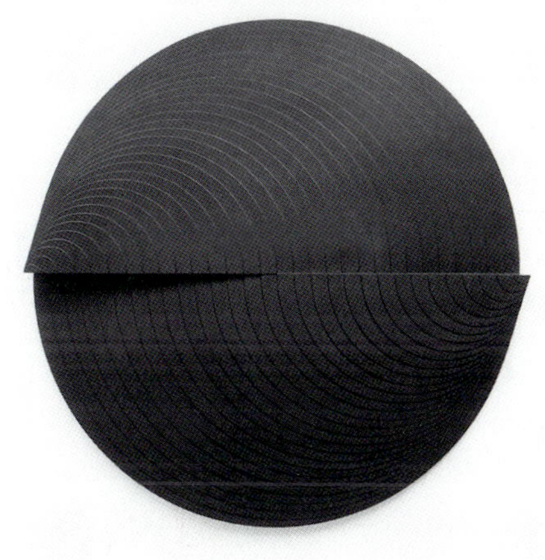

Ad Dekkers *Variatie op cirkels nr. III,* 1965

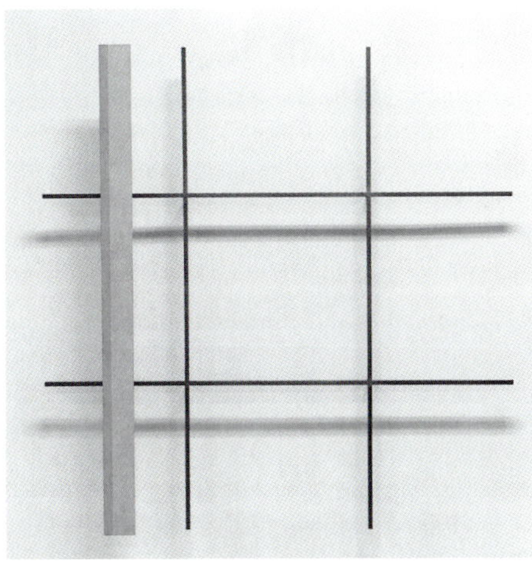

Jan Maaskant *Rasterreliëf met grijs-geel verticaal,* 1975

subject to consistent systematic investigation.

The activities of a number of geometric-abstract artists during the sixties and seventies involved thoroughly personal interpretations of concepts as they had been articulated by the generation from the twenties and thirties. The theories from those years had been necessary in order to create a kind of philosophical background for works which were completely new and unknown at that time. Meanwhile, analytical thought and the resulting methods for painting became an accepted way of making art. The shaping of ideas on the nature of art does take place in dialogue with the abstract-geometric tradition, but it is in the specific work of each artist that these ideas are given coherence and individual meaning.

Analytical thought and the idea of an underlying logical structure dominate throughout the work of sculptor **Jan Maaskant**, but the thoroughly individual intervention that he introduces in that structure on the basis of his own concept, his personal feeling for the manifestation of interrelationships of visual elements, prevents his work from becoming significantly linked with the 'objectivity' of Constructivism.

Furthermore, when Maaskant began to concern himself with sculpture as a self-taught artist in 1961, there were considerably fewer certainties and dogmatic rules than there were in painting. In the early years he was influenced by the work of Henri Laurens and later by that of Brancusi and González, but eventually he developed, on the basis of a

contained, compact form, sculptures and reliefs which display, on the contrary, an open structure, comprised of independent sculptural elements. Maaskant wished to rediscover the actual meaning of sculpture, the extent to which he could bring about a composition in which ordering elements such as scale, distance, direction, division (functioning as a basic plan) take on a meaningful relationship with what he himself called the 'exceptional gesture'. This individual gesture responds to the logical construct and creates a unique situation by removing that construct from its universal order. The reliefs gave Maaskant the potential to work on a space (the wall) that is less disrupted by all sorts of circumstances than the space of a room, for instance, or a outdoor site. In his reliefs, during the early seventies, Maaskant opened up the contained form, no longer placing these against the wall but at a certain distance from it. The materiality (weight) was thereby reduced, and the supportive structure assumed a certain neutrality by consisting of stainless steel or aluminum.

In *Rasterreliëf met grijs-geel verticaal* (1975), the grid (the supportive structure) consists of four equidistant rods of stainless steel which, due to their intersection, form a square in the center. Because no boundaries have been placed on the rods (by establishing a frame along the ends of these, for instance) the structure is opened in all directions; inner and outer space merge. The visual sign (a vertical element stretched with linen and painted in grey and yellow), again set at some distance from the grid, constitutes an instinctive gesture. Though placed asymmetrically in relation to the grid, it fails to throw the entire composition off balance. The choice of color is closely related to the tranparent articulation. The interaction between the universal and the individual gesture represents, for Maaskant, not only a model for sculpture. In his abstract constructions he alludes–by way of groupings, concentrations and combinations of independent structures and tendencies–to the principle on which, in his view, many things in culture and society are organized.

XII

Robert Indiana

Jim Dine

Andy Warhol

Martial Raysse

Arman

Christo

Jean Tinguely

Domenico Gnoli

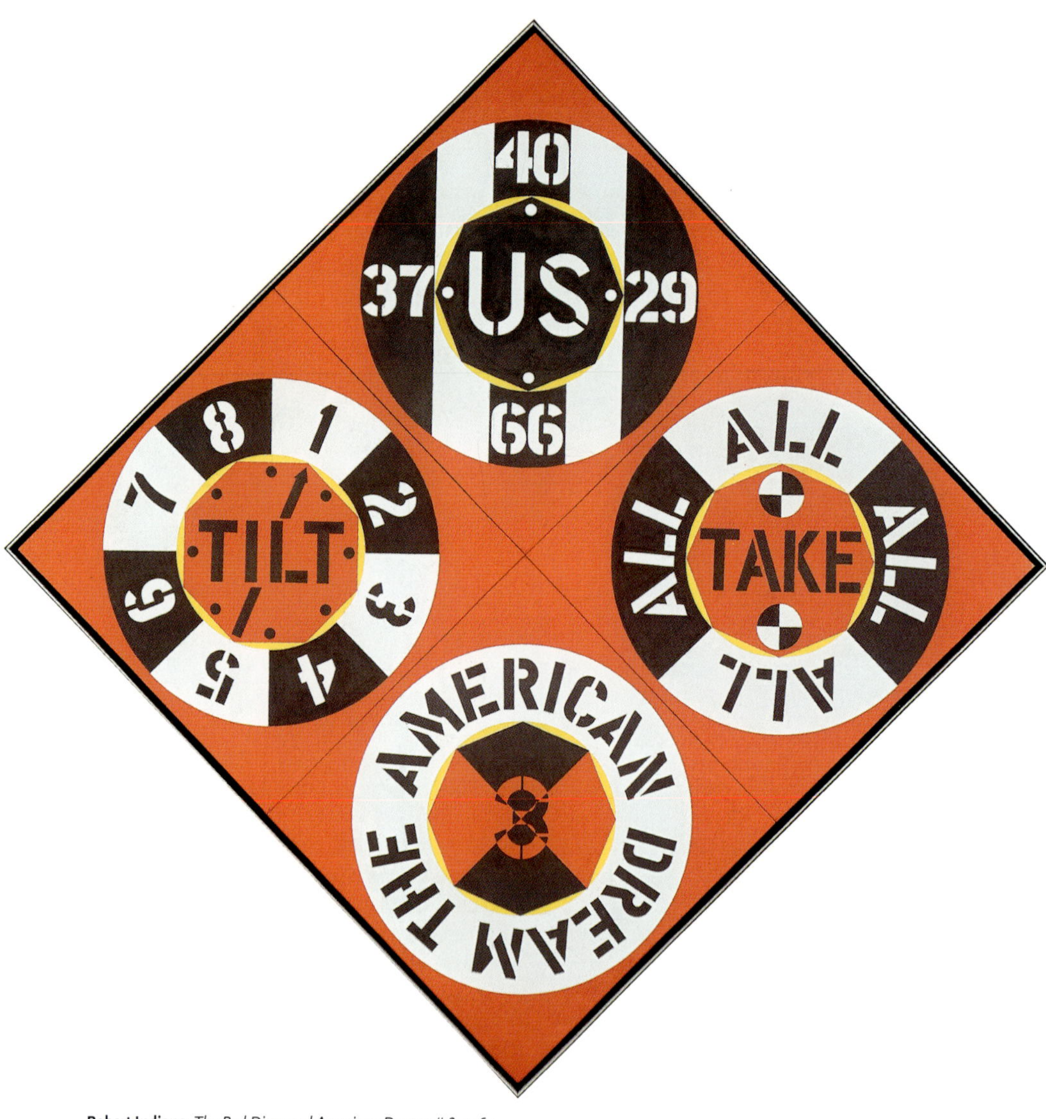

Robert Indiana *The Red Diamond American Dream # 3*, 1962

The late 1940s and early 1950s were completely dominated by abstract expressionist painting. The second half of the fifties could be regarded, however, as a period of reaction and transition. In the United States as well as in Europe, the younger generation was consciously and resolutely relinquishing the overpowering and gradually depleted style. This occurred in a variety of ways, which gave considerable momentum to the development. And so rather than being a simple and straightforward matter, it was something that took many directions at the same time. Even so, in the complex view of this period we can discern two major tendencies: on the one hand, a radical renewal of abstract art–a development which is discussed in another chapter–and on the other, the emergence of a new type of figurative art.

Underlying the new figurative art was a new way of seeing and observing. The younger generation was highly aware of the changing postwar environment and became fascinated with the explosive growth of urban culture–a materialist, populist and blaring culture of consumer goods, publicity and mass media. These everyday surroundings were, for some artists, a captivating source of visual information. They introduced the visual elements around them as the new subject matter of their art. The exploration of unorthodox visual material led, almost automatically, to new visual problems and solutions. This new manner of observation and the changed environment constituted the basis for a formulation of new figurative 'languages': Pop Art (in the U.S. and Great Britain), *nouveau réalisme* (in France) and other forms of realism, such as hyperrealism. An initial figurative reaction to abstract expression could already be seen in the work of Robert Rauschenberg and Jasper Johns. They are often referred to as 'neo-dadaists', because their work involves a certain reorientation to dadaist and surrealist

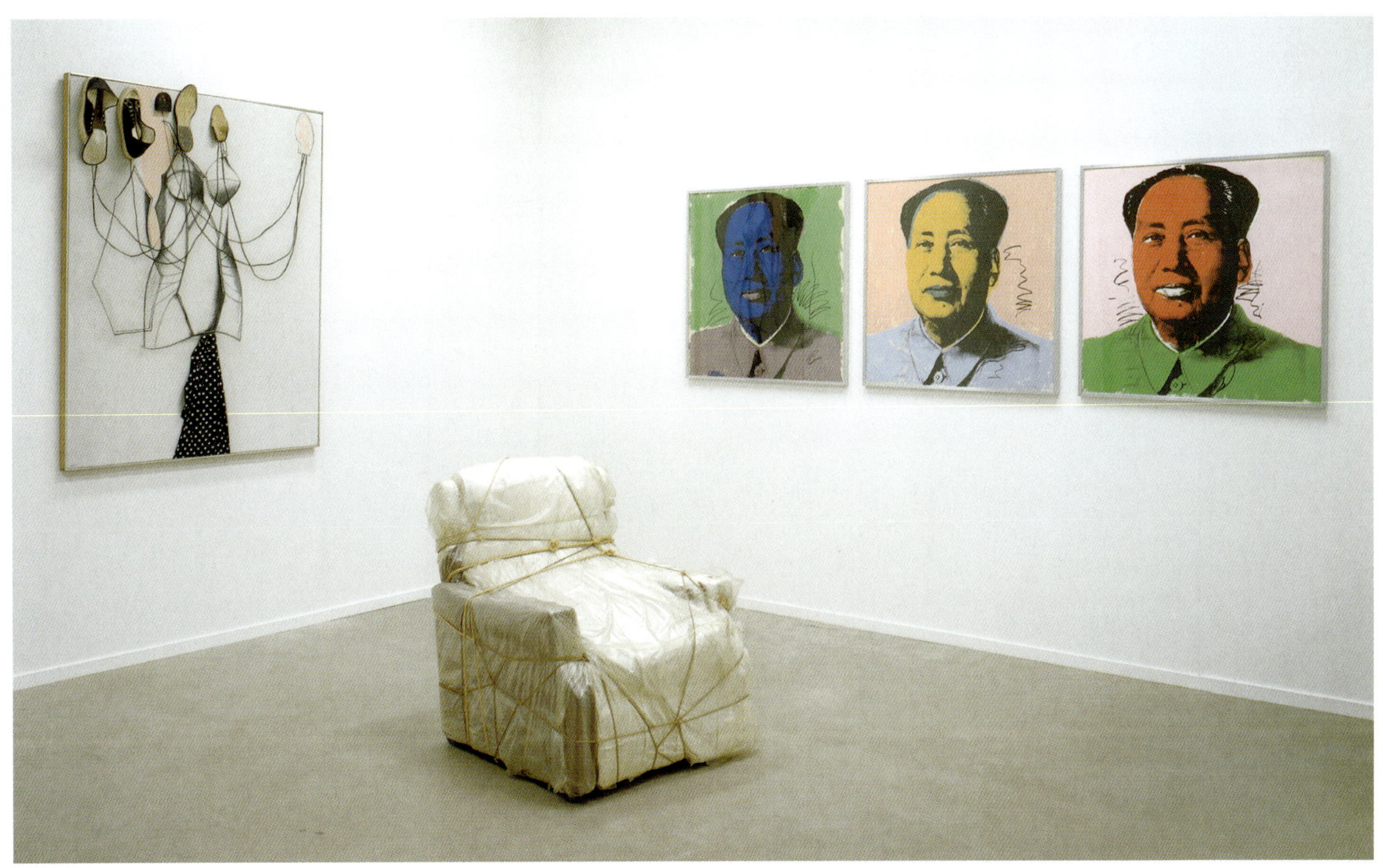

From left to right: **Jim Dine** *All in one Lycra, plus Attachments*, 1965; **Christo** *Packed Arm Chair*, 1964-65; **Andy Warhol** *Mao Tse Tung*, 1972

principles and techniques (the 'readymade' principle of Marcel Duchamp, the collage and assemblage techniques of Kurt Schwitters). In terms of both form and content, they can be regarded as the immediate predecessors to Pop Art.

More or less at the same time, Rauschenberg and Johns brought upheaval to the art scene with extremely controversial works. Around 1955 Rauschenberg exhibited his first 'combine paintings', into which actual objects were incorporated. Jasper Johns painted thoroughly banal subject matter (flags, targets, numbers and letters) in an uncommonly neutral and nonemotional manner. He moreover made use of the 'encaustic' process, in which hot wax mixed with pigment is applied to the canvas. The thick layers of wax cool and harden into a fairly rough, relief-like surface structure, which lends the painting a distinctly object-like character. The 'painting' no longer functions as the familiar, traditional depiction of a target, for example, but becomes a different kind of target by being, as it were, an object unto itself. This autonomous object-like character of Johns's paintings formed the point of departure for

further ideas of abstract artists such as Frank Stella.

Like Jasper Johns, **Robert Indiana** (actually Robert Clark) also introduced banal visual subject matter such as numbers and words in his paintings. He did so in an extreme manner. The numbers and words of slot machines, traffic signs and neon signs were his prime material. Initially, Indiana produced assemblages consisting of all sorts of found objects. At a certain point he came across a great quantity of brass stencils of letters and numbers. From that moment on, his work assumed a definitive form, as he systematically incorporated the stencilling into series of smoothly painted and geometrically ordered canvases. These paintings are made up of brightly contrasting and sharply delineated areas of color, which hint at the influence of 'hard-edge' painters such as Ellsworth Kelly.

The Red Diamond American Dream #3 (1962)–the third version from the *American Dream* series–is a typical Indiana painting in which most of the aforementioned characteristics can be found: the Pop Art idiom in a 'hard-edge' form. The canvas has been divided into four squares, and on each

of these a disc has been painted. Each disc has its own subdivisions and meanings. The disc on the left, for instance, refers to a game board with the numbers one to eight, an arrow pointing to the winning number and the warning 'tilt' in capital letters. The numbers on the uppermost disc are, on the other hand, taken from the American highway code: Indiana's father worked at a gas station on Route 66. Almost all of the visual elements that make up this painting can be reduced to literary/anecdotal connotations. They are part of Pop Art's visual language sheerly because of their visual quality. True Pop Art almost never involves any direct form of social criticism, but Indiana does attach considerable importance to the 'literary' meaning of his paintings–borrowing, incidently, many expressions from nineteenth-century authors such as Melville and Whitman. His work comments, sometimes bitterly, on 'the American way of life'.

Jim Dine also relates to 'pure' Pop Art in his own specific way. He developed a highly personal visual language which was the ultimate consequence, so to speak, of the original 'new figuration' principles, as articulated by Rauschenberg and Johns: a confrontation of reality and illusion, based on new visual material and new techniques. The affinity with the work of Rauschenberg and Johns comes as no surprise when we learn that Dine began to have intensive contact with these two artists in 1961. To an even greater extent than Rauschenberg, he made use of assemblage techniques, constructing occasionally extreme 'combine paintings' in which ordinary utilitarian objects from his daily surroundings (pieces of clothing or, at times, even entire lawn mowers and sinks) are placed in the 'art' context of the canvas, as are the shoes in *All in one Lycra, plus Attachments* (1965). In this respect, he was perhaps the most 'neo-dadaist' of the Pop Art generation. Like Johns, Dine brought reality and illusion face to face. But he did this in a more emphatic manner: his paintings are, as it were, lessons in visual perception and illustrate the different ways in which reality can be represented and presented within the context of visual art.

Andy Warhol comprises a chapter of his own in the history of Pop Art. More than any other Pop artist, he became widely known through his objects, his paintings and silkscreen prints, his underground films and his own personal way of life. Consumer society was his major source of inspiration. Practically anything could serve as a theme for his work. Who doesn't know the Coca-Cola bottles, the Brillo boxes, the Campbell's soup cans that brought him such fame during the sixties? From these supermarket products, Warhol moved on to celebrities such as Elvis Presley, Marilyn Monroe and Elizabeth Taylor, whose photographs he blew up and screenprinted onto paper. One of Warhol's legendary statements is: "In the future, everybody will be world famous for fifteen minutes." In the collection of the Van Abbemuseum are three prints from the series *Mao Tse Tung* from 1972, carried out in different combinations of color. Sensational subject matter, such as accidents, disasters or the explosion of the atomic bomb, also came into his work, usually in series of monotonously repeated images taken from press photographs. Through the use of the screenprint, Warhol eliminated any trace of 'personal handwriting', and by working in editions he deprived the work of its singularity. Without comment, without hierarchy: this is how he depicted the world surrounding him.

In Europe, art was undergoing a similar development. The art scene was centered in the École de Paris: Paris was *the* meeting place for a wide range of artists from all over

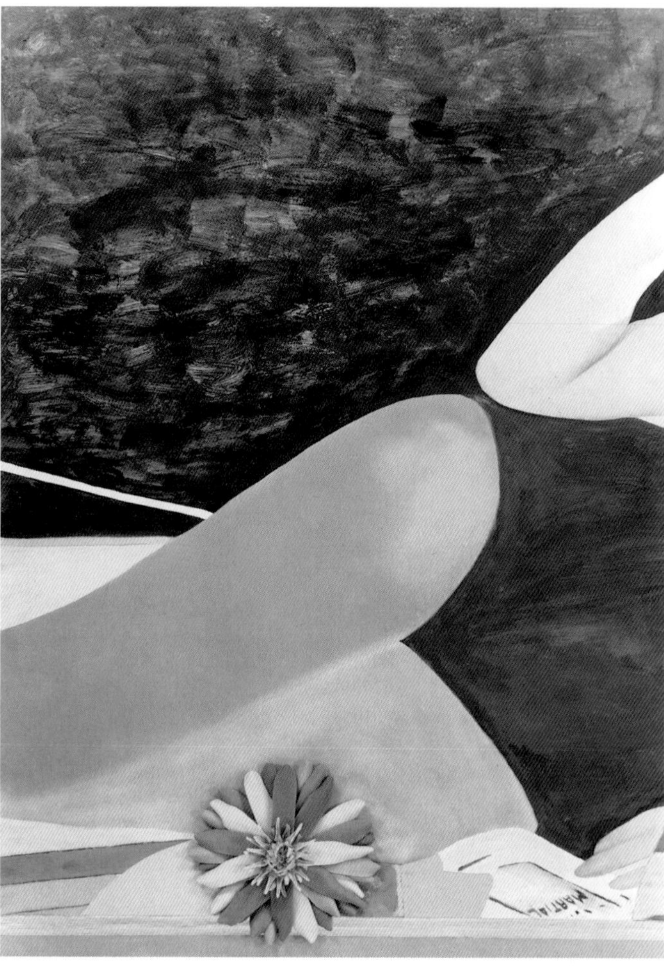

Martial Raysse *Mi-août*, 1962

the continent. Artists such as Wols, Dubuffet, Fautrier and others had set the tone immediately after World War II with stylistic tendencies such as *art informel* and tachism: forms of painting comparable to American abstract expressionism with respect to the combination of abstract-form qualities and a highly emotional, spontaneous treatment of the paint. It is therefore not surprising that an attitude similar to that in the United States arose here as well: a younger generation was rebelling against the dominant trend and laying the foundations for a new type of figurative art.

The art critic Pierre Restany was very influential in France. In 1960 he published a manifesto titled *Les Nouveaux Réalistes* and, somewhat later, formed a group of the same name with a variety of artists such as Klein, Tinguely, Arman, Raysse, Spoerri and the *décollagistes* Hains, De la Villeglé and Dufrêne, joined later by Niki de St.-Phalle, Christo, César and Rotella.

Though a great many differences can be discerned among them, the artists clearly shared common factors: they deliberately dismissed any form of abstract-expressionist painting and, like their American contemporaries, were initially fascinated with the new and rich visual material offered by the day-to-day products of modern society. They, too, once again made use of dadaist principles and techniques such as the readymade and collage/assemblage. Nonetheless, there was a difference in relation to Pop Art: the American artists introduced the everyday utilitarian object in their art while preserving its individual identity, frequently even heightening that identity, as can be seen with Warhol's soup cans. The *nouveaux réalistes*, on the other hand, 'absorbed' the object: they changed its identity through drastic manipulation techniques such as destruction, accumulation and compression (César, Arman) or wrapping (Christo).

Of all the *nouveaux réalistes*, **Martial Raysse** has, in this respect, the strongest ties to Pop Art. The visual material of his assemblages and paintings were simply taken by him from his immediate living environment: the kitschy and snobby vacation culture of the French Riviera, one great euphoria of brimming materialism and mass consumption. He saw the brightly colored abundance of consumer goods as the "quantitative beauty of a wholly falsified nature" and wished to create a similar sort of atmosphere in his work: "a new world that is beautiful, hygienic and artificial." *Mi-août* (1962) is an assemblage painting, consisting of oil painting, silkscreen printing, plastic foam and paper on a wood panel, which can be considered characteristic of Raysse's way of working. The iconographic theme is clearly taken from the 'larger-than-life' billboards along the beaches: the painting speaks the advertising language of beautiful girls recommending, with radiant smiles, the summer resorts, sunglasses or suntan lotion, the perfect world of golden beaches and deep-blue water. Raysse then accentuated and reinforced this unusual imagery by exploiting its own means. The existing material was manipulated by him with the standard techniques of the advertising designer: deliberate cut-outs, photographic enlargements, fluorescent colors. A paint sprayer and stencil were his tools, but Raysse also applied tangible objects (towels, false eyelashes, sunglasses) to his works. He allowed the utilized visual material to maintain its original identity for the most part: the billboard remains recognizable as such.

Arman investigated, in his work, the extent to which the object maintains its identity in an altered context. He took part in exhibitions of the *nouveaux réalistes* from the start and acquired a reputation during the sixties with his accumulations of objects from everyday life–eyeglasses, cogwheels, forks, musical instruments, tubes of paint, coffee grinders. The Van Abbemuseum owns an early work from 1961, *Combien de marins, combien de capitaines*, which is comprised of used coffee grinders that have been packed together in a vitrine. The objects retain their original identity; they are clearly recognizable as being what they are. In addition to this, the jumble of coffee grinders in the glass display case constitutes an intriguing composition of colors and forms, as can be seen in an abstract-expressionist painting. The difference is that Arman's composition has come about on the basis of chance. With respect to the role of chance in his work, Arman himself has said, "My technique of accumulation consisted in allowing [the objects I used] to compose themselves. In the long run, there is nothing more controllable

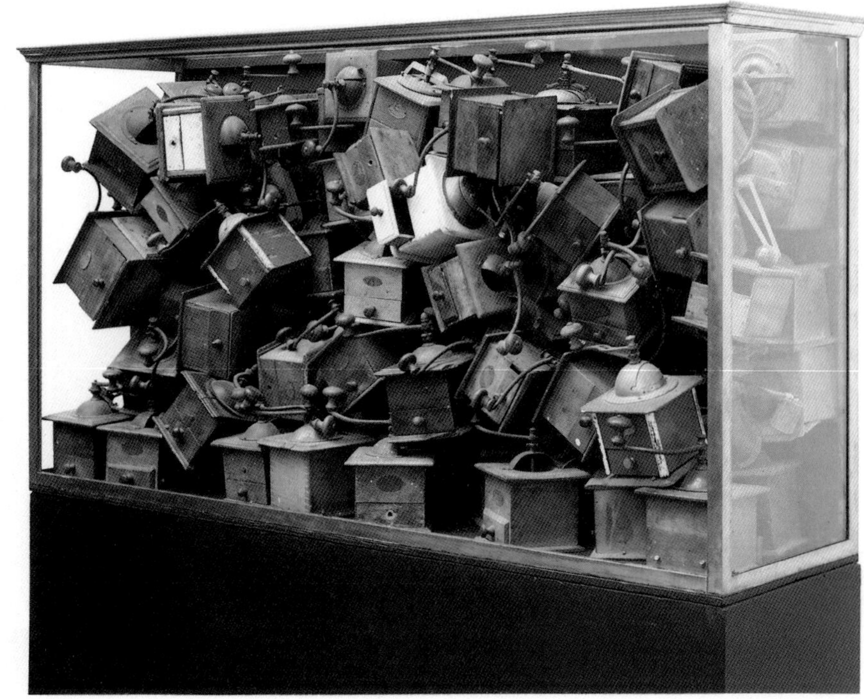

Arman *Combien de marins, combien de capitaines*, 1961

than chance. Since chance depends on laws, on quantity, for instance, it is no longer chance. Chance is my basic material, my blank page."

The object loses its identity in *Packed Arm Chair* from 1964-65, by **Christo**. This originally Bulgarian artist (whose full name is Christo Javacheff) moved to Paris in 1958, at the age of twenty-three; there he soon became acquainted with Yves Klein and the group surrounding Pierre Restany. Under Klein's influence he became more interested, he said, in architectonic realizations than in formal investigation. The beauty of stacked drums of fuel on the Paris docks captured his imagination, and in 1962 he himself produced a similar type of 'stacked' sculpture by closing off a street in the district of Saint-Germain-des-Prés with a 'wall of drums'. Later he attempted to "break through the traditional aestheticism of the object in its spatial potential" by wrapping it. These *empaquetages* attest, in Christo's view, to a conscious artistic stance with respect to reality. He sees his wrappings as comments on today's industrial and materialist civilization. The user becomes the viewer. And the viewer is intrigued but also impeded by this intervention.

With these 'wrappings' Christo appropriates, as it were, the utilitarian object. By way of paper, burlap, canvas and rope he, as an artist, makes his mark on the object and

thereby changes it fundamentally. Wrapping is, to Christo, what accumulation is to Arman, what compression is to César. From this point on, Christo wraps literally anything. At first these interventions were confined to ordinary, small utilitarian objects. But in 1964 he moved to the United States and–perhaps under the influence of the large-scale potential of that country–he developed projects that become increasingly monumental and sensational. For the Van Abbemuseum he designed, in 1966, a gigantic 'air sculpture', which was carried out in the form of a wrapped balloon, measuring eighty-five meters in height, at *documenta IV* in Kassel. In 1968 Christo wrapped the building of the Kunsthalle Bern, and in 1969 a stretch of the rocky Australian coastline. Well-known projects that have taken place more recently include the 1985 wrapping of the Pont Neuf in Paris and that of the Reichstag in Berlin in 1995. With his colossal projects of a temporary nature, Christo has certainly broken through all traditional genres.

The machine is an object which, since its invention, has given rise to admiration but also fear. It symbolizes man's faith in his own knowledge and ability but, at the same time, is the prime object onto which man can project his worst nightmares. The machine is then seen as a threat to man's freedom: it makes him dependent and will one day even come to rule over him. Earlier in history, dadaists such as Picabia and Duchamp used the machine as a visual element due to these controversial connotations. **Jean Tinguely** was also fascinated by modern, industrialized society and particularly by the machine as a symbol of modern life. During the mid fifties he began to use scrap material, including old machine parts, in order to build his own clanking, screeching machines. These machines are parodies of industrial society as well as glorifications of the absurd. They lose their function as production devices and become objects that are doomed–like Sisyphus–to repeat the same pointless movement over and again until death. What remains is the beauty and the poetry of the machine itself and its movement, as can be seen in *Char M.K.* (1967).

Aside from *nouveau réalisme*, there was yet another approach to reality in the European art of the sixties. A number of artists, painting and drawing on the basis of a specific manner of seeing and working, were grouped by Jean Leering under the term *Relativerend Realisme* in connection with an exhibition held at the Van Abbemuseum. Their method consisted of the precise rendering of isolated segments of banal reality.

The painting *Coat* (1968) by **Domenico Gnoli**, for example, may first bring to mind the hyper- or photorealism of painters such as Richard Estes, Malcolm Morley, Ralph Goings or Chuck Close. But there are fundamental differences. The predominantly American hyperrealists aimed for a perfect sort of illusionism: they attempted to imitate reality with as much virtuosity and accuracy as possible, to the point where the painting nearly coincides with harsh photographic illusion. With Gnoli, however, there is an estrangement of reality itself. This effect is achieved by him through a specific way of working: an ostensibly meaningless bit of reality is cut out, enlarged, isolated from its context and portrayed in an extremely accurate, yet oddly stylized manner. This is clearly not about creating an illusion of reality: the aforementioned treatment of the visual material is meant, on the contrary, to yield an alienation of that reality, which leads to a form of 'magic' realism. Gnoli himself has said, "To me the everyday object itself, enlarged by the attention that is lavished upon it, is more important, more beautiful and more terrible than any human invention or imagination could have made it."

Gnoli had already developed this form of figurative painting during the early sixties as a reaction to the *informels*, having been inspired by Surrealism and the work of his friend Hundertwasser. He painted details of reality, blown up larger-than-life: a necktie, shoes, buttons, parts of a suit, a hairstyle. A striking as well as significant factor in the

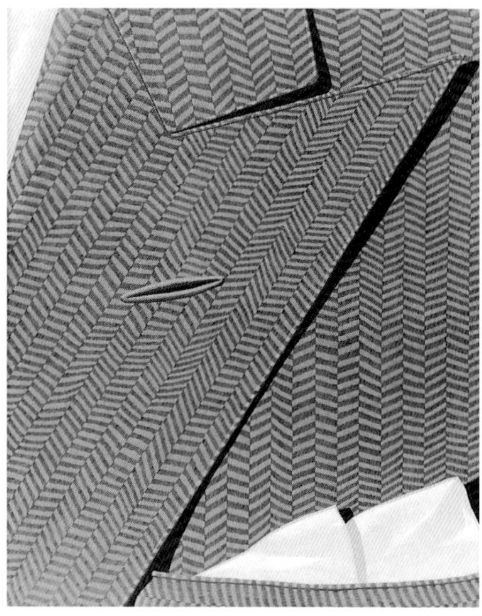
Domenico Gnoli *Coat*, 1968

alienating effect is his handling of space, or rather, the absence of spatial relationships within the painting. Because of this aspect and the extremely trivial nature of the details depicted, any association becomes practically impossible. The only relationship that can be undertaken by the painted detail is that which concerns the fact that it has been painted. The painting's main import is therefore not 'coat', but rather 'a way of painting the coat', the coat as the subject matter of painting. As such, the degree of realism to be found in the coat is hardly relevant, and the painting verges on a type of abstract art, because the elements used have been made free of suggestive or associative connotations.

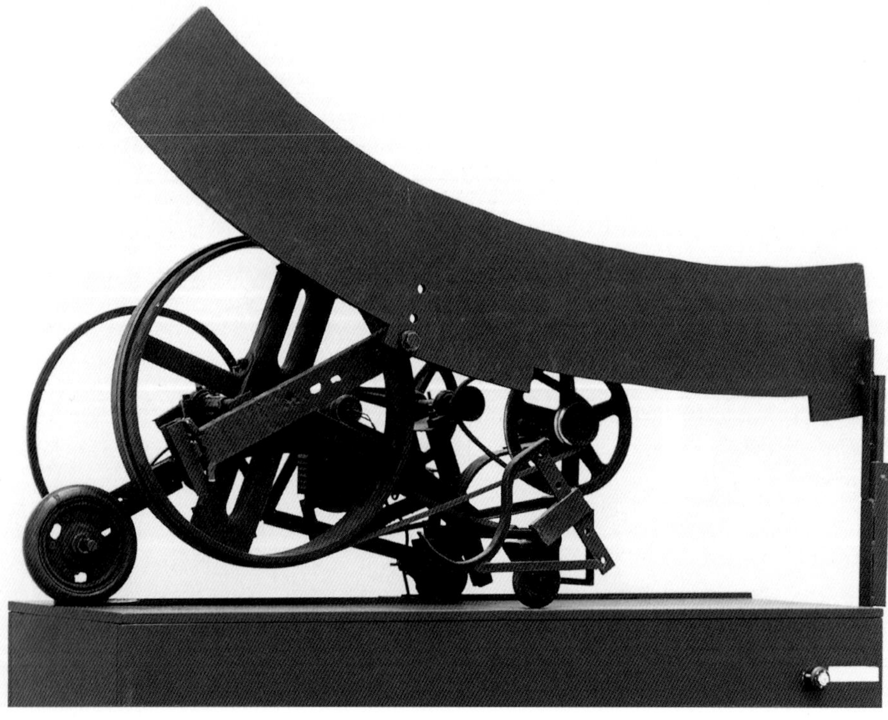
Jean Tinguely *Char M.K.*, 1967

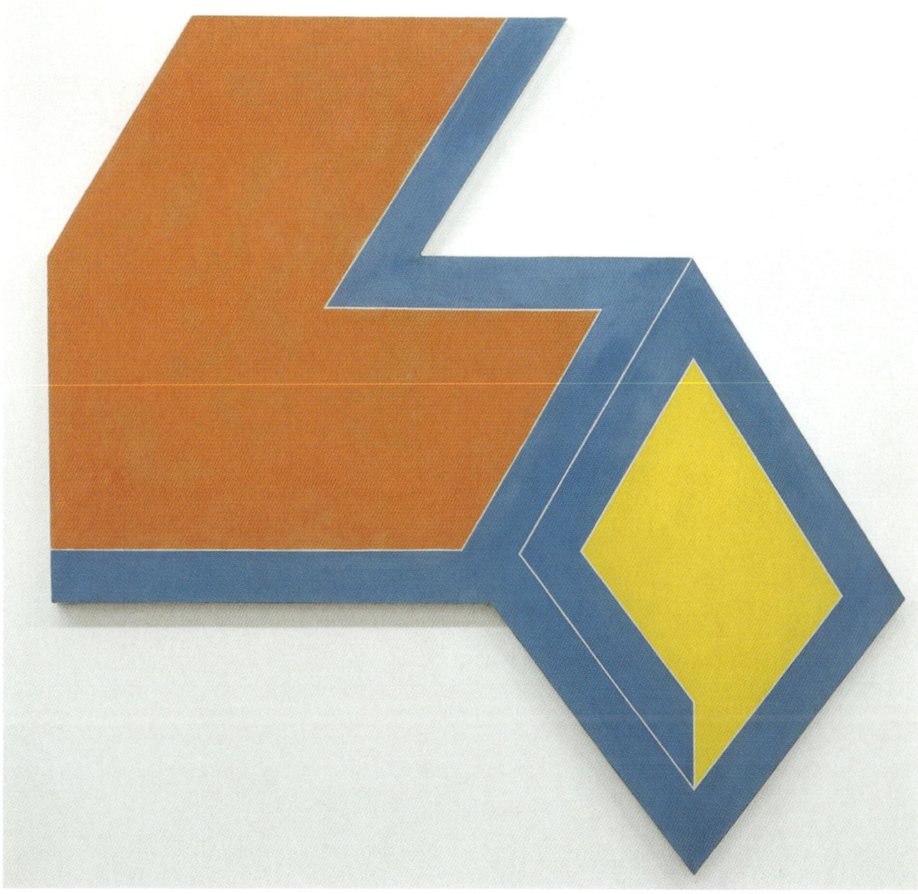

Frank Stella *Effingham I*, 1967

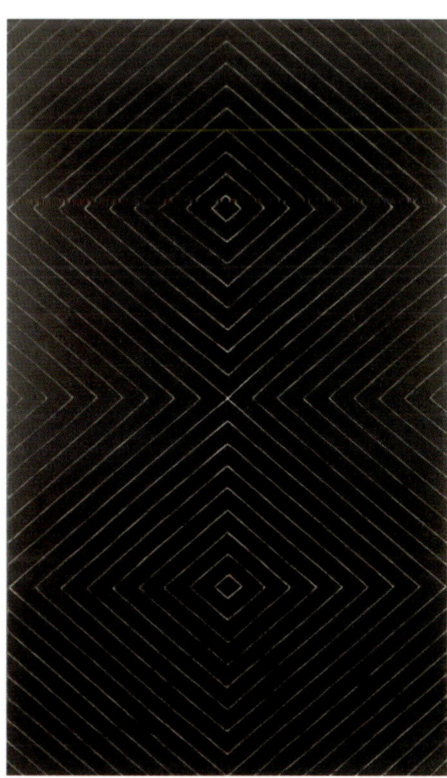

Frank Stella *Tuxedo Junction*, 1960

The legacy of Piet Mondrian, Moholy-Nagy and other abstract artists again took on surprising meaning during the 1950s. Their work, its inherent ideas concerning the painted image, was able to serve, for a number of artists emerging in Europe and the United States during the fifties, as a guiding principle in conquering the fairly ubiquitous abstract expressionism of that time. There had, of course, been other reactions to abstract expressionism, particularly those based on a somewhat neo-dadaist attitude which amounted, with artists such as Piero Manzoni and Yves Klein, to the futile affirmation of the artistic act through the creation of 'futile' paintings. Take, for example, the famous blue monochromes of Yves Klein.

Such figures as Klein and Manzoni could not serve as models for optimistic, perhaps idealistic young artists such as the American Frank Stella. His art was unable to be cynical in this way; he wanted to produce genuine, new art, but on the basis of classical principles.

Regardless of what style the painter chose to work in, there was always that one, inviolable model in classical art: reality, which determined the order of things. Dismissing reality as a model meant that anything was possible. But, on the other hand, painting without discipline is evidently not feasible. And so each painter actually began to seek a substitute model; many painters found the model in the painting as a concrete factor, or in painting itself as a physical act. They opted for a specific point of departure, not in order to defend this as dogma, but for the sake of an orderly procedure by which to create a painting—a model that could provide direction for the painterly act.

Morris Louis emerged from abstract expressionism. His great models were the 'allover' paintings of Jackson Pollock: vast fields covered with a dense web of irregular, colored lines and tendrils, spatters and blotches: veils of color, apparently without structure and without focus. The conception of the painting as an optical field had been passed on to Louis and other colorists of his generation. During a visit to the studio of Helen Frankenthaler, Louis discovered that the optical result to which he aspired could best be achieved by applying diluted paint

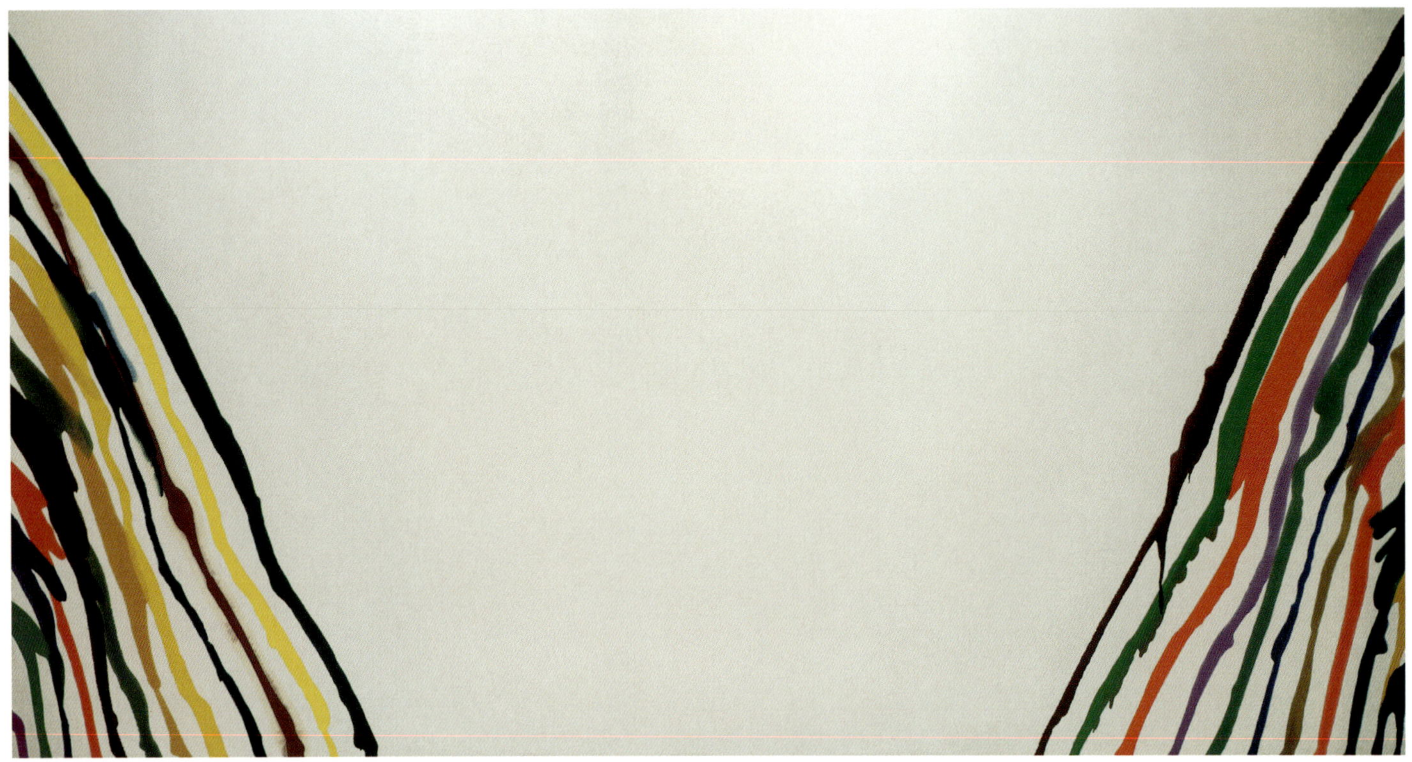

Morris Louis *Alpha Sigma*, 1961

directly to unsized canvas. The paint is so diluted that it has become entirely absorbed by the canvas and is present–as can be seen in *Alpha Sigma* (1961)–merely as color, not as matter.

In order to avoid any trace of the brushstroke whatsoever, Louis allowed the thinned paint to find its own way across the canvas. The bands of color in the two lower corners are, in fact, the remnants of little streams that have trickled down over the canvas. With Louis, therefore, the painting embodies precisely

Ellsworth Kelly *Green White no. 381*, 1967

what it is: the result of the process. The paintings of Louis are intuitive and poetic in character; those of **Ellsworth Kelly**, the leading representative of 'hard edge' painting, are so to a lesser degree. These deal more with an absolute balance of form and color. A painting such as *Green White no. 381* (1967) gives the impression of being the result of a long process of exploration and deliberation, of a gradual discovery of the proper ratio.

In all abstract painting there constantly arose the problem of the surface on which the artist painted and of the form or forms that were placed on that surface–in whatever way this was done. A form painted on a surface easily 'floated'; this disrupted the perfect correspondence of form and ground. Rather than becoming concrete (a word that was used with great frequency during the sixties), the painting became more illusionistic. The American painter **Frank Stella** believed that a painting should be as concrete as possible; one was supposed to see what there was to see, and nothing more. At the end of the fifties he produced a series of paintings, which were later referred to as the *Black Paintings*. One of these is *Tuxedo Junction* (1960), a large, vertical surface filled with a pattern of parallel black bands, created in such a way that one can no longer speak of 'background'. The painting is what one sees.

Other titles, such as *Tuxedo Park* and *Tuxedo Park Junction*, have been used, but *Tuxedo Junction* is the original title which Stella himself gave to the work. It is taken from a jazz song from 1940. Stella attributed the title in connection with Duke Ellington's interpretation of this song. The title refers, like all of the titles of his *Black Paintings*, to a popular jazz club, in this case to a coffee house in Birmingham, Alabama which was popular among the African-American railroad and steel-mill workers.

In later paintings, such as *Effingham I* (1967), Stella began to cut away the parts of the canvas that had no function; here the chosen forms and colors, and their coherence, directly generate the outer shape. This 'shaped canvas' is no longer the neutral, traditional rectangle; the form is determined from the inside out and is no longer imposed in an apriori manner. Both *Tuxedo Junction* and *Effingham I* are significant works, because they demonstrate, in a radical way, a principle which has also played a role in other places–in the Netherlands, with the work of Ad Dekkers and Peter Struycken.

In the paintings that **Larry Poons** produced before painting *Fliegender* in 1967, the oval strokes of color (which float freely across the surface in this painting) are more ordered, like a fixed pattern. In their controlled structure, those earlier paintings can be compared, to a certain extent, to the black paintings of Stella which came about during the same time. But in Stella's work, the emphasis lay completely with the formal structure of the painting; Poons, on the other hand, was more interested in color. On the basis of that initially more rigid way of working, Poons developed a freer painterly style in *Fliegender*. Color is unpredictable: colors enter into relationships with each other, they can, for instance, suggest depth and thereby optically break through the hermetic surface. This is precisely what Poons wanted to prevent–his objective was to find precisely the balance in which both surface and color could become articulated as concrete, independent factors. The demonstration of any sort of intellectual stance, however, was of no concern to him. The aim was always to give rise to a painting with its own distinct and satisfying visual complexity.

One of the issues to be raised time and again in the discussion surrounding the legitimacy of the painting was that of concreteness. Artists were seeking a way of painting in which form and content would coincide completely. **Robert Mangold** and Jo Baer also dealt with this matter. Mangold found a solution by painting lines on the painting in such a way that a second form was created–one which contradicted or was in 'visual conflict' with the original one but which was part of the same surface. The work *A square within two triangles* (1977) consists of two triangles which are juxtaposed in such a way that they yield a new form that is nearly equivalent to a triangle. The outline of a square has been painted on the triangles in such a way that the corners meet the edges of

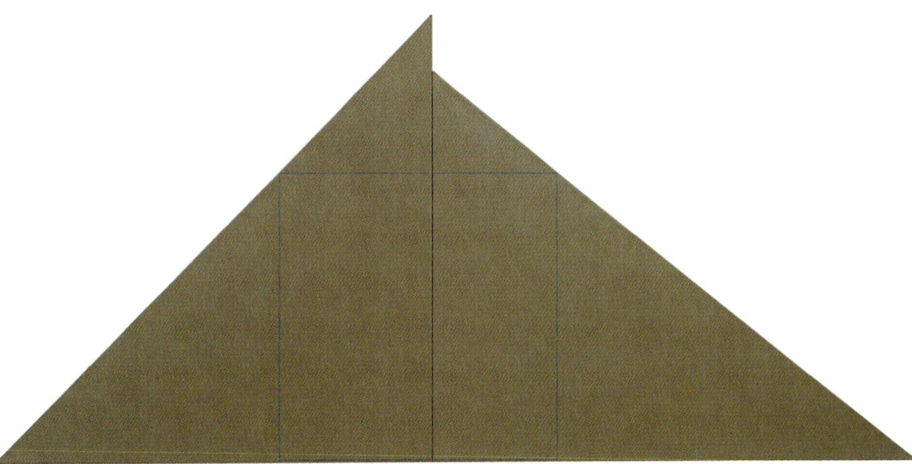

Robert Mangold *A square within two triangles*, 1977

the triangles. Because the two triangles are dissimilar in shape, the square is situated asymmetrically on the triangular plane, and this gives the work an intriguing tension. When one looks at a painting by Mangold, there is always a point at which the initial clarity gives way to ambiguity or even mystery. That moment is essential. The act of looking thereby becomes one of 'seeking': to know precisely what one sees, and yet evidently see something else.

During the sixties **Jo Baer** also arrived, under the influence of her contacts with Sol LeWitt and Donald Judd, at a visual language in which the autonomous nature of the painting was retained; form and color held equivalent positions and thus gave balance to the painting. She painted, on the left and right sides of white or grey canvases, a black geometric form. Running across or along side this is a strip of color which determines the mood of the work and adds a subjective statement to the highly contrasting white and

black. In 1966 she began to produce diptychs–hung in vertical or horizontal rows–and triptychs. In the triptychs she used, in addition to black and white, a different color, as can be seen in *Wrap-around Triptych (blue-green-lavender)* (1970-74). Similarities and differences among the parts interact subtly with each other in this work. The black forms on the left and right seem to 'embrace' the painting. Their well-considered proportions cause them to frame the white surface without stifling it.

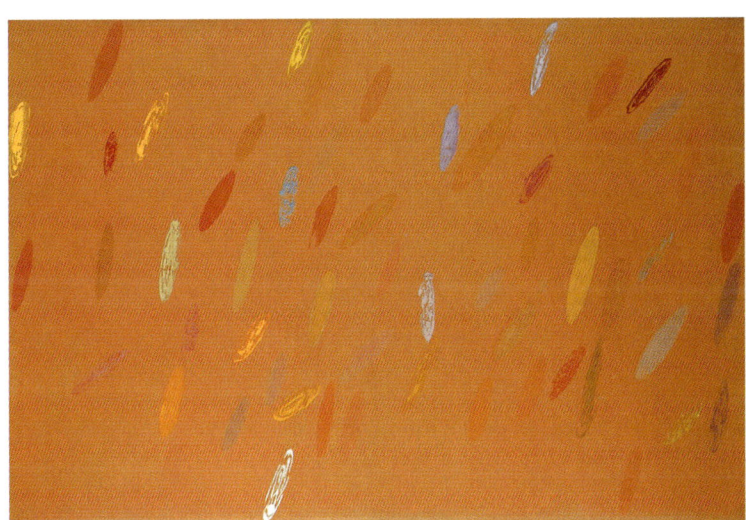

Larry Poons *Fliegender*, 1967

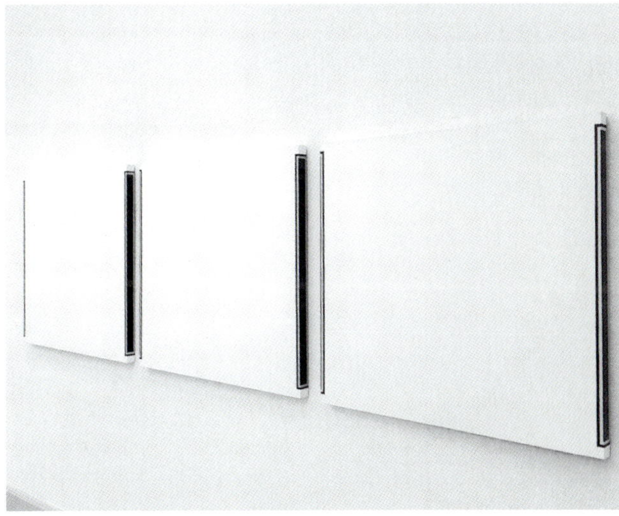

Jo Baer *Wrap-around Triptych (blue-green-lavender)*, 1970-74

XIV

Carl Andre

Donald Judd

Robert Morris

Dan Flavin

Richard Serra

Bruce Nauman

Keith Sonnier

Robert Ryman

Alan Charlton

Sol LeWitt

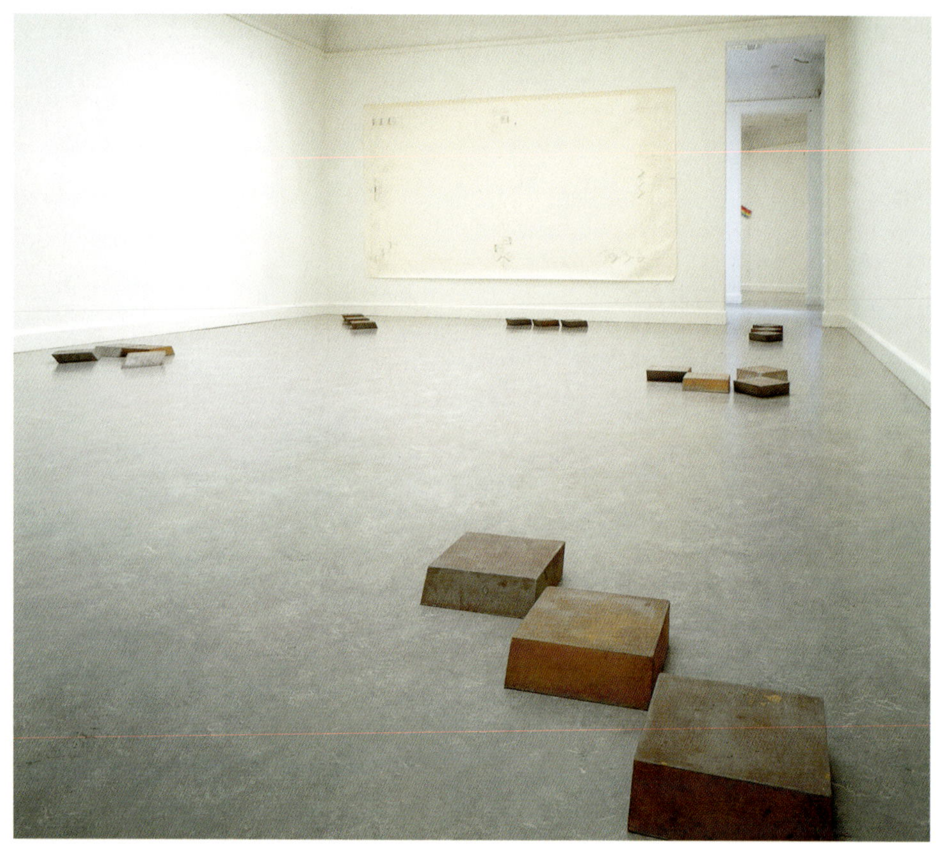

Bruce Nauman *Driven Man, Driven Snow*, 1976

A significant focal point in the collection of the Van Abbemuseum is formed by the sculptures and paintings that are regarded as Minimal Art or art forms closely related to this. Jean Leering discerned the importance of these tendencies at a very early stage, something which is evident from the verve with which he organized solo exhibitions of work by Robert Morris (1968), Donald Judd, Keith Sonnier (1970) and Bruce Nauman (1973).

In 1966 Leering had purchased *Tuxedo Junction* (1960) by Frank Stella. This painting and the series of which it is a part–the *Black Paintings*–are often considered to be a kind of programmatic point of departure for Minimal Art. Averse to painting with existential and metaphysical pretensions, Stella produced these works as a reaction to the watered-down abstract expressionism of the late fifties. As far as the artist was concerned, there could be little confusion as to the subject and the meaning of these paintings: "What you see is what you see." Such a 'detached' statement relates extraordinarily well to Minimal Art, as Minimalist sculptures and paintings allude primarily to their own qualities and not to meanings that lie beyond the work of art. The notion that Minimal Art could, in a certain sense, be regarded as a radical continuation of early twentieth-century avant-garde movements such as De Stijl and Constructivism created, as it were, a foundation for the presence of this type of art in the collection of the Van Abbemuseum. The term Minimal Art, first used by Richard Wollheim in 1965, was practically never something with which artists such as Carl Andre, Donald Judd, Robert Morris, Dan Flavin, Richard Serra or Robert Ryman wished to identify themselves. There was no question of a group, nor of a particular style with accompanying characteristics. Though the term seems to imply otherwise, there is, strictly speaking, nothing minimal about this art. Robert Morris once stated that a simple form does not necessarily coincide with a simple experience, and in that sense, one could say that the means employed are minimal, but certainly not the goal to which they aspired. The similarity of the artworks described in this chapter lies with the significance that all of these very different artists ascribe to the perception of space, based on the direct relationship between the work of art and the body of the viewer. **Carl Andre** once described the development

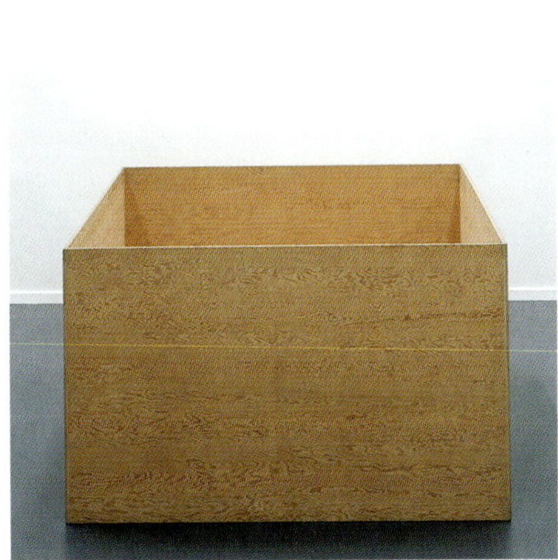
Donald Judd *Untitled*, 1974-76

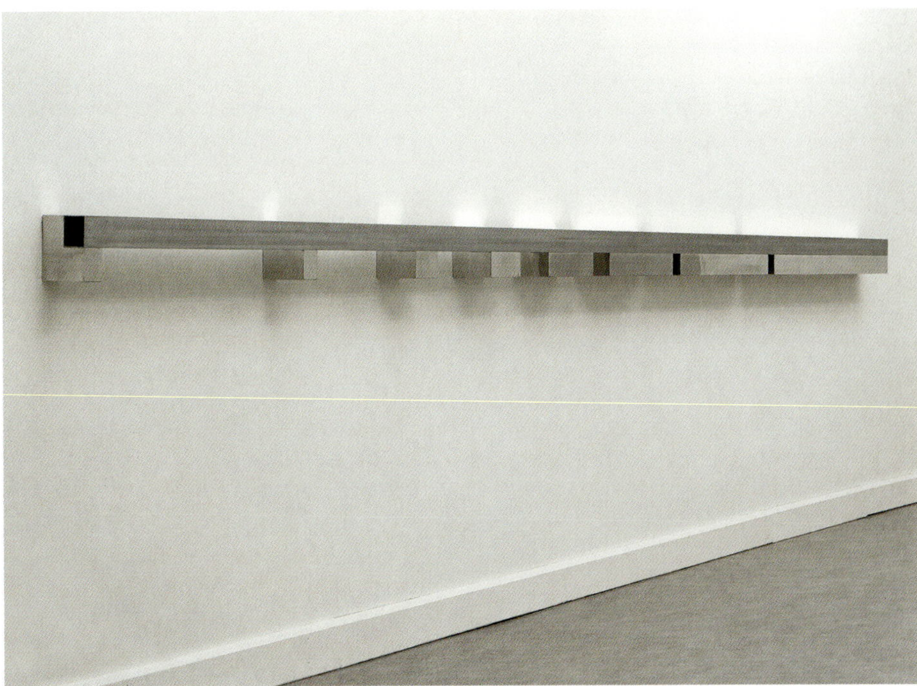
Donald Judd *Untitled (Progression)*, 1969

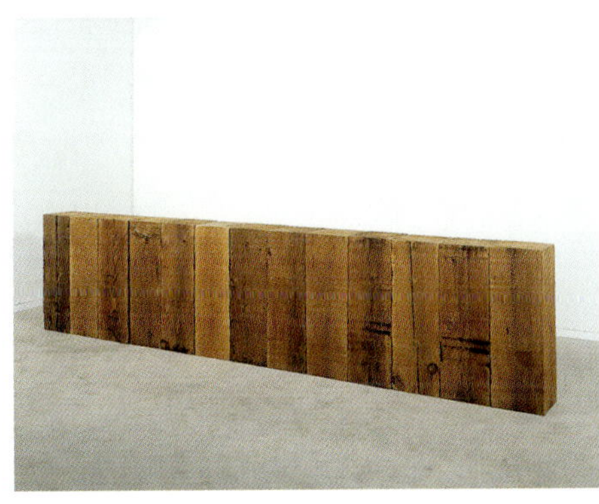
Carl Andre *Palisade*, 1976

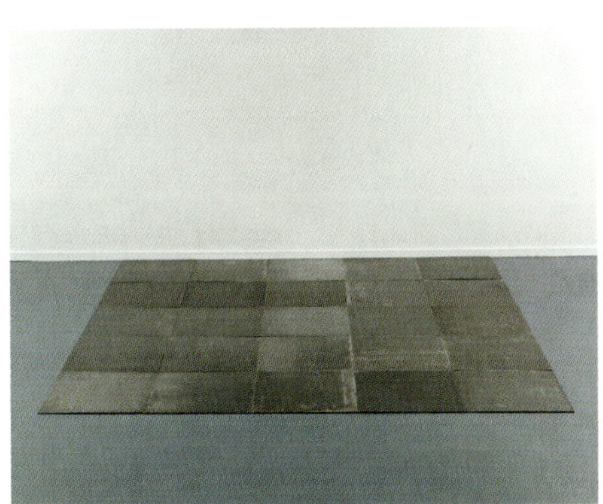
Carl Andre *Twenty-fifth steel Cardinal*, 1974

of his work as consisting of three phases, running parallel to the development of modern sculpture in general: sculpture as form, sculpture as structure and sculpture as place. Inspired by, among other things, *Endless Column* (1938) by Constantin Brancusi, Andre began producing, around 1958, sculptures made of sawed wood (sculpture as form) and, after that, sculptures made of combinations of stacked or connected elements (sculpture as structure). He came to the conclusion, however, that any treatment diminished the quality, and he decided to concentrate, from that point on, solely on the way in which the "sculpture cuts through space." In a manner analogous to that of Stella in the *Black Paintings*, Andre employed, like so many other Minimal artists, symmetry and repetition as principles of order. He created, for instance, floor sculptures from rows of bricks or metal plates, which could be infinitely 'continued' in their seriality. Such sculptures are regarded by him as being a base for the rest of the world, because they lay a foundation, in his opinion, for a new manner of observation and experience of the object in space. Sculptures such as *Twenty-fifth steel Cardinal* (1974) epitomize Andre's notion of sculpture as place. Such works were produced by him in various formats, and in materials that included iron, steel, aluminum, lead, copper and zinc; these floor sculptures seem to exude, above all, tranquillity and balance. The specific nature of works like *Twenty-fifth steel Cardinal* is that they occupy and give shape to a space without filling it. For ultimately, the floor sculptures possess no volume, no depth, thickness, inside or center–simply mass and weight. That sculpture, to Andre, amounts to more than mere observation is evident from the fact that he wants the floor sculptures to be walked upon, whereby tactile and auditory impressions can contribute to the articulation of place.

Donald Judd can be regarded as the most outspoken Minimal artist, a position earned, in part, by way of the sharply formulated essays and criticisms that he wrote between 1959 and 1965. In his influential essay *Specific Objects* (1965) Judd gave primacy, with the new art, to 'real' sculptural space which, in his view, was preferable to the illusionistic reality of painting. Geometry was considered by him to be the most suitable means by which to distance oneself from the anthropomorphic tendencies in sculpture, since the contained, compact form of objects such as cubes can hardly be associated with the human figure. Around 1964 Judd began to concentrate exclusively on the physical and material aspects of the form–volume, surface and, later, color–and he produced, for the most part, box-like sculptures, carried out in various painted and unpainted types of metal, plexiglas, wood or plywood. Judd had a preference for industrial materials and production methods, as these could not easily lead to a personal, 'artistic' signature and could not be linked directly to classical forms of sculpture. Because of this, his sculptures moreover have a virtually perfect finish, which contributes to their precision and visual consistency to a significant degree. That is why they were usually manufactured industrially.

Among the many wall sculptures produced by Judd, the *Progression* series (1969) constitutes one of the highlights. From this series the Van Abbemuseum owns an aluminum piece, which is so prominent due to Judd's clear expression of the 'void' as being an integral part of sculptural space. The way in which the positive and negative volumes interrelate and structure the work could be seen as a reference to the indissoluble link between sculpture and space. An essential aspect of Judd's work is the perception and awareness of spatial conditions and how these are determined by the position of the body with respect to the object. This is especially clear with the observation of *Untitled* (1974-76): an open, wooden cube which, like a great deal of Judd's work, is geared to a human scale.

Like Judd, **Robert Morris** was initially involved with painting in a more or less abstract-expressionist style and he published his views on developments in sculpture in various magazines. Morris's work from the Minimalist period consists of geometric forms–cubes, circles, wedges, L-shaped beams–made of wood, metal or fiberglas; these have been painted, in grey for the most part, and presented in serial arrangements. And with Morris, too, these elements are identical in shape, mass, scale and proportion–truly 'unitary objects', to use the jargon of Minimal Art. Contrary to the work of Judd or Andre, Morris's arrangement of identical elements presupposes a timeless form of stability to a lesser extent, however. This relates to the emphasis which Morris gave to the fact that the experience of a work, as opposed to perception of form, takes a certain amount of time. Already in 1961 Morris had allowed, in connection with a 'proto-minimal' performance in a theatrical setting and within a timed period of seven minutes, a simple column to topple over, thus intending to emphasize the fact that the experience of a form is dependent on the situation or position in which the form is perceived. Such a view also clearly comes across with *9 H-shapes* (1968), which seems to suggest a particular sequence within a period of time (ill. p. 77). The importance that Morris and others ascribed to the factor of time–in combination with space–led to

heated theoretical debates on the essence of sculpture, which included, among others, art historian Michael Fried, who stated, in his essay *Art and Objecthood* (1967), that Minimal Art was essentially "theatrical" as it seemed to be preoccupied with the duration of the experience.

In manner unlike that of any other Minimalist, **Dan Flavin**, whose objects come from the 'real' world, made the institutional context integral to his work. In 1963 Flavin began to work exclusively with fluorescent lighting, which he attached to the walls or floors of exhibition spaces in various configurations. Flavin used, in principle, only four standard lengths and nine colors of fluorescent lighting. By implementing light as a sculptural material, Flavin introduced changes in the way in which the viewer could experience the architecture of the exhibition space. That is why he preferred to speak about his work in terms of "proposals." By situating flourescent lighting in a corner, for instance, he causes that corner to be contradicted and opened up, as it were, by the glow and the double shadow cast by the light. The effect of works such as *Untitled (to a man, George McGovern)* (1972) is radical, not only because the intensity of light emitted by the round fluorescent tubes causes the space to 'disintegrate' to some degree but also because it fills this space with a weightless, immaterial volume. Mindful of the fact that Minimal Art attributes no value to a notion

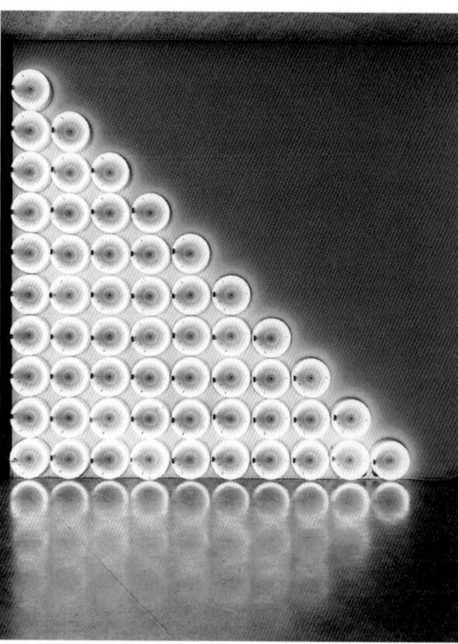

Dan Flavin *Untitled (to a man, George McGovern)*, 1972

such as uniqueness, Flavin usually produced his smaller works in editions of five and the larger ones in editions of two or three.

At the end of the sixties, one could discern a tendency among a number of artists who managed to combine Minimalism's language of forms and principles with a certain degree of emotional intensity. While a wooden cube of Judd can still be described as having a tautological character, the works of Serra,

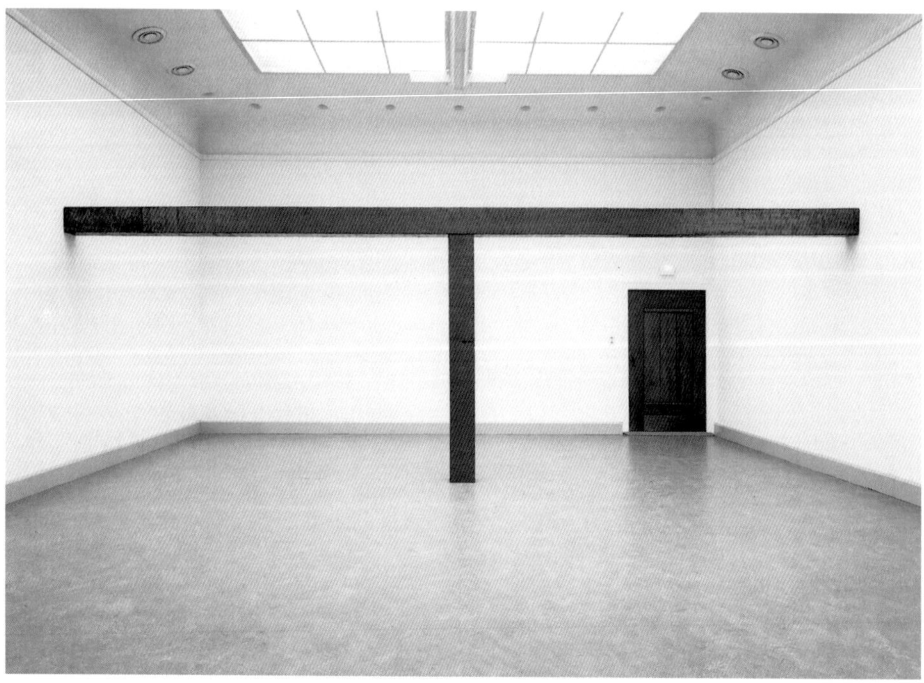

Richard Serra *T-junction*, 1988

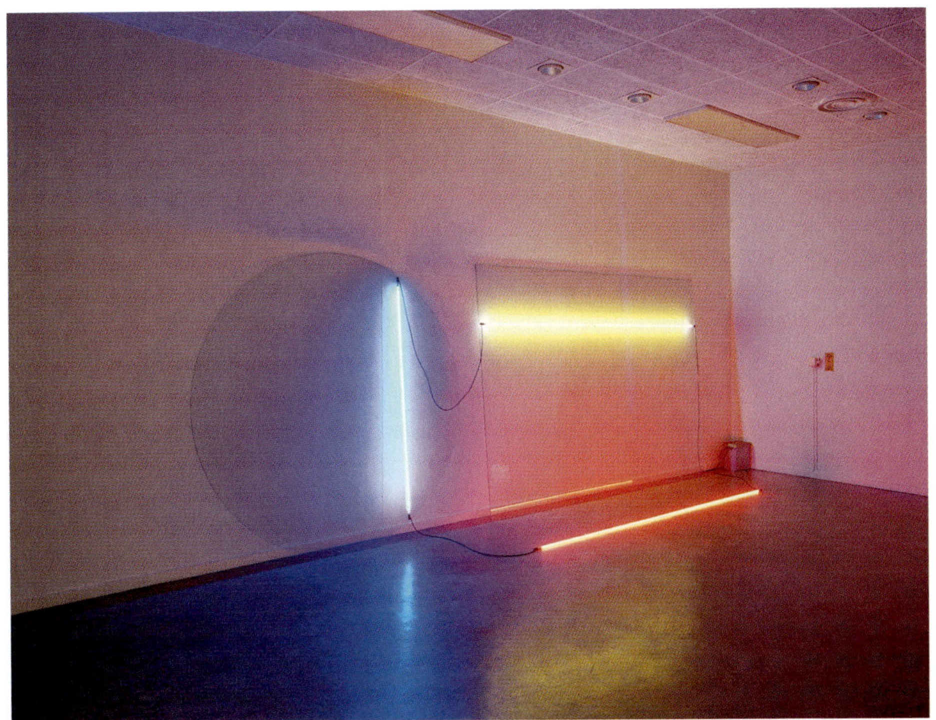

Keith Sonnier *Ba-O-Ba*, 1969

Nauman and Sonnier have that to a far less extent. Also in this development, referred to in the United States as 'Post-Minimal Art', Robert Morris was among the pioneers with his 'anti-form' experiments, which were already demonstrated by the floppy felt works that he exhibited at the Van Abbemuseum in 1968. The generative and transformative processes of the artwork are emphasized as being the consequence of time, for instance, or gravity or, in a more extreme sense, as being influenced by temperature, erosion or other natural processes, aspects that would play a role somewhat later in land art and *arte povera*. Time and impermanence thus become factors of significance and, to an even greater degree than with Minimal Art, there is an endeavor to involve the viewer in the artwork, occasionally in such a way that one could call him a participant.

Since 1969 **Richard Serra** has been making sculptures that usually consist of lead and steel plates and beams, placed at an angle or leaning, often in a precarious balance, against a wall or against each other. Volume, weight, mass and balance are essential concepts in the work of Serra. The generative process remains visible in his sculptures and, in comparison to *Palisade* (1976) by Carl Andre, for instance, they do not have a fixed or timeless appearance. With Serra, instability resulting from a disrupted balance can undermine the existing structure or situation at any moment. The large works, such as *T-junction* (1988), are predominantly site-specific, that is to say designed and intended for a specific location, in this case a particular room of the Van Abbemuseum, of which the sculpture seems to consititute an architectonic part. The work of Serra was purchased only at a late stage, when he presented ten such sculptures geared to specific spaces at the Van Abbemuseum. In *T-junction* gravity, balance and Serra's preference for "construction without arbitrary complications"–the horizontal element simply rests on the vertical without any further connection–are expressed in a nearly programmatic manner. With such works Serra provokes the viewer to walk through the space and to discover how the placement of the sculpture influences one's perception and how its material qualities are inextricably bound to the psychological conditions of perception.

Bruce Nauman can be considered not only one of the most influential artists of recent decades but also one of the most versatile: in addition to sculptures, he has produced neon works, drawings, holograms and worked with video and other audiovisual media. A series of twenty-six video works made during the period 1969-1973, by now of a classic stature, has been purchased by Jan Debbaut in 2000. These video works usually show Nauman himself performing certain actions in his studio: he is stamping on the floor, walking around in an exaggerated contraposto posture, bouncing balls, playing the violin or assuming certain stances. Through seemingly endless repetitions, manipulations of time, framing and uncommon visual angles, Nauman frequently manages to create an alienating effect, which reflects the mental tensions that stem directly from the repetition of certain physical actions.

The work *Driven Man, Driven Snow* (1976), acquired by Rudi Fuchs, is among the less alarming environments by Nauman, but even this work can be described as manipulative in a certain sense. *Driven Man, Driven Snow* is part of a series of sculptures that show configurations of cube-based forms in stone or metal, which are sometimes exhibited in combination with texts or drawings. By way of the arrangement, the interrelationships, the form and the scale of the various elements, Nauman manages to increase the perspectival distortion of the space and the objects and thereby bring about a 'twist' of perception and the psyche. *Driven Man, Driven Snow* seems, at first, to comply with the vocabulary of Minimal Art, but it goes a step further by linking perception to a sense of dislocation.

Keith Sonnier also works with neon lighting, though with entirely different intentions than those of Nauman or Flavin. With Sonnier, the viewer can almost be referred to as a component in the theatrical staging. Like Nauman, Sonnier exhibited at the Van Abbemuseum rather early in his career, namely in 1970. At that point, he had been working for a year on what would later prove to be his most important series of works, the *Ba-O-Ba* series, of which a work was purchased during that same year. The sculptures from the *Ba-O-Ba* series consist of fairly open compositions of neon lighting in combination with plates of glass or aluminum, which are sometimes partially painted black. Because of the radiance, the reflections and the effect of the color of the light on the space and on the viewer's skin–to which the Haitian-Creole title refers–it seems as though the viewer is surrounded by a nearly tangible aura of mysticism and sensuality.

Now, as opposed to during the sixties, Minimal Art is associated primarily with spatial work. Over the years, painting has been classified by exhibition-makers and critics according to a confusing abundance of terms, such as minimal painting, systematic painting, *Geplante Malerei*, analytical painting, fundamental painting and so on.

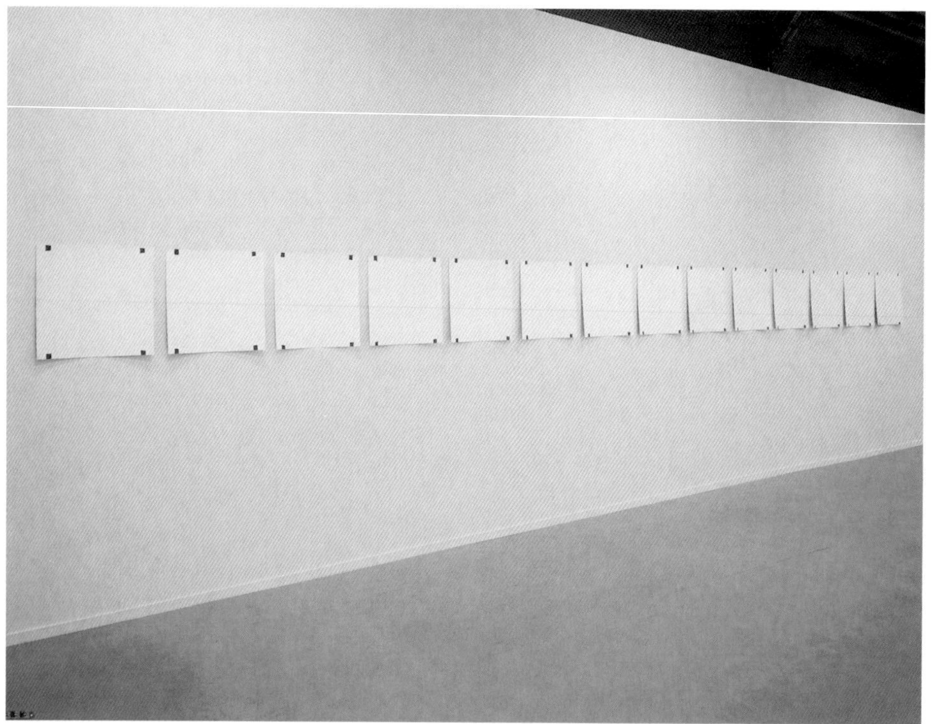

Robert Ryman *Untitled (Brussels)*, 1974

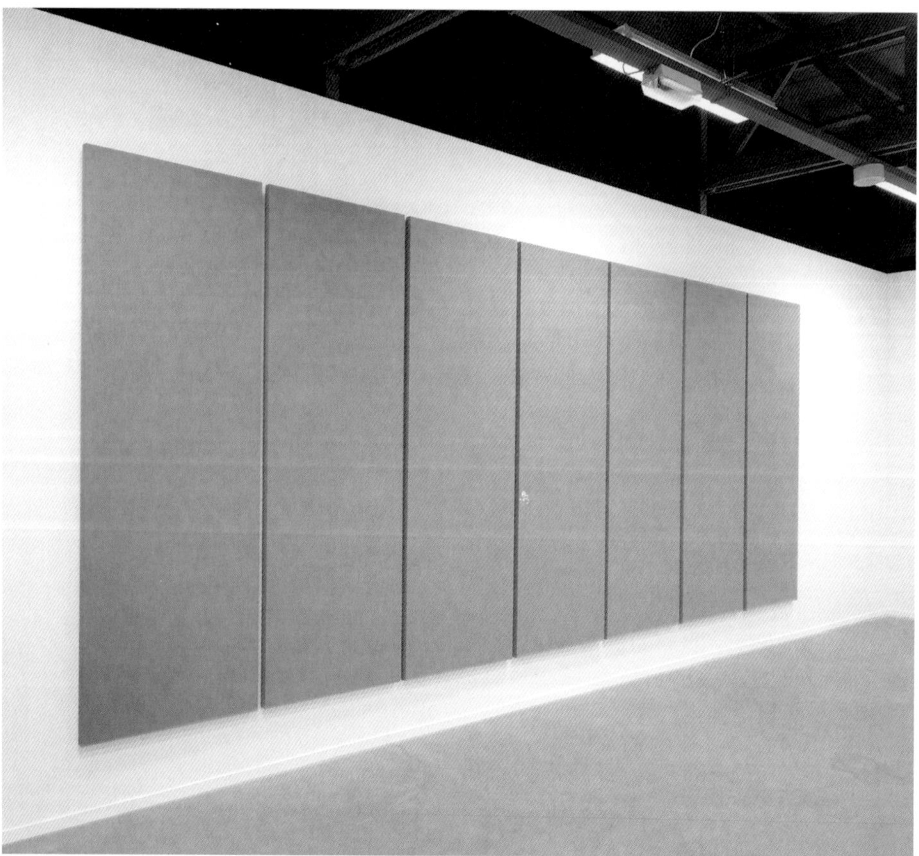

Alan Charlton *Untitled*, 1979

Strikingly, the paintings are often described as though they are objects. This is particularly related to their frequently large format, the monochrome surface and the absence of illusionistic space. In 'minimal painting' there is a focus on a largely analytical investigation of the essence of painting and of the painting itself. This means that material principles such as line, color, form, surface texture, materials, size, scale and the way of working are assessed, like the method and the process of painting, according to their merits. The painting no longer functions, therefore, as the carrier of an illusionistic/realistic or expressive/abstract image but has rather become non-representational, 'concrete' and 'pure'.

All of this is clearly evident from the paintings of **Robert Ryman**. Ryman's motto is simply "to paint the paint," which means that he literally shows that painting is ultimately the covering of a support with paint. Since the second half of the fifties, Ryman has been painting, with a range of brushes and types of paint, on different kinds of supports such as paper, linen, aluminum, plastic, vinyl, steel, copper, plexiglas and the like. For this he has always used white paint, because this is light-sensitive and neutral with respect to potential interpretation. *Untitled (Brussels)* (1974) also appears to be extraordinarily simple and, initially, perhaps even tedious. Further observation shows, however, that a great deal can be discerned in this fourteen-part painting on vinyl: the length, the direction and the regularity or irregularity of the brushstroke, the pressure that is put on the brush, the grittiness or fluidity of the paint, the hardness of the brush, the hue of the white paint, shiny or dull areas that are determined in part by the ground and possible absorption capacity of the support, and so on. The unpainted marks along the lower and upper edges are traces of tape that function as compositional elements.

Alan Charlton—who is roughly a generation younger than Ryman and the only European among this group—has been producing solely grey paintings since the sixties, but contrary to the work of Ryman, the brushstroke plays no significant role here. Charlton's paintings can always be related to a module of four-and-a-half centimeters, derived from the thickness of the support. The sizes as well as the distances between separate parts—as with *Untitled* (1979)—are multiples of the module; even cut-outs in the canvas are related to this. The wall, and therefore the space itself, becomes such a literal part of the painting that the painting immediately becomes part of 'reality'. Like Ryman, Charlton is

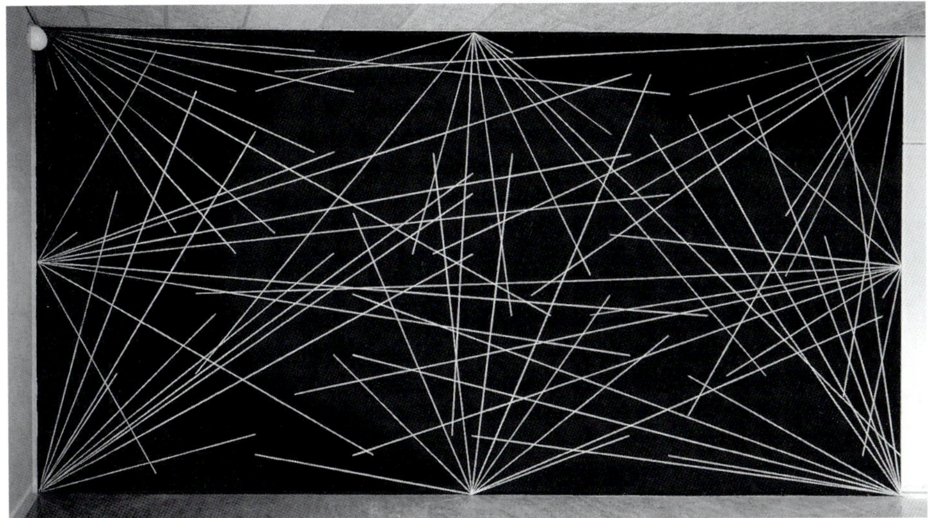

Sol LeWitt *Wall Drawing no. 256, 1975*

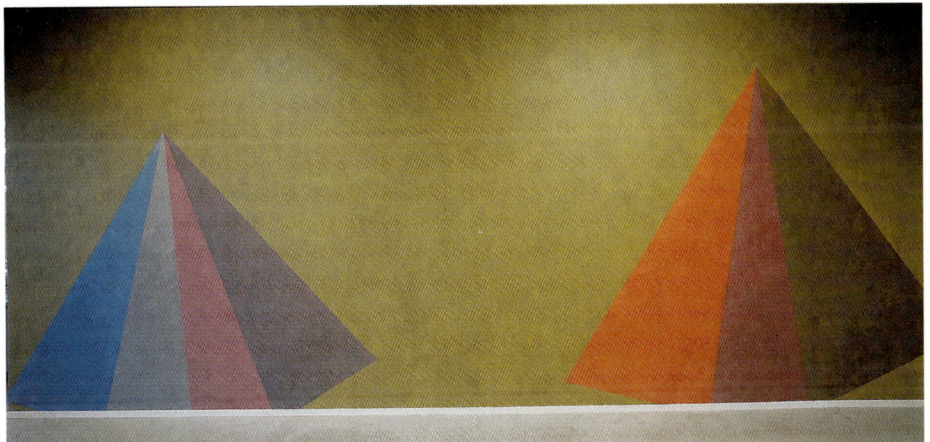

Sol LeWitt *Wall Drawing no. 480, 1986*

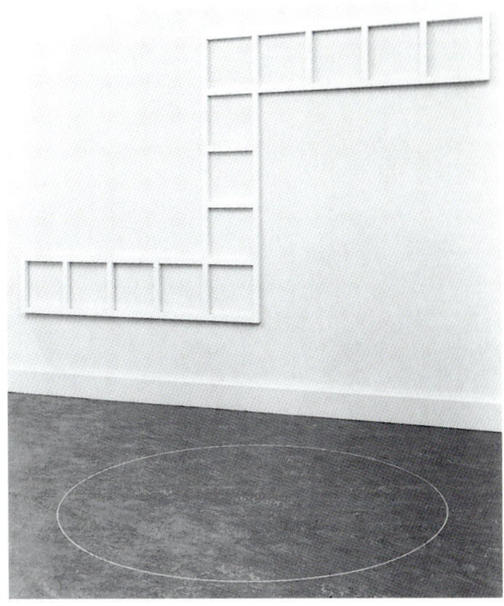

Sol LeWitt *Untitled (wall structure), 1972*
Ian Wilson *Circle on the Floor, 1968*

concerned with 'pure' painting, with tone and surface, light and shadow, with the balance and articulation of space, with a 'silent' form of painting that requires, for both the maker and the viewer, a certain form of contemplation in order to be judged according to its proper merits. The work of Charlton has been purchased primarily in connection with solo exhibitions of his work during the directorship of Rudi Fuchs. On observing the paintings of Ryman and Charlton, one could ask oneself to what extent these have been executed according to a preconceived idea. Though terms such as 'systemic painting' or 'analytical painting' make one suspect otherwise, these paintings are actually the result of an intuitive process and not the product of a 'logical' system. This is different with **Sol LeWitt**, who is among the pioneers of conceptual art, though his wall drawings and sculptures do display common ground with Minimal Art. With

LeWitt, it is no longer the material aspect of the object, but the succinctness of the idea which has prime importance. The sculptures that he began producing during the mid sixties frequently show the 'rib structure' of cubes painted white, or parts of these, in varied series and in arrangements according to certain modules. The system, based on decisions pertaining to elements such as form, structure, order and dimension, is continually written down in concepts, which constitute the points of departure for all of LeWitt's works. "Once the idea of the piece is established in the artist's mind and the final form is decided, the process is carried out blindly," LeWitt has said, implying that the concept is separate from the execution, which therefore does not necessarily have to be done by the artist himself. Such ideas have been explained by him in a number of influential essays on conceptual art, published in 1967 and 1969. Strikingly,

LeWitt attributes value not only to logic, but also to irrationality which can thwart logic and which is considered by him to be necessary for new experiences.
The importance of the concept presupposes a major role for language. The concepts for the wall drawings are therefore meticulously formulated, as with that for the drawing with white lines: "A six-inch (15cm) grid covering a black wall. White lines from the midpoints of four sides to random points on the grid. (The length of the lines and their placements are determined by the draftsman.)" This statement indicates that chance is also a factor of significance and that, on the basis of the concept and an ink drawing by LeWitt, the assistants have their own input on the execution of the wall drawings.
The work of LeWitt demonstrates that there is not simply one way in which reality can be experienced but that an abundance of potential arrangements exist. And it shows how, to conclude with LeWitt's own words, "Conceptual artists are mystics rather than rationalists. They leap to conclusions that logic cannot reach."

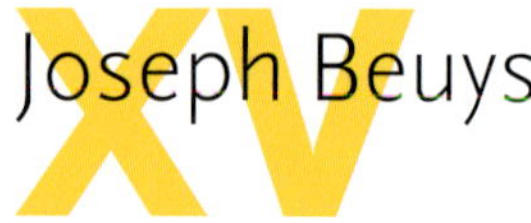

Joseph Beuys

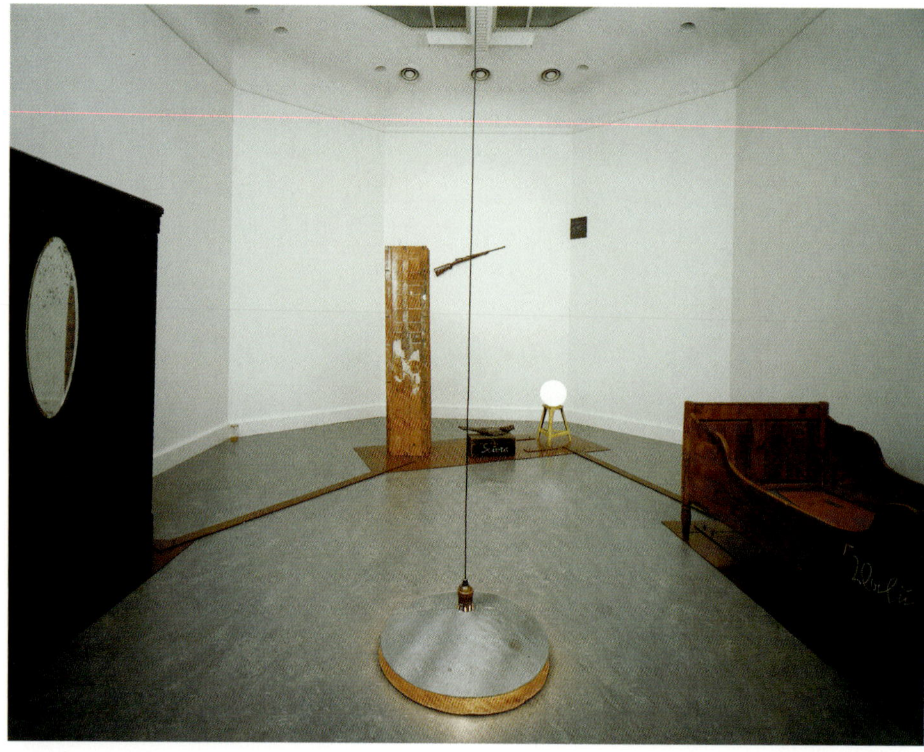

Joseph Beuys *Voglie vedere i miei montagne*, 1971

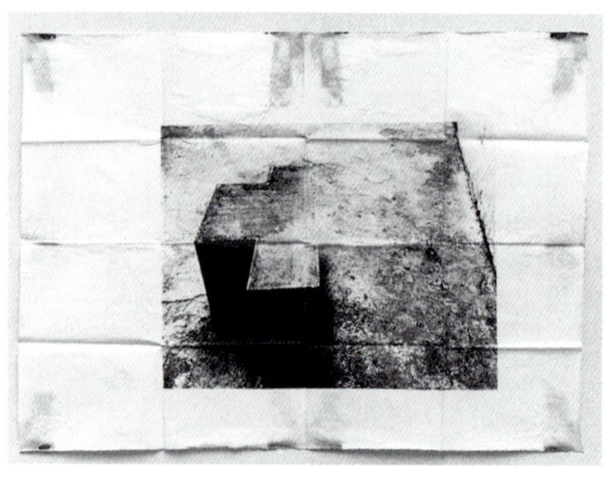

Joseph Beuys *Vakuum <–> Masse*, 1970

A utopian longing for paradise is, according to some critics, one of the key themes in German art. Particularly with artists from nineteenth-century German Romanticism, who excelled in portraying the spiritual, the divine order that lay hidden in nature, we come across this pursuit of the paradisiacal rather frequently. The work of Philipp Otto Runge, for instance, is filled with this longing. A century later it was still distinctly present, as in the paintings of Franz Marc. With him we see a glorification of the animal as an unspoiled creature, living in an idyllic world. In the versatile body of work created by Joseph Beuys, who came from a strict Catholic background, these animal motifs also crop up quite often. The hare is among the animals for which Beuys had a special fondness and to which he ascribed metaphorical meanings. He associated the hare with rebirth and thereby with the cosmic phenomenon of the life cycles. Among his most important performances or *Aktionen* is his appearance at the opening of his exhibition at Düsseldorf's Galerie Schmela on November 26, 1965, at which Jean Leering, then director of the Van Abbemuseum, was present. With his face smeared with honey and gold leaf, Beuys held a dead hare on his lap; he gave the lifeless body of the animal an explanation of the exhibited artworks. The image of the artist with a dead creature on his lap bears a great resemblance to a Pietà, a representation of the Virgin Mary with the body of Christ on her lap–Christ, who will ultimately conquer death and bring salvation to mankind. One of the first sculptures to be produced by Beuys, in 1952, was in fact a Pietà. In another *Aktion* carried out in the space of a New York gallery in 1974, Beuys allowed himself to be caged in with a wild coyote, an animal chosen by him for its symbolization of the untouched North American continent, as it was prior to the arrival of the Europeans; the coyote played an important role in American Indian legendry. With his work Beuys wished to restore, to our world, the harmony which he viewed as being considerably disrupted. He had a utopian belief that art has the capacity to transform everything into a higher spiritual order, into a harmony between man and the earth, between man and life. An often-quoted remark of his is "Everyone is an artist." This stance typifies his enormous faith in the creative potential of man. Only a true utopian could make such a statement.

The work of Beuys is very much linked with his biography. He was born in Krefeld and grew up in Kleef, near the Dutch border. His paternal ancestors were, in fact, Dutch. Beuys himself has said that the circumstances under which he grew up, living along the border, had crucial influence with respect to his artistry. Borders of any kind were always offensive to him. As a result, he always supported the idea of a border-free Europe. An *Aktion* from 1966 bears the title *Eurasia*. Beuys also wished to demolish borders between Europe and Asia, between East and West–borders present in man himself. Another important event in the life of Beuys was his experience as a German fighter pilot during World War II. In 1943 his plane was shot down over the Crimea by Russian artillery. He himself said–though there has never been any proof of this–that the Tartars, a nomadic tribe of The Steppes, took care of him as a badly injured pilot and kept his body warm by rubbing fat on it and wrapping him in felt. This event made a lasting impression on Beuys. Warmth and insulation would continue to be major themes throughout his entire artistic life. Fat and felt were moreover used with great frequency in his sculptures. Beuys also became seriously ill many times during his life. This explains why references to death can be seen regularly in his work. The large installation in the collection of the museum, which was specially conceived for a room in the original building in 1971, also relates to death. The title of the work, *Voglie vedere i miei montagne*, alludes to the words spoken by the nineteenth-century Italian painter Giovanni Segantini on his deathbed. Segantini had, in the course of his life as an artist, developed his own pantheistic vision of nature and was occupied with a triptych that would portray Life, Nature and Death–the theme of the life cycle, which was preeminently part of the Romantic tradition. Segantini, too, was in pursuit of a lost paradise. He eventually sought this by living in a hut in the Swiss Alps, near Pontresina, not far from the Italian border.

Voglie vedere i miei montagne looks like a bedroom and, for some, may give rise to associations with Van Gogh's painting of his bedroom in Arles. This is not far off the mark, since in addition to Segantini, Van Gogh was among Beuys's heroes. The installation includes a bed, a mirror-faced wardrobe, a chest, a lamp, and hanging on the wall are a rifle and a framed photograph. Mountains are nowhere to be seen, not even in the photograph, which shows a bird in a cage. As such, the title stands contrasts sharply with what we actually see. An oppressive room indoors is the opposite of a majestic mountain landscape. But the longing expressed in the title is, of course, articulated precisely because the mountains cannot be seen.

The non-visible constituted a key aspect of Beuys's thinking. "The title of the work does not directly convey what we see," Beuys said in reference to this work. With him, objects always have metaphorical meaning. "There is a visible and an invisible world," he explained. "The invisible world includes the non-perceivable force fields, relationships of form and channels of energy; that which is commonly referred to as 'the inner' belongs to this." Such a statement makes it clear that Beuys was open to the spiritual dimension of existence. Though he had attended lectures on physics, the material, rationalist approach to reality, which is characteristic of scientific thought, was too limited for him. Along with reason, Beuys attached great importance to emotion and intuition.

Voglie vedere i miei montagne is a complex installation, and it was Beuys's first work to fill an entire room. The room in which this work is set up is strikingly changed by it: not only does the lamp hanging in the middle of it obstruct normal passage, but the furniture has been placed on copper plates that do not entirely correspond to the form created by the walls of the room. Because of this, the walls become fluid, as it were, almost unsteady. Copper, to Beuys, moreover had the connotation of being a conductor of energy, just as electricity is conducted by copper wires.

Beuys has written German, Celtic and Rhaeto-Romanic words on the furniture, thereby referring partly to the landscape of the Alps. The word *Vadrec(t)* can be seen on the wardrobe. *Val, vadrec* or *vadret* means glaciated valley, also described as a 'glass-like plain'. The mirror on the wardrobe could be interpreted as such a surface of ice. Opposite the coldness of the mirrored wardrobe, the glacier, perhaps even death (the mirror often symbolizes death in visual art) is the warmth of the glowing lamp. Due to its unusually low position, whereby the rays of light must press their way out from beneath the lampshade via the piece of heat-absorbent felt, the viewer experiences a tension-filled concentration of light, warmth and energy. Energy is one of the key ideas throughout Beuys's work. Warmth, to Beuys, stands for chaos and evolutionary forces, and coldness represents form and intellectual keenness, 'reflection'. On the backside of a chest, we can read the word *Sciora*; behind a mirror on a stool are the words *Cime* and *Pennin*; and on the bed, *Walun*.

They refer, like the word *Vadret*, to the mountain landscape in Segantini's part of Switzerland. Therefore, we could ultimately regard this collection of furniture in various heights and dimensions as the portrayal of a mountain landscape with various peaks and

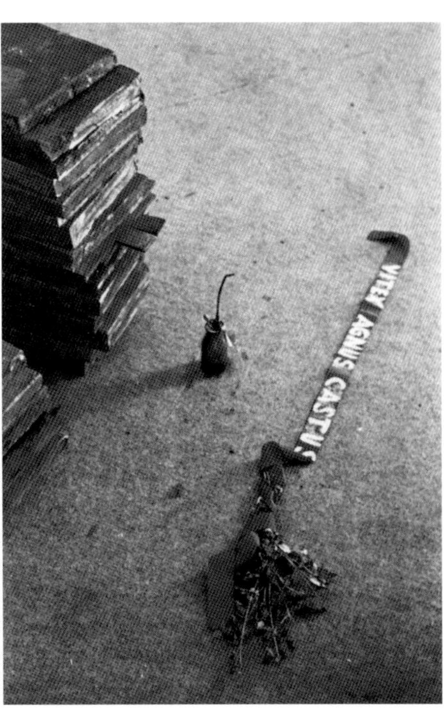

Joseph Beuys *Vitex agnus castus*, 1973

valleys: the nonvisible contained in the visible. The word *Denken* is written on the rifle that is attached to the wall. Its barrel is aimed at the photograph of the bird in a cage. The rifle represents targeted and thus one-sided thinking, a type of thinking which has a limited range of vision, which evidently obstructs freedom, as indicated by the caged bird. This is the antithesis of the freedom in nature, in mountains. To Beuys, mountains signify a higher consciousness. And a higher consciousness implies an emancipation, the ultimate goal that Beuys aims to achieve with his art. An emancipation of the individual, which can lead to a better society: that is where Beuys wanted to play a role.

But before he could undertake this Messianic task, he first had to liberate himself, and he seemed to be thoroughly aware of that. This is probably why he used furniture from his childhood for his first major installation. It makes this work perhaps the most personal of his installations. The large wardrobe with an oval mirror, for instance, is an old family heirloom and had, in fact, already been shown at the Van Abbemuseum in 1968 in connection with the first solo exhibition of Beuys's work to be held outside Germany. According to Beuys, he was born next to this piece of furniture, and it played a terrifying role in many of his earliest dreams. It seems as though Beuys wished to deal with his past, to put that behind him with this installation, even though the work constitutes an ode to

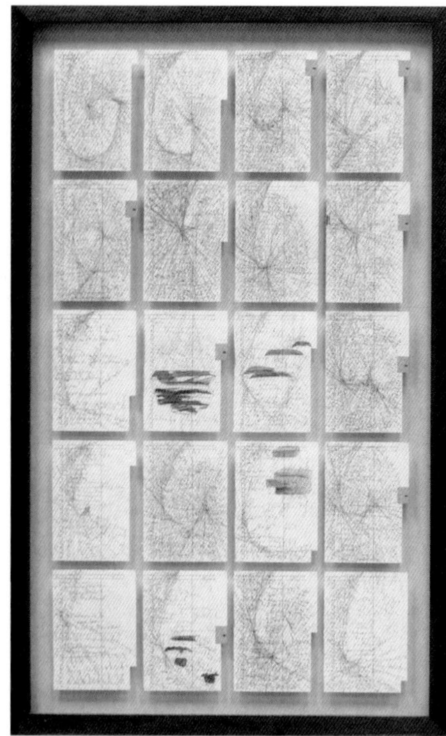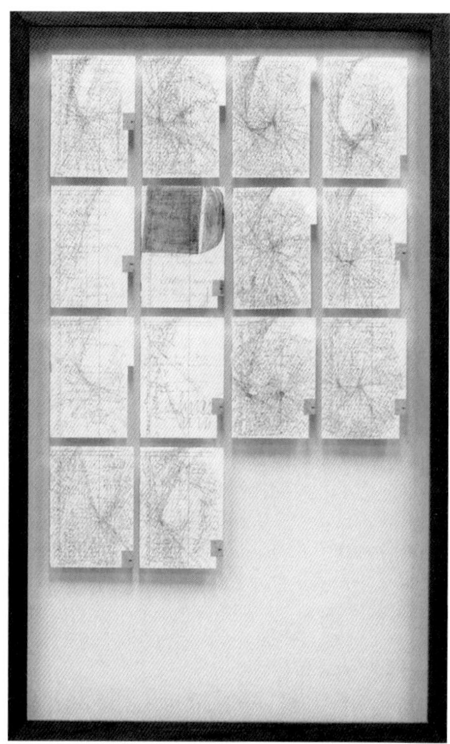

Joseph Beuys *Vorbereitung vor Betreten der Tate Gallery ("Wie Knochen entstehen")*, 1970

that past at the same time. The work portrays the death of his childhood years, of the old forms; that death was needed in order to arrive at a higher consciousness. Juxtaposed with this reality of the oppressive room, the stifling air of family life, is the landscape of the imagination, the unseen mountains. Beuys believed in the existence of contrasts and, above all, in the abolition of these. Heat and cold, life and death, feeling and thinking, inside and outside, nature and culture, man and universe, mass and vacuum, chaos and order: these are opposites that continually crop up in his work, as in *Vakuum<–>Masse* (1970). Disappointed in the excessively analytical and reductionist thinking of the natural sciences, he sought compensation for this in other systems of thought. He became engrossed, for instance, in the writings of Rudolf Steiner, but also in the Romantic philosophy of thinkers such as Schelling and Goethe. The importance that he attached to intuition can be seen in the writings of Schelling. The essence of Beuys's art is characterized by the range of his work, and that partly has to do with his view of man as a universal, whole being. Man is not only reason, but also intuition and emotion, and he is also an operative being, a social creature, who is part of civilization. All of these aspects of man are brought up in the work of Joseph Beuys. He wished to address not only a small part of man, but man in his

entirety. Like no other artist, Beuys broadened visual art's strictly defined realm. Not only drawings, objects and performances or *Aktionen*, but also discussions, the concepts *Soziale Plastik* and *Erweitertes Kunstbegriff,* his active membership in the only ecological party of Germany (one which was hardly taken seriously by the establishment at that time), the founding of the Free International University and his teaching position at the art academy in Düsseldorf, exemplified his versatility and formed, to him, one indivisible whole. Beuys was convinced that man could act freely only when in possession of "insight on the conditions of life in its totality," as Steiner put it. Unlike the Fluxus artists, who opposed the individual and personal nature of art and showed themselves to be advocates of anonymity and collectivity, Beuys had a solemn belief in the creative individual, in the generative power of art and its capacity to save mankind. Beuys's active membership in an ecological party attests to his utopian outlook, his faith in the notion that an artist has the ability to achieve things that are otherwise impossible. A telling measure of this is his accomplishment of an art project, the most prominent part of the 1982 *documenta* in Kassel, which involved the planting of 7000 oaks. The oaks, trees having great mythological significance in Germany, provide a counterweight to ever-expanding

asphalt and concrete surfaces, the 'rationalization' of the city. This costly project was not realized through politics, but with the aid of his many friends and interested individuals throughout the art world. Trees were 'adopted' by galleries and museums. The Van Abbemuseum also supported this project and has two certificates from it. The death of Joseph Beuys in 1986 prompted Rudi Fuchs to say that the greatest artist of the twentieth century had died. Perhaps it is still too early to know whether Beuys indeed was a greater artist than Picasso, for instance, or Mondrian. But there is no doubt as to the fact that he is the most important and most influential German artist since World War II. Beuys liberated art from purely formal thought, from a preoccupation with the aesthetic object. He brought completely new themes and materials to the art world, producing frequently unsightly combinations of objects and materials (such as fat and felt) and showing himself to be a master of bringing things to life. His influence on contemporary art can still be discerned. The unprecedented flourishing of German art during the eighties would have been inconceivable without his charismatic presence.

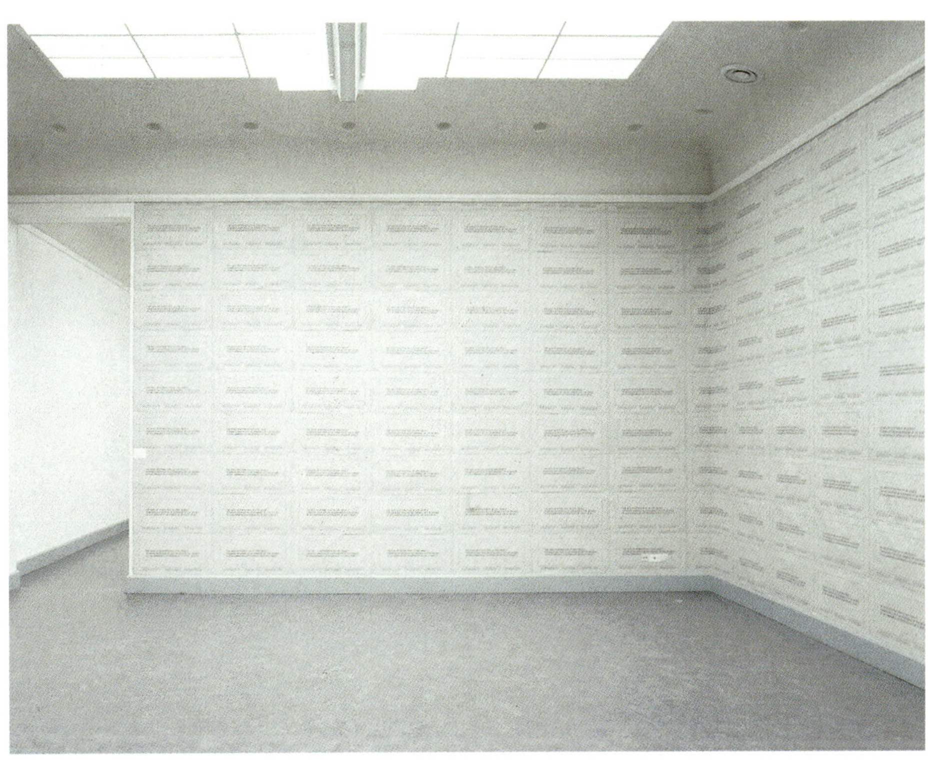

Lawrence Weiner *The rate of attraction of one object towards another as determined by the degree of encumbrance experienced by each object,* 1980

The emergence of conceptual art during the late sixties bears a close relationship to the social and political developments of that time. This was a period marked by unrest, protest and reflection. Young people were demanding to have their own voice and were reacting, in many facets of society, to the status quo, to traditional values and the materialism of the previous generation. In the visual arts, too, one could speak of a radical refusal to conform to prevailing views and of an attempt to redefine the notion of art.

In response to the formalism that dominated the art of the early sixties, the conceptual artists posed the question as to the essence and the nature of art: what makes something a work of art? What determines its value, and what sort of relevance does the work of art have in society? How do meanings come about, and how do the production, the distribution and the reception of art interrelate? The term conceptual art does not, therefore, refer to particular stylistic qualities, but rather to an artistic stance which links a number of artists.

Nevertheless, there are essential differences with respect to the ways in which artists have arrived at a more or less conceptual manner of working. While some underwent a gradual transition into this, others made a clear break. 'Analytical' artists such as Joseph Kosuth and the Art & Language group, for instance, arrived at a rigorous rejection of tradition on the basis of a distinctly theoretical stance. Due to their emphasis on the systematic investigation of the principles underlying the notion of art, theory and practice thoroughly coincide in their work. Contrasting with this are artists such as Lawrence Weiner and Robert Barry, who initially continued to work within the traditional disciplines of art but gradually, by means of a systematic reduction of the visual means, arrived at an advanced degree of dematerialization in their work.

The gradual, almost experimental transition into conceptual art is clearly marked in the work of **Lawrence Weiner**. Weiner began to make art at a point when Abstract Expressionism had reached its peak and Pop Art was on the rise. The investigation on which he focused in his early work relates mainly to the material: why is it that certain materials are, and others are not, specific to visual art? Shortly thereafter came questions regarding the role of the artist and the viewer. During the mid sixties he produced, for instance, monochrome paintings from which a right angle has been cut. The prospective owner of the work would be able to help in determining the size and the color of the work, whereby the role of the artist was reduced.

ON A SMOOTH ——————————
BEING WITHIN THE CONTEXT OF [A] PLACE

OP EEN GLADDE ——————————
BINNEN DE CONTEXT VAN [EEN] PLAATS

ON A ROUGH ——————————————
BEING WITHIN THE CONTEXT OF [A] PLACE

OP RUWE STAAT ——————————
BINNEN DE CONTEXT VAN [EEN] PLAATS

IN THE ROUGH ——————————————
BEING WITHIN THE CONTEXT OF [A] PLACE

IN RUWE STAAT ——————————
BINNEN DE CONTEXT VAN [EEN] PLAATS

Lawrence Weiner, 1975

On the basis of such experiences, Weiner came to the conclusion, in 1968, that the outward appearance of the work was unimportant and that its actual execution by the artist was no longer necessary. The definition of the work by means of language was then considered by him to be sufficient for conveying the concept of a work. From that point on, Weiner has been employing language in such a way that he strives for maximum objectivity and universality. He regards his texts as sculptures which can be conceived or executed through an appeal to the reader's imagination. Clear examples of this are works such as *The salt of the earth mingled with the salt of the sea* (1984) and *Small stones scattered on the ground* (1986). Over the years Weiners works have become more abstract. His instructions are becoming less and less specific, so that the viewer can make them concrete only by association. In this way he makes optimal use of the limitless potential of language–being free of material, time and space–to make images conceivable.

Like Weiner, **Robert Barry** gradually arrived at a more dematerialized form of art. From the need to investigate the limits and the nature of our perception, he experimented during the years 1968-1969 with the most uncommon materials such as magnetic fields, inert gases, radio frequencies and radiation. By filling the exhibition space with FM waves, barium radiation and argon gas, he created 'sculptures' which, though invisible to the eye, are nonetheless real and verifiable. Somewhat later this point of departure brought him to work with phenomena such as telepathy and the possible presence of forgotten thoughts or hidden knowledge in the subconscious. In view of the fact that these immaterial works can actually only be described by words, language constitutes the major component of Barry's work from 1969 onward. By means of word series that he speaks on recording tape or compiles in books and slide projections, he sets off a creative process that follows a different course with every viewer. The slide projection *16th Century* (1974), for instance, consists of a series of forty words–acceptance, celebrate,

enterprise, explain–that appear, one by one, on a dark wall. Each 'word slide' is alternated with a black slide, which serves as a kind of interval.

The words that Barry selects are known to everyone, and so their meanings seem to be preestablished to a degree. At the same time, however, the connection that the artist has made between the words cannot be found. Only on the basis of associations that are continually adjusted can the individual reader arrive at a somewhat coherent and meaningful whole. The end result of the creative process that is set in motion by the work can no longer be controlled by the artist. Barry therefore does not offer the viewer a clear-cut approach to the work, but creates open models that can be completed according to the individual's imagination. Registering, making notes, keeping archives, discussion and documentation are activities undertaken by the conceptual artist in order to question the essence of art and its relationship to the surrounding reality. In the work of **On Kawara** this 'archival' approach is taken to its extreme in a very consistent manner, whereby art and life become nearly indistinguishable.

Kawara takes note of almost every action, movement or encounter within extensive, lengthy projects. Every day between 1968 and 1979, for instance, he sent two postcards with

Robert Barry *Numbers*, 1974 (projection)

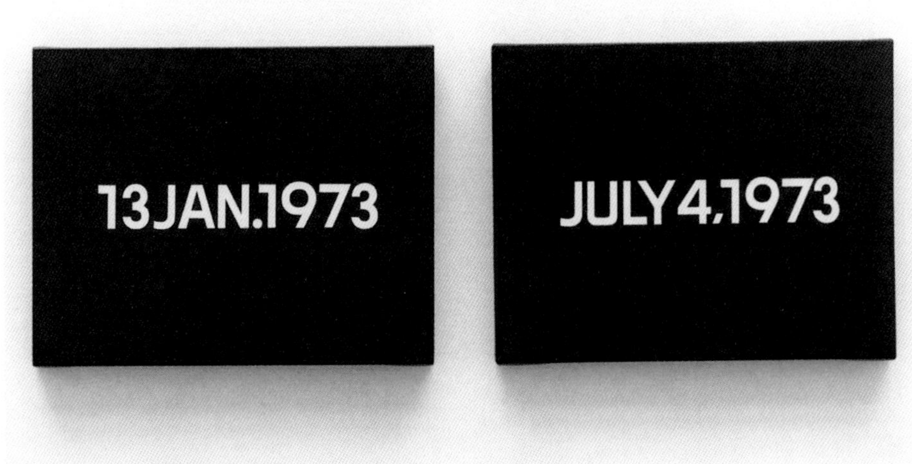

On Kawara *13 Jan.1973 July 4, 1973*

the stamped text "I got up at", followed by the time at which he 'got up' that day. Since 1970 he has been sending telegrams with the initially reassuring statement "I am still alive." The life of the artist is constantly being documented by means of various systems of notation. All of these notes are then stored in archives that gradual come to hold a staggering quantity of registered facts.

A significant part of Kawara's work is comprised of the 'Date paintings', which he has been painting since January 4, 1966 and which collectively make up the *Today* series. These paintings of a date rendered in white letters and digits on a dark, monochrome background are strikingly conventional from a material point of view: two-dimensional and rectangular, they have been painted meticulously, layer upon layer, on canvas. With respect to the subject, however, they are explicitly conceptual. On Kawara paints the date of the day on which he paints the date. If he is unable to complete a work within one day, it is destroyed. On some days he does not produce a single painting, on others he manufactures many. The annual production of the 'Date paintings' is written down in a 'Journal'. In this he lists the date, dimensions, color, subtitle and the serial number. Like the date on the paintings, he makes these notations in the language of the country in which he is staying at the time. When the paintings are finished, they are kept in specially made boxes that often also contain a page from a local newspaper printed on the given day.

The meaning of the 'Date paintings' lies with the fact that Kawara does not simply paint a date, but that he transforms this into the essence of the painting. Rather than dating a

material object, he chooses to materialize the date. Furthermore, the painted date not only refers to the day on which the work was produced; it also functions as a kind of summary of what the artist was doing on that particular day–namely, painting the date. The historic highpoint of conceptual art can be found in the immediate aftermath of its inception, in the agitated period at the end of the sixties and early seventies. During that period the first generation of conceptual artists became known to the public particularly due to the activities of Seth Siegelaub. This New York gallery owner organized important projects and exhibitions that sometimes consisted of no more than a catalogue with essays. In the Van Abbemuseum conceptual art has been actively followed and shown only since Rudi Fuchs became director in 1975. From that point on, extensive consideration, both in the exhibition program and the acquisition policy, has been given to this pioneering art which is often quite difficult for many people to understand.

One of the first conceptual artists, who moreover returned to the Van Abbemuseum frequently, was **Ian Wilson**, whose work can be regarded as extremely radical, from the perspective of that time as well as that of today. In 1968 he produced his last conventional works in the form of circles drawn in chalk, an example of which is *Circle on the Floor* (1968)(see p. 93). Since then, his work has solely consisted of spoken or written words. In reference to this rupture, Wilson later said, "At that point I realized that I could just as easily think that circle or say it, that I didn't need to draw it in order to convey the idea with which I was concerned." From

that time on, Wilson has been producing works into which he allows no trace of materiality and in which the chemistry between the artist and the viewer has prime importance. The traditional visual means are, for this reason, replaced by language, which he uses mainly in spoken form.

On the basis of the question taken from Plato, "Can we know the unknown?", the artist carries on dialogues that actually constitute the work from that point onward. The content of these dialogues is determined by his quest for the (im)possibilities of verbal communication as an art form, their quality by the input of his partners in the discussion. Because Wilson does not allow these conversations to be recorded, from a formal point of view the work vanishes afterwards. No evidence of the postulated stances, arguments and conclusions is left. What

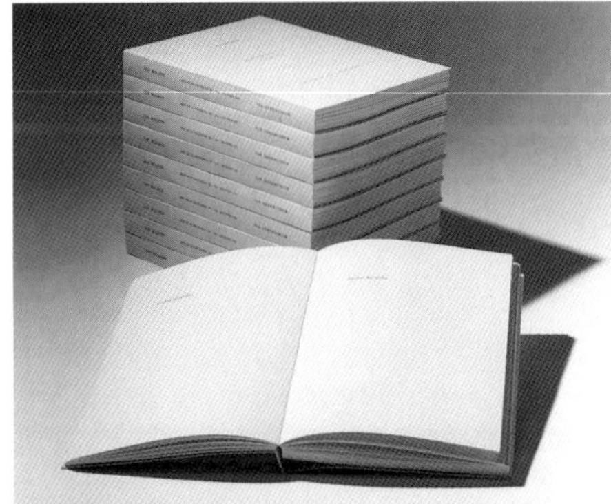

Ian Wilson *The Set of 25 Sections: 90-114, with Absolute Knowledge, 1993*

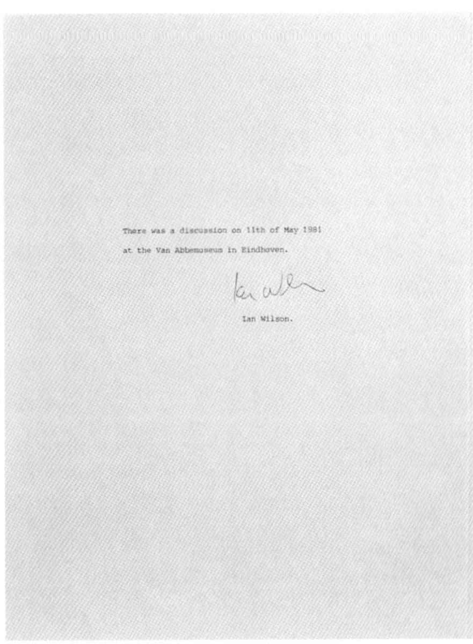

Ian Wilson Certificate of *There was a Discussion, 1981, 11 May*

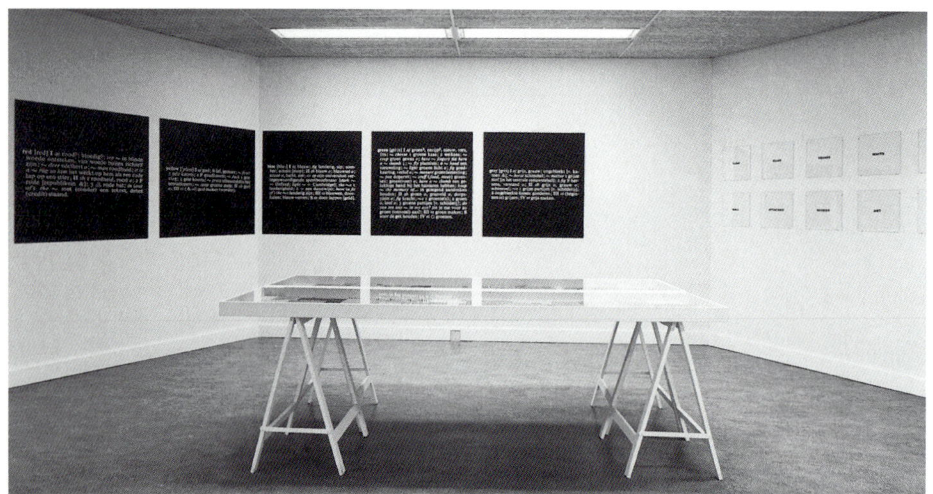

From left to right: **Joseph Kosuth** *Art as Idea as Idea, (The First Investigation)*, 1968; *One and Nine – A Description*, 1965

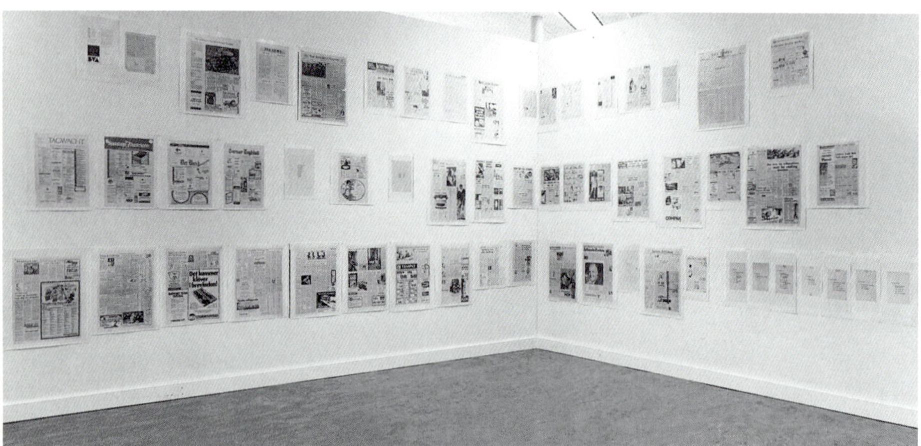

Joseph Kosuth *The Second Investigation*, 1969-74

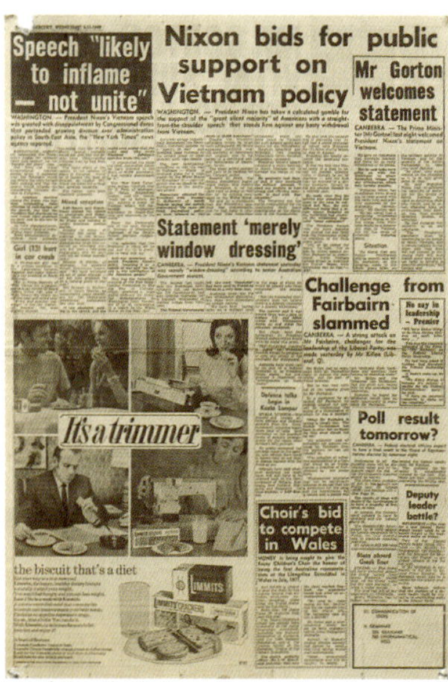

Joseph Kosuth *The Second Investigation*, 1969-74 (detail)

remains is a certificate awarded by the artist; in a concrete sense, this merely consists of a sheet of paper with the words "There was a discussion at the Van Abbemuseum" along with the date and the signature of the artist. The question "Can we know the unknown?" also constitutes the basis of books in which Wilson goes beyond the limitations of visual abstraction and ends up in the formless abstraction of language. The vacuum that he seeks to create, is attained by him through the writing of endless variations on the words 'Known' and 'Unknown', as in *Section 30* (1982) which was published by the Van Abbemuseum. Several years later Wilson went a step further by publishing a series of books in which each page contains only the words 'Absolute Knowledge'.

In the work of the artists mentioned above, one can consistently speak of a more or less experimental transition into a dematerialized form of art, which rather implicitly gives rise to questions as to the nature of the artwork and the role of the artist. There also exists, however, a small group of artists for whom the theoretical analysis of the notion of art constitutes the central and explicitly phrased theme of the artistic activity. Here theory and practice coincide in such a way that one could speak of conceptual art in a more narrow sense.

The work of the predominantly British collective **Art & Language** includes, for instance, polemical and critical writings which deal with ideas related to the foundations of the notion of art, the way in which art functions in society and the conditions for meaningful artistry. The name Art & Language stands for an alternating group of collaborative artists, which was founded in 1968 by Terry Atkinson, David Bainbridge, Michael Baldwin and Harold Hurell. Throughout the early years the activities of the group were centered around the publication of the magazine *Art-Language*, for which Joseph Kosuth acted as the American editor. Ian Burn, Mel Ramsden and the art historian Charles Harrison joined the group in 1971.

The major aim set by the collective was (and continues to be) the abolition of the conventional and hierarchical distinction between art and criticism, between language and aesthetics. The artists therefore adopted a militant stance with respect to modernist ideas such as those conveyed by the critics Clement Greenberg and Michael Fried. Developed on the basis of the Anglo-Saxon philosophy of language, this criticism took shape partly through the production and analysis of texts as art and the presentation of these in archives and indexes. A clear example of this is the twenty-seven-part work *Index 002 (Bxal)* (1973). Art & Language offered, instead of the traditional artwork, a ever-expanding quantity of interrelating quotes and criticisms. The viewer can no longer relate to an aesthetic object in a contemplative manner, but is an active part of the context of the work.

Since the end of 1976, the artistic work of Art & Language has been continued by Michael Baldwin, Mel Ramsden and Charles Harrison. They have been concentrating primarily on a critical analysis of painting and on the role of the museum as an institution which determines value. On the basis of this pursuit, they organized, at the Van Abbemuseum in 1980, an exhibition in which the investigation of the notion of style in modern painting played a significant role. Under the title *A Portrait of V.I. Lenin in the Style of Jackson Pollock*, they presented a series of paintings and photocopies that dealt with the problem of styles which give rise to

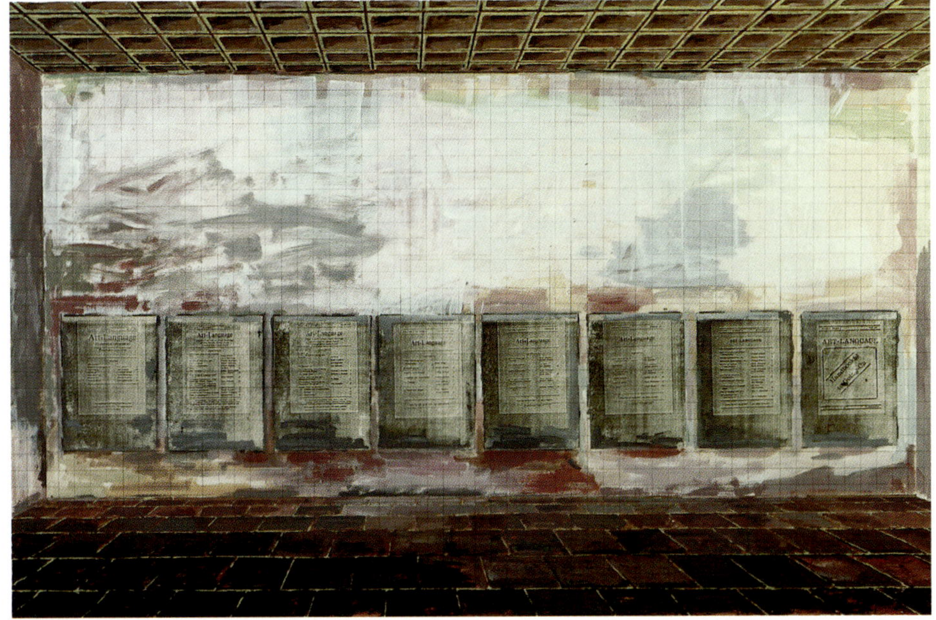

Art & Language *Study for index, incident in a museum II*, 1985

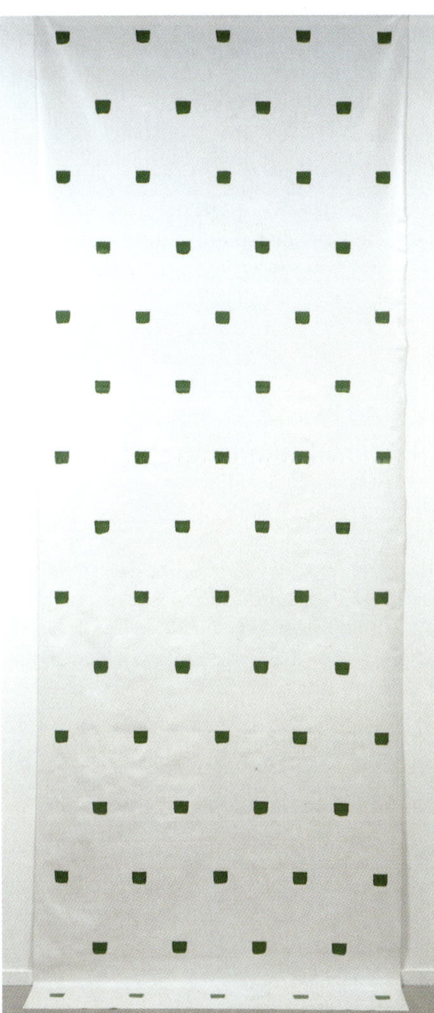

Niele Toroni *Empreintes de pinceau no. 50 répétées à intervalles réguliers (30 cm)*, 1975

idealization, such as Abstract Expressionism and Social Realism.

The analytical investigation into the foundations of art and the conditions under which it can exist also constitutes a key theme in the work of **Joseph Kosuth**. Like the Art & Language artists, Kosuth experienced the art scene of the early sixties as being oppressive and pointless. In order to liberate himself from this situation, it was necessary for the artist to break with the formalist and aesthetic views in which art is defined in terms of forms and colors that serve 'superior taste'.

Kosuth's oeuvre is comprised of texts in which he discusses his theory of art, as well as works that demonstrate this theory. Departing from the idea that art should, on the basis of a logical structure, pose questions and give answers as to what art actually is, he began to produce, in 1966, tautological works that he referred to as "proto-investigations." In these he examined the mechanisms that cause unchanged objects to assume ever-changing meanings. A striking example of this is the work *One and Nine - A description* (1965), which consists of a series of ten identical sheets of glass, each showing a different word in adhesive letters. Each word describes a particular quality of the same object: 'clear', 'glass', 'square' and so on. While the object itself remains the same, we perceive a different quality each time by way of the language that describes it.

Of prime importance in the work of Kosuth is the notion that the essence of something is expressed not so much by its manifestation, but rather by an idea contained in language. *The First Investigations*, for instance, came about on the basis of this notion. In these works Kosuth has taken definitions of abstract ideas from explicative, translating and etymological dictionaries and enlarged them on black panels. Because language has the capacity to be not only what it is–a succession of letters and words–but also that 'to which it pertains', ideas such as 'meaning', 'nothing' and 'abstract' assume the potential to represent themselves. By bringing language into the context of visual art, Kosuth was able to replace the pictorial image with a linguistic definition. Or, to use to Kosuth's own words, "I had the feeling that I had found a way to make art without formal components which could be confused with an expressionistic composition. The expression lay in the idea, not in the form; the forms were merely a means to serve the idea."

All works by Kosuth were given the title *Art as Idea as Idea*. This title makes it clear that, from his point of view, there is an important difference between the artwork/concept and the representation of this concept in the form of an object, a photograph or a definition from a dictionary.

Furthermore, what matters is not the individual work, but rather the notion of art that remains at the heart of all his activities as a constant process which comments on itself. American conceptual art stemmed mainly from the dire need to arrive at a new notion of art which would put an end to the formalism that had dominated art since the start of the twentieth century. In European art, the motivation arose from a different need. For though the social and artistic unrest was no less intense here, the dogmatic modernism of Clement Greenberg and others had much less impact on Europe during the sixties. The break with art movements such as *Zero* was, after all, not radical but nuanced, and it was prompted chiefly by the desire for a new vocabulary that would enable the artist to determine his artistic stance within the social/political scene. Another aspect whereby the European artists distinguished themselves from their American counterparts and contemporaries was the importance given by them to the manual treatment of the visual means which they employed. This aspect is clearly evident with artists such as Niele Toroni and Marcel Broodthaers, whose work holds a prominent place in the collection of the Van Abbemuseum. In addition to this, a great deal of consideration was given, during the seventies, to the work of such artists as

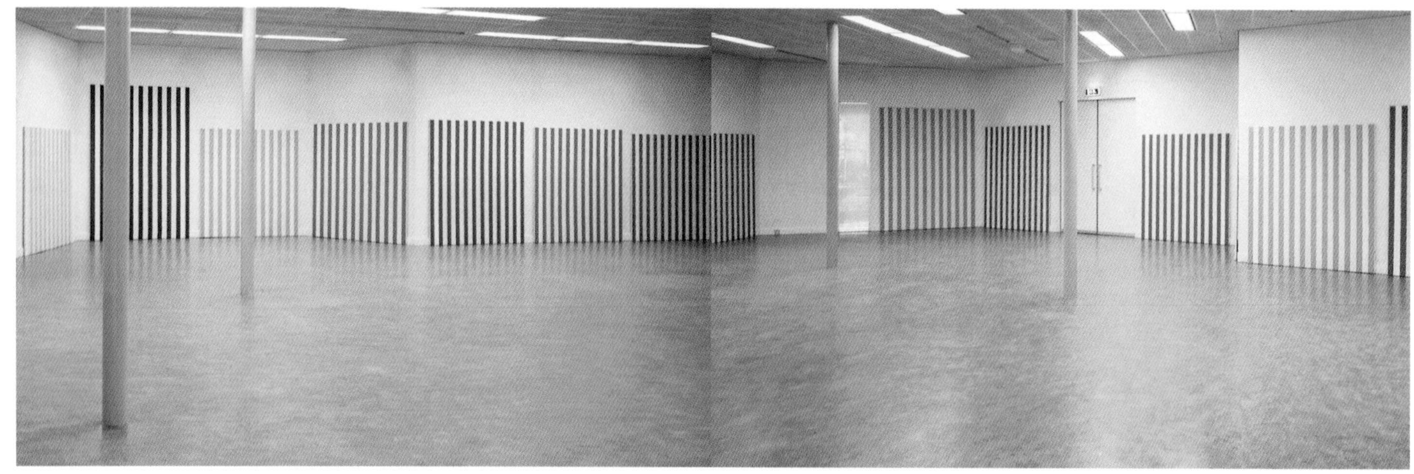

Stanley Brouwn and Hans Haacke, by whom the distinction between art and life is eliminated as much as possible.

The special value that is ascribed to the manual process of making art is emphatically present in the work of **Niele Toroni.** Since the mid sixties he has been concentrating on a form of painting which is intended to be as neutral as possible and which, so far, has remained essentially unchanged. His work was first exhibited in 1967 under the title *Empreintes de pinceau no. 50 répétées à intervalles réguliers (30 cm)*, one which he gave to all of his works from that point on and which already summarizes his way of working: "A no. 50 brush is pressed on the given carrier at regular intervals of 30 cm. The Carrier: canvas, cotton, paper, waxed cloth, wall, floor..., white grounds as a rule. Application: "...to place one thing over another in such a way as to cover it, adhere to it or leave an imprint. No. 50 brush: flat brush, 50 mm wide." The result of this consistently sustained way of working is a body of work that does not display the artistic development that one would expect. The oeuvre of Niele Toroni is therefore a succession of equivalent matters. The interval of thirty centimeters is marked off beforehand by means of a compass. The structure of the work allows for no hierarchical distinction, and thus each mark of the brush has equal value. Within one work, only one color is used, and the way in which the imprint is made also remains the same.

Toroni developed his method, first and foremost, as an anonymous mark of the painted surface. The strict and predetermined definition of his work is aimed at the exclusion of any form of optical effect or lyrical expression. The artistic

freedom of the artist is deliberately kept to a minimum. Toroni is therefore very much opposed to the cult of the genius and to clichés such as progress and originality. Despite this, the imprint of the no. 50 brush is immediately recognized as being that of Toroni. In that sense, the objective act functions as a highly personal signature at the same time. For this reason Toroni's work is often described as being a synthesis between the subjective gesture and the objective mark. In this unique, personal way of working–which is also anonymous and objective–repetition and variation are one and the same. The paintings of Toroni remain essentially the same. What changes is the format, the color, the support and the place in which he makes or hangs them. The correlation of repetition and variation is clearly expressed in two exhibitions organized by the Van Abbemuseum during the late seventies. In 1977 Toroni produced, in four rooms of the museum, an exhibition of works applied high on the wall or low, just above the baseboard. One year later, in the same rooms of the museum, a response to this followed under the title *Autre possibilité.* Whereas the first exhibition dealt with the articulation of the passageways in the museum, the second involved an uninterrupted route along the museum's interior walls.

While Toroni was concerned with the result of an action, **Daniel Buren** prefers to focus on the place and the situation in which his work is made and shown. The works of Buren therefore always bear a direct relationship to the temporal and spatial aspects of the location in which he works. The Latin term 'in situ', which describes this relationship, applies to his entire body of work and emphasizes the importance that the artist

attaches to the context.

Aiming to develop a neutral type of painting in which the problems of form would no longer play a role and in which the painting would function only as a sign of itself, Buren decided, in 1965, to limit the pictorial content of his work to the repeated alternation of white and colored stripes measuring 8.7 cm in width. Through the application of painted or prefabricated stripes, he attempts to question the traditional codes of painting and the social and ideological presuppositions of exhibiting. Convention dictates that art be presented on the wall at eye level and at a distance which allows for an overall view at a single glance. This is the consequence of a painterly tradition in which, by means of a centrally perspective construction, one gains an understanding of the illusory world underlying the painting. For centuries, the painting has been regarded as a contained, framed space that embodies a different, imaginary world.

While titles of works such as *Fragmente einer Rede über die Kunst. 18 peintures sur toile. Tissus rayés blancs et colorés* (1965-81) continue to allude to this historical concept, Buren offers, in fact, an alternative type of painting which is basically limitless and whose form and meaning are determined by the spatial context in which it is made. Buren's works hang in corners, cover entire walls, extend from one space into another or are hung above streets. They assume the shape of the space and, at the same time, constitute an analysis of the location. The works of Buren should therefore not be regarded so much as a negatively based criticism of the tradition, but as a personal strategy aimed at the advancement of painting.

Along with questions that relate to the spatial context of the work, Buren also raises

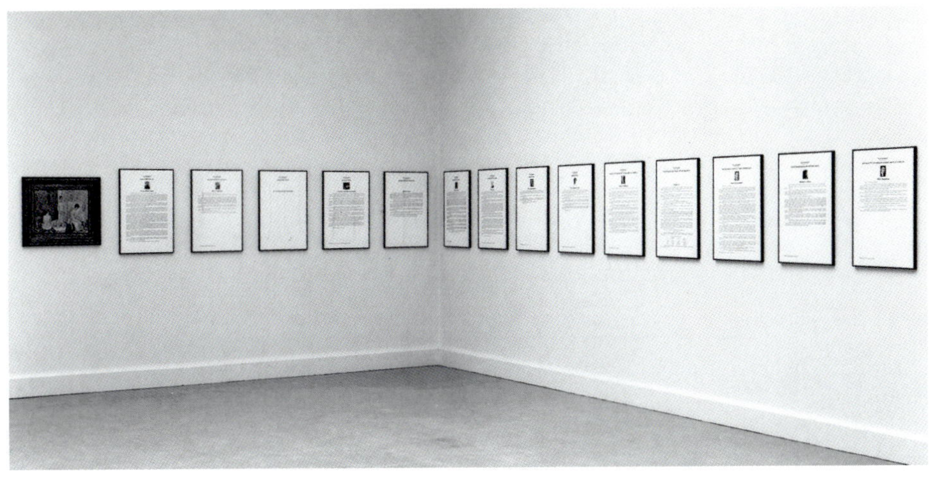

Hans Haacke *Seurat's 'Les Poseuses' (small version) 1888-1975, 1975*

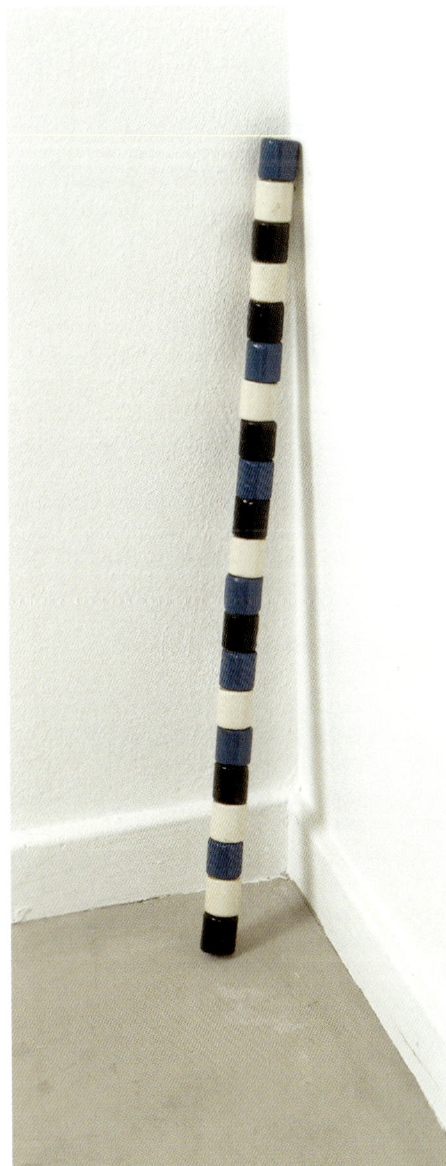

André Cadere *B 12000030 =25= =16x17= Noir Blanc Bleu, 1975*

seventies, however, he began to become more known as he appeared, usually uninvited, at openings of exhibitions of other conceptual artists. He then presented, as a parasite, his own colored wooden bars, carrying them on his shoulder or leaning them against the wall. With this provocative form of infiltration, Cadere irritated both fellow artists and the rest of the art world; for a long time there were highly varied opinions about his work. Nevertheless, he quickly gained a reputation, and–welcome or not–he became part of the network which he criticized but to which he also claimed to belong.

Cadere's round wooden bars are composed of painted segments, whose length is equal to the diameter. The alternation of the various colors is determined by a mathematical system of permutation, and this always contains one error. Each bar has only four variables: color, permutation, scale and flaw. Furthermore, Cadere confines himself to the use of eight colors (black, white, yellow, orange, red, purple, blue and green) and two permutation types, namely A and B. Type A has five variables, type B two. This means that there are seven different types of bars. The qualities of each work can be found in the title, such as *A 12003000 =25= =3x10 = Noir Blanc Rouge* and *B 12000030 =25= =16x17= Noir Blanc Bleu*.

The placement of the wooden bars were described by Cadere as 'displacements' and were primarily intended to show the work. Only later did he begin to make these the object of discussion. "The purpose of my work is to be seen, which means that reactions of indifference, hostility or love are of no interest. I don't collect the public's feeling. My only aim is to put everything into work, in order to show what I'm doing." To this end Cadere visited not only openings of exhibitions; he also carried his work with him almost constantly, through town, in the metro or to a restaurant. In addition to the gallery, the group exhibition and the debate, Cadere also used 'the walk' as a means of 'placing and displacing' his work. Through his walks he was ultimately able not only to show his work outside the context of art, but also to allow the gallery to go beyond its own walls. An exhibition at Galerie MTL in Brussels, for instance, consisted of an officially announced, two-hour walk that was carried out in Paris at a time when the gallery was closed. Cadere hereby gave emphasis to the ordinary gallery's limitations in terms of time and space, as well as to his own struggle to attain a fully independent type of art. Since the mid seventies Cadere made his work, and the context within which it

problems concerning the ideological aspects of exhibiting. Having been involved with his work for more than twenty-five years, Buren continues to be interested in the same fundamental issues on the basis of a changing reality: "Where is one exhibiting? With whom? How? Who has extended the invitation? At which places can something be carried out? And consequently: what is the importance of the place? The importance of the people who have extended the invitation? The importance of the other invited artists with whom one is confronted?"

Because art is largely presented via the museum or the gallery, the critical analysis of the role of these institutions constitutes an ongoing factor in his work. According to Buren, the aesthetic, mythical context of art had long been unquestioningly upheld by them. The museum does possess, after all, the singular power to define anything that is exhibited in it as being art. And though the role of the museum has changed considerably over the years, it is still a theme that he deals with in his work.

At the start of seventies, conceptual art was being shown in a limited number of primarily European galleries and museums. Together these institutions made up an international network, through which artists went on tour, so to speak–from Jack Wendler's Gallery in London to Yvon Lambert in Paris, from Galerie MTL in Brussels to Galerie Sperone in Turin and from Art & Project in Amsterdam to Leo Castelli in New York. For the Rumanian-born artist **André Cadere**, penetrating to the core of this network was one of his prime objectives. On arriving in Paris in 1967, he was an artist without a name or a gallery. For the presentation of his work, he had to rely on the use of public space. During the early

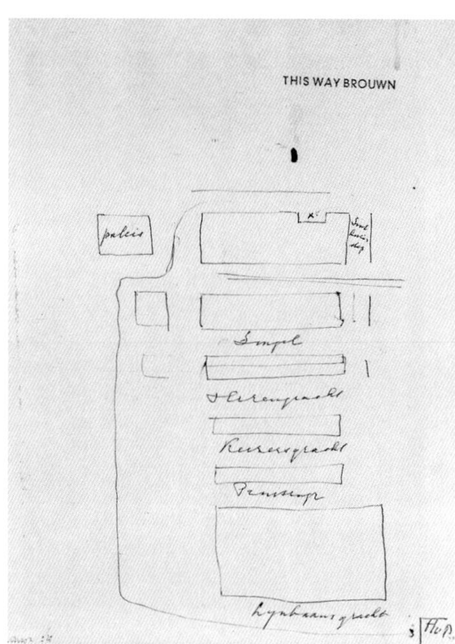

Stanley Brouwn *this way Brouwn*, 1964

functioned, the subject of frequent discussion in spontaneously provoked or organized debates. The main focus of these discussions was usually the social, economic, cultural or political context of the artwork. After having held a series of discussions in galleries and museums, Cadere returned to the public domain in which he began: he opted to use a Paris bus stop as a place in which to exchange ideas with others, invited or uninvited.

The elimination of distinctions between the reality of art and that of life is a theme that plays a key role in the work of **Hans Haacke** as well. Since 1961 Haacke has been making sculptures and installations that he describes as "real time systems"; in them he investigates changes influenced by natural, sociological, economic and political conditions. During the early sixties, he focused mainly on the study of physical and biological processes, such as growth, freezing, condensation and gravity. Fascinated by the fact that all aspects of life interrelate, he has become, since the mid seventies, increasingly dedicated to the analysis of sociopolitical systems and their relation to the art world in particular. From 1969 to 1973, for instance, he took polls in which he asked museum visitors for their opinions on sociopolitical issues and for information pertaining to background, education and profession. The results of these polls were presented by him as works which undermine the idea that the museum is an apolitical institution that serves culture. Art, as Haacke sees it, has never been ideologically neutral. The current state of affairs is therefore not the result of a 'natural' process, but of historic social conflicts that are still going on. The prevailing notion that art and politics have nothing to do with each other is, in his opinion, the consequence of Greenberg's formalist doctrine: "For decades that doctrine has managed to have us believe that art hovers high above us and bears no connection whatsoever to the historical situation from which it emerged. Art is presumed to be something unto itself. The only acknowledged link with history is that of style." Haacke believes that the neutrality of art is a myth that is carefully maintained by those who have a political and economic interest in it.

During the mid seventies Haacke produced several documentary 'provenance' works, including *Seurat's 'Les Poseuses' (small version) 1888-1975* (1975). On the basis of a photographic reproduction framed as a work of art and a 'biographical' description of Seurat's painting, he sketched the history of the work up to the point at which it attained the much-coveted 'museum status'. In the 'biography' of the painting, emphasis is given to the artist's social background and to the routes that he takes in order to gain museum appreciation for his work.

The direct relationship between artistic success and 'big money' is a theme that comes up frequently in Haacke's work. His investigation therefore focuses on the networks that wield power in the art world. He describes his strategy in this as 'subversive imitation', which essentially involves the reorganization of existing systems or structures within changing contexts.

On the basis of an entirely different view and by means of a highly personal approach, **Stanley Brouwn** also opts to eliminate the distinction between art and life. Since the early sixties the central theme of his work has consisted of the bridging and measuring of distances. Initially Brouwn concentrated very much on interaction with the public. He would speak to people who happened to be passing by in the street and ask them to describe how to get from point A to point B. Sometimes he would have them draw the route described and then exhibit this sketch with the words "this way Brouwn" stamped on it. He would also place sheets of paper on the ground, so that people who happened to be walking by left imprints of their soles on them. The works that came about in this manner manifest the notions 'distance' and 'direction', as rendered by the anonymous participants. The fact that the visual result of this way of working is often extremely terse can be seen with the *this way Brouwn* (1964) which is in the collection of the Van Abbemuseum.

Since the early seventies Brouwn has produced a great number of works formed by the counting of footsteps made by him within a particular period of time, at a particular place or in a particular direction. The steps were then multiplied by a metric unit, so that the distance crossed could be expressed in terms of millimeters or meters. The measuring of distances gradually assumed greater importance within his body of work and eventually led to the marking of the length of one step along a line measuring precisely one meter. The distance spanned in the footstep is recorded as a line or a number; such registrations are done on loose sheets of paper, in books, on cards and on graph paper. In *1 stap, 1 el, 1 voet op m², 1 el, 1 voet op 1 stap²* (1989) the relationship between the individual human scale and the metric system plays an important role. Brouwn

From left to right: **Remy Zaugg** *Une feuille de papier*, 1973-86 *Une feuille de papier*, 1973-82 (2 parts) *Une feuille de papier*, 1973-80

refers to old systems in which measurements were expressed in terms of the length of certain parts of the body. Like Buren and Toroni, Brouwn is tremendously consistent in the development of his concept. With the accountant-like precision he records ratios pertaining to space, time, distance and direction and thus accentuates the existential meaning of a simple daily activity such as walking. His work therefore inevitably brings the viewer to a new, conscious experience of the world in which he moves.

Consciousness-raising with respect to aspects usually overlooked by the viewer is a theme that also has prominence in the work of **Remy Zaugg**. Zaugg produces not only visual art; he also writes a great number of essays on art theory in which he deals with issues related to perception. In 1982 the Van Abbemuseum published the book *Die List der Unschuld. Das Wahrnehmen einer Skulptur*, in which he philosophizes on this problem for nearly 300 pages.

The exhaustive manner in which Zaugg articulates his ideas in writing corresponds to the way in which he deals with the same issues in his visual art. Here, too, he brings up all of the facets of making art in a way that makes it impossible to skip over this lightly. The 1984 exhibition *Une feuille de papier…, pourquoi?*, for instance, occupied ten rooms of the Van Abbemuseum in which Zaugg displayed a changing number of sheets of brown paper. Some were written on or painted on, others left untouched. Moreover, the works were presented in different ways: sometimes pinned to the wall, then stacked, or hung behind glass.

The layout of the exhibition attested to a meticulously conceived plan. The uniformity of the works and the almost total lack of color and image stimulated the viewer to abandon his knowledge of an artwork and then allow the work to speak for itself. The viewer was compelled to reconsider his expectations with respect to the work of art: "Now you are looking at sheets of paper (painted, unpainted, behind glass or not, printed with words) many details of which are almost imperceptible. You are looking at sheets of paper with a precision which you never apply when looking other, ordinary paintings. You are looking intently, otherwise you would see nothing."

Zaugg presents the viewer with a model of the artwork, which is completely stripped of its expressive or illusionistic characteristics. From this standpoint, he defines his works as being 'banal': they are things from everyday life, things that are believed to be immediately recognizable and nameable. The lack of visually interesting aspects prompt the viewer, however, to ask questions about the true function and meaning of the work. The 'banality' of the work is therefore merely a device for encouraging the viewer to adopt a reflective and analytical attitude, which gives rise to actual observation. Only through critical perception, after all, can one arrive at relevant questions and, ultimately, at an understanding of the work. Not until the viewer decides to go beyond the banality of the surface and deal actively with the work will art reveal its true meaning.

Dan Graham

Edward Ruscha

Bernd & Hilla Becher

Douglas Huebler

John Baldessari

Ger van Elk

Jan Dibbets

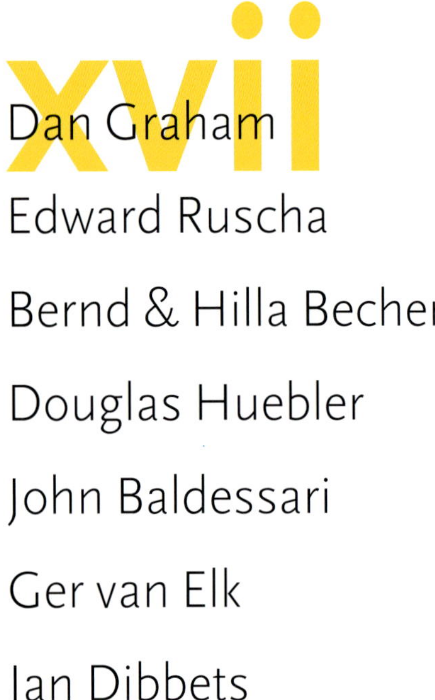

John Baldessari *Subject Matter*, 1967-68

In the period from 1965 to 1975, the development of conceptual art offered unprecedented freedom to experiment with new media and materials. The distinctions among the traditional disciplines were becoming less clear or were being eliminated, which made it possible to pose fundamental questions with respect to art in an entirely new way. It is therefore not surprising that the new media of that time–film, video and photography–began to play an important part in this. Through conceptual art, photography was, for the first time, becoming an integral part of visual art. Represented in the collection of the Van Abbemuseum are a number of artists whose work may not be considered conceptual in the strict sense, though they did engage in the conceptual tendencies of that time and develop them further. A striking and common characteristic of these artists is the fact that they not only make statements on the nature of art and the way in which it operates, but also attach great value to the visual manifestation of their work. Another important aspect of conceptual art is that alternatives were developed in order to present art outside the traditional scene of galleries and museums. This enabled the artist to have an increasing degree of control over the circumstances under which his work was shown. Occasionally, this control became, in itself, part of the work. Such is the case with *Magazine Pieces*, for instance, whereby **Dan Graham** took leave of the 'neutral' space of the gallery during the late sixties. Instead he made use of the ideological and cultural context of the magazine, which causes a work to have different meaning with each publication and thereby eliminates the unambiguous. Furthermore, these works function not only as art, but also as art criticism. By using the art magazine as an alternative context in which to exhibit his conceptual work, Graham was able to prevent his work from becoming 'merchandise'. Normally speaking, artworks are reproduced in the magazine, after having existed first as objects within the context of the gallery. Graham inverted this principle and made works that owe their existence solely to the social and cultural context of the magazine, so that they can be shown in the gallery merely as 'secondhand' art.

In 1969 Graham stopped producing his *Magazine Pieces* and began to concentrate on the production of performances, films and video works. Here the emphasis came to lie more and more with the investigation of the process of perception and with the social and psychological aspects of the interaction between the artist, the audience and the surroundings. Graham was one of the first artists to use the medium of video as an authentic visual means, not only employing it as a means of registration but also exploiting

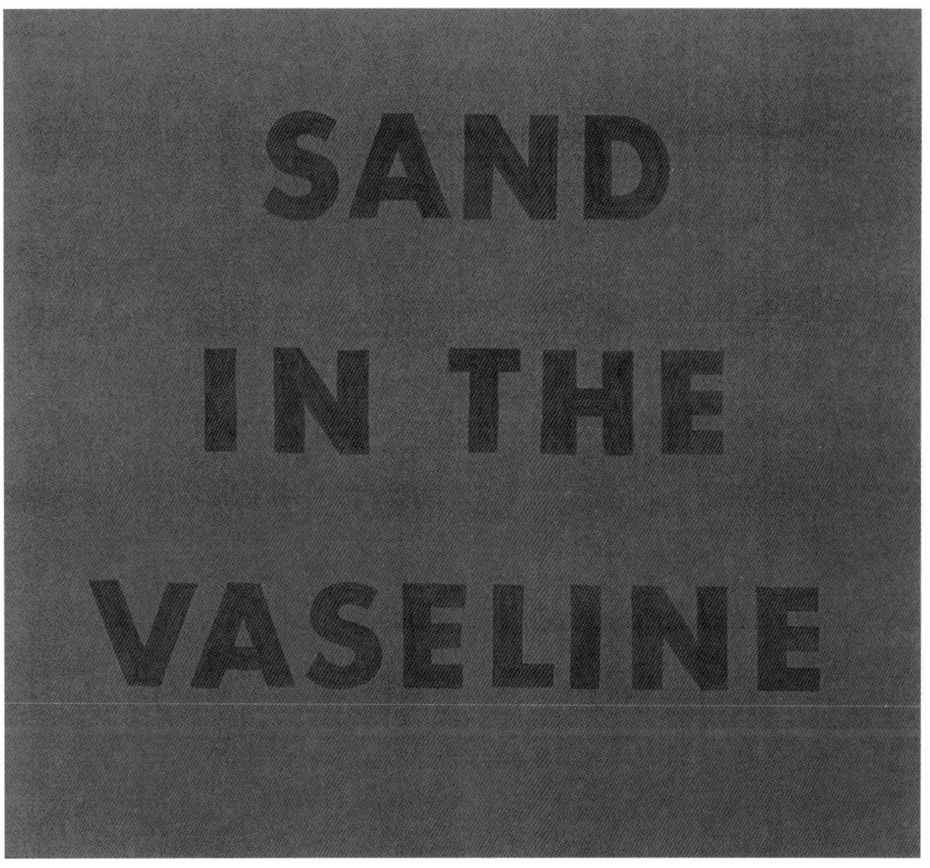

Edward Ruscha *Sand in the Vaseline, 1974*

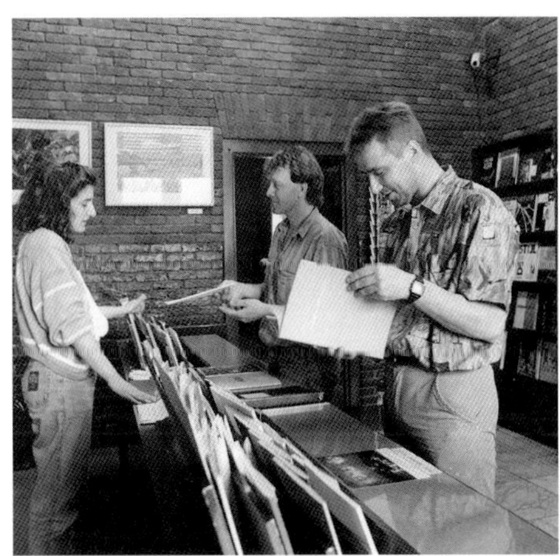

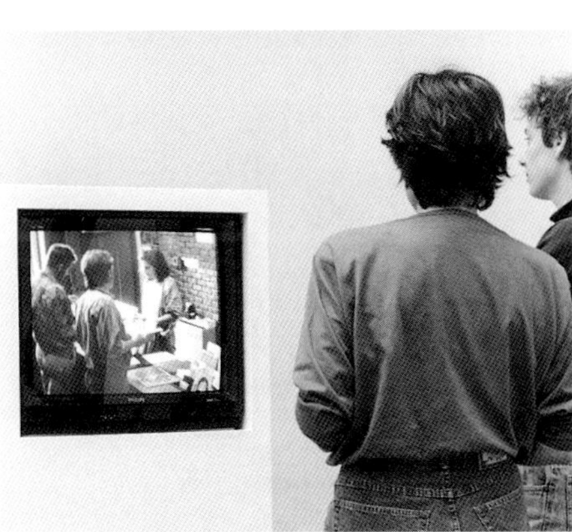

Dan Graham *Yesterday/Today, 1975*

its specific properties in order to expose the viewer's conditioned behavior.

Graham's *Yesterday/Today* (1975) is comprised of a monitor set up in a gallery or museum space which is accessible to the public. On the monitor one sees images that show what is going on in another space of the building at the same time. These include, for instance, scenes from the offices of the museum, the storage rooms, the 'coffee break' area. The sound that accompanies the images has also been recorded in the rooms, but then a day earlier at the same time. Image and sound are not synchronous, yet the two provide insight as to what usually remains hidden to the public. Graham gives the viewer the potential to look (and listen) behind the scenes, and in doing so renounces the presumed neutrality of the art institution. Graham's search for alternative forms in which to produce and distribute the artwork is, to a certain degree, also fostered by **Edward Ruscha**. Due to his preference for what he describes as "the plastic side of life", Ruscha was initially considered a representative of Californian Pop Art. His sources of inspiration are found not in traditionally cerebral matters, but in mass communication and modern urban life. During the early sixties, for instance, he painted subjects such as gas stations, apartment buildings or logos, occasionally combined with words and comic-strip depictions. However, on the basis of his affinity with language, his experiments with peculiar materials and his photo books, his work is being regarded as conceptual art with increasing frequency.

Ruscha gained a reputation during the seventies particularly with his 'word' paintings, drawings and lithographs, in which he experimented not only with the typographical design of words, but also with materials that were entirely foreign to art. A distinct example of this is the work *Sand in the Vaseline* (1974), painted with egg yolk on a surface of silk. In paintings such as this, there is an odd relationship between that which is painted and that which is described. The words are clear but do not refer to the image. Word and image do not concur, but each maintains its own ground, which causes the discrepancy existing between the two languages to become visible in a heightened form.

In addition to these word paintings, Ruscha

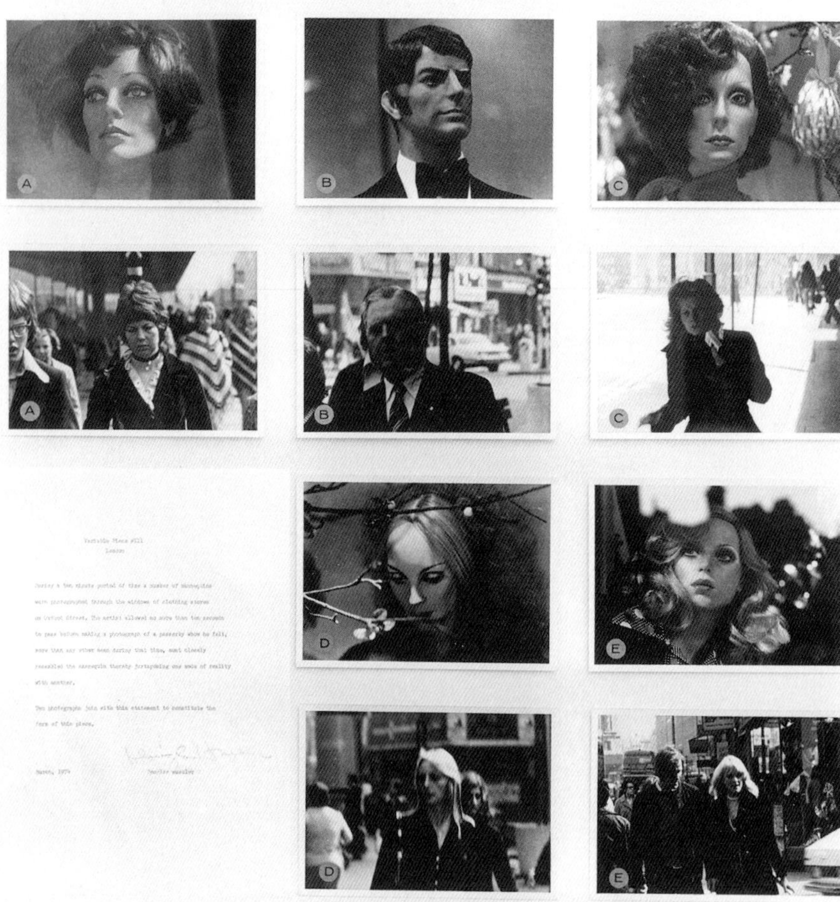

Douglas Huebler *Variable piece no. 111 London*, 1974

has produced a great number of photo books, whose inspiration is taken from the day-to-day culture and architecture of Los Angeles and in which photography is used by him in a nonaesthetic and functional manner.

The neutrality for which Ruscha strives in his photography can be compared to that of the German couple **Bernd and Hilla Becher**, who have been concentrating completely, since 1959, on photographing industrial architecture from around the turn of the century. They record functional buildings, such as gasworks, silos, factories, smokestacks, steelworks as well as half-timbered houses.

The project, which has remained virtually unchanged since the fifties, revolves around collecting, according to fixed guidelines, information that will lead to a better understanding of the form and the function of this architecture. For this purpose they have developed a method which guarantees a high degree of objectivity. They work, for instance, only in black-and-white and avoid coincidental and dramatic effects of light as well as any perspectival distortion. Bernd and Hilla Becher are therefore not interested in providing an artistic interpretation of reality, but rather wish to record this in as neutral a manner possible. The result of this documentary approach appears to be scientific. That idea is further emphasized by the way in which they present and group their photographs. The photographed subjects are classified according to type: criteria such as function, form and material constitute the main factors. Within these typological series, the artists then make groups of nine photographs, and each group serves as a 'display sheet' of the functional construction. "The photo groups have more to do with similarities than with differences. The make-up of the groups is determined by the family to which a photograph belongs. By looking at the photographs at the same time, one stores information as to the ideal type, which can be used the next time. One sees what aspects remain constant and thereby understands more about the function of the structure."

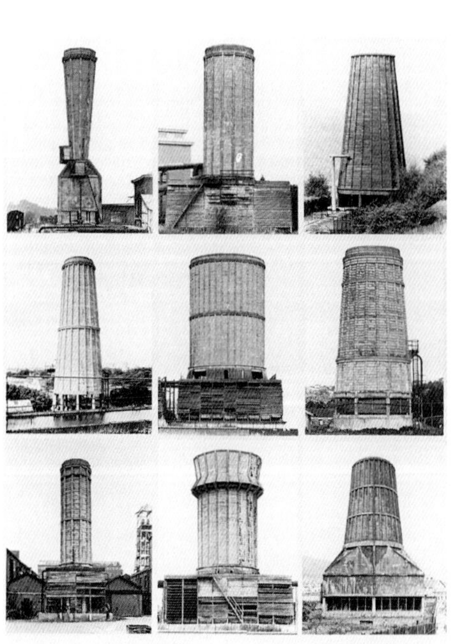

Bernd & Hilla Becher *Kühltürme Beton-Fertigteile*, 1963-75

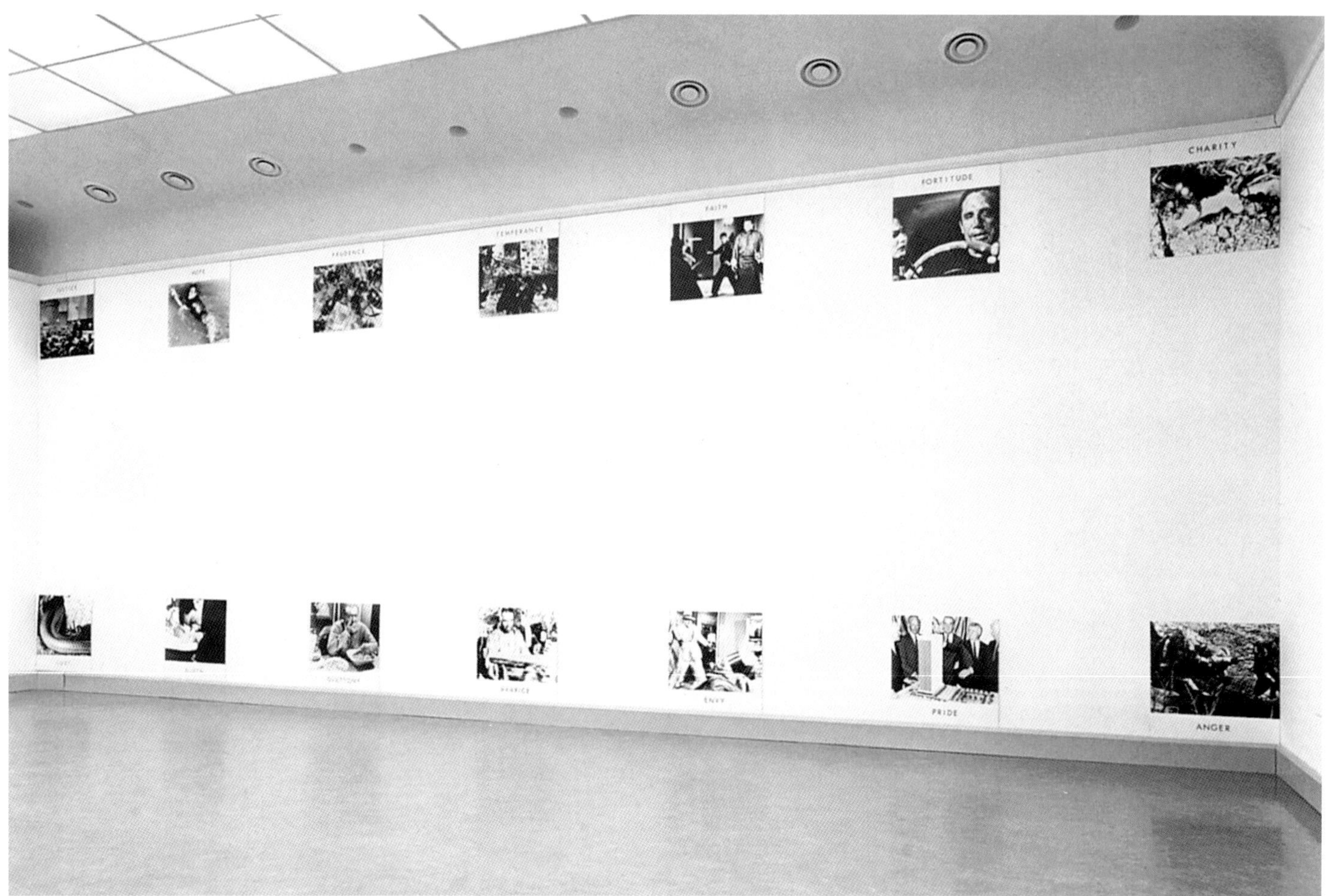

John **Baldessari** *Virtues and Vices (for Giotto)*, 1981

Despite the increasing concern for industrial archaeology in recent decades, Bernd and Hilla Becher attach no moral significance to their work. It does not arise on the basis of a nostalgic longing for the past, nor does it constitute a plea for the preservation of architectonic heritage.

Bernd and Hilla Becher make use of the documentary qualities of photography in order to provide insight on certain facets of reality. In this, they benefit particularly from the photograph's distinct capacity to appear to be a faithful and direct rendering of the visible world.

Other artists use this very quality as a means to manipulate the image of reality and then, within the realm of art and according to their own rules, reconstruct it. This applies, for instance, to the work of Douglas Huebler and John Baldessari, who exchanged the immediate experience of visible reality for the experience of a personal, mythical or potential one.

After having produced, for several years, paintings and sculptures that closely related to Minimal Art, **Douglas Huebler** rejected the artistic approach that led to the making of autonomous aesthetic objects. Instead he began to work in a conceptual manner by compiling a number of thematic series in which he combined various systems of documentation. Language and photography, for instance, function as interdependent systems of representation in Huebler's work; this makes it possible to investigate the way in which forms of communication influence the perception of reality. Furthermore, it enables the viewer to observe reality from many vantage points. Facets of reality that are normally not immediately perceptible are brought to light by being presented as recorded facts.

A clear example of this is the work *Variable piece no. 111 London* (1974) which is made up of ten photographs, accompanied by a typed text in which the artist describes his way of working as objectively as possible. The meanings of the relationships that Huebler registers and analyzes are dictated by these programmatic texts and exist only within the context of the work. Ostensibly coincidental similarities, encounters or occurrences are brought together on the basis of arbitrary criteria and thus allow the entire world to serve as the artist's subject matter. Huebler presents us with the all-encompassing capacity of conceptual art, as opposed to the exclusiveness of modernism. The scope of visual art is limitless; it constantly offers the artist and the viewer new ways in which to look at complex reality from an unfamiliar perspective.

The presentation of an alternative and ambiguous view of reality also plays a significant role in the work of **John Baldessari**. After having studied art history, Baldessari began, during the late fifties, to paint in a manner closely linked with Abstract Expressionism. But less than ten years later, he arrived at the idea that painting had come to an impasse, and he attempted to extricate himself from the stifling confinement of formalism. The continual rearrangement of colors and forms within a rectangular frame could no longer hold his interest: "There must be more to art than just that." Nurtured by this dissatisfaction, Baldessari decided, in 1970, to carry out a

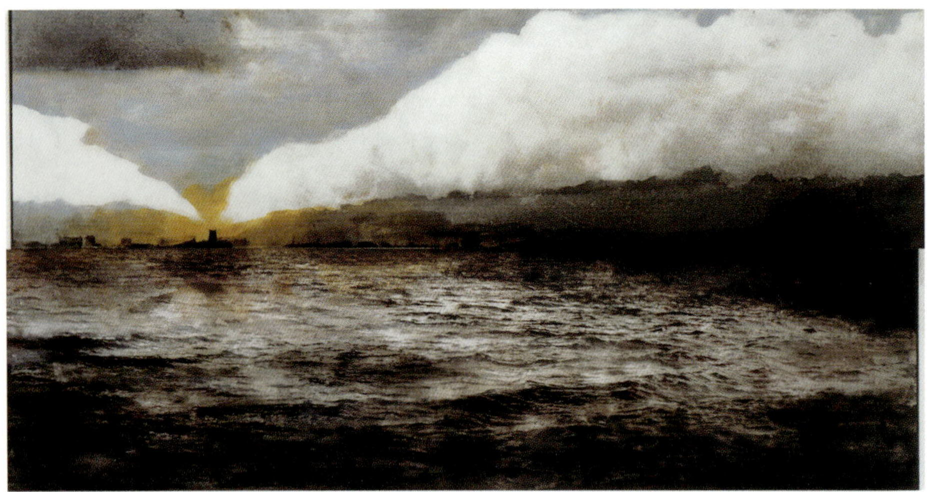

Ger van Elk *Het Kinselmeer (Stompe Toren bij Ransdorp)*, 1996

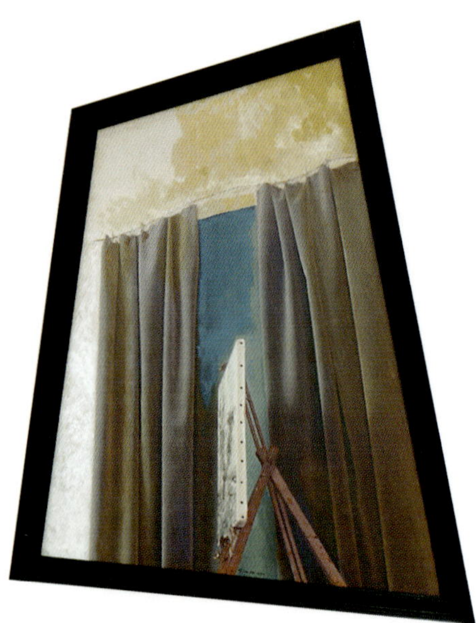

Ger van Elk *Adieu IV*, 1974

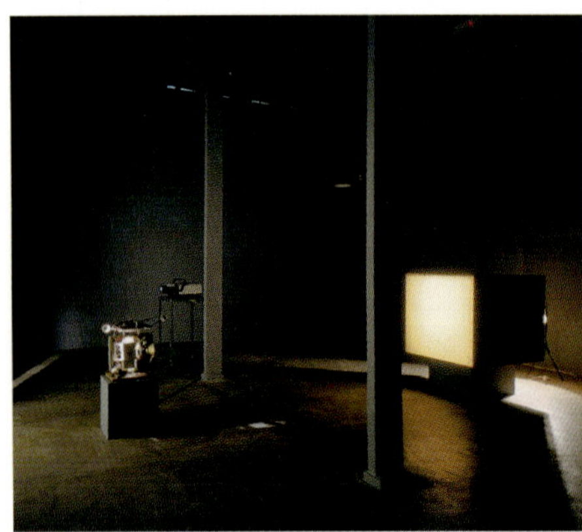

Ger van Elk *The Absorption of the Shadow*, 1969

radical act: he burned all of the works that he had produced from 1953 to 1966. The remaining ash was stored in book-shaped urns bearing the dates of the beginning and end of his painting.

Since deciding, in 1966, never to paint again, Baldessari has been working with texts and images that he takes from magazines, newspapers, the film industry and books. His preference for words and images from the popular visual culture of the twentieth century stems from the wish to undermine the elitist nature of the language of painting in favor of a visual language that speaks to all. This endeavor to democratize art is manifest in the statement-like work *Subject Matter* (1967-68), which resembles a do-it-yourself manual written by the artist. With lighthearted irony, Baldessari appeals to the viewer's imagination and receptiveness, transforming the very act of observation into a work of art.

On the basis of the idea that art is primarily about conveying a standpoint, he poses the question as to whether direct information, without the mediation of images, could equally serve as art. Baldessari uses language, therefore, not as a visual element but as something to be read. Moreover, he says that he is unable to prefer an image to a word, or a word to an image. He regards the two as being equivalent and interchangeable. Despite his refusal to prefer the image to the word, Baldessari began to show an increasing involvement with photography in his work throughout the eighties. In montages made up of photographs that seem similar from a formal point of view, though differing greatly in terms of content, Baldessari attempts to create a suggestive void which causes the

'reality' of the image to become disrupted. In addition to this, the antitheses 'good and evil', 'hate and love', 'truth and lies' frequently recur as themes that contribute to the mythical character of Baldessari's work to a substantial degree. This can be seen with the work *Virtues and Vices (for Giotto)* (1981), where such a polarity is portrayed and developed in a fragmentary series. Baldessari's inclination toward the paradoxical, the ambiguous, toward the mythologizing of reality causes his photographic works to become visual riddles. At first they seem to be fairly simple, yet on further consideration, they prove to be extremely complex. By means of the grouping and juxtaposition of different images, he constructs a new and ambiguous narrative in which truth and fiction can no longer be distinguished from each other. Not only Baldessari, but also **Ger van Elk** has frequently shown himself to be a master in the deliberate confusion of fiction and reality. Van Elk's highly varied body of work includes sculptures, films, photographic works and paintings, in which he aims to decondition perception by playing with the codes and conventions of visual art. More than once he has stressed the importance of the visual manifestation of his work in this respect: "The work must be good in terms of theme, in terms of comment, but I believe that it should be just as good in terms of its visual qualities."

A fascinating work in which Van Elk both analyzes and confuses perception is *The Absorption of the Shadow* (1969). Placed on a pedestal is a box, and across from this, a lamp is directed at the box. At the back of the box is shade. However, Van Elk has lit and filmed the box in such a way that shade can no longer be seen, and this film is projected, on a 1:1 scale, onto the shaded side of the box. As long as the film is running, the shade on the box is 'absorbed' by the projection. As soon as the film stops, the shade returns. Van Elk plays with twin concepts such as reality and illusion, eternity and ephemerality by briefly eliminating their contradiction, at least to the eye.

The work of Van Elk is primarily aimed at the manipulation of reality and its forms of representation. In order to disrupt the coded expectations with respect to the image, he has been making increasingly frequent use of photographic means since 1972. The characteristic *Adieu* series, for instance, is comprised of five paintings in gouache and ink on a photographic surface. The format of these works is not traditionally rectangular but trapezoidal, which emphasizes the

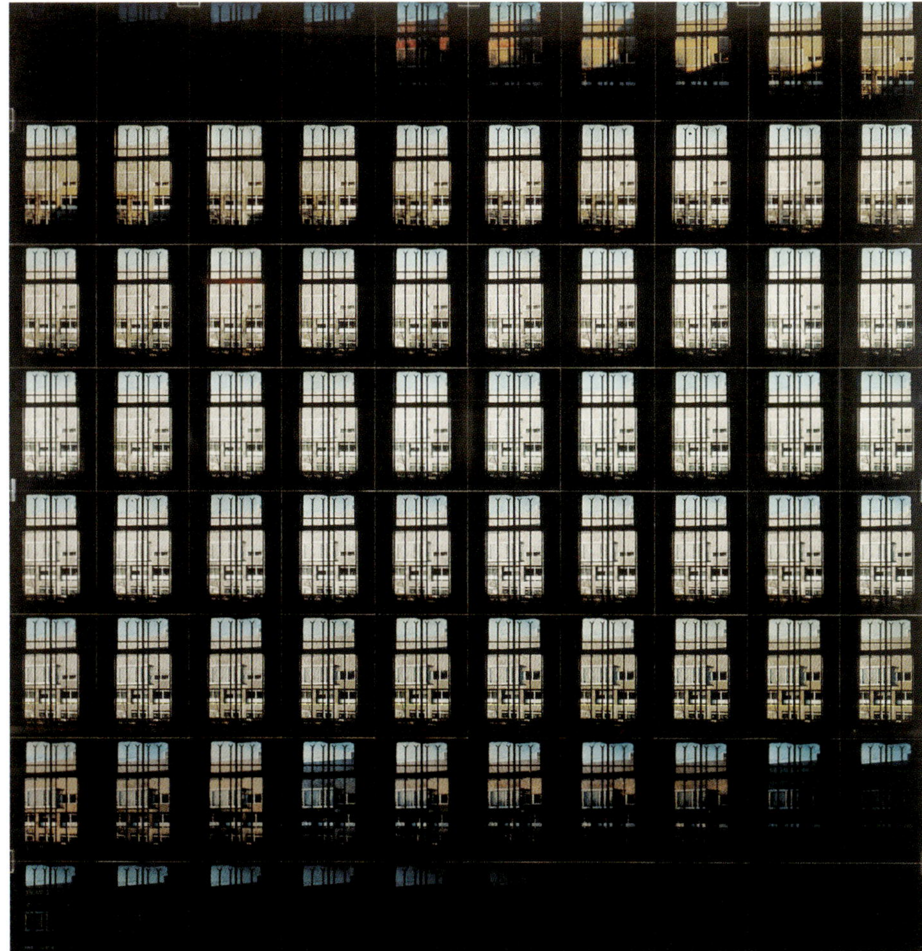

Jan Dibbets *The Shortest Day at the Van Abbemuseum*, 1970

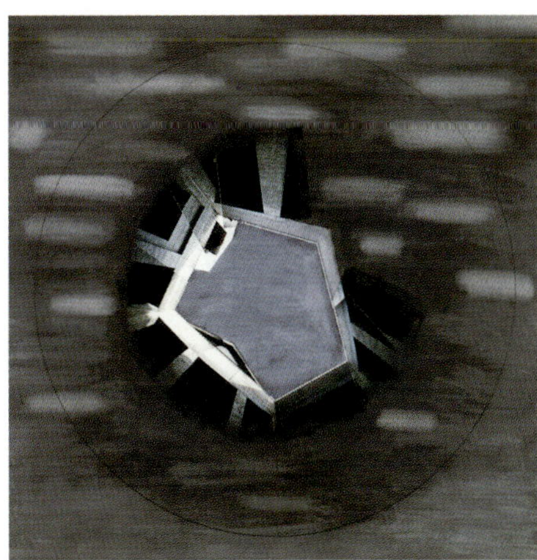

Jan Dibbets *Claustra I*, 1986

layer of light-sensitive substance on paper. Van Elk is fascinated with the artificial character of photography and with its capacity to evoke an impression of realness despite its shiny surface. By contrasting the photographed image with abstractions in paint, he wishes to expose the deceptiveness of photography.

Whereas the work of Van Elk deals primarily with art historical conventions that influence perception, that of **Jan Dibbets** focuses mainly on the process of perception. Since 1967 Dibbets has been producing photographic works in which the perception of reality and the portrayal of space, color, light and structure constitute the main themes. He is particularly concerned with problems of visual perception that have determined, to a significant degree, the development of the painterly tradition. The most important aspects of this are the organization of space and perspective within the flat surface, nuances of color, visual structure and the treatment of light. With the aid of photography's specific qualities, Dibbets deals with these classical themes in an innovative manner.

Dibbets began his career as an abstract painter, influenced by such figures as Giotto, Vermeer, Saenredam and Mondrian. His last paintings were serial geometric works in space, whereby he attempted to record the observation simultaneously from changing vantage points. In 1967 he spent six months studying at the St. Martin's School of Art in London, where he came to know artists such as Richard Long, Hamish Fulton and Gilbert & George. Shortly after this he began to produce sculptural interventions in the landscape.

By photographing his sculptural interventions, Dibbets developed his concept of 'perspective correction'. The perspective corrections consist of trapeziodal forms which have been applied to the floor, the wall, in grass or in dirt and which seem, from the fixed viewpoint of the camera, to be perfect squares. Once photographed, these squares hover, as it were, above the ground and constitute part of the surface of the photograph. In these works Dibbets investigated the paradoxical nature of illusion and reality. The reality of the seemingly natural observation is juxtaposed with a physical or conceptual reality.

Another important aspect of Dibbets's work is his fascination with ideas such as movement, light and time. During the seventies, for instance, he produced a series of works in which the notion of time is made visible as the movement of light. Dibbets

object-like status of the painting. The combination of gouache, ink and photography gives Van Elk, at the same time, the ability to underscore the artificial character of the work. By ingeniously toying with the various levels of reality, Van Elk shows the artwork as being a staged and suggestive reality. This idea is taken further in *Adieu IV* (1974) with the rendering of a painting within a painting, which is in turn is partly hidden behind a stage curtain. While the format and the form of the painting emphasize the fact that the artwork is an object unto itself, the image affirms its fictitious nature.

In works such as these Van Elk uses painting not to create an image, but rather to deconstruct the apparent reality of the image. Photography's outstanding suitability with respect to this endeavor has to do with the contradictions that lie at the very heart of this medium. While the photograph provides, on one hand, a faithful, objective depiction of reality, it is, on the other, no more than a thin

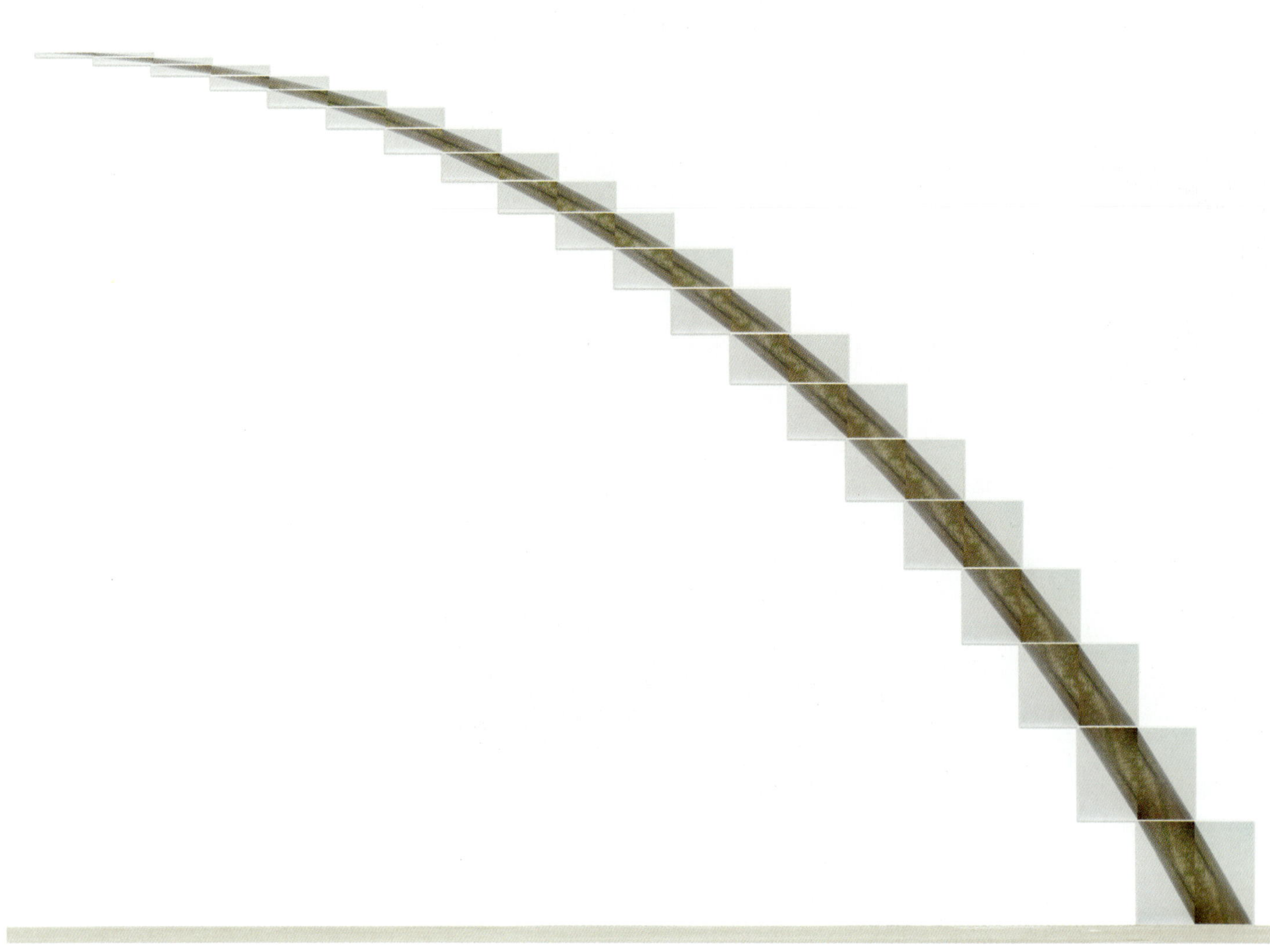

Jan Dibbets *Big Comet 3°-60°, sky / land / sky,* 1973

registered the passing of time by photographing, at set intervals, the incidence of light in a space and arranging these photographs into series. This principle is also inherent in the work *The Shortest Day at the Van Abbemuseum* (1970). The subject of this work is the perception of a visual element–the window–throughout changes in the incidence of light. In order to gain control of the passage of time, Dibbets mounted the photographs into a series which makes that sequence readable.

Closely related to this is a work in which the relationships between time, space and movement constitute a key element: *Big, Comet 3°-60°, sky / land / sky,* (1973). Here the artist produced a series of photographs of the horizon, where land and sky part. For each new photograph of this typically Dutch,

almost abstract landscape, the camera was turned a single degree. He then mounted the photographs, two by two, upside down and right-side up, causing the sky to be at the top and then at the bottom of the image surface. The slightly curved line of the horizon thus became an elongated spiral. Eventually Dibbets printed the pairs of photographs in various sizes and mounted them into a long, upwardly tapering curve. The form of the work and the movement suggested by the montage correspond to the image of a comet streaking across the sky. The formal structure of such works is not dependent on direct perception, but is abstract and, in that sense, corresponds to Dibbets's pursuit of a thoroughly optical art, which is completely abstract at the same time.

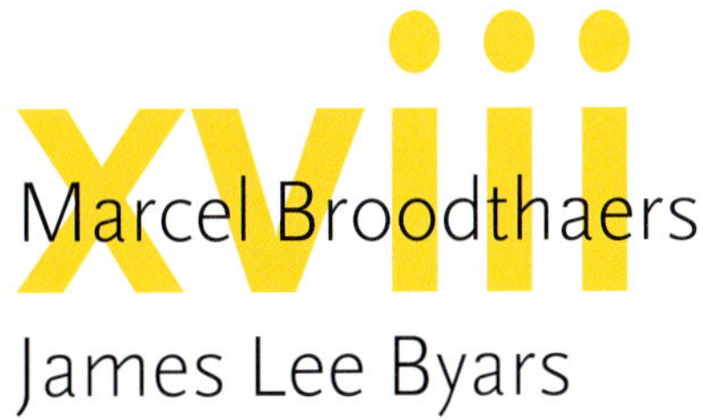

Marcel Broodthaers
James Lee Byars

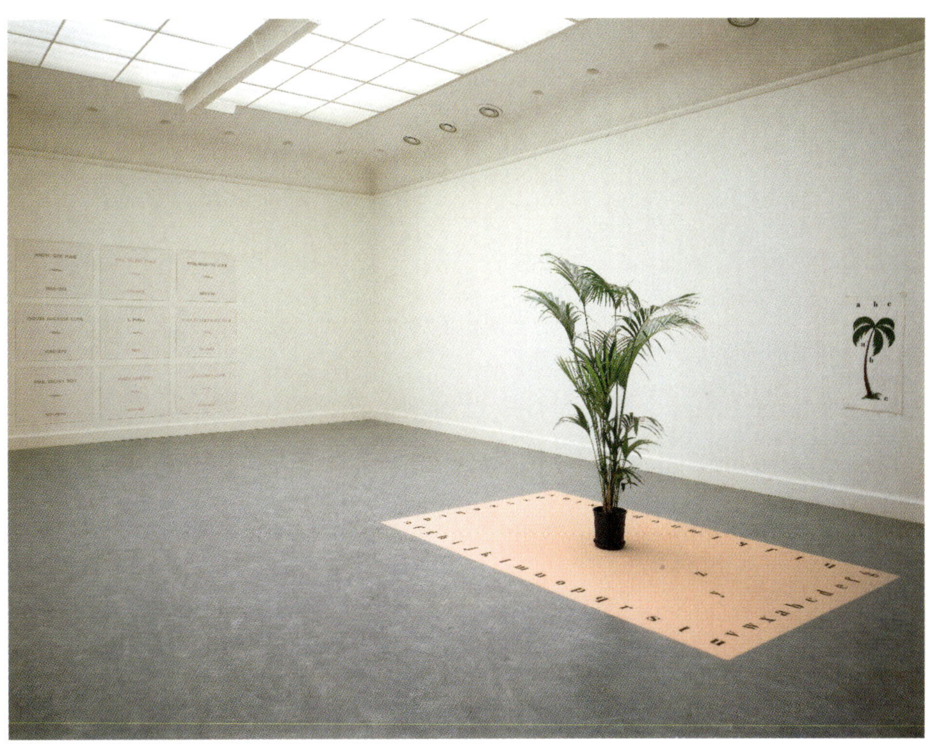

Marcel Broodthaers *Série de neuf tableaux*, 1972; *Tapis de Sable*, 1974

Marcel Broodthaers, the poet who became a visual artist yet always remained a poet, the saboteur, the artist on the fringe or the charlatan: these are only a few of examples of attempts to pinpoint Broodthaers's position within contemporary art. His comprehensive body of work consists of the highly varied products of his work as a journalist, painter, filmmaker, photographer and visual artist. The choice of one particular profession, as he said, was something he preferred to put off until after his death.

Even so, in 1964 Broodthaers took the decisive step to become a visual artist and announced his carefully staged debut in this world with the following words: "I, too, wondered if I couldn't sell something and have success in life. For quite a time now, nothing has worked for me. I am forty years old…Ultimately, the idea of thinking up something unusual gave me strength, and I immediately got to work. After three months went by, I showed my work to Ph. Edouard Toussaint, owner of the gallery Saint Laurent. 'Why, this is art,' he said, 'and I'd even be glad to exhibit it.' Okay, I answered him. If I sell something, he gets 30%. Those are, it appears, normal terms; certain galleries get 75%. What are they? Objects actually."

These provocative words already set the tone that would characterize the greater part of his work: ironic, critical, humorous and complex.

With this statement he mocked not only the object-like character of the artwork or the presumed integrity of the artist, but also the commercial interests that control the art world. Until his death in 1976 Broodthaers dealt with, in a distinct but disguised way, the current circumstances that determine the way in which art functions. This was done by him, however, not from an external point of view by means of written art criticism, but from an internal one, by way of his own work. Like a wolf in sheep's clothing, he became involved in the art scene in order to be able, at just the right moment, in front of the right audience, to cast off his disguise and terrify the people of that world. An important aspect of this, though, was Broodthaers's refusal to give priority to his undermining strategies, to sacrifice the artistic and poetic qualities of his work for an effect. Because of this, his work is never heavy-handed or moralistic, but playful, poetic, elegant and intelligent.

In his short career of twelve years, Broodthaers managed to assume a key position within the history of contemporary art. He did so not as a representative of a particular movement, but as an artist on the fringe–as an artist who appropriated the visual means of his time while maintaining, at the same time, a certain distance. And it is this very distance which gives his art its pointed character.

Despite his preference for the topical issues related to the making of art, the work of Broodthaers conveys a nostalgic atmosphere, which is brought about to a significant degree by the many references to Western art of past centuries–to that of the nineteenth century in particular. He made, for instance, frequent use of literary forms that proved, during that century, to be preeminently suited to critical reflection on man and nature. Examples of these are the bestiary, the fable and the fictional account of a journey.

In addition to this, he often referred to nineteenth-century writers, poets and artists whom he regarded as kindred spirits from the past. In *Série de neuf tableaux* (1972) the names Gide, Valéry, Baudelaire, Ducasse and Lautréamont appear along side those of Magritte and Broodthaers himself, who is concealed behind the personal pronoun *il*. The names have been combined with years indicating the particular person's year of birth and year of death and with verbs alluding to particular activities: *fume, boit, écrit, peint, parle* and *copie*. While the combination of the name and year is acknowledged as being a 'true' fact, Broodthaers seems to have erred with respect to the verb. Although…is it not true that Magritte was just as much a writer as he was a painter, that Baudelaire painted with words and that Lautréamont and Ducasse were actually copyists because they are one and the same person? Broodthaers punishes our desire for the unambiguous by organizing things on the basis of his own criteria. Broodthaers's fascination with the nineteenth century is expressed not only in these '*Peintures litteraires*' but also in the slide projections, which served as the basis for a series of five exhibitions held at the Van Abbemuseum from 1992 to 1993. A great many of these slide works consisted of pictures and illustrations that have their origins in nineteenth-century lithography. The title *Images d'Epinal*, for example, refers to the countless series of images produced at the Pellerin picture-card factory in the French town of Epinal. The popularity of these series is evident not only from the huge numbers of them that were produced, but also from the term *image d'Epinal* which continues to be used in French as a synonym for the stereotypical image. In Broodthaers's slide series, the nineteenth-century illustrations are extracted from their original contexts, whereby they become not only whimsical, comical and absurd but also literally seem to demand a new story. By bringing them together on the basis of personal associations and a logic of his own, the artist transformed his projections into visual poems that occur in time.

The same can be said about the series *Ombres Chinoises* (1973-74) whose images come from the world of visual art, the comic strip, the adventure story and the popular-science book. A great number of slides show fascinating natural phenomena such as meteorite craters, volcanic eruptions and solar eclipses. There are also all sorts of references to natural and mechanical forms of reproduction, such as the reflection, the shadow, photography and lithography. Broodthaers alternates these images with slides containing the text '*Verboden te fotograferen*' (Photography Prohibited). The irony of these words becomes clear when one realizes that the entire projection consists of reproductions of borrowed images. Broodthaers has ignored the prohibition and used the reproductions for the assemblage of an authentic and original work of art. Furthermore, the combination of images from different realms causes the series to have the appearance of a visual analysis of the imagery. For while they refer to the same things, the image presented to us by science is of a completely different nature than that of the comic strip or of visual art.

The analysis of language, by which the world is not only designated but also interpreted, is equally central to the slide work *ABC-ABC Image* (1974). In this simultaneous projection, Broodthaers shows letters and images as they are used in order to familiarize children with language as a way of attributing meaning. By means of language, one can become acquainted with the world. Things are designated, distinguished from each other and classified: one is able to speak about them. Language determines the way in which reality appears to us and provides us, on the level of that very language, with the ability to share meaning. Broodthaers constantly aimed to show the subjectivity of language and to end its domination of the world of things and images. The strategy that he employs in order to achieve this includes, among other things, the portrayal of language as an arbitrary convention, in which chance plays a essential role. The order of the letters projected in *ABC-ABC Image* seem so arbitrary that chance could, in fact, almost be outruled. The slide images, in which letters are joined to form the words 'Fine Arts', constitute an exception to this. Several letters in these words have been replaced by a depiction: the 'e' is substituted with an 'eagle', the 'a' with an 'ass', the 'i' with an 'inkstand' and the 't' with a 'toy'. The choice of these substitutions is indeed prescribed by the letter blocks themselves, but this is by no means arbitrary. The eagle is, after all, frequently used by Broodthaers as a symbol

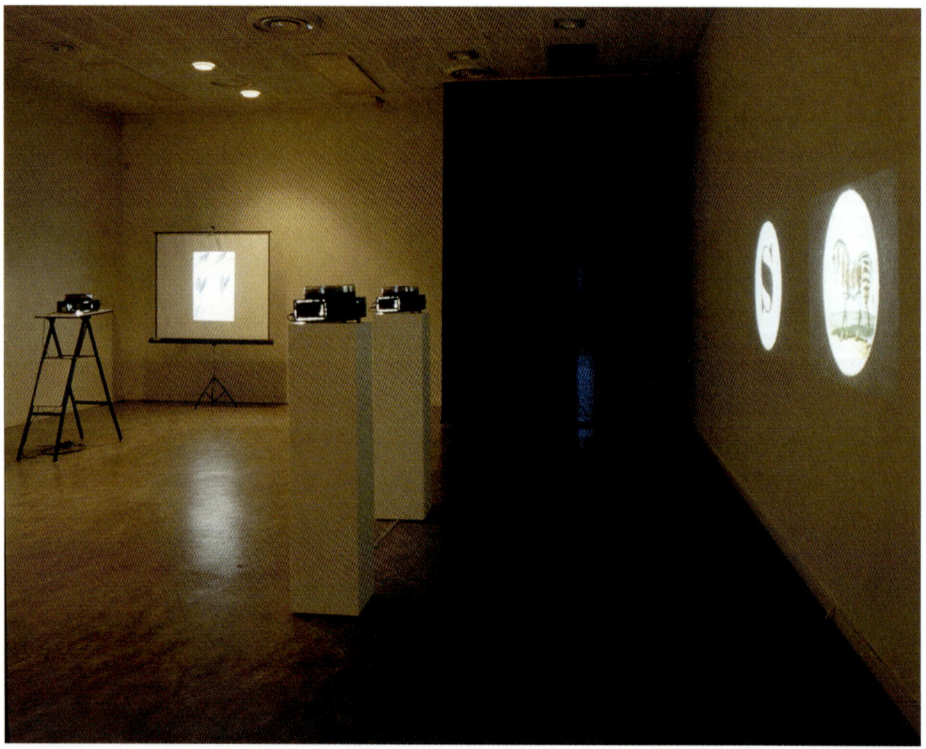

Marcel Broodthaers *ABC – ABC Image*, 1974; *Sex-Film*, 1971-72

of power and domination, whereas the ass, or donkey, is generally regarded as a metaphor for stupidity. The toy moreover alludes to the game and to chance, and the inkstand to the language of the written word. In this virtually offhanded manner, Broodthaers turns his slide projection into a cryptic game that demonstrates both the power and the capriciousness of language.

Broodthaers's fondness for the concealment of meanings also lies at the heart of his projection *Sex Film* (1971-72) which rouses the curiosity of many viewers by way of its title. The projection does not consist of pornographic images, however, but of slides containing words, abbreviations, punctuation marks and symbols, all written or drawn by hand. Texts such as 'Sex-Film', '25 D.M.' and 'Museum' are accompanied and alternated by arrows seeming to point the way to a world of sex, money and art, were it not for the fact that they constantly contradict each other with their opposing directions. In this series Broodthaers plays cunningly with the expectations of the viewer, leaving him empty-handed time and again. The frequent indication 'Fig.', for instance, is normally used in didactic literature in order to bring about a connection between the word and the depiction. In Broodthaers's work the term only gives rise to uncertainty. Symbols, signs and words appear to have been robbed of their usual meanings due to the absence of a meaningful context. The slide series of Broodthaers consequently resembles a riddle that suggests all sorts of solutions, though it remains ambiguous and unsolvable at the same time.

His slide projections constitute visual poems, for which the keys to interpretation are largely missing. Because the basis on which the images have been brought together remains unknown and can never be explained in full, there emerges a poetic and wondrous universe that evokes many associations for the viewer. At the same time, there is always room for the critical ideas that are raised by the artist in his works. Broodthaers seems, therefore, to be constantly looking for new forms of language that enable him to express both his critical and his poetic spirit.

It was most likely this same aspiration which gave rise to the work *La Pluie (Projet pour un texte)*. In this two-minute film, Broodthaers is seen writing at a small table in his garden. The rain is falling more and more heavily, so that writing gradually becomes impossible. The paper is wet, the ink is running and the artist becomes completely drenched. Nevertheless, he steadfastly goes on writing,

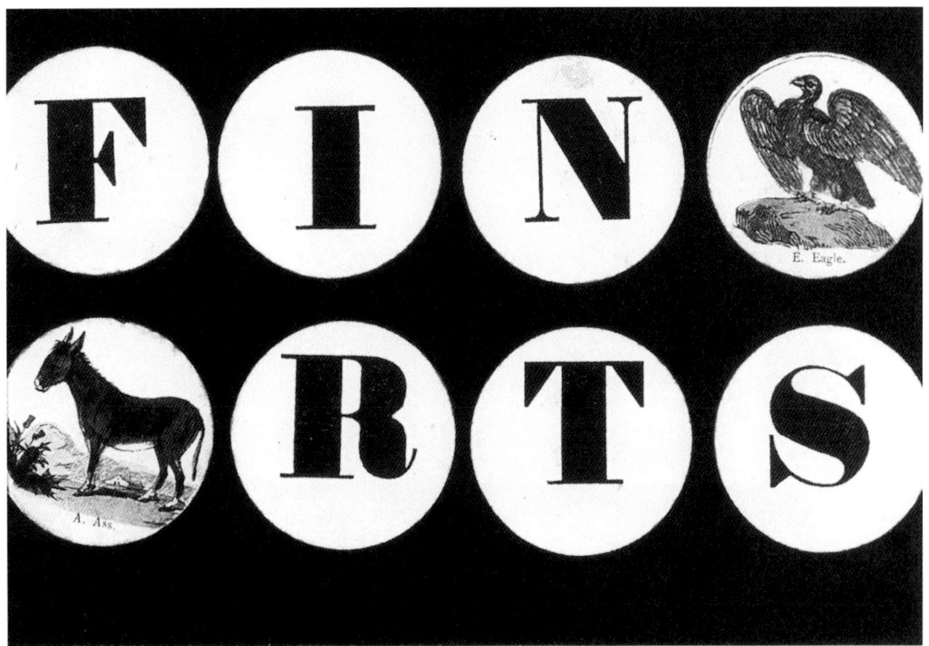

Marcel Broodthaers *ABC-ABC Image*, 1974

signs the text that has disappeared in the meantime and, only then, puts down his pen. The film *La Pluie (Projet pour un texte)* can be regarded as a metaphor for the transition undergone by Broodthaers from being a poet to becoming a visual artist. The impossibility of finding an audience for his poetry becomes the subject of a film, which tells this story at a rate of twenty-four images per minute.

At the same time, this work clearly shows how Broodthaers ignored or crossed the boundaries between the different disciplines and always refused to conform to prevailing traditions or views. In response to the question as to whether film still had a future, Broodthaers defined his position as an artist as follows: "I do not believe in film or in any other form of art. I do not believe in the unique artist or in the unique work of art. I believe in phenomena and in people who bring ideas together."

As a key figure within the conceptual tendency in art history, Broodthaers plays a significant role in the collection of the Van Abbemuseum. In addition to a great number of prints, several multiples of embossed plastic and the works mentioned above, the museum has owned, since 1993, the very important and massive installation *Tapis de Sable* (1974).

Broodthaers's work is characterized by enormous complexity and multiple levels of meaning, which makes it difficult to isolate works. He was constantly building on the basis of previous works or themes, regarding his exhibitions as works in themselves and presenting his poems, open letters, interviews and catalogues as essential aspects of his art. Just as the poet has the capacity to use the same words, over and again, for the creation of poetry, Broodthaers drew upon his body of work, as a visual vocabulary which remained at his disposal. Due to the continual reworking of material, one can speak of a constant deepening and often very subtle shift of meanings.

Broodthaers believed that a new notion of art could arise from a critical investigation of the context in which the artwork functions. During the years 1974-1975, this principle took shape in a series of six retrospective exhibitions, which can be seen as the highlights of this investigation. In these exhibitions, to which he referred as *Décor*, he presented his own works in the most explicit manner, as elements of an open discussion. On various levels and in various forms, new and existing works were brought together within the comprehensive context of the exhibition. In display cases, installations and rooms Broodthaers created complex ensembles in which he revived the function of his works.

The idea of *décor* brings to mind the world of theater and film. It alludes to the temporal and spatial background against which events take place and from which things as well as actions derive their meaning. Broodthaers's décors are, similarly, not an end in themselves but, rather, have come about on

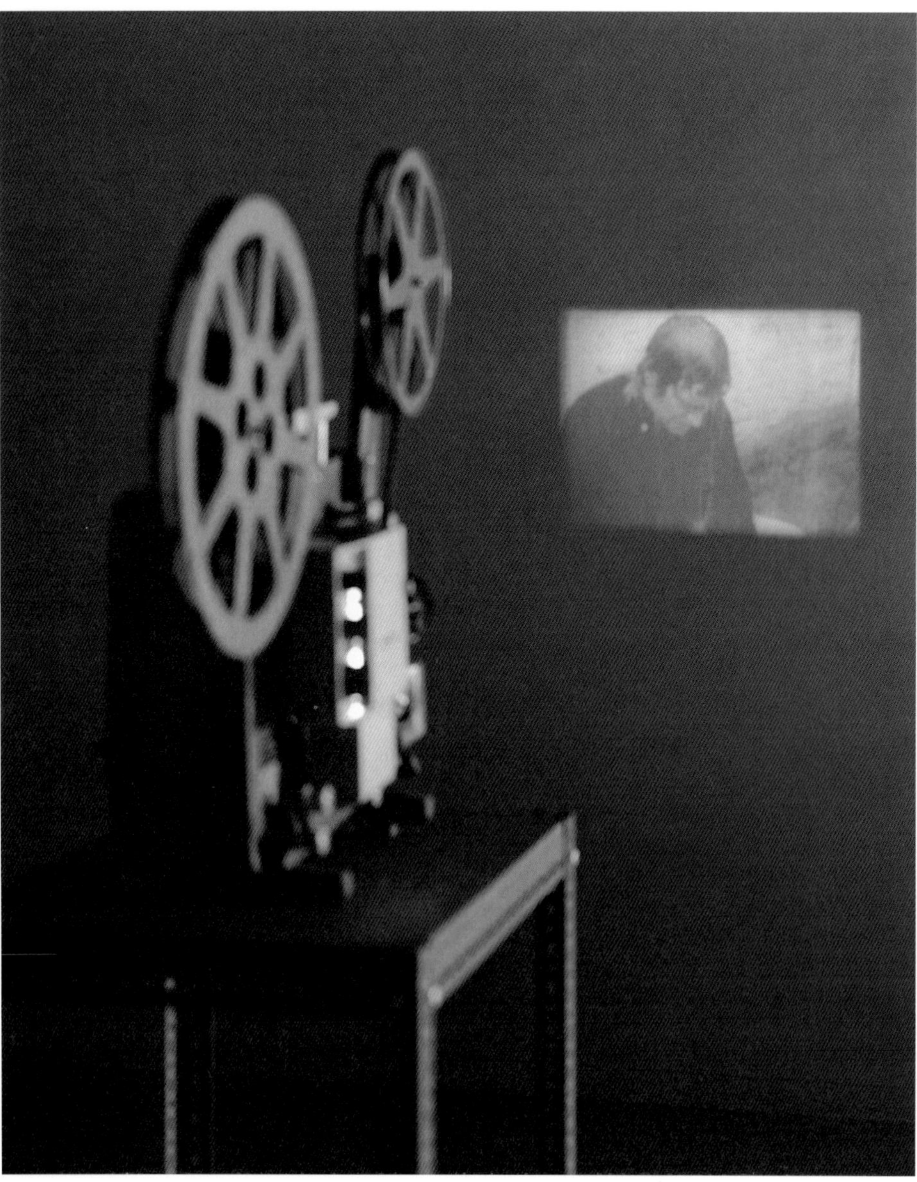

Marcel Broodthaers *La Pluie (Projet pour un texte)*, 1969

the basis of the historical and social context within which he wished to give his work new topicality.

The installation *Tapis de Sable* has its origins in Broodthaers's first décor exhibition, held at the Brussels Paleis voor Schone Kunsten in 1974. The work consists of a rectangular carpet of pale-pink sand, in the center of which a large palm has been placed. The letters of the alphabet have been applied in dark-brown sand along the edges of the carpet. Hanging on the wall is a terry-cloth 'canvas' displaying the image of a palm tree and, two times, the first three letters of the alphabet.

A number of aspects of Broodthaers's work come together in *Tapis de Sable*. There is, for instance, his fascination with the interrelationship of words, images and objects which, as representatives of different notational systems, refer to the same world. In this work he brings about an encounter between the real object (the palm), its depiction (on the terry-cloth canvas) and the letters of the alphabet that are used for the naming of things. At the same time, he shows the letters as being independent elements, detached from the conventional context of language. By treating words, images and objects as equivalent elements, Broodthaers undermined the potential for immediately recognizable and clear-cut meaning.

Along with this, one could consider the work a criticism of the role of the museum and of the presumed autonomy of the artist. *Tapis de Sable* conjures forth an image of emptiness and associations with a deserted island. It is the image of an isolated world in which one is scarcely reminded of the social, economic or political reality that lies beyond it. Broodthaers transformed his work into a metaphor for the museum, as the very place in which the separation of life and art, of the social and the artistic, is upheld.

In 1974 the work was carried out by a sand-carpet artist from Hekelgem, in Flanders, where this particular discipline has been practiced since the nineteenth century. In an interview Broodthaers stressed that the work was a result of a fusion of creative powers which, in fact, can be found anywhere. And from this point of view, the work could be seen as a reaction to the myths of originality and authenticity, which continue to dominate the history of art to this day. This idea is manifest time and again with each presentation of the work, because afterwards the palm vanishes into someone's living room and the sand is carefully swept up. Broodthaers may have remained a poet, but his vocabulary consists of images. The theoretical implications of his critical and ironic art are therefore also evident through the images, on the basis of the visual and poetic qualities of the work itself.

The raising of issues related to the fundamentals of modern art characterizes not only the work of Marcel Broodthaers, but also that of his equally controversial fellow artists and friends Joseph Beuys and James Lee Byars. None of these three artists can be classified under one particular term or movement; they were artists as well as critics, and it was not only through their work but also by way of their fascinating personalities that they influenced the history of twentieth-century art in a significant manner. But while poetry, wonder and irony were key elements for Broodthaers, the life of Byars was centered around the attainment of absolute beauty, perfection, the sublime.

James Lee Byars was an exceptional, sensational figure who stood out wherever he went by being dressed in monochrome suits of white, pink, red, black or gold material, a matching hat and a mask covering all or half of his face. In this extravagant garb he would appear, like a magician, at almost every opening of an important international exhibition and carry out his performances or 'actions'. And yet, despite his striking and unforgettable appearance, few people have ever spoken with him or even heard him speak, for Byars preferred to remain silent or to whisper almost inaudibly. It was as though he wished to be as far away as possible,

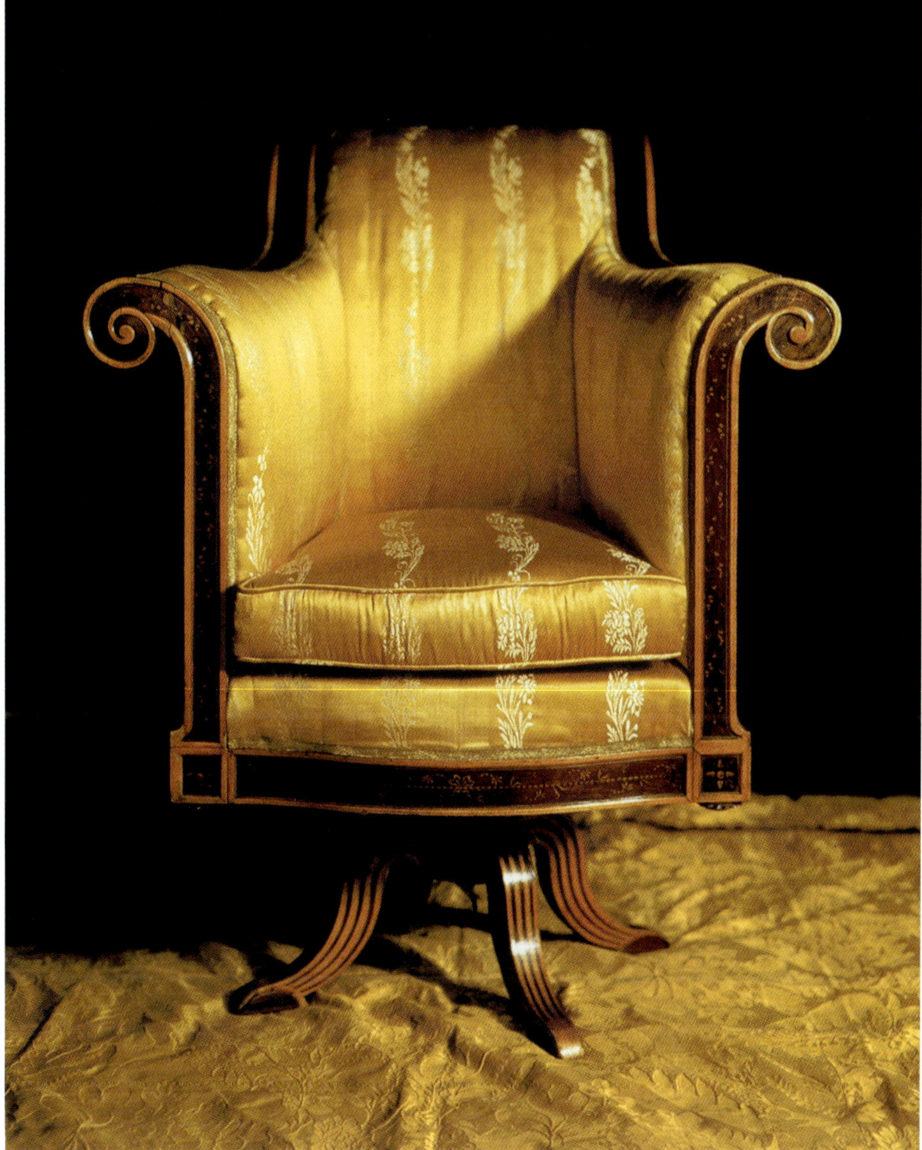

James Lee Byars *Hear TH FI TO IN PH Around This Chair (Hear The First Totally Interrogative Philosophy Around This Chair)*, 1978

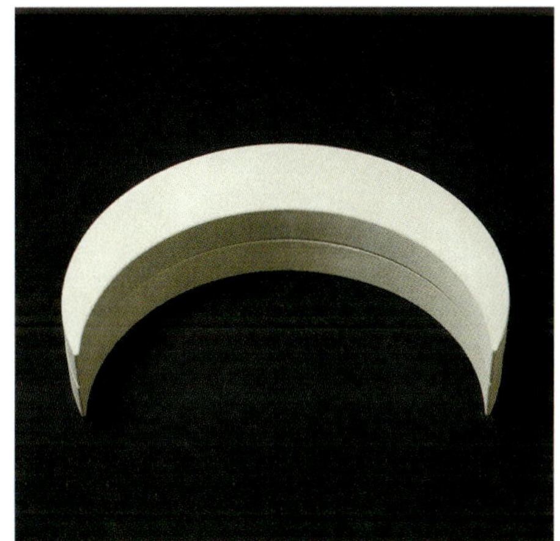

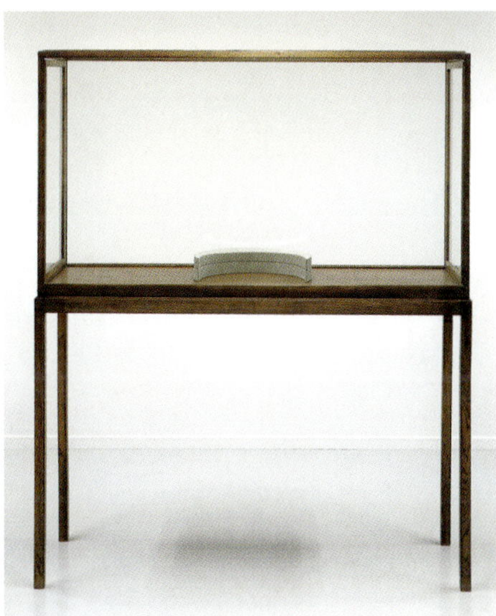

James Lee Byars *Moonbook*, 1980

regardless of the visual impression evoked by his presence. In the eyes of Byars, presence was no more than a particular form of absence–and not the most interesting one. The soundless convergence of his persona and his work became an evident choice; at the Venice Biennial of 1980, for instance, he appeared in a pink suit and handed out small pink slips of paper on which the words 'Be Quiet' were written by hand.

The sculptures and installations of Byars are never mundane, but tranquil and solemn in character, whereby he underscores the aural aspect of his art. He had a fondness for refined and costly materials, such as gold, silk, marble, velvet, glass and gems. Moreover, he preferred to exhibit his work in elegant display cases on long legs, as can be

seen with the sandstone sculpture *Moonbook* from 1980. The 'book' consists of two crescent-moon-shaped stones, one on top of the other, which would form a perfect circle or full moon when 'opened'. The smoothly polished shapes, which seem to hold cosmic mystery, are the result of Byars's continual search for perfect and absolute form and for the right way in which to present it. Aside from this, the performances and 'actions' of Byars were also carried out, by himself or others, with a great feeling for atmosphere, ceremony and theatricality. His many years of residence in the Japanese city of Kyoto, where he studied art and philosophy and became familiar with Zen Buddhism and Nō, undoubtedly contributed to the development and refinement of his magical and mystifying language of forms.

The art and the life of James Lee Byars were completely devoted to a quest for perfection, as evident from the titles, for instance, that he gave to his works and exhibitions: *The Perfect Moment*, *The Perfect Thought*, *The Perfect Whisper* or *The Perfect Smile*. In 1960 he spent twelve days poring over one hundred white eggs until he had found the roundest and the whitest one. And later, in Munich, he placed one hundred identical, white marble balls at equal distances on the floor of a whitewashed museum space. The work, given the title *Thinking Field*, has a commanding presence due to the purity of the marble, the absolute uniformity of the balls and the extreme precision of their placement.

Byars has sought perfection by asking or raising the right questions. The question, to him, is preferable to the answer, because it is open and indeterminate. By placing a question mark at the end of a statement, he imbues it with life and poetry. This is perhaps the reason for his affinity with Plato, who wrote his dialogues by allowing a new question to follow every answer. It may also be the reason for his preoccupation with death, which is, after all, the greatest question of all.

Included in the collection of the Van Abbemuseum is the majestic work *Hear TH FI TO IN PH Around This Chair*, or 'Hear The First Totally Interrogative Philosophy Around This Chair', from 1978. This installation was shown for the first time at the Marian Goodman Gallery in New York, concurrently with an exhibition of work by Marcel Broodthaers. In a completely darkened space closed off with a black curtain, the floor is covered with glistening gold silk and a stately chair is upholstered in this gold silk. The black color of the curtain surrounding the chair seems to absorb any thought generated or any question posed here. In the infinite black and the absolute silence lies full knowledge.

When a long-anticipated death came to Byars in 1997, he left behind relatively few concrete works of art. The greater part of his work was made of perishable material or had a temporary character, like the performances and 'actions' which were documented only on rare occasions.

Furthermore, he had confined himself for many years to working with paper or cloth, and the writing of cryptic letters and short poetic statements had become integral to his life and work. Every day he had written to friends, colleagues, collectors and curators throughout the entire world. The elegant letters of his school handwriting, which he liked best in gold on a black background, are decorated with five-point stars that make reading difficult. It is as difficult to read his words as it is to hear his whispers; the utmost concentration is required.

James Lee Byars was a shaman, an aesthete, a magician and a philosopher. In the present-day history of art, he has always remained an outsider, however, because the absolute beauty to which he aspired is a quality regarded with distrust. In the art of today, the magic word is, after all, not beauty but meaning, and the artwork is subject to elaborate examination, analysis and interpretation. The work of Byars does not ask to be understood, however, but experienced. It demands our complete attention and obtains this by way of its tranquil form and simplicity. The reward for this follows in sublime moments of enlightenment.

XIX

Barry Flanagan

Hamish Fulton

Richard Long

Ian Hamilton Finlay

Gilbert & George

Tony Cragg

Anish Kapoor

Boyd Webb

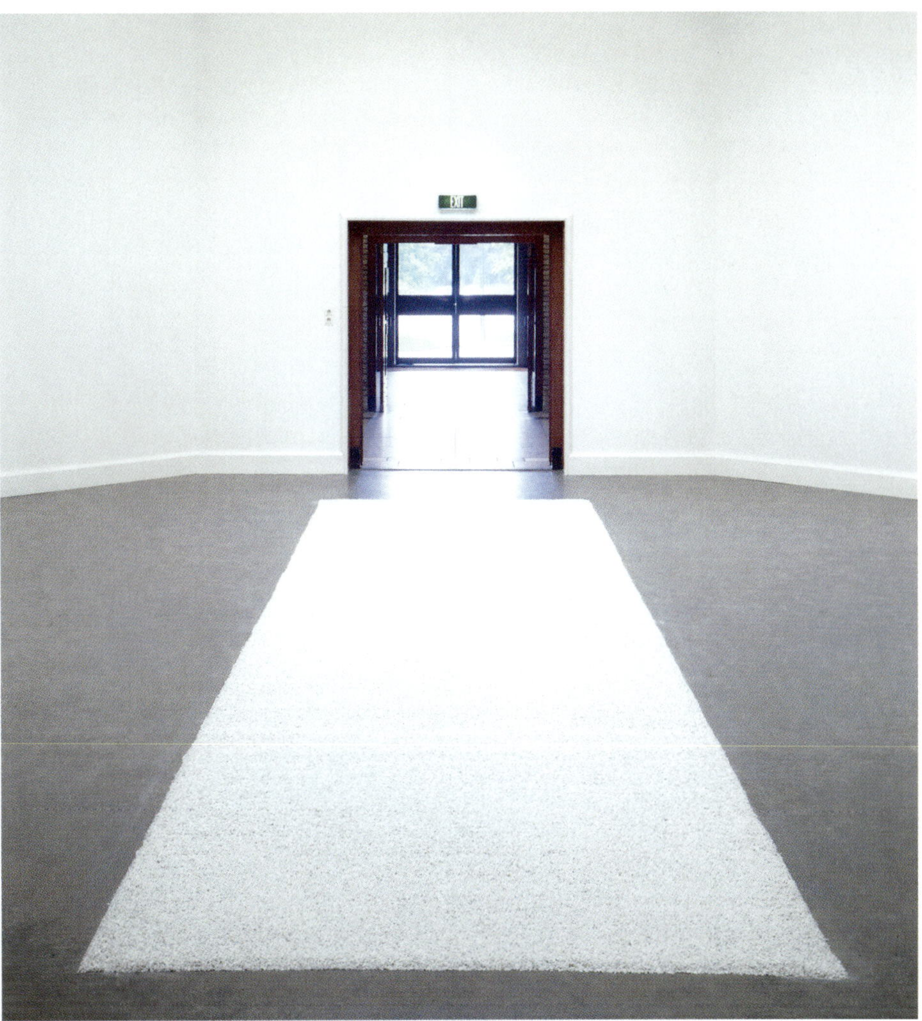

Richard Long *White Marble Line*, 1986

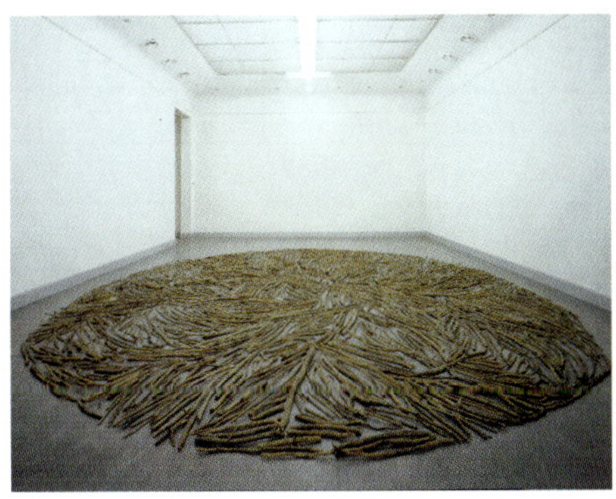

Richard Long *Wood Circle*, 1977

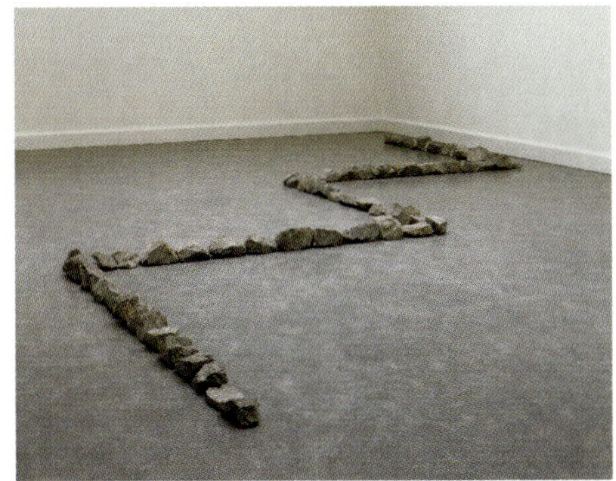

Richard Long *Sixty Stones*, 1975

Though there has certainly been no lack of good painting from Great Britain since the Second World War, it is nevertheless British sculpture which has drawn the most attention from an international point of view. This is moreover discernible in the collection of the Van Abbemuseum, in which British sculpture is amply represented. Not included in the collection is work by the older artists, such as Henry Moore, Barbara Hepworth and Anthony Caro, but indeed present is the sculpture of the somewhat later artists, who developed their work on the basis of a strong opposition to that tradition and took inspiration from tendencies such as Minimal Art, Conceptual Art and Land Art.

It was particularly the formal and aesthetic conventions of Anthony Caro that drew a strong reaction from younger artists. Since 1953 Caro had held a teaching position at London's St. Martin's School of Art, among whose students were Gilbert & George, Barry Flanagan, Hamish Fulton, Richard Long, Victor Burgin, Bruce McLean as well as Jan Dibbets.

Stimulated in part by the great social changes of the late sixties, sculpture and photography involved a range of new possibilities. Sculpture no longer appeared to be tied to a particular use of material or to an aesthetic form but, instead, could show a process or articulate a particular place, enter into a relationship with nature, with photography and with language, with human activities or with life itself. Those revolutionary ideas led to the radical expansion of the domain of sculpture, which had been circumscribed in a formal sense up to that point.

The Van Abbemuseum's concern for British sculpture (contrary to that shown for Minimal Art) began to gather momentum at a relatively late stage, namely in 1977, with solo exhibitions of work by Barry Flanagan and Hamish Fulton. It should be said, however, that the acquisitions date, in some instances, from several years prior to this.

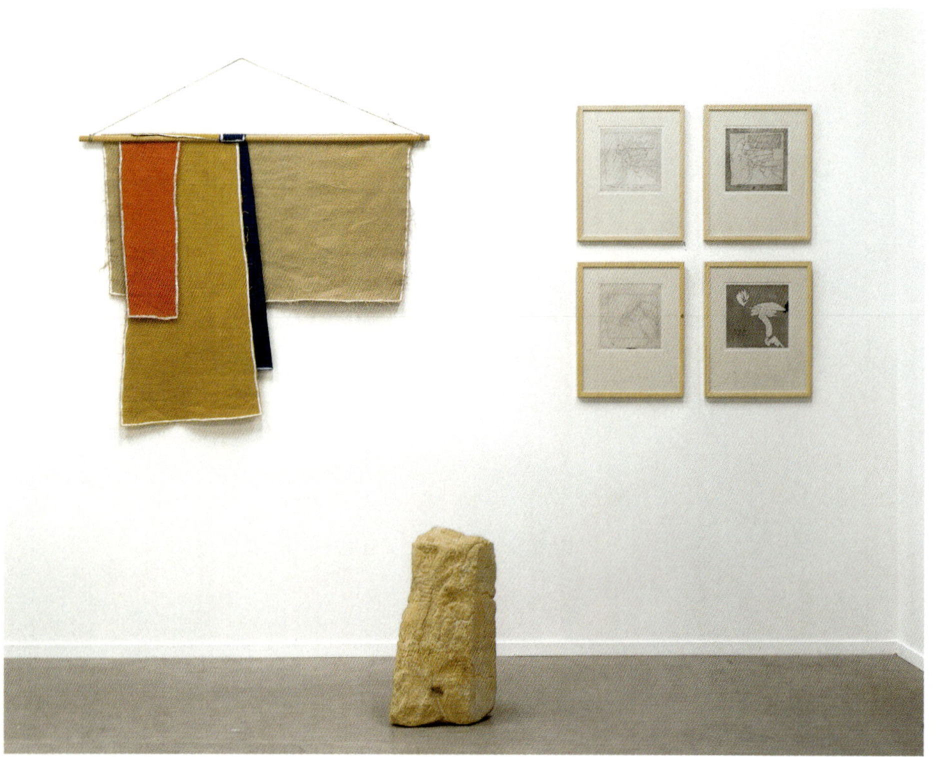

Barry Flanagan *Untitled Once*, 1973; *Withdrawal from Stone Wall Street*, 1970; *Left Hand by Left Hand*, 1971; *Withdrawal from Stone Wall Street*, 1970; *To Draw Fire*, 1970; *Figures*, 1976

By about the end of the seventies, a new generation of British artists was again making its international debut with such figures as Tony Cragg, Anish Kapoor and, somewhat more on the sidelines, Boyd Webb. With only a few exceptions, their work was acquired for the collection from the late eighties onward.

As of 1965, the work of **Barry Flanagan** is characterized by an incessant and playful search for the essence of sculpture, in which the use of material, the significance of language and views on the autonomy of the sculptural object serve as a constant guideline.

As became evident with Flanagan's solo exhibitions in 1977 and 1983, this led to an extremely versatile body of work, ranging from sculptures made of burlap bags filled with plaster, wigwam-like tents and pieces of furniture, to rough lumps of stone and bronze animal figures. As far as the use of material is concerned, there occasionally seems to be a resemblance to *arte povera*: the parallel between the igloos of Mario Merz and Flanagan's tent-like sculptures made of branches and cloth is particularly striking. *Untitled Once* (1973)–a wall piece consisting of lengths of cloth thinly painted in different colors of acrylic–seems to stem directly from the ostensibly simple issue as to where painting ends and sculpture begins. Such a formal and truly 'St. Martin-like' problem was provided with ironic commentary by Flanagan. *Untitled Once* is not comprised of volumes but of edges, lines and planes. The irony lies partly with the fact that Caro's metal assemblages could also be described in such a manner.

During the early seventies, Flanagan became interested in traditional sculptural techniques and materials, such as stone, clay, bronze and wax, but he implemented these in a thoroughly unconventional way. Stones and boulders were given sparing incisions that suggest natural or prehistoric origins, but from which a rudimentary sort of figuration in the form of animal or human figures often emerges. In that sense *Figures* (1976) does have the look of a natural *objet trouvé*, which raises the question as to what intervention must be carried out by an artist in order to transform an object into an image.

Flanagan's graphic work–largely comprised of etchings and linoleum cuts–contains 'borrowed images' in a relaxed, naturalistic style and shows portraits of friends, animals, landscapes and studies after Rembrandt. While, with Flanagan, the form can still be associated with what could be called the classical notions and materials of sculpture, this is not the case with **Hamish Fulton**: in his work the idea of sculpture is inextricably linked with the physical and mental experience of nature. Going on the principle 'no walk no work', Fulton has been making walks since 1969 through largely uninhabited and sometimes treacherous landscapes all over the world. Through the course of these walks, which vary greatly in terms of distance and duration, he takes photographs, and these are occasionally furnished with several words containing factual information and with haiku-like bits of text that suggest an atmosphere. Usually he exhibits only one photograph or a small series from each walk; his aim in this is not to show particular qualities of the landscape or to employ certain photographic techniques, but to form a poetic image, in which observations, memories and experiences are brought together. With the walks and with the occasionally considerable physical effort involved in them, Fulton creates a receptiveness to nature, a concern for perception and how this is influenced by specific circumstances. He therefore does not produce sculpture in the traditional sense of the word, but in his work he does focus on the observation and experience of space, distance and time which he continues to stage and evoke, as it were, by means of his photographs. The photographic works, fifteen of which are owned by the Van Abbemuseum, are no more than a residue; the walk itself is the work, and the photograph is a memento of this. One could even maintain that the actual sculpture consists of all of the walks undertaken by Fulton over the years.

Fulton's work initially bears a great similarity to that of **Richard Long**, which the Van Abbemuseum began to be exhibit on a regular basis in 1979. Both artists make walks, sometimes in each other's company, and Long, too, produces photographs of the landscape that he crosses. With Fulton, however, the photograph is the only proof of his presence in it; Long, on the other hand, leaves traces of this in the landscape. The work of Long is, like that of Fulton, scarcely imaginable without the developments of Minimal Art and Conceptual Art, and yet in both cases it also stems from an English tradition of experiencing nature which goes back to Wordsworth, Turner and Constable. Using, for the most part, stones and branches, Long creates sculptures–often in the form of straight lines, circles, squares or spirals–which eventually disintegrate through the course of time and through the effects of natural circumstances. Photographs such as *Circle in Africa* (1978)

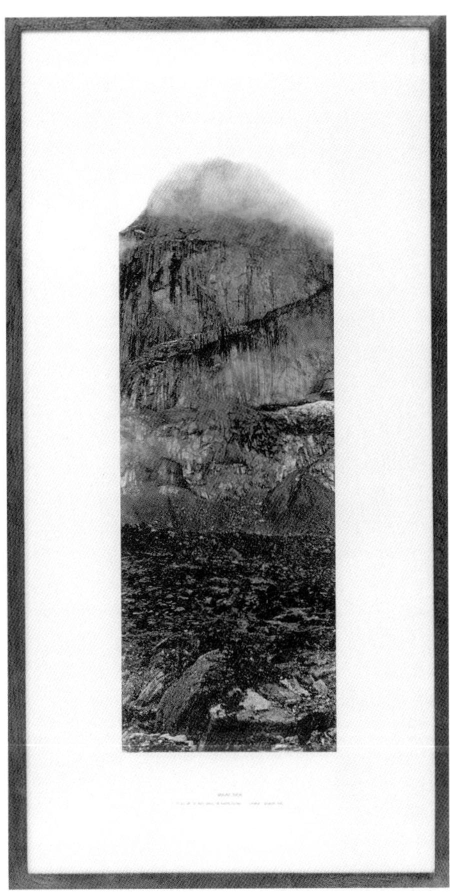

Hamish Fulton *Mount Thor, a six day 70 mile walk on Baffin Island Canada, Summer 1976*, 1976

show images of this kind; these can be interpreted as the marking of a specific place, traces of human activity, of occupation and movement in a landscape which is totally deserted for the rest. It has been said that Long's work gives expression to "man's presence by his absence." *Meeting Place* (1977) shows the walking route of Long and Tony Cragg, who proceed in opposite directions, nonstop, following a more or less circular course, so that they eventually meet at a certain point. By presenting the walk on the basis of topographical maps, Long emphasizes the conceptual character of his work and attempts to make the experience of distance, time and space observable and ordered, though it cannot be experienced. Since the early seventies Long has not only been creating sculptures in nature, but also presenting these in exhibition spaces, where the contrast between nature and culture becomes even more distinct. Although his work is, as he says, about "real stones, real time and real actions"–and real, authentic experience could be added to this–there is a strong emphasis, especially in the museum presentations, on the formal elegance of his sculpture. That formal refinement, which is undeniably part of his photographs as well, is clearly expressed in *White Marble Line* (1986), in which the scale, the texture, the differences in color among the stones and the distinction between light and dark are of essential importance.

In the work of the poet and visual artist **Ian Hamilton Finlay**–a generation older than the previously discussed artists and a loner in this group (or any other, in fact)–major significance is once again given to landscape, more specifically the typically English phenomenon of a landscape garden. In Stonypath, near Edinburgh, Finlay has created a landscape garden, which he has named 'Little Sparta', containing a temple devoted to Apollo, commemorative stones with inscriptions and other objects. This is where he produces almost all of this work–poems, graphics and objects–which frequently exudes an air of neoclassicism and in which views on aesthetics mingle with morality, politics and poetry. During the fifties Finlay was concerned with 'concrete poetry', and so it is not surprising that his work–both the graphic and the sculptural–is largely made up of 'word sculptures'. He often refers to figures from the French Revolution, such as Robespierre and Saint-Just, and to the French Revolution in general, which functions, in his view, as a philosophical model of extremes: virtue, individual freedom and beauty versus violence, terror and destruction. The rugged contours of the stone blocks in *De huidige orde is de wanorde van de toekomst Saint-Just* give rise to the suggestion that these are fragments from an 'enlightened' past, and whether the age of chaos, to which the text refers, may have already begun is open to interpretation. Due to the location of the sculpture, originally situated in front of the entrance to the museum building, there is furthermore a suggestion that the values represented by the museum are anything but timeless.

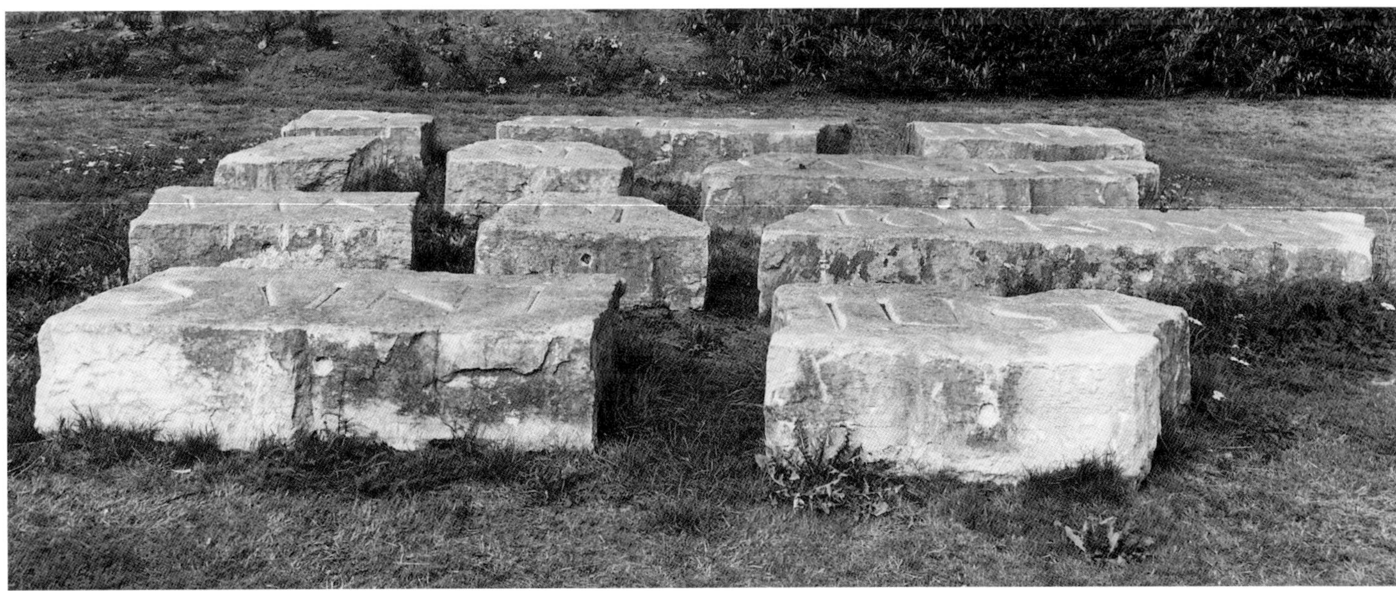

Ian Hamilton Finlay *De huidige orde is de wanorde van de toekomst Saint-Just*, 1986

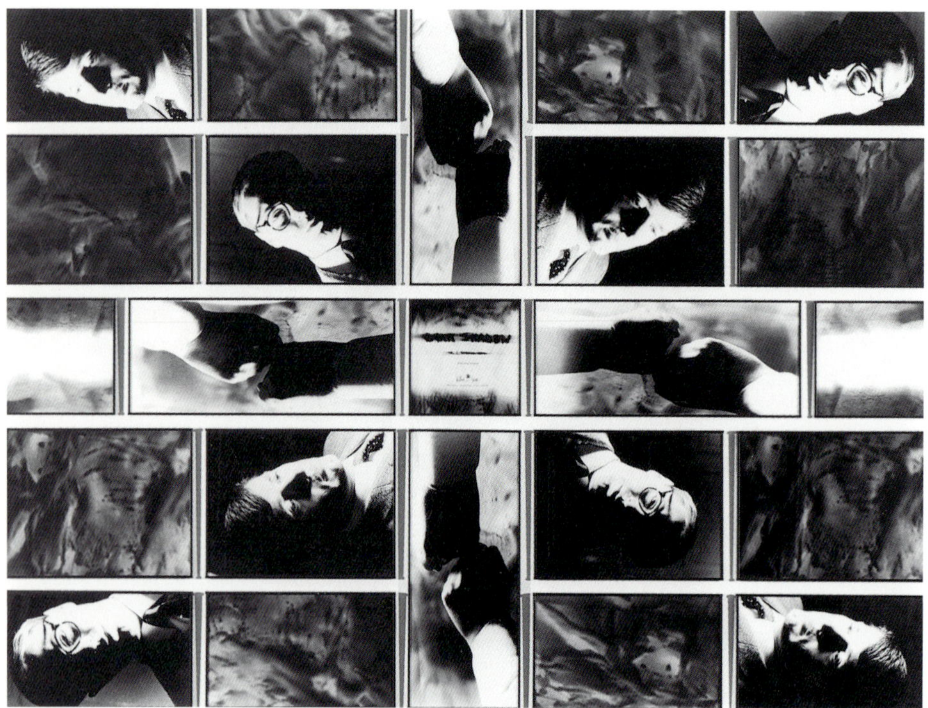

Gilbert & George *Dark Shadow no. 8*, 1974

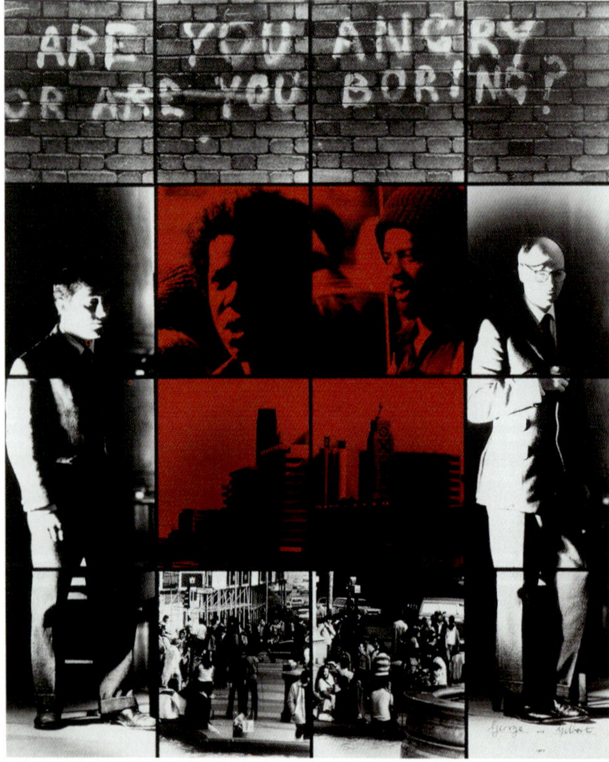

Gilbert & George *Are You Angry or Are You Boring?*, 1977

with modern life in all its forms. The motto of Gilbert & George is 'Art for All'; art is not simply for the elite but should be comprehensible to everyone and have life itself as its theme. Gilbert & George met each other while studying at the St. Martin's School of Art and decided, in 1969, to start presenting themselves as 'living sculptures'. Dressed in very conservative and inconspicuous-looking suits, they would pose, sometimes for hours, at all sorts of locations–their faces and hands covered with bronze powder–or would perform a little dance and mime to music-hall songs. Since then they have referred to all of their work as sculpture, whether it be postcards, films, drawings or photographs, and have been giving aesthetic form to their life together in a manner reminiscent of nineteenth-century dandyism. In 1971 the photo pieces began to assume prime importance as an expressive means. Initially these were series of black-and-white photographs, varying in size and arranged in different patterns, which displayed the artists in nature, in domestic surroundings or in a pub, sometimes in a distinctly melancholy mood or in an advanced state of drunkenness. By about 1975 the photo pieces had become comprised of series of separate, rectangular photographs that were now being colored in by hand; due to their color intensity and grid pattern, these bear a certain resemblance to stained-glass windows. The photo piece *Are You Angry or Are You Boring?* (1977) represents a significant point in their body of work. Not only is color being used as an expressive element for the first time, but the subject is also different in the sense that the artists now adopt a stance as observers of modern urban life; and in this they are surrounded by signs of power and powerlessness, such as graffiti, impersonal buildings, minorities, alcoholics and the homeless. In *Red Fists* (1980) their stance is less aloof, and they surround themselves with strong yet innocent-looking 'working-class' boys, thus giving rise to undertones of homosexual eroticism. The importance of the work of Gilbert & George in the collection of the Van Abbemuseum should not be underestimated, because, like many younger artists, they make allegorical reference to human existence in all its dramatic, religious, sexual, sentimental and even banal forms of expression and, in that sense, continue to emphasize art's function and place in society.

As mentioned earlier, a younger generation of British art can also be found in the collection. That division into various generations is based not so much on

Whereas in the photographs of Long and Fulton man is actually absent yet, by way of the introvert experience of nature, still the implicit subject, in those of **Gilbert & George**, it is the two artists themselves who are almost always playing the main role. Their work deals very explicitly with human nature and

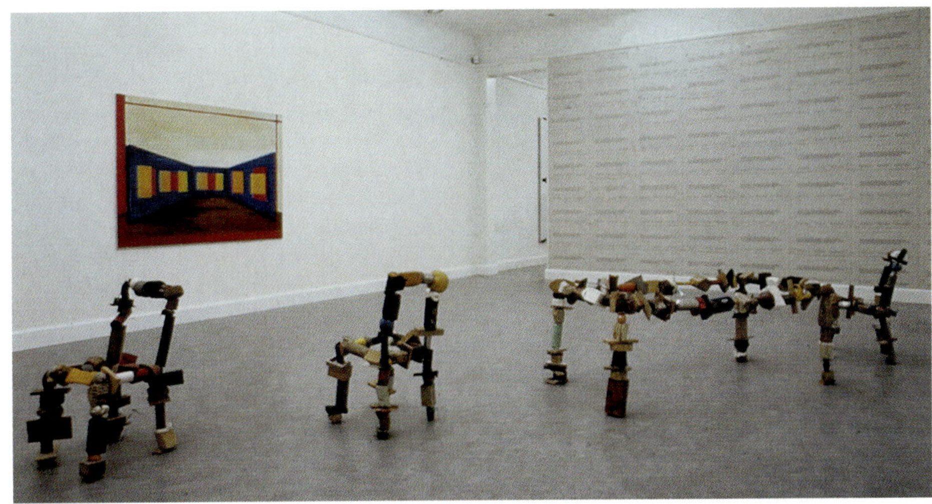

Tony Cragg *One Space, Four Places*, 1982; **René Daniëls** *Painting on the Bullfight*, 1985

differences in age–these are not very great–but on differences in intention. Tony Cragg can certainly be considered the leading artist of what was referred to during the early eighties as 'New British Sculpture', and included in this were also Anish Kapoor, Bill Woodrow, Shirazeh Houshiary, Julian Opie, Anthony Gormley and Richard Deacon. All of them have made free use of metaphors and an associative, poetic vision, and the meanings that seem to lay hidden in the work often remain ambiguous.

Like Flanagan's work, that of **Tony Cragg** can be described as highly varied, especially as far as the use of material is concerned. Cragg became known during the late seventies for his floor and wall sculptures in different figurative forms and consisting of colored, plastic waste material. With such work, including *Red Skin* (1980), Cragg obviously alludes to the work of Richard Long, but the romantic experience of nature is hardly evident. It would be wrong, however, to interpret *Red Skin*, whose form is derived from a found plastic toy Indian, solely as a type of social commentary or as a criticism of the consumer society. Cragg's work embodies a much broader, more ambiguous and poetic pursuit, namely the portrayal of man's relationship to his new, less-than-natural

environment. He regards his sculptures as conveyors of experience and emotion; from that point of view, his objects can contribute to a greater knowledge and understanding of the world around us. That is why his work often contains allusions to chemistry, biology, geology and their processes and why his sculptures often seem to consist of man-made objects in materials ranging from clay, bronze, plaster, glass and wood to found objects which he groups, stacks, outlines, enlarges or perforates. Cragg's early sculptures are often made up of separate elements, and in them he creates the suggestion that the ultimate form or construction may be only a temporary one and a consequence of internal fragmentation. Or one could think that the main form, such as the four chairs and one table in *One Space, Four Places* (1982), is comprised of 'molecules' which collectively provide the object with its own identity or 'place'. Cragg's interest in the relationship between the natural and the artificial was clearly expressed in his two solo exhibitions at the Van Abbemuseum, in 1989 and in 1991. Here he showed, for instance, a giant shell, apparently on the verge of devouring a number of instrument cases, and a sculpture titled *Eroded Landscape* (1991): various levels of milky, sandblasted glass bottles and vases that seem to have come from a laboratory but, at the same time, have a 'classical' look, the whole of which conjures up associations with the diagrammatic inserts of cell structures

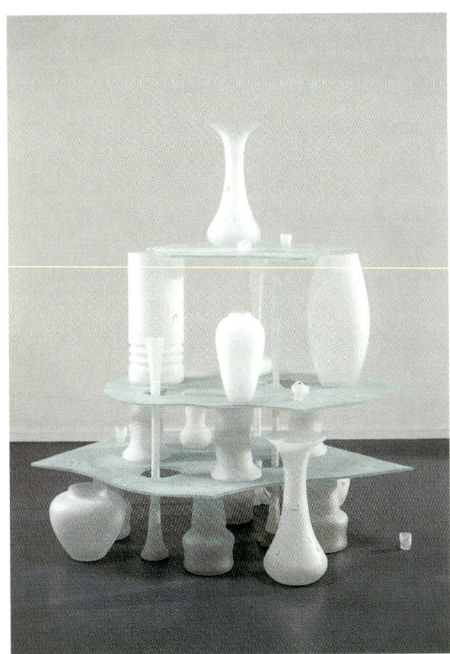

Tony Cragg *Eroded Landscape*, 1991

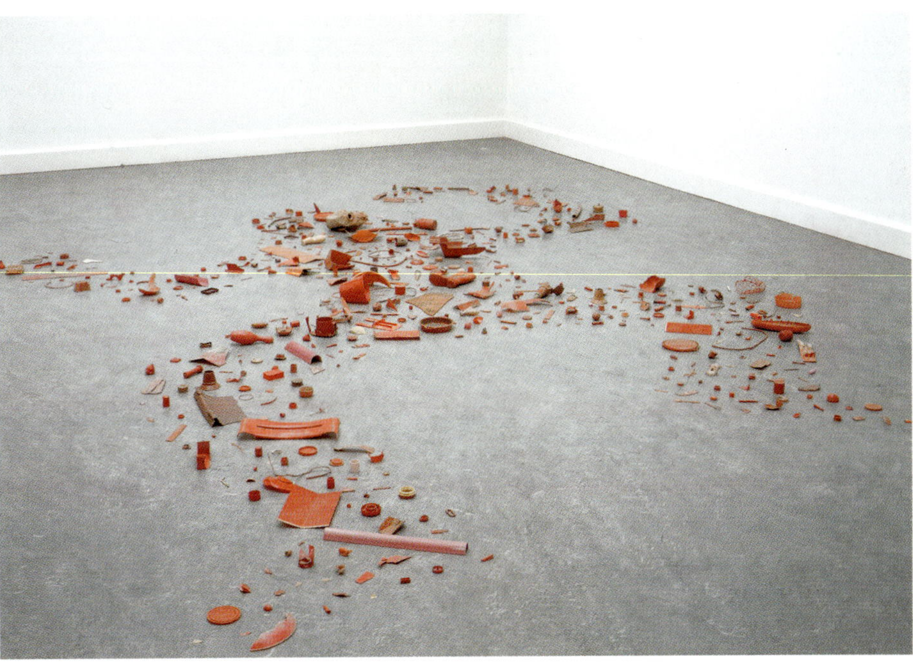

Tony Cragg *Red Skin*, 1980

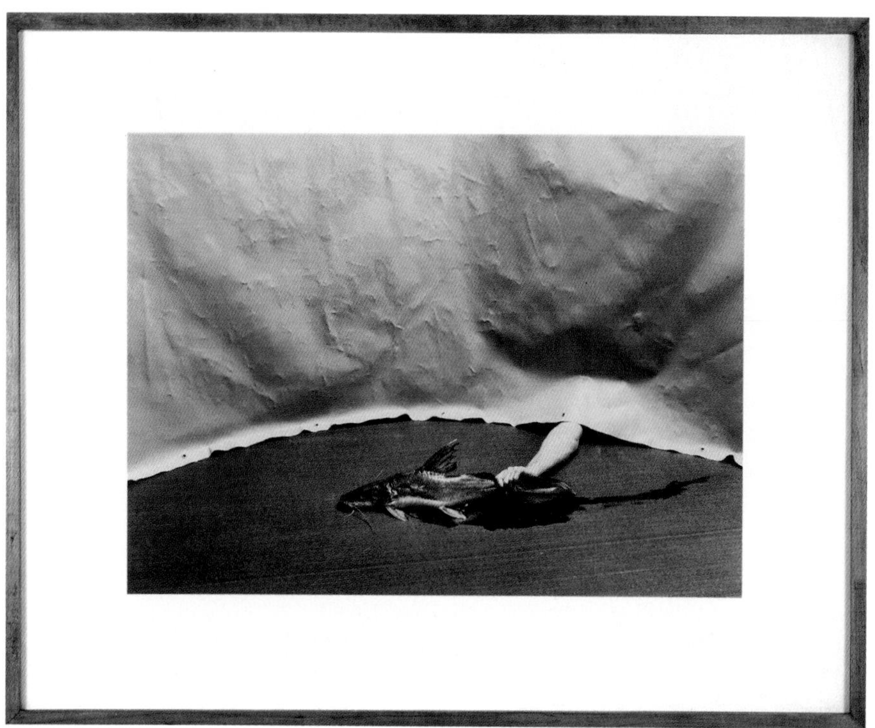

Boyd Webb *Untitled*, 1981

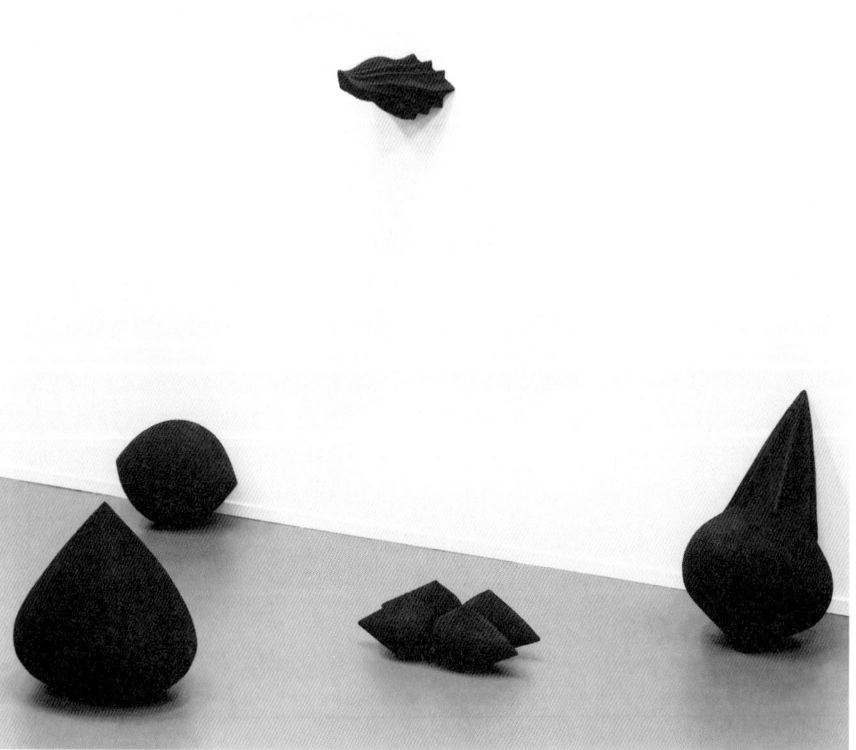

Anish Kapoor *Tongue no. 2*, 1982

that are found in physiology books.
Of an entirely different nature, the sculptures of **Anish Kapoor** manage to evoke metaphysical ideas in a unique way. Characteristic of his earlier work, *Tongue no. 2* (1982) is a grouping of isolated, abstract as well as organic-looking forms, which have been dusted with pigment and which thereby possess an almost unreal type of serenity. Due to the pigment, *Tongue no. 2* has a timeless appearance, as though it has not been made by human hands but simply 'is'. Kapoor is of Indian origin, and his use of red, blue, black, white and yellow pigment can indeed be linked with Hindu rituals, in which pure color symbolizes divine presence. But in Western art, too, color functions as a vehicle for the transcendent and the absolute, as in the monochrome-blue paintings of Yves Klein. A striking aspect of Kapoor's work is his portrayal of antithetical principles: spirituality and materiality, the formed and the unformed, light and dark, the feminine and the masculine, absence and presence. While Long and Fulton used photography in order to represent nature and reality, each in his own way, the photography of **Boyd Webb** is, to a great extent, aimed at conjuring forth an artificial, staged world. In his work sculpture is present only in order to be photographed. A tension is created between photography as an objective, registering medium–a photograph, after all, never lies, and everything that has been photographed has 'actually' existed–and as an artificial, fictional reality which has a very enigmatic and, at times, absurd appearance. *Untitled* (1981) constitutes a transition from Webb's earlier, more narrative scenes and the later still lifes, landscapes and seascapes (made of carpet, plastic and paper) in which actors often carry out mysterious acts. The notion of 'staged photography' practically seems to have been invented with Webb's *Untitled* in mind: in a clearly theatrical setting, there appears to be, hiding behind the white screen, a person whose manner of behavior cannot exactly be explained, as in a dream or in a surrealist film: it exemplifies mystery.

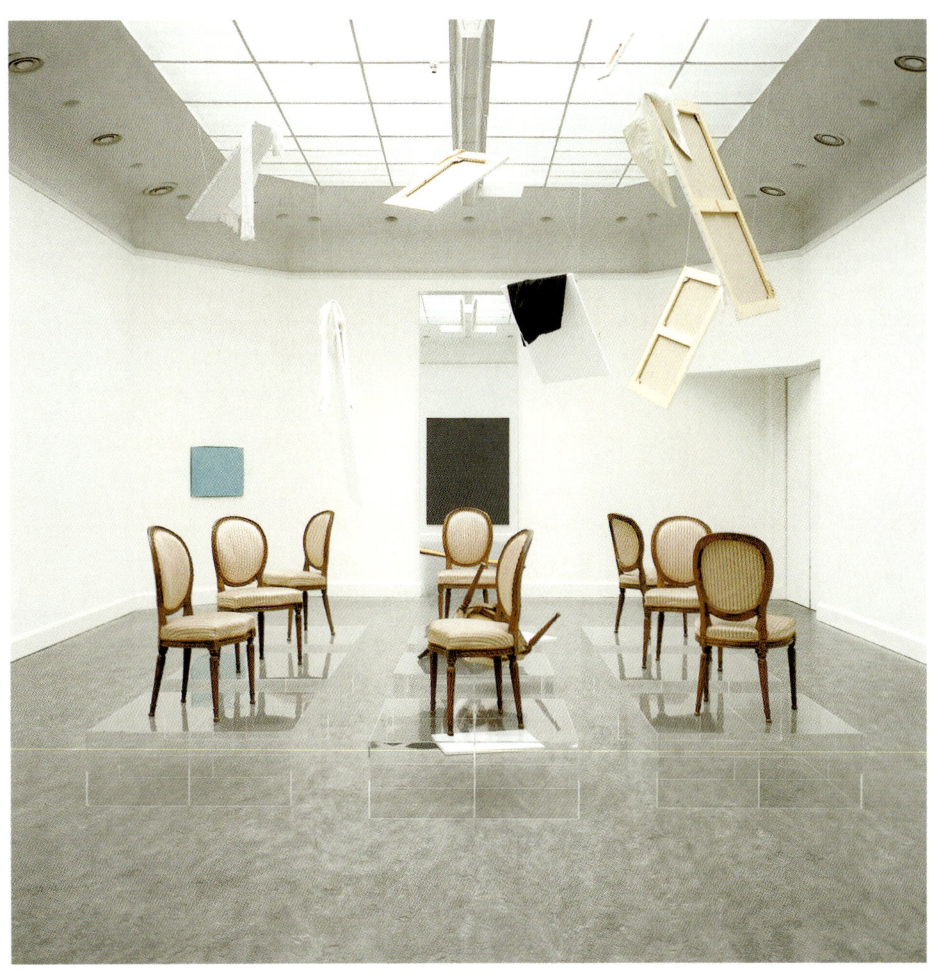

Giulio Paolini *La caduta di Icaro*, 1982

Nomadism, the recording of reality, the elimination of demarcations between art and life: these are terms which one encounters in texts on *arte povera* written at the time of its development. In 1967 Michelangelo Pistoletto rolled an enormous ball of newspaper through the streets of Turin; during that same year, Luciano Fabro cleansed an area of floor, rubbed wax over it and then placed a newspaper on it; rather than showing artworks, Jannis Kounellis had twelve horses stabled at a gallery in Rome in 1969. The artists of *arte povera* wanted nothing to do with the supposition that art had to be suited to a museum and made of imperishable materials. Having emerged during the second half of the sixties–a period of social protest, flower power, hippies and Vietnam demonstrations–*arte povera* was a child of its time. Art's old order was disrupted, because now it was possible to incorporate into the artwork all sorts of materials, even the most unpretentious–and this what is meant by the term *art povera*, or poor art. Soil, bundles of branches, coal, hair, plants, live animals: in short, ordinary materials, uncommon to art, constitute an essential part of *arte povera*.

The term *arte povera* is somewhat misleading. Some artists do, in fact, use lasting materials, such as marble and bronze, which have already been tried and tested in art for centuries. Furthermore, the diversity of the work by these artists is so great that one can justifiably wonder whether all of these artists should be regarded as a single group. *Arte povera* clearly differs, however, from the rational, unambiguous and neutral American art of the sixties, such as the Minimal Art of Carl Andre and the paintings of Stella. Though the term 'poor art' itself suggests an affinity with the term 'minimal art', the differences between the two movements are enormous, in terms of content as well as form. Unlike the neutral and formal Minimal Art, *art povera* stands for complexity, for content, for the human aspect, for nature and culture.

Even so, the work *Luci* (1968) by **Gilberto Zorio** clearly displays Minimalist traits. It is,

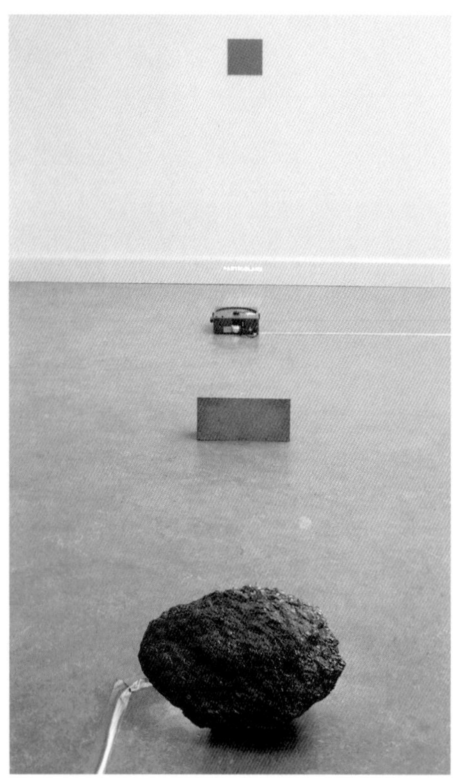

Giovanni Anselmo *Un disegno e un particolare a est, trecento milioni di anni a ovest*, 1967-78

in fact, the oldest *arte povera* piece in the collection, as well as the first and only work of this group to be acquired in 1970, while Jean Leering was still director of the museum. Leering focused mainly on the Americans, and he may have viewed this work by Zorio as a European variant of Minimal Art. The six identical concrete building elements that make up part of *Luci* could indeed be part of a work by Carl Andre. But due to the fact that Zorio has placed two rows of three concrete elements across from each other and has aimed, in each row, six lamps at six other light sources opposite these, the work takes on a distinct character of its own, also because the wiring of the lamps is a prominent part of the work. An enormous tension, typical of all Zorio's work, is evoked between the two rows of lamps that are aimed at each other. Though *Luci* is a relatively early work, which in formal terms is still atypical of Zorio, one can already discern his fascination with energy, which lies at the heart of his artistry. While *Luci* deals with electric energy and the tension between two rows, the other works are also about physical, psychic and especially chemical energy.

Giovanni Anselmo is the first of the group to whom Rudi Fuchs dedicated a solo exhibition in 1980. His work, too–involving the frequent use of granite blocks and monochrome-blue, square surfaces–bears a certain resemblance to Minimal Art. In addition to this, it has strong conceptual characteristics, as when a granite block is furnished with a compass which determines its orientation in space, not only in relation to the museum but in relation to the earth. By doing so, Anselmo relates his 'humble' artwork to the enormous mass of the earth and its iron core which creates its geomagnetic field. The four-part *Un disegno e un particolare a est, trecento milioni di anni a ovest* (1967-78) contains such a stone block with compass as well as a 300-million-year-old anthracite block, to which the title refers. Also part of the work is a light projection of the word *particolare* (detail) on the wall. With this Anselmo also directs our attention to both the small, the detail, and the large, the whole, of which the detail is a part, for instance the wall of the museum as part of the whole building, but also–in a broader sense–part of the entire world or even the entire universe. There is a certain similarity to the work of Manzoni, who placed in a landscape a stone cube with the upside-down inscription *Socle du Monde*. While Manzoni transfigures, with a simple yet grand gesture, the entire globe into his own work of art, Anselmo, on the other hand, minimizes the magnitude of his work in relation to that of the earth.

More remote from Minimal Art is the concern for mythology, which pervades the work of **Guilio Paolini**. Paolini is the most

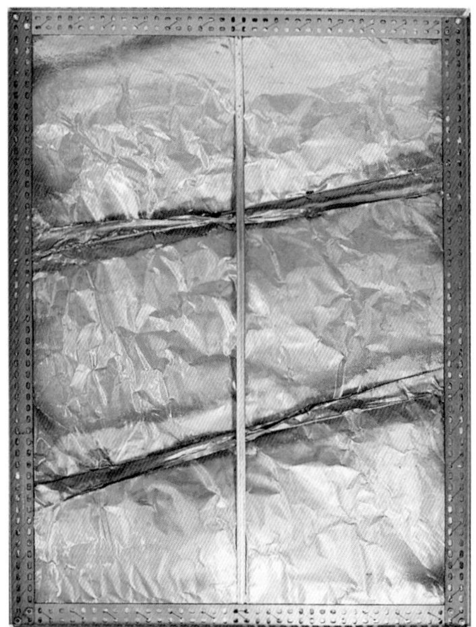

Luciano Fabro *Mercurio*, 1982

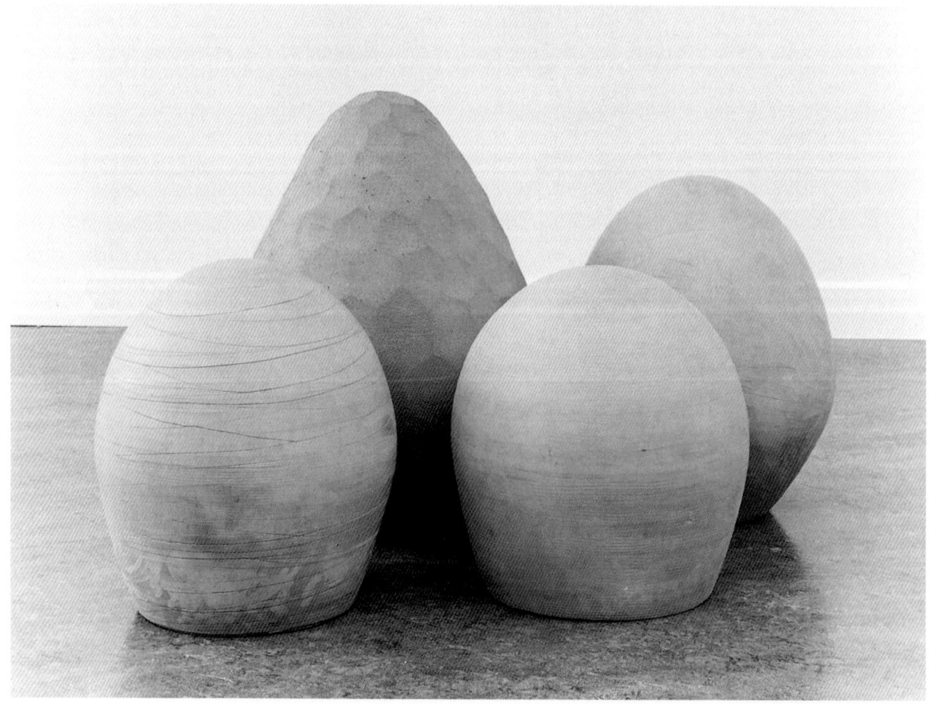

Luciano Fabro *Il guidizio di Paride*, 1979

classical, but also the most analytical artist of the group. His sculptures are full of allusions to the French writer Raymond Roussel, for example, and to architecture and perspective. In the collection of the Van Abbemuseum, he is represented with the large installation *La caduta di Icaro* from 1982. In the well-known story from Greek mythology, Icarus, son of the architect and engineer Daedalus, flew off with wings created by his father and came too close to the sun; the wings, held together with wax, thereby melted and Icarus plummeted into the sea. Not only from a formal standpoint is Paolini's version of this story peculiar–we see empty canvases, partly wrapped in articles of clothing, hung from the ceiling at a low level, as well as nine antique chairs on plexiglas platforms–but in terms of content, there is also something strange going on. The artist himself describes the work as follows: "The work consists of nine paintings, which are marked with the common symbols of the nine planets of our solar system. The size and location of each canvas moreover corresponds to the position of the particular planet in the solar system. The protagonist (Icarus), who enters this *scena di conversazione*, falls to the canvas on the floor (the Earth) on his attempt to touch Venus." Paolini presents us with a liberal adaptation of the myth. It is not the sun, but the planet Venus, that causes Icarus to fall. Between 'Earth' on the floor and the eight hanging canvases, there are nine chairs, one of which has toppled over, thus heightening the effect of Icarus's fall–which is symbolized by the black dress suit lying on the floor along side the canvas, which represents the planet Earth. All of this makes *La caduta di Icaro* one of the most dramatic works of *arte povera*. The mythological figure Venus also plays a role in one of the works by **Luciano Fabro** which is present in the collection. *Il guidizio di Paride*, from 1979, is comprised of four egg-shaped terracotta sculptures, one of which is distinctly larger than the other three. Is this one perhaps meant to symbolize Paris? It is, after all, a bit more pointed and thus more masculine than the other, rounder and thus more feminine forms that probably represent the three goddesses. The title refers to the Greek myth of Paris, the Trojan prince who was told to give a golden apple to the one goddess whom he thought was the most beautiful of the three: Juno, Minerva or Venus. His choice of Venus, who promised to reward him with marriage to the beautiful Helen of Troy, would lead to the Trojan War. But Fabro did not choose this story in order to make a work about it. Unlike Paolini, who works according to a preconceived plan,

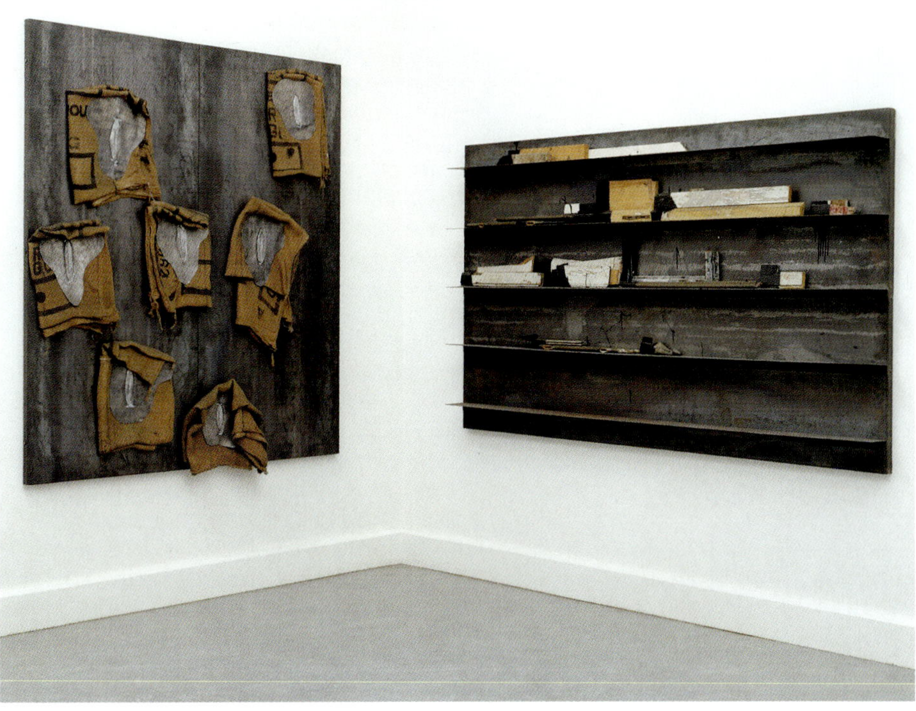

From left to right: **Jannis Kounellis** *Senza titolo*, 1986; *Senza titolo, Roma*, 1983

Fabro is mainly concerned with forms and with sensuality. The titles are conceived only after he finishes his sculptures, which makes it clear that the issue is not such literal reference, but rather the associative power of the artwork. Those who give closer consideration to *Il guidizio di Paride* will also see that Fabro has given each of the four forms a character of its own by way of subtle differences in the drawing of the skin. The skin of the larger form is, for instance, given a honeycomb pattern, and one of the smaller ones is decorated with a spiral motif. Fabro's concern for detail and visual enjoyment is clearly evident in this work.

Arcobaleno, dating from 1980, shows another aspect of this magician among the *arte povera* artists. This rainbow, measuring nearly nine meters in length, is made of cotton wadding that has been painted with acrylic. In the cheerfully colored arc form, the soft cotton evokes associations with a cloudy sky onto which the rainbow is projected. *Arcobaleno* is a fine example of Fabro's preoccupation with color, which is shared only by Mario Merz and Alighiero e Boetti in the *arte povera* movement. Fabro is the most sensual and poetic of these artists. In his work one is immediately struck by the perfect control of technique, the artistic command of the material from which the work is made, despite the surprising and matter-of-fact

manner of expression. What makes this all the more amazing is his use of very diverse materials, from the fragile to the relatively lasting, including cloth, glass, various kinds of metal, marble, ceramics, cotton wadding and plants. Sometimes he works like a classical sculptor, bringing the marble to life, other times as a skillful ceramist, producing perfect forms in clay.

In *Mercurio* from 1982, Fabro shows that he has taken inspiration from the material (iron and copper). Primarily having the form of a painting, *Mercurio* displays a greater emphasis on structure. It is more angular and, with its sharp metal edges, much more resistant than the other two works in the collection.

It is not the mythological past, but history and human nature that play a prime role in the work of Greek-born **Jannis Kounellis**, who has been living in Rome since the age of twenty. The materials used by Kounellis–coal, iron, gas flames, soot, burlap bags–conjure up associations with old industries. A work in a Swiss collection literally consists of a brick chimney which actually did produce smoke as well as soot; another work is a toy train on a spiral-shaped track. Industry and transport, like the fragment and the past, are major themes throughout Kounellis's work. It has once been pointed out that the artist was born in Piraeus, where ships come and go,

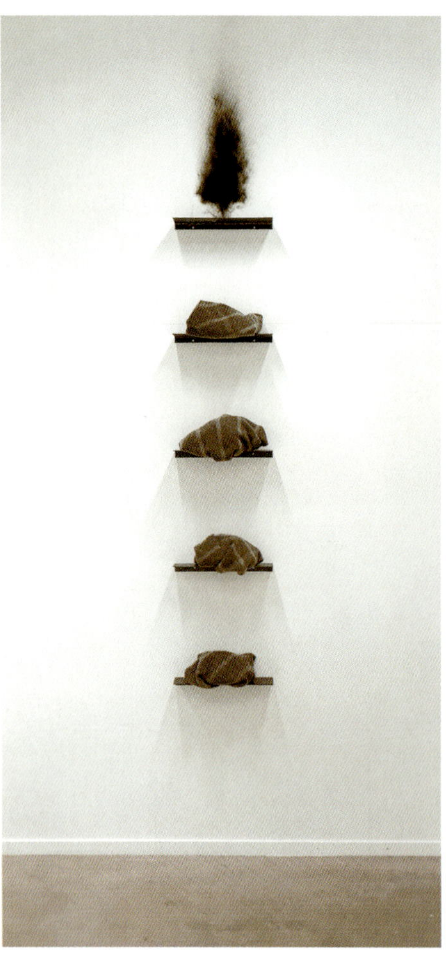

Jannis Kounellis *Senza titolo*, 1980

transporting cotton, coal, coffee beans and the like–materials that appear in his work quite often. But Kounellis himself seems to want to renounce his Greek past. He calls himself an Italian artist, and ever since his arrival in Italy he has refused to speak any Greek.

A striking aspect of his work is that it often appeals to many senses. Aside from the eye, the nose and the ear are also frequently roused in many of his works, as in the previously mentioned case of the horses in the gallery, giving off a strong body odor and whinnying. When he uses fire, there is a hissing of flames as well as the smell of gas fumes. Fire has played a significant role in his work since 1967. To Kounellis, it represents transformation and punishment. The latter gives rise to associations with the medieval practices. Kounellis moreover characterizes himself as a medieval monk. His ideas, which involve a renewed interest in European culture and its traditions, have had considerable influence on the ideas of Rudi Fuchs. In one of his most important exhibitions at the Van Abbemuseum, *Het ijzeren venster / The Iron Window* of 1985, which included only three living artists, Fuchs juxtaposed the work of Kounellis with the paintings of the Russian artist Kazimir Malevich, who is considered to be among the greatest figures in modern art. By doing this,

Fuchs wished to point out that Kounellis, like Malevich, is a major representative of the Eastern European, or more specifically, the Byzantine culture.

Soot, that is to say the traces of fire, constitutes part of *Senza titolo* (1980) which is among the works by Kounellis in the collection. The work consists of five iron shelves that are 'stacked' vertically on the wall. Four plaster casts of statue fragments, wrapped in wool cloth, are placed on four of the shelves. Above the fifth shelf, a spot of soot is visible on the wall, as though a statue fragment has literally gone up in smoke. This element contributes to the dramatics of the work, as it suggests that something is lost forever. As such, smoke alludes to the past, to the disappearance of something. In Kounellis's thinking, there is a key focus on the dissolution of totality, of the whole. He believes, along with others for that matter, that we are now living in a world that is made up of fragments. The shelves with the remnants of the past seem to express Kounellis's attempt to preserve the remains of what had once been a whole. Another work in the collection, *Senza titolo, Roma* (1983), is comprised of a collection of fragments, in this case wood from Roman buildings, which have been placed in a wardrobe-like construction of iron.

The theme of time, touched upon with a somewhat melancholy undertone in the work of Kounellis, is expressed with *joie de vivre* in the work of **Mario Merz**. Growth and vitality form a key theme in his work which, despite its thematic coherence, is highly varied in its execution. The materials used by Merz are very diverse, ranging from soil, bundles of branches, stuffed animals and stacks of newspapers to neonlighting and automobiles. The matter-of-factness with which Merz manages to join 'primitive' and advanced materials in a harmonious whole brings to mind the ideas of Claude Lévi-Strauss, who ascribed just as much value to the 'mythical thinking' of so-called primitive peoples as to Western scientific thought. In his book *La Pensée Sauvage* he examines his 'mythical thinking' which, in comparison to our analytical thought, is based more on sensory intuition. Lévi-Strauss makes a connection between mythical thinking and the *bricoleur*, or tinkerer, "someone who still works with his hands and, in doing this, uses very different means than the skilled craftsman. The typical trait of mythical thinking is that, in order to express itself, it makes use of a collection of means which are heterogeneous and, no matter how extensive, nonetheless remain limited. (...)What

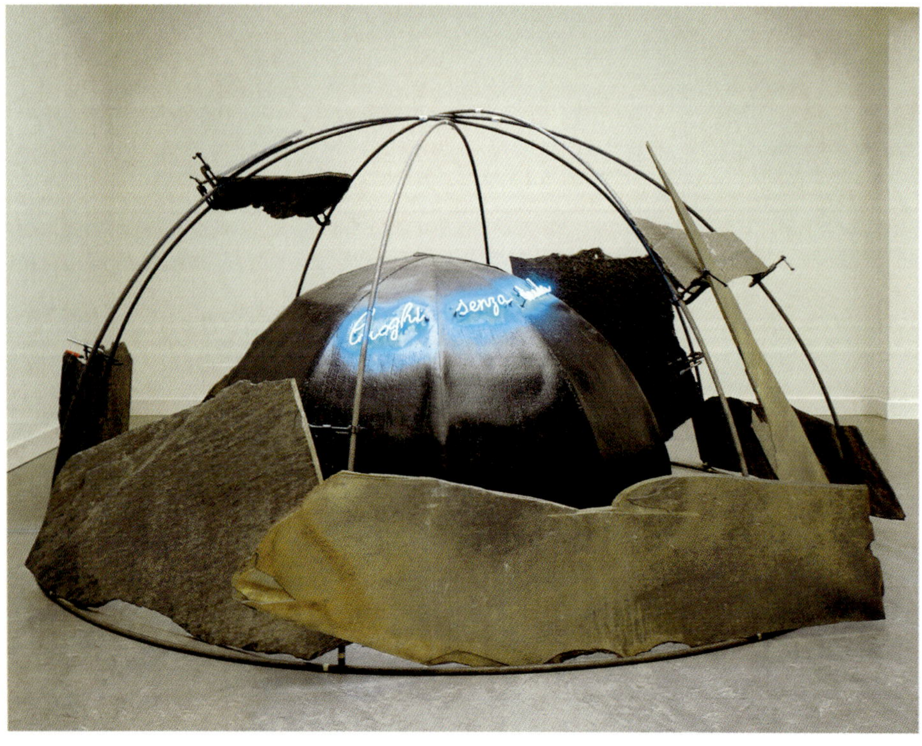

Mario Merz *Igloo Nero*, (1967-79), 1994

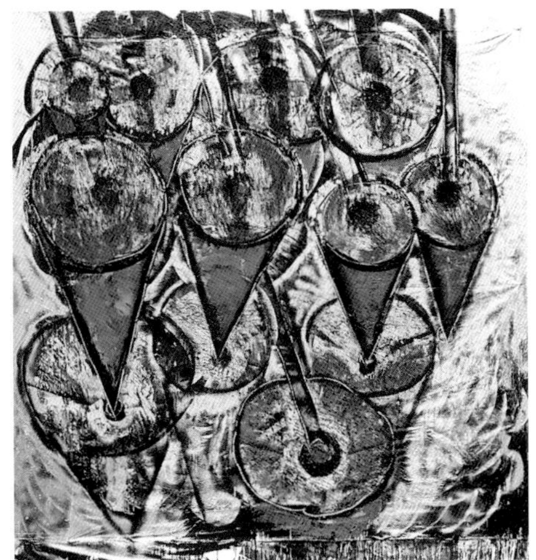

Mario Merz *Senza titolo*, 1984

particularly characterizes mythical thinking is its capacity to generate a structured whole (...) through the employment of remnants and remains of events." Merz is an outstanding example of a *bricoleur*. He implements very diverse materials in order to provide his typical structures with continually different appearances. The igloos, tables and spirals that can be seen in his work with great frequency always have a surprisingly new look.

Merz's body of work is characterized, in part, by 'primitive' imagery, as evident from the igloo form which begins to appear regularly in his work as of 1967. The igloo symbolizes the 'primordial dwelling', but also the world or even the universe. Merz makes frequent use of archetypes such as spirals, prehistoric animals such as the crocodile, but also tables and plants. His work is based on the Fibonacci numbers, the unending sequence 1, 1, 2, 3, 5, 8, 13, ...where each number is defined as the sum of its two predecessors. It is a simple number sequence, devised by the thirteenth-century Italian mathematician and monk Fibonacci and based on the reproductive speed of rabbits. In its simplicity, the sequence is also complex and wide-ranging. Not only does it give expression to the growth and propagation of plants and animals, but the ratio of the two successive numbers comes closer and closer to the golden section. Consequently, this sequence has a certain magical quality. The form of the igloo is, to Merz, moreover a translation of the Fibonacci numbers. In addition to a colorful painting into which the cone motif has been incorporated, the Van Abbemuseum also owns an igloo, titled *Igloo Nero* (1967-79, 1994). In 1994 this work was expanded by the placement of a larger igloo form, made of other materials, on top of it. The words *Luoghi senza strada* written in blue neon lighting on the inner igloo's surface of black tar, evokes the image of a primitive settlement without streets. In retrospective exhibitions of his work, Merz has been known to bring together a large number of igloos and thereby give rise to an image of some exotic nomad village, or an 'unreal city',

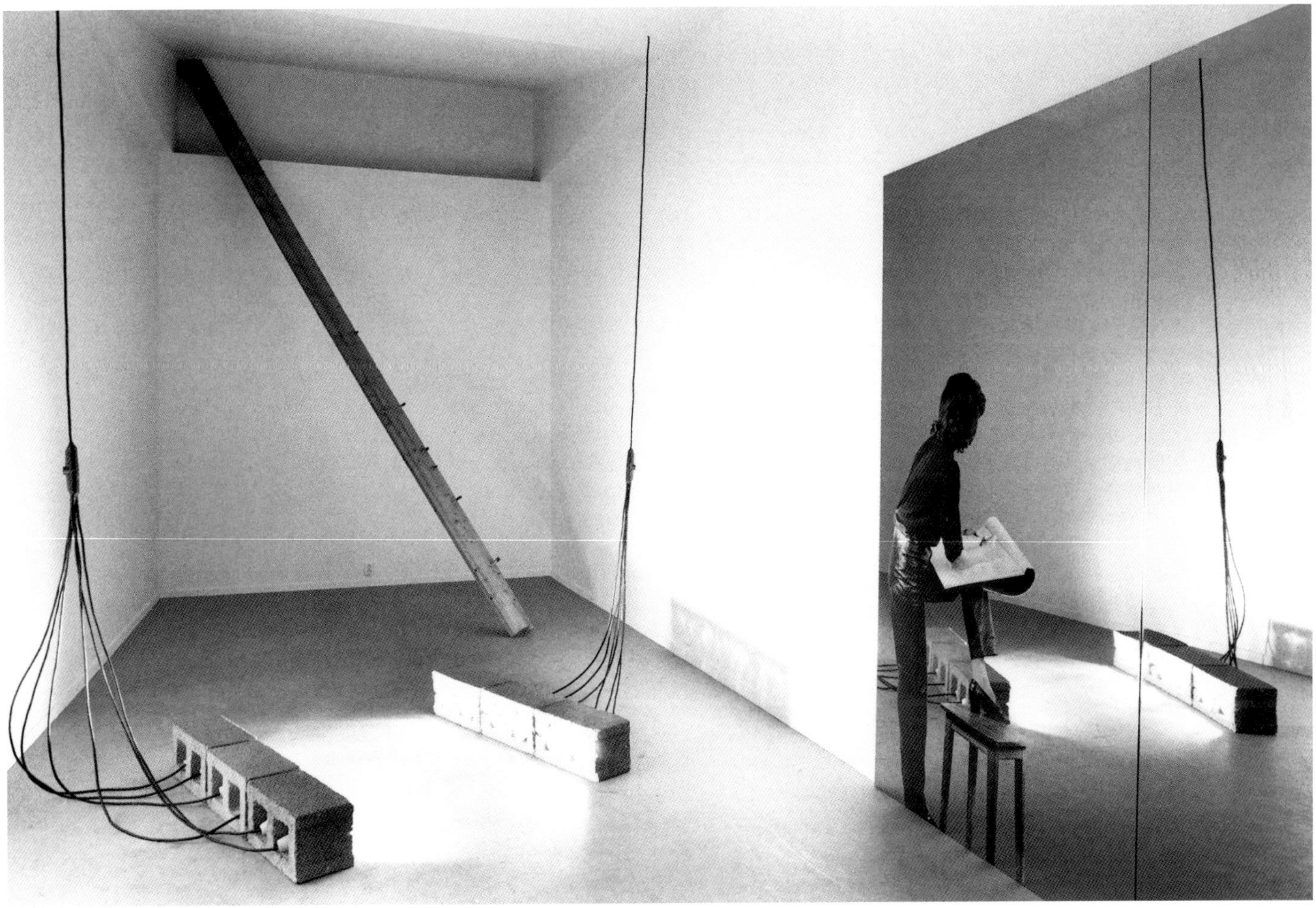

From left to right: **Gilberto Zorio** *Luci*, 1968; **Giuseppe Penone** *Un albero di sei metri*, 1969; **Michelangelo Pistoletto** *Donna che disegna*, 1962-75

as an early neon work in the collection of the Stedelijk Museum in Amsterdam is called. In the art world it is not very common for an artist to alter a work years after it has been made. This act of adding, however, is pre-eminently suited to Merz's artistic vision, which is centered around the principle of growth. *Igloo Nero*, which had previously undergone one change, has been given a new, larger shell. It is striking how the added igloo, with its different materials and openness, has completely transformed the character of the original work. Whereas the black *Igloo Nero* comes across as being very contained and resistant, the new, open igloo gives the whole a more aesthetic appearance with its metal frame, filled in here and there with anthracite-colored slabs of stone. Though the work continues to be predominantly black, it is now particularly characterized by a play of contrasts. There are now open and closed elements, rough (stone) and smooth (tar) surfaces as well as hardness (again stone) and softness (the canvas on which the tar has been smeared) along with the contrast already present in the old work, that of light (the neon words) and dark.

Growth also plays a crucial role in the work of **Giuseppe Penone**, the youngest artist representing *arte povera*. But Penone is concerned only with the growth process in nature. One of his first artistic endeavors, in 1968, was to clasp the trunk of a young tree with a bronze cast of his hand. Over the years the tree has grown over the bronze cast, and the two have merged into one. The Van Abbemuseum owns one of his *Alberi. Un albero di sei metri* from 1970 is, like all of these, made from a thick wooden beam, in this case one which is six meters tall. From this beam the artist has partially peeled away the growth rings, so that the tree (or rather, the negative of the original tree) comes into view again. The irregularity of nature is thus exposed in the 'abstract' straight beam. It is as though Penone tries to bring the 'dead' beam back to life, as though he wishes to bring culture and nature closer together. Penone's work is about the union of man and nature, which seems to be disintegrating more and more in Western society. Tactileness is an important part of this. The cautious way in which he must have removed the growth rings in order to show, intact, that one tree of that height, in all its irregularity (knots, etc.), attests to great patience and respect for nature. The smooth surface of the 'exposed' tree makes the polishing done by the artist almost palpable. It is therefore not surprising that Penone has made enlargements of fingerprints, not only his

own but those of others as well.

In the work of **Michelangelo Pistoletto**, nature plays no role whatsoever. Pisoletto makes frequent use of the mirror, which he produces himself and usually combines with photographs, life-size portraits, as in *Donna che disegna* (1962-75). His first mirror painting was produced in 1962, and with the dating of the later mirror works, reference is always made to this first year; thus the dual date. In his mirror paintings Pistoletto links the static quality of the photograph, which moreover represents the past, with the active and coincidental quality of the present: the viewer being reflected in the mirror. He himself says the following about this: "I began using the mirror because everyone must take responsibility for self-knowledge...Through its particular characteristics, the mirror escapes all problems of change in pictorial art. And photography, among all the ways of representing mankind, comes closest to the mirror. The sole important difference lies in the fact that the mirror renders the image instantly, whereas the photograph takes the past as its departure point. Thanks to photography, two related but asynchronous realities can be made to figure in the same picture, and although totally independent,

they contribute to each other's affirmation. Thus, avoiding any artificial deformation, I arrive at the maximum concentration of elements separated in time and space." For Pistoletto, the mirror is evidently a means by which to arrive at self-knowledge, not only for the artist–he has produced many self-portraits–but also for the viewer. In *Donna che disegna* the concentration of observation is portrayed by the photograph of the drawing woman, who is looking into the empty mirror. We do not see her face, but those who stand in front of the mirror can have the impression that she is studying their image in the mirror. Since 1980 Pistoletto has also been producing sculptures in polyurethane and stone. *Scultura nera*, from 1983, is such a sculpture, made of light foamed plastic over which black acrylic paint has been applied. The black makes the vague silhouettes even more impersonal and unapproachable than they already are, and this gives the work an elusive and thus intriguing quality. The Van Abbemuseum's interest in *arte povera* began to develop at a relatively late stage. It was not until 1979, with a group exhibition including work by Merz and Zorio, that Fuchs started to give regular and intensive attention to this group. The outstanding and broad representation of *arte povera* in the museum's collection, among the most complete in the Netherlands, is an indication of the importance that the museum gives to this movement.

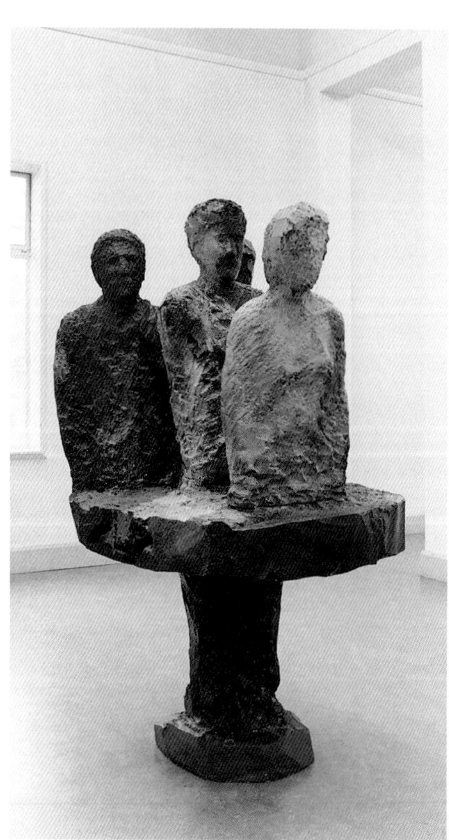

Michelangelo Pistoletto *Scultura nera*, 1983

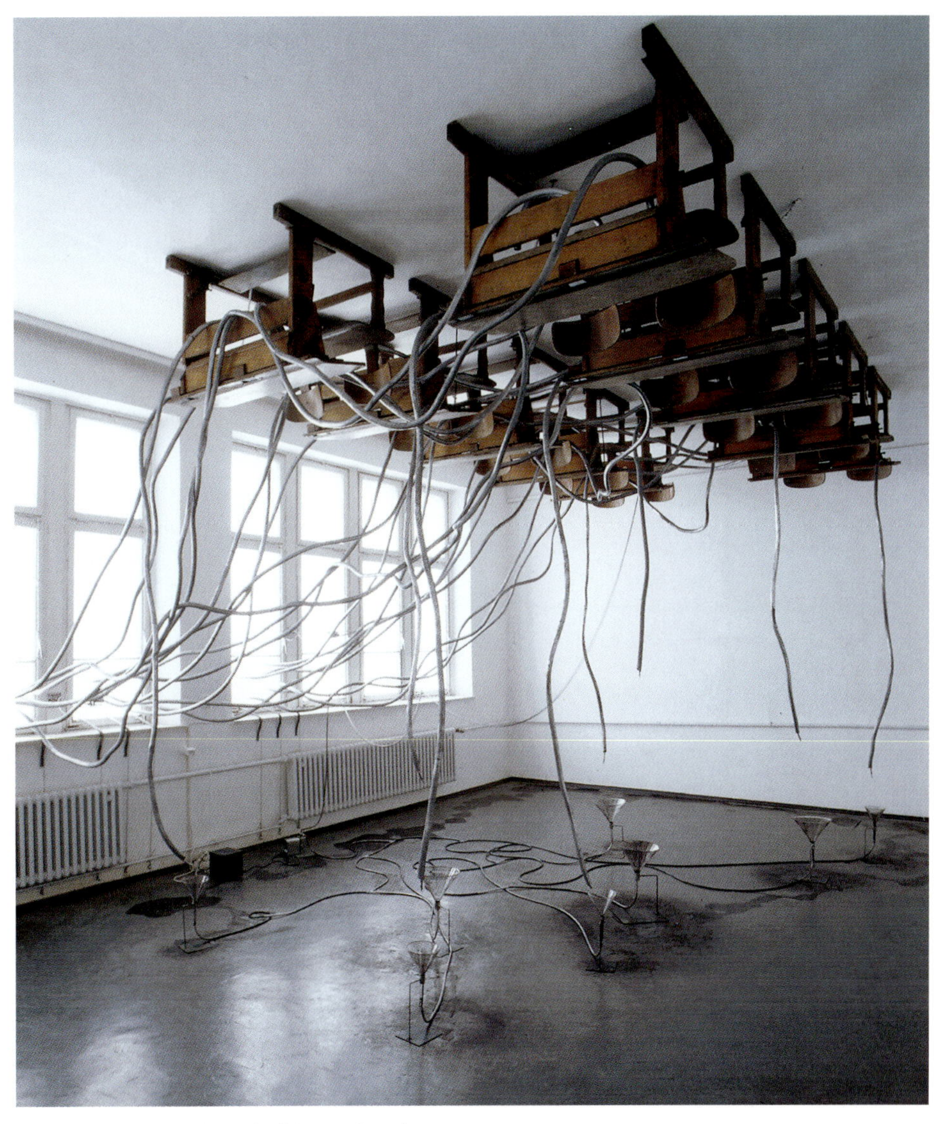

Rebecca Horn *The Moon, the Child and the River of Anarchy*, 1992

The common factor among the artists to be discussed in this chapter is that they have all been influenced by Joseph Beuys to some degree. Most of them have studied at the Staatliche Akademie in Düsseldorf, where Beuys taught. His inspiring presence has no doubt contributed to the fact that this academy has, within a brief period, produced a great number of artists who have managed to gain considerable recognition on the international art scene. Walter Dahn, one of his pupils, says that Beuys taught him "how you can make something without lapsing into ideology." From him he learned about "openness, respect and solidarity", about "how you can relate your own biography, the commonplace, to your work and how a one-to-one relationship can come about between the author and the work: how you can create something that arises from this inner need."

Remarkably, none of these pupils of Beuys have become imitators of their teacher. On the contrary. Each has gone his or her own artistic way. Therefore, this chapter is about anything but a group of kindred spirits; it deals, rather, with the diverse approaches of artists who have, sometimes by chance but usually very deliberately, taken inspiration from the same source.

In Beuys's work there is a fusion of the autobiographical and the universally mythical, linked with a political awareness. Energy is a key notion in this. These are ingredients that can be found, for instance, in the work of **Katharina Sieverding**. And yet there is a world of difference between this and the work of Beuys. Sieverding's medium is photography, which scarcely played a role of significance for Beuys. In Sieverding's work there is a frequent use of the self-

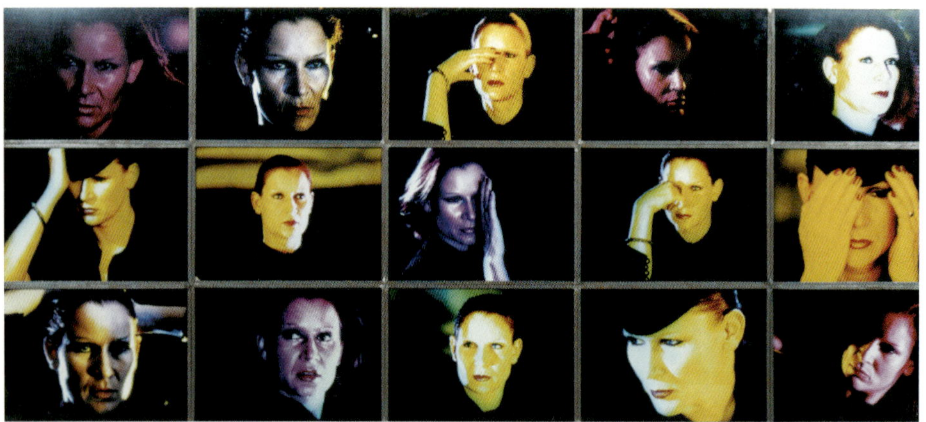

Katharina Sieverding *Nachtmensch*, 1982

portrait, but this does not necessarily mean that the work is autobiographical. She shows her own face, sometimes enlarged to enormous dimensions, or combines a number of smaller portraits to form one large work, such as *Nachtmensch* (1982), which is made up of fifteen photographs. Her self-portraits are not about herself, however, but seem rather to be generalized portraits. Her face is lit, made up or dressed in a different manner, so that it constantly changes in appearance and seems to represent us all. Formally speaking, these portraits bear a resemblance to the work of Andy Warhol, but Sieverding's work is not about stardom, like that of Warhol, but about alienation and a sense of danger. Sieverding's photographs are characterized by unnatural colors and a dark background, as can be seen with *Nachtmensch*, in which her face is lit by lamps of different colors. Artificial light dominates throughout her work and gives it a nocturnal atmosphere. In this one could detect an influence related to the profession of her father, a radiologist. The tension between light and dark constitutes an important theme. Her choice of the medium of photography, which would not exist without light and darkness, therefore has

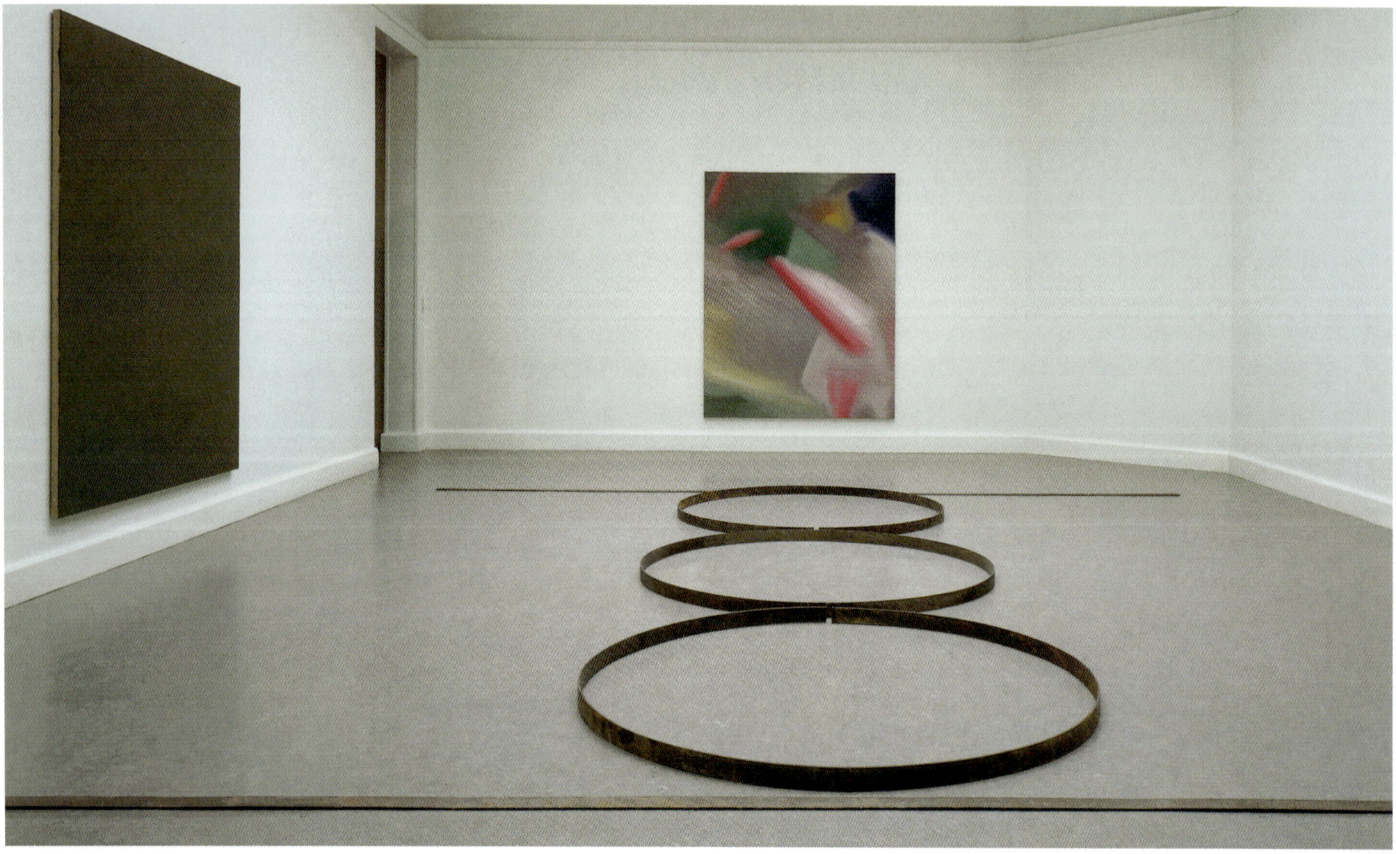

From left to right: **Gerhard Richter** *Grau (Nr. 365/2)*, 1974; **Ulrich Rückriem** *Ohne Titel*, 1972; **Gerhard Richter** *Abstraktes Bild (Nr. 421)*, 1977;

significance in more than a mere formal sense. In addition to self-portraits, Sieverding makes use of images from newspapers, television and film, which reflect, as in a photograph of the atomic bomb being dropped on Hiroshima, her criticial view of world events, Western supremacy, the controversy between East and West, and our way of dealing with the earth. On the other hand, she also shows concern for various forms of energy which manifest light: the nuclear energy of the atomic bomb, solar flares, volcanic eruptions. Sieverding herself describes her work as "energetic photography."

While Sieverding's work maintains a certain autobiographical element, that personal dimension is completely absent in the paintings of **Gerhard Richter**. His work is even explicitly void of any one style and is diverse, without an ideology. In this latter aspect, one can discern the influence of Beuys. A refusal to adhere to any one style constitutes the common characteristic of the four following painters to be discussed. Richter strives for neutrality, and this is precisely what enables him to paint anything. "I have no motif, only motivation," he writes. Richter's motifs vary from photorealist landscapes and portraits to a collections of enlarged color samples from paint stores, from monochrome-grey canvases to explosions of color in alluring jungles of planes and lines. For a time he may paint newspaper photographs or pornographic pictures, then go on to take inspiration from images in art history. His work is actually an exploration of painting's wide range of possibilities; it is as though he is presenting us with samples of painting, showing us what can be done with this art form. His quiet landscapes with snowy mountain tops, desolate seascapes or cloudy skies are sometimes associated with the Romantic tradition in painting, that of Caspar David Friedrich, while the grey monochromes seem to speak the language of Minimal Art. Richter says the following about these, which he began to produce at the end of the sixties: "Grey has no definite character; it doesn't give rise to emotions or associations; grey is neither visible nor invisible. Because of its neutrality, grey is highly suited to serving as a mediator, as elucidation. And it clarifies 'nothingness' better than any other color." The grey monochromes are the best illustration of Richter's neutral stance with respect to painting.

The neutral and even grey of *Grau (Nr. 365/2)* (1974) stands in sharp contrast to the colorful *Abstraktes Bild (Nr. 421)* (1977), which has an almost cosmic, spatial effect. *Abstraktes Bild (Nr. 421)* belongs to the series of colorful works in which forms and fields of color run together. At the time it must have come across as being totally new; nothing of the kind had ever been shown before in painting. Though it may conjure up some vague reminiscence of American abstract expressionism, there is an important difference: the paint is applied smoothly. This smoothness can be explained by the fact that the work is, in fact, a meticulously painted copy (250.5 x 202 cm) of a small painting from 1976 which measures only twenty-six by twenty-three centimeters. The method came to be used frequently by Richter, and it further emphasizes the neutrality that characterizes Richter's work. The small work that has served as a model does have a spontaneous and messy appearance, in the tradition of abstract-expressionist painting by figures such as Hans Hoffman and Willem de Kooning. With the meticulously painted enlargement, involving a blurring of color and form, the distance between the artist and the artwork is greater.

A transcendence of style is also the aim of **Walter Dahn** and **Jiří Georg Dokoupil**, who were part of the group *Mülheimer Freiheit*, named after a street in Cologne where its six members had their studios. These are artists who wish to be restrained by nothing. "Everything is open," says Dahn, while Dokoupil attributes his dislike of fixed programs to the fact that he grew up in the former East bloc country Czechoslovakia. *Maler ohne Idee* is the title that Dahn has given to several paintings. But, even so, Dahn's early paintings have a clearly expressive, spontaneous style with images that can best be described as exalted figuration: human figures that have been anatomically distorted for the sake of heightened expression. Dokoupil makes much more graphic work and puts more emphasis on drawing and on imaginative forms. Dahn's 'stylelessness' mainly consists of an openness to a variety of cultural atmospheres. His work is a melting pot of influences that vary from pop music, ethnographic objects to everyday life. Dahn's art is as complex as life itself: layered and chaotic. If any guiding principle can be found in his motifs, it is to be found in the frequently ironic tone of his work, which always harbors a certain seriousness nevertheless, as can be seen with *Trinken, trinken, er trinkt (Posada)* from 1982. The works that he produced shortly following this period were much more graphic in character: a thick, black line drawing is set against a colorful background. In order to stress their freedom from any personal style, Dahn and Dokoupil have also made paintings together. In 1984 the Folkwang Museum in Essen initiated a travelling exhibition of the work of Dokoupil. Typical of the 'stylelessness' to which Dokoupil aspired, the exhibition was comprised of sixteen groups of paintings that differ from each other thematically as well as formally. There were dark, cosmic paintings, referred to collectively as *Scenes from the Postnuclear World*; there were the *Amsterdammer Bilder*, distorted portraits in a 'psychedelic' style; and there were paintings dominated by a nocturnal color of blue. The two 'mask' paintings from 1982, *Masken IV* and *Masken V*, are among the most subdued groups. These elongated images are reminiscent of abstract African masks. But the painting itself is also 'masked', because the white paint covers a large part of the colorful ground layer. This is a stratified work in which the artist plays with depth and flatness, with color and the absence of color, with abstraction and figuration.

If there is any artist whose work is stratified, then it would have to be **Sigmar Polke**. In a connotative as well as in a formal, painterly sense, his paintings are composed of many levels. Time and again, Polke paints layer upon layer, image upon image, in a manner not unlike that of the earlier Francis Picabia, though Polke's work is more complex. Occasionally Polke also combines different types of grounds, existing fabrics that he pastes on top of each other, fabrics that often have a pattern of their own, such as curtain fabric, tablecloths or blankets, over which he applies an image of his own, be it abstract or figurative. By now he has also built up a body of work that stands out by way of its enormous diversity. Whereas neutrality prevails throughout the work of Richter, irony and magic are Polke's points of departure. But his irony does contain a high degree of seriousness and depth. The painting *Höhere Wesen befahlen: rechte obere Ecke schwarz malen!* from 1969 is characteristic of this interweaving of seriousness and irony. On the one hand, he parodies the hard-edge painting of someone such as Ellsworth Kelly, who paints planes of color that are void of personal 'handwriting'. Moreover, there is an ironic reference to the German Romantic tradition, in which 'the higher', the transcendent, played a central role. But with the countless allusions to the 'higher', to mysticism and alchemy in his work, Polke does suggest that he at least takes these metaphysical aspects seriously. Sigmar Polke's art fluctuates not only between irony

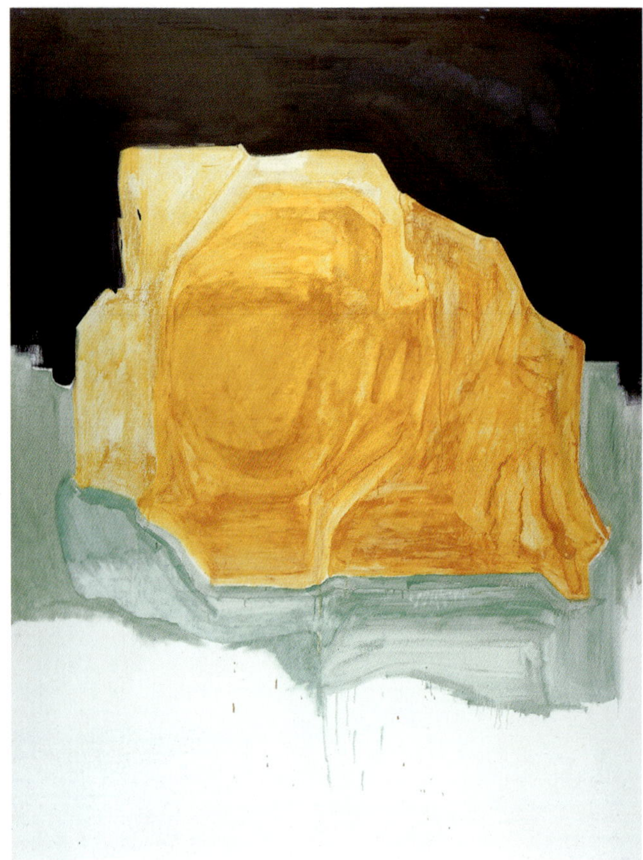

Sigmar Polke *Goldklumpen*, 1982

Sigmar Polke *Höhere Wesen befahlen: rechte obere Ecke schwarz malen!*, 1969

and magic, but also between anarchy and alchemy, the barrenness of conceptual art and the sensuality of abstract-expressionist painting. In short, his work possesses a great richness and does not allow itself to be reduced to a clear-cut category.

Some of Polke's paintings are subjected to changes, whether these be chemical changes that occur over the course of time or changes brought about by a varying concentration of humidity in the space. To Polke, the painting is sooner a natural process than a static object. This is why the gist of the artwork cannot be conveyed in a photograph. Because the toxic *Schweinfürter* green and the yellow (gold pigment), which also contains an arsenic compound, are incorporated in the work *Goldklumpen* (1982), it cannot be reproduced properly. Like *Höhere Wesen befahlen: rechte obere Ecke schwarz malen!*, this is a key work, since Polke was making deliberate use of the meanings of materials for the first time. Polke says the following about *Goldklumpen*: "In search of magnificent colors, I discovered that they were toxic. Certainly where *Schweinfürter* green (containing arsenic) is concerned. This pigment is no longer being produced,

because it is so poisonous. There are quite a few things that you can't get anymore, because they've found ways to make them less harmful. Just as they did with art." Polke does not want art that is 'harmless' or noncommittal in terms of meaning.

At the end of the sixties, **Lothar Baumgarten** also began to produce art that indicated his dissatisfaction with innocuous, 'easy' and commercialized art. This is why he created sculptures of pure pigment powder; being touched would cause them to disintegrate and thereby make them ill-suited to commercial ends. In the large installation *Projektion*, from 1971, this principle is still evident. It shows an actual-size slide projection of a wall in his kitchen which at the time, in 1968, was still serving as a studio as well. There are all sorts of objects–photographs, a table with all kinds of things on it, some artworks and articles of clothing. Several other projected objects have also been added, in concrete form, to *Projektion*, so that the projection and the object sometimes coincide. In this work the influence of Marcel Broodthaers's projections can be sensed to a considerable degree. It is a work that deals with

appearance and reality, with illusion and ephemerality. When the light is switched off, the projection ceases to exist and the single objects placed against the bare wall of the museum suddenly seem homeless. Baumgarten is especially known as being the artist who spent a year-and-a-half, from 1978 to 1979, living among the Yanomamö Indians in Venezuela. Before setting off on this journey, he had acquainted himself thoroughly with their culture. The period spent with these people had a profound influence on his work. Later he would give expression, in his work, to a critical standpoint with respect to the Western, colonialist view of this culture. But even before this Baumgarten took inspiration from this Indian culture. The Van Abbemuseum owns a number of 'staged' photographs, in which there is a suggestion that these have been taken by an anthropologist in the rain forest, while they were actually made in Germany.

For **Rebecca Horn**, visual art is equally unimportant as a source of inspiration. Writers such as Franz Kafka, Raymond Roussel, and film world figures such as Luis Buñuel and Buster Keaton have greater significance to her. One of the main themes of her work is the tension of contained energy, which sometimes explodes. The machine-like objects that she produces bring to mind the curious machines that one encounters in the books of the French writer Roussel. Horn began her career as a performance artist, giving her body prosthesis-like additions and extensions that were used in actions resembling rituals. In her later work as well, the human body continues to play a key role, though it is no longer visible in a literal sense, at least if one excludes the various films made by her. In her performances she treated the body as though it were a machine; the machines evoked in the later work resemble bodies, living creatures that begin to move now and then. Fluids ooze, hammers suddenly start to bang away and threaten to break large mirrors, rifles are aimed at the viewer and then move toward each other and shoot off red liquid. Like the later work of Polke, Horn's work cannot be captured in a reproduction; it is dependent on the experience of the viewer, who will immediately feel the tension on entering a space where Horn's work is present. That tension may not be so immediately visible in the early sculpture *Das Goldene Bad* from 1980. Due to its severe, rectangular iron form, it might seem to relate to the tradition of Minimal Art, but the text printed on the glass cover plate indicates that this work, too, refers to the body. The text comes from a book by the famous Florentine artist and historian Georgio Vasari (1511-1574). In his renowned book on the lives and work of

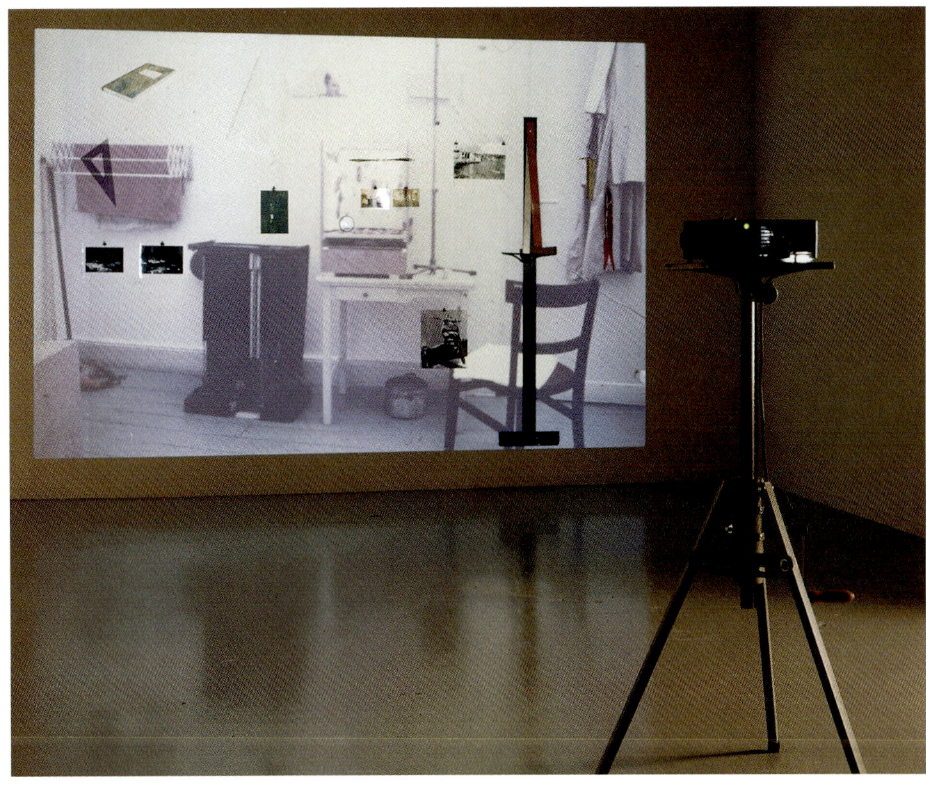

Lothar Baumgarten *Projektion*, 1971

Italian painters, Vasari tells about a boy who, in a procession, was to portray the rise of the Golden Age. The body of the naked boy was gilded. Vasari wrote, not without irony, "Let me not fail to mention that, as a consequence of the discomfort suffered for the gain of ten scudi, the gilded little fellow, the son of a baker, died shortly thereafter."

Horn's dark iron case does, in fact, have the look of a tomb. The bin is filled with water, whose condensation forms beneath the plate of glass and then drips, as though tears, back into the basin. The work was exhibited in Florence in 1980.

Like *Das Goldene Bad*, the large installation *The Moon, the Child and the River of Anarchy* was also made for a specific place, namely for a former school building in Kassel. It was among the most impressive works to be seen at *documenta IX* in 1992. The location gave rise to an unpleasant memory that Horn had from her school days, of standing in front of the class and wetting her pants from nervousness. *The Moon, the Child and the River of Anarchy* is far from being an illustration of this experience. There is indeed a flowing of liquid, but rather than urine we see black ink. A number of school desks are hung upside-down from the ceiling, defying gravity and evoking enormous tension. A tangle of lead pipes sprouts from the desks. Some are short and remain in the space itself, but the majority work their way outdoors and, along the outside wall, descend several floors to reach the ground. Ink flows through the pipes and into funnels. Most of it is pumped up again, thus bringing about a cycle of ink, which symbolizes energy here. The whole of this

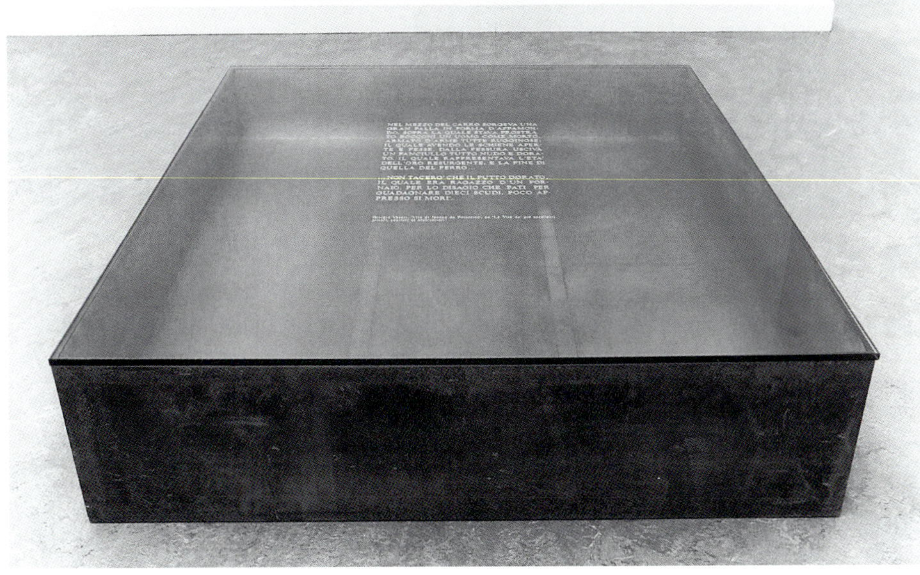

Rebecca Horn *Das Goldene Bad*, 1980

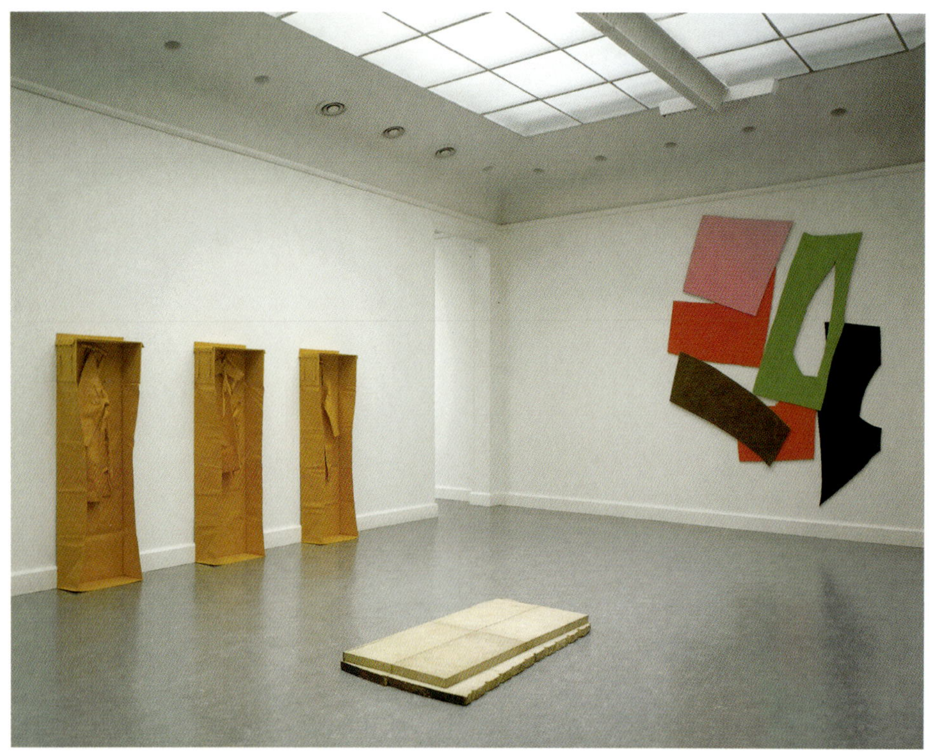

From left to right: **Franz Erhard Walther** *Gelber Plastischer Gesang (einzeln zusammen)*, 1984; **Ulrich Rückriem** *Sandstein geteilt und zugeschnitten*, 1976; **Imi Knoebel** *Ohne Titel*, 1978;

boards enter, as it were, into a human relationship with each other. As simple and formally reduced as the two wooden boards may be, Lohaus manages to animate them, or to be more precise, he manages to emphasize that the used, old materials contain a soul and a history.

Such a romantic approach to materials is not at all evident in the equally austere sculptures of **Ulrich Rückriem**. Rückriem began his career as a stonecutter employed to make copies of antique Gothic sculptures for the restoration of Cologne's cathedral. There he became aware of his concern for the qualities and tooling potential of materials, and he came to dislike the way in which such stone is 'enfeebled', as he describes it. To Rückriem, it is important that stone remains stone after it has been worked. Purity is therefore his theme. "Stone," he says, "is often surrounded by a kind of myth that it doesn't hold." Rückriem takes, in fact, a highly objective approach to his work. For his own purposes, he has drawn up an overview of, first, the various materials that he uses (e.g. dolomite, granite, cast iron, steel), secondly, the

creates the impression of a machine, or even a factory, which leads a life of its own, has its own bloodstream, so to speak, and is a contained organism. For Rebecca Horn, though, it is not so much the clear symbolism of the work, but rather the experience of this by the public which matters.

The experience undergone by the public is also central to the work of **Franz Erhard Walther**. With Walther as well, the body constitutes a main element, but that is where any similarity to the installations of Rebecca Horn ends. Horn is interested in energy and in mechanical and alchemistic aspects, while Walther seeks the tranquillity and meditative aspects of art. Contrary to Horn's increasingly baroque language of forms, that of Walther seems to relate more to the work of Donald Judd in its quietness. Walther, however, does not use the hard materials of Judd and Horn, but soft woven materials such as cotton and linen.

In 1963 Walther started on the series *I. Werksatz*, which he finished in 1969, when it had come to consist of fifty-eight pieces of work. The museum owns thirteen of these works, produced between 1966 and 1969. In addition to this, the collection includes three later works and a portfolio of graphics. The objects from *I. Werksatz* are actually utilitarian objects. They are meant to be used by the visitors. One can lie in them and

unwind, half covered by the soft materials. Unlike the restless sculptures of Horn, those of Walther offer a place for relaxation. Walther is an artist who resists the speed and superficiality of contemporary society, the speed with which art is consumed. With his work he wishes to urge people to slow down. More than stimulating a physical experience, Walther's objects actually serve a mental purpose, and that makes them comparable to ritual objects.

The humanization and vitalization of the artwork as it is brought up by Horn and, in a different way, by Walther can also be seen with the wooden sculptures of **Bernd Lohaus**. Lohaus, who has lived in Antwerp since 1966, makes use of weathered wooden beams that wash up along the shores of the Schelde River, for instance, wood that bears marks of the past. The beams and the boards are altered only minimally by Lohaus: "I saw up or shorten the beams, or I work away the flaws and the superfluous elements. I add nothing." His simple sculptures consequently seem, at first, to be related to Minimal Art. But while Minimal Art refers only to itself according to the principle of 'what you see is what you get', the plain boards of Lohaus are given personality. The word *Ich* is written in chalk on one of the upright boards of *Ich-Du* from 1973. The word *Du* appears on the other. The two upright

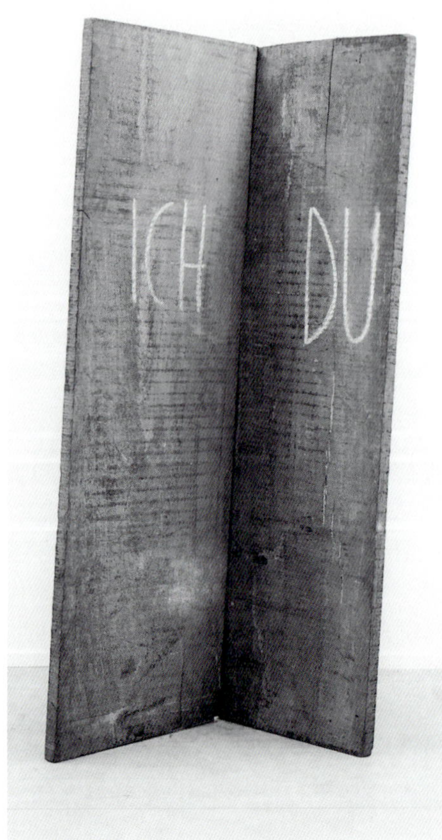

Bernd Lohaus *Ich - Du*, 1973

different tools that can be used (e.g. hammer, chisel, cutting torch, crowbar) and finally the range of tooling methods that can be employed (e.g. hacking, carving, sawing, splitting, forging). Furthermore, Rückriem makes a distinction between three main themes in his sculpture. One of these is the division of volume: a volume of stone or steel, for instance, is divided into segments and then joined together in the original volume. The second theme involves the change of volume, as when steel volumes are altered by beating, embossing or forging. And last of all, volumes can be supplemented or completed, as when additional beams extend across the width of a particular space. The working process and the recognizability of this in the end result are essential in his view. We see the chiselled holes in the stone, the lines of fracture, the smooth, polished surface of one sculpture, the roughness of another. Rückriem shows the wealth of traditional sculptural techniques. And the visual effects of the various tooling methods are done justice by the very simplicity of the forms. The Van Abbemuseum owns a number of sculptures, which illustrate the different materials and techniques employed by Rückriem.

Starkly contrasting with the ruggedness and the elementary nature of Rückriem's sculptures are the elegant and seemingly weightless works that **Isa Genzken** produced during the late seventies and early eighties. At that time she was making, for the most part, reclining and elongated sculptures of wood, concealing this material beneath a smooth, colorful layer of paint. The curved form of these streamlined sculptures, among them *Feuervogel* from 1981, gives them a dynamic appearance. Having been calculated by a computer, this form was carved from the wood in an extremely precise manner and then polished. Its artificial character strikes the eye immediately, certainly when the work is juxtaposed with that of Rückriem. Along side the stones of Rückriem, which have been worked by human hands, we see smooth, computer-drawn forms that look more like industrial design than sculpture. These sculptures are based on three geometric figures: the parallelogram, the hyperbola and the ellipse. *Feuervogel* is a hyperboloid and has an incision which shows an 'interior' of the sculpture in another color. This 'inside' form is a thinner hyperboloid, and it suggests that the outside form is moreover present in the core, like growth rings in a tree. Because the sculpture broadens at the two ends, it is as though it is only a fragment of a larger, endless form, this being antithetical to the

closed ellipsoids. Later in the eighties Genzken produced, among other things, grey concrete sculptures placed on tall iron structures; these have the appearance of architectural models, though they look more like models of building ruins than of new housing. With these new, more existential works, the gap seems to have narrowed in relation to Rückriem's sculpture, despite the fact that concrete is an artificial material, unlike stone and iron. But Rückriem is a true sculptor, who combines all sorts of sculptural techniques and materials as tersely as possible, while Genzken produces sculptures that deviate from the traditional.

The work of **Imi Knoebel** is also colorful and painted smooth. Knoebel produces painting which is spatial and which can just as easily be interpreted as sculpture. And when he creates an installation with various objects–sometimes with paintings, too, that are stacked on the floor or leaning against the wall as they are in a studio–then the spatial arrangement itself can be seen as a three-dimensional painting. The distinction between painting and sculpture is blurred. Along with Beuys, Malevich is also an

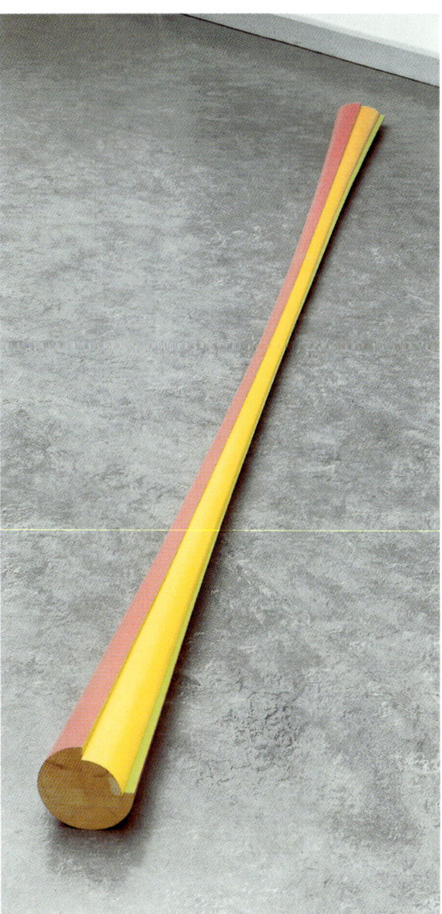

Isa Genzken *Feuervogel*, 1981

important source of inspiration for Knoebel. In his free, unconstrained implementation of an abstract language, Knoebel is perhaps most comparable to Domela and Van Doesburg, two artists whose work developed within the strict tradition of De Stijl but who deal with form and color in a more liberal manner than Mondrian. Knoebel began his career with white canvases on which straight, parallel lines have been painted. But his work quickly became more 'unregulated' when he began showing immaterial projections of light on the wall. By way of these light projections, he arrived at the making of hovering forms, by hanging a square monochrome painting slightly askew for instance, which altered not only the experience of the work but also that of the space. Dynamics thereby come into the picture.

Since 1973 Knoebel has been using color in his work. His palette includes a broad range of colors. Furthermore, his abstract visual language is very free, though not lacking in clarity. Knoebel's work is a combination of harmony and movement. *"Offenheit, kein System!"* (Openness, No System!) is written somewhere on a drawing from 1975.

The six irregular monochrome forms of Knoebel's *Ohne Titel* (1978) are like abstract elements which, when placed against the white wall of a museum, transform that wall, as it were, into a white painter's canvas. They are slightly reminiscent of Matisse's most abstract *papiers découpés*, which he made while bedridden at the end of his life. The careless edges of *Ohne Titel* could indeed have been caused by scissors. But *Ohne Titel* is cut from wood, not paper.

Knoebel's body of work is varied. In it one can discern a freedom that is also sought by such artists as Richter and Dokoupil. But unlike Richter and Dokoupil, Knoebel opts not for 'stylelessness' but for a broad notion of painting as a manifestation of this freedom. Knoebel has a distinct style, which is a distant echo of Russian Constructivism. Playing a role in this are personal experiences and visual impressions, which may be the reason why the work projects, despite its massiveness, a certain intimacy.

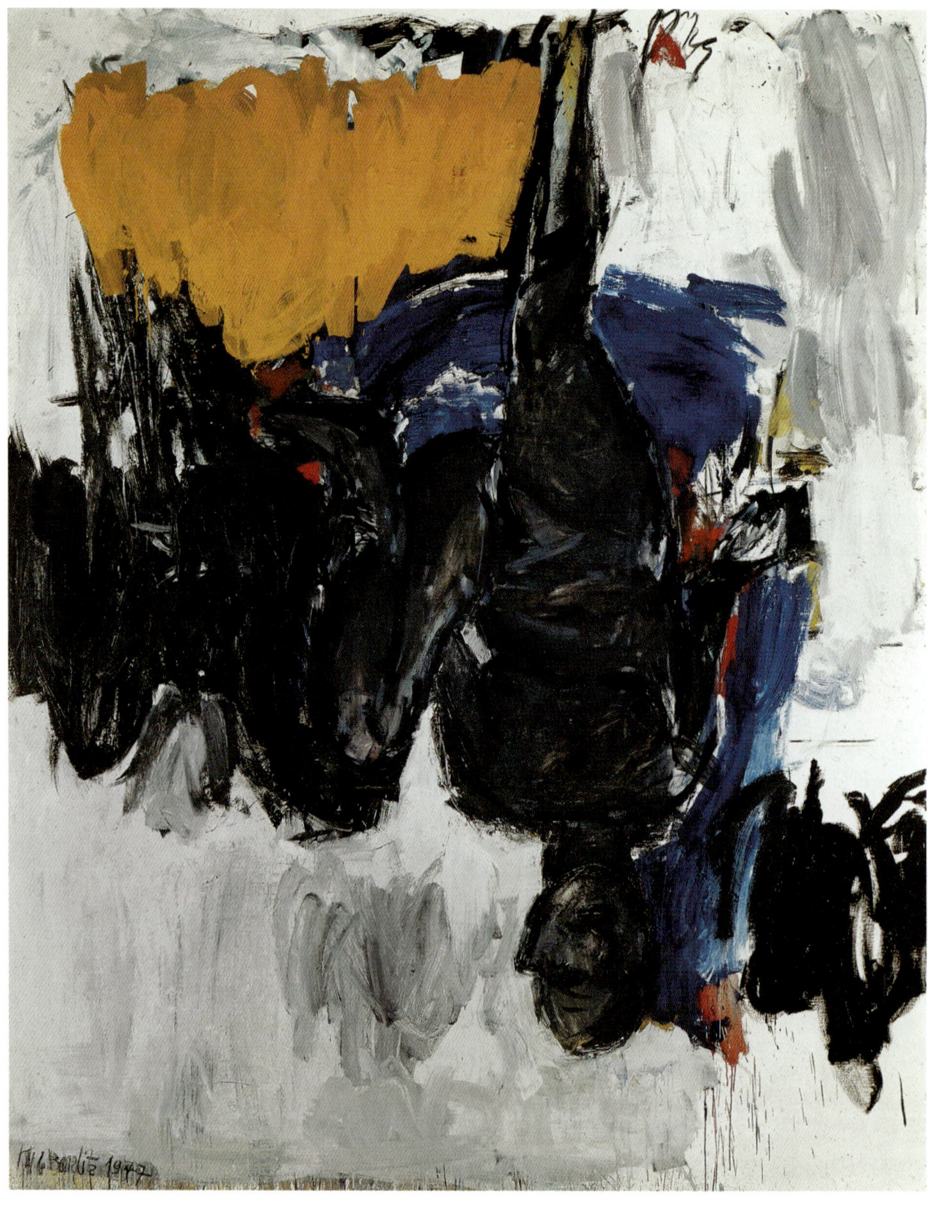

Georg Baselitz *Akt Elke*, 1977

"The tradition of German painting is the tradition of ugly paintings." This statement by Georg Baselitz does hold an element of truth. German artists such as Dürer, Grünewald and Holbein seem, after all, to have had little concern for beauty. The suffering of Christ, for instance, has never been depicted so gruesomely and intensely as in German painting. Emotion, expression and symbolism are, in that art, more prominent than formal beauty, and this can still be said with respect to the contemporary art. When Rudi Fuchs first saw the somber work of Anselm Kiefer in 1974, he opposed it vehemently: "It was an enormous slash at what I had always believed, namely that Ryman was the greatest painter in the world, directly followed by Mangold." The painting which was setting the tone at that time was abstract and minimalist. Ryman made entirely white paintings, Mangold monochrome fields of color, all without representation, minimalist, pleasantly clear and void of any personal 'handwriting'. Moreover, (non-minimal) painting had, in fact, been declared dead.

But like a thunderbolt, it seemed, a new generation of painters had appeared on the scene, reintroducing figuration and applying the paint with wild gestures. Gone was the clarity and calm. To some, this reintroduction of the depiction was a step backward. The American Minimal artist Donald Judd railed against this in his writings. And in 1981, in the influential ideological magazine *October*, Benjamin Buchloh launched a fierce attack on the return of figuration and expression in European painting, which he regarded as a dangerous regression. Buchloh discerned a relationship with the *rappel à l'ordre* of the 1920s, a reversion to the past, to which avant-garde artists such as Picasso and Severini also fell prey–a new conservatism that he linked with the rise of fascist dictatorship during that time. Those are serious insinuations, though not entirely incomprehensible, in view of the motifs that were being dealt with on the canvases of these German artists: facets of German history, including some of its darkest pages. While the norm of those days said that art should be international, in Germany paintings obviously manifesting their German roots were being produced. Kiefer, for instance, did not shy from broaching heavy themes associated with the Nazi era, such as German mythology, the glorification of heroism and Nazi architecture. Lüpertz and Baselitz depicted soldiers and the attributes of war. These neo-expressionist paintings were consequently described by another critic as being "acts of aggression."

In many cases, the work is certainly painted in an aggressive manner, not only in terms of subject matter but also in a painterly sense. Many pieces of work come across as being raucous and restless, either in the painterly technique or in the overall atmosphere. Kiefer's palette is somber, like the (German) soil. Sometimes he even literally attacks the painting with fire, so that the paint is scorched black in certain areas. In Baselitz's earliest works, bloody, amputated parts of bodies were depicted. The image thus deviating from the rule, evoked by the paintings of Kiefer and the other Germans, nevertheless made a lasting impression on Fuchs. During the first half of the seventies, while most museums of modern art were still concerned with the United States, where the modernist tradition was purest, the newly appointed young director of the Van Abbemuseum, Rudi Fuchs, had already set his sights on Germany in 1975. A crucial factor with respect to his acquisition and exhibition policy was his friendship with Johannes Gachnang, director of the Kunsthalle in Bern and former exhibition-maker at the Goethe Institute in Amsterdam, where Gachnang had exhibited work by some of these German artists. Already in his first year as director, Fuchs took over an A.R. Penck exhibition that Gachnang had organized for his museum in Bern. In 1977 an exhibition was dedicated to Markus

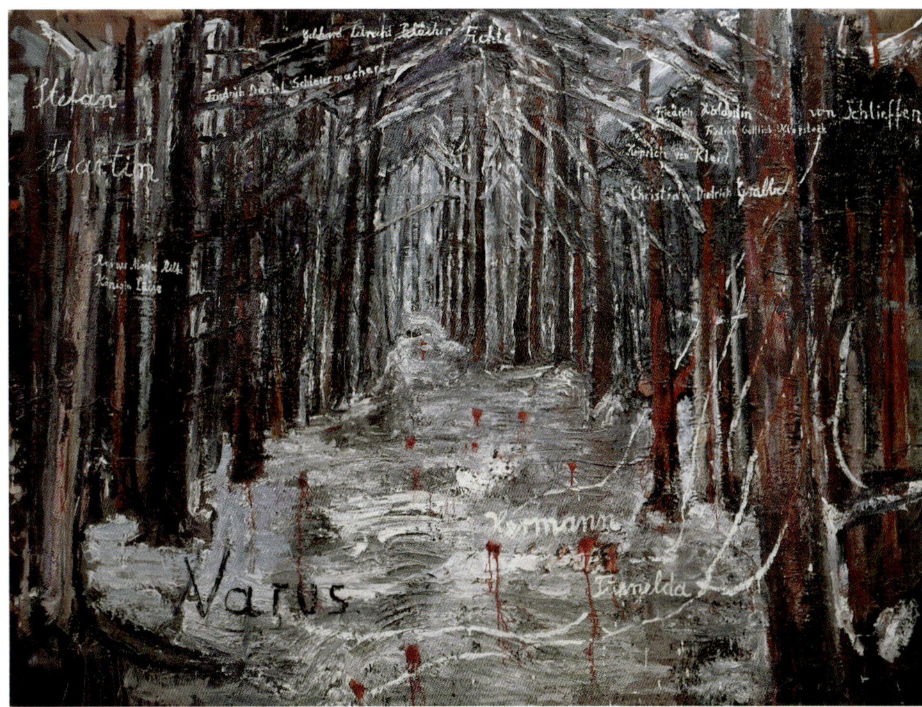

Anselm Kiefer *Varus*, 1976

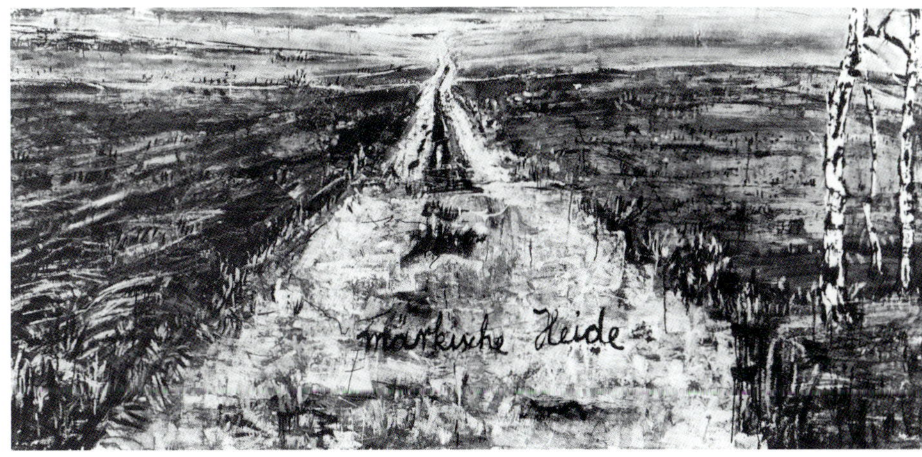

Anselm Kiefer *Märkische Heide*, 1974

Lüpertz, also a good friend of Gachnang. Thanks to the early involvement that Rudi Fuchs had with the leading figures of the new German painting, this is outstandingly represented in the Van Abbemuseum. The museum is even fortunate enough to own a number of key works, such as Polke's *Höhere Wesen befahlen: rechte obere Ecke schwarz malen!* from 1969, Jörg Immendorff's *Hört auf zu malen* from 1966 and several early paintings by Anselm Kiefer. The Van Abbemuseum was also the first museum ever to purchase a work by Baselitz.

The German identity constitutes an important source of inspiration for **Anselm Kiefer**, who was born in the last year of the war. Kiefer's treatment of the darkest pages from German history attests to a certain audacity, as this theme was never discussed during those years. *Märkische Heide* (1974) is an early painting. The composition, a dirt road that vanishes into the horizon from the middle of the canvas, is faintly reminiscent of Meindert Hobbema's *Het laantje van Middelharnis* from 1689. But rather than the rural idyll presented to us by Hobbema, Kiefer shows an unattractively barren and scorched heath. Only three bare trunks of birches, along the right side, hint at any sort of life and hope. Moreover, Kiefer has hardly depicted any sky in the painting, only the dismal earth, so that the road seems endless.

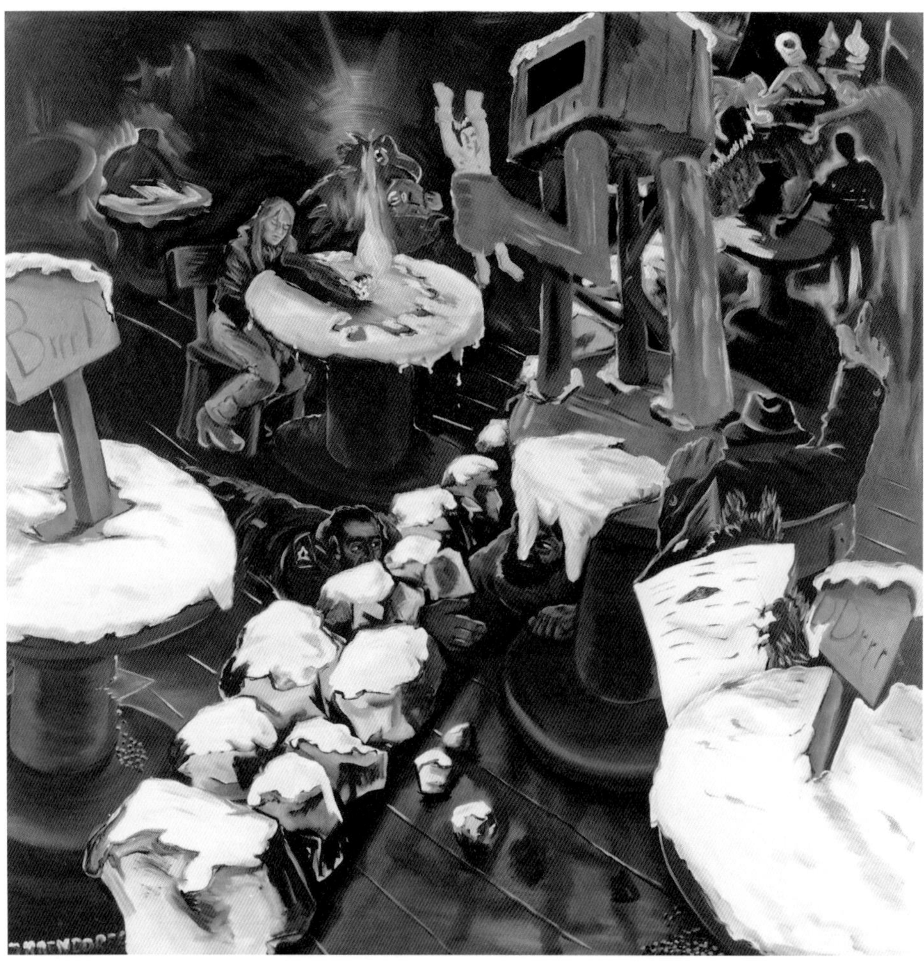

Jörg Immendorff *BrrrD-DDrrr Café Deutschland*, 1978

The title refers to the Mark Brandenburg, the area around Berlin, in former East Germany, which is fraught with historical meaning. The painting, the first of the series relating to the landscape of Brandenburg, conjures forth the image of a country ravaged by war, withered and desolate.

Varus (1976) is also an empty landscape, gloomy and bloodstained, a dense forest of tree trunks through which a road cuts. Just as little life can be discerned here, though various names have been written on the canvas–'Varus' in black at the lower left. At the lower right we see the names 'Hermann' and 'Thusnelda'. These refer to the *Hermannschlacht*, a battle which, according to tradition, took place in the Teutoburger Wald in 9 A.D. between the Roman general Varus and the German leader Armin or Arminius, a name which became Germanized into 'Hermann' during the seventeenth century. Thusnelda was his wife. Because the Romans were defeated in this battle, various authors have identified it with the birth of the German nation. By adding the names of writers and philosophers such as Friedrich Hölderlin, Heinrich von Kleist and Martin Heidegger, who wrote about this battle in their works and thus contributed to the creation of the legend, Kiefer makes it clear that he is concerned not only with historical fact itself but particularly with the interpretations of this, the cultural preservation of the myth. A work such as *Varus* suggests that Kiefer is a well-read man, who makes art that is fraught with mythological and historical meaning. However, the work also consists of images that have a strong visual character, with absorbing perspectives and sharp contrasts–in *Varus*, for instance, between the dense forest and the emptiness of the road running through it. The museum also owns two other works by Kiefer. These deal with the theme of painting itself, the struggle that it involves, both culturally (iconoclastically) and personally (the artist as a 'falling angel'). *Hört auf zu malen* from 1966 by **Jörg Immendorff** also relates to combat, the combat that he wages against current painting. The work is, in fact, a 'pamphlet' that holds a paradox, because it orders, as a painted work of art, a halt to painting. A large cross has been painted over the bright red of this work in a darker color, and on top of this are the words *Hört auf zu malen*. One can also discern the hat of Joseph Beuys, the father figure of postwar German art, who argued very much for the social involvement of the artist and, in doing so, went far beyond the bounds of painting. The work was done at a turning point in Immendorff's oeuvre. He wished, as he himself put it later, to express his disgust "at the self-congratulatory nature of painting that takes no stance. It is aimed at painting that can be interpreted arbitrarily." Immendorff, a former pupil of Beuys, is an artist with distinctly leftist sympathies. Like Beuys, he has been a member of *Die Grünen*. Immendorff does not wish to produce art for an elite, but works that will also be understood by the masses. His motto: "The work must assume the function of the potato." Unlike the mythical works of Kiefer, Immendorff's art is clear-cut. With six paintings, one of which consists of six parts itself, Immendorff is among the most extensively represented artists from this German group. The museum also owns a work from the important series *Café Deutschland*, which was started by him in 1978 and established his reputation. Immendorff's inspiration for this series was taken from Renato Guttoso's painting *Caffè Greco*. In these paintings, where he places all sorts of figures from the German art world in a disco-like setting, Immendorff's work seems to have become more complex and less clear-cut. There is usually a reference to the dichotomy of Germany. Also in *BrrrD-DDrrr Café Deutschland* from 1978, whose title alone alludes to the country still divided at that time, a snow-covered partition runs through the depicted space. We see the artist extending his hand, straight through this wall, into the DDR, the German Democratic Republic: a sign of protest against the division of his country and a gesture of friendship toward his friend Penck, who was still living in East Germany.

A.R. Penck–the pseudonym of Ralf Winkler, who was born in Dresden in 1939–is not only a painter, but a poet and a jazz musician as well; he has also used other pseudonyms, such as Mike Hammer, Theodor Marx, Y, each with its own background and meaning. The real Albrecht Penck was a geologist who specialized in the Ice Age. The highly simplified, pictogram-like figures that are painted by the artist A.R. Penck bring to mind the drawings of cave men. Penck seeks a universal language in which man is the central focus. His paintings are inhabited by

sign-like figures and symbols that are
sometimes reminiscent of the work of Paul
Klee, but then with the verve of Jackson
Pollock. The theme of identity continues to
crop up in his work, as is already evident
from the different pseudonyms that he has
adopted. That use of pseudonyms,
incidentally, has had to do with his
difficulties, as an artist, in encounters with
the East German authorities. The identity of a
divided Germany, that of himself and of the
artist in East Germany, shut off from the
Western culture of which it was once a part,
are among the themes in his work. His
Torquato Tasso (1976), painted in the year
after his exhibition at the Van
Abbemuseum–a work in which a green
silhouette of a naked woman (a muse, a lover,
perhaps both?) is prominently visible–alludes
to the famous Italian poet from the fifteenth
century, to whom Goethe devoted a play. In
this play the romantic poet elaborates on the
obstinacy and maladjustment of the artist:
society and the artist are simply unable to get
along with each other. Penck seeks
communication with his art. Penck has
experienced how the Communist authorities
manipulate information. That is why his
symbols and signs have the appearance of a
primitive visual language, a language that is
universal and unadulterated. He wishes to
produce images that are so general that
anyone can reproduce them, which to him
would be the ultimate democratization of art.
Penck consequently does not approach his
work in an arbitrary manner. He has become
deeply engrossed in cybernetics, the study of
the structures of control systems in living
creatures, organizations and technology,
particularly with respect to communication
and information-processing. "I think in
themes," says Penck, "and after that I think
about how to depict them." Over the years his
work has become increasingly personal,
though he does continue to respond to world
events, such as the Gulf War and the fall of
the Berlin Wall.

Georg Kern was also born in East Germany
and he, too, makes use of a pseudonym,
Baselitz, taken from the town of
Deutschbaselitz, where he was born in 1938.
In 1957 he moved to West Berlin, long before
Penck, who did not leave for the West until
1980. With his fierce colors and rough
brushstroke, Baselitz can be considered the
most expressive artist of the group. His early
works full of gruesome images show
influences from Antonin Artaud and
Lautréamont; later Dubuffet and the art of
the mentally ill were important to him as
well. In order to concentrate better on the

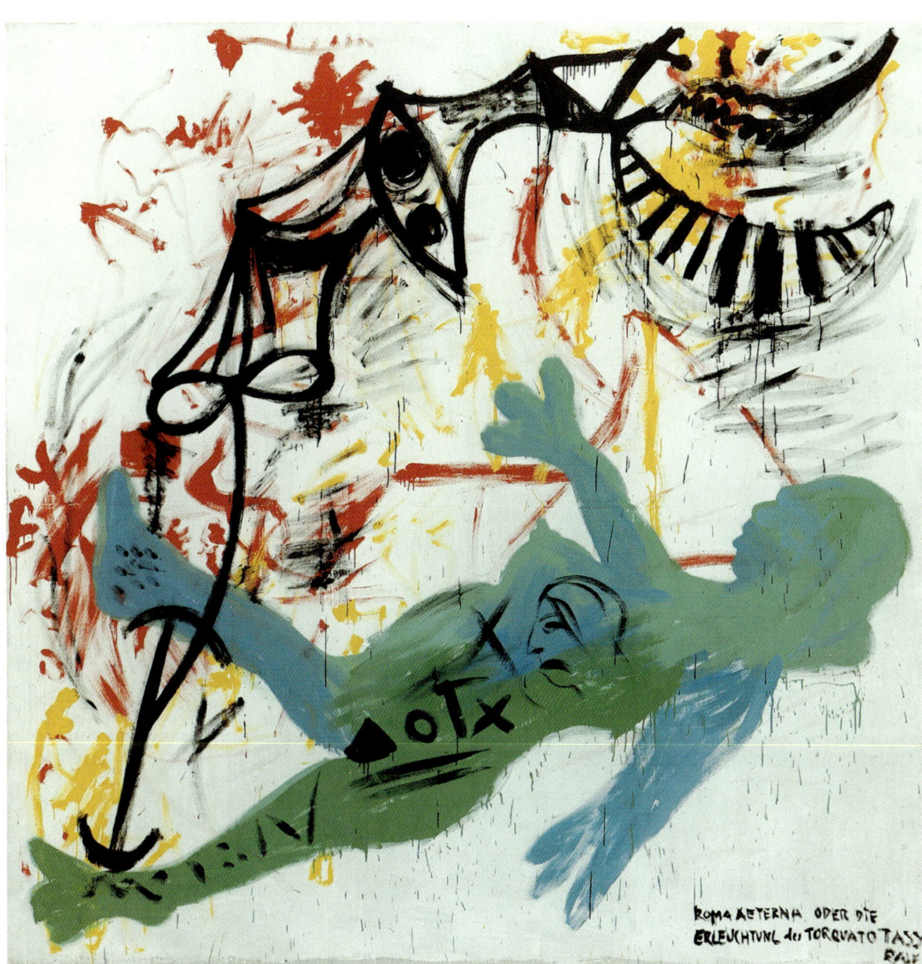

A.R. Penck *Torquato Tasso,* 1976

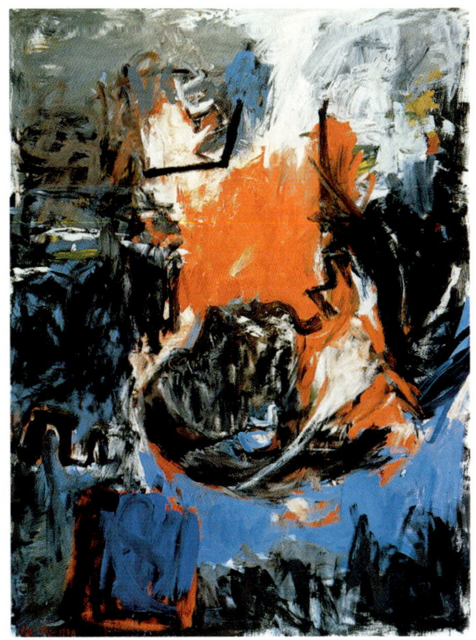

Georg Baselitz *Trümmerfrau,* 1978

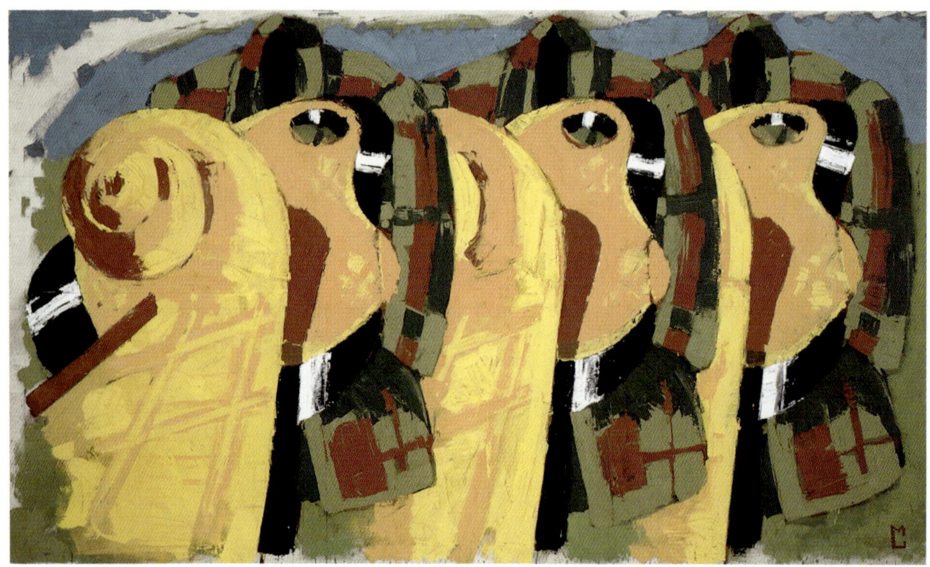

Markus Lüpertz *Eskalation - dithyrambisch,* 1973

painterly aspects than on the depiction, Baselitz has been painting his motifs upside down since 1969. Furthermore, since this time he has been depicting primarily classical, universal themes from painting: the nude, the landscape, the portrait and the still life, trivial and uncommonly old-fashioned subjects that contrast sharply with the powerful expressiveness of his brush and the large format of the canvases. The early paintings having this peculiar rendering of the world, upside down, are still fairly light in color and brushstroke. *Akt Elke* (1977), a nude portrait of his wife, already shows a slightly looser stroke and a greater expressiveness in comparison to previous works, while *Trümmerfrau* from 1978 represents a much bigger step toward an independence of the brushstroke and color. In this work, there is hardly anything left to make it recognizable as a portrait. It seems to be made up of scarcely coordinated sweeps of the brush. Strikingly, the bright red in the middle–juxtaposed with blue, grey and especially a great deal of black–manages to be very imposing, while it actually portrays nothing. As of 1997 he is still painting his subjects upside down, and yet there is a clearly discernible development in his body of work and he remains open to different influences, to which he gives shape in his own inimitable way. At times one can see the influence of Munch, then Nolde seems to be a source of inspiration, and this gives way to Jawlenski–all artists who used color expressively.

That which Baselitz aims to achieve can be compared to what **Markus Lüpertz** claims to be concerned with: painting about painting.

And in this Lüpertz, too, makes use of figuration. But for him, figuration and abstraction do not constitute separate worlds. Whereas, with Baselitz, the figuration sometimes vanishes behind the vehemence of the painterly gesture, with Lüpertz it remains more present, though it is often not clear exactly what the form is supposed to be. In addition to this, his brushstroke is less turbulent and his use of color is more subdued and gloomy. At times Lüpertz combines certain images without giving a clear indication as to why this is done, as with the combination of the snail's shell, palette and soldier's uniform, repeated three times in *Eskalation - dithyrambisch* from 1973. There

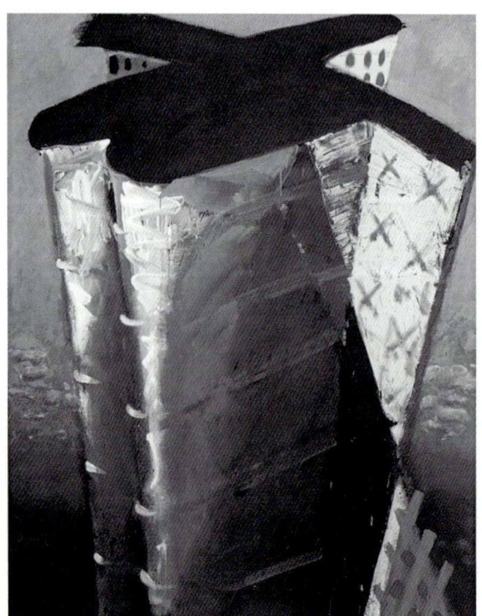

Markus Lüpertz *Babylon - dithyrambisch XII,* 1975

are two smaller, related versions of this with a single combination of the uniform, palette and snail's shell, which have been titled *Tod und Maler - dithyrambisch.* The term *dithyrambe,* or dithyramb in English, was introduced by Lüpertz in 1964. A dithyramb, in Greek antiquity, is a choral song or chant in honor of Dionysus. The importance thus ascribed by him to the ecstatic, which is linked with the ritual worship of this god of wine, or Bacchus, is thoroughly consistent with the expressionist style. To Lüpertz, the dithyramb stands for a vital, autonomous visual language. Nietzsche, who wrote an extensive treatise on the cult of Dionysius, states that the Dionysian urge is the engine of the creative process, and he places this in contrast to the outward charm and forced shape of the cult of Apollo. Even so, Lüpertz does not wished to be called an expressionist. He admires, on the contrary, Mondrian, and in his paintings he quotes the styles of figures such as Picasso, Corot and Poussin. Lüpertz strives, above all, for a continuation of the European painterly tradition, and that is why he wants to measure up to these old masters. His *Babylon - dithyrambisch XII* from 1975 is a prime example of the convergence of figuration and abstraction in his work. On the one hand, it seems as though an architectonic mass is being depicted from a bird's-eye perspective, but on the other, the mass is so scantly defined and sooner decorative in layout that it could just as easily be interpreted as a nonrepresentational motif. With both works, however, the forms can be described as robust, which is typical of all work by Lüpertz.

Though **Per Kirkeby** is a Danish artist whose work displays strong Scandinavian traits, he does have close ties with Germany. Beuys, Baselitz, Immendorff and Penck are among his friends, and he teaches at several art academies in Germany. Furthermore, his brush technique is closely related to the neo-expressionist style. Having a degree in geology, Kirkeby has taken part in a number of scientific expeditions to, among other places, Greenland and Central America. In addition to paintings and drawings, he makes unique sculptures of brick, directs plays and films, publishes articles and books on various topics and writes poetry. In his paintings he evokes a sense of landscape, that is to say almost abstract impressions of this, as can also be seen with the late work of Willem de Kooning and with some paintings of Asger Jorn. While De Koonings evocations relate to the play of light and water in the landscape, Kirkeby's brushstrokes seem to depict mainly dark woods, tree trunks, rocks and

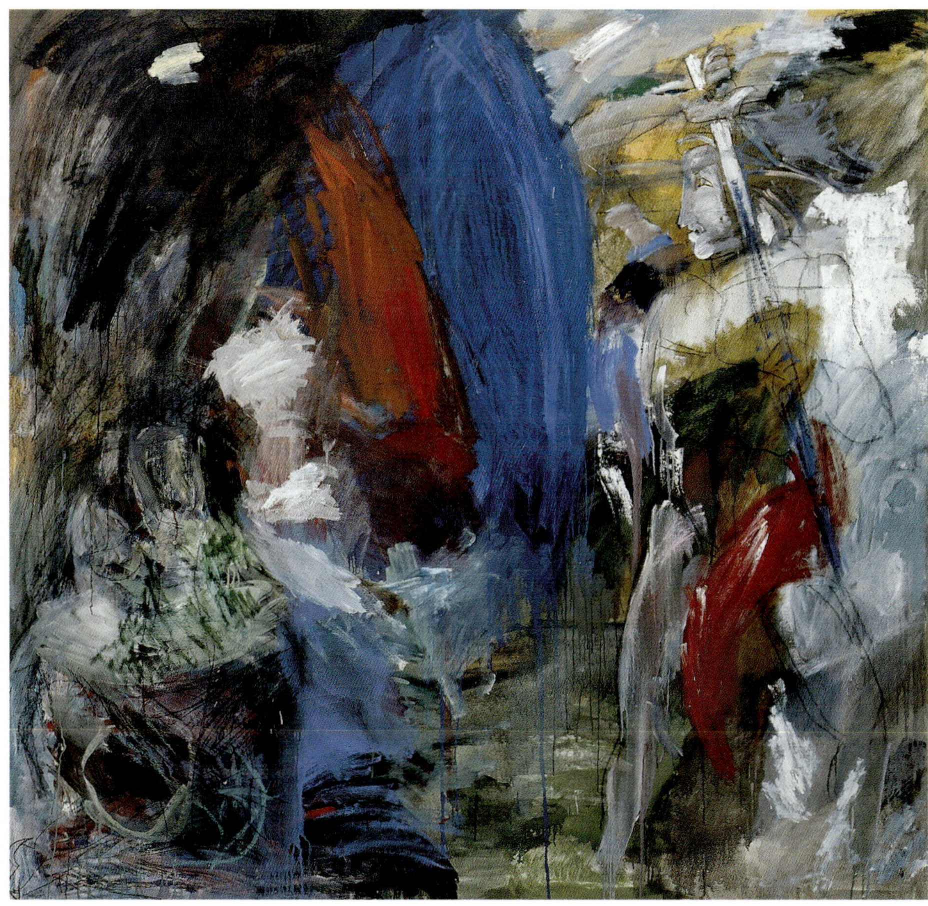

Per Kirkeby *Ohne Titel*, 1979

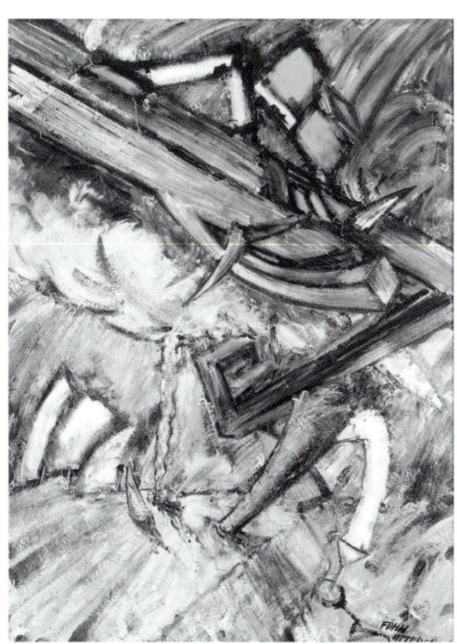

Christian Ludwig Attersee *Föhn*, 1984

caves–with intermittent rays of light that make the colors flare up against the somber background. The Van Abbemuseum owns three works by Kirkeby, two from 1979 and one from 1985.

Compared to the expressionism in Germany, the Austrian variant of this movement (if it can be called that) is much more physical and psychological. It is as though the ideas of Sigmund Freud, the great Viennese psychoanalyst, continue to give Viennese art a powerful impulse. Perhaps it is **Christian Ludwig Attersee**, born in 1940 in Slovakia, who makes work that can still be described as expressive in the usual sense, with respect to his loose handling of the brush, the dynamics and the bright hues of his palette. Even so, one can discern in his work a concern for the physical and especially the erotic, which seems characteristic of Austrian art, such as that of Klimmt and Schiele has been in the past. Attersee, who also produces music and poetry–some of his paintings also have a poem as a pendant–frequently paints absurd scenes. A church in a champagne glass, a dancer whirling away on top of two mountain peaks, a woman with a horse's head above a surface of water. But the colors and brushstrokes always seem to explode into a cheerful orgy of movement.

This cheer forms a glaring contrast with the profoundly psychological and dead-serious ritualistic activities of **Hermann Nitsch**, with whom Attersee has worked however. Nitsch, then one of the representatives of the *Wiener Aktionismus*, drew considerable attention with his *Orgien Mysterien Theater*, which began in 1963. These were happenings to which the term Dionysian applies unconditionally. Sometimes going on for several days, the mystical stagings–often involving hundreds of extras and musicians, dozens of dead and living animals, and the pouring of literally thousands of liters of blood–form a *Gesamtkunstwerk* which holds such a wealth of meaning and allusions that it can scarcely be explained in a few words. These were ritual sacrifices directed by Nitsch, accompanied by various assistants and musicians. In 1983 Nitsch carried out such a work at De Fabriek in Eindhoven, in connection with his retrospective exhibition at the Van Abbemuseum. These performances usually start with peculiar music and end with the crucifixion of a previously slaughtered lamb and the flow of blood and animal organs onto undressed assistants, who were frequently bound to crosses as well. Christian symbolism plays an obvious role, but there are also references to other types of ritual sacrifice. And blasphemous provocation is involved. But, to Nitsch, provocation also implies devotion. Like all rituals, these acts are ultimately, to Nitsch, a liberation, a victory over that which is gruesome and an exaltation of life. The clothing and other objects that have been stained at these rituals are later, together with his paintings (canvases drenched in blood-red paint), exhibited as relics of sacred events. The museum owns a stretcher that was used in such an *Aktion* in 1985 and a large red painting titled *Schüttbild* from 1982.

The work of **Arnulf Rainer** is also physical, though less extreme than that of Nitsch. A ritualistic element can be discerned here as well, but this is a ritual that the artist carries out on his own. Rainer sometimes paints over existing paintings, often reproductions of old masters, and refers to these as *Übermalungen*. This can result in an entirely monochrome work. At first such paintings may seem related to the monochromes of Ryman or Klein, for instance. But the difference is dramatic. To Ryman and Klein, it is ultimately the visible surface that has importance–and with Klein this can even portray the universe. Rainer, however, is interested in the gesture, in the process of

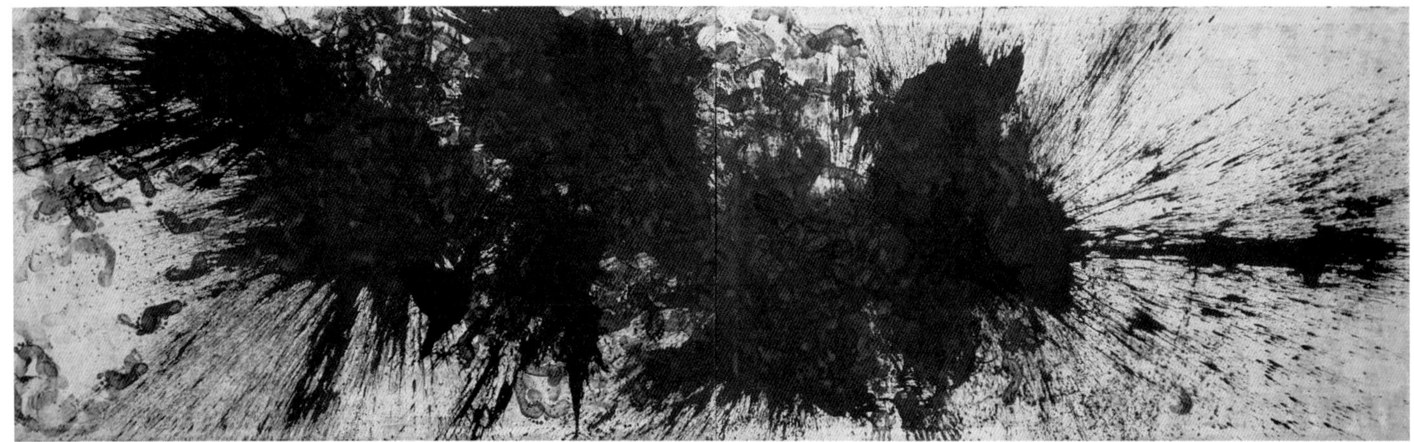

Hermann Nitsch *Schüttbild*, 1982

painting layer upon layer as a ritual, obsessive activity, in which the paint's concealment of what lies beneath it remains palpable. It is a process of internalization, aimed at attaining the expression of complete calm.

But Rainer has also produced paintings where the paint has been applied with his fingers. Contrary to the *Übermalungen*, which are often somber in color, these *Fingermalereien* are colorful, exuberant and spontaneous. They are mostly reminiscent of the wild works produced by primates who have been allowed to play around with paint and paper. Here it is important that the paint ends up on the canvas directly via the body, without the use of a tool. Spontaneity is the main thing. That is why Rainer shows great concern for art made by the mentally ill; they are not impeded by norms and restraints. In Rainer's view, everything produced by man stems from madness, an idea that brings to mind the theories of Freud, who considered human activity to be determined more by irrational, subconscious urges than by reason. And it is this very Dionysian element in man that appears to be a significant source of his creative capacities. At times this is expressed in an aggressive manner, as in the provocative themes chosen by Kiefer, Baselitz and Lüpertz (though this, of course, is not provocation alone), in the sadomasochistic performances of Nitsch and in Rainer's 'painting over' of someone else's work. The aforementioned works, however, point to a clear distinction between the German and the Austrian expressiveness. The provocative element of the Germans is extrovert in character, while the Austrians display an introversion based on depth psychology and the collective subconscious.

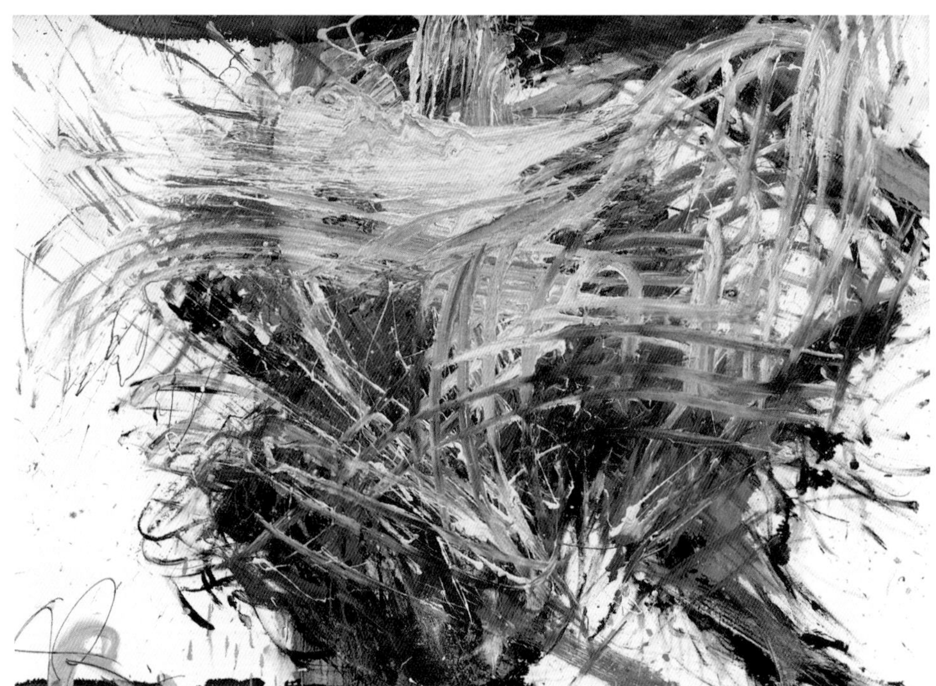

Arnulf Rainer *Fingermalerei*, 1984

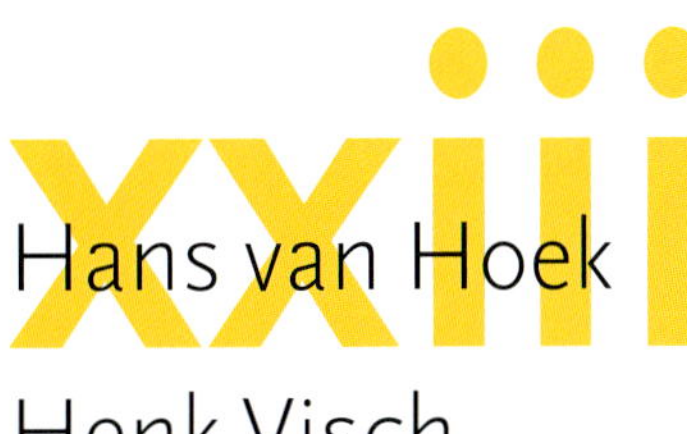

XXIII

Hans van Hoek

Henk Visch

Gerrit van Bakel

Marinus Boezem

JCJ Vanderheyden

Marlene Dumas

Toon Verhoef

Carel Visser

Ulay & Marina Abramović

JCJ Vanderheyden *Blauw kader*, 1966-80

By now there have been many attempts to explain the return of figurative painting. The most obvious explanation relates, of course, to the generation gap. Young artists were supposedly reacting against the conceptual art of the sixties and seventies. The transformation of visual art into theory and philosophy would make the desire for an expressive and distinctly visual art inevitable. Another explanation involves the commercial art market, for which the craving of the 'new' is vital. Fashion imposes its rules on art as well. A third explanation is found in the socioeconomic crisis which affected Europe since the late seventies and which is, in fact, regarded as being the main factor leading to the 'me' generation. Artists were allegedly no longer interested in universal values or fundamental issues, but in personal experiences and highly individual expression. The return of figuration is much less universal or absolute, however, than the aforementioned explanations lead one to suspect. Giving virtually no consideration to the visual art itself, this portrayal of the situation largely has to do with the way in which linear art history writes itself. There are, after all, countless artworks in which figuration merges easily with the conceptual investigation into the specific nature of art. A clear and important example of this is the work of Georg Baselitz, discussed in the previous chapter.

In the Netherlands, too, the gap between abstraction and figuration, or between perceptual and conceptual art, is not extreme. The Netherlands has an art tradition which is not continually being rejected and

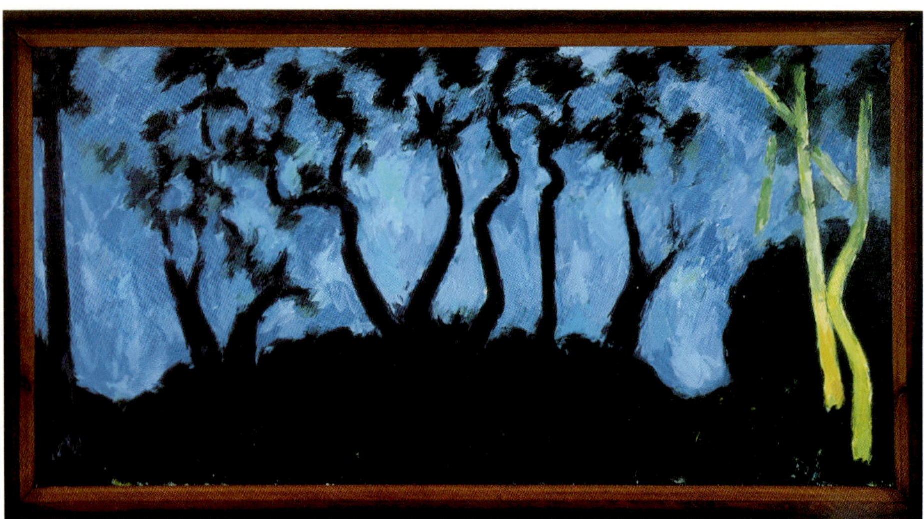

Hans van Hoek *Klein landschap,* 1980-81

rediscovered, but which prompts artists, rather, to contemplate its fundamental aspects. The many Dutch artists represented in the collection of the Van Abbemuseum provide a broad and varied impression of the developments that were taking place in art during the seventies and eighties. That the division between painting and sculpture has vanished entirely here probably only shows that the traditional distinctions among disciplines are indeed no longer relevant. **Hans van Hoek** emigrated to Canada during the early seventies in order to "escape the compromises of the art world," as he himself has put it. In the Netherlands, his expressive and figurative painting was consistently misinterpreted and was seen as being conservative and lacking originality. But when he returned in 1977, there appeared to be an international revival of expressionist painting under way, and his paintings proved to be ahead the new figuration in a number of respects.

Hans van Hoek concentrates on classic painterly conditions, such as composition, invention and the use of color. Along with this, he quotes from art history, which he investigates by means of his work. Like nature, the works of old and modern masters constitute sources of inspiration which he studies with respect. In the work of Van Hoek, there is consequently no real difference between his love of nature and that which he has for painting: "I learn about nature by studying, for instance, the works of El Greco and Rubens; and conversely, I gain greater insight into their art by working, myself, from the nature that surrounds me." After returning to the Netherlands, Van Hoek began to paint landscapes based on observations made outdoors. An essential

problem which arises as a result of this is the issue as to how to express the virtually religious exaltation that he experiences with regard to nature. For the painting which he envisages offers no impression of visible reality, but is rather a painterly re-creation of nature.

In a work such as *Klein landschap* (1980-81) it becomes clear that nature, to Van Hoek, is not limited to the world of people, animals and plants, but also includes the natural properties of materials, colors and light. Like the still life painted by him in Canada, *Chinese bowl on Indian tablecloth* (1974), this landscape is characterized by deep, vibrant colors and fluid lines that imbue the work with a mysterious strength. Hovering between figuration and abstraction, this mysteriousness involves a blend of his own personal symbolism and that of Christendom.

The paintings of Van Hoek are, without exception, set in immense wooden frames that have been carefully worked, varnished and polished. Sometimes they have been decorated with carved ornamental or floral motifs and inscriptions that add to the visual information. Due to the great contrast between the mass of the frame and the immaterial quality of the painted depiction, the frames emphasize the idea that this is a form of painting which is meant to be seen as a kind of relic.

The enigmatic quality that characterizes Van Hoek's paintings can also be found in the sculptures of **Henk Visch**. An important difference, however, is that the work of Visch is not based on a religious experience of art and nature, but on a poetic awareness which is nurtured by memories, dreams, associations and impressions.

Visch's work as a whole is extremely diverse, consisting of drawings, graphics, abstract constructions and figurative sculptures. A overview of the works in the collection of the Van Abbemuseum clearly shows, however, that this diversity is present not only in his equal use of various disciplines, but also in the stylistic appearance of his sculptures. He produces, for instance, massive wooden sculptures, airy constructions, stylized human figures and humorous assemblages made of all sorts of materials. Frequently, a sculpture of his may be comprised of no more than a framework over which paper or cloth has been stretched. Moreover, he has special concern for the surface of a work, which has always undergone some sort of treatment. By notching or painting the surface of the sculpture, or by adding materials such as feathers, wood chips or horsehair, he instills the works with a variety of subtle connotations that are difficult to define. The titles of Visch's works are equally poetic and unfathomable, prompting the start of an interpretation but never pointing in one specific direction. The impulses that give rise to a work are, in Visch's view, innumerable and often impossible to pinpoint or trace. They are simply there, as the result of his urge to produce images. The sculptures of Visch appeal not only to the visual sensibilities of the viewer, but also to his sense of balance. Because the sculpture's contact with the ground is confined to a minimum, its balance is often extremely precarious. In addition to this, the works are occasionally so airy and fragile that wind and weather have free rein and can thus affect the material. Qualities such as vulnerability and transitoriness, which are traditionally foreign to sculpture, are shown with emphasis in the work of Visch.

Contrasting with Henk Visch's belief that the origins of a image can no longer be traced is the aim of **Gerrit van Bakel** to create forms that make the origins of his work evident: "I want to show the form and, at the same time, the way in which I arrived at it–which means that the sketch books are just as important as the machines and the other things, and that everything becomes one and the same."

The works of Gerrit van Bakel stem from his personal ideas about technology and its history, about specific properties of materials and about physical phenomena. With this he has always sought a harmony between these matters and the emotional experience of man. His objects can best be described as machines, even though they do not function as such in a strict sense. After all, Van Bakel's 'machines' produce no material products, but

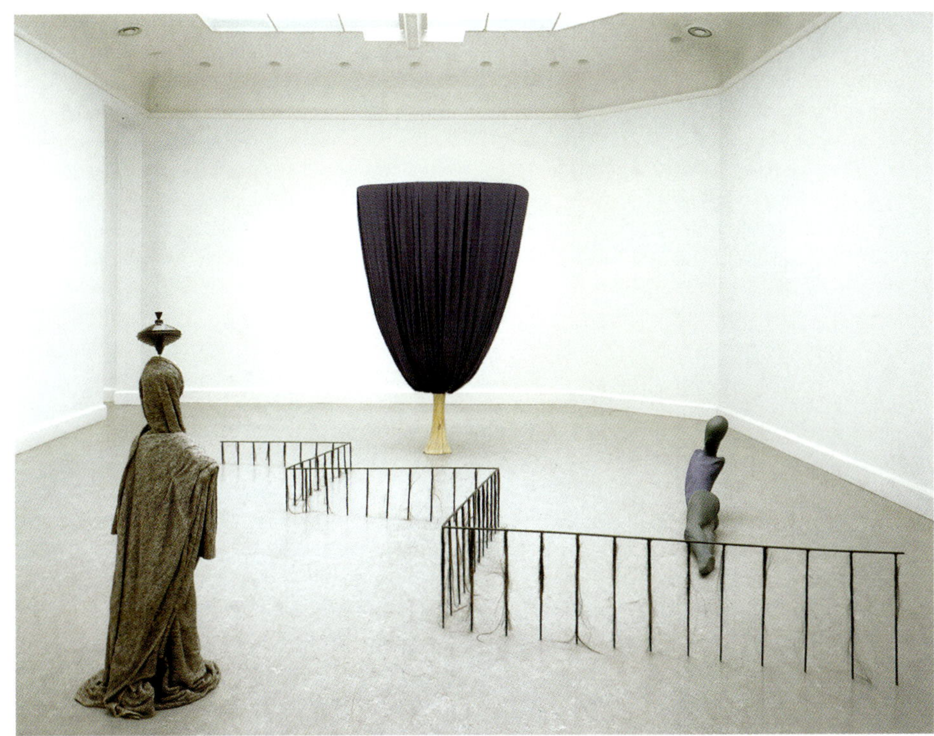

From left to right: **Henk Visch** *Idle thoughts for idle men*, 1992; *Stay Close*, 1984; *Voor dat wat blijft*, 1985; *The artist model*, 1984

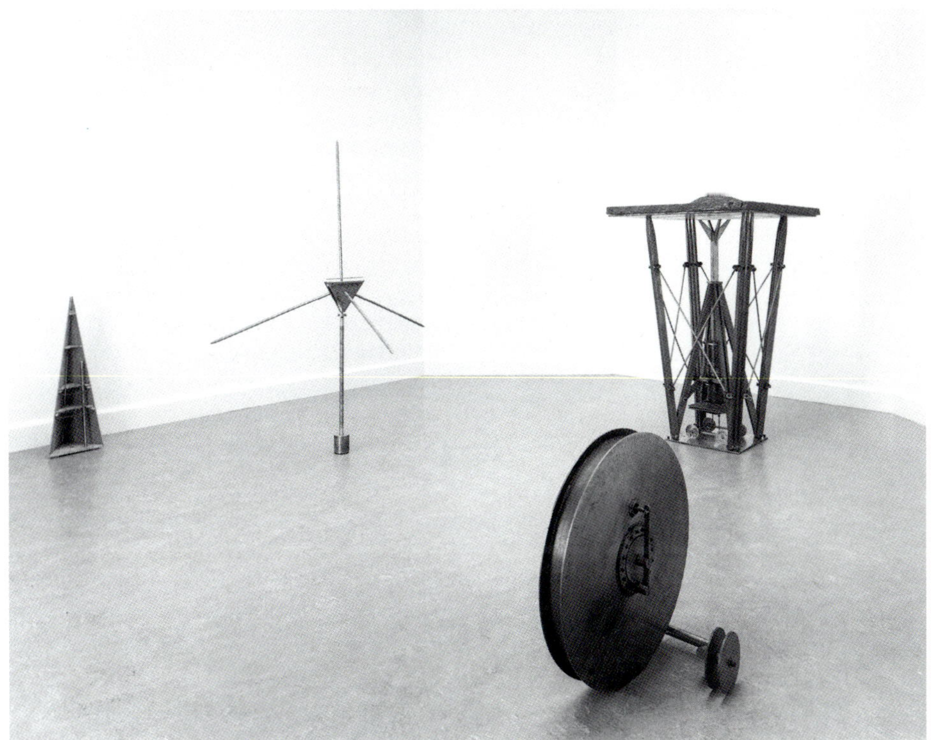

From left to right: **Gerrit van Bakel** *Tetraëder*, 1982; *Een nieuwe mogelijkheid van de vreugde van Papin*, 1981; *Utah-machine (behorend bij de Utah-Tarim connectie)*, 1980

rather awareness, poetry and imagination. They are the materialization of a personal interpretation concerning the relationship between man and nature. In order to attain this, the artist has combined scientific facts and observations with personal experiences and desires.

Themes such as movement, energy, time and temperature are central to the work of Van Bakel. In addition to this, many of his works constitute fundamental criticisms of advanced technology, which has led, for instance, to the fact that we move forward with increasing speed. The ingenious but also humorous nature of this criticism can be seen in a global work such as *Utah-Tarim Connectie*, which he designed in 1980-1982. This was prompted by the news that the three-wheeled rocket 'Blue Flame' had reached a record land speed of about 1000 kilometers per hour on the salt flats of Utah. The first segment of Van Bakel's 'connection' is the *Utah-machine* (1980), which consists of a large, solar-driven wheel that is kept on balance by a smaller auxiliary wheel. Van Bakel would have preferred to set up his machine along side the rocket, in order to have it move across the same salt flats in Utah at a speed of eighteen millimeters per day. The counterpart to this work is the caterpillar-like *Tarim-machine* (1982), which was to start from the other side of the world, in the Tarim Basin of Tibet, also at a speed of eighteen millimeters per day. According to the artist's calculations, it would take thirty million years for the machine to cross the basin. In contrast to the speed record of the Blue Flame, Van Bakel sets a kind of natural record for slowness. His fascination therefore applies not so much to speed as to the phenomenon of time and the way in which man attempts to elude this.

Van Bakel's *Utah-Tarim Connection* was followed by a number of works in which he sought a closer connection with sciences such as mathematics, physics and chemistry. The crucial points at which discoveries or inventions were made by scientists constituted a very important source of inspiration in these. A prominent and clear example of such work is *Een nieuwe mogelijkheid van de vreugde van Papin* (1981), which was shown for the first time at *documenta 7*. The origins of this work lie with Kassel's memorial for Denis Papin, inventor of the steam cylinder. This work by Van Bakel consists of a heap of earth on a granite table, which is lifted by the power of compressed steam. The title, the form and the function of this 'machine' allude to the delight with which the scientist was probably overwhelmed on discovering that he had developed a force many times greater than that of people or horses. As such, the work could be interpreted as a 'reexperience' of the moment of discovery. The fact that the work refers not only to the French scientist and the history of technology, however, is manifest by way of the heap of earth that Van Bakel has placed on the granite table. This earth comes from his birthplace in the province of Brabant and from the field on which his father died. Because of this, the work can be considered not only a monument to Papin, but also an 'altar' for his father and a tribute to the origins of his own, or perhaps even all life.

The 'machines' of Gerrit van Bakel are ingenious, amazing and simple at the same time; in an effective manner, the viewer is faced with an alternative outlook on ordinary matters such as the passing of time and movement through space. The same can be said, to a certain degree, about the works proposed–and carried out on request–by **Marinus Boezem** during the 1960s: a wind tunnel set up in a landscape, a room with the foam floor full of bubbly 'air pockets', a rotating panel driven by fans or a room whose space is suggested by curtains that are moved by air currents.

Since 1960 Boezem's work has no longer consisted of paintings but of acts, demonstrations and stagings in which physical phenomena such as wind, light and gravity are his materials. He has made, for instance, video recordings of himself while breathing onto a monitor; he attempted to map out a particular area by means of sound; he signed fans or registered the humidity of a gallery space by means of a hydrometer. Due to the enormous diversity of materials used, the work of Marinus Boezem has never had the appearance of a formal entity. This does not alter the fact that his work is founded on a number of conceptual principles. It continually focuses on the idea of space in the broadest sense of the word. He is therefore not interested only in the physical space of his art, but also in the historical and present-day contexts which influence the experience and the meaning of the work.

Furthermore, the work of Boezem is largely constructed on the basis of polar notions such as the visible and the invisible, the object-like versus the contextual, or the perceptual versus the conceptual. Such polarity is particularly evident in works from the seventies, in which the experience of scale and the contrast between light and dark play a significant role. Whereas the works involving light deal with the contrast of absence and presence, those involving scale focus on the relationship between the subjective experience of a particular scale, on the one hand, and the concrete, objective facts pertaining to this scale, on the other. An unusual example of a convergence of these two aspects can be seen with *Visual Research* (1970). This installation is essentially made up of an uncovered canvas stretcher leaning against the wall and bright lamp which is directed at it. This causes a shadow to be cast on the wall, at a diagonal behind the concrete stretcher. The dimensions that are projected by Boezem between the wall and the stretcher relate to an invisible form located somewhere between the wooden object and its shadow. Boezem shows the viewer three ways in which he can approach the artwork: on the basis of materiality, on the basis of the immaterial shadow, or on the basis of a definition imposed by the metric system. The freedom to which Boezem aspires, particularly in his early works, also plays a role in the work of **JCJ Vanderheyden**. In the work of Vanderheyden, however, the idea of freedom relates not only to his own position as an artist, but also to that of the viewer. "With respect to the outside world, I primarily honor the principal of freedom, that is to say the freedom of perception as well. One simply cannot force the observations of others, nor would that make any sense in my opinion."

Vanderheyden's work from the early sixties is characterized by analysis and experiment; here he concentrates on the perception and experience of the world, in which he sees all things as being interrelated. That the same can be said about his own work is evident from his continual reuse or reproduction of it, which gives rise to a kind of condensation of time. By means of elementary divisions of space, frames and grids, he attempts to arrive at minimal, sometimes even void forms which have maximal connotations at the same time. Because motifs such as the horizontal division, the checkerboard grid and the frame continually recur, they have assumed an almost mystical absoluteness in his work. Vanderheyden paints the same compositions in various formats. At times he also combines a number of existing works or reproductions of these in order to attain new meaning. Each work does maintain its own autonomy, but is also part of a new, heterogeneous whole. Around 1967 Vanderheyden's interest in painting began to wane for a time, and he experimented with works in which the perception of light and space and the experience of time play a prominent role. Dark rooms that brought the outside world 'inside' were built, for instance, and moving video cameras and monitors were installed in his studio, so that perception would become visible as each portrayed the other.

Around 1975 Vanderheyden began to paint again and immediately reverted to work from earlier days, producing revised versions of previous works by incorporating experience

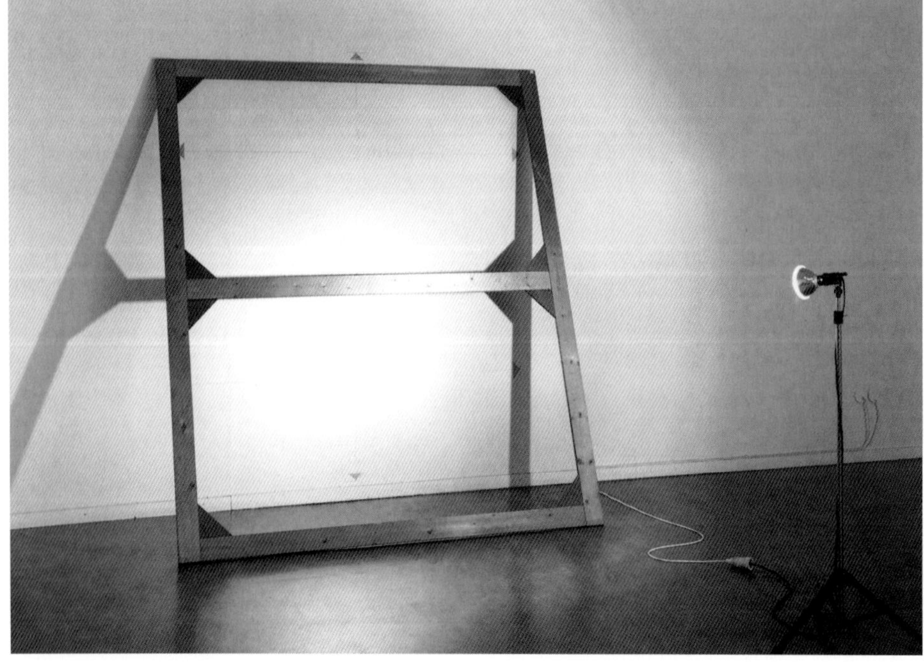

Marinus Boezem *Visual Research*, 1970

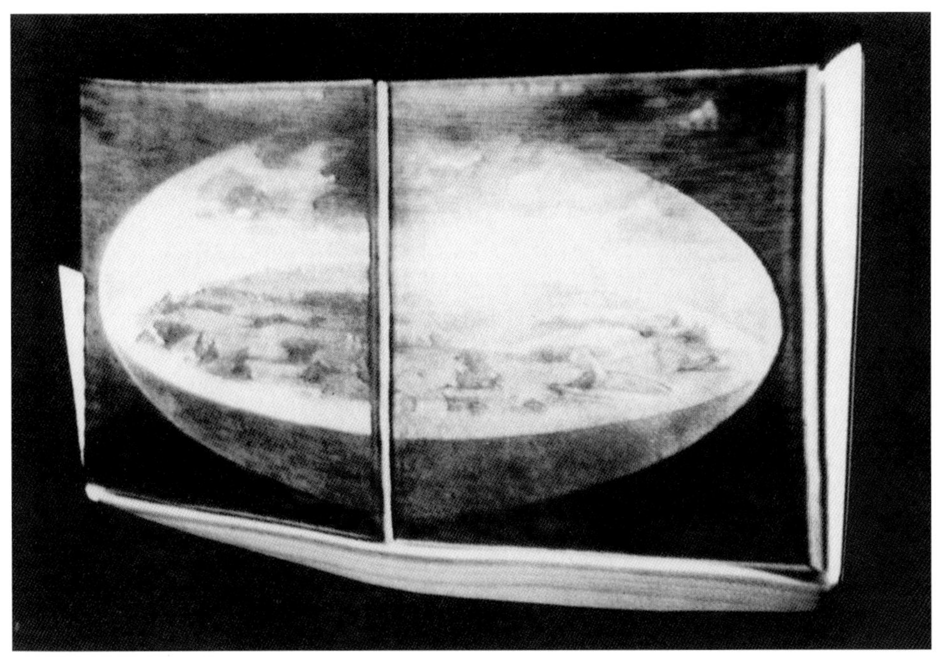

JCJ Vanderheyden *Day of Creation after Hieronymus Bosch*, 1990

that had been acquired during the interim. Moreover, it often takes years before he considers a work finished or strong enough to be presented to the outside world. This holds true for the work *Blauw kader* (1966-80) whose large, evenly white surface is framed by a broad blue edge that beams like a clear summer sky. After 1975 this bright blue became a feature of a great number of works produced by Vanderheyden in connection with his travels to such countries as India, China, Japan and Nepal.

Vanderheyden is fascinated with the process of perception and regards the eye as an instrument through which he can arrive at an understanding of reality. By means of the mechanical eye of the camera, he photographs his work, after which he then paints this photograph and photographs himself while painting. In this way the potential difference between the original and the reproduction is examined in all of its facets. To Vanderheyden, the reproduction is a form of interpretation which involves

change not only in terms of color, form and dimension, but also in the content that the original derives from its own specific context. The almost scholarly perseverance with which Vanderheyden concentrates, in his art, on several specific aspects of painting and perception forms a considerable contrast with the broad pursuit of **Marlene Dumas**: to transform individual experience into a model for collective awareness. The work of Dumas deals with the relationship between art and reality, intention and interpretation, the process of attributing meaning and communication by means of language and images. While the images in her work are often derived from images gathered from mass media, she portrays themes such as love, fear, cruelty, eroticism and death on the basis of personal memories, emotions and experiences.

Though the problems that Dumas raises in her work are wide-ranging, they always relate to her preference for painting as the medium in which the tension between depiction, on the one hand, and representation, on the other, is most strongly expressed. She comments on her own work by means of written statements and essays, fragments of which are then incorporated into her paintings or collages. These texts are not only an integral part of her visual art; they also provide the work with a broader context. Like the titles of her works, the fragments of text steer the viewer in a particular direction, from which the work can be considered. Under the title *Miss Interpreted*, Dumas focused on the problem of interpretation in

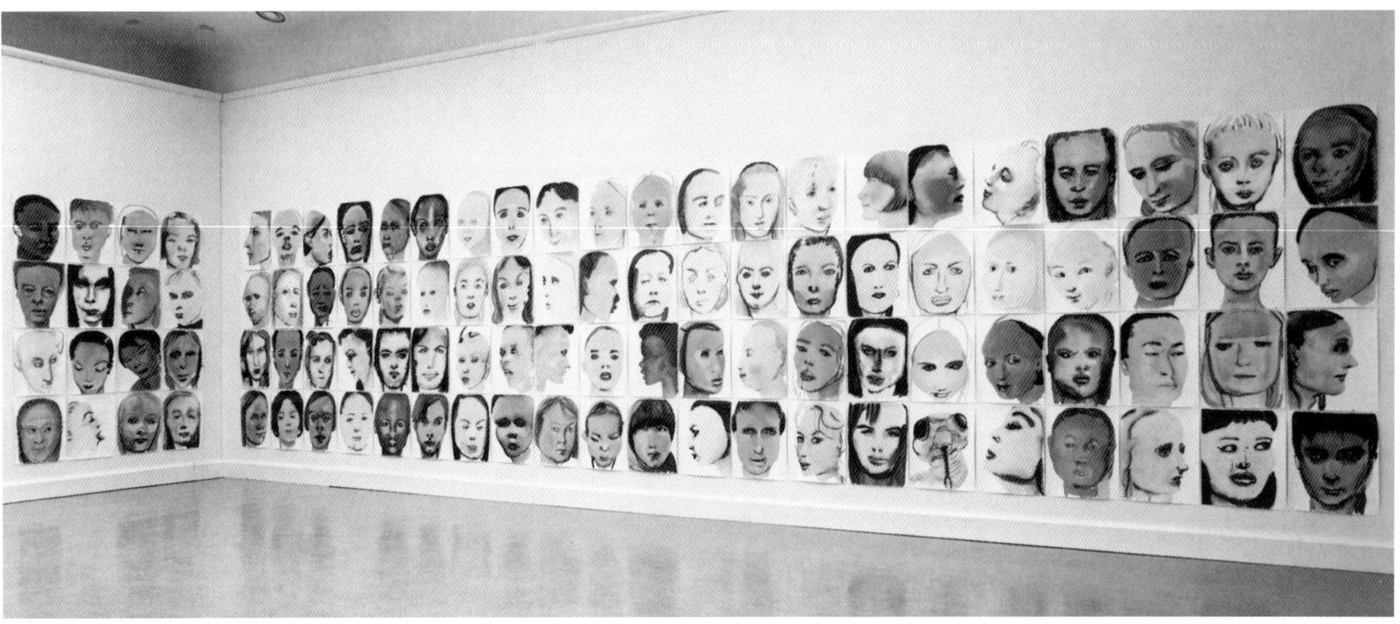

Marlene Dumas *Models*, 1994

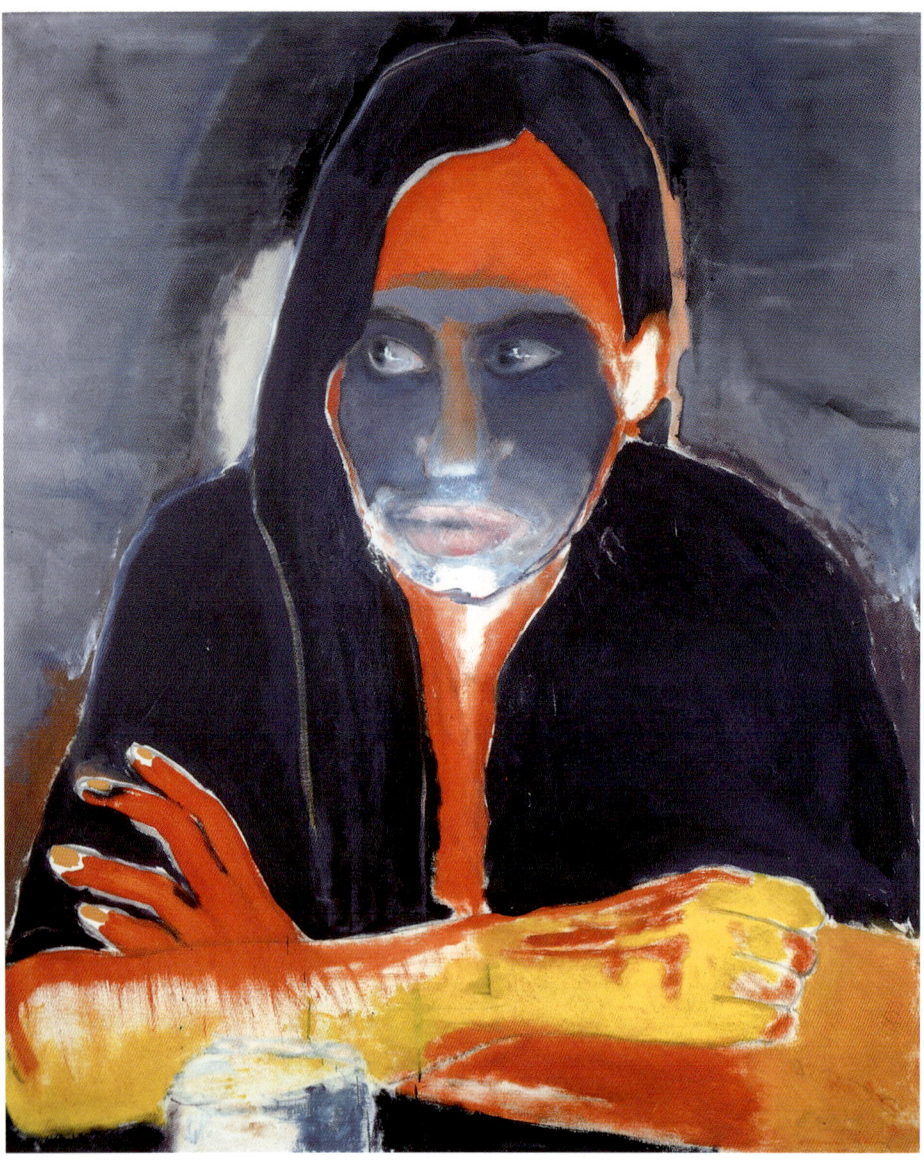

Marlene Dumas *Genetiese Heimwee*, 1984

the retrospective exhibition organized by the Van Abbemuseum in 1992. From essays and quoted statements in the catalogue, it is evident that Dumas has no faith in fixed meanings, but in the interdependence of the cultural context and the experiences and memories of both the artist and the viewer. Her paintings show conflicting inner experiences and truths which continually become reversed. Within a single painting, beauty and ugliness become interchangeable, good and evil happen to be two aspects of the same thing, and life and death are so intertwined that the distinction begins to fade.

The human figures in the work of Marlene Dumas therefore often give the impression of being tormented, as though they are struggling with themselves and with the

situation in which they find themselves. This is very apparent in *Genetiese Heimwee* (1984), whose bright, aggressive colors contrast with the penetrating, though empty gaze of the portrait subject. With its macabre and ominous character, the painting manages to 'invade the soul' of the viewer. Like all of the paintings of Dumas, this work has not been painted from a live model, but via polaroids that she places as a kind of buffer between herself and the model. The emotions captured by Dumas are predominantly her own and not those of the person portrayed. As such she has actually been able to refute the persistent misconception that the portrait conveys the subject's state of mind.

The work of **Toon Verhoef** deals with yet another, entirely different realm. Since 1975 he has been painting abstract works that could be regarded as prime examples of Stella's 'what-you-see-is-what-you-see' idea. The works by which Verhoef established a reputation are characterized by verticality, distinct forms and contrasting colors. The forms often bear a clear relationship to the elongated format of the canvas. Diagonals or parts of circles and ovals extend, for instance, to the full height of the painting. At times they seem to continue beyond the canvas; in other works they are compressed within the confines of the painting.

Due to the way in which he employs the visual language of forms, lines, colors and structures, Verhoef distances himself from the theory and practice of twentieth-century abstract art. Artists such as Malevich, Kandinsky or Mondrian attached great value to the metaphysical qualities of abstraction, which, in their view, revealed the true nature of reality. The work of Verhoef, however, deals purely with painting. He does not believe in the power of the image to convey specific meaning and wishes to deal only with that which is intrinsic to painting. As an artist he presupposes nothing and attempts, with each work, to start from the very beginning. What ultimately concerns him is the experience that unfolds during the making and the observation of the work: "If you want to know what a painting is about, you have to stand in front of it and look at it."

The importance that Verhoef attaches to discoveries that appear along the way is evident not only from the compositions but also from his way of working, which involves the continual exploration of possibilities. Each painting is the result of a lengthy process of applying paint, scraping it away and painting over areas, of working the surface with the palette knife and scaper and of using different sorts of brushes. The traces

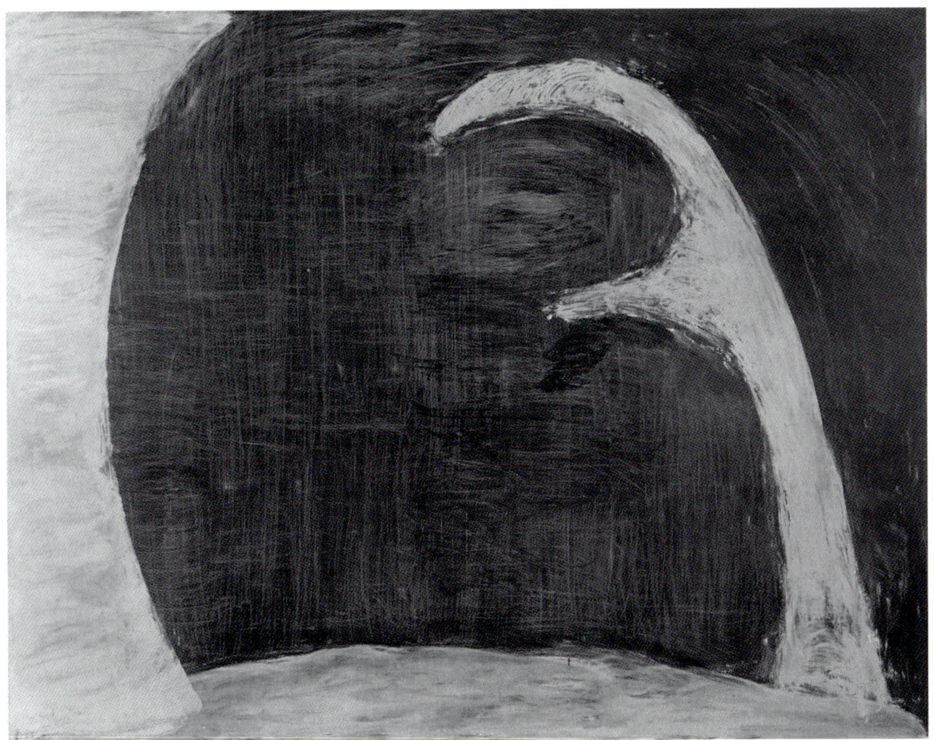

Toon Verhoef *Zonder titel*, 1984

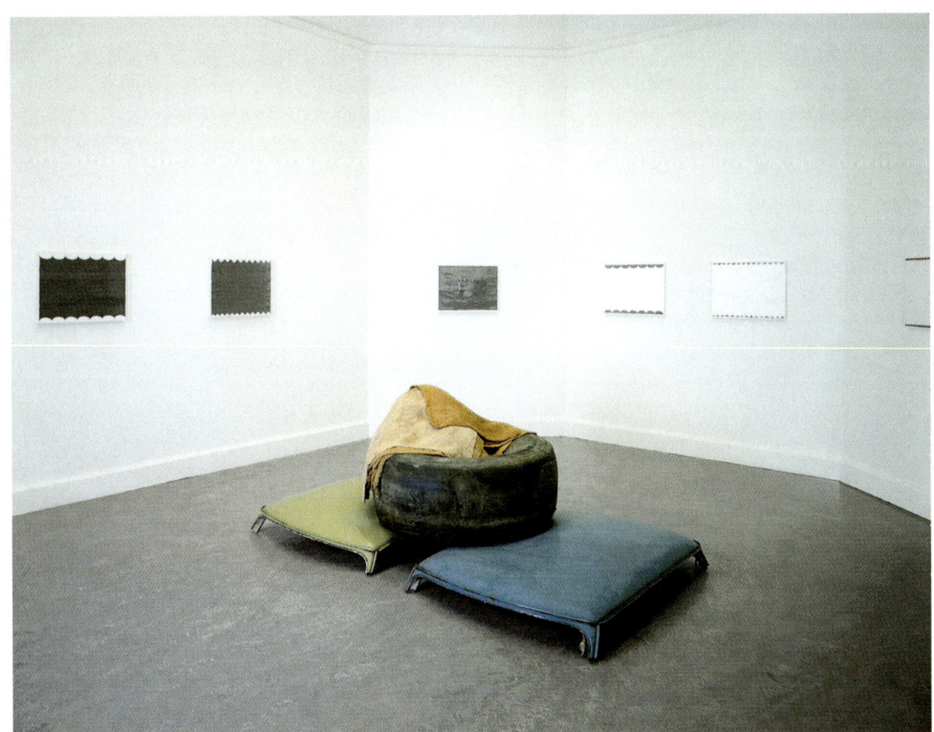

Carel Visser *Op het balkon*, 1985; *Zonder titel*, 1977

of this process that attest to the genesis of the work are thus discernible in the smallest details.

In 1984 Verhoef was given the use of a large studio in the storage space of the gallery Art & Project in Amsterdam. From that point on, his paintings are no longer elongated and vertical, but quite immense. Verhoef has had a distinct preference for out-of-the-ordinary formats which hold a particular image in themselves. Due to the 'chemistry' between the format and the image, his way of painting changed as well. The work *Zonder titel* 1984), which is in the collection of the Van Abbemuseum, came about during this period; it suggests a new desire for space and openness. The composition seems to have greater freedom and spontaneity, because the forms are no longer bumping into each other but standing along side each other in a state of calm. This makes the work, to use Verhoef's own words, less "cramped" and more "generous." Furthermore, the striking hues of bronze and green heighten the tranquillity that compels the viewer to see the work as a totality. The image, the material and the technique constitute an entity whose parts correspond thoroughly.

The Van Abbemuseum's collection of Dutch art has its main focus, in which aspects such as personal preferences and geographic definition are expressed. No collection in the Netherlands, however, can ignore the work of **Carel Visser**, which has not only determined the high regard for Dutch sculpture to a considerable degree, but also linked it with developments abroad.

Visser strives to create autonomous sculptures that relate not only to grown forms in nature, but also to forms constructed by man. To this end he produces both abstract and figurative sculptures. The extent to which the relationship with nature and the visible world emerges varies, but this is never entirely absent. In the work from the sixties, for instance, Visser systematically investigated the way in which he could disrupt the severity of a square or a cube and thereby give the form a more natural or human character. As a result, the geometric works of Visser, carried out in steel or aluminum, have a less rigid and composed appearance than works by minimalist contemporaries such as Judd or Morris. Since the second half of the seventies, Visser has been using, aside from traditional materials such as stone and metal, 'frugal' materials and 'found' objects that make his works more suggestive and poetic. From that time on, his sculptures have consisted of stackings and assemblages of diverse

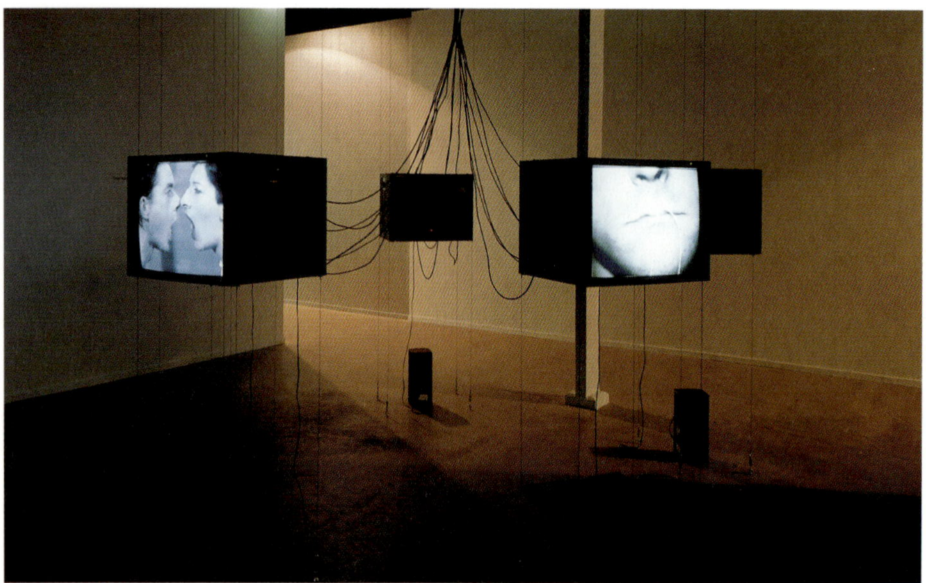

materials including dirt, wood, eggs, automobile tires, iron, tin, plate glass and unprocessed wool. These are works imbued with both the beauty and the vulnerability of nature and human existence. Along with the abstract elementary forms, one also finds 'figurative' references in these works: to a landscape, for instance, a house or a river. Characteristic of this is the work *Op het balkon* (1985), which is made up of burlap bags, one large car tire and two car roofs. Unlike the abstract works from the early seventies, this work is not so much a construction as a composition in which perfectly ordinary and recognizable things come together in a peculiar manner. Visser appears to have gradually shifted the focus from analytical and architectonic abstraction to the poetic portrayal of his personal thoughts, experiences and memories. Just as our view of Dutch sculpture is inconceivable without the work of Carel Visser, so has the history of the European performance been greatly influenced by the figures **Ulay and Marina Ambramović**. Since the start of their collaboration in 1976, the two regarded themselves as an 'androgynous whole' in which the oppositions of the masculine and the feminine are joined. The tumultuous performances carried out by them in the first half of this collaboration were marked by vehement confrontations in which they explored the limits of each other's physical and mental endurance. In the performance *Relation in Space* (1976), for instance, they continued to crash into each other until both collapsed in exhaustion. A year later came the work *Light/Dark* (1977), in which they strike each other's faces with the flat of the hand until one of them stops. Through the course of time, their work became less violent, though the exploration of limits by a defiance of their own and each other's resilience and endurance remained a central theme. Furthermore, their own bodies continued to be their most important material.

During the early eighties, Ulay and Abramović made countless trips throughout the world. With the Aboriginals in the Australian desert or with the Buddhist monks in Tibet, they became acquainted with the enormous energy that can be generated by motionlessness. From that point on, long periods of motionlessness and of slow, concentrated movement became a means to control energy. This radically changed the nature of their performances. The audience was no longer confronted with the physical battle of two lovers but witnessed, instead, hours of silence as they remained still. Violent emotions, aggression and rivalry seem to have been banned here. But the effort yielded by the artists was no less impressive.

A great number of the performances of Ulay and Abramović have been recorded on video or film. Because these were not rehearsed or repeated and were, in a certain sense, unplanned, this actual registration was primarily of importance to the artists themselves. Later there arose a desire to allow their earlier work to live on in a form which was as authentic as possible, and the original material was adapted for the creation of wall-sized video installations during the 1990s.

The collection of the Van Abbemuseum includes sixteen of these works and thus gives extensive consideration to the unique collaboration that ended in 1988.
In addition to the performances, Ulay and Marina Abramović produced works which are less linked with time and place, but which also transcend personal experience and convey universal meaning. Personal signs, for instance, are invariably rooted in the magical contexts of the circle (cosmos, spirit) and the square (earth, matter). In both the overall design and the details, one can discern these universal symbols. As a result, their concern for rituals and magic is clearly expressed in works such as *China Ring* (1987). This photographic work consists of a series of sixteen large polaroids that form a kind of diptych. The first eight photographs show yellow template forms of a crested tower, a square, a dagger, a crescent moon, an open circle and a square surrounded by a circle divided into four segments. The yellow templates have been set against a black background and seem to be made of skin covered with fine hair. The next eight photographs show the portrait of an Asiatic woman who, concealed beneath a black veil, reveals only her eyes to us. The portraits seem to be identical, were it not for the principle of the polaroid, which makes this impossible. This photographic process is, after all, characterized by the direct print which is developed without a negative. It is therefore the reflection of light in the eye which tells us that these are photographs taken at eight different moments. This gradually gives rise to the awareness that the photographs display certain parallels with the motionless performances of the artists. With the exception of inevitable blinks of the eye, the model has remained completely still for an extended period of time.

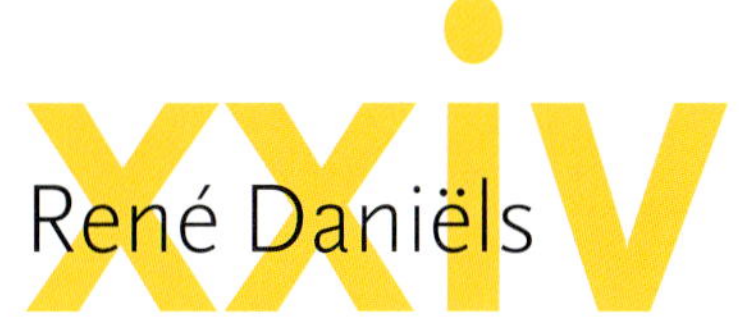

René Daniëls

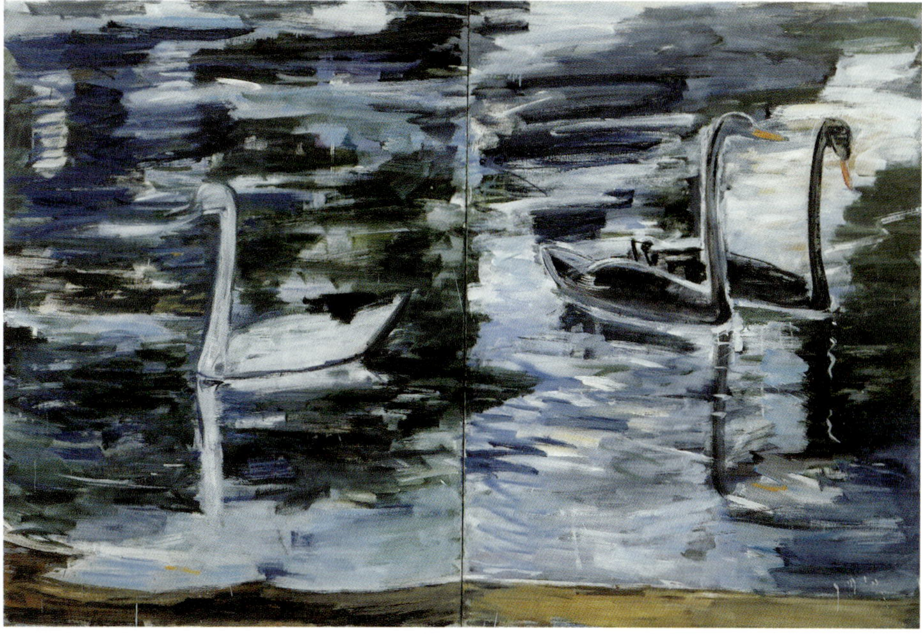

René Daniëls *La Muse Vénale*, 1979

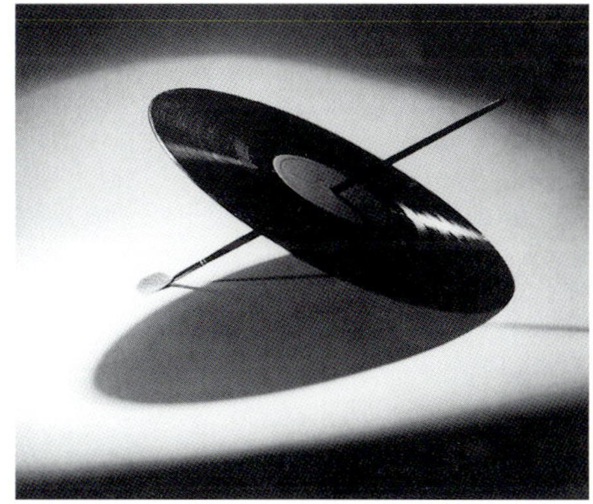

René Daniëls *L'objet*, 1980
Coll. René Daniëls Foundation, Eindhoven

Born in Eindhoven in 1950, the artist René Daniëls was granted only a short time in which to build an artistic reputation. His first exhibition was held in 1977, and ten years later a severe stroke put an end to his career as a painter. During this brief period, though, he created a unique and fascinating body of work, which draws national as well as international attention. Moreover, he continually managed to surprise his audience with new changes in the course of his visual thinking, never contenting himself with the clearing of a single path, but always seeking adventurous lateral routes that led to yet other paths. This gave diversity to his oeuvre without detracting from the coherence among the individual works.

Initially Daniëls painted with a fair amount of impasto, with broad and separate brushstrokes that filled the entire image surface. While fundamental painting was setting the main trend at that time in the Netherlands, a clearly expressive use of paint could be discerned in this early work of Daniëls. At the start of the eighties, when Daniëls was producing chaotic-looking paintings filled with diagrammatic images along side and on top of each other, some relegated him to the camp of neo-expressionist painting, which was flourishing especially in Germany. But the nearly abstract representation of his earliest works–the rectangular form of a book or a camera, the round shape of a phonograph record,

generally geometric forms, in fact–already indicates that expressiveness is not a significant factor in the work. As early as 1979, he was astonishing the art world with paintings in which swans or mussels were depicted; little trace of expressiveness could be found in these. The museum owns two of these early works. Such paintings, named after the poem *La Muse Vénale* by Charles Baudelaire, have a lyrical and succinct rather than a wild quality. And so it is not German gravity but lightness and a thin application of paint that ultimately come to characterize the painterly style of Daniëls.

The title, meaning 'the corrupt muse', suggests that the beauty of the painting is questionable. Baudelaire's poem touches on the difficult existence of the artist. It is about the muse's outward appeal, which masks something else–something painful. With Daniëls, too, there is the idea of stratification: in the literal sense, with depictions being painted on top of each other, and in a figurative one, with his use of ambiguities in words and images. Furthermore, Daniëls maintains a vagueness and a sense of weightlessness in the painterly space, as though it were a world under water. The painted forms hover in areas of color; like fish in water, they are not anchored in a clearly defined environment. Water is, for that matter, a theme that often recurs in his work. We see it in the paintings of *La Muse Vénale*, in the various *Salles Pacifique* works,

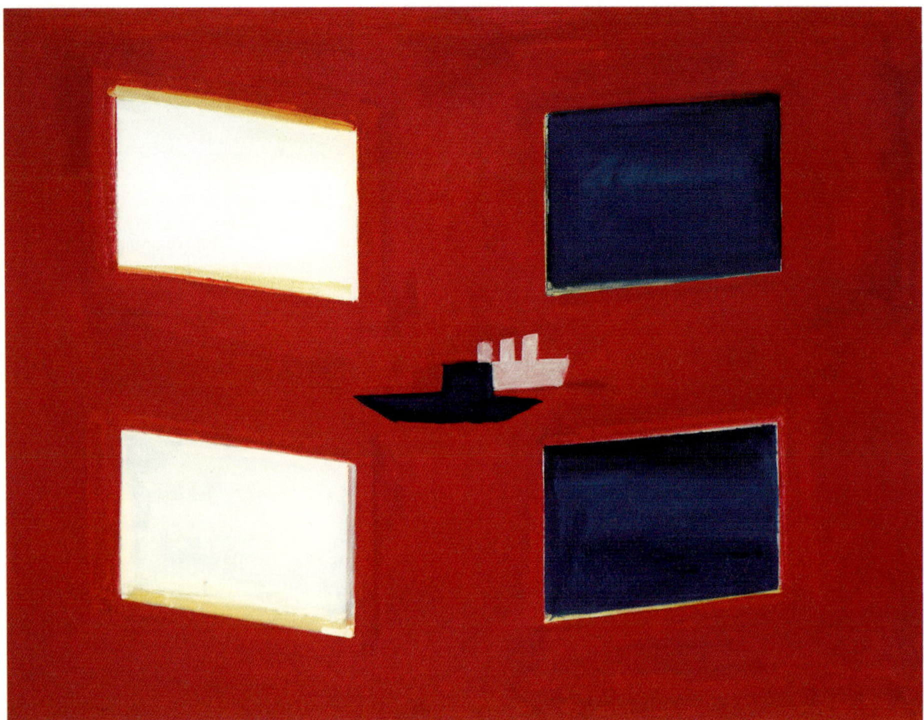

René Daniëls *A Hot Day in the Lighthouse*, 1984

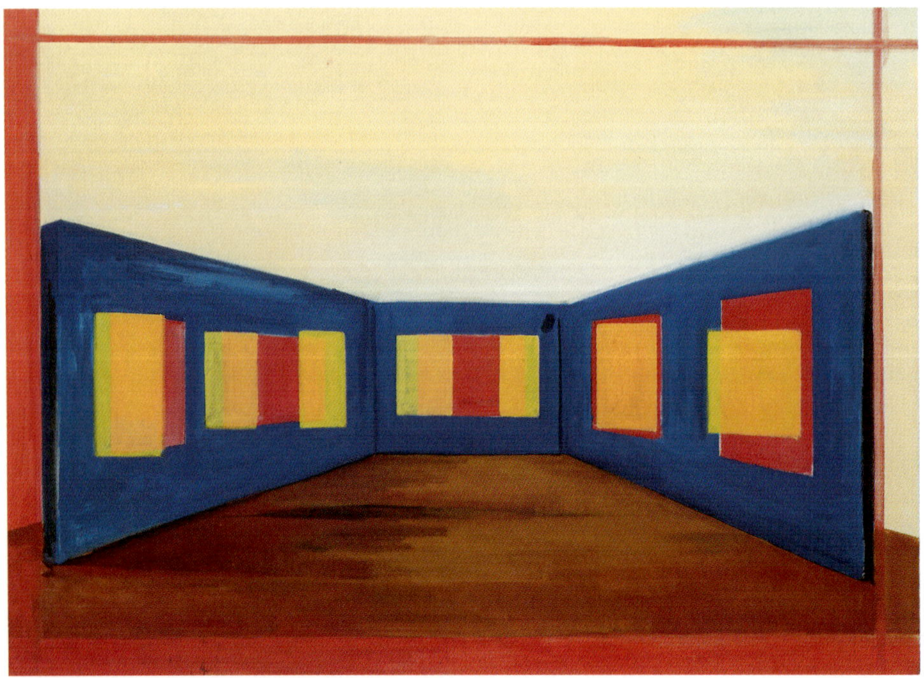

René Daniëls *Painting on the Bullfight*, 1985

and in *A Hot Day in the Lighthouse* (1984) there is, with the little ship in the center, also a reference to water, though that element itself is not depicted. The fluidity and indeterminate quality of water must have fascinated him.

In 1982 Daniëls painted a school of herring, one consuming the other after having discovered just how appetizing they were. This work, titled *Hollandse nieuwe*, was soon interpreted as a criticism of the art world, a portrayal of the new generation of artists, the *nieuwe wilden* who were cropping up all over Europe and begrudging each other's existence. Daniëls himself dismissed this interpretation and pointed to paintings of Bosch and Brueghel and a text by Picabia. Nevertheless, the painting is strikingly reminiscent of a photograph of one fish threatening to devour another, published in connection with a text written by the French philosopher Georges Bataille in 1930. *"L'espace peut devenir un poisson qui en mange un autre,"* was Bataille's caption–rather fitting in relation to the work of Daniëls. His paintings are about space. Just as space, with Bataille, is materialized and consumes itself, the spatial depictions in the paintings of Daniëls interlock in a complex manner. With *A Hot Day in the Lighthouse*, for instance, there is no clear indication of foreground or background, of space or objects. The bright-red surface is, on one hand, the maritime space in which the boat rocks, but it could also be a fragment of the lighthouse whose four windows are depicted. Are we looking from the inside out via two light windows, at open space, or are we looking, instead, from the outside in, at the blinding beacon? In his work it is frequently unclear as to what is 'inside' and what is 'outside'. Spatial ambivalences are characteristic of Daniëls. Also because his paintings seem to be unfinished–the forms are scarcely filled in and the paint is applied thinly–the elusiveness of the representation is heightened. As his career progressed, Daniëls began to hover more and more between figuration and abstraction.

After 1984 Daniëls produced paintings that dealt primarily with the subject of exhibitions. This had somewhat vague beginnings in the painting *De slag om de twintigste eeuw* (1984), where a 'bow-tie' form is shown floating above a blustery sea. Only in later paintings, when this 'bow-tie motif' develops into an independent element despite many variations, does it become evident that the motif represents an exhibition space, with walls at each end and two sides on which paintings are hung. The paintings on the wall are designated merely as planes, so that they could just as easily be interpreted as windows. *Painting on the Bullfight* (1985), in the collection of the Van Abbemuseum, is a beautiful example of such work. An extra dimension is created by the peculiar addition of semitransparent yellow planes that have been shifted, as it were, over the red 'paintings' and almost literally illustrate the stratified quality of his paintings. But the refined use of color, the juxtaposition and overlapping of yellow, red and blue (which naturally brings to mind the painters of De Stijl) gives such radiance to the colors and shows such painterly consideration that any banal interpretation of the work is immediately silenced. These are moreover paintings which, because they refer to the rooms of a museum, inherently relate to the space in which they are hung. Sometimes a semitransparent screen seems to be stretched over his paintings, as in *Het huis* from 1986. In such works, the ambiguity of the space is heightened even further. Often we see an exhibition space depicted with something resembling a microphone in the center and, next to this, a piano. In front it are 'silhouettes' of walls, but now in shapes which, within the space of the depicted room, sooner resemble television sets. In this painting, too, all sorts of graphic bow-tie motifs are floating about. It is as though we are looking at two paintings at the same time, as though hidden behind one painting is another, which will reveal the true force of its colors only when the foremost painting is removed.

In 1987, his last productive year, Daniëls made a series of paintings which initially seem to deviate entirely from his previous work. One sees a schematic rendering of a blossoming tree. *Lentebloesem* is the title given to these works. At first the series appear to be modern, more abstract versions of Van Gogh's flowering trees. But on further consideration, the blossoms evidently consist of words. With some works these words are titles of his paintings. As though sensing the approaching end of his artistic career, he summed up his entire oeuvre within an organic structure in these final paintings. The collection of the René Daniëls Foundation, which is managed by the Van Abbemuseum, owns a work from this series. In this particular version, the blossoms consist of words in Swahili. Those who look carefully will recognize one word that happens to be the title of a painting: alzumeazume. It seems related to Swahilian words such as 'hakukuwa nawatu' that it hardly strikes the eye. This epitomizes the

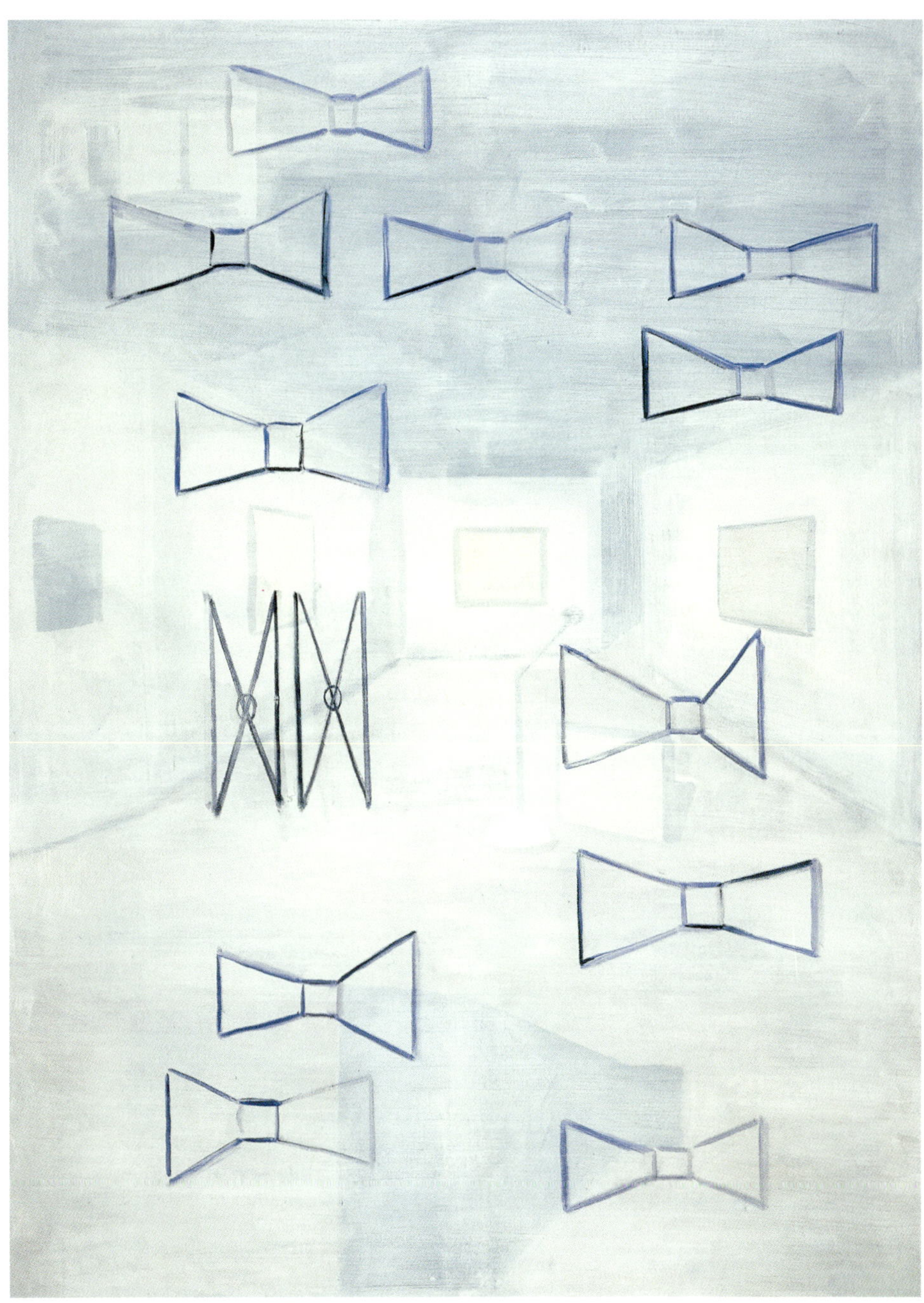

René Daniëls *Het huis*, 1986

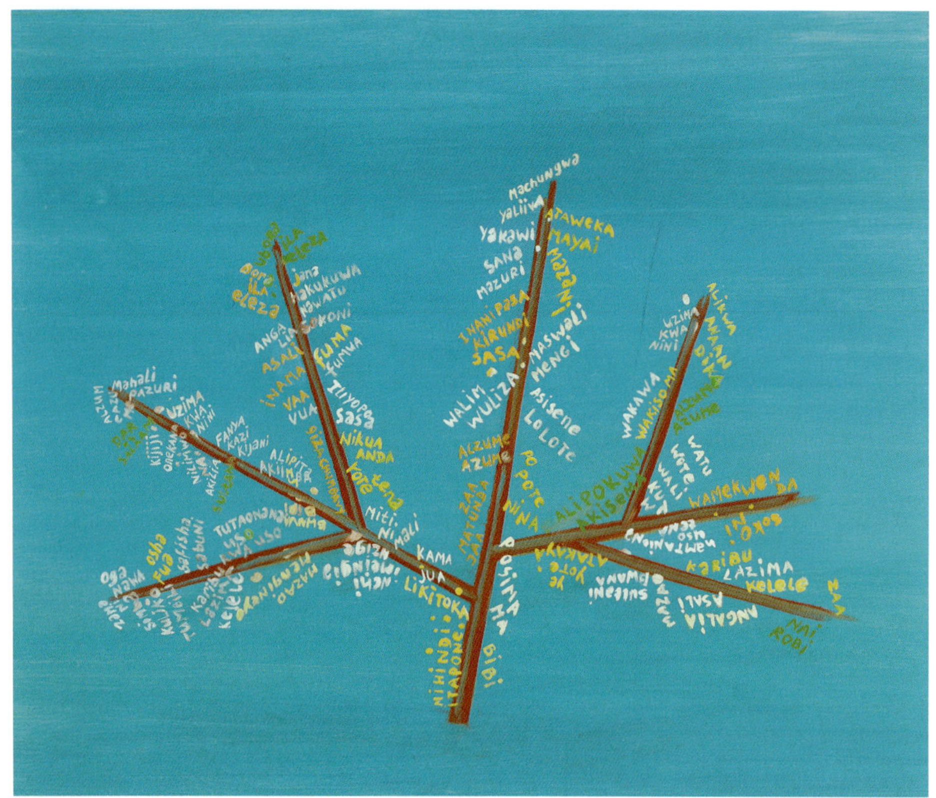

René Daniëls *Lentebloesem*, 1987 Coll. René Daniëls Foundation, Eindhoven

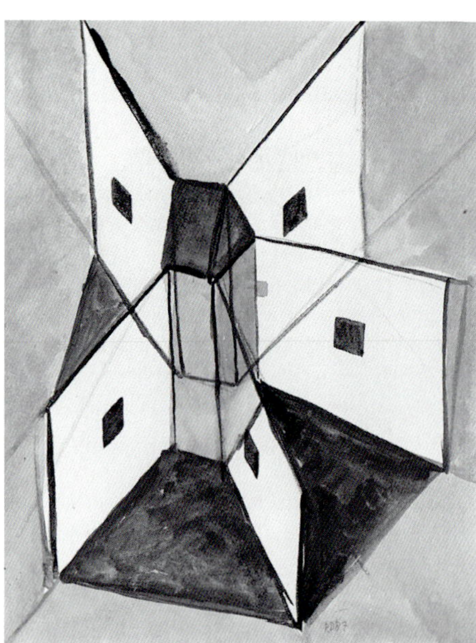

René Daniëls *Zonder titel*, 1987 Coll. René Daniëls Foundation, Eindhoven

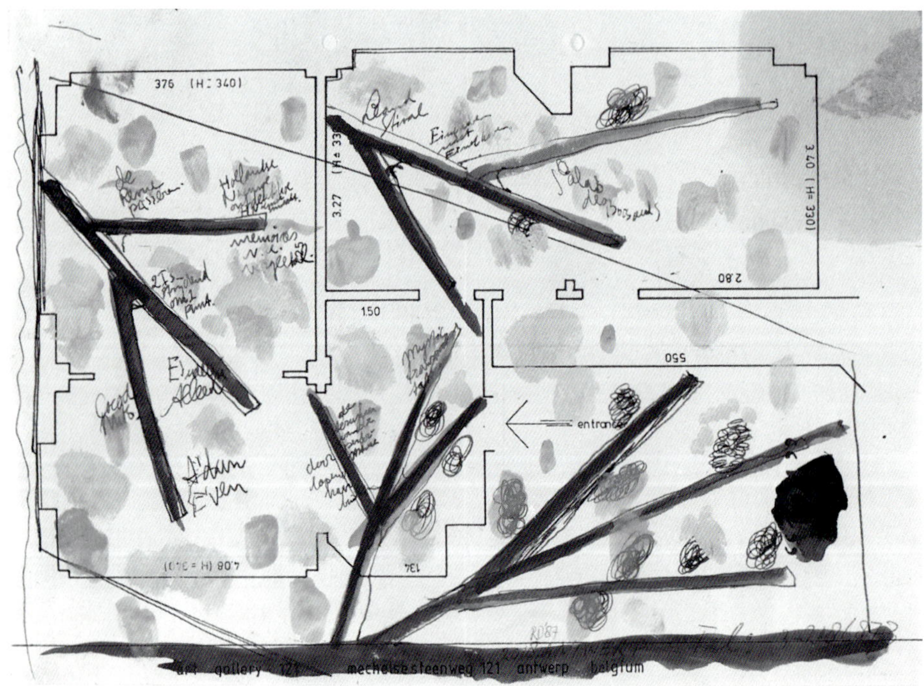

René Daniëls *Zonder titel*, 1987 Coll. René Daniëls Foundation, Eindhoven

refinement of Daniëls, for the word 'alzumeazume' is derived from 'La muse amusée'.

The muse of this artist has a poetic disposition. Daniëls strives for a combination of visual poetry and painting. Just as a poet plays with words, Daniëls allows one image or word (titles such as *La muse amusée* and *Alzumeazume*, which can be read as a kind of 'open Sesame') to lead to other (word) images by way of free association. Once introduced, themes are later placed in other contexts, and meanings begin to shift. Motifs undergo a continual metamorphosis. The floor plan of an exhibition space can thus be transformed into the layout of a harbor with wharves, which in turn can become the structure of a tree. A depiction of three walls of an exhibition space can become a bow-tie, the shutter of a window, an open book or a triptych. Shifts of the image give rise to plays on words that are present in the title or written on the painting itself. Maze-like and whimsical, and thereby also layered and elusive, spatial and flat: perhaps these words most aptly describe the character of his intriguing body of work.

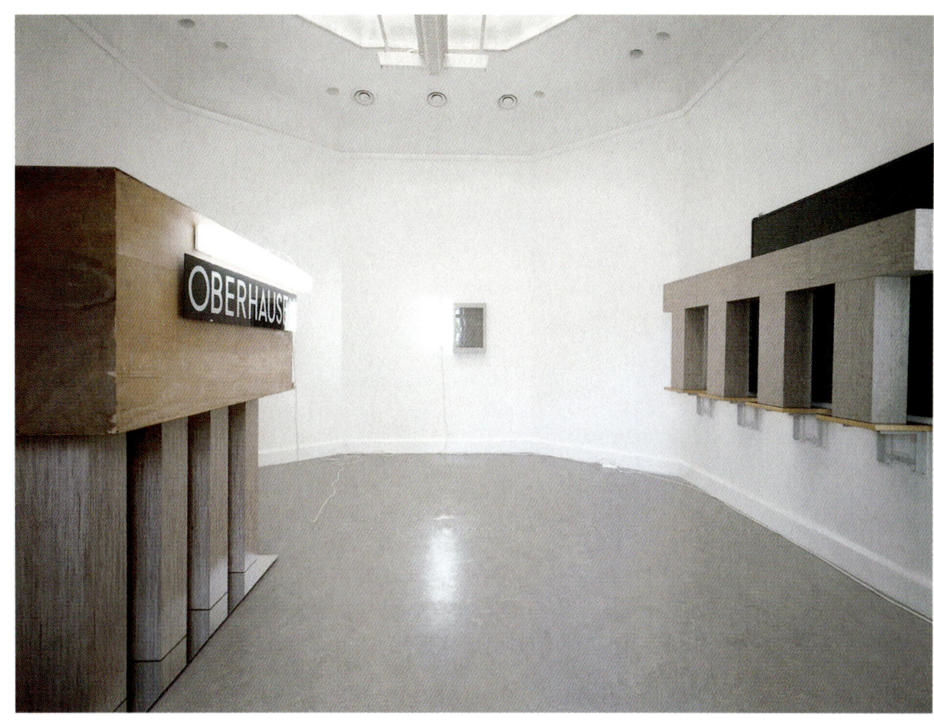

From left to right: **Reinhard Mucha** *Ohne Titel (Oberhausen)*, 1983; *Vechta*, 1982; *Ohne Titel (Wülfrath Wo)*, 1983

On close consideration, one may find more differences than similarities among the predominantly spatial works of the artists discussed here. There is, however, one common factor to be discerned in their work, but this has more to do with cultural-philosophical than with stylistic aspects. Various cultural philosophers have argued that reality has become fragmented and our coherent view of the world has collapsed under the influence of new technologies, the media and an unbridled consumer society. Universal truths and ideologies seem to have lost their validity, and what remains, in a cultural/social sense, is doubt and instability. Visual art has been equally unable to escape this ongoing restlessness and has, at least in the opinion of some, gone adrift. Modernism—once so vital, the autonomy of the artwork having been its most cherished possession—seems finished once and for all. The question is: what credible place and meaning can still be granted to art, now that it has lost its utopian potential? Obviously, the answer to such a complex question can never be straightforward, and it moreover requires an analysis of the codes and conventions that determine both the production and the appreciation of the artwork.

The spatial work of **Fortuyn/O'Brien** is often characterized as 'domestic art': art is part of the day-to-day reality and should be just as important as walking, eating or sleeping. And so Fortuyn/O'Brien strives, by way of very explicit stagings, for a new experience of that reality. The means employed are emphatically artificial. The objects seem to be tasteful yet peculiar props, derived from such elements as a banister, a mirror, oval frames, shutters, ornaments, a sofa or a bower. Works such as *Melancholia* (1986) or *Venetian Blinds* (1987) call to mind, partly through the use of seductive materials including silk, an undefined world of illusion. The precise meaning of the object remains hidden, however, since both the artist and the viewer are no longer able to ascribe a fixed, definitive meaning to a form.

Since the early eighties, **Harald Klingelhöller** has been drawing attention with sculptures in which the ambivalent relationship between language and image is investigated. This principle is expressed most clearly in the post-1985 sculptures made from cardboard, mirrors, metal, plaster and basalt. These compact works, which invariably seem to maintain a fragile balance, consist of parts, leaning against each other, which often display letters and banister-like forms. Sometimes the sculptures are leaning diagonally against the wall, or they obstruct the passage from one room to another as though barriers or 'guards', as seen with the solo exhibition of Klingelhöller's work in 1990. By incorporating mirrors into them, Klingelhöller relates the immediate surroundings, including the viewer, to the sculptures in a fragmentary way and thereby suggests that the sculpture cannot be regarded as something separate from the viewer and the space. A striking aspect of this is the titling of the sculpture in the form of metaphors or frequently used expressions. These often allude to human actions or states of being, as do *Schweigen bricht* (1991) or *Zur Konjugation von 'fallen'* (1991). At first glance, one may think that Klingelhöller's sculptures can literally be read, because the letters so clearly determine the appearance of the image. But that impression is misleading. Letters, after all, acquire meaning only when they form, in a particular sequence, a word or a sentence and when they can be interpreted by a reader. In the work of Klingelhöller, there is the idea that language is, in fact, always misleading and, like the image, has its own reality–and that an irreconcilable gap exists between a description in language and that which is described visually. Klingelhöller maneuvers within that gap, in the fluid realm between language, image and meaning. Unlike Klingelhöller, **Thomas Shütte** does not confine himself solely to spatial work. Many of Schütte's works are based on watercolors, which he himself regards as a kind of 'gymnastic warm-up'. In 1990 the Van Abbemuseum purchased an important 141-part series of watercolors for the collection. In this *Athener Tagebuch* (1984) ideas and plays on words are written down, and Schütte has tried out images and themes to which he frequently returns during the years that follow. A good deal of his work appears to be staged or makeshift, as though it amounts to no more than a proposal or an experiment where changes can still be made in accordance with the situation. A number of figurative sculptures, which he presented at his solo exhibition in 1990 and which

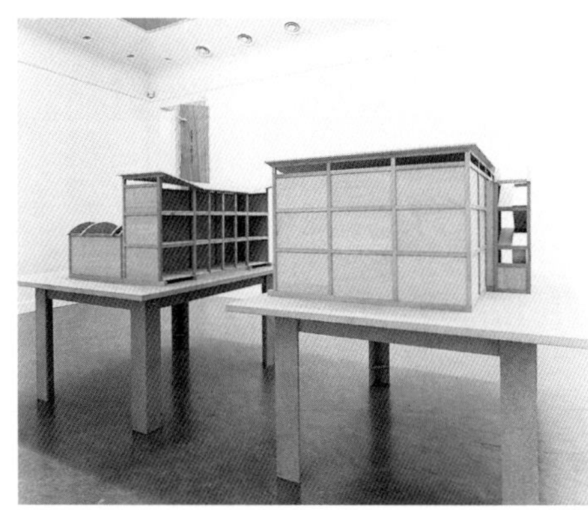

Thomas Schütte *Collector's Complex*, 1990

function as models for work in public space, could even be described as awkward in terms of their finish and detail. With this, Schütte manages to evoke a tension between evidently no longer be able or wanting to comply with certain accepted conventions and rules and the search for new possibilities and forms of representation. Many of his sculptures are literally scale models, and one could say that his work–due to the

ambivalence with respect to reality–always embodies a *potential* reality.

The architectural models could be built if this were desired, but Schütte regards them as sculpture to an equal degree. *Collector's Complex* (1990) is a two-floor, externally closed and inwardly directed space where a collector, being isolated from and undisturbed by impulses from the outside world, can 'enjoy' his collection. The staged, theatrical character of Schütte's 'thought models' can also be seen with *Blauer Bunker* (1984): a sky-blue bunker which, in terms of form, seems to have been inspired by utopian, eighteenth-century architecture and which most resembles a memorial with its radiant decor of orange paintings displaying floral motifs.

In the work of **Reinhard Mucha**, art also appears in a 'staged' form. Mucha–who, like Schütte and Klingelhöller, also studied at the academy in Düsseldorf during the early eighties–has been building sculptures and installations since the very start of the eighties. These initially consisted of objects which, for the most part, came from the

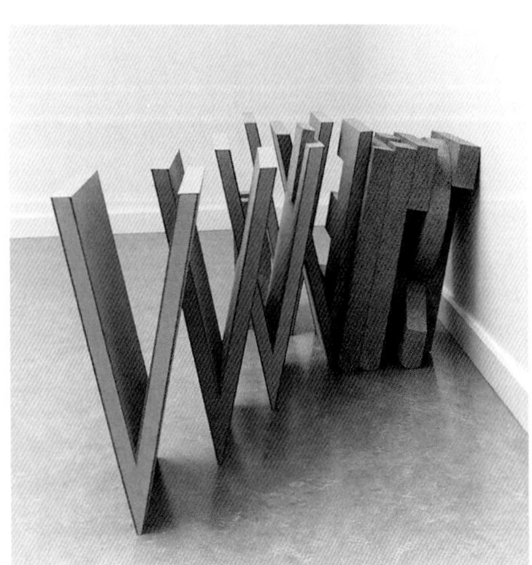

Harald Klingelhöller *Zur Konjugation von 'fallen'*, 1991

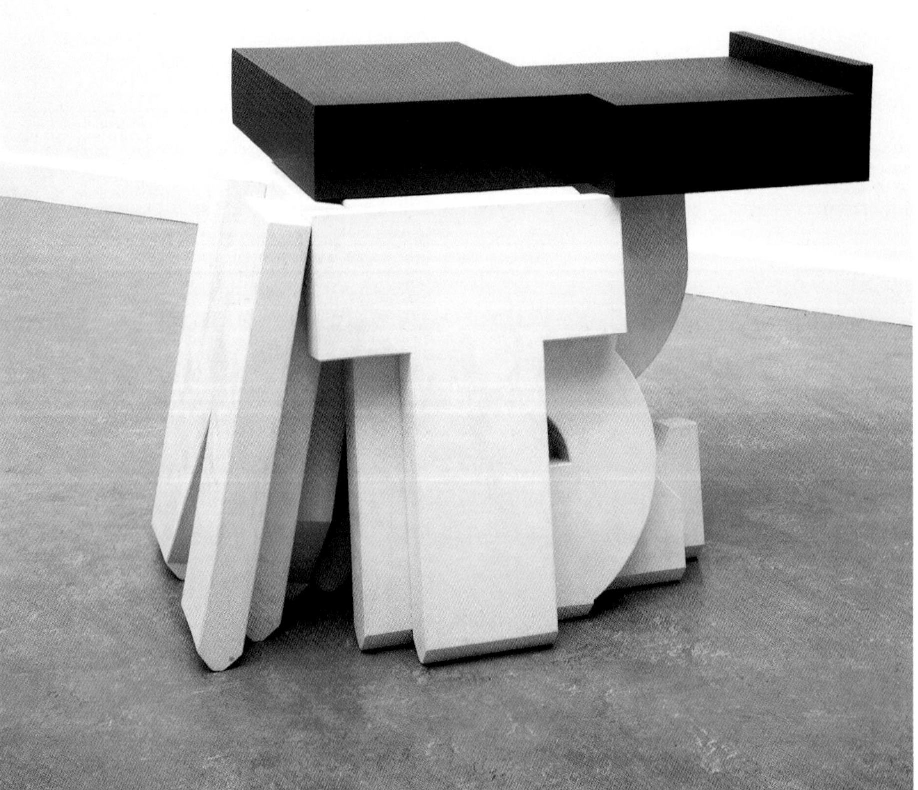

Harald Klingelhöller *Schweigen bricht*, 1991

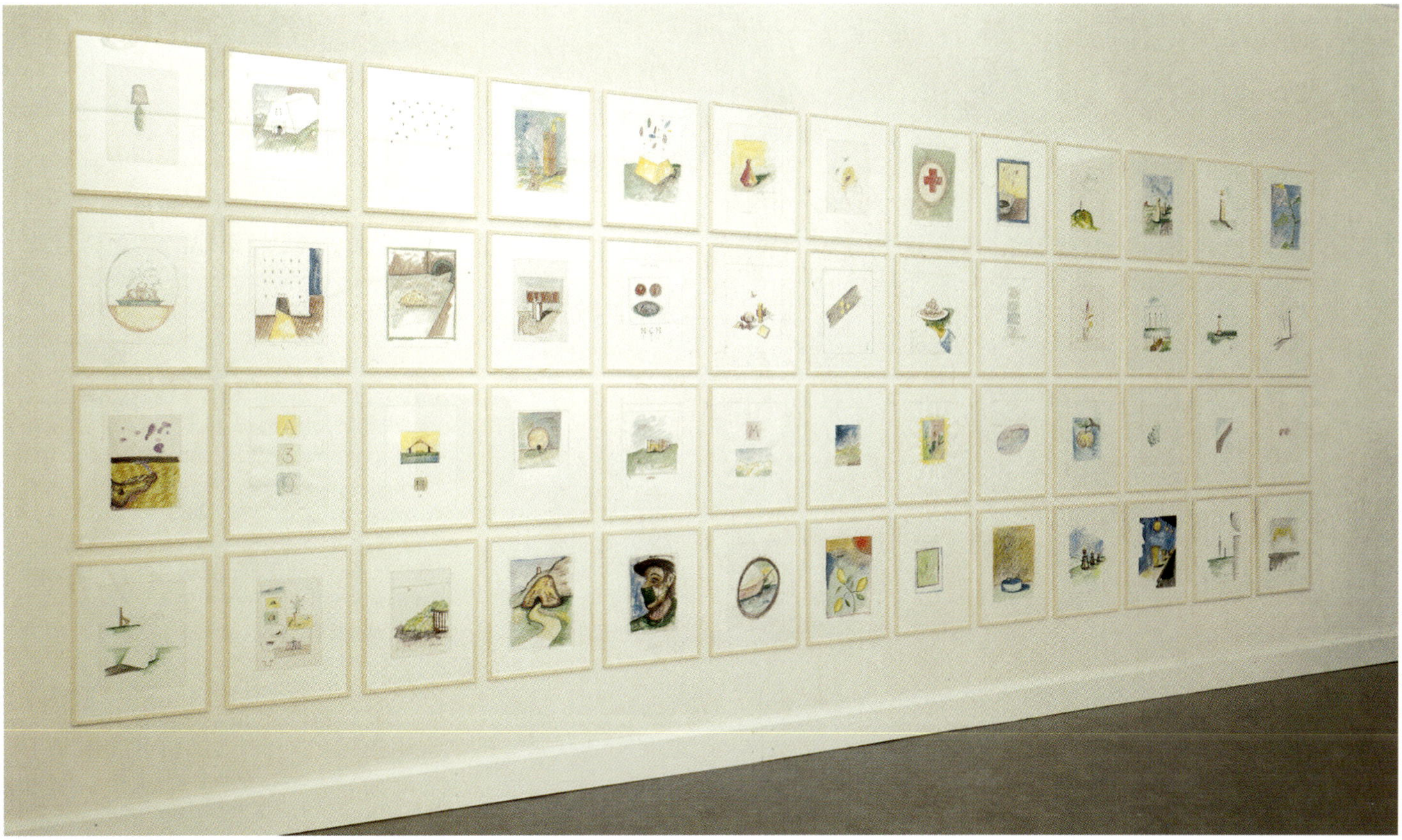

Thomas Schütte *Athener Tagebuch*, 1984 (detail)

inventory of an exhibition space: tables, chairs, scaffolding, pedestals and fluorescent lighting. Because of this, there is a sense that the whole of it is temporary and can easily be dismantled, but a shift has also occurred in the sense that utilitarian objects, which previously– in their 'original state'–were intended as a means for presenting art, now function as artworks. This notion of mobility is further heightened by the fact that Mucha has incorporated train-station signs of German places into a number of works, as with that of 'Oberhausen' in *Ohne Titel* (1983). The flat vitrines used by him are sometimes empty, and their glass covers reflect the viewer and the space, in a way similar to the continual alternation of inside and outside views during train travel due to the movement and the reflecting windows. Mucha's work seems to suggest that art is deprived of a permanent place and has become homeless, as it were. The physical presence of Mucha's work in the museum alludes to its very opposite, namely to a metaphorical form of absence; the work is both 'there' and 'not there'. Evidently even museums are unable, despite their forced efforts, to provide art with a permanent, meaningful place, and they have been

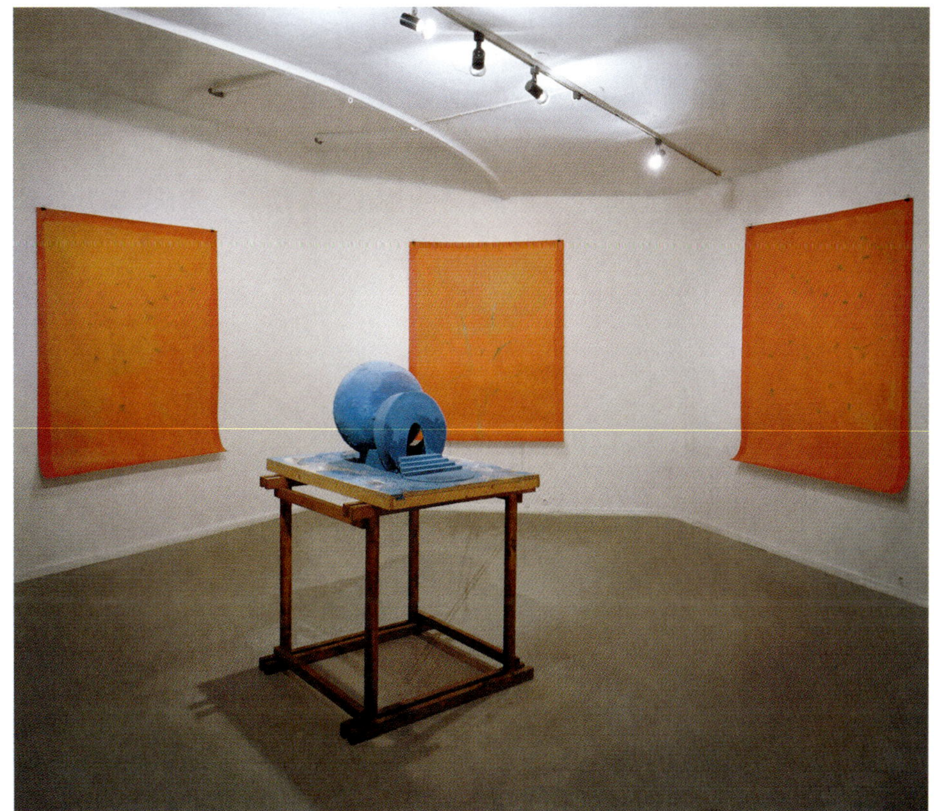

Thomas Schütte *Blauer Bunker*, 1984

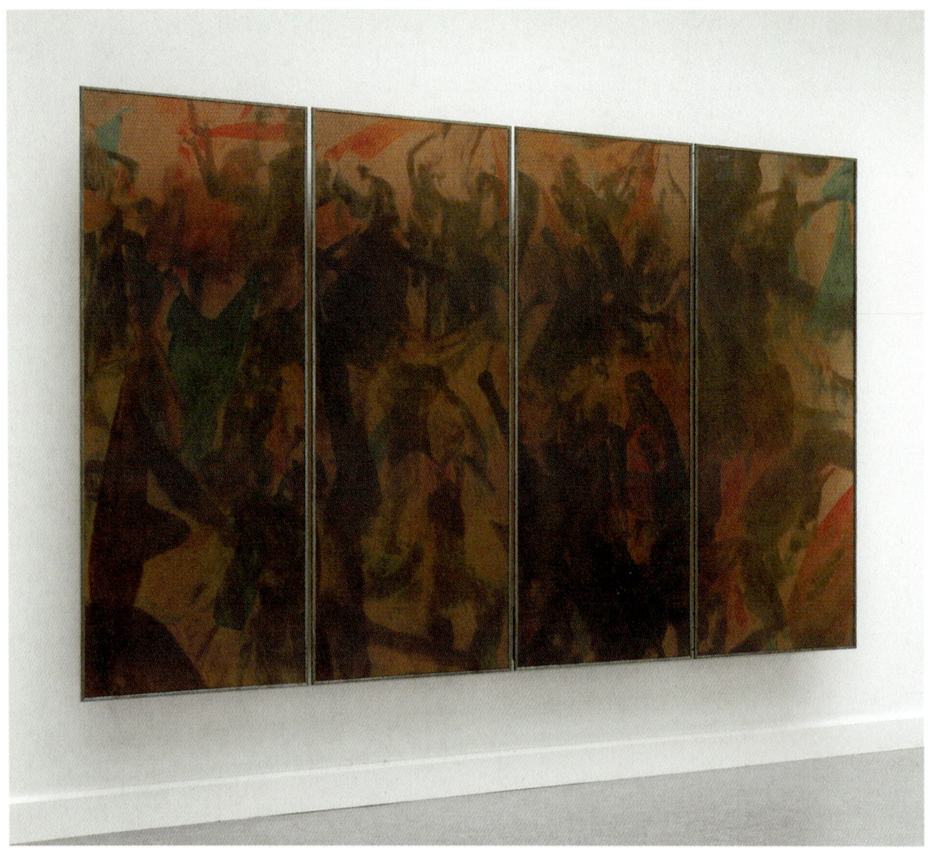

Niek Kemps *Sevillanas I-IV*, 1992

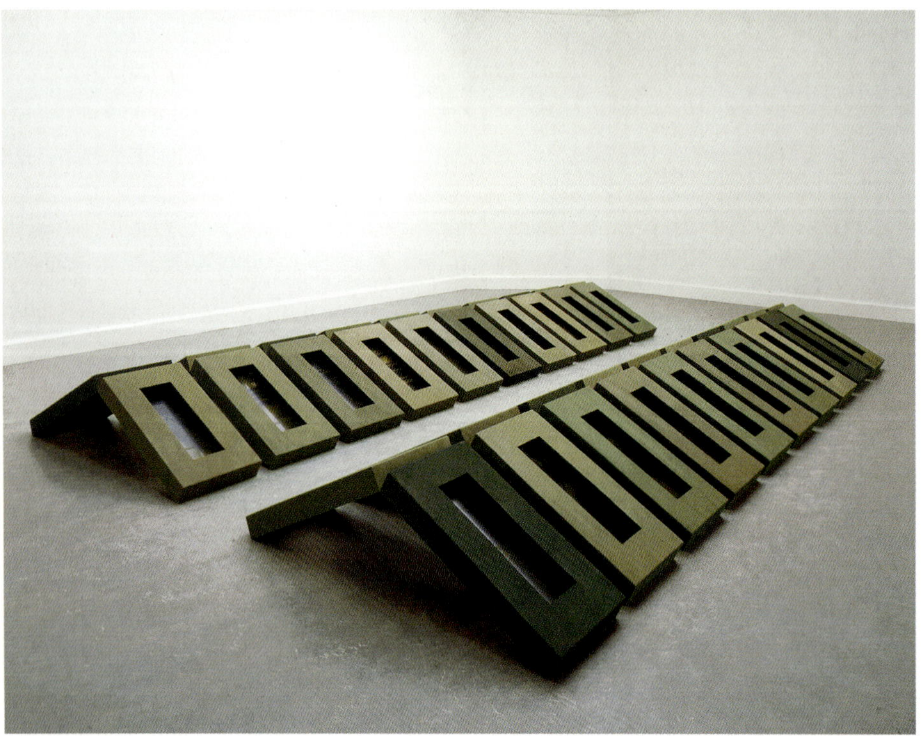

Niek Kemps *Les privilèges de la promenade*, 1992

reduced to serving merely as 'distribution centers' between which the nomadic artworks circulate endlessly.

In a certain sense, that hectic quality is also expressed in a great deal of work by **Niek Kemps**. His sculptures never simply manifest themselves, because they cannot be seen from a single vantage point, for instance, or because their surface consists of reflective glass or lacquered wood from which the eye seems to be somewhat deflected. On further observation it appears that photographic images of landscapes or buildings lie hidden beneath this almost impervious and resistant exterior. Kemps's complex way of dealing with perception, with emptiness, attraction and repulsion, transparency and reflection is a metaphor for the experience of a fragmented reality, the discernment of which moreover depends on the position that one occupies. By confronting the viewer with countless impressions, Kemps prompts him or her to abandon established ideas and actively seek new meanings. Catalogue essays, written by the artist himself or by other authors, are less explicative than they are allusive to a parallel experience of image and text. In *Les privilèges de la promenade* (1992) the illusive effect and the unrest have given way to a certain tranquillity. Inside the box-like forms covered with felt, one can see photographs of a fragmented, 'park' landscape with a labyrinth of hedges that evoke–as though a vague memory–a flowing image of relaxation, calm and aimlessness. A sculpture titled *Entre deux boîtes qui sont des maison VI* (1993) functions in a similarly 'inviting' way: the viewer is meant to find calm and shelter in the soft surroundings of light that filters in through the pallid, skin-colored polyester.

Also in the work of **Jean-Marc Bustamante**, the sharp distinction between the search for meaning and meaninglessness is poignantly expressed. Initially he produced photographs of landscapes referred to as *Tableaux*–vacant lots, sun-drenched cypresses or buildings on the outskirts of cities–in which there is actually nothing unusual to see. In 1988 he began to create a number of hybrid objects that are remotely reminiscent of nameless pieces of furniture. Characteristic of both the photographs and the objects is their continual reference to places that are definite as well as indefinite, foreign and familiar at the same time. Titles such as *Intérieur*, *Paysage* and *Site* seem to underscore this quality of presence and absence, of detachment from time and space. With *Bac à Sable* (1990) Bustamante suggests an 'inner' landscape' of childhood days, referring to

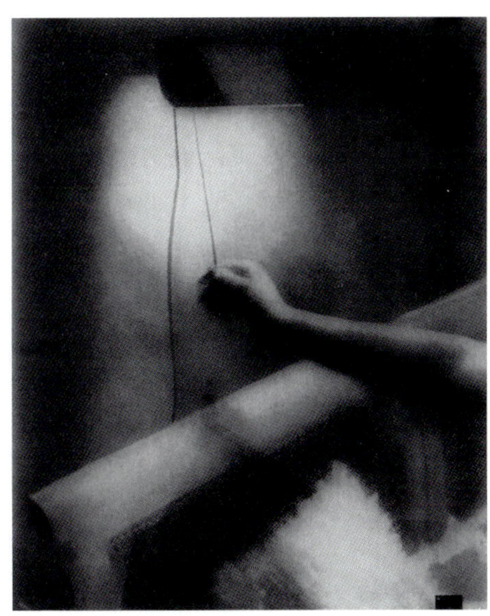

Jean-Marc Bustamante *Lumière no.1, 1988*

play, to physical and social activities. The contrast between interior and exterior, between mental space and concrete reality is also dealt with in a wall sculpture of bricks and wood, whose title bears a dual location: *Ici, Là* (1990). Bustamante constantly seeks, by means of his sculptures, the outermost limit at which a recognizable form changes into an abstract form. It is here that meanings arise and memories are conjured up, though these are never specific. It is as though we reach for the things around us by way of perception, by interpreting them anew again and again, while the 'reality' is constantly on the verge of slipping away from us. The same sort of idea, prompted by the awareness of an irreconcilable gap between subject and object, also constitutes the point of departure for *Sans Titre (diptych)*, (1993): both heavy and gracious, painted metal plates with an 'open' form make one think of leaves or hearts.

Jan Vercruysse endeavors to evoke, by means of his sculptures and photographic works, an awareness of the fact that there is no longer any sort of "idea of a place for art in this world." *Chambre (IV)* (1986) can be regarded as a room or a 'house' which can be entered only with a certain amount of difficulty. In the dark interior one manages to find a number of steps that lead nowhere, as well as a vacant picture frame that shows nothing. Absence and emptiness prevail here: that much is

certain. The notion of absence or of a non-place surfaces again in another series of sculptures, referred to as *Atopieën, atopie* meaning 'non-place'. *Atopies (N.N.)* (1987), in the collection of the Van Abbemuseum, is comprised of empty panels and a 'hearth' of mahogany plywood–a virtually archetypal image of a 'home' which assumes poignant meaning due to the loss of its function. It is important to mention that, despite the clear sense of melancholy, Vercruysse does not resign himself to the emptiness and absence that he evokes, but rather uses these qualities as starting points from which to reconsider the conditions of art. By confronting the viewer with all sorts of artistic, aesthetic and, in his photographic works, linguistic codes and conventions, he provokes interpretation, however, whereby the mysterious character of his work always remains intact. *TOMBEAUX (1988)* from 1991 has an exceptional place within this series. The cold and indefinable rack- and cabinet-shaped constructions have given way to a form that could almost be called figurative: it seems as though the two fragile glass chairs, hung on a coatrack, have been set aside for the time being. The title of this series refers not so much to death or to grief as it does to a piece of work inspired by the memory of something or someone. This implies a degree of calm, reflection and creative energy–conditions which Vercruysse considers essential for the production of

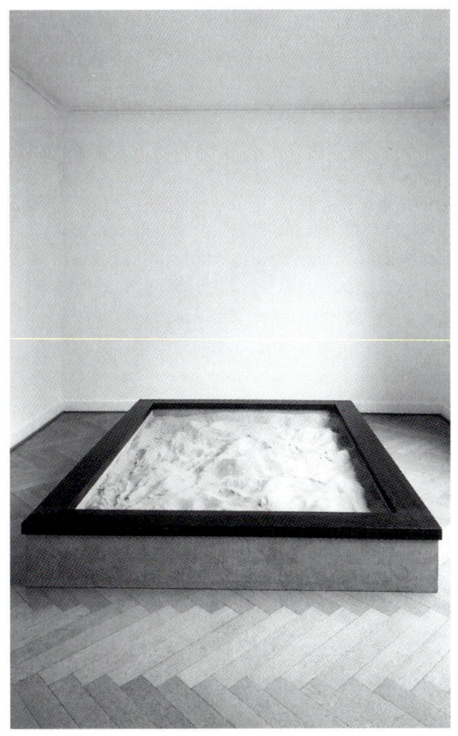

Jean-Marc Bustamante *Bac à Sable*, 1990

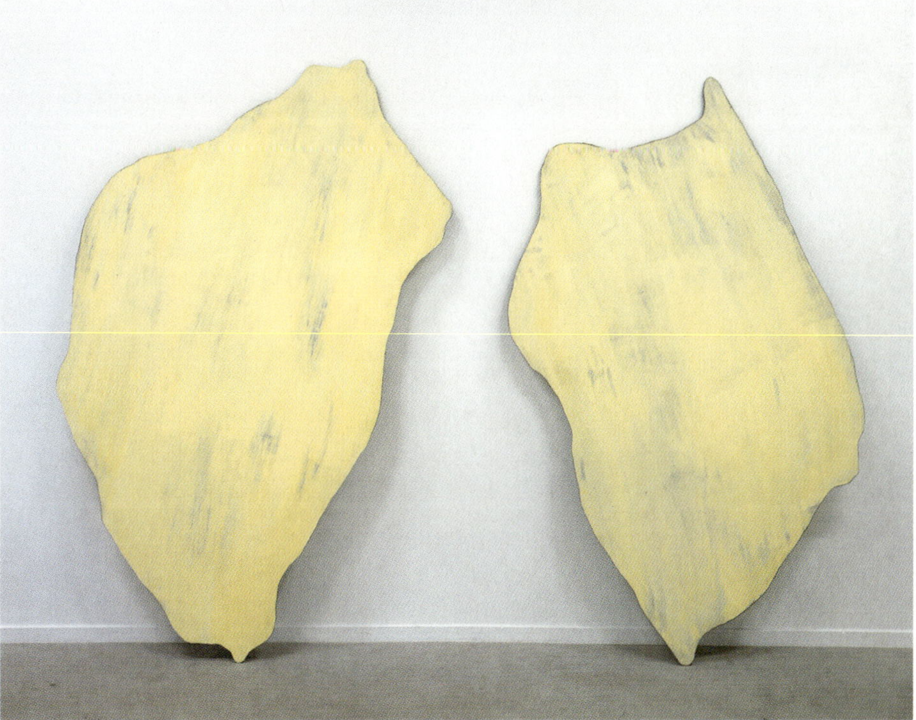

Jean-Marc Bustamante *Sans Titre (diptych)*, 1993

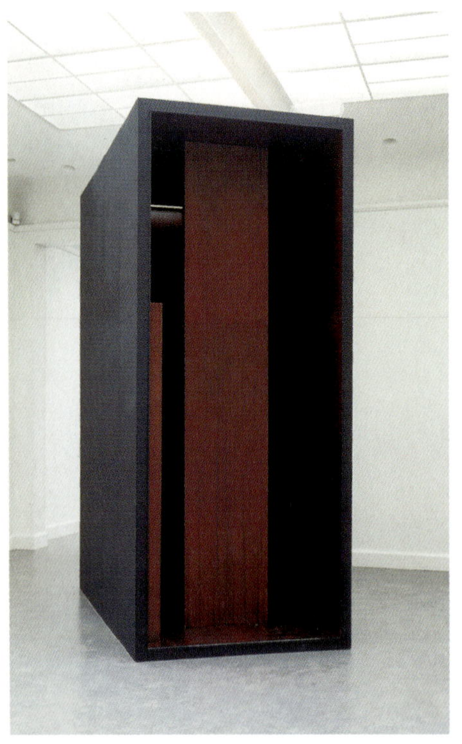

Jan Vercruysse *Chambre (IV)*, 1986

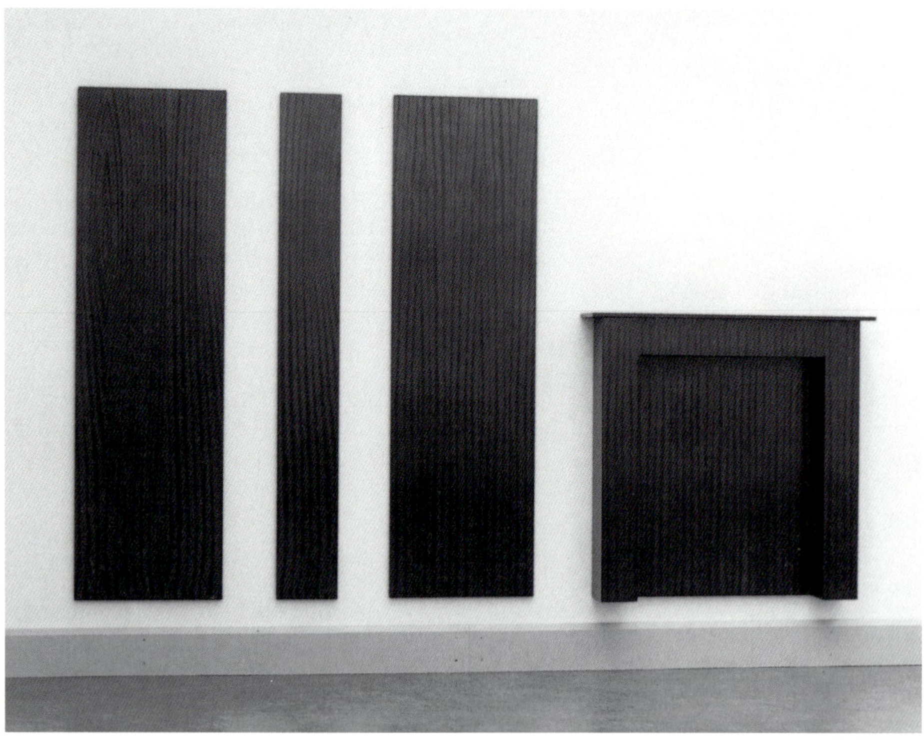

Jan Vercruysse *Atopies (N.N.)*, 1987

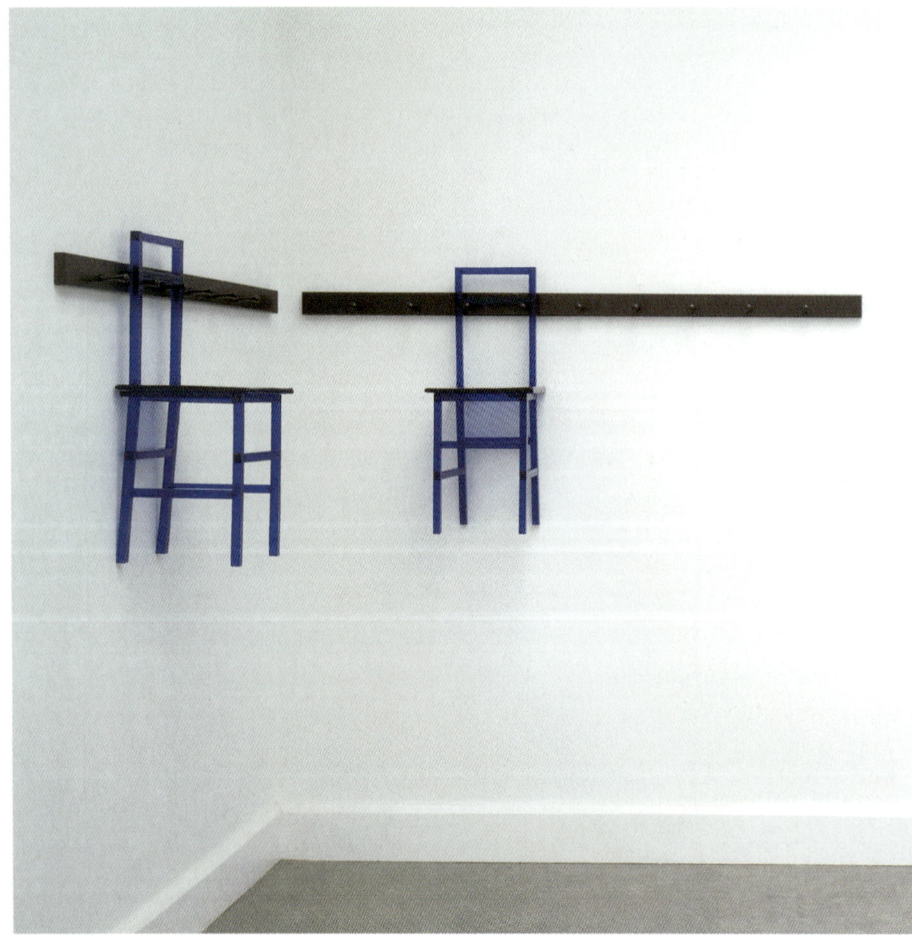

Jan Vercruysse *TOMBEAUX*, (1988) 1991

meaningful art.

The point of departure for the sculptural work of **Didier Vermeiren** is the classical pedestal. This serves as the basis of Vermeiren's investigation into the characteristics of modern sculpture and how it relates to tradition. The decision to carry out this investigation on the basis of the pedestal is not so peculiar. In traditional sculpture, the pedestal literally raises the image to the level of 'art', while in Minimal Art the pedestal is no longer relevant because that image is part of the viewer's own space and reality. *Sculpture* (1982) could be seen as a programmatic point of departure; due to the doubling of the base, the distinction between the sculpture and the pedestal is abolished. *Socle du Monument à Sarmiento* (1986) is a casting of the pedestal of Rodin's *Monument à Sarmiento* (1895). By showing the mold together with the casting, Vermeiren gives emphasis to such a classical sculptural principle as 'negative' and 'positive' form, but also to the serial character of Minimal Art. And by making use of the same material and often imitating the surface structure of the image to which he refers, he 'stages' it in a new, condensed form. That such an investigation has everything to do with sculpture's literal as well as metaphorical place in space and in the world is evident from *Untitled* (1989): a geometric volume is indicated by means of thin rods, and the

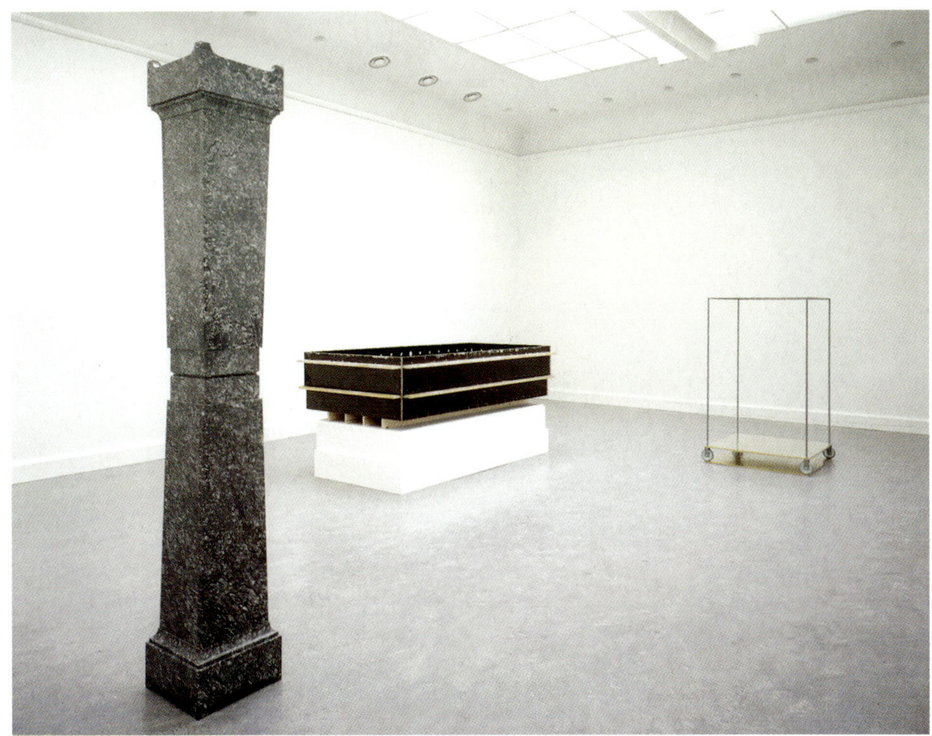

From left to right: **Didier Vermeiren** *Sculpture*, 1982; *Socle du Monument à Sarmiento*, 1986; *Untitled*, 1989

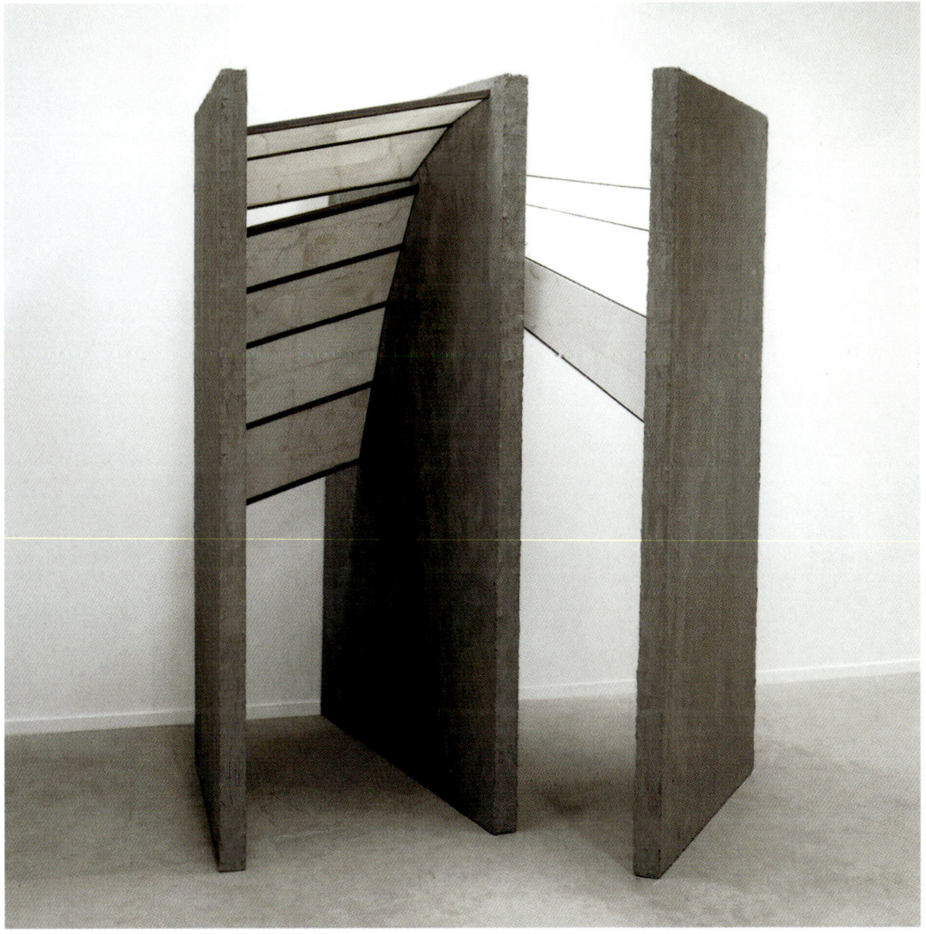

Cristina Iglesias *Untitled*, 1994

swivelling wheels, beneath the copper base plate, that suggest mobility and freedom are limited by a second base plate or pedestal. Like some works of Klingelhöller, the sculptures of **Cristina Iglesias** also frequently require the walls of the exhibition space, since they lean against these or are related to them in some other direct manner. The sculpture *Untitled* (1994) is chiefly reminiscent of an architectonic construction. At times her works are accessible only to the eye, often causing fairly high walls to bend in toward the space. This creates an inner space, and the sculpture becomes a space within a space. There is a striking contrast between interior and exterior. Whereas the exterior consists of wood, aluminum or somewhat rough cement, the interior is bathed in a soft glow as the light is filtered or colored by alabaster or glass at the top of the construction. Iglesias also occasionally provides the interior with depictions of trees, landscape, tapestry or floral motifs. Because of this, her work could be described as a mental or an interim realm, an inaccessible place where a transition can occur independently of time and space.

Rodney Graham produces not only sculptures, but also books, films, photographs, architectonic maquettes and even pieces of music. One distinguishing characteristic of this artist is his frequent appropriation of the work of other artists in order to add to that and present it again. *Lenz, Pamphlet* (1983), for instance, is an adaptation of a novella by Georg Büchner; here Graham creates a 'loop' based on the original text, thus causing the reader to remain stuck in the same passage. This principle also plays a role in the video work *Vexation Island* (1997). Here the artist is lying on the beach of a tropical island, dressed in eighteenth-century clothing, evidently in a state of profound rest. At a certain point, he wakes up and begins to shake a palm tree: a coconut hits him right on the head, and he falls flat onto his back, unconscious. From this point on, the film is back at its beginning. This apparently simple sequence remains intriguing and could be interpreted as a metaphor for the artist as a modern Robinson Crusoe, caught in the endless cycle of the art 'system'.

In the aforementioned novella of Büchner, the experience of nature plays a significant role–an aspect which also predominates in photographic works such as *Flanders Trees* (1989). Our conception of nature, Graham seems to say, is primarily a romantic construction, and it is impossible to provide a 'faithful' registration of the reality of

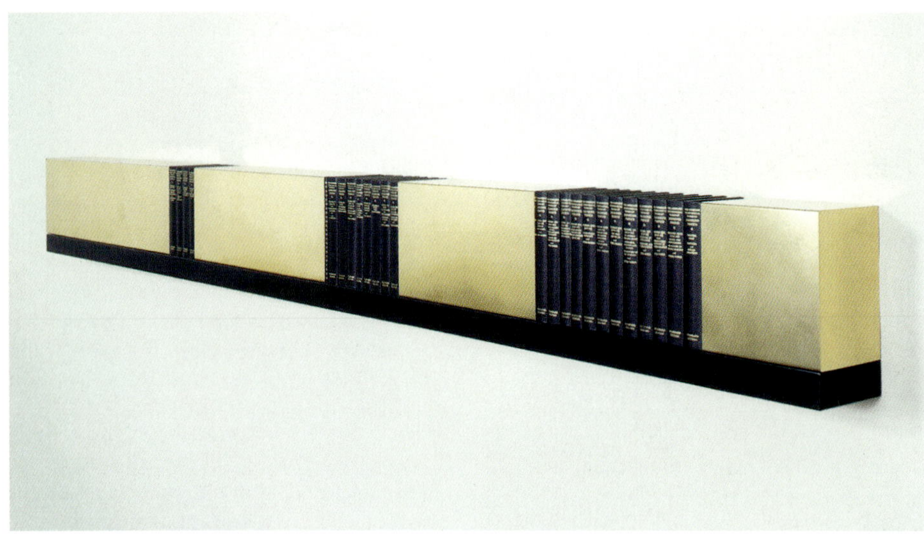

Rodney Graham *Supplemented Standard Edition with Prussian Blue Shelf (for Eindhoven)*, 1990-91

nature–including the spiritual connotations ascribed to the experience of nature–by means of art. Of an entirely different nature, *Supplemented Standard Edition with Prussian Blue Shelf (for Eindhoven)* (1990-91) involves Graham in an ironic dialogue with modernism. Here Graham has added several pages to volume four of Freud's collected writings, and the entire series is presented by him on a kind of bookshelf which bears a suspicious likeness to a work from Donald Judd's *Progression* series. As a result, the objectivity and 'empty space' of the quasi-Judd becomes crowded, as it were, by the subjective and associative language of Freud.

Ideas such as authenticity and uniqueness are also raised by **Allan McCollum** in his work. McCollum does this by presenting his work in various groups of objects, photographs, drawings and paintings, which sometimes consist of more than ten-thousand separate items. His *Plaster Surrogates* (produced from 1982 onward) have the appearance of small paintings with black surfaces, but these can just as easily pass as objects due to the fact that they are cast in plaster. McCollum sells these plaster object-paintings in bulk quantities; the Van Abbemuseum has owned, for instance, two gross of *Plaster Surrogates* since his solo

exhibition in 1989. With his work McCollum responds to the conventions of art production and reception and to how these are dictated explicitly by commercial tendencies. One could deduce, from the *Plaster Surrogates*, that the artist can respond to the increased demand for his work only by switching to mass production. The uniqueness of the artwork is an illusion, for this is ultimately based on arbitrary differences in color and size, plus the fact that McCollum furnishes his *Plaster Surrogates* with a signature and inventory number. The buyer of the *Plaster Surrogates* can be regarded as a true consumer in the modern-day capitalist sense of the word; the desire to distinguish oneself by means of exclusive products implies a loss of identity and functions as a surrogate for other unfulfilled desires. Furthermore, this desire only *seems* to be fulfilled by the purchase of the product, since the production method has been standardized to a considerable degree. McCollum's *Perfect Vehicles* (produced from 1985 onward) function as symbols, in this case for sculpture. *Perfect Vehicles* exist in two sizes and resemble urns or vases–the form is derived from that of Chinese ginger jar–which exude a distinctly 'human' quality due to their helmet-like tops and rigid arrangement in rows. Like the black, 'void' surface of the *Plaster Surrogate*, the form of the *Perfect Vehicle* invites an endless interpretation and projection of meaning and emotion.

Matt Mullican produces banners, posters,

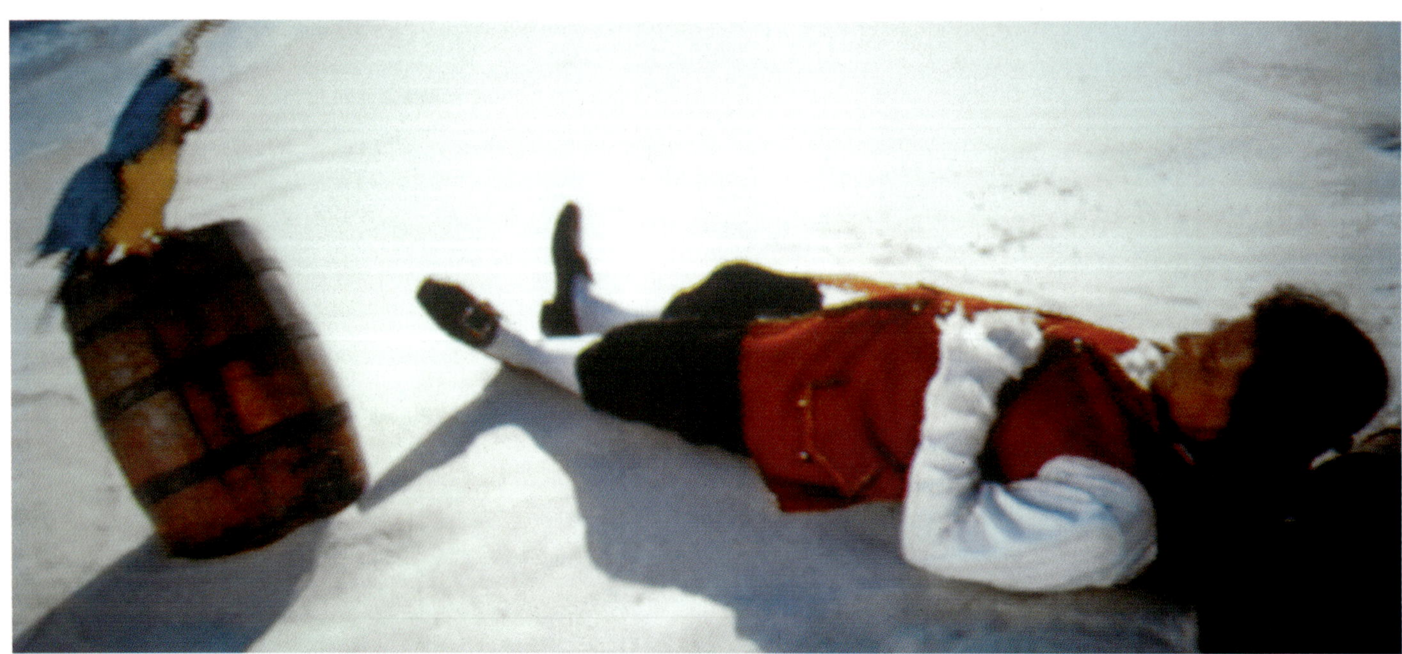

Rodney Graham *Vexation Island*, 1997 (video still)

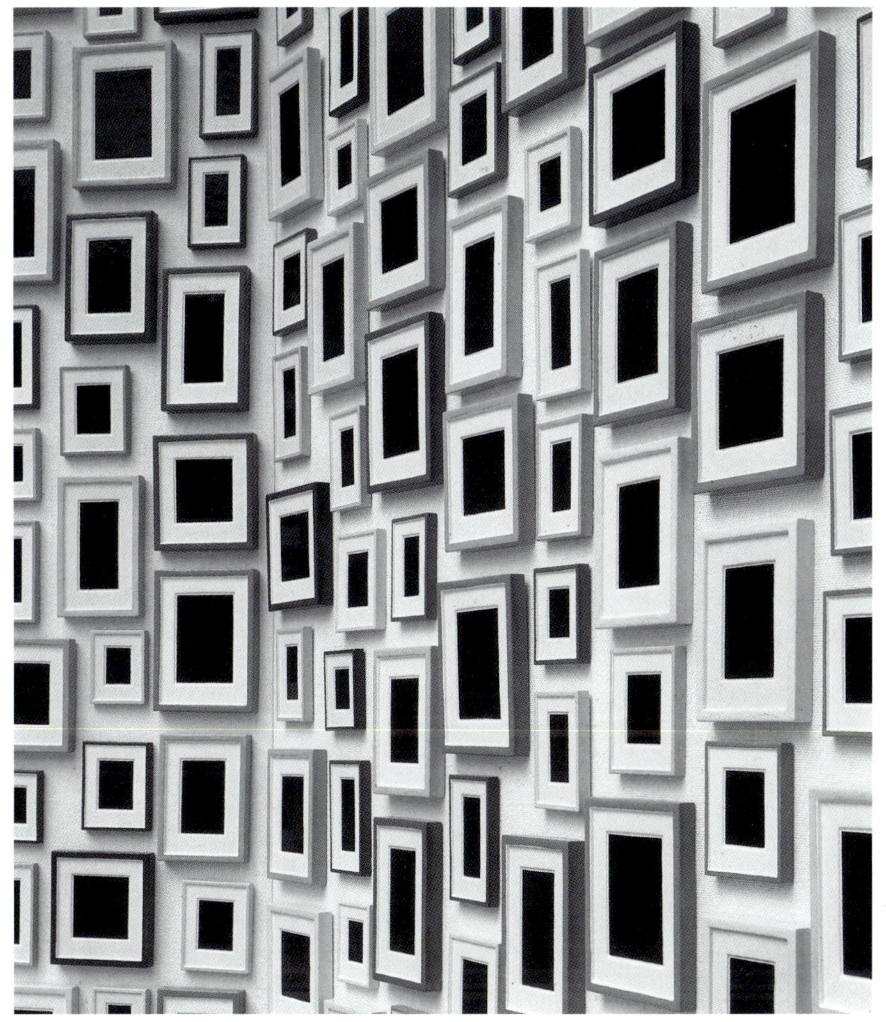

Allan McCollum *Plaster Surrogates*, 1989

drawings, 'bulletin boards', plaques, computer images, sculptures and installations. He is also involved in performances, in which he sometimes has himself placed under hypnosis. A characteristic feature of Mullican's work is his use of pictograms, which he develops and applies to paper, canvas, stone or to glass, as is the case with *Untitled* (1992). These pictograms call to mind the signs found at airports and train stations, though the images of Mullican encompass a much broader range of meaning. Over the years he has, for example, introduced signs for ideas such as God, the world, subject, object, heaven, hell, death, art, history and so on. Mullican's 'cosmology' is a model in which subjective experiences, artistic activities, empirical knowledge and philosophical ideas converge. His computer images in light boxes show a desolate, fictitious city that also serves as a model for the way in which man deals with objects, signs and abstract notions. Mullican's system of semi-abstract signs seems easily readable–should one hold the key to deciphering this–but this readability is frequently undermined by Mullican's juxtaposition of subjective meanings ascribed to the pictograms. A consideration of Mulllican's work leads one to believe that the attribution of meaning is not an objective process, but a construction–and that every individual has his own way of coding and decoding an image of the world.

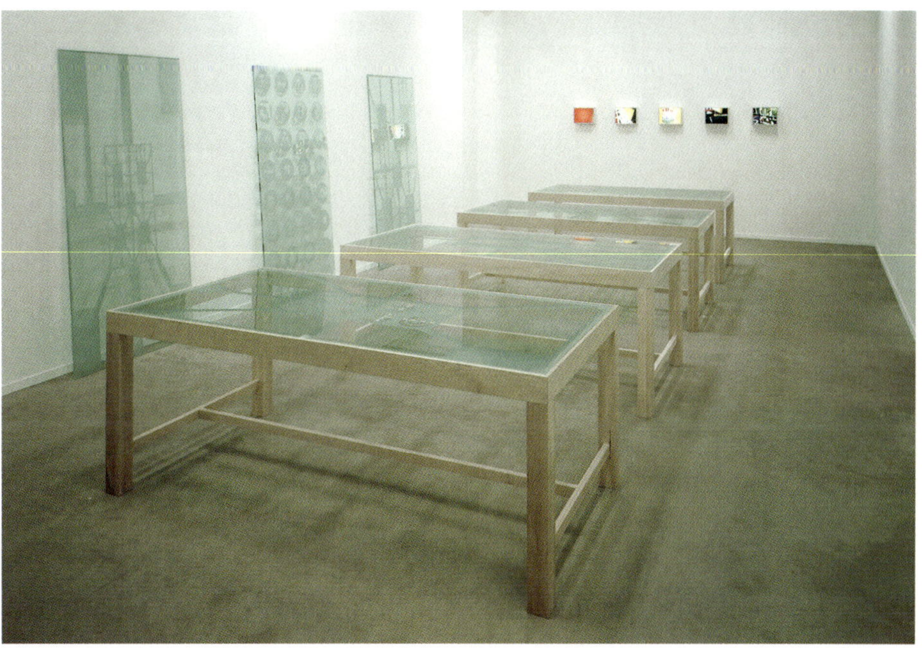

Matt Mullican *Untitled*, 1992; *Untitled*, 1996

Miroslaw Balka

Christian Boltanski

Juan Muñoz

Rachel Whiteread

Julião Sarmento

Ann Hamilton

Thierry De Cordier

Pieter Laurens Mol

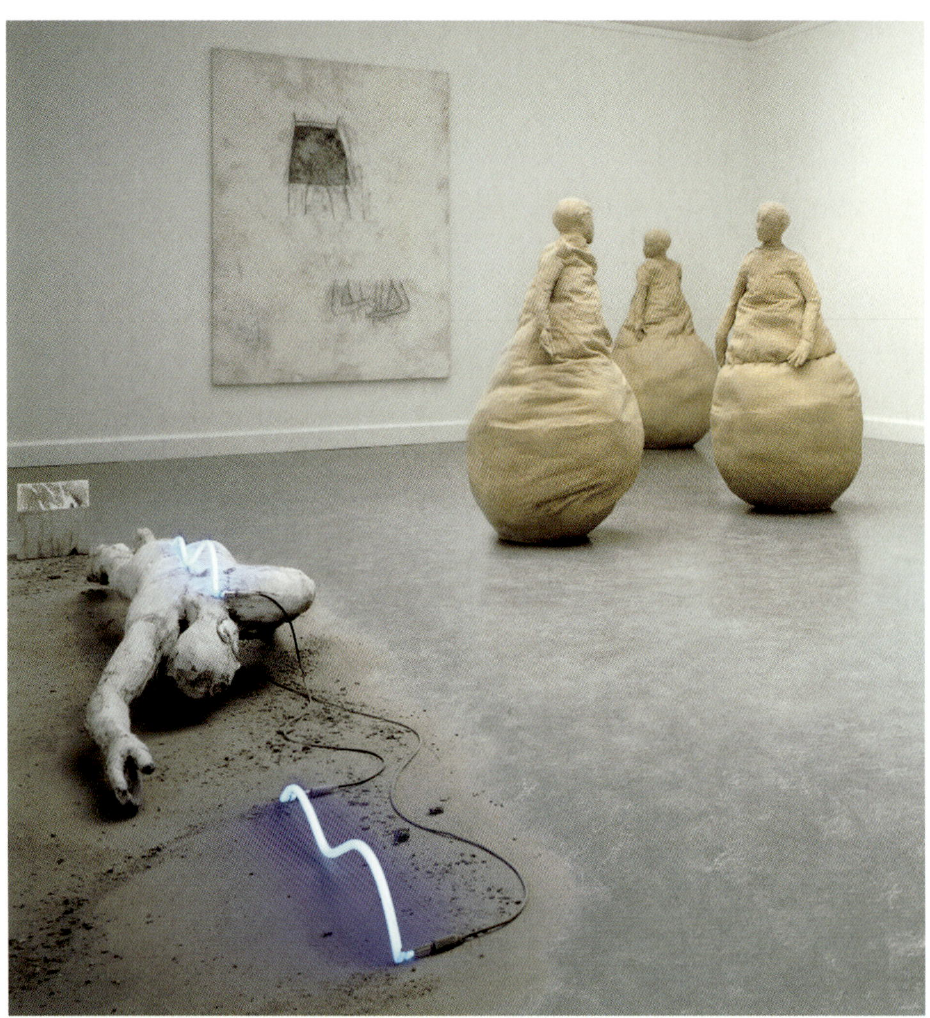

From left to right: **Miroslaw Balka** *River*, 1988-89; **Julião Sarmento** *Metropolis*, 1991; **Juan Muñoz** *Conversation Piece*, 1994

Under the directorship of Jan Debbaut, the Van Abbemuseum's area of concern has shifted toward a new generation of artists, most of whom were born during the fifties. Part of this generation produces work which often refers to the human body and the activities that it is able to perform, such as sleeping, eating, standing, playing, learning and also dying. The balconies of Muñoz, Bustamante's sandbox, Balka's beds, Boltanski's articles of clothing, Whiteread's bath: these are works that evoke all sorts of aspects of human activity and existence. In many cases they do so in a subdued, serene manner, though not without underlying and sometimes overt dramatics. The human figure itself is usually absent. Or it is of such an uncommon form (like the tumbling figures of Muñoz) that a high degree of alienation, a remoteness from the normal, is created.

It is striking that, during the late eighties and early nineties, many artists are interested in such traces of the human body; in literature,

as in the novels of Paul Auster and Patrick Modiano, we find similar preoccupations. Singular in relation to this is a general renewed concern for the absurdist plays of Samuel Beckett, who created, with the work *Waiting for Godot*, the prototype of an absent character who influences events on the stage. Juan Muñoz has expressed his own feeling that his work is about waiting, waiting until something–which may never happen–happens, and the paradoxical fear that it will happen: this parallels what one finds in *Waiting for Godot*. Balka, too, discerns an affinity between Beckett's work and his sculptures.

Why this tendency, this concern for absence and vestiges of presence happens to surface at this point is a complex philosophical issue which can scarcely be dealt with in a brief manner. It may have to do with the increasing influence of technology and media on society; these make the physical presence of the laborer, for instance, more and more superfluous. Or it may be related to the

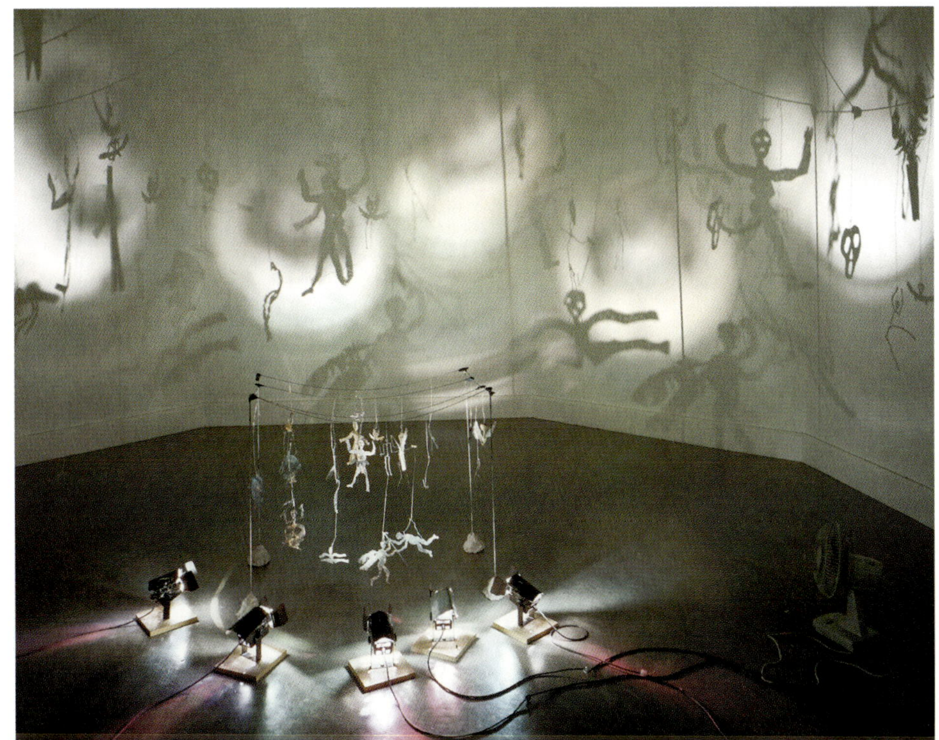

Christian Boltanski *Les ombres*, 1986

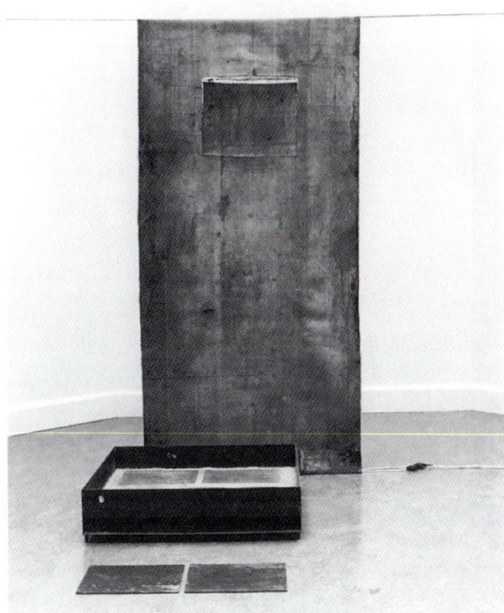

Miroslaw Balka *40x30x1, 40x30x1, 99x90x25, 250x126x1, 117x91x11,*
1992

growing degree of individualization in society and the loss of contact and communication that is linked with this. Such a vast topic cannot, however, be discussed at length here. Our focus is the way in which artists raise this matter.

The child is the subject of the final-exam work of Polish artist **Miroslaw Balka**. This sculpture shows the artist himself as a boy at his First Communion. The work from 1985 is a three-dimensional interpretation of a photograph. The boy is standing on a low platform, his right hand resting on a simple table, into which the photograph that has served as a model has been incorporated. This early sculpture deals with themes that continue to crop up in later work. The reference to his own body, for instance, occurs in later work in a more abstract and invisible manner, due to the fact that only the dimensions of his body, such as his height of one meter ninety, determine the appearance of the otherwise abstract sculptures. Another aspect is the representation of a ritual moment of transition, namely Holy Communion. In his later work, cleansing rituals are evoked and sometimes literally performed. For his exhibition at the Van Abbemuseum in 1993 he created transitional areas between the spaces where his older figurative sculptures were shown and those containing more abstract work. These 'transformation' zones consisted of two

corridors, the walls of which were smeared with soap. The soap symbolizes cleansing, a process of purification through which the visitor must pass before entering the tranquil, serene spaces with the abstract works that have 'transcended' figuration. The sculptures themselves are largely comprised of secondhand utilitarian objects and dilapidated items from his grandmother's house.

River (1988-89) is Balka's last figurative sculpture. It shows a tall human figure making a swimming motion, with one arm stretched forward. The water is suggested by waves of neon lighting in front of him and on his back. Water is a purifying element, and the surface of the water actually divides two worlds: that of water and that of air. Water is of vital importance, but it can also be deadly. The figure must swim so as not to drown. Immediately after *River* Balka produced a coffin, intended for the sculpture of the swimming figure which is, in fact, already an abstract form referring to the human body–a characteristic of Balka's abstract sculptures. Balka himself describes the transition into abstraction as follows: "I became interested in the forms that accompany the body and in the vestiges left by the body: a bed, a coffin, a funerary urn. In a certain sense, the earlier human figures had died. Then there arose the problematics of dimensions, which only truly become important after death, when a coffin has to be made."

The importance that Balka ascribes to measurement is also expressed in his titles, which are nothing other than the measurements of the sculpture. This initially appears to be straightforward information that corresponds to the frugality and drabness of the materials used. The relationship between these measurements and the body of the artist himself, as well as that between the shabby and worn materials such as linoleum, felt and ash–in the work *40x30x1, 40x30x1, 99x90x25, 250x126x1, 117x91x11* (1992) for instance–and his grandmother's house which has become his studio, gives soul and subdued tension to the abstraction. Autobiographical aspects play a significant role in Balka's work.

Death, the ultimate absence, which is brought up indirectly in the work of Balka, usually comes up in an unconcealed manner in that of **Christian Boltanski**. Boltanski has a preoccupation with death. "The fact that all of us will die at some point is so bizarre. We are such complex creatures, and then we die. Now you're an individual, with vanities, affections, worries, but before you know it you are, at least if you aren't religious,

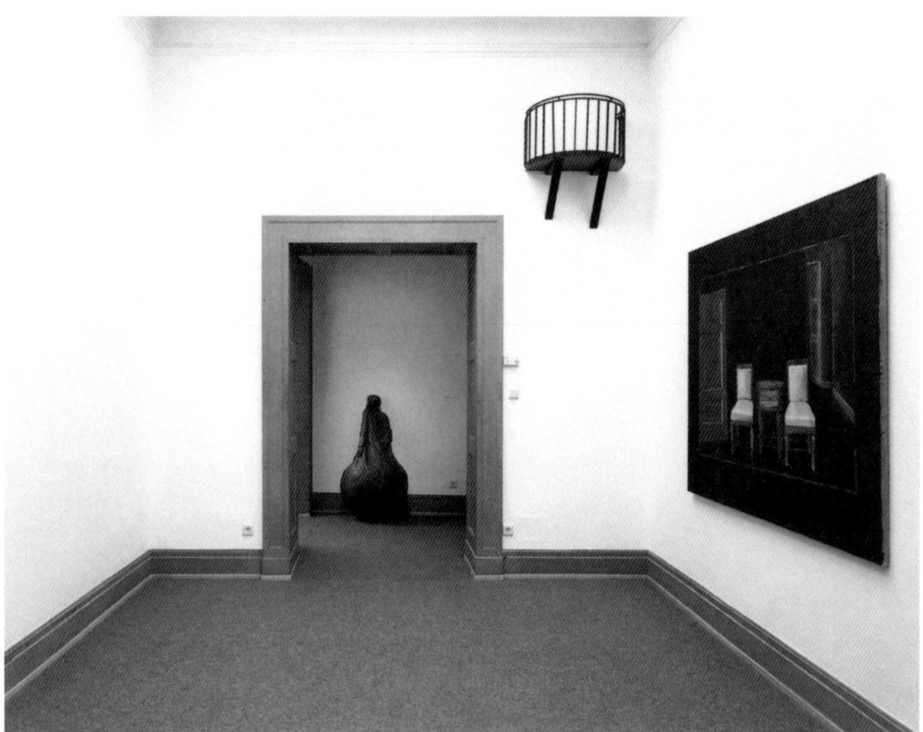

From left to right: **Juan Muñoz** *Listening Figure,1991; Balcony, 1991; Large Raincoat Drawing III, 1989*

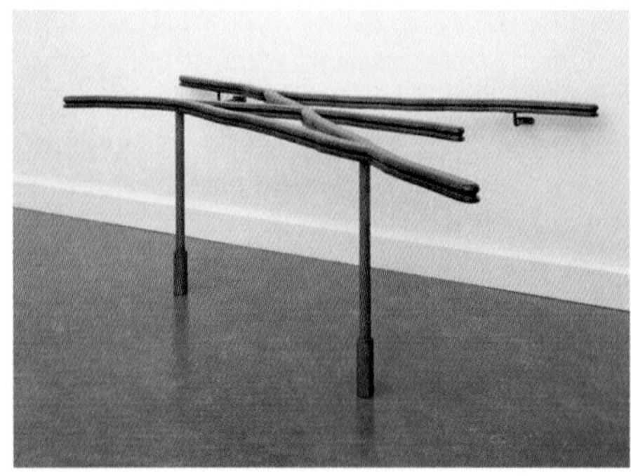

Juan Muñoz *Lines of my Hand, 1990*

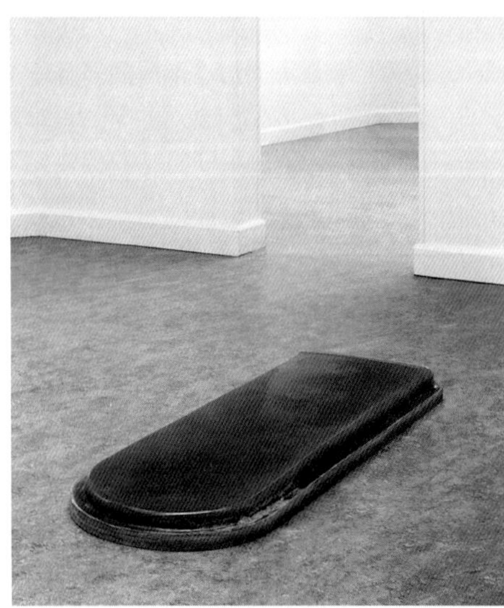

Rachel Whiteread *Untitled (Slab II), 1991*

reduced to a revolting pile of shit." With the aid of such things as tin boxes, articles of clothing, photographs and light, Boltanski creates theatrical stagings that may evoke a religious atmosphere with 'altarpieces' or a commemorative one with clothing and photographs depicting holocaust victims. His early work deals largely with the evocation of a bygone childhood. In 1970, for instance, he attempted to reconstruct lost objects from his youth–his childhood slippers, toys and pocket knives–in materials such as clay and paper. These reconstructions of the past are not faithful renderings; fiction and fact are always intertwined here. In *Les ombres*, from 1986, a number of important themes throughout Boltanski's work come together: childhood, with references to puppets; the theater, with dramatic effects of movement and light/dark contrasts; death, with darkness and skulls, skeletons, a hanged person and the Grim Reaper, all of these dangling like puppets and lit from below by three lamps, so that enormous shadows of them are cast onto the walls of the museum. The figures are made of plain materials–cork, wire, wood, paper. A fan causes movement, which is heightened in the greatly enlarged projection on the wall. It is actually all very simple. In *Les ombres* Boltanski even allows the sources of light and the fan to remain visible. But the simple means have a huge impact. The work moreover contains a wealth

of references. Plato's cave, Asian shadow puppetry, children's games, early films, a magic lantern, a scene from hell: an virtual pandemonium of allusions is conjured forth by this magical play of light, darkness and movement.

A theatrical aspect can also be found in the world that **Juan Muñoz** show us, but this is one of absolute calm; if any sound is suggested, it involves no more than a soft whisper. The figure depicted with his ear against the wall in *Listening Figure* (1991) is concentrating in order to pick up any sounds that can be heard. The balconies have the look of abandoned stage sets. Muñoz himself says that the empty balconies are about the absence of the human figure. The absence of language is also a theme of his. He refers to the silence that surrounds the figures in Seurat's paintings and the distance between these people with his remark "the image of the soul looking at the desert"–which could just as easily relate to his own work.

Lines of my Hand (1990) has the appearance of a strange banister along a stairway. Anyone familiar with the curved railings in the Barcelona apartment buildings of architect Antoni Gaudí will discern an echo of these in *Lines of my Hand*. But the form of this work has been determined, as the title indicates, by the lines in the palm of Muñoz's hand. The hand that seeks support from the railing has become fused with it, so to speak. Like Balka, Muñoz establishes a direct link between his body, in this case his hand, and the sculpture that this hand has produced. A railing invites the hand to touch, and it is this tactile quality that Muñoz has managed to convey by way of another sense, namely that of sight which is the sense of the visual arts, by allowing the imprint of his groping hand to become part of the work.

In work by the English artist **Rachel Whiteread** there is also reference to the imprint. Her sculptures resemble objects from a household environment: a bathtub, a wash basin, a mattress, a door. It is not the object itself but a cast of this, in negative form, that we see. Sometimes she also makes imprints of interior spaces, such as the inside of a closet or even an entire house before this has been torn down: the invisible becomes visible, space becomes mass, the inside outside, the ordinary is elevated to the status of a monument. Not only the absence of the object is made palpable here, but the absence of man (who has left his mark on the utilitarian object) can be discerned; evidence of his presence appears in the castings, as in the form of chewing gum that someone has tucked under a table, and thereby literally

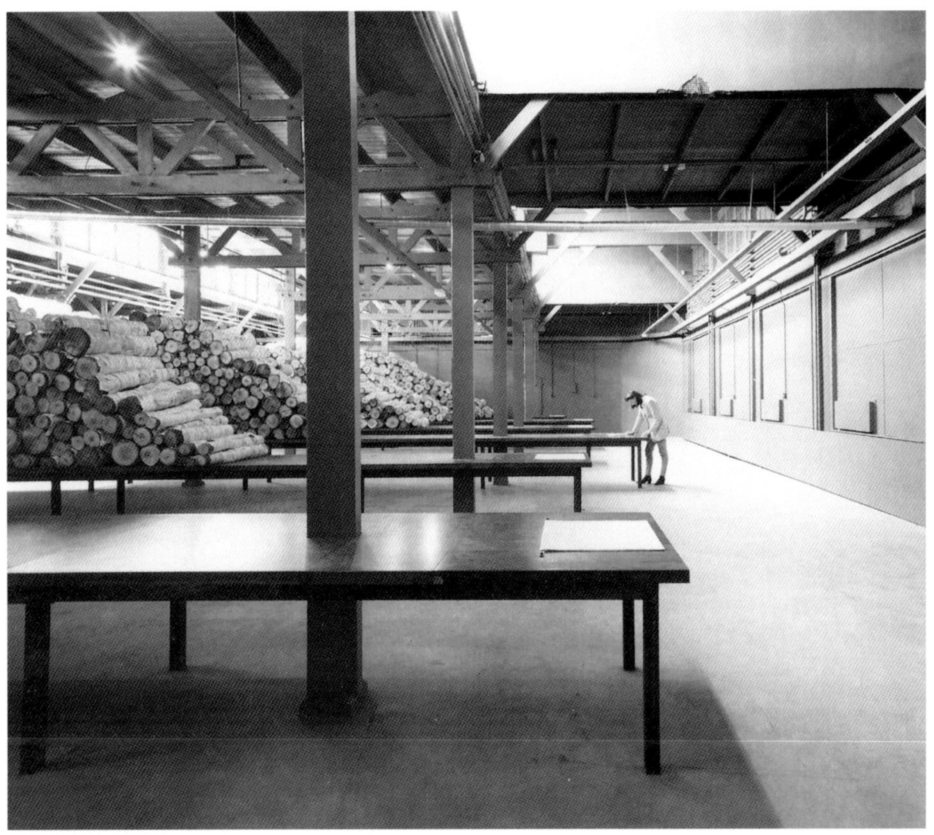

Ann Hamilton *Reserve*, 1996

comes to the surface of her work. Furniture, to Whiteread, is a metaphor for the human being. Because the original objects are no longer discernible in reality, only as imprints, her sculptures have become mental pictures of extinct things. Whiteread usually makes use of plaster, casting resin, rubber and wax–materials from which molds are usually made. Therefore one can speak of a reversal in this. She allows the utilitarian object to function as the mold and produces a cast of this in a material used for molds. After having been transposed into the negative, the object itself is usually ruined.

Valley (1990) is a casting of the underside of a Victorian cast-iron bathtub. Two additional castings of this same object were also made by her. The three works differ in terms of material and color, and they bear different titles. *Valley*, which is covered with a sheet of glass, looks very much like a sarcophagus. The glass refers to water, on the one hand, but Whiteread herself associates it with the glass coffin of Snow White and the glass under which bodies excavated from peatbogs are preserved. With Whiteread's two other sculptures in the collection, *Untitled (Marble Slab)* and *Untitled (Slab II)*–both from 1991–the connection with death is made more direct. The forms are derived from

dissecting tables on which corpses are laid out. But the relationship with death can also be seen in her way of working. The filling of empty spaces in order to give mass to an invisible form is reminiscent of the way in which body shapes of victims from the archaeological site at Pompeii were made visible again. Like these casts of individuals from the past in the throes of death, Whiteread's sculptures are silent witnesses of a bygone world.

The white paintings of **Julião Sarmento** resemble walls on which someone has made unfinished drawings in a childlike yet illustrative manner. The fragments of figures, in which previous mistakes in the drawing have been left visible, could also be mysterious tomb paintings found on the walls of a burial chamber from an ancient civilization. The most adequate present-day comparison would be the experience of entering a classroom where evidence of the previous lesson can still be seen on the chalkboard: parts of this have been erased and other areas filled in with yet other details. What the lesson was about is no longer entirely clear. One recognizes the visual fragments but does not know the narrative that is meant to connect them. The center of *Metropolis* (1991) shows the lower body of

(probably) a woman wearing a tight skirt; to the lower right one sees an upper body in which the position of the hands strikes the eye: a finger of the right hand is pointing to the flat of the left hand. At the lower left, a streamer making a circular movement has been drawn. What connection exists between the title and these three fragments remains a mystery, and that may even make the experience of the work disappointing. But it is this very sense of disappointment which the Portuguese artist wishes to express, because he believes that it is impossible to fully portray or to gain a grasp of reality or the object of one's desires.

Like Boltanski, the American artist **Ann Hamilton** incorporates large quantities of clothing into some of her installations. But while Boltanski is concerned with used clothing that refers to the former wearers of it, Hamilton focuses on massiveness. Great amounts of starched and folded work clothing or scorched white shirts are stacked, on a table, into an enormous and somewhat peculiar form. There is no reference to the user, but indeed to the human body for which it is intended. What matters, though, is the great amount of physical labor required for the starching, scorching or other processing of this huge quantity of clothing. Hamilton's work often involves an almost endless repetition of an action, whereby the aspect of time but also–due to the repetition–that of inertia becomes palpable. *Reserve* (1996) deals with the great number of trees that were felled and sawed into certain dimensions for the installation, along with video images of more minor activities.

Reserve is part of the large installation that Hamilton produced for the Van Abbemuseum's temporary location. In the main space she had placed six long steel tables parallel to each other. On one end, extending well beyond the middle of each table was a towering stack of poplar trunks. Each trunk was wrapped in pages of secondhand books. At the other end of each table was a built-in monitor, covered by a cloth, on which a video image of an endlessly repeated action could be seen, including a hand scratching with a piece of chalk across a surface of glass, the sound of which could be heard in the space. Water leaked from the roof onto the wood. The work was created specifically for the room, even specifically for the Netherlands. The division between language (the writing) and image (the tree trunks) refers to the distinction between the Protestant North and the Catholic South. It is typical of Hamilton's way of working that she becomes immersed in the cultural context of

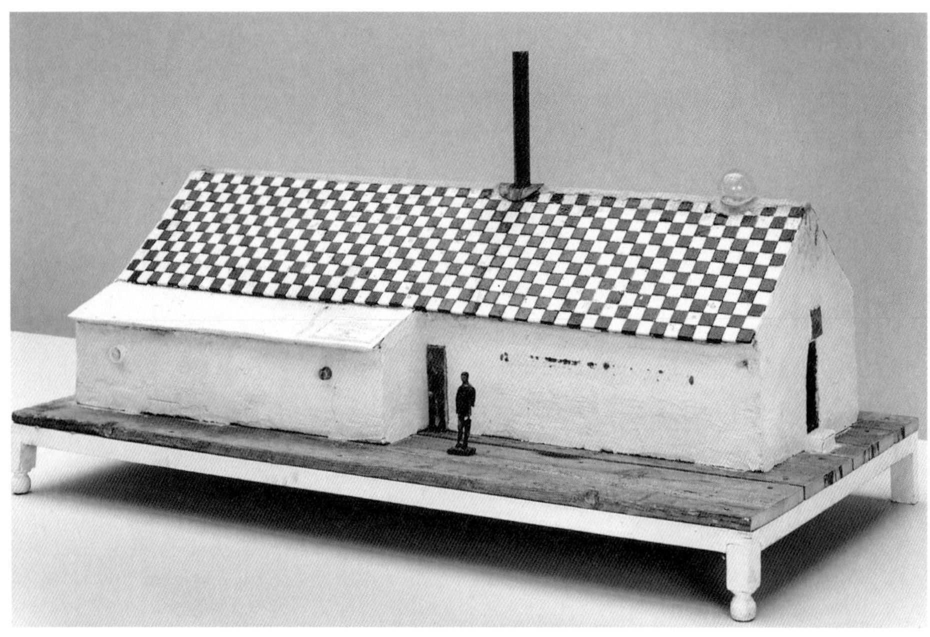

Thierry De Cordier *La Cuisine (maquette)*, 1988

the place for which the work is being made. The tree trunks symbolize, however, the importance of forests for cultural history. Poplars are used a great deal in the paper industry. Nature and culture, Protestantism and Catholicism: Hamilton reconciles various oppositions in her work. Extremes, too, such as the intimate (the video images) and the massive (the stacks of tree trunks), production and consumption, verticality and horizontality, moisture and dryness are juxtaposed in *Reserve*. Furthermore, many of the viewer's senses are stimulated–the scratching sound, the smell of wood and the lifting of the cloth in order to see the video image–but the experience of the imposing totality of the work remains intact, so that one can never speak of a fragmentation of focus. Whereas Hamilton allows us to sense the complex cultural condition of life, the Flemish artist **Thierry De Cordier** is more concerned with a return to the individual. De Cordier is an artist who seeks isolation. During the eighties and nineties, he lived a secluded life in the village of Schorisse, in the Flemish countryside. The contact with the earth, with the seasons is of great importance to him. In this way of living he deliberately distances himself from present-day society, even from contemporary art, because he wishes to remain as independent as possible

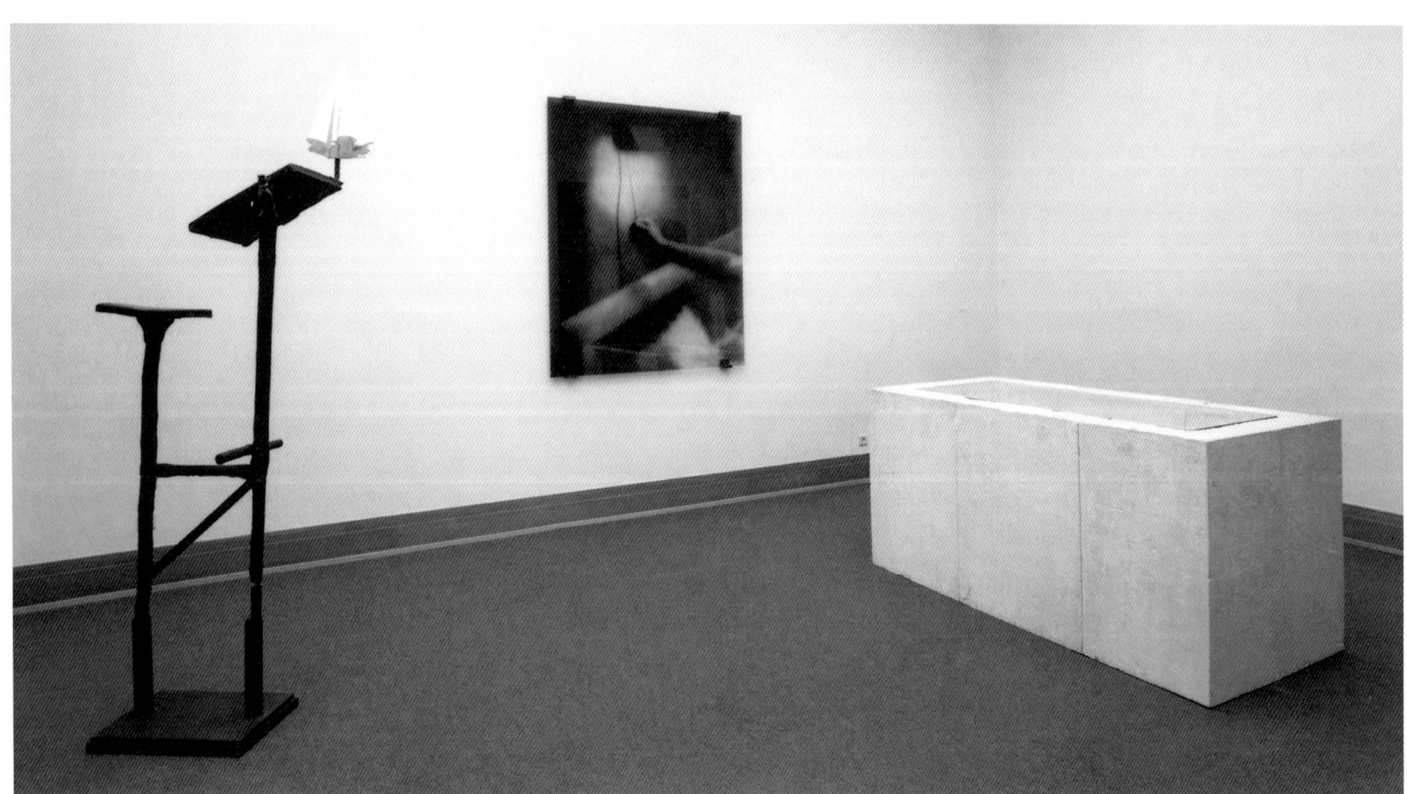

From left to right: **Thierry De Cordier** *Écritoire, I (schrijfgestoelte)*, 1988-93; **Jean-Marc Bustamante** *Lumière I*, 1988; **Rachel Whiteread** *Valley*, 1990

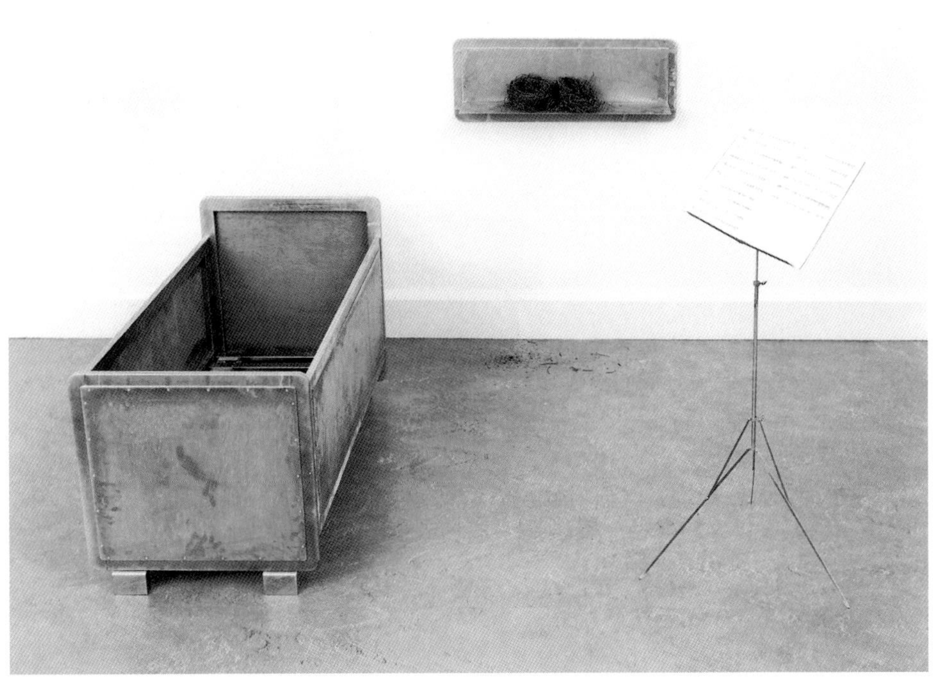

Pieter Laurens Mol *Lament Superior*, 1991

from external influences. "Our current culture is completely uprooted," is the gist of his conviction. "It builds Towers of Babel. The models employed generate patterns of automatism and of greedy, blind behavior that leads to illusions. Like the ethnologist who wanted to study the Indians. Until he realized the total absurdity of his study: he stopped and began to describe his room." De Cordier, too, is actually occupied with describing his room to us. *La Cuisine (maquette)* (1988) is a model of De Cordier's own studio/farm in the Ardennes–not as it appears now, but as it should appear in his imagination. It is a space which scarcely has any windows and thus expresses his need for seclusion and contemplation.

Though his work differs enormously from that of Hamilton, a certain similarity can nonetheless be discerned. Hamilton brings time to a standstill, or to put it more aptly, stretches it out and thereby takes time to consider the culture from which we come. De Cordier withdrew into a reclusive existence in order not to participate in the hectic nature of present-day life, but to take time for being able to "conceive of the world from his own backyard." Both depart from the notion that human culture is rooted in nature. While Hamilton ultimately places the accent on culture, De Cordier opts for a life that is as close to nature as possible. Many of his sculptures are made of materials that he has found in or around his farm, such as

earth, plant remains and ash.

Contrary to De Cordier, who turns his own backyard into a universe, **Pieter Laurens Mol** makes the entire universe his playground. For instance, Mol 'writes' with moonlight: the words 'I love you' are captured by his moving camera. We also find references to various planets such as Mars and Saturn and the stars, but with the symbolic meanings that are linked to these in European culture and history. Saturn, for instance, is regarded as the planet of artistry, but also that of death and the melancholic temperament. Melancholia is a recurrent theme throughout Mol's work. His use of material is also pregnant with meaning. With the 'melancholic' works, for example, Mol uses heavy metals such as lead and zinc, and with the 'Mars' works, which are linked with the sanguine temperament, mainly iron. This highly varied and rich body of work also includes references to seventeenth-century Dutch culture, in which figures such as Van Leeuwenhoek, with the invention of the microscope, and Huygens, with that of the telescope, made major contributions to science. It is actually not the vestiges of man as an individual, but rather that of European cultural history and of generally human qualities that interests Mol.

While De Cordier has withdrawn from the world to his farm, Mol seems to make all sorts of attempts to leave this world by defying gravity. But the work is also filled

with the awareness that one cannot escape gravity. This is why the fall, particularly the fall of high-flier Icarus, constitutes a central motif. *Schacht der Vergetelheid* (1987), with its five glass funnels, deals with this theme of the fall. The title, however, also refers to death. The black tar covering the background can be obtained only by digging deep into the earth, a descent that also symbolizes a progression into deeper layers of oblivion. The funnels primarily evoke chemical or perhaps one should say alchemistic processes. But the varying sizes of the glass funnels, combined with the three long saw blades, also allude to sound waves. As such the classical idea of a 'harmony of spheres' is called to mind–the universe seen as an expression of musical harmony–so that earth and the heavens are joined in the work. The very essence of Mol's oeuvre may have to do with the place that man occupies between these two great variables: his restriction to the earth, his desire and inability to escape this and thus his insignificance with respect to the universe.

With the exception of Mol and the painter Sarmento, the artists discussed in this chapter make work that is often presented in the form of installations; it defines the space in which it is being shown. Muñoz's *Listening Figure* and *Balcony*, for instance, involves the entire wall in the work, and the balcony moreover transforms this into an exterior wall. Hamilton's *Reserve* was specially conceived for the main space of the temporary building of the Van Abbemuseum. Boltanski's *Les ombres* fills the entire space with its terrifying shadows, though it is actually small in size. Despite the installation-like character of the work, however, a basic intimacy remains, and this makes the experience of absence, of death, of longing or melancholy all the more moving.

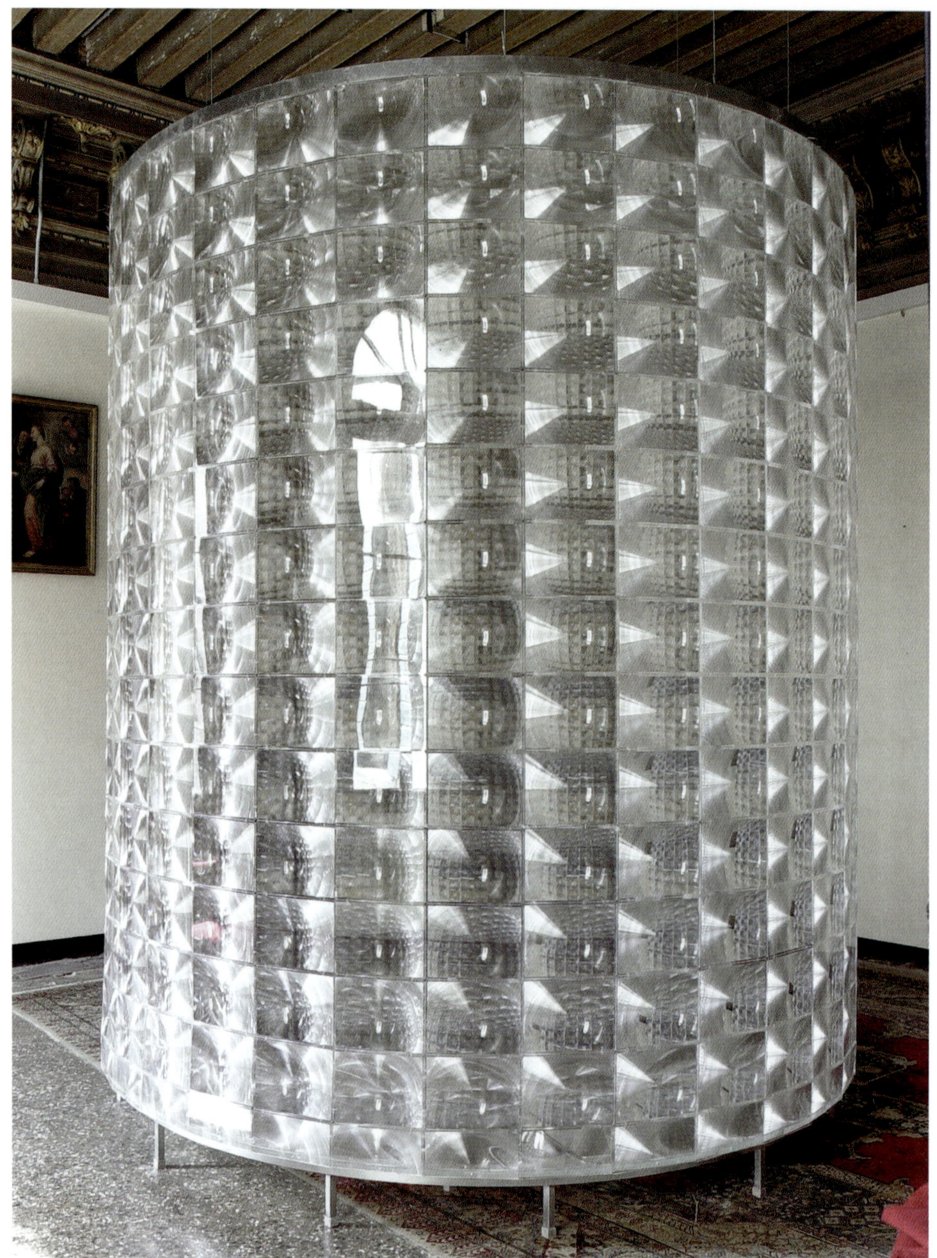

Job Koelewijn *Kaleidoscoop*, 2001

In the spring of 1992, on bidding farewell to art school, Job Koelewijn had the glass pavilion at the Rietveld Academy cleansed by four women in traditional Spakenburg costume. Armed with buckets and rags, ladders and brooms, soap and water, his mother and aunts scrubbed the building spick-and-span in just a few hours. The spring-cleaning ritual was an ode to Gerrit Rietveld, based on a respect for his austere and functional architecture. At the same time, this thorough cleaning was intended as a gesture to the world–a symbolic purification, a plea for casting away ballast and making a fresh start.

Koelewijn's plain statement attests to a childlike radicalness and matter-of-fact attitude, which contrasts sharply with the philosophical reflections of artists who arrived on the scene during the eighties, such as Arno van der Mark, Fortuyn/O'Brien and Niek Kemps. Koelewijn sooner speaks the language of the street. The endless introspection of art and scepticism with regard to its political or social claims gradually gave way, toward the end of the eighties, to pragmatism and a more expectant, sometimes straightforwardly idealistic approach to the world. The act of looking outward is then considered more

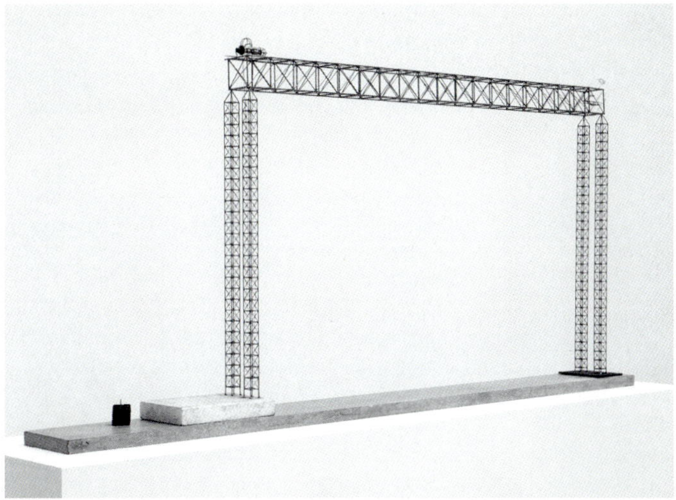

John Körmeling *Pier voor Zeeland*, 1985

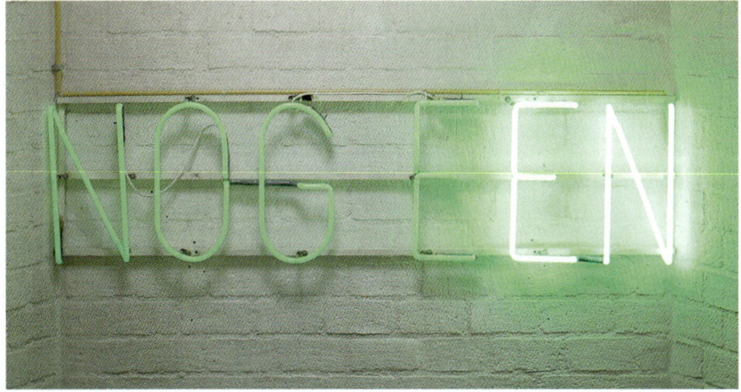

John Körmeling *Nog een*, 1990

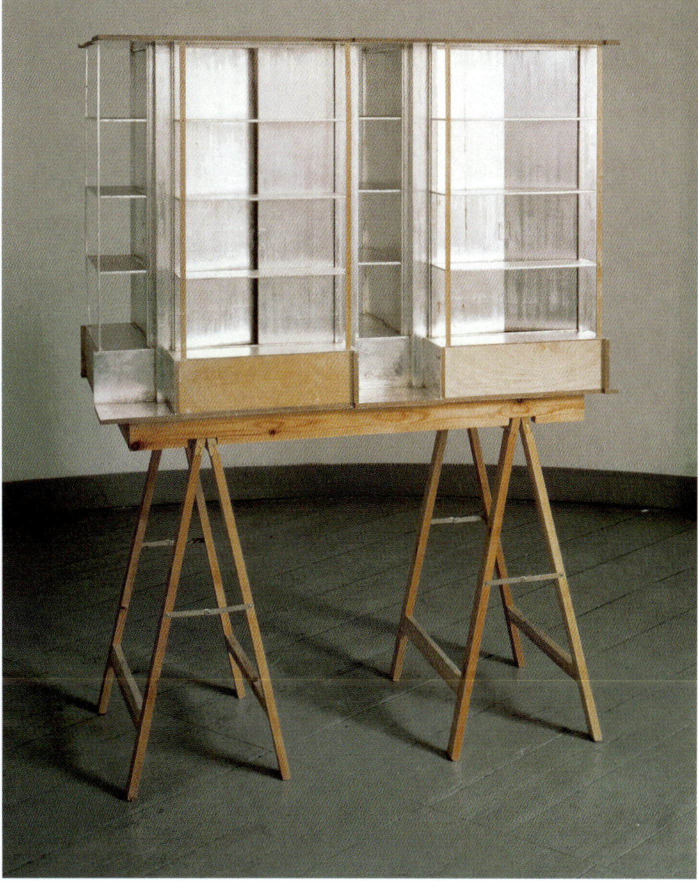

Jan van de Pavert *Segment uit een bibliotheek voor eindeloze tekst*, 1989

important than that of looking inward, and it is not the past but the future which concerns many artists. Some believe that the artist can bring progress to the world (John Körmeling) or that art can revive a numbed and crippled society (Tiong Ang). Others withdraw into an insular world which evolves according to their own laws and has its own language, as seen with the self-portraits of Mark Manders. A few express critical views on the great degree of self-reflection in art. **Jan van de Pavert**, for instance, writes, "I am turning against that intellectualist irony which later came to be called postmodernism, against sculpture that is about sculpture, photography that is about photography, etc. (...) It makes no attempt whatsoever to develop anything for the future."

Van de Pavert's *Segment uit een bibliotheek voor eindeloze tekst* (1989) is not meant to be a play of optical illusions; it appeals, rather, to our ability to imagine that which is all-encompassing, to the potential of mental resources. The segment refers to a larger, imaginary library. In a similar manner, the works *Voorgevel* and *Erker* from 1993 depict

fragments of an imaginary house conceived by Van de Pavert. The dwelling does exist as a entity, but there has indeed been consideration for the potential to build it. That the design must actually be feasible is even a condition, because this in particular is what gives things their meaning or justification. This is how the shelter for a homeless person, a motif that appears in various exhibitions and individual works of Van de Pavert, gives a symbolic place, and thereby meaning, to the anonymous thinker with no address–"as someone who is there, a factor that has its place."

Van de Pavert prefers to work in terms of models, maquettes and plans, due to their open and mediating character. The table, which serves as a base for the sculpture of two girls embracing each other, also plays a mediating role. The modelling wax of which the work is made moreover suggests changeability. It is as though the table is emphatically claiming not to be presenting an autonomous work of art, but rather a possible starting point for one. The embrace could be a sculptural translation of the dinner

which Van de Pavert and Frank Mandersloot prepared in 1993–as an exhibition–for a few dozen guests. *Geen tafel voor twee* was primarily meant to generate an encounter, to give rise to a discussion.

Many artists are no longer sceptical about the reformative power of art. Some are absolutely convinced that art can contribute to the improvement of the world. **John Körmeling** even says, "I do good for the world." Not that he opposes certain social tendencies; he is not a critic in that sense. But through his work he exposes the conformism in our ways of thinking and acting, patterns that can be disrupted only when we adopt a different attitude.

Körmeling is an inventor, architect and visual artist all rolled into one. His designs subvert a number of steadfast presumptions. His open, square car from 1994, whose primitive appearance inspires little trust with regard to speed and comfort, is a great deal more aerodynamic than vehicles seen on the highway. The idea that a round and streamlined model constitutes the only possible condition for speed is therefore

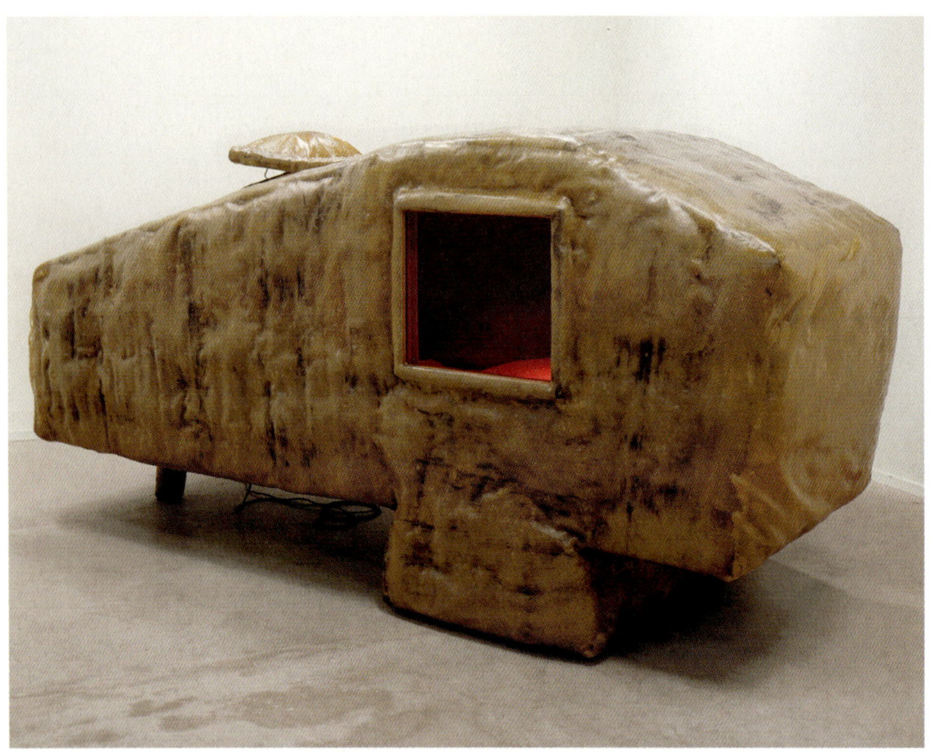

Atelier van Lieshout *Orgone/Sleep/Dinette Skull*, 1998

incorrect. He also applies, out on the street and in public buildings, marks which bring attention, in a caricatural way, to something we already knew or offer an alternative, point to a change. This aspect of affirmation and change is the basis of the neon work *Nog een* (1990), in which the words *een*, *en* and *nog een* light up alternately. In one of his drawings, he situated the neon letters on the roof of a building, but they can just as easily be placed at the entrance to an exhibition space.

Such models and one-liners are reminiscent of industrial prototypes and the engaging power of advertisements. Körmeling thus recommends his own work as new, improved products by which he hopes to bring about a change of mentality. The series of thirty-two drawings purchased by the Van Abbemuseum in 2001 provide an idea of his wide range of approaches and ways of using work. A striking aspect is that he always elaborates on a given reality, whether this be a building, a trend in fashion or a ritual, such as the giving of compliments or birthday presents. His statement "I believe that you can consider a building a place on which to build further" relates, in that sense, not only to his proposals for architectonic additions to existing buildings but also indirectly to all of his work.

Through the course of the nineties, more and more artists present alternatives to products, production processes or forms of service. **Joep van Lieshout** is one such artist. During the late eighties he made the switch–from sculptor to independent contractor. The multiple became the focus of a new marketing strategy, a strategy that took into consideration the context in which art was being presented, sold and discussed. In 1989 he presented his first furniture collection: tables and cabinets in various standard sizes, manufactured in polyester and available, in various colors, by order. The texture of reinforced polyester has become his trademark.

Since the mid nineties, under the business name Atelier van Lieshout, he has rendered services as a designer/contracter of all sorts of building extensions, mobile homes and furniture suites. The Atelier offers "practical solutions to everyday problems," not only in the realm of interiors and housekeeping, but also with respect to psychology and a philosophy of life. His *Orgone/Sleep/Dinette Skull* (1998) is, for instance, a caravan as well as a relaxation space. Van Lieshout took his inspiration from the ideas of the psychoanalyst Wilhelm Reich, who conceived of the Orgone Energy Accumulator in 1940. This was a booth, partly constructed in metal, which was said to have healing and bioenergetic properties. Van Lieshout's first

booths offered enough space for one person and had the shape of an orb or a coffin with an adjoining chaise longue. The more recent, organically shaped models can be used for different purposes: sleeping, eating and studying. The mobile home–a workman's hut, sex caravan, study cubicle and lounge space all in one–corresponds to Van Lieshout's ideas about a self-providing community.

Driven by the notion that man is responsible for his own actions and that he should be able to provide for himself in order to survive, the artist has taught himself elementary, often traditional skills. In instruction manuals that can be understood by all, Van Lieshout passes on knowledge. By now he is not only able to design and build things, but also to slaughter pigs, brew beer and carry out simple techniques for the processing and preservation of food. He manufactures weapons and designs systems for the reuse of waste matter. In less-than-reassuring images, Atelier van Lieshout builds on an 'autarkic' existence, on a form of survival. With this, there is an anticipation of a potential deluge. The act of secluding oneself from the world relates to the work of painter **Tiong Ang** in a different way. Ang regards his images as compensation for a human shortcoming, the inability to communicate any longer: "The new images present a conflict; they are there to promote communication among people and things, not to be 'seen' as images. While John Körmeling makes productive use of technology, Ang considers technology to be the very cause of social problems. He takes a critical stance toward the influence of technological developments on the general behavior of people. The profusion of images, sounds and increasing automatization make us numb and incapacitated, Ang believes: "The projections have blinded us, the loudspeakers have made us deaf, clogged infrastructures have numbed our skins and crippled our limbs. (...) Our bodies are left in a new natural state, that of invalidity."

As a model of the virtually autistic condition in which modern man lives, Ang situated, at the Van Abbemuseum in 1993, a television set with its screen facing the wall, onto which it projected a silent stream of rapidly alternating images of light. A similar aura of numbness also characterizes Ang's paintings, which are shielded from the world by a tautly stretched voile screen. Behind this, there appear images taken from the media: images from film or television, photographs from newspapers, magazines and encyclopedias. These images have not been chosen in an arbitrary manner. They show dramatic events–mutilations of eyes and ears through surgery or initiation rites–or oppressively vacant spaces, such as waiting rooms and stairwells. They represent extremes in life, such as passivity, loneliness, death and blindness. Even so, Ang suggests an opening in the apparently secluded world. The slight optical vibration that is caused by passing the voile surfaces activates the static images and implies a small promise of perspective–that is to say life, light, a future. The artwork, which requires concentration and tranquillity, functions as an aid in regaining an understanding of reality. Or, to use the words of Ang: "The artwork as a prosthesis through which reality can be seen differently (better, more beautifully, more shamelessly?)–in order to compensate for the invalidity of our thinking."

The paintings of **Michael Raedecker** also portray the world in terms of extremes. The barren landscapes, suburban neighborhoods and interiors that he conjures up by way of paint and textile materials are ghostly no man's lands. Any trace of human presence is missing. The greys, blues and greens are chilly and toneless, as though they have lost strength through the course of time. The uncanny nature of this imaginary world is nurtured by a systematic distortion of visual statements. The paintings are thereby constantly contradicting themselves. Perspectives are opened, on the one hand, with broadly applied areas of paint–a bungalow in a suburban area, the corner of a room or a bird's-eye view of a landscape–and on the other, garish details undermine the illusion of space. Thick lumps or marblings in the paint and bits of textile, such as loose threads, stitching, tangles of yarn or scraps of carpet, emphasize the material properties of the painting, as an object in the 'here and now'. Along the perspectival lines set out in textile material, new vantage points open up and thereby change a preexistent one, as though this were the portrayal of a mental leap. The row of trees with tops of jumbled thread seen in *pitch*, for instance, intensifies the sloping of the green landscape and tones it down at the same time. The word 'pitch', with its various meanings, also refers to this dual effect.

Raedecker relates ambiguity to the inability to find firm ground, to arrive at a something definite. The marble-like lumps of paint represent stones as fluid substance. In that form they actually bring to mind the 'fluid' world view of computer animations: dead and alive at the same time. *kismet* shows how that animation can be captured in a motionless surface. The tongue of white

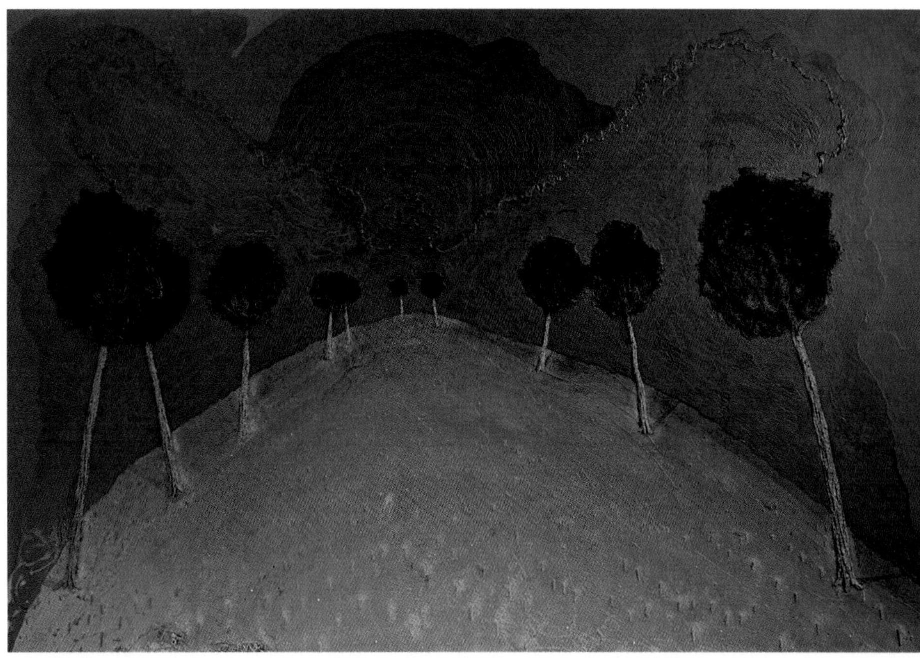

Michael Raedecker *pitch*, 2000

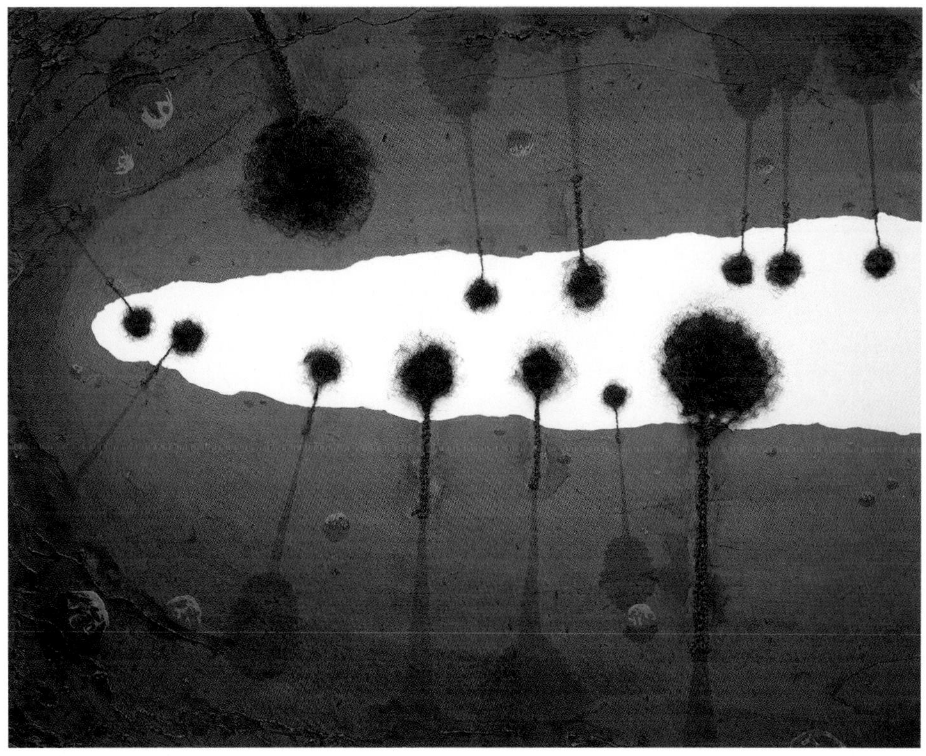

Michael Raedecker *kismet*, 1999

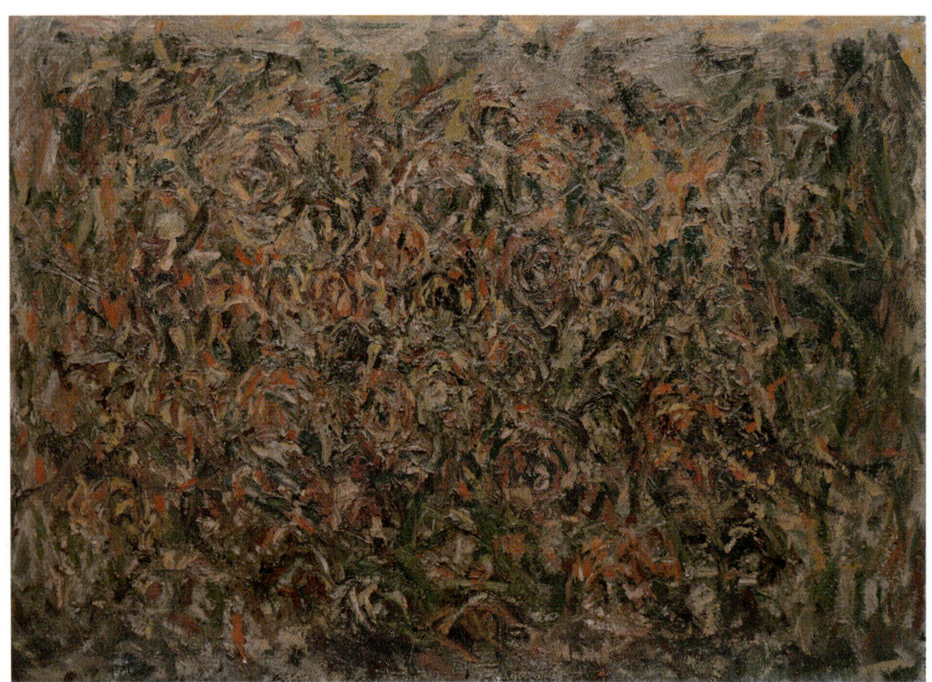

Marc Mulders *Rozen XIV*, 1992

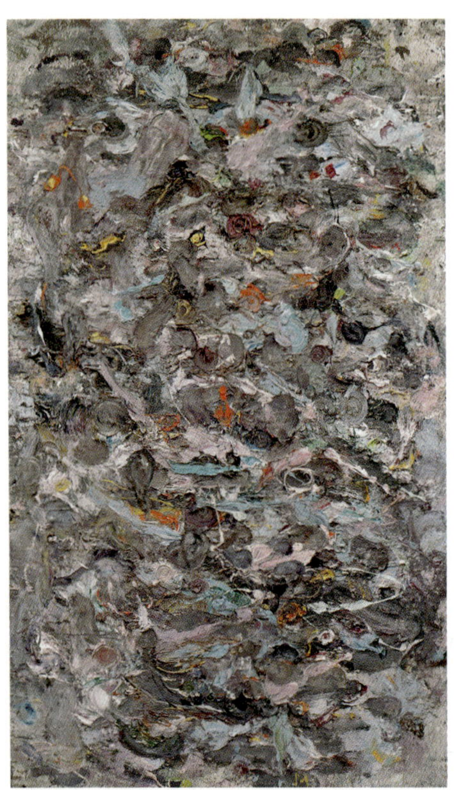

Marc Mulders *Picardie*, 2000

paint gives the impression that there is a source of light located behind the painting and that the world revolves around this. Here the cinematographic side of Raedecker's work plays a role: he is showing us the present as a projection of the past or the future, of memories or desires, realms in which we can wander but never live.

Film and computer images are not the beacons by which the painter **Marc Mulders** sets his course. Conversely, tradition is the inexhaustible source of inspiration from a painterly point of view. Classical motifs such as flowers, 'vanitas' still lifes of dead game and pietàs reflect themes that are just as classical. Mulders displays a preference for dramatic subjects: suffering, death and persecution. Having in mind the powerless or resigned attitude with which we still face, to this day, gruesome mass murders such as those in former Yugoslavia, he puts up a visible battle with thick layers of paint that seem to cling to the canvas like mire. The world has not become any less cruel or more beautiful over thousands of years. Like Tiong Ang, Mulders believes in the persuasive power of art, in the purifying effect that can come from images when they confront us with both the vulnerable and the extraordinarily dramatic aspects of existence.

Frank Mandersloot takes a more reticent stance with regard to the meaning and influence of art. "Art's force as a reformative principle is negligible," Mandersloot says emphatically. Nevertheless, he has been trying to tighten the link with everyday reality in recent years, and his work has gradually become less autonomous. Since 1993 Frank Mandersloot has been making exhibitions in which he literally offers the viewer a chair and, as such, allows him to become part of his work. In this way he seeks a connection with the everyday experience of people. During the eighties he was constructing tables, chairs, beds and cabinets with plywood and linen. Initially, these were sawn into pieces and jumbled together to form small interiors, but later, in a more stylized form, they began lead a life of their own. The continual play of form and negative form, gluing and stacking, the forces of pulling and tightening attests to an intensive and craftsmanly labor process. To Mandersloot, the process of making something and the motives underlying it are more important than the ultimate product, which he views as a negative form that can be 'exhausted' at a certain point. He has an ambivalent relationship with the work of art. Some furniture is simply put back in his own household or surfaces again more in other works. It is as though he refuses to be content with the inanimate status of artworks and wishes to put them in constant circulation. The meaning of his work is not determined particularly by iconography, by 'the picture', but by the idiom of physical experience: looking, listening, drinking, walking, sitting, making love. Mandersloot is more interested in the single-mindedness of the action, in daily rituals and the mental and social implications of our occasionally mechanical behavior. The sculptural play of curves and doublings, as in the works from the series *Jogos de Cama* (1990), which means 'bed play' or 'bedding', refers to the curvatures and the symmetry of the human body. The tension evoked by the tautly drawn linen and the curved forms has an erotic connotation. The concise language of forms alludes, like many of Mandersloot's sculptures, to the origins and the cycle of life. Mandersloot 'undresses' life and shaves the body bare and gaunt.

Along side Mandersloot's recognizable works that refer to collective behavior, the personal creations of **Mark Manders** form a stark contrast. *Zelfportret als gebouw*, on which he has been working since his art-school days, shows a completely insular world. Though this world does not propagate 'art for art's sake', it is confined in the sense that the language that is spoken there and the rules that apply in it do not go beyond the walls of the imaginary house. The self-portrait shows the materialization of Manders's thoughts and emotions and the place that these have in the whole of his experience. Manders has even designed a storage cabinet for his collection of unsuccessful ideas: "They're real ideas, so I do have to store them." The building exists and, at the same time, doesn't exist. There are countless plans of it, which on paper easily change in terms of form, division and scale, depending on the moment and the needs of the maker. At exhibitions, those interested are given a glimpse at several reconstructions of various furnished rooms. The building as a whole, however, exists only in Manders's imagination, which he experiences as a truly inhabitable world and which he can leave only for a day every now and then. The spaces are inhabited by countless unsightly objects in the most amazing combinations: dice on castors, pencils stuck into erasers, and wires that connect coffee cups, pieces of wood, bottles and batteries with each other, slung across the floor, passing chairs and thresholds. Residing in them are also human and animal figures fired in clay, twins, sexless or fetus-like creatures. For Manders, they are offshoots of himself, characters or children bred by 'mental intercourse' with illustrious women from art history, such as Lucas Cranach's Venus.

The space at the foundations of his house contains an encyclopedia in which all knowledge and stories about life are stored, and on top of this is a large and inaccessible room that Manders has reserved for all unused possibilities and unproductive ideas. From both of these, the artist draws the ingredients for his personal theory of evolution, a semi-scientific and philosophical investigation of the twists of the mind and the caprices of life–a theory which seems to have been conceived with the earnestness and delight of a child.

While, with Manders, the shape and the effect of thought constitute the subject matter of his work, **Job Koelewijn** is sooner

fascinated by symbolism and the power of enthusiasm. His work appeals strongly to the senses. They stimulate the nervous system which directs all parts of the body, its organs and functions. In 1995, for instance, he smeared the entrance doors of De Appel with inhalation salve. The scent of eucalyptus penetrates into one's head and chest and opens the body, as it were, to new impressions. For the exhibition 'Post Nature' shown at the Venice Biennial of 2001, Koelewijn created a gigantic kaleidoscope. This space resembling a shower cubicle, screened off on all sides by a curtain of plastic fish-eye lenses, offers a fragmented and richly varied view of the immediate surroundings from the inside out. The world is experienced as a wave that absorbs, distorts, heightens, reduces and enlarges everything–prismatic poetry in a shower of lapsing images.

Koelewijn believes in the force of the immaterial and the beneficial effect of art. The works make connections, are temporary and often fleeting, because images, to the artist, are nothing but ballast. The religious references in his work are countless. The transition from a fixed to an ephemeral state has a parallel in other forms of sublimation, such as mental edification through words or

in the devotional air of incense. With the exhibition 'Blow', held at the Van Abbemuseum in 1995, Koelewijn sent three 'messages' into the world. The words of one of these works, titled *Drink* (1995)–taken from a poem by Marsman, (a Dutch writer from the vitalist movement)–descend upon the world on a parachute: *Vlam/ schuimende morgen/ en mijn vuren lach/ drinkt uit ontzaglijke schalen/ van lucht en aarde/ den opalen dag.*

The sense of breathing new life into things, which Job Koelewijn represents, relates to a significant degree to the optimism of this fairly young generation of artists. They opt for openness and the fleeting nature of the street as a laboratory for their ideas, rather than the relatively insular and inward world of the museum.

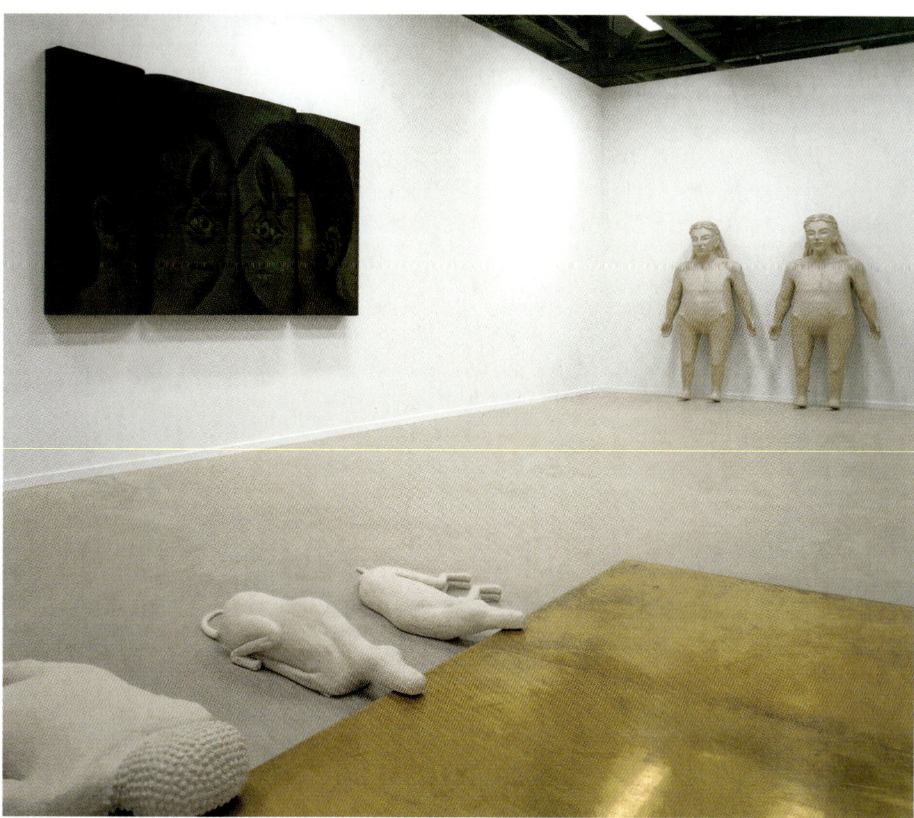

Frank Mandersloot *Jogos de Cama IV*, 1990

From left to right: **Tiong Ang** *Portret van twee jongens (initiatie/chirurgie)*, 1991; **Mark Manders** *Zelfportret (fragment uit 'Zelfportret als gebouw')*, 1994 en 1992

XXVIII

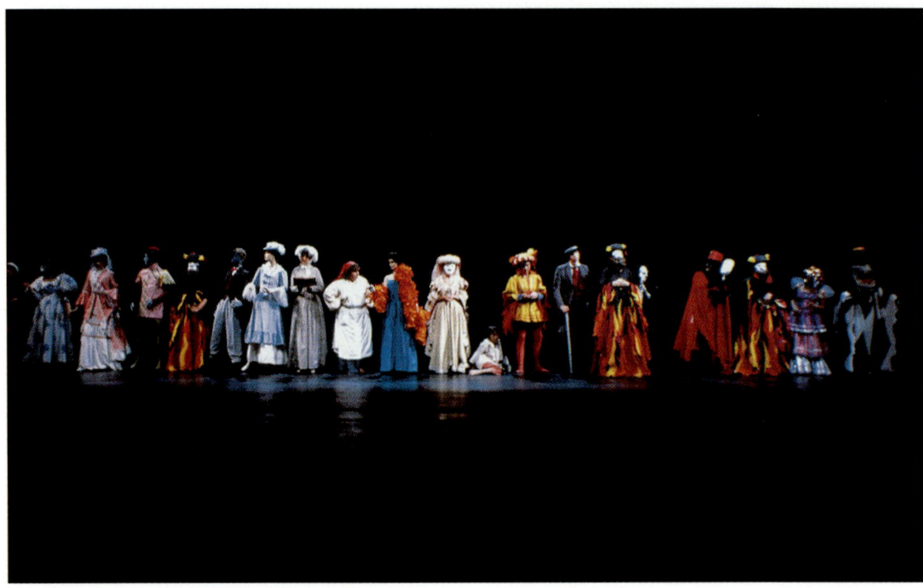

James Coleman *Living and Presumed Dead*, 1983-85

The impressive presentations of Gary Hill, Tony Oursler and Bill Viola at the 1992 *documenta IX* in Kassel have contributed to the public recognition of artworks produced with audiovisual means. They were referred to as 'video artists', but that term is somewhat misleading. In addition to video, these artists do make use of other techniques, working with film or sound installations; these are, in turn, often part of an all-encompassing spatial staging. More important than the experiments with modern technology are the cultural implications of the new media: how people think and act in an age where the 'media' image is for granted and audiovisual means are within everyone's reach. It is not the medium of video or film, but mainly the reality represented, hidden or revealed by it that fascinates these artists. Video as a means of registration and observation is a medium suitable, for instance, for works that focus on the social behavior of people and on the manipulative potential of the media, on tendencies toward voyeurism, control and domination. Many young artists who have grown up with television and the camcorder utilize the collectively experienced world of popular radio and television programs. With their work they often explore the vague distinction between fiction and reality. Strikingly, both the younger and older generations of these artists resist or minimize rather than emphatically display the 'high-tech' aspect. At times the very shortcomings of the material–the scratches on the film, blurred images or the rattling of the projector–are revealed in an attempt to show the reality behind the scenes and to offset this with the fictitious content of the images. As far as the tradition of the new media is concerned, these artists tend to follow in the footsteps of renowned cultural critics such as Bruce Nauman, John Baldessari and Dan Graham rather than those of 'media man' Nam June Paik, whose obsessive interest in technology and mass consumption occasionally displays fetishistic traits.

With the works of the nine artists discussed here, who differ vastly in terms of age and style, the Van Abbemuseum has built a modest but richly varied collection that offers a good impression of the direction taken by much of this 'media art' during the nineties. These artists are not particularly involved in the propagation of ideological stances. When critical statements are made, they are distinguished by an exposure of the ways in which mass media manipulate reality and control the credibility of the images. They are sooner concerned with the camera as an instrument for reflection on the human condition than with recording and commenting on all sorts of social developments. In that respect these artists have an affinity with the philosophical and psychological approaches of conceptual art, though the definition of art does not constitute a theme for them and there is no distinct allusion to the tradition of the classical disciplines of art, such as painting and sculpture. The history to which they refer, namely that of the popular media–television, radio, film and home video–is a relatively young one. They deal with the common identity derived from this

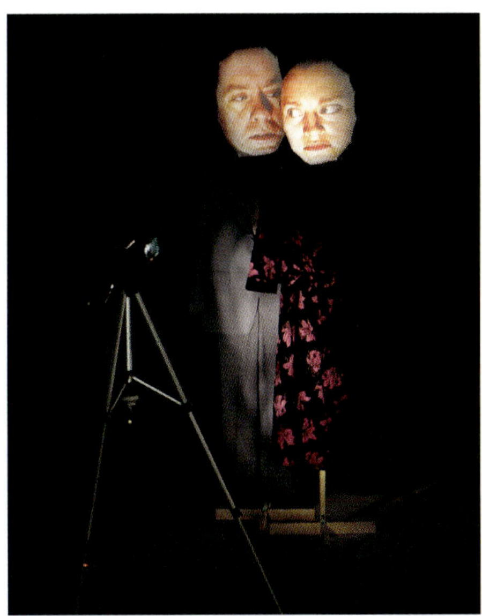

Tony Oursler *Autochthonous Alien*, 1995

and how that takes shape in privacy. Their work manifests just how much influence modern media have had on our consciousness, on the image that we have of ourselves and of others.

What these artists share in particular is the creation of an experiential realm. The presentations are seldom confined to a monitor set up in the corner of an exhibition space. The viewer is absorbed into a decor that fills the entire room, and a visit to the exhibition thereby becomes a physical experience which steers the mind, as it were, in a particular direction. Gary Hill and Tony Oursler lead the visitor, for instance, through a nocturnal darkness in which luminous images flit about like ghosts, this alluding to an inner or supernatural world. The sound of lapping waves in Marijke van Warmerdam's installation *Golf* (exhibited at the Van Abbemuseum in 1997) gives rise to a sense of melancholy. While wandering through the corridor and hearing the sloshing water, one imagines being on the waterfront. Compared to such installations, the earlier experiments with new media from the beginning of the seventies are of a much more detached nature and analytical approach. Audiovisual media had, for the most part, a purely registrational function or were explored on the basis of their typical qualities. An early work by the Irish artist **James Coleman**, *Loudspeaker Piece*, from 1972 is a study of the process of observation, of the way in which the eye and ear influence each other. How the lone loudspeaker on the wall is 'seen'–as a concrete object or in terms of its function as a transmitter–depends on

something as simple as a minimally audible signal.

The calculating and abstract character of this work still attests to a considerable influence from the conceptual art of the sixties and seventies. Coleman's later works, two of which are in the collection of the Van Abbemuseum, have theatrical settings, and their frame of reference has extended into more visual and literary realms. On closer analysis, though, the artist still appears to be playing with various levels of observation and the way in which they converge into a meaningful entity in our minds. The detached and regulated character of his work has given way to narrative elements with intrigue-like dramatics, as in detective stories or mythological tales.

In *So Different...and Yet* (1979-80) two narratives overlap with each other. One deals with a glistening green dress which is admired as though part of a fashion show, and the other tells the tale of a crime intertwined with a romantic plot. Meanwhile, a woman in a fluorescent-green garment is nestling provocatively on a sofa–an image that we know from Manet's *Olympia* or Titian's *Venus of Urbino*. Commercial, fashion report and crime: the narratives portray various images that cannot be reduced to a single image or story, let alone a particular place or moment in time. They assume a unity of time and space only in the imagination of the viewer, who creates his own image on the basis of the given 'scripts' in combination with the background of his own personal experience.

Tony Oursler and Gary Hill go a step further in terms of these psychodramatics. They, too, have woven various levels of image and sound with each other but involve all sorts of spatial and sculptural aspects in this. Contrary to the presentations of Coleman, one can cross the stage as a viewer and become a more engaged participant in the events that take place there.

Tony Oursler became known during the early nineties particularly for his makeshift décors consisting of stuffed articles of clothing, rag dolls, hovering clouds of cotton wool and jars containing organs, all of these serving as projection screens for videos of moving body parts or of faces that often express feelings of despair, doubt, frustration or pleasure. Lifeless and amorphous material is given a soul, as it were, this being reminiscent of the way in which children bring their stuffed animals to life or adults can sometimes regard the faltering of a motor as the capricious behavior of an object with a will of its own. The expressions that are literally

projected by Oursler onto his models or the stories that he 'puts in their mouths' appeal to archetypal emotions and desires. The woman in *Autochthonous Alien* (1995), who responds in an increasingly restless and vehement manner to the whispering of the man next to her, is the embodiment of a phobia. The feelings of distrust and unease that gradually transform into constrictive fear are so tersely portrayed and so recognizable that it is impossible to remain unaffected by the sight of this. Even so, it is not the phobia but the process of (re)presentation and identification which actually constitutes the theme of this work and the leitmotif throughout Oursler's entire oeuvre. When the video comes to an end, there do remain only a few unsightly articles of clothing on poles, but those primitive likenesses are essentially the point of the matter. Oursler refers to them as effigies or stand-ins. The magic that we unintentionally ascribe to such innocuous signs–whether it be a scarecrow or a cloud formation–can have a positive or a negative effect, depending on our personal experience: it can be fascinating, conjuring or repellent. The works themselves do not convey a moral but rather alert us to the enormous power of archetypes.

Like Tony Oursler, **Gary Hill** is fascinated with the effect of the psyche and its physical manifestation. But Hill's approach is much more abstract and poetic, and it betrays his affinity with linguistics and philosophy. With Oursler, the narratives or dialogues spoken by the various stand-ins are important for a better understanding of the work. The texts that appear in Hill's work are, on the contrary, scarcely intelligible audible or almost illegible. Voices murmur, human figures are blurry and coherence is practically indiscernible in the undulating lines of text. It is mainly the sensitive orchestration of language, image and sound that lends the work its poetic strength.

With *Tall Ships*, the silent and interactive video installation presented by Hill at *documenta IX*, everything revolves around the language of the body and the mental state linked with this. Shrouded figures loom forth from the profound darkness that surrounds the visitor and eliminates any awareness of time and space. They come closer, seem to seek contact and to ask, "Who are you?" But at a certain point (generated by an invisibly interactive electronic system geared to the movements of the visitor) they withdraw again.

According to the American sound poet George Quascha, a friend of Hill's, these encounters are not about a depiction of, but

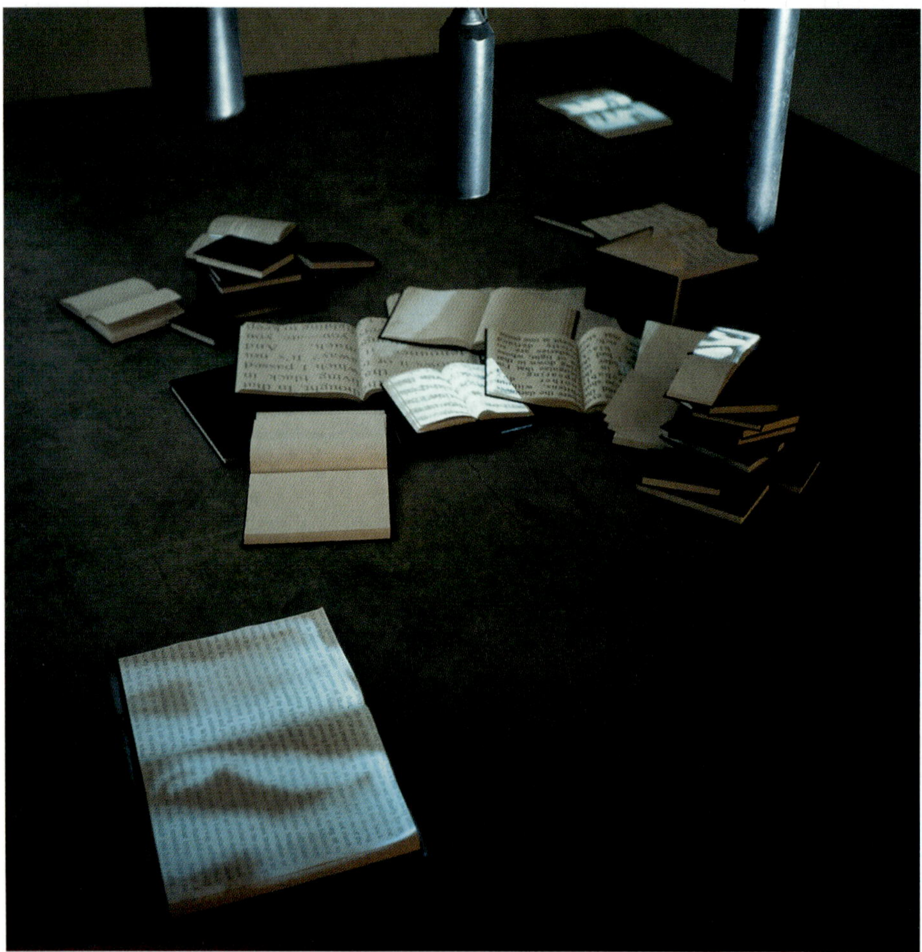

Gary Hill *I Believe It Is an Image in Light of the Other*, 1991-92

about an evocation of a particular state of awareness which he describes as 'living on the edge'. It is a kind of self-balancing capacity which can be experienced at a 'dead' moment–while one is waiting for the starting shot at the beginning of a race. Hill calls it a 'majestic kind of buoyancy', by which he is referring to the grandness of a ship at sea. On the level of thought, this deceleration is comparable to reflection: the world as it is projected onto a screen in the mind, a sort of 'inner video'.

Reference to this reflective capacity–similar to the immediate 'feedback' of the video–is also made in the title of the installation *I Believe It Is an Image in Light of the Other* (1991-92). Seven projectors are concealed in cylinder-shaped lamps that hang from the ceiling like oxygen tanks. They project images of naked body parts (face, hands, mouth and torso) and printed text onto books scattered across the floor, some of them lying open. Here the senses have been presented physically, bulging and fluctuating across the pages in thin, sharp or fat, blurry letters. The

fragments of the body are, in turn, rendered as text: as flat, graphic patterns. The sound of raspy breathing heightens the suggestion of an invisible world, a space where the amorphous, the diffuse and the subconscious take shape. The segments of text are taken from *Le dernier homme* by the French writer and philosopher Maurice Blanchot. Like Blanchot, Hill is not interested in what a text or body represents or says about reality, but in how the two convey meaning together and assume a form. Hill regards video as a form of 'thinking out loud'. Those who think aloud are actually speaking indirectly to themselves. Words echo back to the source in a slightly estranged form. The image that corresponds to this continuous movement is both circular and linear, like a spiral.

Closed circular movements appear on various levels in the work of the Dutch artist **Marijke van Warmerdam**. Whereas Hill's videos deal with the contemplative effect of an inner world, Warmerdam's films are rooted in day-to-day reality, where their endless loops defeat the principle of cause

and effect. She takes her motifs from concrete, often banal occurrences. Nothing mysterious. This is also true of the open, barefaced manner in which she presents her work. One sees and hears the film running through the projector. But in the montage of successive images that form a loop, the concrete action loses its original purpose and meaning. In the perpetual cycle, the action itself becomes the objective.

Van Warmerdam's *Kring* (1992), which is owned by the Van Abbemuseum, combines many themes dealt with in other works. More than any other work by Van Warmerdam, it shows, in an attempt to grasp reality, how the process of attributing meaning can become one grand circle dance.

In a darkened room a film projector is rotating on its axis, thereby echoing the original movement and central viewpoint of the camera during the filming. On a marketplace in North Africa, people standing in a circle were filmed by Van Warmerdam as though they were watching a dancing bear. The motif of the circle surfaces in different ways, namely in the movement of the camera during the filming, in that of the projector during the presentation, in the film loop itself and in the circle of people being filmed. The viewer is situated at the location of the filmmaker during the filming, at the center of the circle, and is thus transferred to another moment in recent history, as though in a time machine. At the same time, this limitless panorama places the temporary gathering of people on a marketplace in the perspective of eternity. Indirectly, through references to non-Western culture and documentary reporting, *Kring* becomes a silent document of exoticism and voyeurism, or a small media circus at the intersection of anthropology and art criticism.

Like Hill, Oursler and Van Warmerdam, the Scottish artist Douglas Gordon and the Finnish Eija-Liisa Ahtila are ultimately more concerned with the process of attributing meaning than in the actual meaning of the images, more interested in the 'how' than in the 'what'.

Douglas Gordon is, like Oursler, moved by the issue as to what mechanisms steer the consciousness. In this he gives consideration to physical aspects, such as the effect of the memory, but also to our behavior and to the images or language that can influence that behavior. He refers, for instance, to film classics, to songs heard on the radio or confronts us with familiar expressions. His earlier works based on text, which consist of cliché statements applied to walls or sent out into the world as phone messages or letters,

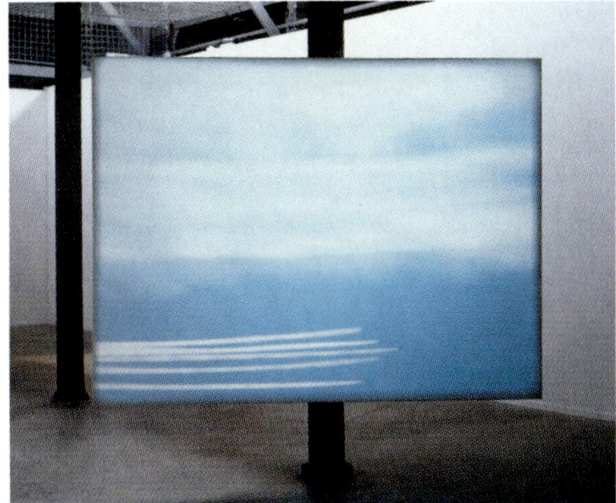

Marijke van Warmerdam *Skytypers*, 1997

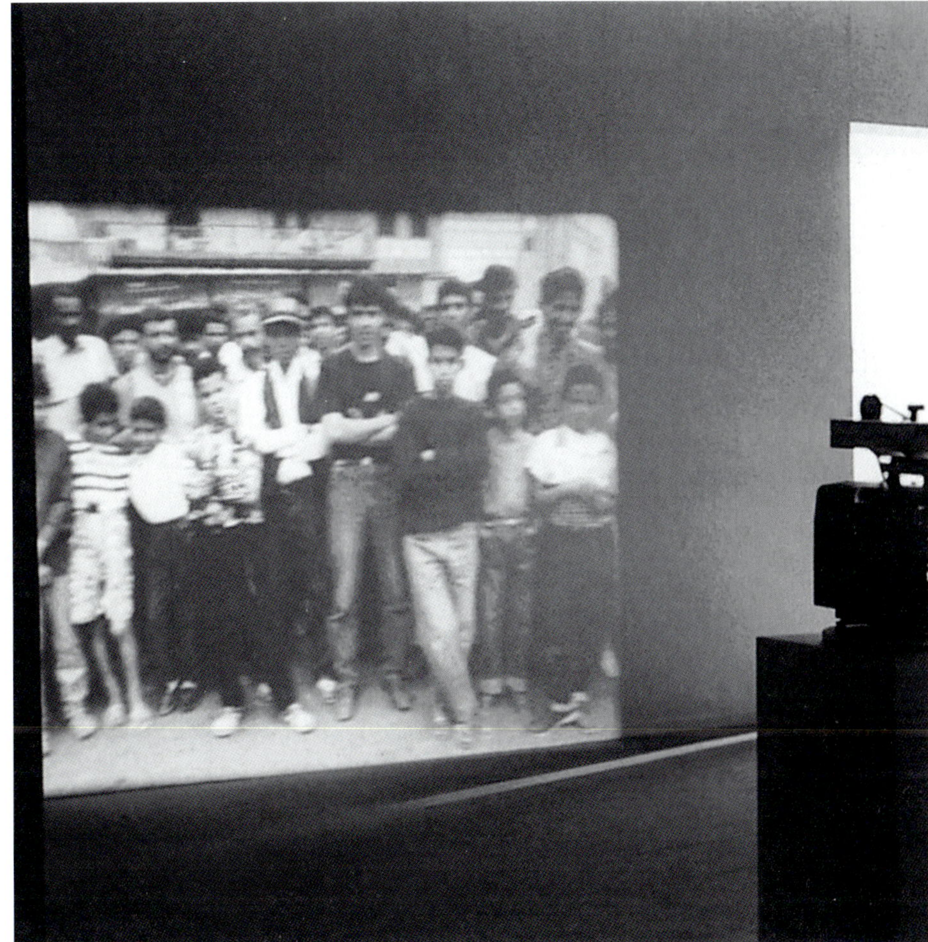

Marijke van Warmerdam *Kring*, 1992

Douglas Gordon *Untitled (Text for someplace other than this)*,
1996

are about the personal way in which meaning is given to a collective use of language. *List of Names* (1990-97) is sooner a test for the individual memory, yet it actually raises the question as to how the past comes about and how history is 'made'. The work comprises more than 2500 names of individuals whom Gordon once met and whose names he remembered. These impressively long–and obviously incomplete–lists of names constitute a monument to the memory of the individual but, at the same time, attest to its failure. The brain manifests itself as a system which we understand only in part, a construction full of gaps that involuntarily allow all sorts of information to enter it–or to escape it.

10ms⁻¹ (1994), which is in the collection of the Van Abbemuseum, shows the fierce battle of an unwilling body. The man's futile attempts to stand up–he seems to be suffering from a physical or psychological abnormality–reflect the viewer's mental struggle to place this image: What is happening here? What is wrong with this

man? What sort of film is this? This is a fragment of a film on neuropathology taken from a medical archive. The document was found in a virtually forgotten area of our cultural heritage and, in itself, also represents a kind of struggle, namely for the right to a few seconds of existence in history.
In the endeavor to instill meaning, to form a coherent whole, the processes of identification play a significant role. One could say that this identification with the other or with that which is different is the main subject of the films of **Eija-Liisa Ahtila**. The short film *Me/We* is about a family situation, where confusion is introduced with respect to who plays what role in the context of this family. The father tells the story of a minor household mishap, involving a cup of coffee spilling across the table and things having to be laundered. The events take place at a quiet, almost dream-like pace. Everything seems to be under control, except that the daughter is speaking with the voice of her father. The feeling that nothing is wrong begins to wane as a result. This brief 'spot' of

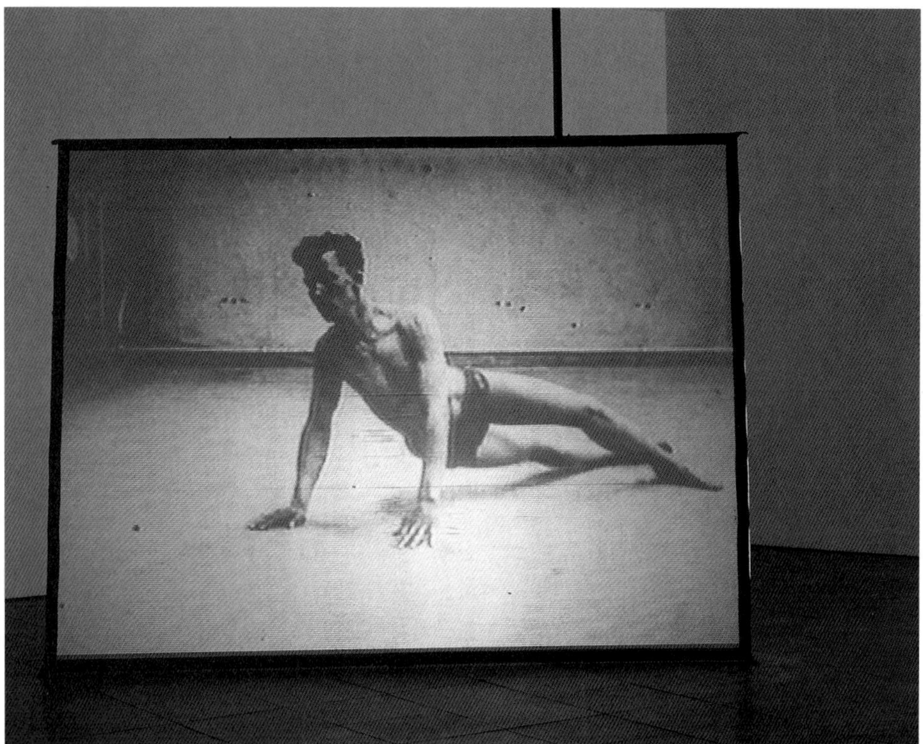

Douglas Gordon *10ms⁻¹*, 1994

ninety seconds was intended for television. It was broadcast as a 'stopper' between a block of commercials and subsequent programs. The fluid style and the condensed narrative of *Me/We* corresponds to that of many advertising spots, but the message does not fulfill our expectations. It defies them. One can also speak of such an alienating role reversal in *If 6 was 9* (1995) in which five teenage girls reveal their sexual fantasies. In this they address the viewer directly. The script, written by Ahtila, is based on conversations that she had with (older) friends and acquaintances. The apparently personal disclosures do not concur with the images. Words and images clash with respect to age and experience, articulated and demonstrated emotions. They cannot be reduced to a single person, maker or character. Ahtila couples documentary journalism with fiction and with the outpourings of popular 'emotion TV'. One can view the images from a comfortable three-seat sofa, which reconstructs something of the household environment and thereby reinforces one's capacity for empathy. Is this not a depiction of the adult's reminiscence of adolescent feelings? Due to the distance in time, experiences are fragmented, exchanged and tainted, subject to fictitious direction. Life is experienced as fiction.

Also in the work of Aernout Mik and the French artist **Pierre Huyghe**, there is often a fine line between fiction and reality. Both artists make the observer a participant in their presentations by forcing him to assume a particular role or stance. To this end, the environment of practically every exhibition is changed in such a way that rooms or experiential spaces are created. As such, the establishment of specific links among individual works adds a unique level of experience. Pierre Huyghe frequently opts to center his presentations around the video game *Pong*, which he builds into the ceiling. With the aid of remote control, visitors are thus able to play 'tennis' with each other. Smirking, as it were, at this recreational aspect, Huyghe hereby raises the issue of interactivity, which constitutes a main part of his work. Huyghe often uses existing material–whether it be motion pictures, television programs, computer animations or video games–in order to give them a new life in a totally different setting created by him. He reproduces them or makes 'tales' of them by isolating an element that supported the fiction in the original version and bringing this into the spotlight. *Dubbing* (1996), for instance, shows a panoramic view of a recording studio where the dubbing of a particular film takes place. The film can be envisaged only on the basis of the translated and enacted dialogues which the dubbers, the voice performers, carry out at their computers. Here fiction is unveiled and re-created, the difference being that the reality of the studio forms the point of departure. In *Les Grands Ensembles* (1994-2001) precisely the opposite occurs. In the eight-minute film, we see how two apartment buildings seem to communicate with each other by way of lights that switch on and off behind the countless windows. Time passes, judging from the changes in weather and light: day transforms into night, rain gives way to snow. The speed with which the lights switch on and off makes one suspect that the film is accelerated, yet that factor conflicts with the absence of any traffic in the immediate vicinity of the apartment buildings and the fluid transition into a different type of weather. Actually, the film is completely staged–recorded in a studio by means of a maquette. The soundtrack that accompanies the film is adapted with each presentation. Here a piece of reality has been made a model and transformed into a *tableau vivant* which

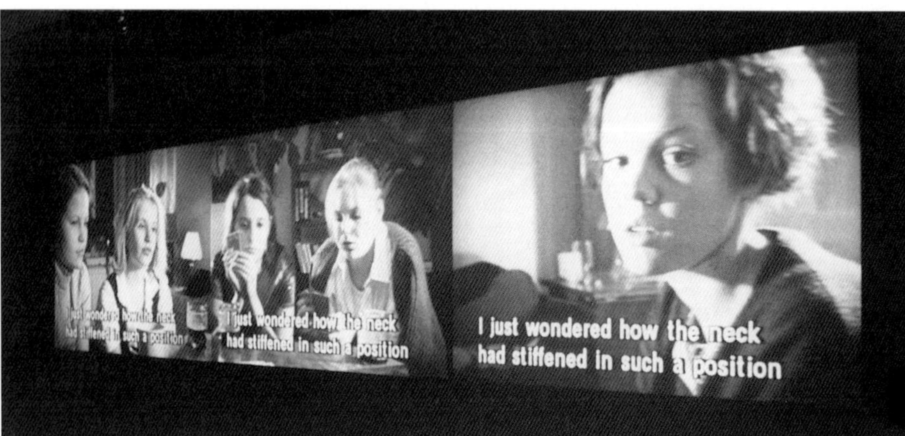

Eija-Liisa Ahtila *If 6 was 9*, 1995

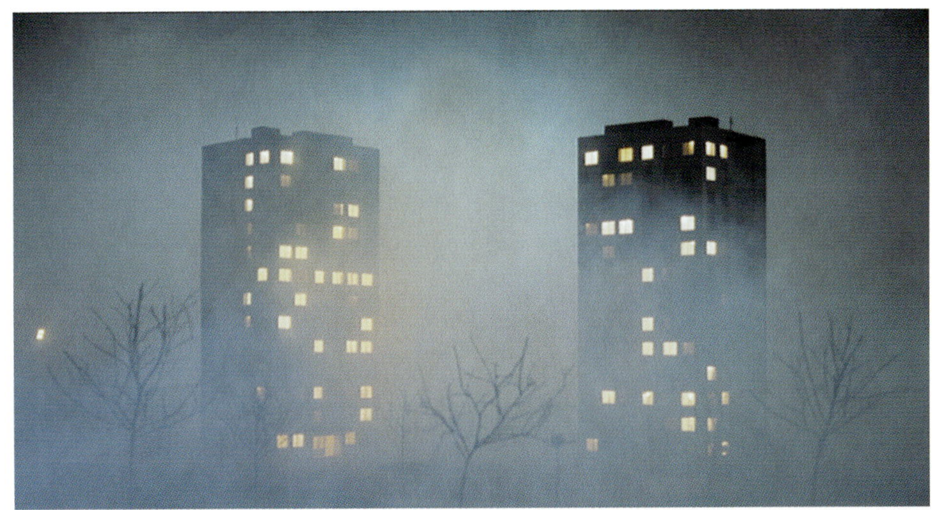

Pierre Huyghe *Les Grands Ensembles*, 1994-2001

speaks to the imagination to such a degree that one longs for its realization.

Aernout Mik prefers to create his spatial stagings at locations with a public or semi-public character: the police station, the airport, the conference resort–places where people stay for a short time. The museum is only one example of such a place. In such places, where an artificial order prevails, the extent to which man is conditioned–how he is manipulated and follows rules and fixed

patterns–becomes very evident. Mik accentuates this mechanical behavior by juxtaposing it with other forms of conditioning which allude to stupor or addiction, such as sleeping, smoking or drinking coffee. In 1993, in the Utrecht conference center 'La Vie', Mik placed people on beds to sleep during working hours and, as a dramatic reduction of this scene, introduced cages containing hamsters. For the presentation of his video work Mik

designs special spatial structures. In *Hongkongoria* (1998), a project where Mik collaborated with the filmmaker Marjoleine Boonstra, the viewer is led along low walls with video projections. The transparent screens, placed low, can be seen from various angles and jointly make up a mildly alienating visual environment. The way in which Mik converts the existing museum space and thereby forces viewers to take alternative routes and approaches is comparable to the way in which he records situations from daily life (like that of the metropolis Hong Kong) and controls them by subjecting them to an alienating choreography. The title *Hongkongoria*–a combination of 'Hong Kong' and 'phantasmagoria'–alludes to this intertwining of reality and illusion. *Miscellaneous Exits for Smaller Animals* (1991), an elongated glass case which displays an oppressive dream situation in a business-like environment, is an early forerunner of these later stagings and video installations. The limbless cloth dummies with photographic imprints on their torsos seem, in turn, to anticipate the later interim figures that Mik constantly produces. The interim figures or 'assistants' are conveyors of all sorts of functions and thoughts. They are people in uniform, such as police officers and guards, or people of Asiatic origins whose

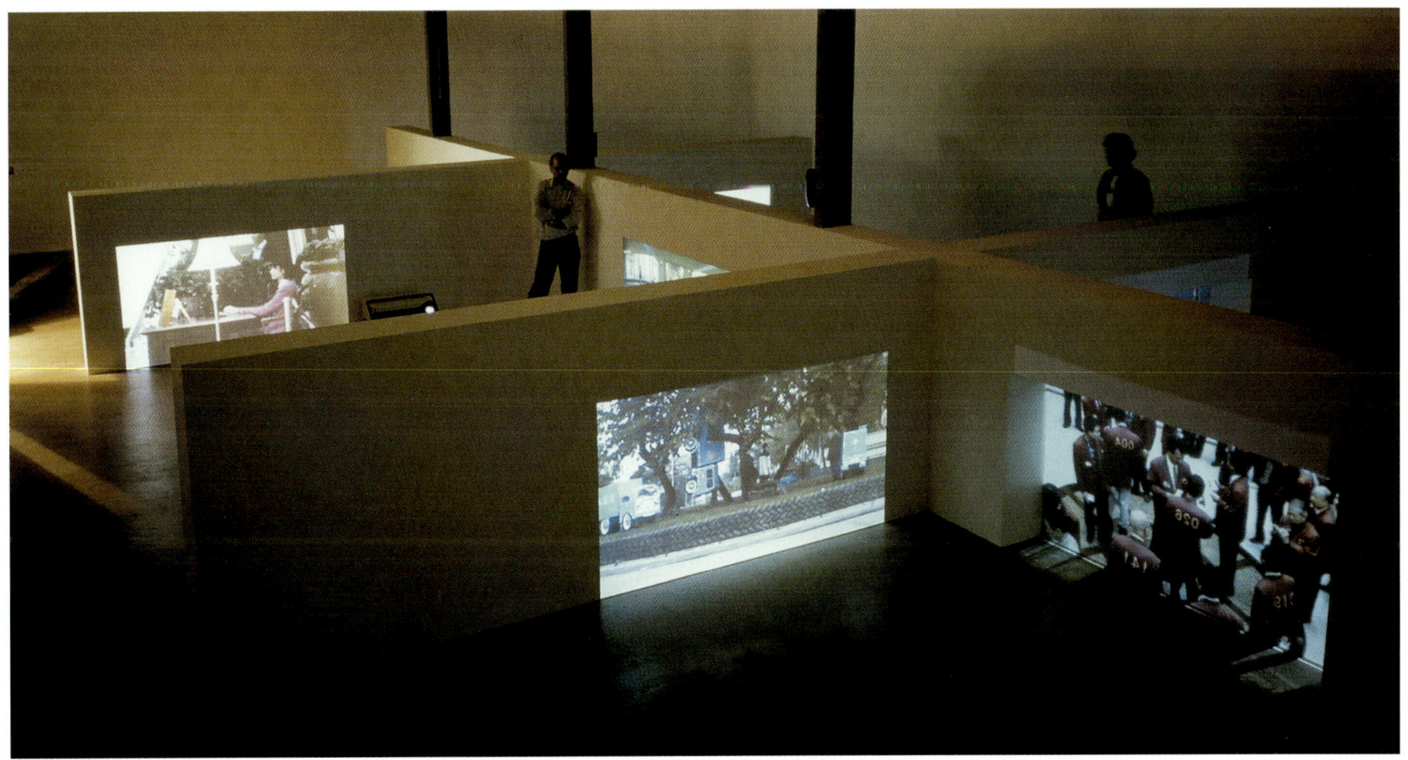

Aernout Mik and Marjoleine Boonstra, *Hongkongoria*, 1997-98

appearance and behavior are somewhat foreign, otherworldly or picturesque to us. Mik frequently makes use of semi-automatic (mechanically driven) dolls or animal figures. The repetitive actions which they carry out stand for conduct, functions and circumstances that mark daily life–from 'going to bed' or 'holding a meeting' to 'smoking' and 'playing billiards'. According to Mik, the individual actually does not exist, because he is exposed to all sorts of tendencies that drive him externally and internally. Man is, in his view, a "conglomerate of urges and impulses." In a work such as *Suck* (1997) machines assume human characteristics and vice versa. Something as ordinary as vacuuming nearly becomes science-fiction. The household appliance guzzles and sucks as though it leads a life of its own, threatening or caressing people, while the men, frozen and lifeless, sooner resemble machines. Not infrequently, such scenes take on nightmarish proportions with Mik.

The photographs and video works of **Rineke Dijkstra** deal with identification in the broadest sense of the word. Dijkstra acquired an international reputation during the nineties with her series of portraits of teenagers on the beach, several of which are in the collection of the Van Abbemuseum. Against a neutral background, a sea view in soft focus, the adolescents are shown from head to foot–alone or in small groups. The depictions are roughly all the same, as are the beaches, which scarcely differ from New York to Kolobrzeg in Poland. These are children from the same age group, all scantly clothed in bathing suits or beach dresses. All of them look directly into the camera, which is always set up at knee height, this bringing the subject closer. This uniformity serves, however, as a means to capture the highest degree of individual expression in terms of stance and gesture, color and textural expression. Down to the last detail, the ruthless eye of the camera registers the cocktail of traits that distinguish the person: red blotches from the cold, a cramped finger, the folds of a slightly oversized bathing suit or the bulge of the navel under a wet, clinging dress.

At the same time, these unique registrations of basically ordinary people display classical poses and gestures. It is as though the portrait subjects have consciously or unconsciously complied with a model: a venus, a madonna, an athlete. That same aspect emerges in the realm of character or cultural identity: distinct examples of classifications in terms such as 'tough',

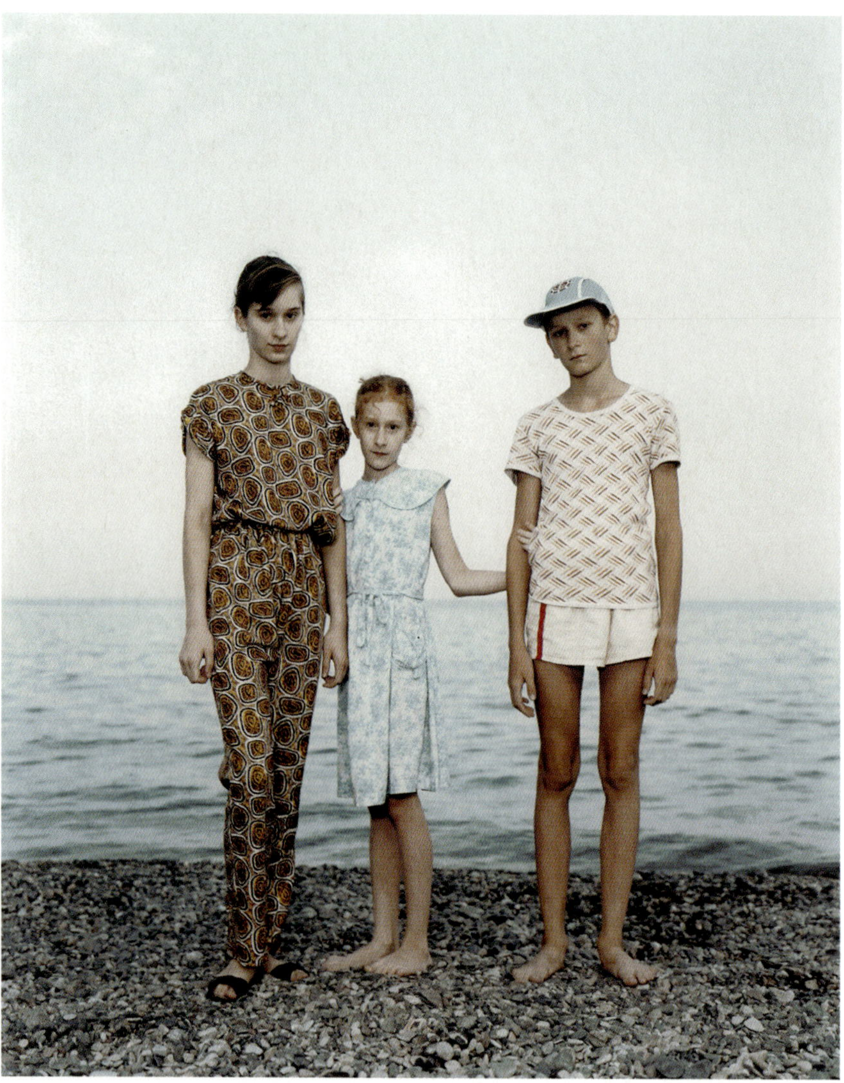

Rineke Dijkstra *Jalta, Ukraine, 30 July 1993*

'phlegmatic' or 'East European' present themselves. The perception of all of those similarities gives tangibility to that which is individual and that which is not, to that which is known and unknown–for the person posing, but also for the viewer. The sharpness with which Rineke Dijkstra manages to bring that undefined and complex identity to the surface with the aid of extremely simple means has moving beauty and attests to sublime mastery.

List of illustrations

With each chapter you will find the names of artists listed in alphabetical order. Works are listed chronologically under the names.
To the extent that such information is available, the artist's place and year of birth, and if applicable the year of death, are indicated. Titles are listed in the original language. English translations have been provided only with titles in Dutch and in Russian.
The title is followed by the date of the work. When a year is placed in parentheses, it represents the year in which the work was conceived. The year which follows this is the year in which the work was executed.
Unless otherwise stated, dimensions are given in the order of height-width-depth.
An asterisk (*) stands for 'dimensions including frame'.

i
pp. 33 - 35

Hendrik Chabot
Sprang 1894 - 1949 Rotterdam (NL)
Slapende boer, 1936
Sleeping Farmer
oil/canvas
137,2 x 152,7 cm *
p. 34

Leo Gestel
Woerden 1881 - 1941 Blaricum (NL)
Drie Huizer vrouwen, 1929
Three Women from Huizen
gouache/cardboard
89,7 x 119,3 cm *
p. 33

Herman Kruyder
Lage Vuursche 1881 - 1935 Amsterdam (NL)
De varkensdoder, ca. 1925
The Pig Killer
oil/canvas
71 x 83,5 cm *
p. 34

Albert Servaes
Ghent (B) 1883 - 1966 Luzern (CH)
Portret van Henri van Abbe, 1937
Portrait of Henri van Abbe
charcoal/paper
103 x 97,5 cm *
p. 33

Jan Sluijters
's-Hertogenbosch 1881 - 1957 Amsterdam (NL)
Lezende vrouw, 1911
Woman Reading
oil/canvas
78 x 54,7 cm *
p. 34

Vrouwenportret, 1929
Portrait of a Woman
oil/canvas
189 x 147 cm *
p. 33

Charley Toorop
Katwijk 1891 - 1955 Bergen (NL)
Zelfportret met wintertakken, 1944-45
Self-Portrait with Winter Branches
oil/canvas
67,9 x 58 cm *
p. 35

Carel Willink
Amsterdam 1900 - 1983 Amsterdam (NL)
Schilder met zijn vrouw, 1934
Painter with his Wife
oil/canvas
172,5 x 122,5 cm *
p. 33

Stadsgezicht, 1934
Townscape
oil/canvas
87,5 x 112,5 cm *
p. 35

ii
pp. 36 - 39

Max Beckmann
Leipzig (D) 1884 - 1950 New York City (USA)
Winterbild, 1930
oil/canvas
87,2 x 78,9 cm *
p. 38

Jean Brusselmans
Brussels 1884 - 1953 Dilbeek (B)
Le bain des vagabonds, 1936
oil/canvas
164,5 x 164 cm *
p. 39

Heinrich Campendonk
Krefeld (D) 1889 - 1957 Amsterdam (NL)
Boerderij, 1919
Farm
oil/canvas
137 x 59 cm *
p. 37

Gustave De Smet
Ghent 1877 - 1943 Deurle (B)
Danslokaal, 1921
Dance Hall
oil/canvas
122,5 x 112,2 cm *
p. 39

Wassily Kandinsky
Moscow (RUS) 1866 - 1944 Neuilly (F)
Blick auf Murnau mit Kirche, 1910
oil/canvas
110,5 x 120 cm *
p. 36

Oskar Kokoschka
Pöchlarn (A) 1886 - 1980 Montreux (CH)
Die Macht der Musik, 1918
oil/canvas
103 x 154,5 cm *
p. 37

Constant Permeke
Antwerp 1886 - 1952 Oostende (B)
De zaaier, 1935
The Sower
oil/canvas
153 x 178 cm *
p. 39

iii
pp. 40 - 45

Georges Braque
Argentueil 1882 - 1963 Paris (F)
La Roche-Guyon, 1909
oil/canvas
116 x 96,2 cm *
p. 40

Marc Chagall
Vitebsk (BY) 1887 - 1985 Saint Paul-de-Vence (F)
Hommage à Apollinaire, 1911-12
oil/canvas
203,5 x 192 cm *
p. 40

Robert Delaunay
Paris 1885 - 1941 Montpellier (F)
L'équipe de Cardiff, 1913
oil/canvas
198,5 x 135,3 cm *
p. 44

Juan Gris
Madrid (E) 1887 - 1927 Boulogne-sur-Seine (F)
Nature morte, 1920
oil/canvas
80,9 x 65,4 cm *
p. 44

Fernand Léger
Argentan 1881 - 1955 Gif-sur-Yvette (F)
L'accordéon, 1926
oil/canvas
134 x 92,5 cm *
p. 43

Jacques Lipchitz
Druskieniki (LT) 1891 - 1973 Capri (I)
Marin et guitare, 1917-18
bronze
91,5 x 37 x 36 cm
p. 44

Pablo Picasso
Malaga (E) 1881 - 1973 Notre-Dame-de-Vie (F)
Femme en vert, 1909
oil/canvas
100,3 x 81,3 cm
p. 41

Buste de femme, 1943
oil/canvas
100,2 x 81,3 cm
p. 42

Ossip Zadkine
Smolensk (PL) 1890 - 1967 Paris (F)
Saint Sébastien, 1929
wood
height: 260 cm
p. 45

iv
pp. 46 - 51

Theo van Doesburg
Utrecht (NL) 1883 - 1931 Davos (CH)
Compositie XXII, 1922
Composition XXII
oil/canvas
78,5 x 76 cm *
p. 47

Ontwerp kleurbeeld van een bloemenkamer, 1924-25
Design for flower room
gouache, ink, pencil/tracing paper
102,2 x 82,2 cm *
p. 46

Interieur grote feestzaal van l'Aubette Strasbourg, 1928
Interior of large banquet hall l'Aubette Strasbourg
wood (reconstruction 1968)
276 x 379 x 255 cm
p. 47

Bart van der Leck
Utrecht 1876 - 1958 Amsterdam (NL)
Compositie (bloeiende tak), 1921
Composition (blossoming branch)
oil/canvas
49,5 x 66,5 cm *
p. 49

László Moholy-Nagy
Bács-Borsod (H) 1895 - 1946 Chicago, Illinois (USA)
Die grosse Gefühlsmaschine, 1920
oil/canvas
115 x 95 cm *
p. 50

Licht-Raum-Modulator, 1922-30
metal, wood, glass (replica 1970)
201,7 x 78,8 x 69,7 cm
p. 46

Piet Mondrian
Amersfoort (NL) 1872 - 1944 New York City (USA)
Compositie XIV, 1913
Composition XIV
oil/canvas
93,8 x 64,7 cm
p. 48

Composition No.II, 1930
oil/canvas
50,5 x 50,5 cm
p. 48

Kurt Schwitters
Hanover (D) 1887 - 1948 Ambleside (GB)
Isle of Man, 1941
oil/paper/linoleum
112 x 93,5 cm
Purchased with support of Vereniging Rembrandt
p. 51

Friedrich Vordemberge-Gildewart
Osnabrück 1899 - 1962 Ulm (D)
Komposition no.176, 1949
oil/canvas
111,2 x 111,4 cm *
p. 51

v
pp. 52 - 55

El Lissitzky
Polschinok 1890 - 1941 Schodnia (RUS)
Italiaanse stad, 1913
Italian town
pencil, chalk, gouache/paper
24 x 32,4 cm
p. 52

Venezia, 1913
watercolor/cardboard
26,6 x 34,5 cm
p. 52

Proun P23, no. 6, 1919
gouache/canvas
77,5 x 62,9 cm
Purchased with support of the Van Abbemuseum Promoters
Foundation, the Mondriaan Foundation, Vereniging Rembrandt
and the Province of Noord-Brabant
p. 52

Klinom krasnym bej belych, 1919-20
Beat the Whites with the red wedge
offset/paper (reprinted 1966)
48,8 x 69,2 cm
p. 54

Ontwerp voor Proun G7, ca.1922-23
Preliminary study for Proun G7
pencil, gouache/paper
78,2 x 62,7 cm
p. 53

Prounenraum, 1923
wood, oil, metal, cheesecloth (reconstruction 1965)
320 x 364 x 364 cm
p. 54

Vladimir Majakovski, Dlja golosa, 1923
Vladimir Majakovski, For the voice
letterpress/paper
19 x 13,5 cm
p. 55

*Figurinen. Die plastische Gestaltung der elektro-mechanischen
Schau Sieg über die Sonne, Neuer*, 1923
litho/paper
53,5 x 46,2 cm
p. 55

Der Konstrukteur (Selbstbildnis), 1924
black-and-white photograph
61,3 x 44,4 cm *
p. 55

vi
pp. 56 - 59

Jean Bazaine
Paris 1904 - 2001 Paris (F)
Écorce de chêne-liège, 1949
ink/paper
41,8 x 31,4 cm
p. 57

L'orage au jardin, 1952
oil/canvas
101 x 82 cm *
p. 57

Roger Bissière
Villeréal 1886 - 1964 Boissiérettes (F)
Composition, 1955
oil/canvas
51 x 70,7 cm *
p. 56

Edgar Fernhout
Bergen 1912 - 1974 Bergen (NL)
Herfst, 1962
Autumn
oil/canvas
82 x 117 cm *
p. 58

Sam Francis
San Mateo, California 1923 - 1994 Santa Monica, California (USA)
Peinture, 1957
oil/canvas
192 x 105,5 cm *
p. 58

Hans Hartung
Leipzig (D) 1904 - 1989 Antibes (F)
Composition, 1956
oil/canvas
164 x 123 cm *
p. 59

Alfred Manessier
Saint Ouen 1911 - 1993 Orleans (F)
Barabbas, 1952
oil/canvas
202,5 x 152 cm *
p. 56

Serge Poliakoff
Moscow (RUS) 1906 - 1969 Paris (F)
Composition, 1956
oil/canvas
92 x 133,5 cm *
p. 57

vii
pp. 60 - 63

Pierre Alechinsky
Brussels (B) 1927
Malone meurt, 1962
gouache/paper, canvas
151 x 323,5 cm *
p. 61

Karel Appel
Amsterdam (NL) 1921
Paard en fluitist, 1951
Horse and flute player
oil/canvas
92,2 x 119,5 cm *
p. 63

Le cavalier, 1957
oil/canvas
147 x 114,5 cm *
p. 62

Sculptuur, 1961
Sculpture
painted wood
187 x 104,5 x 74,5 cm
p. 62

Constant
Amsterdam (NL) 1920
De oorlog, 1950
The War
oil/canvas
125 x 117 x 4 cm
p. 63

Corneille
Liège (B) 1922
Fin des terres, 1955
oil/canvas
67,5 x 83,5 cm *
p. 63

Asger Jorn
Vejrum 1914 - 1973 Vejrum (DK)
Le monde perdu, 1960
oil/canvas
117,5 x 90 cm *
p. 60

Le creux au ventre, 1960
oil/canvas
130,4 x 97,4 cm *
p. 61

Lucebert
Amsterdam 1924 - 1994 Bergen (NL)
Prinsenpaar, 1962
Royal couple
oil/canvas
151,5 x 101,5 cm *
p. 63

viii
pp. 64 - 66

Francis Bacon
Dublin (IRL) 1909 - 1992 Madrid (E)
Fragment of a Crucifixion, 1950
oil, cotton wool/canvas
158 x 127 cm *
p. 65

Max Ernst
Brühl (D) 1891 - 1976 Paris (F)
Interrogation (what kind of bird are you?), 1956-58
oil/canvas
147,5 x 115,5 cm *
p. 65

Wilfredo Lam
Sagua la Grande (C) 1902 - 1992 Paris (F)
Figure, 1962
oil/canvas
130 x 98 cm
p. 65

Joan Miró
Barcelona 1893 - 1968 Palma de Majorca (E)
Composition avec des cordes, 1950
oil, plaster, rope/canvas
123,5 x 103 x 10 cm *
p. 64

Pieter Ouborg
Dordrecht 1893 - 1956 The Hague (NL)
Figuur, 1947
Figure
oil/canvas
64,5 x 56 cm *
p. 66

Schutter, 1950
Marksman
chalk, gouache/paper
83,5 x 63,5 cm *
p. 66

Zwevend op elkaar stoten, 1950
Floating and colliding
gouache, pencil, paper/paper
63,5 x 83,5 cm *
p. 66

Bram van Velde
Zoeterwoude (NL) 1895 -1981 Grimaud (F)
Zonder titel, 1961
Untitled
gouache/paper
133 x 138 cm *
p. 66

ix
pp. 67 - 69

Gaston Chaissac
Avallon 1910 - 1964 La Roche-sur-Yon (F)
Le masque, 1959
oil/paper/linen
103,7 x 73 cm *
p. 67

Jean Dubuffet
Le Havre 1901 - 1985 Paris (F)
Barbe des solitudes, 1959
oil/canvas
131 x 97 cm *
p. 68

La main dans le sac, 1961
oil/canvas
165,5 x 133,5 cm *
p. 67

Antonio Saura
Huesca 1930 - 1998 Cuenca (E)
Ada, 1962
oil/canvas
164 x 132 cm *
p. 69

Antoni Tàpies
Barcelona (E) 1923
Blue outremer, 1958
oil, sand/canvas, panel
164 x 132 cm *
p. 69

Double porte beige, 1960
oil, sand/canvas
98,5 x 131,3 cm *
p. 68

Jaap Wagemaker
Haarlem 1906 - 1972 Amsterdam (NL)
Sable gris, 1960
mixed media/canvas
131 x 121 cm *
p. 69

x
pp. 70 - 75

Armando
Amsterdam (NL) 1929
Zwarte bouten op zwart, 1960
Black bolts on black
metal, oil/wood
122 x 100 cm
p. 75

Fahne, 1980-81
oil, sand/canvas
165 x 240 cm
p. 75

Lucio Fontana
Rosario di Santa Fé (RA) 1899 - 1968 Varese (I)
Concetto Spaziale, 1955
mixed media/canvas
125 x 84,5 cm
p. 72

Concetto Spaziale: Attese, 1960
oil/canvas
130,5 x 97 cm
p. 71

Yves Klein
Nice 1928 - 1962 Paris (F)
Monochrome bleu, sans titre (IKB 63), 1959
pigment, phenolic resin/canvas/wood
117,3 x 68 cm *
p. 70

Heinz Mack
Lollar (D) 1931
Silberrotor, 1965
glass, aluminum, electric motor
122 x 123 x 29 cm
p. 73

Piero Manzoni
Milan 1933 - 1963 Milan (I)
Achrome, 1958
kaolin/linen/jute
136 x 103 x 5 cm *
p. 71

Henk Peeters
The Hague (NL) 1925
62-01, 1962
cotton wool, synthetic gauze, cotton, synthetic foil
200 x 90 cm
p. 75

Otto Piene
Laasphe (D) 1928
Rauchzeichnung, 1959
soot/paper
75 x 105 cm *
p. 73

Jan Schoonhoven
Delft 1914 - 1994 Delft (NL)
R 68-6 (Reliëf VI), 1968
latex/papier-mâché/wood
104,5 x 104,1 cm
p. 74

Günther Uecker
Wendorf (D) 1930
Bewegtes Feld, 1964
nails, oil/linen/wood
117 x 116,5 cm *
p. 73

xi
pp. 76 - 79

Joost Baljeu
Middelburg 1925 – 1991 Laren (NL)
Synthetische constructie W-II, 1957
Synthetic Construction W-II
oil/wood
56 x 72,8 x 33 cm
p. 77

Bob Bonies
The Hague (NL)1937
Dyptiek, 1972
Diptych
acrylic/canvas
(2x) 200 x 160 cm
p. 79

Ad Dekkers
Nieuwpoort 1938 - 1974 Gorinchem (NL)
Variatie op cirkels nr. III, 1965
Variation on circles no. III
polyester/panel
Ø 120 cm
p. 79

Richard Paul Lohse
Zurich 1902 - 1988 Zurich (CH)
Bewegung von Gelb über Grün und Blau zu Violett, 1958-73
oil/canvas
120 x 120 cm
p. 77

Vier gleiche asymmetrische Gruppen innerhalb eines regelmässigen Systems, 1962-63
oil/canvas
120,2 x 120,2 cm
p. 76

Jan Maaskant
Woluwe, St. Pieter (B) 1939
Rasterreliëf met grijs-geel verticaal, 1975
Grid relief with grey-yellow vertical
stainless steel, acrylic/linen
128,5 x 128,5 cm
p. 79

François Morellet
Cholet (F) 1926
32 Rectangles, 1953
oil/wood
80 x 79,8 cm
Gift of the artist
p. 77

Néon moderne en état de marche, 1973
neon, plywood, switchbox
286,5 x 286,5 x 6,4 cm
p. 77

Robert Morris
Kansas City, Missouri (USA) 1931
9 H-shapes, 1968
aluminum
(9x) 91,5 x 91,5 x 91,5 cm
p. 77

Peter Struyken
's-Hertogenbosch (NL) 1939
Cluster 12, 1971-75
synthetic paint/plexiglas
200 x 134 cm
p. 78

Victor Vasarely
Pécs (H) 1908 - 1997 Paris (F)
Silur, 1952-58
oil/canvas
134 x 101 cm *
p. 76

xii
pp. 80 - 84

Arman
Nice (F) 1928
Combien de marins, combien de capitaines, 1961
glass display case, coffee grinders
81,5 x 154 x 43,5 cm
p. 83

Christo
Gabrovo (BG) 1935
Packed Arm Chair, 1964-65
arm chair, plastic, textile, polyethylene
93,7 x 85 x 93,4 cm
p. 81

Jim Dine
Cincinnati, Ohio (USA) 1935
All in one Lycra, plus Attachments, 1965
mixed media/canvas
156,5 x 122 cm
p. 81

Domenico Gnoli
Rome (I) 1933 - 1970 New York City (USA)
Coat, 1968
oil, sand/canvas
153 x 124,5 cm *
p. 84

Robert Indiana
New Castle (USA) 1928
The Red Diamond American Dream # 3, 1962
oil/canvas
187,5 x 187,5 cm *
p. 80

Martial Raysse
Golfe-Juan (F) 1936
Mi-août, 1962
plastic, foam rubber, oil, offset/paper, wood
185,5 x 134,5 cm *
p. 82

Jean Tinguely
1925 Fribourg 1925 - 1991 Bern (CH)
Char M.K., 1967
iron, wood, electric motor
120,5 x 208,5 x 77 cm
p. 84

Andy Warhol
Pittsburgh, Pennsylvania 1928 - 1987 New York City (USA)
Mao Tse Tung, 1972
serigraphy/paper
(3x) 91,5 x 91,4 cm
p. 81

xiii
pp. 85 - 87

Jo Baer
Seattle, Washington (USA) 1929
Wrap-around Triptych (blue-green-lavender), 1970-74
oil/canvas
(3x) 91,5 x 99 cm
p. 87

Ellsworth Kelly
Newburgh, New York (USA) 1923
Green White no. 381, 1967
oil/canvas
217,1 x 217,4 cm *
p. 86

Morris Louis
Baltimore, Maryland 1912 - 1962 Washington, D.C. (USA)
Alpha Sigma, 1961
acrylic/canvas
262 x 487 cm
p. 86

Robert Mangold
North Tonawanda, New York (USA) 1937
A square within two triangles, 1977
acrylic/canvas
122,2 x 257,5 cm
p. 87

Larry Poons
Tokyo (J) 1937
Fliegender, 1967
acrylic/canvas
259,5 x 389 x 3,2 cm
p. 87

Frank Stella
Malden, Massachusetts (USA) 1936
Tuxedo Junction, 1960
synthetic paint/canvas
312 x 187 cm *
p. 85

Effingham I, 1967
acrylic/canvas
327 x 335,5 x 10,1 cm
p. 85

xiv
pp. 88 - 93

Carl Andre
Quincy, Massachusetts (USA) 1935
Twenty-fifth steel Cardinal, 1974
steel
(25x) 0,5 x 50 x 50 cm
p. 89

Palisade, 1976
wood
(13x) 90 x 30 x 30 cm
p. 89

Alan Charlton
Sheffield (GB) 1948
Untitled, 1979
acrylic/canvas
(7x) 266,5 x 89 cm
p. 92

Dan Flavin
New York City 1933 - 1996 New York City (USA)
Untitled (to a man, George McGovern), 1972
fluorescent tubes
316 x 316 x 10,3 cm
p. 90

Donald Judd
Excelsior Springs, Missouri 1928 - 1994 New York City (USA)
Untitled (Progression), 1969
aluminum
20 x 647 x 21 cm
p. 89

Untitled, 1974-76
wood
91,4 x 152 x 152,4 cm
p. 89

Sol LeWitt
Hartford, Connecticut (USA) 1928
Untitled (wall structure), 1972
painted aluminum
194,1 x 345 x 4 cm
p. 93

Wall Drawing no. 256, 1975
graphite, chalk, latex/wall
various dimensions
p. 93

Wall Drawing no. 480, 1986
ink/wall
various dimensions
Gift of the artist
p. 93

Bruce Nauman
Fort Wayne, Indiana (USA) 1941
Driven Man, Driven Snow, 1976
cast iron, pencil/paper
(26x)10 x 31,4 x 31,1 cm, (1x) 272 x 491 cm
p. 88

Robert Ryman
Nashville, Tennessee (USA) 1930
Untitled (Brussels), 1974
acrylic/plastic
(14x) 53,5 x 53,5 cm
p. 92

Richard Serra
San Francisco, California (USA) 1939
T-junction, 1988
iron
(1x) 240 x 25 x 25 cm, (1x) 25 x 788 x 25 cm
p. 90

Keith Sonnier
Marmon, Louisiana (USA) 1941
Ba-O-Ba, 1969
neon, glass
(1x) Ø 216,8 cm, (1x) 218 x 322,6 cm, (1x) 313 cm
p. 91

Ian Wilson
New York City (USA) 1924
Circle on the Floor, 1968
chalk line
Ø 183 cm
p. 93

xv
pp. 94 - 96

Joseph Beuys
Krefeld 1921 - 1986 Düsseldorf (D)
Vakuum <—> Masse, 1970
color photograph/linen
151 x 200 cm *
p. 94

Vorbereitung vor Betreten der Tate Gallery ("Wie Knochen entstehen") (aus der Serie: Words Which Can Hear), 1970
pencil, ink/paper
(2x) 126,3 x 78,6 cm *
Gift of the artist
p. 96

Voglie vedere i miei montagne, 1971
various materials
460 x 585 x 788 cm
p. 94

Vitex agnus castus, 1973
offset/paper
60,3 x 44 cm
p. 95

xvi
pp. 97 - 105

Art & Language
Study for index, incident in a museum II, 1985
gouache, pencil/paper
144 x 625,5 cm
Gift of the artist
p. 101

Robert Barry
New York City (USA) 1936
Numbers, 1974
slides
projection: variable dimensions
p. 98

Stanley Brouwn
Paramaribo (SME) 1935
this way brouwn, 1964
ink/paper
32,9 x 25,5 cm *
p. 104

Daniel Buren
Boulogne-Billancourt (F) 1938
Fragmente einer Rede über die Kunst. 18 peintures sur toile. Tissus rayés blancs et colorés, 1965-81
acrylic/canvas
224 x 198 cm
Purchased with support of Vereniging Rembrandt
p. 102

André Cadere
Warsaw (PL) 1934 - 1978 Paris (F)
B 12000030 =25= =16x17= Noir Blanc Bleu, 1975
enamel/wood
48,6 x Ø 2 cm
p. 103

Hans Haacke
Cologne (D) 1936
Seurat's 'Les Poseuses' (small version) 1888 - 1975, 1975
offset, black-and-white photo/paper, color photo
(14x) 70,5 x 60,5 cm, (1x) 60,5 x 70,5 cm *
p. 103

On Kawara
Kariya (J) 1933
13 Jan. 1973, 1973
acrylic/canvas
25,5 x 33 cm
p. 99

July 4 1973, 1973
acrylic/canvas
25,5 x 33 cm
p. 99

Joseph Kosuth
Toledo, Ohio (USA) 1945
One and Nine - A Description, 1965
synthetic paint/glass
(10x) 30,3 x 30,3 cm
p. 100

Art as Idea as Idea; (The First Investigation), 1968
photographs/aluminum
(5x) 100 x 100 cm
p. 100

The Second Investigation, 1969-74
black-and-white photographs
various dimensions
p. 100

Niele Toroni
Muralto (CH) 1937
Empreintes de pinceau no. 50 répétées à intervalles réguliers (30 cm), 1975
synthetic paint/oilcloth
380 x 140 cm
p. 101

Lawrence Weiner
New York City (USA) 1940
ON A ROUGH __________
BEING WITHIN THE CONTEXT OF [A] PLACE, 1975
language
p. 98

ON A SMOOTH __________
BEING WITHIN THE CONTEXT OF [A] PLACE, 1975
language
p. 98

IN THE ROUGH __________
BEING WITHIN THE CONTEXT OF [A] PLACE, 1975
language
p. 98

The rate of attraction of one object towards another as determined by the degree of encumbrance experienced by each object, 1980
poster
42,5 x 85,5 cm
p. 97

Ian Wilson
New York City (USA) 1924
Discussion, 1981, 11 May
language
p. 99

The Set of 25 Sections: 90-114, with Absolute Knowledge, 1993
letterpress/paper
(25x) 27,3 x 18,8 cm
p. 99

Remy Zaugg
Courgenay (CH) 1943
Une feuille de papier, 1973-80
pencil, serigraphy, oil/paper/canvas
200 x 175 cm
p. 105

Une feuille de papier, 1973-82
pencil, serigraphy, oil/paper/canvas, oil/paper/canvas
(1x) 200 x 175 cm, (1x) 199,5 x 175 cm
p. 105

Une feuille de papier, 1973-86
pencil, serigraphy, oil/paper/canvas
200 x 175 cm
p. 105

xvii
pp. 106 - 112

John Baldessari
1931 National City, California (USA) 1931
Subject Matter, 1967-68
acrylic/canvas
172 x 143,5 x 2 cm
Purchased with support of the Mondriaan Foundation
p. 106

Virtues and Vices (for Giotto), 1981
black-and-white photographs
(14x) 76 x 76 cm
p. 109

Bernd & Hilla Becher
1931 Siegen (D), 1934 Potsdam (D)
Kühltürme Beton-Fertigteile, 1963-75
black-and-white photographs/paper
147 x 107 cm *
Gift of the artists
p. 108

Jan Dibbets
Weert (NL) 1941
The Shortest Day at the Van Abbemuseum, 1970
color photographs/wood
178,5 x 171,5 cm *
p. 111

Big Comet 3° - 60°, sky / land / sky, 1973
color photographs/paper
450 x 600 cm
p. 112

Claustra I, 1986
gouache, pencil, color photograph/paper/wood
183 x 182 cm
Gift of the artist
p. 111

Ger van Elk
Amsterdam (NL) 1941
The Absorption of the Shadow, 1969
cardboard, wood, metal, color film
p. 110

Adieu IV, 1974
acrylic/color photograph
120 x 91 cm
p. 110

Het Kinselmeer (Stompe Toren bij Ransdorp), 1996
Kinsel Lake, Truncated Tower at Ransdorp
color photograph/cibachrome between plexiglas
76 x 145 cm *
Purchased with support of the Mondriaan Foundation
p. 110

Dan Graham
Urbana, Illinois (USA) 1942
Yesterday/Today, 1975
concept for a video work
p. 107

Douglas Huebler
Ann Harbor, Michigan (USA) 1924
Variable piece no. 111 London, 1974
color photographs, stickers
68,5 x 68,5 cm *
p. 108

Edward Ruscha
Omaha, Nebraska (USA) 1937
Sand in the Vaseline, 1974
egg yolk/satin
91,5 x 101,4 cm
p. 107

xviii
pp. 113 - 118

Marcel Broodthaers
Brussels (B) 1924 - 1976 Cologne (D)
La Pluie (Projet pour un texte), 1969
16mm film (black-and-white), no sound, 0:02 min.
projection: variable dimensions
Gift of Marcel Broodthaers Estate
p. 116

Sex-Film, 1971-1972
color slides
projection: variable dimensions
Gift of Marcel Broodthaers Estate
p. 114

Série de neuf tableaux, 1972
serigraphy/linen
(9x) 79,5 x 100 cm
p. 113

Tapis de Sable, 1974
quartz sand, pigments, palm in a pot, printed terrycloth
(carpet) 337 x 220 cm, (terrycloth) 107 x 52,4 cm
Purchased with support of the Van Abbemuseum Promoters
Foundation
p. 113

ABC-ABC Image, 1974
color slides
projection: variable dimensions
Gift of Marcel Broodthaers Estate
p. 114 - 115

James Lee Byars
Detroit, Michigan (USA) 1932 - 1997 Cairo (ET)
Hear TH FI TO IN PH Around this Chair, 1978
chair, carpets, silk tent, spotlight
ca. 357 x 355 x 368 cm
p. 117

Moonbook (stonebooks), 1980
sandstone, display case
(2x) 3,7 x 41,3 x 29,4 cm, (1x) 175,5 x 146 x 46 cm
Gift of the artist
p. 117

xix
pp. 119 - 124

Tony Cragg
Liverpool (GB) 1949
Red Skin, 1980
plastic
646 x 450 cm
p. 123

One Space, Four Places, 1982
various materials
(4x) ca. 102 x 65 x 65 cm, (1x) 87 x 215 x 113 cm
p. 123

Eroded Landscape, 1991
glass
150 x 120 x 125 cm
Gift of the artist
p. 123

René Daniëls
Eindhoven (NL) 1950
Painting on the Bullfight, 1985
oil/canvas
170,4 x 240,5 cm
p. 123

Ian Hamilton Finlay
Nassau (BS) 1925
De huidige orde is de wanorde van de toekomst Saint-Just, 1986
The Present Order is the Disorder of the Future Saint-Just
sandstone
various dimensions
p. 121

Barry Flanagan
Prestatyn, Wales (GB) 1941
Left hand by left hand, 1970
etching/paper
52,5 x 42,5 cm *
p. 120

Withdrawal from stone wall street, 1970
etching/paper
52,5 x 42,5 cm *
p. 120

Withdrawal from stone wall street, 1970
etching/paper
52,5 x 42,5 cm *
p. 120

To draw fire, 1970
etching/paper
52,5 x 42,5 cm *
p. 120

Untitled Once, 1973
painted jute, wood
114 x 139,5 cm
p. 120

Figures, 1976
Clipsham stone
60 x 35 x 25 cm
p. 120

Hamish Fulton
London (GB) 1946
*Mount Thor; a Six Day 70 Mile Walk on Baffin Island Canada
Summer 1976*, 1976
black-and-white photograph
199 x 103 cm *
p. 121

Gilbert & George
San Martino (I) 1943 & Totnes, Devon (GB) 1942
Dark Shadow no. 8, 1974
black-and-white photographs
151 x 205,5 cm
p. 122

Are You Angry or Are You Boring?, 1977
black-and-white photographs, color photographs
242 x 202 cm *
p. 122

Anish Kapoor
Bombay (IND) 1954
Tongue no. 2, 1982
pigment, polystyrene, cement
ca. 195 x 325 x 220 cm
p. 124

Richard Long
1945 Bristol (GB)
Sixty Stones, 1975
flint
ca. 720 x 480 cm
p. 119

Wood circle, 1977
wood
ca. Ø 700 cm
p. 119

White Marble Line, 1986
white pebbles
220 x 1000 cm
Gift of the artist
p. 119

Boyd Webb
Christchurch (NZ) 1947
Untitled, 1981
color photograph
120,5 x 151 cm *
p. 124

xx
pp. 125 - 130

Giovanni Anselmo
Borgofranco d'Ivrea (I) 1934
Un disegno e un particolare a est, trecento milioni di anni a ovest,
1967-78
graphite/cardboard, granite, compass, anthracite, electric light,
slide projection
variable dimensions
p. 126

Luciano Fabro
Turin (I) 1936
Il giudizio di Paride, 1979
terracotta
(3x) 45 cm, (1x) 55 cm
p. 126

Mercurio, 1982
iron, brass, wood, bitumen
138,5 x 106,5 cm
p. 126

Jannis Kounellis
Piraeus (GR) 1936
Senza titolo, 1980
metal, cloth, plaster
335 x 40 x 20 cm
p. 128

Senza titolo, Roma, 1983
metal/wood
145 x 244 x 20 cm
p. 127

Senza titolo, 1986
metal, jute
200 x 190 cm
Gift of the artist
p. 127

Mario Merz
Milan (I) 1925
Zonder titel, 1984
Untitled
mixed media/panel
277 x 265 cm
p. 129

Igloo Nero, (1967-79), 1994
iron, asphalt, neon tube, slate, gluing clamps, tube clamps,
transformer
251 x Ø 490 cm
p. 128

Giulio Paolini
Genoa (I) 1940
La caduta di Icaro, 1982
plexiglas bases, chairs, stretched canvases, dinner jacket
dimensions variable
p. 125

Guiseppe Penone
Garessio Ponte (I) 1947
Un albero di sei metri, 1969
wood
561,5 x 19,5 x 11,6 cm
p. 129

Michelangelo Pistoletto
Biella (I) 1933
Donna che disegna, 1962-75
serigraphy/polished metal
(2x) 230 x 125 x 3,7 cm
Gift of the artist
p. 129

Scultura nera, 1984
painted polyurethane
210 x 121 x 100 cm
p. 130

Gilberto Zorio
Andorno Micca (I) 1944
Luci, 1968
cast concrete, lamps
(2x) 21 x 19,5 x 121,5 cm
p. 129

xxi
pp. 131 - 137

Lothar Baumgarten
Rheinsberg (D) 1944
Projektion, 1971
slide projection, various objects
ca. 227 x 346 cm
Gift of the artist
p. 135

Isa Genzken
Bad Oldesloe (D) 1948
Feuervogel, 1981
synthetic paint/wood
(length) 520 cm
p. 137

Rebecca Horn
Michelstadt (D), 1944
Das Goldene Bad, 1980
iron, messing, glass, water
45 x 180 x 180 cm
p. 135

The Moon, the Child and the River of Anarchy, 1992
school desks, ink, glass funnels, lead tubes,
variable dimensions
Purchased with support of the Van Abbemuseum Promoters
Foundation and the Province of Noord-Brabant
p. 131

Imi Knoebel
Dessau (D) 1940
Ohne Titel, 1978
acrylic/wood
380 x 260 cm
p. 136

Bernd Lohaus
Düsseldorf (D) 1940
Ich-Du, 1973
white crayon/wood
210 x 110 x 5 cm
p. 136

Sigmar Polke
Olesnica (PL) 1941
Höhere Wesen befahlen: rechte obere Ecke schwarz malen!, 1969
synthetic paint/canvas
151 x 126 cm *
p. 134

Goldklumpen, 1982
gold pigment, Schweinfurter green with arsenic/canvas
261,5 x 202 cm *
p. 134

Gerhard Richter
Dresden (D) 1932
Grau (nr. 365/2), 1974
oil/canvas
250 x 200 cm
p. 132

Abstraktes Bild (nr. 421), 1977
oil/canvas
250,5 x 202 cm
p. 132

Ulrich Rückriem
Düsseldorf (D) 1938
Ohne Titel, 1972
steel
7,5 x 600 x 600 cm
Gift of the artist
p. 132

Sandstein geteilt und zugeschnitten, 1976
sandstone
10 x 95 x 180 cm
permanent loan
p. 136

Katharina Sieverding
Prague (CS) 1944
Nachtmensch, 1982
color photographs
(15x) 43 x 61 cm *
p. 132

Franz Erhard Walther
Fulda (D) 1939
Gelber Plastischer Gesang (einzeln zusammen), 1984
textile, wood
p. 136

xxii
pp. 138 - 144

Christian Ludwig Attersee
Pressburg (CS) 1940
Föhn, 1984
acrylic/canvas
212,5 x 163,5 cm *
p. 143

Georg Baselitz
Deutschbaselitz (D) 1938
Akt Elke, 1977
oil/canvas
252,5 x 203 cm *
p. 138

Trümmerfrau, 1978
oil/canvas
330 x 250 cm
p. 141

Jörg Immendorff
Bleckede (D) 1945
BrrrD-DDrrr Caf, Deutschland, 1978
synthetic paint/canvas
291 x 291 cm *
p. 140

Anselm Kiefer
Donaueschingen (D) 1945
Märkische Heide, 1974
oil, acrylic, shellac/jute
118 x 254 cm
p. 139

Varus, 1976
oil/canvas
200 x 270,5 cm
p. 139

Per Kirkeby
Copenhagen (DK) 1938
Ohne Titel, 1979
oil/canvas
203 x 250 cm *
p. 143

Markus Lüpertz
Liberec (CS) 1941
Eskalation - dithyrambisch, 1973
oil/canvas
218 x 365 cm *
p. 142

Babylon - dithyrambisch XII, 1975
oil/canvas
167,5 x 135,5 cm *
p. 142

Hermann Nitsch
Vienna (A) 1938
Schüttbild, 1982
acrylic/canvas
200 x 652 cm
p. 144

A.R. Penck
Dresden (D) 1939
Torquato Tasso, 1976
acrylic/canvas
285 x 285 cm *
p. 141

Arnulf Rainer
Wiener Neustadt (A) 1929
Fingermalerei, 1984
oil/cardboard
84,3 x 112,9 cm *
p. 144

xxiii
pp. 145 - 152

Gerrit van Bakel
Ysselstein 1943 - 1984 Deurne (NL)
Utah-machine (behorend bij de Utah-Tarim connectie), 1980
Utah-machine (belonging to the Utah-Tarim connection)
iron, rubber, petroleum, brass
81 x 81 x 66 cm
p. 147

Een nieuwe mogelijkheid van de vreugde van Papin, 1981
A new possibility of Papin's Joy
granite, steel, soil, fiberglass filament, brass
184 x 147 x 104 cm
p. 147

Tetraëder, 1982
iron, multiplex, rubber, leather
(closed) 108 x 37,5 x 30 cm, (open) 199 x 169,5 x 144 cm
p. 147

Marinus Boezem
Leerdam (NL) 1934
Visual research, 1970
wood, artificial lighting
242,5 x 209,5 x 2 cm
p. 148

Marlene Dumas
Capetown (SA) 1953
Genetiese Heimwee, 1984
Genetic Longing
oil/canvas
130 x 110 cm
p. 150

Models, 1994
ink wash, crayon/paper
(100x) 62 x 50 cm
p. 149

Hans van Hoek
Deurne (NL) 1947
Klein landschap, 1980-81
Small Landscape
oil/canvas
185 x 345,5 cm *
p. 146

Ulay/Abramović
1943 Solingen (D) 1943 / Belgrado (YU) 1946
Talking about similarity, 1976
video registration/laser disc, black-and-white, sound, 9:20 min.
Purchased with support of the Mondriaan Foundation
p. 152

AAA-AAA, 1978
video registration/laser disc, black-and-white, sound, 9:19 min.
Purchased with support of the Mondriaan Foundation
p. 152

JCJ Vanderheyden
's-Hertogenbosch (NL) 1928
Blauw kader, 1966-80
Blue Frame
polyvinyl, tempera/canvas
240 x 197 cm
p. 145

Day of Creation after Hieronymus Bosch, 1990
inkjet, acrylic/canvas
130 x 200 cm
p. 149

Toon Verhoef
Voorburg (NL) 1946
Zonder titel, 1984
Untitled
oil, alkyd/canvas
270 x 351,5 cm
p. 151

Henk Visch
Eindhoven (NL) 1950
Stay Close, 1984
iron, horsehair
55 x 550 x 150 cm
p. 147

The artist model, 1984
painted wood
71 x 160 x 22 cm
p. 147

Voor dat wat blijft, 1985
For what remains
wood, textile, iron
252 x Ø 165 cm
p. 147

Idle thoughts for idle men, 1992
textile, plaster, metal, spinning top
153 x 54 x 44,5 cm
p. 147

Carel Visser
Papendrecht (NL) 1928
Zonder titel, 1977
Untitled
pencil/paper
(8x) 52 x 67 cm *
p. 151

Op het balkon, 1985
On the Balcony
jute, tire, car tops
120 x 160 x 240 cm
p. 151

xxiv
pp. 153 - 156

René Daniëls
Eindhoven (NL) 1950
La Muse Vénale, 1979
oil/canvas
200 x 300 cm
p. 153

L' objet, 1980
phonograph record, brush, paint
ca. 20 x 30 x 30 cm
coll. René Daniëls Foundation, Eindhoven
p. 153

A Hot Day in the Lighthouse, 1984
oil/canvas
150 x 200,5 cm
p. 154

Painting on the Bullfight, 1985
oil/canvas
170,4 x 240,5 cm
p. 154

Het huis, 1986
The House
oil/canvas
180 x 130 x 2 cm
Gift of the artist
p. 155

Lentebloesem, 1987
Spring Blossom
oil/canvas
100 x 200 cm
coll. René Daniëls Foundation, Eindhoven
p. 156

Zonder titel, 1987
Untitled
watercolor, ink, black chalk/paper
26 x 20 cm
coll. Foundation René Daniëls, Eindhoven
p. 156

Zonder titel, 1987
Untitled
watercolor, ink/paper
21 x 29,5 cm
coll. René Daniëls Foundation, Eindhoven
p. 156

XXV
pp. 157 - 165

Jean-Marc Bustamante
Toulouse (F) 1952
Lumière no.1, 1988
serigraphy/plexiglas
174 x 144 cm
p. 161

Bac à Sable, 1990
concrete, wood, sand
28 x 231,5 x 182,5 cm
p. 161

Sans Titre (diptych), 1993
alkyd/steel
(1x) 201 x 135 x 1 cm, (1x) 196,5 x 125 x 1 cm
Purchased with support of the Van Abbemuseum Promoters
Foundation
p. 161

Rodney Graham
Vancouver (CDN) 1949
Supplemented Standard Edition with Prussian Blue Shelf (for Eindhoven), 1990-91
books, brass, painted aluminum
28 x 286 x 14,5 cm
Gift of the artist
p. 164

Vexation Island, 1997
video projection, color, sound, 13:40 min.
projection ca. 155 x 365 cm
Purchased with support of the Van Abbemuseum Promoters
Foundation
p. 164

Cristina Iglesias
San Sebastián (E) 1956
Untitled, 1994
cement, wood, alabaster, iron
240 x 215 x 220 cm
p. 163

Niek Kemps
Nijmegen (NL) 1952
Sevillanas I - IV, 1992
glass, photograph, textile fiber, iron
251 x 409,1 x 6,5 cm
p. 160

Les privilèges de la promenade, 1992
wood, glass, serigraphy, felt
50 x 385 x 590 cm
p. 160

Harald Klingelhöller
Mettmann (D) 1954
Zur Konjugation von 'fallen', 1991
cardboard, basalt lava
119 x 305 x 181 cm
Purchased with support of the Van Abbemuseum Promoters
Foundation
p. 158

Schweigen bricht, 1991
plaster, cardboard
119,5 x 126 x 127 cm
p. 158

Allan McCollum
Los Angeles, California (USA) 1944
Plaster Surrogates, 1989
enamel/solid-cast Hydrocal
ca. 175 x 675 cm
p. 165

Reinhard Mucha
Düsseldorf (D) 1950
Vechta, 1982
lacquered wood, felt, glass, metal, cardboard, rubber, synthetic
material, fluorescent lights
(1x) 70,2 x 48,5 x 9,2 cm, (1x) 62,1 x 14,4 x 6,1 cm
p. 157

Ohne Titel (Wülfrath Wo), 1983
glass, metal, wood, linoleum, fluorescent light, name plate
262 x 480 x 36,7 cm
p. 157

Ohne Titel (Oberhausen), 1983
wood, mirror, linoleum, metal, plexiglas, rubber,
fluorescent lights
197,3 x 207,5 x 88,5 cm
Purchased with support of the Mondriaan Foundation
p. 157

Matt Mullican
Santa Monica, California (USA) 1951
Untitled, 1992
glass, wood
(7x) 203,5 x 102 cm, (7x) 79 x 105,5 x 207 cm
Purchased with support of the Van Abbemuseum Promoters
Foundation
p. 165

Untitled, 1996
ilfochrome print/plexiglas in metal box
(5x) 23 x 31,7 cm
p. 165

Thomas Schütte
Oldenburg (D) 1954
Athener Tagebuch, 1984
watercolor/paper
(141x) 58,5 x 48 cm *
Purchased with support of the Van Abbemuseum Promoters
Foundation
159

Blauer Bunker, 1984
synthetic paint/paper, latex, plaster, wood
(3x) ca. 200 x 157 cm, (1x) 161 x 108 x 126 cm
p. 159

Collector's Complex, 1990
wood
267 x 500 x 178 cm
p. 158

Jan Vercruysse
Oostende (B) 1948
Chambre (IV), 1986
multiplex, hardboard, mahogany veneer
389,5 x 167 x 305 cm
Purchased with support of Vereniging Rembrandt
p. 162

Atopies (N.N.), 1987
mahogany veneer/multiplex
(1x) 115 x 120,3 x 23 cm, (2x) 200,5 x 60 cm, (1x) 200 x 25 cm
p. 162

TOMBEAUX, (1988) 1991
glass, iron
(2x) 89,5 x 38 x 38 cm, (1x) 8 x 160 x 10 cm, (1x) 8 x 200 x 10 cm
p. 162

Didier Vermeiren
Brussels (B) 1951
Sculpture, 1982
marble
242 x 47,5 x 43 cm
p. 163

Socle du Monument à Sarmiento, 1986
plaster, wood
115,5 x 147,5 x 260 cm
p. 163

Untitled, 1989
brass, steel, synthetic material
166,5 x 100 x 108 cm
p. 163

xxvi
pp. 166 - 171

Miroslaw Balka
Warsaw (PL) 1958
River, 1988-1989
painted jute, neon lighting, ashes, wood
variable dimensions
p. 166

40x30x1, 40x30x1, 99x90x25, 250x126x1, 117x91x11, 1992
steel, linoleum, heating cables, ashes, felt, paper, plaster
variable dimensions
p. 167

Christian Boltanski
Paris (F) 1944
Les ombres, 1986
puppets of wood, cardboard, tin and cork/metal frame, projectors, transformer, fan
variable dimensions
Purchased with support of the Van Abbemuseum Promoters
Foundation
p. 167

Jean-Marc Bustamante
Toulouse (F) 1952
Lumière no.1, 1988
serigraphy/plexiglas
174 x 144 cm
p. 170

Thierry De Cordier
Oudenaarde (B) 1954
La Cuisine (maquette), 1988
plaster, glass, ceramics, metal, wood
73,5 x 138 x 64,5 cm
p. 170

Écritoire I (schrijfgestoelte), 1988-93
wood, rubber, metal, glass, textile
243,5 x 44,5 x 81 cm
p. 170

Ann Hamilton
Lima, Ohio (USA) 1956
Reserve, 1996
steel, tree-trunks, paper, rubber bands, monitors, textile, laser
discs
dimensions variable
p. 169

Pieter Laurens Mol
Breda (NL) 1946
Lament Superior, 1991
steel, wood, iron, red lead, paper, birds' nests
(1x) 84,5 x 76,5 x 123 cm, (1x) 32,5 x 87,5 x 21,5 cm, (2x) › 16 cm
p. 171

Juan Muñoz
Madrid 1953 - 2001 Ibiza (E)
Large Raincoat Drawing III, 1989
crayon, ink/canvas
150 x 200 cm
p. 168

Lines of my Hand, 1990
wood, metal
90,5 x 247 x 183,5 cm
p. 168

Listening Figure, 1991
patinated bronze
129 x 74 x 73 cm
Purchased with support of the Van Abbemuseum Promoters
Foundation
p. 168

Balcony, 1991
iron
85,3 x 73 x 45 cm
Purchased with support of the Van Abbemuseum Promoters
Foundation
p. 168

Conversation Piece, 1994
fiberglass, polyester, sand
(3x) ca. 155 x 82 x 85 cm
Gift of the artist
p. 166

Julião Sarmento
Lisbon (P) 1948
Metropolis, 1991
mixed media/canvas
285 x 205 cm
p. 166

Rachel Whiteread
London (GB) 1963
Valley, 1990
plaster, glass
94 x 96,5 x 185,5 cm
p. 170

Untitled (Slab II), 1991
rubber
13,5 x 75,5 x 197 cm
p. 168

xxvii
pp. 172 - 177

Tiong Ang
Surabaya (RI) 1961
Portret van twee jongens (initiatie/chirurgie), 1991
Portrait of two boys (initiation/surgery)
veil, alkyd paint/linen/wood
140 x 247 cm
Purchased with support of the Mondriaan Foundation
p. 177

Job Koelewijn
Spakenburg (NL) 1962
Kaleidoscoop, 2001
Kaleidoscope
metal, plexiglas, Fresnel lenses
min. 293 / max. 377 x Ø 300 cm
p. 172

John Körmeling
Amsterdam (NL) 1951
Pier voor Zeeland, 1985
Pier for Zeeland
metal, stone
89,5 x 109,5 x 18,3 cm
p. 173

Nog een, 1990
Another one
neon lighting, iron
52,2 x 201 x 9,5 cm
p. 173

Atelier (Joep) van Lieshout
Ravenstein (NL) 1963
Orgone/Sleep/Dinette Skull, 1998
wood, polyester, orgone substance
175,5 x 362,5 x 166 cm
Purchased with support of the Mondriaan Foundation
p. 174

Marc Manders
Volkel (NL) 1968
Zelfportret (fragment uit 'Zelfportret als gebouw') 1992
Self-Portrait (fragment from Self-Portrait as a Building)
brass, wood, acrylic/ceramics
18,5 x 300,5 x 251,5 cm
p. 177

Zelfportret (fragment uit 'Zelfportret als gebouw') 1994
Self-Portrait (fragment from Self-Portrait as a Building)
acrylic/bronze
(1x) 193,5 x 109,5 x 40 cm, (1x) 192 x 107,5 x 40 cm
Purchased with support of the Mondriaan Foundation
p. 177

Frank Mandersloot
Utrecht (NL) 1960
Jogos de Cama IV, 1990
plywood, linen
(2x) 80 x 90 x 195 cm
p. 177

Marc Mulders
Tilburg (NL) 1958
Rozen XIV, 1992
Roses
oil/canvas
170 x 240 cm
p. 176

Picardie, 2000
oil/canvas
240 x 140 cm
p. 176

Jan van de Pavert
Zeist (NL) 1960
Segment uit een bibliotheek voor eindeloze tekst, 1989
Segment from a library for unending text
silver leaf/wood, wood
173,5 x 126,5 x 64 cm
p. 173

Michael Raedecker
Amsterdam (NL) 1963
kismet, 1999
acrylic, thread/canvas
204,5 x 255 cm
Purchased with support of the Mondriaan Foundation
p. 175

pitch, 2000
acrylic, thread/canvas
203,5 x 305,5 cm
p. 175

xxviii
pp. 178 - 184

Eija-Liisa Ahtila
Hämeenlinna (SF) 1959
If 6 was 9, 1995
video installation, color, sound, 0:10 min.
projection dimensions variable
p. 182

James Coleman
Ballaghaderreen (IR) 1941
Living and Presumed Dead, 1983-85
multiple slide projection, sound, 0:25 min.
projection dimensions variable
p. 178

Rineke Dijkstra
Sittard (NL) 1959
Jalta, Ukraine, 30 juli 1993
C-print/paper
149,5 x 125,5 x 4,7 cm *
Purchased with support of the Mondriaan Foundation
p. 184

Douglas Gordon
Glasgow (GB) 1966
10 ms-1, 1994
video projection, b/w, no sound, 10:37 min.
229 x 304,5 cm
p. 182

Untitled (Text for someplace other than this), 1996
vinyl or painted letters/wall
text: 247 x 197 cm
p. 181

Gary Hill
Santa Monica, California (USA) 1951
I Believe It Is an Image in Light of the Other, 1991-92
video installation, b/w, sound, video projectors, books
ca. 369 x 290 x 332 cm
p. 180

Pierre Huyghe
Paris (F) 1962
Les Grands Ensembles, 1994-2001
video installation, color, music by Pan Sonic, graphic/light box,
7:51 min.
projection dimensions variable
Purchased with support of the Mondriaan Foundation
p. 183

Aernout Mik, Marjoleine Boonstra
Groningen (NL) 1962, Groningen (NL) 1959
Hongkongoria, 1997-98
video installation, color, sound, 7 projections
various dimensions
Purchased with support of the Mondriaan Foundation
p. 183

Tony Oursler
New York City (USA) 1956
Autochthonous Alien, 1995
video installation, color, sound
(1x) 206 x 33 x 33 cm, (1x) 190 x 33 x 33 cm
p. 179

Marijke van Warmerdam
Nieuwer Amstel (NL) 1959
Kring, 1992
Circle
16mm film, color, no sound, projection stand, base with
rotation platform, loop system, 0:45 min.
height ca. 240 cm
Purchased with support of the Mondriaan Foundation
p. 181

Skytypers, 1997
16mm film, color, no sound, projector, projection table,
loop system
ca. 260 x 350 cm
Purchased with support of the Mondriaan Foundation
p. 181

Since 1989, the foundation Promoters of the Van Abbemuseum has donated the following works:

1990
Thomas Schütte
Athener Tagebuch, 1984
ill.p. 159

1991
Christian Boltanski
Les ombres, 1986
ill.p. 167

James Coleman
So Different...and Yet, 1979-80

Harald Klingelhöller
Zur Konjugation von 'fallen', 1991
ill.p. 158

1992
Juan Muñoz
Listening Figure, 1991
ill.p. 168

Juan Muñoz
Balcony, 1991
ill.p. 168

1993
Marcel Broodthaers
Tapis de Sable, 1974
ill.p. 113

Jan Vercruysse
M (M6), 1992

1994
Rebecca Horn
The Moon, the Child and the River of Anarchy, 1992
ill.p. 131

1995
Jean-Marc Bustamante
Grand Miroir, 1991

Jean-Marc Bustamante
Sans Titre, 1993
ill.p. 161

Jean-Marc Bustamante
Tableaux, 1991

Matt Mullican
Untitled, 1992
ill.p. 165

1997
El Lissitzky
Proun P23, no. 6, 1919
Purchased with support of the Van Abbemuseum Promoters
Foundation, the Mondriaan Foundation, Vereniging Rembrandt
and the Province of Noord-Brabant
ill.p. 52

1998
Rodney Graham
Vexation Island, 1997
ill.p. 164

2000
Mike Kelley
Categorical Imperative and Morgue, 1999
Purchased with support of the Van Abbemuseum Promoters
Foundation and the Mondriaan Foundation
ill.p. 31

On the occasion of the Van Abbemuseum's
fiftieth anniversary in 1986, the museum
received the following works.
All gifts have been made by the artist, unless
stated otherwise.

Armando
Fahne, 1986
Schenking Galerie Turkse & Turkse

Art & Language
Study for index, incident in a museum II, 1985
ill.p. 101

Christian Ludwig Attersee
Tischreise, 1986

Georg Baselitz
Grüner Baum, 1986

Günter Brus
Das Augenbeet, 1983

James Lee Byars
Moonbook (stonebooks), 1980
ill.p. 117

Alan Charlton
Panel Painting, 1978

René Daniëls
Het huis, 1986
ill.p. 155

Ad Dekkers
Twee fasen van cirkel naar vierkant, 1971
Schenking R.H. Fuchs

Jan Dibbets
Claustra I, 1986
ill.p. 111

Edward Dwurnik
Widzialem go !, 1984

Edgar Fernhout
In herfst, 1971
Schenking R.H. Fuchs

Barry Flanagan
Chess Piece, 1973
Schenking Galerie Art & Project

Hamish Fulton
Walking South for Seven Days England Winter, 1980

Gilbert & George
Doers, 1984

Jörg Immendorff
Kampfpause, 1983

Per Kirkeby
Flugten til Aegypten, 1985

Joseph Kosuth
Intentio (Project), 1984-1985

Jannis Kounellis
Senza titolo, 1986
ill.p. 127

Sol LeWitt
Wall Drawing no. 480, 1986
ill.p. 93

Thomas van der Linden
Følsom Tålmodighet - the complexity of symmetry, 1986

El Lissitzky
Der Konstrukteur (Selbstbildnis), [1924]
Schenking J. Leering
ill.p. 55

Bernd Lohaus
Ich..Tod, 1977

Richard Long
White Marble Line, 1986
ill.p. 119

Markus Lüpertz
Orpheus in der Unterwelt II, 1982

Hermann Nitsch
Tragbahre (Aktionsrelikt), 1985

A.R. Penck
Was ist Gravitation? I, 1984

Michelangelo Pistoletto
Donna che disegna, 1962-1975
ill.p. 129

Arnulf Rainer
Mumienkopfübermalung, 1984

Roger Raveel
Man op stoel, 1986

Ulrich Rückriem
Granit bleu de Normandie coupé et scié, 1985

Niele Toroni
Empreintes de pinceau no. 50 répétées à intervalles réguliers, 1986

JCJ Vanderheyden
Horizon, 1983-1986

Toon Verhoef
Zonder titel, 1986

Alex Vermeulen
De ruil van zee, voor zand was briljant, 1985
L'eaujean, 1985

Henk Visch
Be to one another true, 1984

Carel Visser
Wilde Bok, 1986

Franz Erhard Walther
Gelbe Antwort, 1984

Lawrence Weiner
SMALL STONES SCATTERED ON THE GROUND, 1986

Remy Zaugg
Une feuille de papier, 1973
Une feuille de papier, 1973-1985
Une feuille de papier, 1986
ill.p. 105

Colophon

Edited by
Jan Debbaut, Monique Verhulst

Photo editing
Arlette Brouwers, Jan Debbaut,
Monique Verhulst

Coordination and production
Monique Verhulst

Translation
Beth O'Brien

Design
Arlette Brouwers, Koos van der Meer

Texts
The texts on the collection have been written
by staff members of the museum and outside
authors, partly on the basis of existing material (published in *Van Abbemuseum Eindhoven*;
[Dutch Museums IV] Haarlem, 1982) written
by Jaap Bremer (chapters **iii, vi, vii, ix, x**),
Jan Debbaut (chapter **xii**), Rudi Fuchs (chapters **iii, viii, xiii**), Margriet Suren (chapters **ii,
iv, xi**).

Authors
Christiane Berndes (**ii, v, x, xii, xiii**)
Jaap Guldemond (**i, ix**)
Anna Hakkens (**xvi, xvii, xviii, xxiii**)
Henriëtte Heezen (**xxvii, xxviii**)
Frank Lubbers (**iii, iv, vi**)
René Pingen (**xiv, xix, xxv**)
Bert Steevensz (**xv, xx, xxi, xxii, xxiv, xxvi**)
Monique Verhulst (**vii, viii, xi**)

Photography
Ruud Balk, Eindhoven
Louis van Beurden, Eindhoven
Van den Bichelaar, Eindhoven
Hans Biezen, Sunne
Marente Bloemheuvel, Amsterdam
James Coleman, Dublin
Martien Coppens, Eindhoven
Peter Cox, Eindhoven
François Eyck, Eindhoven
Francesca Giovanelli, Weiningen
Tom Haartsen, Ouderkerk a/d Amstel
Intercolor bv, Eindhoven
Benjamin Katz, Cologne
Jannes Linders, Rotterdam (cover)
Mark McLoughlin
Attilio Maranzano, Montalcino-Siena
Cary Markerink, Amsterdam
Ernst Moritz
Dirk Pauwels, Ghent
John Riddy, London
H.J. Schröfer, Eindhoven

The Van Abbemuseum would like to thank
Lecturis BV, Eindhoven,
Karel van de Laarschot, Eindhoven
Van Abbemuseum Promoters Foundation

Lithography and printing
Lecturis BV, Eindhoven

Binding
Boekbinderij de Ruiter BV, Zwolle

Paper
135 grs. Go! Matt

Typeface
FF Scala, FF Scala sans

Publisher
Van Abbemuseum, P.O.Box 235,
NL-5600 AE Eindhoven

Distribution
NAi Publishers, architecture, urban planning,
visual arts
Mauritsweg 23, NL-3012 JR Rotterdam
www.naipublishers.nl

Available in North, South and Central America
through D.A.P./Distributed Art Publishers Inc,
155 Sixth Avenue 2nd Floor, New York, NY
10013-1507, Tel. 212 6271999 Fax 212 6279484

Available in the United Kingdom and Ireland
through Art Data, 12 Bell Industrial Estate,
50 Cunnington Street, London W4 5HB,
Tel. 181 7471061 Fax 181 7422319

For works of visual artists affiliated with a
CISAC-organization the copyrights have been
settled with Beeldrecht in Amsterdam.
©2002, c/o Beeldrecht Amsterdam.
It was not possible to find all the copyright
holders of the illustrations used. Interested
parties are requested to contact the
Van Abbemuseum, P.O. Box 235,
NL-5600 Eindhoven, The Netherlands

Printed and bound in The Netherlands
ISBN 90-70149-85-0

Van Abbemuseum
Bilderdijklaan 10
5611 NH Eindhoven
The Netherlands
(t) +31 (0)40 238 10 00
(f) +31 (0)40 246 06 80
(e) info@vanabbemuseum.nl
(i) www.vanabbemuseum.nl